TORTURED LOGIC

COLUMBIA STUDIES IN TERRORISM AND IRREGULAR WARFARE

COLUMBIA STUDIES IN TERRORISM
AND IRREGULAR WARFARE

Bruce Hoffman, Series Editor

This series seeks to fill a conspicuous gap in the burgeoning literature on terrorism, guerrilla warfare, and insurgency. The series adheres to the highest standards of scholarship and discourse and publishes books that elucidate the strategy, operations, means, motivations, and effects posed by terrorist, guerrilla, and insurgent organizations and movements. It thereby provides a solid and increasingly expanding foundation of knowledge on these subjects for students, established scholars, and informed reading audiences alike.

For a complete list of titles in the series, see page 319.

TORTURED LOGIC

WHY SOME AMERICANS SUPPORT THE USE OF TORTURE IN COUNTERTERRORISM

ERIN M. KEARNS AND
JOSEPH K. YOUNG

Columbia University Press
New York

Columbia University Press
Publishers Since 1893
New York   Chichester, West Sussex
cup.columbia.edu
Copyright © 2020 Columbia University Press

Library of Congress Cataloging-in-Publication Data
Names: Kearns, Erin M., author. | Young, Joseph K., author.
Title: Tortured logic : why some Americans support the use of torture in
counterterrorism / Erin M. Kearns and Joseph K. Young.
Description: New York : Columbia University Press, [2020] | Series: Columbia
studies in terrorism and irregular warfare | Includes bibliographical
references and index.
Identifiers: LCCN 2020000774 (print) | LCCN 2020000775 (ebook) |
ISBN 9780231188968 (cloth) | ISBN 9780231188975 (paperback) |
ISBN 9780231548090 (ebook)
Subjects: LCSH: Torture—United States—Public opinion. | Torture—Government
policy—United States. | Terrorism—United States—Prevention.
Classification: LCC HV8599.U6 K43 2020 (print) | LCC HV8599.U6 (ebook) |
DDC 363.325/165—dc23
LC record available at https://lccn.loc.gov/2020000774
LC ebook record available at https://lccn.loc.gov/2020000775

Columbia University Press books are printed on permanent and
durable acid-free paper.
Printed in the United States of America

Cover design: Lisa Hamm

TO OUR PARENTS, WHO INSTILLED
A LOVE OF READING AT A YOUNG AGE
AND WHOSE LIMITLESS SUPPORT AND
ENCOURAGEMENT MADE US BELIEVE
WE COULD WRITE THIS BOOK.

CONTENTS

ACKNOWLEDGMENTS

We presented earlier parts of this book at the American Political Science Association and the American Society of Criminology annual meetings, George Washington University, the University of Denver, the University of Essex, and the University of Pittsburgh. During these talks and through other discussions, we received valuable feedback from many colleagues, including Victor Asal, Michael Becker, Brandon Behlendorf, Mia Bloom, Erica Chenoweth, Christian Davenport, Laura Dugan, Cullen Hendrix, Daren Fisher, Oliver Kaplan, Michael Kenney, Gary LaFree, Yonatan Lupu, Erin Miller, James Piazza, and Burcu Savun, that helped us shape later parts of the book project and unquestionably improved our argument. We have also received invaluable feedback from a number of our colleagues at American University and the University of Alabama.

Through the design and writing process, many colleagues provided instructive feedback and guidance. We are grateful to Courtenay Conrad and Casey Delehanty for their comments on draft chapters; Shana Gadarian for feedback on experimental design; Chris E. Kelly for comments on our overall framing and how to think about various interrogation styles; Brendan Nyhan for help on the persuasion literature; Darius Rejali for his suggestions on broader framing and pioneering work on torture; Brian G. Stults for comments and assistance with survey design and execution; James Igoe Walsh for comments on conjoint experimental design; Thomas

Zeitzoff for feedback on our survey and experimental design; and Will Moore for his mentorship and his revolutionary work on torture and state violence. Finally, we are thankful to Brad Bartholomew, Peter Krause, and James Igoe Walsh for helping us pilot surveys in their classes.

A number of our former students at American University and the University of Alabama provided helpful research assistance on these projects from start to finish: Evan Padulla, Hannah Pruden, Caitlyn Sanders, Carol Ann Sharo, Taylor Windsheimer, and the students in Kearns's *Torture* courses at both universities.

We are indebted to our Columbia University Press editor, Caelyn Cobb, for encouraging us to undertake this project as a book and shepherding us through the entire process.

Joe is grateful for Melissa Scholes Young's example on how to write a book. Her advice and guidance were invaluable in turning these ideas into a manuscript.

Data collection for the survey-experiments in this book was made possible with funding from the American University School of Public Affairs Scholars Award, the American University Faculty Research Support Grant, and funding from the University of Alabama.

TORTURED LOGIC

INTRODUCTION

What Impacts Public Perception of Torture in Counterterrorism?

Should any American soldier be so base and infamous as to injure any [prisoner] . . . I do most earnestly enjoin you to bring him to such severe and exemplary punishment as the enormity of the crime may require. Should it extend to death itself, it will not be disproportional to its guilt at such a time and in such a cause . . . for by such conduct they bring the shame and disgrace and ruin to themselves and their country.

—GEORGE WASHINGTON, CHARGE TO THE NORTHERN
EXPEDITIONARY FORCE, SEPTEMBER 14, 1775

As George Washington's words illustrate, Americans were debating the treatment of enemy soldiers even before the founding of the United States. Washington, a general and the first president of the Republic, makes both a moral and a strategic argument against mistreatment. The issue of torture is legally settled in the United States. Domestically, torture is forbidden under the Eighth Amendment. Furthermore, the United States Criminal Code prohibits torture.[1] Internationally, torture is prohibited under the Universal Declaration of Human Rights, the Geneva Conventions, and the United Nations Convention Against Torture and Other Cruel, Inhuman or Degrading Treatment or Punishment, among others.

Opinion polls suggest that an overwhelming majority of Americans support basic political rights, such as freedom of expression and assembly. Even contentious rights, such as a minimum standard of living, receive support among the American public.[2] What many observers would seem to know anecdotally, however, is that when the country is under threat Americans are often willing to trade more security for fewer civil and political rights.[3] After the terrorist attacks of September 11, 2001, or the attack on Pearl Harbor on December 7, 1941, a majority of Americans supported policies they were unlikely to have supported during peace time. More recently, Colonel Tony Nadal, who served in Vietnam, stated succinctly, "So the enemy is my enemy, until he's my prisoner, then he's my responsibility." Part of this responsibility is how to treat people who we have detained.

Given the long history of humane treatment of the detained enemy, why do some people support torture, and under what conditions, whereas others do not support this practice? This is the central question motivating our book.

One easy answer is that people's views are fixed and unmovable. Similar to views on abortion or other controversial social policy issues, some suggest that our beliefs about torture are inflexible. The problem with this claim is that views on torture have fluctuated a great deal.[4] Within the United States, public support for torture varies across demographics,[5] time,[6] and how the question is worded.[7] Globally, public support for torture varies greatly as well. In a 2015 Pew Research Center survey, support for torture in one's own country ranged from roughly 15 percent for Argentines and Ukrainians to more than 70 percent for Lebanese and Ugandans. Here, too, support for torture in one's own country often differed from support for torture in the United States.[8] These polls demonstrate that—at least for some—support for torture is fluid and context dependent. For others, however, support for torture may be fixed.

Some have argued that a majority of Americans support the use of torture or enhanced interrogation.[9] A 2017 Pew Research Center study found that roughly half (48 percent) of Americans felt that torture was "acceptable under some circumstances" but that the other half (49 percent) oppose this action.[10] In the Pew study, a majority of men and Republicans supported the use of torture. In 2016, the International Red Cross global survey found that 46 percent of Americans supported the use of torture to extract information from an enemy combatant, and only 30 percent disagreed with its use.[11]

In 2005, after the Abu Ghraib scandal, only 38 percent of those polled supported torture if it could prevent a future terrorist attack.[12] By 2009, a Washington Post/ABC news poll found that support for torture in interrogations had risen to 48 percent. Political scientist Paul Gronke and colleagues aggregated polling on support for torture in the United States from July 2001 to July 2009.[13] They argue that a majority of Americans oppose the use of torture or enhanced interrogation and that majorities of Marines and Army soldiers also oppose the use of these techniques.

Political scientists Joan Blauwkamp, Charles Rowling, and William Pettit took issue with public polling on torture support after the 2014 Senate Torture Report was released.[14] In a survey-embedded experiment, they found that support for torture varies widely depending on how the question is framed. For example, a slim majority support torture when it is framed as a response to 9/11, whereas nearly two-thirds of participants oppose torture when it is framed as sleep deprivation.

So, do a majority of Americans support or oppose torture? Does it matter? We are, in some ways, going to sidestep these questions. What really matters for our purposes is this: whether support for torture among Americans is 20 percent or 60 percent, opinions *can* change. As the above examples show—depending on time period, how questions are asked, and a number of other factors—there is a great deal of variation in support for the use of torture in the United States. A skeptic might argue that this variation is just an artifact of the many ways the question has been asked over different surveys and different years. If this were accurate, then our attempts to shift opinion on this issue will not work.

Major events such as 9/11 seem to change people's beliefs and actions. In the aftermath of that major attack, support for torture in response likely rose. A few years later, photographs from Abu Ghraib prison in Iraq showed American servicemembers abusing prisoners in their custody. These photographs drew public outrage; Abu Ghraib likely shifted opinion away from the use of so-called torture-lite techniques once people could visualize the horrors involved. Aside from unexpected events, can media influence decisions? What about messages from elites? Especially elites that share similar ideological beliefs. When a Democratic politician suggests torture is an acceptable tactic to gather information from a terrorism suspect, does that influence a liberal person more than a conservative? Is support for torture conditional on the ethnicity of the person being subjected to the punishment? Or is it conditional on the person's religion?

For our study, we want to know whose views on torture are fixed and whose are fluid. For those with more fluid views on torture, when and why do they change? Is it related to personal factors? Major events? Context? And how much do opinions change?

It is important for academics to understand support for public policies to see why and when these policy decisions will be made. For policymakers, it is helpful to know why opinions on seemingly fixed issues change substantially in relatively short time periods.

In this book, we argue that people are inclined to support torture as a natural response to meet violence with more violence, but we propose that support for torture can be constrained and swayed in predictable ways. We expect that support for torture is influenced by whether or not it works, what type of torture is used, who is being tortured, how salient threats are, and one's own political views.

WHAT IS TORTURE?

Unlike defining terrorism,[15] more scholarly and public consensus can be found around defining torture, and differences in definitions between various governmental and nongovernmental bodies are minimal. We use the UN Convention Against Torture (UN-CAT) definition of torture as our guideline.

> Any act by which severe pain or suffering, whether physical or mental, is intentionally inflicted on a person for such purposes as obtaining from him or a third person information or a confession, punishing him for an act he or a third person has committed or is suspected of having committed, or intimidating or coercing him or a third person, or for any reason based on discrimination of any kind, when such pain or suffering is inflicted by or at the instigation of or with the consent or acquiescence of a public official or other person acting in an official capacity. It does not include pain or suffering arising only from, inherent in or incidental to lawful sanctions.[16]

There are several important pieces to highlight in this definition. First, to be torture, the pain involved can be physical or psychological. As political scientist Darius Rejali details,[17] much of the more recent torture perpetrated by democratic countries does not leave scars and is sometimes referred to as *torture lite*. We consider an act as torture if it inflicts pain through stress positions, exposure to extreme temperatures, exposure to extreme sounds, et cetera, as well as the more conventional forms that inflict extreme pain, such as punching or removing fingernails. Again, this pain can be physical or psychological. We examine variations in how people support an act based on this difference in the following chapters, but we do not rule out an action as torture if it is only psychological. Second, to be torture, the pain must be inflicted either by or with the consent or acquiescence of a *public official*. In short, we are not examining why serial killers torture their victims, nor are we examining the reasons rebel groups or nonstate actors use torture. This phenomenon is worthy of study, but we are interested in state-sanctioned or state-allowed personal integrity rights violations. These are actions that citizens in any political system, but especially in a democracy such as the United States, should be able to influence through support or opposition.

Finally, the UN-CAT defines *ill treatment* as "other acts of cruel, inhuman or degrading treatment or punishment, which do not amount to torture."[18] Torture and ill treatment are acts that both state and nonstate actors can perpetrate.[19] Throughout history, torture has occurred both inside and outside of state-sanctioned behavior (such as lynchings in the U.S. South by the Ku Klux Klan during the late nineteenth and early twentieth centuries).[20] However, for the purposes of this book, only torture by state actors is examined and discussed.

Some politicians and members of government in the United States attempted to redefine torture after the events of 9/11. Lawyers for the George W. Bush administration argued that actions in which military and intelligence officers have engaged do not meet the definition of torture or that laws against torture do not apply to detention centers overseas. The so-called Bybee memos attempted to redefine torture and argued that the use of *enhanced interrogation techniques* such as sleep deprivation and waterboarding[21] (which had long been considered torture) may not constitute torture and are permissible in the *war on terror*. U.S. Attorney General Alberto Gonzales argued that the Geneva Conventions did not apply to the war on terror because it was a new kind of war. Gonzales also stated that U.S. laws against torture did not apply to detention centers overseas that, in his view, were not subject to the due process protections of the U.S. Constitution.[22] In an August 1, 2002, memo written for the attorney general by Assistant Attorney General Jay Bybee, he argues that

> for an act to constitute torture . . . it must inflict pain that is difficult to endure. Physical pain amounting to torture must be equivalent in intensity to the pain accompanying serious physical injury, such as organ failure, impairment of bodily function, or even death.[23]

This is a fairly narrow definition of what constitutes torture, and it provided a great deal of flexibility for an administration wanting few restrictions on acceptable interrogation practices. President Bush claimed that allowing the CIA to use any method necessary in interrogations was essential to the war on terror.[24]

For our purposes, it is not important whether enhanced interrogation *is* or *is not* torture. More important for us is whether people *believe* there is a difference between the two terms. We piloted chapter 1's survey with both "torture" and "enhanced interrogation techniques" and found no difference in support when we use these terms interchangeably. In chapter 3, we specifically ask participants about their level of support for a variety of techniques and found little difference in support for techniques that might be more commonly associated with enhanced interrogation than with torture. In sum, respondents in our experiments largely consider torture and enhanced interrogation synonyms and we use them as such. In the actual experiments, we used the term *torture* but we would, based on the pilots and interviews, expect results to be identical if we used the term *enhanced interrogation*.

We hope what we mean by torture is clear when we use the term. Next, we discuss a brief history of the use of torture in the United States that focuses on the state-sanctioned use of torture.

A BRIEF AMERICAN HISTORY OF TORTURE

The United States has long thought of itself as exceptional. Sometimes that exceptionality is due to amazing innovation, progress, or concern for human rights. The United States has also been exceptionally violent. Some scholars credit the high levels of violence in the United States compared to other developed democracies to the culture of honor in the American South,[25] to the availability of guns in the United States,[26] to guns in the hands of the wrong kind of people,[27] and to many other factors.

The United States, to the storied time of the Founding Fathers, was brutal to native populations.[28] Mass killings, forced displacement, and torture were commonplace among colonial Americans and the native populations. Torture, in this context, was not about gathering information but was used as punishment or deterrence. One factor cited as slowing down the eventual westward expansion of the nascent United States was the brutality of the Comanche people,[29] who were known to torture, murder, and disfigure any male adversary and enslave any female. A nomadic people, they could not afford to take prisoners and benefited from having settlers fear them. Historian Wayne Lee argues that part of the reason for brutality among both the native populations and the European settlers was the difference in accepted norms of warfare across continents.[30] Lee claims that this uncertainty for colonists created a dichotomy between *brothers* (other Europeans) and *barbarians* (Native Americans), with the latter group receiving the most inhumane treatments.

In this milieu, what has been the history of state use of torture? The trans-Atlantic slave trade and the massive system of slavery in North America led to the brutal treatment of enslaved African people that ranged from whippings to killings. We could have, and many scholars have, written an entire volume detailing the violence associated with the system of slavery in the United States.[31] Historians John Hope Franklin and Loren Schweninger suggest that torture in this system was often used as punishment for resistance.[32] They detail a story of an enslaved woman who questioned the master's treatment of other enslaved people. As punishment, the master sold the enslaved woman's children to another plantation far away. Other examples of whipping, torture, and intense violence against enslaved people often coincided with insurrection or rumors of insurrection from enslaved individuals or groups. In this context, torture served as punishment or deterrence not information gathering, which it is often associated with in modern times.

The conclusion of the Civil War formally ended the system of slavery but did not end other means of violence toward both Native and African

Americans. In the early 1900s, the United States turned to consolidating state and global concerns and began to establish a global empire as the power of Great Britain and other European countries began to wane. One of the sites of U.S. imperialism was the Philippines, which attempted a revolution and independence from Spain and then from the United States around the turn of the century. Filipino resistance was often unconventional and employed guerrilla tactics. Similar to other nonconventional battles for independence, such as that of Algeria, counterinsurgents used harsh tactics. Torture as a tool for information gathering was detailed in the conflict. For example, testimony in subsequent congressional hearings about the conflict stated that the *water-cure*[33] was used "in order to secure information of the murder of Private O'Herne of Company I, who had been not only killed, but roasted and otherwise tortured before death ensued."[34]

In World War II, Americans were more often the subjects of torture. The Japanese government took tens of thousands of U.S. prisoners and subjected many to torture from water-curing to operations without anesthesia to other depraved experiments. The United States was usually more measured with enemy detainees, and incidents of torture were notable in their infrequency. Historian Philip Lundeberg detailed one instance in which American authorities tortured a German submarine crew to extract information about future missile attacks.[35] Japanese soldiers were told of potential harsh treatment of POWs by Allied forces, which may have prompted kamikaze attacks by Japanese pilots. In the aftermath of World War II, the United States and its allies sought to build global institutions to mitigate future violence, and the Geneva Conventions of 1949 were developed to establish humane treatment of adversaries during war. They do not necessarily outline treatment during times of peace. It has been a cornerstone of both codified and customary international law that there is an inherent difference between what is deemed acceptable in times of peace versus times of war,[36] and this became an important point of debate later in the U.S. Global War on Terrorism.

During the Cold War in the 1950s and 1960s, the CIA experimented with tools we would define as psychological torture, or *clean* torture.[37] As Rejali details, clean torture has been the preferred and most frequently used approach by developed democracies in the modern era such as France and the United States.[38] For example, MK-Ultra was an illegal

CIA mind control experiment used on U.S. and Canadian citizens in an attempt to alter the subject's brain state through drugs, sleep deprivation, and other tactics.

At the same time, American soldiers in Korea were exposed to debilitating torture at the hands of their communist captors. The U.S. Air Force's SERE (Survival, Evasion, Resistance, and Escape) program used information from these detainees to reverse engineer their interrogations to train future soldiers to endure and resist similar treatment.[39] With the Cold War winding down in the late 1980s, torture became less of an issue.

The optimism about global affairs in the 1990s was brought to a halt on September 11, 2001. Many Americans were blindsided by the most destructive terrorist attacks in the history of humanity. Policymakers and many other Americans were uncertain about how to handle a nonstate adversary that operated as a transnational network. U.S. policymakers and the military knew how to fight large conventional opponents but struggled with both the strategy and tactics of dealing with Al-Qaeda and the Taliban. The Bush administration declared a Global War on Terrorism that critics and supporters claimed had no boundaries and an indefinite time horizon. Utilizing this "war" paradigm, some politicians and members of the media in the United States told the public that punishment—including methods such as enhanced interrogation techniques—is necessary to control the behavior of terrorists, to gather actionable intelligence, and to protect our national security.[40]

In 2003, at the outset of the Iraq War, the Bush administration had an easy conventional military victory over the Iraqi regime, but that was followed by an unconventional insurgency that avoided conventional pitched battles.[41] When military casualties among the United States and its coalition partners began to mount, the Bush administration asked the military to ramp up intelligence collection efforts to thwarting insurgency. Meanwhile, suspected Al-Qaeda and Taliban members and sympathizers collected from Pakistan, Iraq, and Afghanistan were detained around the world—most notoriously at the U.S. military base in Guantanamo Bay, Cuba. News stories began to leak about rough treatment of Guantanamo detainees and detainees at Bagram Air Force base in Afghanistan. In late 2003, the Associated Press reported on detainee mistreatment at the Abu Ghraib detention facility in Iraq. These and other stories did not gain much public attention until April 2004, when an episode of *60 Minutes*[42] coupled with a *New Yorker* article[43] exposed pictures of the prisoner abuse, which spurred a large scandal over how the military was prosecuting the war.

Since 9/11, torture has been an increasing part of public discourse.[44] Amplified discussion has led to an uncertain conventional wisdom that more people in the United States support torture than is actually the case.[45] The lack of awareness of torture in the United States prior to 9/11 has led to an (incorrect) assumption that torture is now more prevalent worldwide. Although the public was largely unaware of it, torture has been widely practiced around the world and in the United States since World War II despite the conventions and treaties prohibiting it. Amnesty International found that 96 countries practiced or tolerated torture in 1996.[46] By 2000, 150 countries had used ill treatment and torture in the previous three years.[47] In 2010, Amnesty International reported that 111 countries used ill treatment and torture.[48] Contrary to the general assumption that torture is more commonplace today, Amnesty International's reports indicate that there was a significant reduction in the number of torture regimes and in the number of torture allegations in the decade after 2001. Nonetheless, many countries, including the United States, have continued to use torture despite signing treaties against this practice. As Rejali notes, the types of torture have varied as the United States and other democracies have increasingly used nonscarring physical and psychological techniques, but their use of torture has not declined.[49]

WHY TORTURE?

Torture violates most national and international laws, but it persists in the United States often in the name of counterterrorism. Countries use terrorism to justify the use of torture, or at least to turn a blind eye to torture.[50] Scholarly literature on the topic identifies two types of torture that are used in the name of counterterrorism: interrogational torture and deterrent torture. *Interrogational torture* aims to extract information and is seen as "preventative."[51] *Deterrent torture* aims to discourage similar acts of terrorism by raising the cost of engaging in this form of violence.[52]

Interrogational justifications have been the strongest motivation for torture throughout recent history. This presupposes that the individual being tortured possesses information and that this information will only be divulged via torture.[53] Political scientists Leonard Wantchekon and Andrew Healy state that torture can be a rational action for both the state and the individual torturer to extract information.[54] Building on classical criminology theory, the decision to commit a crime, including torture, is influenced by an evaluation of its rationality (costs/benefits) and utility (usefulness). Criminologists Derek Cornish and Ronald Clarke emphasize bounded rationality to explain law breaking, the idea that rationality is constricted by the information available, and that behavior is ultimately about utility.[55] In response to terrorism in which information is constricted, torture can be appealing as a way to gather intelligence that potentially prevents future attacks because it is quick and has a low financial cost.[56] It is unclear, however, whether torture is effective for gathering information (an issue we discuss in more depth later in the chapter).

According to classical deterrence theory, crime is a choice based on weighing costs and benefits, and increasing the costs is likely to deter the action. The idea of deterrence has been applied to a range of criminal offenses, including terrorism.[57] Philosopher Christopher Tindale discusses deterrent torture as a mechanism to raise the costs of terrorism to individuals in an attempt to dissuade future offenders.[58] Some argue that terrorists are rational actors,[59] and others argue that terrorists are more altruistic and are more concerned about their larger goal and less worried about their own physical punishment than a traditional criminal may be.[60]

Deterrence theory assumes that punishment deters offenders and that humans are rational and self-interested. The expected utility of perpetrating a terror attack is a function of the perceived probability of being punished, anticipated benefits, and severity of the penalty if caught. Because terrorists have collective goals, however, deterrence involves more than the impact on an individual. To date, deterrence research has largely focused on the cost-benefit analysis of crimes at the individual level as opposed to the group level.[61] In addition, deterrence sometimes fails not only to deter future acts of violence but leads to increased incidents of the very crime deterrence is trying to reduce.[62]

In the post-9/11 context, torture has often been justified as a quicker, more efficient approach to defeating the ticking time bomb scenario. In an interview with us on September 14, 2018, Tony Lagouranis, a former

Army interrogator who served in the Iraq War and was stationed at Abu Ghraib prison in 2004, argued that in

> post-9/11, you don't have a ticking time bomb scenario. But post-9/11, where we're under siege, we have to infiltrate these cells. . . . So if you have someone in custody who you believe has information, then your resource is his mind and your access to it . . . with torture you're going to scramble that information. It makes it very hard for him to recall or to describe things if he's sleep-deprived, or if he has hypothermia, or whatever other ways you're going to perturb his psyche, right? So you're destroying your own information base . . . that's a problem. . . . This is somebody that you want to continue to have a relationship with to continue to get information. . . . You want to cultivate this source. It's just really, really bad intelligence work to do this [torture].

As this former interrogator highlights, torture is a poor form of information and intelligence gathering. Rather, torture is likely to compromise memories, scramble cognitive function, and decrease the likelihood that a person would cooperate with interrogators in the future.

IS TORTURE EFFECTIVE?

The reasons states have used torture vary over time and context, and depending on what the goal of using torture might be, what it means for torture to be "effective" may change. If the purpose of torture is punishment, it can be quite effective at inflicting unbearable pain on an individual. Even clean torture, such as exposure to extreme temperature—one of the tools used on Abu Zabaydah, a high-value Al-Qaeda detainee held in a CIA so-called black site and then transferred to Guantanamo—can be extremely painful when an individual is subjected to it for long periods of time. Torture was effective at deterring enslaved people from revolting and for punishing them for attempting an insurrection. It is less clear whether torture is effective at deterring other behaviors, such as terrorist attacks. Political scientists James Igoe Walsh and James Piazza found evidence that respecting human rights reduces terrorist attacks at a cross-national level.[63] To be confident that torture or respect for human rights influences individual decisions to use terrorism requires a fairly high level of abstraction. For obvious ethical reasons, we do not have good controlled experiments that can shed light on this problem. In addition, studying deterrence is a difficult empirical task because the researcher needs evidence of the absence of a behavior. In criminological research, little evidence supports deterrence methods such as harsh penalties for crimes.[64] In part this could be due to the difficulty of gathering evidence at the heart of the issue—an individual's perception of the likelihood of sanctions.[65] That is, we need to gather perception-based data from individuals likely to be affected by deterrence. In our case, we would need individual surveys or interviews from potential terrorists on how likely torture would be to either dissuade or encourage future violence. It is fair to say that the aggregate evidence we do have casts doubt on the idea that torture is an effective deterrent.[66]

In the post-9/11 world, the use of torture has often been justified as an effective information gathering tool, but it is difficult both practically and ethically to design an experiment to assess the validity of this claim. However, interviews with former U.S. interrogators and other experts in this area cast doubt on the value of torture in gathering actionable intelligence. Former NCIS deputy assistant director for counterterrorism and commander of the USS Cole Task Force Mark Fallon noted in an interview with us on July 20, 2018, that "if you talk about high-value interrogations, or high-end counterterrorism interviews, which everyone highlights when you talk about this stuff, there are very few people who have actually generally been in the room with terrorists."

James Mitchell, one of the proponents and architects of the CIA enhanced interrogation program, would agree with Fallon but would claim the opposite about efficacy.[67] Fallon's statement highlights one of the key issues when discussing torture and its efficacy. Very few people have the firsthand knowledge of how counterterrorism interrogations actually operate. It is nearly impossible, for example, to know whether information gleaned from a particular source who was tortured could have been obtained in other ways, and if torture failed to elicit the desired outcome from a detainee, it is improbable that we could examine alternative methods that might be more effective. We cannot systematically test whether or not torture works as an information gathering tool, so we must rely on information from interrogation professionals who have real-world experience in this area. Many politicians and members of the media discuss torture, but how would they know about its efficacy? In our interviews with some of these interrogation professionals, we heard strong arguments against the general efficacy of torture for intelligence gathering purposes.

Retired FBI Special Agent Joe Navarro, an expert in nonverbal communication, told us that torture is ineffective because it creates stress for the subject of the interrogation. In our interview on September 18, 2018, Navarro said: "Anytime you create stress, it inhibits the ability to remember. The more stress you create, the less useful that person's memory is. So, we avoid anything that creates stress because you want facts . . . you don't torture, you don't call names, you don't harass."

In an interview with us on September 14, 2018, Tony Lagouranis argued against torture in the specific scenario most used to justify the practice—the ticking time bomb.

[The ticking time bomb scenario] seems like a compelling thing. Like, "Oh, if my child were in danger and I had somebody who had information, I'd do whatever it takes." Right? Throw morality out the window. And you could make a moral case for that. . . . But in terms of efficacy, it just doesn't work. Especially a ticking time bomb scenario . . . If you have a dedicated terrorist who's willing to do these horrible things, if it is a ticking time bomb scenario, he knows he just has to hold out for the 45 minutes or whatever it is until the bomb goes off. That makes him pretty resilient. He can give you false information or no information for 45 minutes, and he can hold out. So that scenario makes it very hard for harsh interrogation to work.

The closest thing we have to causal research in this area is on plea bargaining in criminal cases. Faced with harsh sentences, innocent people sometimes accept blame for crimes they did not commit. These false confessions can be motivated by a number of things—long interrogations, intensity of potential prison sentences—but they do sometimes occur.[68]

Researchers Melissa Russano, Christian Meissner, Fadia Narchet, and Saul Kassin designed a novel experiment that involved falsely accusing college students of cheating on a test administered by the researchers.[69]

The experimenters then threatened sanctions against the students. They randomly assigned each student to one of four interrogation approaches: a deal was offered to student; the offense was minimized; deal + minimization; and no tactic (control). They were able to elicit false confessions from many of the innocent subjects, although the rate varied with the interrogation approach used (6 percent for no tactic and 43 percent for deal + minimization). Other researchers have replicated and expanded this approach with similar results.[70]

We cannot be sure that torture never works at eliciting accurate confessions, but we are left with a great deal of doubt. Experts disagree about the efficacy of the approach, research in this domain is difficult both practically and ethically, and related criminological research is doubtful even though it is not directly about torture. Without a more definitive basket of empirical research, we cannot directly answer this question. That is a task for future research. We hope that future research on torture will do what we are doing here—address this issue using experimental or causal research.

THE INSTRUMENTAL, LEGAL, AND ETHICAL CASE AGAINST TORTURE

As social scientists, we hope to bring data and evidence to the discussion about torture and policies related to its use. With that said, many people advocate against the use of torture for practical, legal, and moral reasons that have little to do with the data and evidence we provide in this book. As Lagouranis's statement typifies, some people oppose torture for instrumental reasons. They argue, in Lagouranis's case from experience, that torture does not work. In short, even though they may or may not have qualms with poor treatment of detainees, they oppose torture because they see it as counterproductive to policy goals.

George Washington's statement at the beginning of the chapter is not about whether torture works or does not. Washington is concerned with the moral fabric of America. Washington is making a moral claim and arguing that torture is not what Americans do as a people or as a country. Finally, human rights lawyers, such as Kenneth Roth, have made the case regarding the legality of torture, especially in the context of the U.S.

Global War on Terrorism that began during the Bush administration.[71] They cite both domestic and international law that advocates against torture and for humane rules for treating enemy combatants when detained.

These reasons—instrumental, ethical, and moral—are all valid perspectives to support or oppose the use of torture. People may rely on one or more of these reasons to inform their initial beliefs about the practice. We encourage readers to develop their own perspective and to read beyond our book to gain a better understanding of each of these motivations.

WHY EXPERIMENTS

What Americans know about support for torture generally comes from public opinion surveys, moral philosophy, and punditry. Our approach is different. In the social sciences, we are in the midst of an experimental revolution.[72] We by no means started this revolution, but we would like this book to take part in it. These experiments can be done in a lab setting or in the real world (field experiments). Some field experiments[73] are novel and increase the real-world application of the experiment, but serious issues related to ethical challenges and the ability to generalize to other places and contexts have arisen. We think both kinds of experiments (lab and field) are incredibly useful and have done each.[74] In this book, we use lab experiments because it is challenging to create a field design that will pass ethical considerations dealing with torture. In one of the most famous experiments in social science, psychologist Stanley Milgram's series of studies on obedience to authority in the 1960s helped explain to the world how ordinary people could do unbelievable acts of violence when prompted by authority. This work was lauded for explaining some of the banal acts of violence that occurred in the mass killing of Jews during World War II. In *Eichmann in Jerusalem*,[75] Hannah Arendt reported that "the Israeli court psychiatrist who examined Eichmann found him a 'completely normal man, more normal, at any rate, than I am after examining him,' the implication being that the coexistence of normality and bottomless cruelty explodes our ordinary conceptions and present the true enigma of the trial."

In Milgram's experiments, subjects were asked to administer shocks (that they believed to be real) to another person to potentially fatal levels.

Many of the subjects were willing to take the shocks up to maximum levels due to the presence and commands of a man in a lab coat. Of course, no one was actually receiving the shocks; the cries from the other subject were prerecorded. Milgram's study raised important ethical questions about research, including when is deceiving subjects appropriate in scientific research.[76] In the videos from the experiments, participants were clearly distressed, nervously laughing, smoking, and uneasy. Milgram's experiments—along with more clearly unethical interventions (or lack thereof) such as the Tuskegee syphilis experiments or the Willowbrook State School experiments—helped usher in an era of more careful controls over social science research. Universities across the United States now have institutional review boards that oversee and guide researchers to protect human and animal subjects. Field experiments dealing with torture are extremely difficult to devise.[77] We used survey and lab experiments in an ethical manner to help us isolate the causal effects of some of the key drivers of support for torture within the United States.

Experiments serve as the main form of evidence in this book, but we also draw on original interviews with pundits[78] and experts and on public opinion polling where available. However, this is not a moral philosophy text and should not be read as such. We, of course, have views on the morality of torture, but our goal is to examine *why* people support torture and *how* views might change. Both sides of the moral debate may find evidence that supports an argument on their side. The strength of an experimental approach is the ability to assign causation to the levers that we pull. In short, we are more confident that the factors we manipulate influence people's decisions than the information you may gather from opinion polls and talking to experts or pundits alone. We absolutely cannot say what is the *right* thing to do. That is the job of moral philosophers like Michael Walzer.[79]

On some issues, such as abortion, for example, people tend to have fixed views. On other issues, such as marijuana legalization or marriage equality, people's views have become more fluid in recent decades. It is not clear where views on torture fall on the fixed to fluid scale. As Scott Edwards, senior advisor at Amnesty International, told us on August 1, 2018,

any given threat is going to catalyze changes in attitudes and behaviors. The extent to which we actually are able to capture measurements in changes and attitudes regarding torture . . . it's a difficult thing to measure in itself. . . . That said, attitudes . . . can be structural. Depending on how ingrained they are and how many generations they persist, you have processes. You have dynamics that have more to do with demographics than they have to do with world events or institutions. That'll perpetuate those attitudes and those opinions.

Data on public support for torture come from polls and surveys. These public opinion surveys generally ask about support for torture in abstract ways that do not account for other factors that may influence perceptions of the practice. For example, a 2005 Gallup poll asked people, "Would you be willing—or not willing—to have the US government torture suspected terrorists if they might know details about future terrorist attacks against the US?"[80] Similarly, a Pew poll from 2015 asked people if the "use of torture by our government could be justified against people suspected of terrorism to try to gain information about possible attacks in our country."[81] Public opinion questions like these have two main limitations: (1) they lead participants to believe that torture works, and (2) they do not account for other factors that also may influence support for torture.

Our overarching argument is that people support torture as a base response to being attacked. Simply put, you hurt (or may hurt) us, so we will hurt you. However, we propose that—at least for some—support for torture is not fixed. Rather, support for torture can be tempered in predictable ways. We test this argument using a series of experimental studies. In each study, people are randomly assigned to a condition (or treatment video or vignette). This approach is the gold standard for isolating and identifying the causal impact that each factor—efficacy, for example—has on support for torture.

The main focus of our argument rests on a series of experimental studies, but we also interviewed a number of former members of the intelligence community to better understand real-world counterterrorism interrogations and public perceptions of them. Using our networks and a targeted list of former interrogators or other members of the intelligence community, we reached out to potential interviewees to participate in this project. In total, we conducted ten semistructured interviews that lasted between thirty minutes and an hour. Each interview was conducted by one or both of this book's authors in the summer and fall of 2018 (see appendix for list of interviewees, their professional qualifications, and the dates of each interview). The general questions we asked all interviewees appear in the appendix, but we also allowed for interviewees to supplement our questions with information they deemed relevant. Throughout the book, we include quotes from these interviews to highlight our experimental findings, provide deeper insight into counterterrorism interrogations, or contextualize counterterrorism efforts more broadly.

ROADMAP FOR THE BOOK

In chapter 1, "Media and Perceptions of Torture," we begin with a discussion of media depictions of terrorism and counterterrorism practices. How do dramatic depictions of counterterrorism practices—specifically torture—influence public opinion and policy? We examine how framing the problem affects support for torture. In this chapter, we introduce and describe an experiment in which participants were randomly assigned to watch a dramatic depiction from TV's 24 showing torture as (1) effective, (2) ineffective, or (3) not present (control). Participants who saw torture as effective increased their stated support for it. Participants who saw torture, whether effective or ineffective, were more likely to sign a petition to Congress related to torture than those in the control group. We discuss the policy implications of our findings that showing dramatic depictions of torture influences opinion and action regarding torture, and we outline additional questions that our findings raise.

The nature of the threat from terrorism can have a significant impact on support for the use of torture. In chapter 2, "Fear, Death, and TV," we show how thoughts of dying and media depictions of various types of counterterrorism interrogations influence support for torture. In this chapter, we build on the experiment in chapter 1 by examining how a person's feelings of imminent death, or *mortality salience*, influence support for torture. Here we manipulate two factors: (1) mortality salience and (2) media depictions of counterterrorism interrogations. By priming on mortality salience, we can identify the extent to which threat drives support for torture. In addition, we build on the idea that exposure to violence generally pushes people toward more violent responses to threats to national security. We are able to identify whether our previous findings about media depictions are specific to torture or merely that seeing violence in general increases support for violent practices. We also examine whether media framing can increase support for *rapport-building interrogations*, the alternative to torture. In this chapter, we ask about support for interrogation practices and ask participants to allocate a portion of the federal national security budget to various areas as a way to disentangle belief from action. Results here support the findings from chapter 1 and demonstrate the different impacts media depictions of violence, generally, and counterterrorism interrogations, specifically, have on views of torture. We discuss the implications of these findings and suggest additional avenues for research on public support for torture.

Chapter 3, "Context Matters?," outlines the contextual factors that may influence perceptions of and support for torture. We review previous work on how identity, type of torture, and location affect opinions about torture. Using a mixed within-subjects and between-subjects experimental design, we presented participants with vignettes to examine how three factors influence views about torture by varying (1) the ethnicity of both the interrogator and the suspect, (2) whether the event took place domestically or internationally, and (3) whether the torture was psychological or physical. We collected data for this study a few months before the 2014 Senate Torture Report was released and then again immediately after its release. This provided a natural experiment on how salience affects perceptions of torture. Results show that proximity and type of tactic used influenced views on the interrogation, whereas social identity and issue salience largely did not influence views. We again discuss how our findings support the overarching argument of this book, the policy implications of these results, and what additional questions they raise.

The previous chapters demonstrate how malleable perceptions of torture can be—at least for some people. In chapter 4, "Elite Cues, Identity, and Efficacy," we explore ways to change support for torture. We use a relatively new kind of experiment to test how support is influenced by expert/elite cues. *Conjoint experiments* allow for comparison of multiple factors simultaneously and iteratively, meaning that a person can evaluate multiple scenarios without issue. Here we manipulate four key factors: (1) the expert (military interrogator, Supreme Court justice, academic researcher, Republican member of congress, Democratic member of congress, and a friend); (2) the suspect's nationality (U.S. citizen, similar country, nonsimilar country that is not associated with terrorism threats, and nonsimilar country that is associated with terrorism threats); (3) the suspect's goal (animal rights, anti-abortion, Antifa, neo-Nazi, armed militia, and ISIS); and (4) the expected outcome (actionable intelligence, mix of information, inaccurate intelligence). We found that support can be manipulated depending on who is endorsing the action, who the suspect is, and what the likely outcome will be. We also discuss both the academic and policy implications of the results.

Having demonstrated that aggregate support for torture is conditional on contextual factors and that framing can increase or decrease support for torture, in the conclusion, "Torture, Terrorism, and the Future," we explore what this means for public opinion and policy, and for American democracy more broadly. We outline how our results compare with previous research on perceptions of torture. Namely, we find that some people have fixed views on torture and that others have more fluid views. We then discuss how our findings can inform politicians and media. Last, we discuss the implications of our findings among the public. We address the areas of disconnect between the general public and the experts, how to rectify these differences, and why this matters to a broad audience. As Scott Edwards told us, "torture is . . . really the only prohibition on behavior that crosses human right's law, humanitarian law, that's universally a truth. That's universally a proscription. So, by definition, when you see torture you see a problem with [the] rule of law."

———— ∞ ————

In this book, we use experimental research to probe the bounds of public support for an unlawful practice. Specifically, in chapters 1, 2, and 3, we manipulate a number of factors—media depictions of counterterrorism interrogations, the suspect and perpetrator's identity, the type of harm done to the suspect, and the outcome of the interrogation—to see how contextual factors influence differences in public support for torture across American adults. In chapter 4, we examine how elite cues, suspect nationality and ideology, and interrogation outcome influence support for torture across incidents. Here we are able to see how an individual's support for torture varies based on contextual factors and also identify factors that have the strongest influence on support for torture across American adults. Throughout the book, we include quotes from the experts we interviewed to help contextualize the findings of our experimental studies based on their experiences. Unless otherwise indicated, all uncited quotations are from these interviews and will not appear in the notes.

1

MEDIA AND PERCEPTIONS OF TORTURE

People are conditioned, and have been for a long time, to believe that harsh interrogation is an effective method of gaining information. . . . I think that the impact of shows like 24 can't really be overstated.

—TONY LAGOURANIS, FORMER ARMY INTERROGATOR DURING THE IRAQ WAR

For most Americans, torture is an abstract action far removed from their daily lives. Prior to 9/11 and the subsequent photographs of U.S. service members engaging in torture against prisoners at Abu Ghraib prison in Iraq, it is doubtful that many people in the United States thought about torture much at all. What people do know of torture, however, largely comes from media. TV and movies often depict torture as a tool to effectively and efficiently extract information from the dramatized bad guy.

In the television show 24, which first aired less than two months after the 9/11 attacks—a time when fear and nationalism were stoked—the show's protagonist, Jack Bauer, regularly bent the rules and tortured suspects, often with tacit, or even explicit, support from high-ranking government officials, including the fictional president. In the first five seasons of 24 alone, torture was shown more than sixty times.[1] Bauer's tactics were depicted as unsavory but often effective at subverting terrorism and destruction of the United States and its people. From these images, people saw that torture worked. Elizabeth Grimm Arsenault, a former member of the intelligence community and now a professor at Georgetown University, expressed concern with media depictions of torture:

> By presenting torture as a quick, easy, and effective means to acquire intelligence, it not only stifles public debate around these practices but it obscures what the real work of counterterrorism and intelligence show (methodical, slow, obscure, and often conflicting).

Beyond 24, torture scenes in entertainment media jumped in the four years following 9/11,[2] and the majority of top grossing movies during the last decade—including almost half of children's movies—depict at least one torture scene.[3] For example, movies like *Zootopia* and *The Secret Life of Pets* depict coerced interrogations. Although these interrogations are mostly conducted by and against animated characters, children are primed from a young age to think that harsh interrogations are acceptable and often effective. In short, torture is increasingly depicted in media and is often shown to be an effective method for gathering actionable intelligence.

The situations that Bauer and other protagonists find themselves in are often outlandish. Many fans argue that 24 and similar media are entertainment only and have no bearing on real-world opinions or policies.[4] Indeed, even deceased former senator from Arizona John McCain, a staunch opponent of torture, was a self-proclaimed fan of 24 and had a cameo appearance in an episode.[5] The extent to which people believe that 24 or similar media provides any insight into counterterrorism is unclear. Research has long shown that media frames public perception on a host of issues.[6] Steven Kleinman, retired Air Force colonel and career military intelligence officer and interrogator, expanded on the impact media has on perceptions of torture:

> When you have an emotionally laden content, such as the television show 24, it's very difficult to differentiate . . . that the events observed were fictional rather than reality. What we know from research on the influence of narratives is that a fictional scenario can be deeply persuasive and shift opinions as long as that scenario is considered to be realistic.

In the years immediately following 9/11, terrorism was certainly a salient public concern. Because most Americans had no experience with interrogations, people received their information about counterterrorism from television shows like 24. With nothing to compare it against, it is reasonable to expect that media depictions provide accurate information.

Some military leaders also took Bauer's actions seriously. In 2007, Brigadier General Patrick Finnegan, along with former interrogators and human rights groups, traveled to Hollywood to meet with 24's producers. They attempted to convince the show's producers to remove torture and other illegal actions from the show for fear that they were having a negative impact on troops in Iraq and Afghanistan. Furthermore, Finnegan encouraged producers to show scenes in which torture is used but fails.[7] Tony Lagouranis attended these meetings and told us that "they sent me out to Hollywood to actually talk to the producers and writers of 24. . . . Their answer was great, actually, and I can't really fault them for it. . . . 'Well, we have a formula that we're making tons of money on and there's no way it's going to change.' "

Building on concerns from General Finnegan and other military interrogators, how do dramatic depictions of torture impact the American public? Finnegan's argument was that both military interrogators and the public, more broadly, are influenced not merely by torture's depiction on television but also by its depiction as an effective method for gathering information. Our broad argument for this book is that people support torture for retaliatory reasons—we respond to violence (or the threat of violence) with more violence. We agree with Finnegan's assumption that seeing torture work on television makes people more supportive of the practice. Finnegan urged television producers to show torture not working, but it is less clear that doing so would decrease support for the practice. Rather, merely showing torture at all—regardless of its efficacy—may push people to respond more harshly.

In this chapter, we are interested in how dramatic depictions of torture—either effective or ineffective—influence public views of the practice and the public's willingness to take action on those views. To preview, we find that media depictions of torture *do* influence people. As Finnegan and others expected, when people see torture work, they are more supportive of the practice and more likely to sign a petition about torture. Contrary to expectation, however, seeing torture fail does not reduce support for the practice but increases the public's willingness to sign a petition on the topic.

This chapter is organized as follows. First we review the current state of the literature on public perceptions of torture. Next, we discuss how media affects attitudes in general and how this pertains to views of law enforcement and torture more specifically. We then discuss our methodological approach, experiment, sample, and analyses. We conclude with a discussion of how our results pertain to policy and what is yet to be learned.

HOW CONTEXTUAL FACTORS IMPACT PUBLIC OPINION ON TORTURE

The 9/11 terrorist attacks in the United States generated opposing views on the best response to these events. These events also increased scholarly attention on torture, especially in the context of counterterrorism. In recent years, researchers have examined public perceptions of and support for torture.[8] Studies have also examined how identity shapes perceptions of torture;[9] what people think counts as torture;[10] why torture persists despite prohibitions on its use;[11] and how people perceive both torture's efficacy[12] and its legality.[13]

Scholars have examined how institutions can change public perceptions of and support for torture. Conventional wisdom suggests that democracy should have a palliative effect. But political scientist Darius Rejali found that democratic institutions often influence the type of torture used rather than constrain its use altogether.[14] In response to this, political scientists Courtenay Conrad, Daniel Hill, and Will Moore argue that institution type does matter.[15] They begin with the assumption that governments generally torture individuals who voters view as threatening. From this they demonstrate that institutions further removed from public opinion—a strong, independent judiciary, for example—are linked with lower levels of torture, whereas institutions that reflect public opinion—electoral contests, for example—are linked with greater levels of torture.

Experimental research has examined how situational factors impact support for torture. This growing body of research clearly demonstrates that perceptions regarding torture can be swayed by factors such as the suspect's identity, perceived guilt of the suspect, location, and the type of torture being used. Our study builds on this research by systematically examining factors that influence public support for torture. We argue that people support torture for retaliatory reasons when it is an ingrained response to being attacked. Early research on aggression suggested that there were natural/biological reasons for supporting and using violence.[16] Having any behavior, including violence and support for violence, be completely biologically determined is unsatisfying for many reasons. Most important, if human behavior is determined by biological/neurological reasons, it seems to take much of the choice out of decisions. More recently, scholars have not engaged in the so-called nature (biology) versus nurture (experience) debate. Instead, evolutionary psychological theories that take into account both human experience over generations as well as context and adaptation have gained prominence.[17] What is important for our study is that violence and support for violence can be viewed as an evolutionary adaptation to dealing with issues such as defending your group from attack against another group and attempting to build a reputation to deter rivals from future aggression. These processes can be seen at both a group and an individual level. Studies of honor culture in the American South, for example, often make related claims to explain why individuals in this region exhibit more violence than those in other regions of the United States.[18] Support for torture may be a group response rooted in a desire to defend one group (Americans) and to deter future rivals (terrorists). There are other reasons violence might be an evolutionary adaptation at the individual level, such as sexual fitness; however, we don't believe these other reasons for the adaptation are applicable in this context.

We argue that support for torture can be tempered in predicable ways. We expect that aggregate support for torture can be bolstered or constrained and that context will have an influence on some but not others. In short, some people should have more fixed views on torture, and their support will be nearly impossible to change. For others, however, we expect that support for torture will be more fluid and thus dependent on how the issue is framed.

Social identity theory suggests that people have more positive views of their in-group (people like them) and more negative views of out-groups (people different from themselves), which are often based on nationality, race, or religion.[19] Research shows that people are more supportive of torture when the suspect is a member of an out-group, including being of a different race,[20] political group,[21] or nationality.[22]

Beyond suspect identity, views on the suspect's guilt—or the extent to which torture might be deserved—affect support for the practice. People are more supportive of torture if they think the suspect is guilty.[23] Using perceived guilt as a proxy for torture justification is also mirrored in support for punishment more broadly.[24] Furthermore, framing the suspect as a "terrorist" increases support for torture.[25]

Location also impacts support for torture. Psychologists Kurt Gray and Daniel Wegner found that people were more supportive of torture when there was greater geographic distance between them and the suspect.[26] It may be that people use the "out of sight, out of mind" logic to justify torture when it is more of an abstract action happening far away as opposed to in one's own backyard. It is also possible that Western democracies hold our democratic institutions and their agents to a higher human rights standard and thus are less tolerant of using torture domestically.

Finally, people tend to support psychological torture more than they support physical torture.[27] Despite medical evidence to the contrary, people tend to think that physical torture causes more pain and has longer-lasting effects than psychological torture.[28]

To summarize, some people may have fixed views on torture, whereas others' views are fluid. Various contextual factors can, and often do, sway support for the practice, although people are largely unaware of their reasons for supporting torture. People who support torture often justify this view on utilitarian grounds; that is, the pain of a few is acceptable if it keeps the larger population safe.[29] Although research shows that people may abstractly support utilitarian torture policies, their actions often contradict their stated views in favor of retributive justifications for torture. People who are more supportive of torture are also more supportive of other physically punitive approaches such as spanking children[30] and the death penalty.[31] Simply put, torture is seen as an acceptable form of punishment.

For some, support for torture is malleable, which is a double-edged sword. If views on torture are easily swayed, this suggests that people can be convinced to oppose torture. However, research suggests that support for torture is often predicated on prejudice and a desire to harm or punish others. These ingrained responses can be difficult to overcome and may constrain our ability to shift views on torture.

POLITICAL RHETORIC, EXPERT OPINION, AND EVIDENCE ON THE (IN)EFFICACY OF TORTURE

Although most Americans lack direct experience with torture or interrogations, vigorous debate over appropriate counterterrorism practice has taken place in the public sphere, primarily among politicians and pundits. Some politicians, including President Trump, have advocated for torture as a necessary evil in the war on terror.[32] President Trump boldly pronounced in a July 27, 2016, press conference that "I am a person that believes in enhanced interrogation, yes. And, by the way, it works." Beyond politicians, pundits also share views in support of torture. As retired FBI Special Agent Joe Navarro told us,

> every talking head out there had an opinion on how to interview a terrorist but they had never sat across from one, they'd never smelled one, they'd never cried with one, they had never seen one much less interviewed one. . . . We're primarily affected by these images of somebody torturing somebody on TV where it always seems to magically work. We're ignorant of history. We're ignorant of how the brain works. Most people are ignorant of the fact that torture does not work. That all torture guarantees is pain and suffering not the truth.

Similarly, Tom Parker, a former MI5 officer who has written extensively about terrorism and counterterrorism, stated:

> When a former senior official . . . shows up on TV trading off his old title this doesn't necessarily mean the guy's actually got any investigative experience. . . . The guys who work in the trenches don't usually have time to play the kind of political games that take you to the top, they're too busy catching bad guys.

Although politicians and pundits sometimes assert that torture works, they largely have not conducted counterterrorism interrogations themselves, so how would they know? Those who do know, such as military interrogators, state that torture is an ineffective way to gather accurate and reliable information from a suspect.[33] Donald Canestraro, a former interrogator, claims that torture "didn't prevent any attacks and/or gain information that couldn't have been gained legally through rapport-based interrogations."[34] Furthermore, many argue that torture is strategically counterproductive, wastes resources, and may well destroy opportunities to gather accurate intelligence.[35] Former FBI interrogator Ali Soufan downgrades the importance of information gathered through torture from one of Osama bin Laden's trusted lieutenants: "There was no actionable intelligence gained from using enhanced interrogation techniques on Abu Zubaydah that wasn't, or couldn't have been, gained from regular tactics."[36] The 2014 Senate Torture Report corroborated these expert interrogator accounts, explicitly stating that CIA torture did not elicit actionable intelligence. In response to President Trump's 2017 comments in support of waterboarding, then Secretary of Defense James Mattis spoke out against torture in favor of rapport-building techniques.[37] Deceased former Senator John McCain, who was tortured during the Vietnam War, and human rights groups Amnesty International and Human Rights Watch are other vocal opponents of torture.

For a host of legal, ethical, and practical reasons, researchers cannot torture research participants to see what interrogation approach yields the most accurate information and the least false information. To proxy this, however, scholars have examined the efficacy of various legal interrogation methods. Law enforcement interrogations often use either an accusatorial or an inquisitorial style of questioning. In accusatorial interrogations, the suspect is barraged with questions in hopes that the suspect will implicate him- or herself in the crime. Inquisitorial interrogations, in contrast, focus on information gathering.

Experimental research shows that the accusatorial method increases both true and false confessions when compared with the inquisitorial method.[38] In addition, people are more likely to give false information when exposed to physical pain,[39] and confessions obtained under duress have long been regarded as unreliable and unconstitutional in the United States.[40] Some evidence indicates that using torture can increase the risk of terrorism—the violence that torture is purportedly used to prevent[41] — but this outcome is rarely communicated clearly to the public. Despite general expert consensus that torture does not yield accurate intelligence and may even be counterproductive, many in the public still think that it can or does work. Gallup and Pew polls worded in a way that presumes torture's efficacy find that approximately half of American adults support the use of torture in counterterrorism.

We have established that contextual factors influence support for torture. We can also be reasonably confident that torture in the real world is ineffective despite how it tends to be portrayed in entertainment media. Yet approximately half of the American public still support it.[42] Why is this? And what role do media depictions of torture's efficacy or inefficacy play?

MEDIA AND TORTURE

Media provides information about the world beyond our own experience and plays a critical role in the perceptions people form on issues.[43] Through media's lens, people develop opinions on many issues they do not personally experience in their daily lives. When people lack firsthand knowledge or personal experience—which certainly is the case for most Americans and torture—they rely more heavily on media to process and interpret the topic.[44] Media depictions can help create a perspective that is an inaccurate reflection of reality.[45] Issue framing can lead to a noticeable shift in opinion, at least on some topics and among some people. At the aggregate level, even subtle changes in framing can produce a shift in views on a topic.[46]

Television is a common form of media through which issues are framed. The average American adult spends an entire day each week watching television.[47] Turning first to news media, the adage "if it bleeds, it leads" suggests that coverage tends to focus on more negative, threatening, and bloody stories. Indeed, recent research shows that news media heavily cover terrorism and mass violence, and they often do so in stereotyped ways that highlight racial and cultural differences.[48] In part, these news media depictions may explain why the public dramatically overestimates the risk of negative events such as crime and terrorism.[49] But news media tend not to show negative reactions to terrorism including torture, suggesting that news may not play as key of a role in public views on torture.[50]

Although torture is rarely discussed in news media, it is prominently featured in entertainment media that rely on sensational, compelling, and attention-grabbing story lines to attract and hold viewers' interest. When asked about the influence of entertainment media on support for torture, Curt Goering, executive director of the Center for Victims of Torture, speculated on this influence while reiterating that media depictions of torture do not reflect the reality of this practice.

> I think 24, Homeland . . . [these kind of] programs shape public opinion. The story often was that it's the good guys doing the bad things, ultimately for a larger public good or purpose. And somehow therefore it's justified and acceptable. And the shows don't depict what actually happens in the world of torture—that so often, it's the wrong people who are picked up, interrogated, and tortured. That it isn't effective, it doesn't produce accurate or reliable information. The kinds of situations that are depicted in the most dramatic scenes are absent in the real world. The ticking bomb scenario, for example, is something that in the real world never happens.

Retired FBI Special Agent Joe Navarro echoed Goering's comments, "probably the biggest factor, at least I saw around the 2003 time frame, was the media, what you saw on television. For instance, the show 24, which tended to both glorify violence and simplify it, and that had a tremendous effect."

Supporting this perspective, in the nearly two decades since 9/11, television shows and movies on terrorism and counterterrorism have flourished (e.g., 24, Homeland, Quantico, Blindspot, Person of Interest, Sleeper Cell, Zero Dark Thirty). Torture scenes are present in many movies, including animated children's films, even when a terrorist threat is not imminent.[51] Navarro expounded on why such media may have proliferated after 9/11.

> We didn't need torture to talk to people and get information prior to 9/11, and we still don't. All of a sudden we have 9/11. . . . I think it made people feel good in the same way that, you know, every week you can watch the show Seal Team Six rescue somebody. I think it makes us feel good.

In response to a major terrorist attack, Navarro suggested that people find comfort in entertainment media that depict the "bad guys" being harmed while the "good guys" save innocent civilians. Intuitively, this makes sense. People want to feel safe from their rivals, and this type of aggressive response may deter future challenges.

Torture is generally depicted as an interrogation tactic necessary to yield information about a ticking time bomb or some other time-sensitive scenario in which information is required to stop a bad outcome. Psychologist Ronnie Janoff-Bulman notes that depictions like this "seem to fundamentally define how we think about and react to torture interrogations."[52] Scholars have argued that dramatic depictions of torture may impact perceptions about its efficacy and thus alter support for these tactics under the false assumption that they work, even if they are bad. When people see torture work on TV, they may assume that torture works in real life as well.[53] Beyond the public, Mark Fallon suggests that media may impact members of the armed forces as well. He told us: "In spite of the training, in spite of their teachings, in spite of what the academies are trying to instill in these young professionals, in their heart of hearts, they just seem to intuitively think that it'll work, and if they had to do it, they'd do it to save their country, not realizing that it actually jeopardizes our country."

Despite much speculation on the influence of media depictions of torture on public perceptions, there is little evidence to date.[54] However, many scholars have examined the influence of media on perceptions of law enforcement practices more broadly, which can inform our expectations here. In recent years, there has been a boom of pop-culture media—namely, television shows—focused on crime and reactions to crime. This growth of media attention has sparked a debate on the impact television and movies have on public perceptions of law enforcement and other topics related to criminal justice.[55] Some argue that crime dramas do not impact public opinion on law enforcement or their practices.[56] Numerous other studies, however, show that news and entertainment media depictions of police do impact public perception of law enforcement.[57] Entertainment media can prime people toward more authoritarian views.[58] In a recent article, Matthew Dolliver, Jennifer Kenney, Lesley Reid, and Ariane Prohaska found that watching crime-related violent media increases support for punitive criminal justice policies.[59] This effect is amplified when media consumption is also associated with fear of crime. In short, entertainment media influence views on crime and responses to it, often pushing people toward harsher policy stances.

Much of the general public has limited interaction with the criminal justice system. Thus perceptions of law enforcement and crime control are derived in part from media depictions.[60] Media depictions should have the strongest influence on people who have not had direct, personal contact with police.[61] Taken further, a drastically smaller subset of the American population has experience with and knowledge of interrogations, particularly in the context of counterterrorism. In short, very few people know what it is like to be a real-life Jack Bauer standing before a terrorism suspect to interrogate him or her. From this discussion, we expect that media depiction of torture's efficacy will impact support for the practice. Specifically, we expect that people will be more supportive of torture when it is depicted as effective. Conversely, people may be less supportive of torture when it is depicted as ineffective (as Finnegan proposed), or merely seeing violence could increase support for the practice. Finally, support for torture should remain unchanged when torture is not depicted at all.

LINKING PUBLIC OPINION AND POLICY

Beyond public perceptions of torture, we are interested in how media depictions ultimately impact policy. The *CNN effect* proposes that media impact public policy in the context of war. Simply put, how media frame an issue can shift opinion and lead to changes in foreign policy.[62] Scholars have debated and contextualized the extent of these impacts, which appear to be strongest when the policy is uncertain.[63] Public opinion polls, policy discussions, and legal arguments demonstrate that views on torture fall into this uncertain category.

Deliberately hurting someone is generally considered to be wrong, but there are contexts in which people think it is allowable.[64] For example, many states still allow the death penalty, and police are allowed to use force when needed. In both examples, pain is permissible because it is ostensibly a "necessary evil" to remove harm from the community. Similarly, some view torture as a "necessary evil" in counterterrorism.[65] As we have discussed, media like *24* perpetuate the ticking time bomb paradigm whereby torture is the only option to save a city from destruction at the hands of a terrorist who is in law enforcement custody. Although this trope is fictional and quite unlike real life, this persistent story line may impact public opinion on torture as well as its actual practice.[66]

There is little evidence that exposure to violent media inspires the average viewer to engage in criminal or aggressive behavior,[67] but violent media may impact support for aggression and policies that allow law enforcement to use aggressive tactics. There is a robust, ongoing debate about the influence of media violence on aggressive thoughts and actions. Some argue that exposure to violent media increases both short- and long-term aggressive thoughts.[68] Others argue that violent media can decrease aggression[69] or has no impact on aggression.[70] Individual-level factors may explain variance in these findings.[71] On balance, there is more debate than consensus at present.[72]

Regardless of the influence of violent media on action among the general public, legal scholars have used 24 to justify torture. For example, deceased former Supreme Court Justice Antonin Scalia used a story line from 24 in which Bauer saved Los Angeles from a nuclear attack as a justification for torture.[73] Scalia further suggested that a jury wouldn't convict Jack Bauer for his use of torture because it prevented an attack on the American public.[74] John Yoo, legal scholar and author of the so-called Torture Memos justifying U.S. interrogation policy in the early years post 9/11, cited 24 as support for torture.[75] Furthermore, Mark Fallon told us that

> policymakers . . . were influenced by television shows and movies and pop culture. Shows and movies seem to always depict that the good guy can resist torture and the good guy can always apply just the right amount of torture to absolutely the right person to get the exact information they need to save the day and be a hero. . . . Shows like 24 and others were highly influential in the periods after 9/11 because they were frequently cited by policymakers that I was talking to, trying to convince them that torture doesn't work.

Steven Kleinman echoed Fallon's sentiments. Kleinman recounted an interaction he had while testifying before the House Judiciary Committee subcommittee: "A representative challenged my position on torture by referring to events he has seen on the television show 24. I heard it later reported that this was a favorite show for Vice President Cheney and Supreme Court Justice Scalia." Kleinman continued:

> Among those who were shaping policy on interrogation and detention, it seemed there wasn't a senior official in the government, in the White House, or serving in Congress who had even seen a real-world interrogation. Their opinions—and therefore policies—were informed by fictional portrayals on televisions and in the movies that were, I must add, written

by people who likewise had never seen an actual interrogation. They were written for entertainment, not for national strategy. In these Hollywood-based scenes, torture is frequently portrayed as particularly effective and key to saving innocent lives. And the visceral reaction it arouses can be difficult to escape. Add to this the post-9/11 desire for revenge, the anger, and the fear, and we have a calculus for the creation of insidious choices.

Although anecdotal, Kleinman's experiences suggest that U.S. policymakers were influenced by 24 and dramatic depictions of torture. Policymakers and elites are more influenced by media than by the perspectives of experts such as Fallon and Kleinman.

If legal experts Scalia and Yoo and other policymakers to which Fallon and Kleinman refer are swayed by media depictions of torture, it is reasonable to expect that the general public is also influenced by media. Public opinion about torture can then indirectly impact policy. Furthermore, elite opinions—such as those held by Scalia and Yoo—also impact public opinion about terrorism and counterterrorism policy.[76] It is particularly concerning that media depictions may impact action, not just attitudes.

People often say one thing and do another.[77] Researchers are concerned with social desirability bias—the idea that people will say what they think others want them to say or what is more socially acceptable as opposed to what they actually think. When the topic is contentious, such as views on torture, social desirability bias may be more prevalent. To address this issue, researchers sometimes measure behaviors in addition to more traditional attitude questions. For example, in a study on public worry about election violence in Nigeria, researchers gave participants a postcard to mail in if they had concerns.[78] People should be more likely to give the socially acceptable response to an attitudinal question, but we expect they would be less likely to take action that contradicts their true beliefs.

METHODS

SAMPLE

To test these claims for how entertainment media can influence perceptions and actions on torture, we use experimental methods. In this chapter, we are interested in how entertainment media depictions of torture's efficacy impact both stated support for the practice and willingness to commit to that support vis-à-vis signing a petition to Congress. We can assess support for torture before and after viewing this content. It is a bit more difficult to then directly view how this influences behavior. One way to do this is to examine whether viewing content impacts political behavior. One of the basic behaviors in a democratic society is signing a petition or lobbying a congressperson.

Data for this chapter were collected between April 17 and June 18, 2014, from a sample of 150 students at American University. The study was open to undergraduate and graduate students across the university. Appendix table 2.A1 shows participant demographics for the sample discussed in this chapter.

Most social science laboratory experiments have sampled from student populations. The obvious concern with this approach is that university students are not representative of the larger population, which may limit researchers' ability to generalize their findings more broadly. Although this is a concern, the experimental approach does allow us to identify causal mechanisms from this convenience sample. Furthermore, one core component of the study is to measure not just attitudes but also behaviors. Here we use petition signing as a measure of behavioral commitment to a perspective about torture. Measuring behaviors like this is much more challenging, if not impossible, with online national samples.[79] (We discuss these challenges in detail in chapter 3.) For these reasons, we use a convenience sample of university students for the study in this chapter. The studies in the next three chapters come from national samples, which allow us to make more generalizable statements about our results.

EXPERIMENTAL DESIGN AND PROCEDURE

Experimental research's largest benefit is that we can identify and isolate cause and effect. In short, we can see the impact (or lack of impact) that a particular factor or set of factors has on people. Experimental research allows us to identify a causal relationship without interference from other factors. For example, in this chapter we are interested in the impact of entertainment media depictions of torture on perceptions of the practice. But in the real world, people can select what kind of shows they watch.

Some people like violent shows, crime dramas, and thrillers. Some people don't. If we just asked people what shows they watch and whether or not they support torture, we couldn't say that the shows cause those views. Perhaps people who watch violent shows are predisposed to (or at least desensitized to) violence. However, if we randomly assign people to watch different clips, we can isolate the impact each clip has on average perceptions.

We know that about 50 percent of the general population is male and about 50 percent is female. The benefit of random assignment is that each treatment group should also be about half male and half female, so we can be confident that gender is not influencing our results. Each treatment group should roughly approximate the larger sample on a host of demographic variables, whatever those variables may be. Thus each treatment group (meaning which torture clip they were assigned to watch) should have roughly the same proportion of people who like violent crime shows as those who don't like them. Each group should also contain about the same proportion of people who vary on other factors that could impact support for torture, for example, gender, age, political views, and military experience.

To date, most research that has looked at media and perceptions of crime and crime control have used surveys. These studies show correlational relationships, but we cannot know if media causes people's views on crime and crime control or if their views impact what media they decide to watch. Or something else entirely may impact this relationship. Our design in this chapter (and throughout the rest of the book) mitigates these concerns because we use a randomized controlled trial design to expose people to one treatment. This is a popular approach in the social sciences, which gained prominence from its use in medical studies.

To attract participants, we advertised a study on "current events" using email LISTSERVs and flyers hung up around campus. Potential participants then emailed us to sign up for a session. Each session lasted approximately forty-five minutes, and participants were given a $10 Amazon gift card for their time.

To mask the true purpose of our study, participants were first asked about their level of support for five potentially contentious current event topics from 2014: legalization of marijuana, legalization of same-sex marriage, teaching intelligent design/creationism in public schools, the Keystone Pipeline, and, of course, the use of torture in interrogations.[80] Participants rated their support for each of these five issues, which gives us our pretest measure of support for torture. Participants were then shown a series of five video clips from entertainment media, one related to each of these five policy areas.[81] Every participant saw the same four videos for the filler issues. Participants were randomly assigned to see one of three possible experimental videos that shows torture as either *effective, ineffective,* or *not depicted* (our control condition).[82] After watching the video clips, participants were again asked to rate their support for each of the five policy areas, which gives us our posttest measure of support for torture.[83]

We are interested both in what people say and what they are willing to actually do. To measure behavior, at the end of the study participants were given the option to sign petitions either in support or in opposition to each of the five policy issues discussed in the study. Each participant was presented with ten possible petitions to sign, one in support of and one in opposition to each issue. We made it clear that, should the person decide to sign any petitions, they would be sent to the chairman of the U.S. congressional committee related to that issue and that this would waive confidentiality for this portion of the study. We also made it clear that the petitions were optional and that there would be no incentive or penalty based on signing or nonparticipation in this portion of the study.[84] A full version of our survey is included in the appendix.

In summary, we expect that some people will be more likely than others to take action vis-à-vis signing a petition that aligns with their stated views on torture. We expect that seeing a clip of torture—regardless of its efficacy—will sway what people say, but we do not expect that people will be as likely to act on these views. People who see a clip in which there is no torture—meaning we have not manipulated their views—should be most likely to sign a petition. Participants in the treatment conditions either see torture work or see torture fail. We expect that seeing torture work will push people to be more supportive of it, although social desirability bias may play a role in reducing the desire to sign a petition in line with the posttest supportive view on torture. From this, we expect that people in the *ineffective* condition will be more likely to sign a petition than people in the *effective* condition.

DEPENDENT VARIABLES

There are two main outcomes of interest in this study: participants' stated views on torture and whether or not participants will commit to their stated view by signing a petition. We measure stated views on torture pretest and posttest using a 4-point Likert scale in which response options are an ordered ranking ranging from "completely disagree" to "completely agree" each time.[85] This allows us to compare two things. First, we can examine within-subject changes in support for torture after watching the video clips. Basically, does a person's level of support for torture change after seeing a torture clip, and if so, how? Second, we can compare average support for torture posttest across treatment conditions. In short, does the average level of support for torture in the group who saw it work differ from the average level of support for those who saw it fail or didn't see torture at all? We measure behavior commitment by whether or not a person is willing to sign a petition on torture. Because people were given the option to sign a petition either in support of or in opposition to torture, we can also compare factors that impact who is more likely to sign a petition supporting versus opposing torture.

MANIPULATED INDEPENDENT VARIABLES

We manipulated one variable in this study: how torture is depicted in the video clip. Participants were randomly assigned to one of three conditions: *torture effective*, *torture ineffective*, or *no torture* (control). For all three conditions, we use video clips from the TV show *24*. Each clip shows a ticking time bomb scenario in which the main character, Jack Bauer, has a suspect in his custody, there is an imminent threat, and he knows that the suspect has information about the potential attack.

For our two treatment conditions, we used the exact same clip but varied the ending to control for any situational factors that may impact how people view the interrogation. In this episode, Bauer has a suspect in custody and uses torture in an attempt to find the bomb's location. Bauer uses both psychological and physical torture against the suspect. First, Bauer has the suspect's two sons on a live-stream television. Bauer threatens to kill the children if the suspect doesn't divulge the bomb's location, and then he orders one of the children to be shot when the suspect refuses to give information.[86] Bauer also physically tortures the suspect by breaking his fingers when he won't divulge information. In the *effective* condition, the clip ends with the suspect finally giving Bauer information about the bomb's location in enough time for Bauer and his team to thwart the plot. For the *ineffective* condition, we stop the clip with the suspect yelling "I will never tell you" and remove the final scene in which the suspect divulges the bomb's location.

The control condition shows a clip of Bauer interrogating a different suspect about the location of a different bomb. In this clip, Bauer does not use torture against the suspect. It is also unclear whether or not the interrogation was successful at eliciting information about the imminent attack.

MEASURED INDEPENDENT VARIABLES

Public opinion polls routinely show that views on torture are conditioned by partisanship. Democrats or liberals tend to be less supportive of torture than Republicans or conservatives. Random assignment to treatment means that there should be a relatively equal proportion of any political ideology in each condition,[87] so there is no reason to think partisanship would impact support for torture between groups. However, general opinion polls do show that views on torture are correlated with partisanship, and roughly 70 percent of conservatives support torture whereas the same proportion of liberals oppose it.[88] Thus we do expect that partisanship will impact *which* petition a participant signs. Regardless of treatment condition, liberal participants should be more likely to sign a petition opposing torture and less likely to sign a petition supporting torture. The reverse should be true for conservative participants. To test this, we ask participants to rate their political ideology on a 5-point scale from very liberal to very conservative.

ANALYSES

STATED SUPPORT FOR TORTURE

We asked people about their level of support for torture twice: once before watching the video clips and once after. Responses were measured on a 4-point Likert scale ranging from "completely disagree" to "completely agree" each time.[89] Of the 146 participants who answered both the pretest and posttest questions measuring support for torture, 36 (24.66 percent) changed their level of support. This suggests that support for torture is fixed for some and fluid for others. From this, we can compare the average difference in support for torture pretest and posttest for each of the three conditions (torture effective, torture ineffective, and no torture). Figure 1.1 shows the percentage change in support for torture from pretest to posttest by condition.[90]

We expected that entertainment media depictions would impact support depending on whether or not torture was shown to be effective. We expected that, when torture works, people should support it more, and when it fails, people should support it less. To test this, we compare the pretest average level of support to the posttest average level of support for each of the three conditions using a t-test,[91] which is a method for comparing the average score of one group to the average score of another group to see if they are statistically different. Here we compare the average pretest level of support for torture (group 1) to the average posttest level of support for torture (group 2) by treatment condition. So, we conduct three t-tests, one for each condition. Beyond caring if there is a statistical

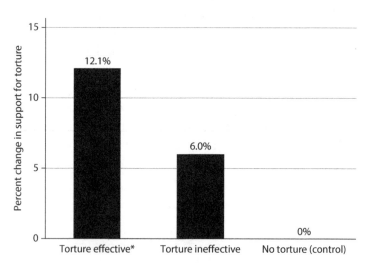

FIGURE 1.1 Percent change in support for torture from pretest to posttest

Note: * Indicates significant change.

difference in average support for torture from pretest to posttest in each treatment group, we also care how large or small the effect size of that treatment is on support for torture.

As we expected, people are more supportive of torture after watching a clip in which torture works to gather intelligence and stop a terrorist attack. The effect size indicated that our pop-culture clip has a small impact on support for torture. Our expectation (and Finnegan's) was that people would be less supportive of torture if they saw it fail. However, we did not find this. People who saw ineffective torture were slightly, but not statistically significantly, more supportive of torture after watching the video clip. Showing people that torture does not work does not reduce support. It is possible that showing people violence, regardless of the outcome, primes support for aggression. We come back to this notion and test it in chapter 2. Finally, as expected, there was no difference in pretest and posttest support for torture among participants in the control condition.[92]

ARE PARTICIPANTS WILLING TO TAKE ACTION?

As we mentioned previously, most research on public perceptions focuses on attitudes—what people say. However, we know that people often say and do different things. We are interested in what people will actually do, not just what they say about torture. To measure behaviors, we gave participants the option to sign petitions either in support of or in opposition to each of the five current event issues in our study.

The 150 participants decided whether or not to sign a petition on each of the five issues, creating a total of 750 possible actions to take (150 people × 5 issues). Participants signed a total of 460 petitions (61.33 percent).[93] We are only interested in whether or not people signed petitions about torture. Figure 1.2 shows the percentage of people in each condition who signed a petition that lined up with their stated views on torture after watching the video clips.[94]

Beyond signing any petition, we are also interested in which petition participants signed and how this may vary across conditions. We consider petition signing in general (0 = did not sign a petition on torture; 1 = signed a petition on torture). We also look at the three possible petition

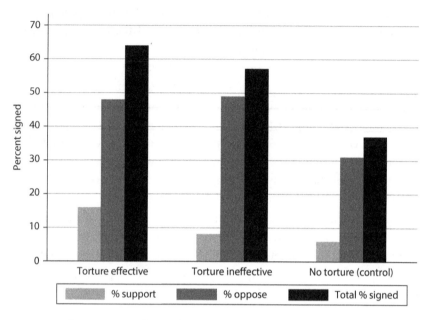

FIGURE 1.2 Petition signing by condition

options (0 = no petition signed; 1 = signed petition in opposition to torture; 2 = signed petition in support of torture).[95]

We expected that participants who did not see torture would be most likely to sign a petition because we did not prime them in a way that would impact their opinion. However, we found the opposite (see appendix table 1.A3). People who saw torture work were most likely to sign a petition, followed by people who saw it not work, and finally people who didn't see torture. The probability of signing any petition by condition is 69.3 percent for the effective condition, 64.8 percent for the ineffective condition, and only 37.5 percent for the control condition. Furthermore, this finding holds for petitions both in support of and in opposition to torture. Our findings here suggest that salience matters. When you see torture, regardless of whether or not it works, you're more likely to take action. We return to the impact of salience on opinions about torture in chapter 3.

Random assignment to treatment—a hallmark of experimental research—should ensure that various demographics, views, and other participant-level factors are evenly distributed across conditions. However, we know that views on torture are strongly divided on partisan lines, so we should expect some differences in petition signing as a function of a person's political views regardless of treatment received. To examine this, we look at how both treatment condition and a measure of political ideology (5-point scale ranging from 1 = very liberal to 5 = very conservative) influence petition signing.

Political ideology does not impact *if* a petition as signed. However, political views do impact *which* petition a person is willing to sign (see appendix table 1.A4). As expected, people who are more conservative were less likely to sign a petition in opposition to torture and more likely to sign a petition in support of it.

SUMMARY AND DISCUSSION OF THE FINDINGS

Our overarching argument in this book is that people support torture for retaliatory reasons; violent experiences lead to increased support for retaliatory violence. However, this support can be tempered in some cases. Results here show that aggregate support for torture is not fixed, and the issue's salience impacts willingness to take action about it. There are a few main takeaways from this chapter that support our argument and also lead to additional questions that we explore in the following chapters.

First, when people see torture work, they are more supportive of its practice. Building from our discussion of media's impact on how people perceive the world, particularly for unfamiliar topics, this finding is not surprising. Most Americans lack direct personal experience with torture, so media should have a stronger impact here. Media showing that torture is effective should lead people to believe that this is the case, which increases support for its use.

Second, and contrary to both Finnegan's expectation and ours, when people see torture not work, their support for it does not decrease. In fact, this group was slightly, although not significantly, more supportive of torture after seeing that it was ineffective. With a larger sample, this difference may be statistically significant. Because torture is often justified on the grounds that it's a necessary evil to prevent a terrorist attack, seeing it not work should decrease support for the practice. There are a few potential explanations for this finding. Perhaps merely priming people on torture makes them think it works. Our results may also support psychologists Kevin Carlsmith and Avani Sood's finding that people say they support torture for utilitarian reasons but that their actions suggest their motivations are punitive. It is also possible that merely seeing violence primes people to respond in a more aggressive manner. Psychology research has long shown that witnessing violence can lead an observer to mimic those actions.[96] These arguments also fit with an evolutionary psychological perspective on the roots of aggression. We return to these explanations and test them in chapter 2.

Third, and also contrary to our expectation, people who saw torture were more likely to sign a petition about it regardless of whether or not it worked. Across conditions, a little over half of the participants signed a petition on torture. This demonstrates that people do not always act on their beliefs. So what does increase action? We found that issue salience— meaning that the person has been primed to think about the topic— increases petition signing. It is interesting that people who saw torture work were more likely to sign *either* petition. In short, people were more likely to be galvanized to action when torture was made salient.

Fourth, some people have fixed views on torture, and others' views are more fluid. In this sample, about 25 percent of people changed their views on torture after our experimental manipulation in framing, and about 75 percent were unchanged. If people have either fixed or fluid views on torture, understanding people whose views are fluid can help explain the slight shifts in aggregate support for torture across time and context. We continue to investigate fixed versus fluid views on torture throughout the book.

WHY IT MATTERS

Finnegan feared that media depictions of torture may impact troops who are in a position to actually engage in this violence. Our results show that priming people with torture may suggest that it is effective, which influences support for the practice.

Dramatic depictions of torture may also have an unintended influence on practitioners—interrogators and elites who are in a position to create an environment in which torture is permitted. Speaking about the influence of media on counterterrorism practices specifically, Lagouranis told us:

> I saw with my own eyes that in our planning meetings, on talking about how to approach a particular detainee, people were taking ideas for harsh interrogations from television shows that we had just watched together. We had just watched a DVD, and they were formulating ideas on how to bring that sort of interrogation into the interrogation booth. . . . You can't come up with a clearer connection there.

From this, we see how media depictions of torture had a direct, nearly immediate impact on interrogations in real life. Lagouranis is correct; there is no link more clear than between media depictions of torture and torture in practice.

Our treatments were short, but media depictions of torture are numerous, and torture works in most of these scenes. Results from this chapter show that seeing torture work can impact both attitudes and actions. It is possible that prolonged exposure to dramatic depictions of torture harden views on the topic and desensitize viewers to this violence over time.[97] Echoing this concern, Mark Fallon told us this:

> They're glorifying torture, and I've spoken in the last year at Annapolis as well. And the concern is they get these cadets and midshipmen and try to train them to be officers in the United States Military and United States Naval Academies; and they're trying to undo what twenty, twenty-one years of conditioning has embedded in them that no matter what you're told, when the chips are down, you gotta do what you gotta do. And you gotta do these things to save lives.

Fallon, too, is concerned with the impact media depictions of torture have, not just on the general public but on those who may one day be in a position to actually conduct counterterrorism interrogations and—if they are so inclined—engage in torture.

The policy implications of our findings are troubling. Exposure to pop-culture media depictions of torture working makes people more supportive of the practice. One policy recommendation could be to limit media depictions of torture. Of course, constraining media would be an affront to our free and open society and its democratic values. Legal prohibitions on media depictions are out of the question, but are requests from the public, academics, or political leaders appropriate? In his meeting with the producers of 24, Finnegan is said to have asked that they "do a show where torture backfires . . . [because] the kids see it and say, 'If torture is wrong, what about 24'?" However, our findings show that depicting torture as ineffective may actually backfire. So what can be done to minimize the impact of media on public perceptions of torture?

For over a decade, the public has debated whether and when torture is acceptable in counterterrorism. Consensus among scholars and high-level military officials is that torture does not lead to accurate, actionable intelligence. In fact, torture may be counterproductive in at least three ways: (1) inaccurate information wastes time and resources; (2) suspects who have information may have divulged it under a different interrogation approach but will not after they are tortured (Abu Zubaydah, for example); and (3) when the United States uses torture, this can serve as a recruitment tool that leads to further violence (for example, Abu Ghraib).

Despite the general consensus among scholars and military leaders, approximately half of the American public think it is acceptable to torture terrorism suspects. Academic research and policy papers are inaccessible to much of the public, whereas television is not. As our results suggest, media depictions of torture help drive public support for the practice. To narrow the gap between expert and public opinion, we must change the narrative on torture. Finnegan's recommendation to show torture as ineffective for gathering information is simply not enough. We need more nuanced portrayals of torture. For example, Jack Bauer does not face psychological or physical struggles based on his actions. Real-life interrogators who have conducted or witnessed torture, however, do face long-lasting effects.[98] Media also do not show the damage that torture does to victims who face myriad long-term physical and psychological struggles.[99] Perhaps depicting torture's impact on both victims and perpetrators would be a step toward making the damage of this practice more real for the public. Humanizing torture can make it less abstract, which could erode public support for the practice.

Media depictions of torture rarely show its reality from an intelligence perspective. Media could depict torture as producing inaccurate information that wastes valuable time, as a tactic that once used leads to suspects no longer talking, or as a potential recruitment tool for the very groups whose violence we are trying to stop. These more accurate portrayals of torture could change minds.

WHAT'S NEXT

Our results from this chapter set the stage for our next experiments. As we see in this chapter, when torture is made salient, people are more willing to take action by signing a petition. For many Americans, torture is generally not a topic of consideration or discussion. In chapter 3, we explore how issue salience impacts views of and support for torture using a national sample.

Contrary to expectation, seeing torture as ineffective did not reduce support. We have identified three possible explanations for this finding, which we test in the next chapter. First, as is true with all experiments on subpopulations, these results may not generalize to the larger public. It is possible that this finding is an artifact of our university student sample. To explore this, we replicate the study from this chapter with a national sample of participants. Second, it is possible that merely priming people to see violence—regardless of its outcome—increases support for a violent response. To test this, we include a treatment that shows general violence rather than torture. Third, the clips that we used for treatments here were constrained by how torture is depicted in 24. We had to alter the effective clip to show torture as ineffective; however, this may not have been clear. To test this, we include another treatment group that is shown a scene at the end of the current ineffective clip in which a bomb is detonated to make it explicit that torture did not work.

2

FEAR, DEATH, AND TV

We need a TV show that shows very thoughtful interrogation and why the other ones don't work.

—COLONEL STEVEN KLEINMAN (RET.), FORMER SENIOR INTELLIGENCE OFFICER
WITH THIRTY YEARS OF OPERATIONAL AND LEADERSHIP EXPERIENCE IN
HUMAN INTELLIGENCE, SPECIAL OPERATIONS, AND COUNTERTERRORISM

In the nearly two decades since 9/11, terrorism and counterterrorism story lines are prevalent across entertainment media. The shows *24, Homeland, Quantico, Jack Ryan,* and many more explicitly focus on terrorism and counterterrorism. In addition, these are peripheral story lines in many other shows such as *Criminal Minds* and *Designated Survivor.* Across television and movies, counterterrorism interrogations often depict some level of force. As Tony Lagouranis told us:

> On television and movies . . . every [suspect] talks, ultimately. That's just something that everyone believes. Everyone's going to talk if you just torture them hard enough. Right? That's repeated on television shows over and over and over again, right? So, it's a hard thing to fight against. It happens to not be true, but people have been hearing that their whole lives.

In short, these media depictions of torture are predominant and influence public perceptions, as we discussed in chapter 1.

In discussing unrealistic media depictions of counterterrorism interrogations, Mark Fallon told us he asked screenwriters, "Why in these interrogations do you always make it so controversial? . . . I've never seen a television show where the bad guys don't say 'we're done here.' . . . No one's ever told me that 'we're done here' and walked out of the room. But on television shows I see that all the time." Fallon was one of the interrogators who accompanied Brigadier General Patrick Finnegan to Hollywood in 2007 in an attempt to convince producers of 24 and other entertainment media to stop showing torture as being effective. Beyond this concern, Fallon's quote highlights another disconnect between media depictions of counterterrorism interrogations and how these interrogations transpire in real life. In short, media sensationalize counterterrorism interrogations and depict events in ways that are wholly incongruent with real-life practice.

Sometimes media show interrogators using a different approach— rapport-building—to elicit information from a suspect. Rapport-building interrogations in which the interrogator builds trust with and shows respect toward the suspect are commonplace in the real world. To be effective, this approach requires more skill, time, and cultural awareness on the part of the interrogator. Related approaches, such as the Scharff technique, are shown to be more effective than the direct approach of interrogations.[1] Many law enforcement agencies favor the rapport-building approach because it tends to generate more information. Research shows that social strategies and rapport-building can increase both the disclosure of information and the speed with which that occurs.[2]

Media depictions of interrogations, especially in counterterrorism, don't often show the rapport-building approach. Rapport-building takes time and may not be as dramatically satisfying for the viewer; however, entertainment media sometimes do show rapport-building. For example, the recent miniseries Looming Tower—based on Lawrence Wright's award-winning book of the same name—depicts the real events leading up to 9/11. Here the audience sees FBI agents (including Ali Soufan) use rapport-building when interrogating suspected members of Al-Qaeda, and it is shown to work—as it did in the actual event.

As we saw in chapter 1, when shown media depictions of torture, this can influence both people's attitudes toward the practice and their willingness to act in support of torture. If we can push people to support torture in this way, can we pull people away from supporting torture? When we show people dramatic depictions of counterterrorism interrogations that involve rapport-building, will this reduce support for harsh approaches?

In chapter 1, we discuss the results of a study in which college students were randomly assigned to watch one of three videos that showed either torture as effective, torture as ineffective, or a control condition with no torture. As a reminder, we found that people who saw torture work were subsequently more supportive of it. Contrary to expectation, however, seeing torture fail didn't reduce support for the practice. In fact, support was slightly, although not statistically significantly, higher on average. In addition, people who saw torture—regardless of its efficacy—were more likely to sign a petition on torture. In short, salience impacts actions, which we discuss in chapter 3.

A few questions arise from the original study in chapter 1. First, it is possible that our results are not about torture specifically but about violence generally. Perhaps priming people with violence in general will make them more supportive of violent responses, including torture. Second, if seeing a dramatic depiction of torture impacts both attitudes and actions, how do people respond to interrogations using rapport-building approaches? Does it matter whether rapport-building is effective or not? Third, how does threat perception impact responses? Do people shift the range of acceptable responses based on the saliency of threat and their own mortality?

In this chapter, we are interested in how both dramatic depictions of interrogations and threatening environments impact public views of torture. We recognize the limitations of doing these experiments with a sample of college students. With this in mind, can our findings from chapter 1 be replicated with a national sample? With a nationally representative sample a few years later, do we see a similar breakdown of people who have fixed versus fluid views on torture? We discuss how dramatic depictions of both torture and rapport-building in counterterrorism interrogations impact support for torture. We discuss and test whether results from chapter 1 may be a function of violence generally rather than torture specifically. We also discuss how mortality salience—thoughts of one's own death, which creates a threatening environment—impacts support for torture. After outlining our argument, we discuss our methodological approach, the experimental design, the sample, and the analyses. We conclude by discussing how our results relate to police and other forms of interrogation and outline remaining questions.

Our overarching argument for this book is that support for torture is explained through a base need to meet violence with violence, but that this impulse can be curtailed in some cases or contexts. In this chapter, we test our argument by manipulating both the threat environment and how entertainment media depict a counterterrorism interrogation. We expect that people in aggregate will increase their support for torture when they see torture work or violence generally. Conversely, we expect that people will be less supportive of torture when they see an alternative interrogation approach, that of rapport-building. Regardless of the video clip shown, we suggest that people should be more supportive of harsh policies when they are primed to think about a threatening environment in which their own mortality is salient. Furthermore, we expect that some people will have fixed views on torture and not be influenced by our manipulations, whereas others with more fluid views will shift their opinions with framing.

Results from this chapter, however, do not support a number of our expectations. We do replicate results from chapter 1, specifically that seeing torture work increases support and seeing torture either fail or not occur has no impact on support. Contrary to our expectations, however, seeing general violence decreases support for torture, whereas seeing rapport-building, regardless of its efficacy, increases support for torture. Furthermore, priming people to think about a threatening environment does not have a clear impact on support for torture across video treatments. At the end of the chapter, we discuss why we think these results are contrary to our expectations and foreshadow a discussion in the concluding chapter of the book.

The experiment in this chapter builds on and expands from chapter 1. Much of the literature focused on media influence is the same, and we provide a short review of that literature here. We then discuss how dramatic depictions of both rapport-building and general violence may influence support for torture. Following that, we discuss how responses to interrogation approaches may be conditioned by the level of threat a person is feeling. Next we outline our sample and methodological approach, and we discuss our results and how these findings tie into our main argument in this book and the findings from other chapters. Finally, we outline additional questions raised in this chapter.

MEDIA AND PERCEPTIONS OF INTERROGATIONS

In chapter 1, we provide a detailed discussion of media's influence on perceptions and public opinion broadly and how this relates to law enforcement and torture specifically. As a quick refresher, media frames influence what people think about and how they think about those topics.[3] When people lack direct personal experience with a topic—as is the case for most Americans and torture—they rely more heavily on media to form opinions.[4]

In the context of law enforcement more broadly, research has clearly shown that media depictions influence perceptions of police.[5] Legal experts Justice Scalia and John Yoo used 24 anecdotally in an attempt to justify torture. Tony Lagouranis, the former Army interrogator we spoke with, described how soldiers in Iraq watched 24 and then suggested adopting Jack Bauer's methods to use on prisoners.

In chapter 1, we systematically evaluated how media depictions of torture influence attitudes and actions toward the practice. We randomly assigned participants to watch one of three videos showing torture as effective, torture as ineffective, or a control clip in which torture was not used. Our results from chapter 1 show that dramatic depictions of torture influence public support for torture as well as their willingness to act on torture policy. Specifically, people are more supportive of torture when they see it work. Furthermore, people who see torture, regardless of whether or not it works, are more likely to take action by signing a petition on the subject.

DEPICTIONS OF ANOTHER INTERROGATION
APPROACH: RAPPORT-BUILDING

In the real world, rapport-building approaches to interrogations involve the interrogator building trust and mutual respect with the suspect. This process can take hours, days, or even weeks. By building rapport with the suspect, the interrogator hopes to increase the suspect's future willingness to cooperate.[6] Furthermore, rapport-building takes skill on the part of the interrogator. Many people possess the sheer ability to engage in harsh practices, as we saw from psychologist Stanley Milgram's famous shock experiments[7] and psychologist Philip Zimbardo's Stanford Prison study.[8] Rapport-building with a suspect, however, takes more skill and practice.

When counterterrorism interrogations are depicted in television and movies, they often involve torture. Despite military leaders trying to convince screenwriters to eschew this trope, it has persisted. Mark Fallon, author of *Unjustifiable Means: The Inside Story of How the CIA, Pentagon and U.S. Government Conspired to Torture*, and who has published op-eds in newspapers and magazines, told us that this is "just journalistic laziness."

> It's much easier to create that kind of physical drama, slamming your hand on a table, than it is to create the emotional drama that occurs in an actual real-world interrogation or interview, where it's this kind of mental chess match. . . . fictional authors have told me it's much more work to replicate that type of emotional drama than it would be with a physical type drama. So they take a shortcut, and they don't put as much attention into it.

Occasionally entertainment media do show counterterrorism interrogations that use alternative methods such as rapport-building. The shows *Looming Tower* and *Criminal Minds* have depicted rapport-building interrogations in response to terrorism threats. More broadly, police procedural dramas such as *Law and Order* routinely depict rapport-building with everyday criminals. How do these depictions influence public perceptions of and support for various interrogation practices?

GENERAL DEPICTIONS OF VIOLENCE

When presenting the results of our research to public and scholarly audiences, one of the most frequent comments about our findings in chapter 1 has been, "well, isn't this just priming people on violence?" There is a debate over the influence media violence has on both support for and engagement in criminal behavior and in violence more broadly. Some suggest that media violence causes people to be more violent, whereas others suggest that media violence provides an outlet that constrains real-life aggression.[9] Although this debate has yet to be settled, considerable evidence suggests that media influence perceptions not just of crime and criminal justice but also of acceptance of punitive policies more broadly.[10]

EMOTIONS, THREATS, AND RESPONSE TO TERRORISM

When discussing American support for torture, Mark Fallon stated that "fear is an incredible motivator." A growing body of political psychology research examines how emotions such as fear, anger, and anxiety influence perceptions of and responses to crime generally and terrorism specifically. Scholars Matthew Dolliver, Jennifer Kenney, Lesley Reid, and Ariane Prohaska found that watching crime-related violent media increases support for punitive criminal justice policies and that this effect is amplified for people who are more fearful of crime.[11] Using a field experimental design after 9/11, psychologist Jennifer Lerner and colleagues found that fear increased estimates of terrorism risk, whereas increased anger reduced perceptions of risk.[12] Another emotion, anxiety, also influences views on terrorism and terrorism threats.[13] When people are anxious, they make more stereotyped associations between terrorism and people of Middle Eastern descent.[14]

Beyond emotional states, threat perceptions also influence views of terrorism. When asked about threat salience and perceptions of terrorism, Leslie Parsons, commander of the Criminal Investigations Division of the Washington, D.C. Metropolitan Police Department, told us, "your answer would probably coordinate with current events too. You ask people that on September 12, 2001, you'd probably get a much different answer than you would today." Similarly, Tricia Bacon, former member of the intelligence community and current professor at American University, told us that post-9/11 an urgent need to "prevent another major attack was so strong that it justified doing things that hadn't been done in the past. . . . if there was any utility to using harsher tactics, then it was fine to do it because there was such an intense fear of any other attack and such an intense sort of feeling against those actors."

Research supports Bacon's and Parsons's hunch. When people feel greater threat, they are more likely to use stereotypes to make decisions about how to respond.[15] Terrorism salience, in particular, increases hostility toward minorities.[16] Stereotyped views of terrorism suggest that the threat comes from Muslims or Arabs—characters who often portray terrorists in media.[17] Furthermore, people who think terrorists are rational and could be persuaded by reason are less supportive of harsh responses.[18] But media depictions of terrorists are often stereotyped and do not suggest rationality by the perpetrators. Supporting this, political scientist Shana Gadarian found that people who both felt threatened and watched more television had more hawkish views on counterterrorism.[19] Conversely, reducing threats can decrease support for policies intended to combat terrorism.[20] In short, emotional states can influence perceptions of threats that can, in turn, influence perceptions of terrorism and support for counterterrorism policies.

Nearly half of Americans are afraid that they or someone in their family will die in a terrorist attack, and support for torture is often justified on the ground that it would save lives. We explore the impact a particular type of threat—mortality—has on support for torture. Priming people to think about their own mortality is associated with many possible correlates of support for torture. Specifically, mortality salience increases nationalistic worldviews,[21] fosters a stronger preference for in-groups and disapproval of out-groups,[22] increases intolerance of those who threaten one's worldview,[23] pushes people to support more hawkish counterterrorism policies,[24] and increases support for harsh criminal justice policies.[25]

We expect that mortality salience will strengthen support for harsh responses such as torture. We do not have public opinion polls on torture immediately before and after 9/11; however, it is reasonable to expect that support for torture would have increased dramatically. As Curt Goering, executive director of the Center for Victims of Torture, told us:

> people felt under threat. There was an unknown. There was a desire for revenge, and there was an anger and all that. Fear played into it. The whole combination of emotions, I think, led to an acceptance of torture, and how it was discussed by officials, of course, was that it's not exactly torture; we're going to go to the dark side, but it's gonna be limited, it's gonna be contained. Even the debate on being waterboarded. Dozens and dozens of times. The graphic sort of detail of what that is and what that involved—we weren't confronted with that.

Our overarching argument is that support for torture is a response to violence with more violence but that this support can be tempered in predictable ways. In this chapter, we expect that people will respond more aggressively when they are primed to a threatening environment where primal violent responses are more likely. We expect to replicate our findings from chapter 1. Specifically, people should be more supportive of torture when they see it work, and their support shouldn't change when they see it either fail or not be depicted. We also expect that seeing violence not related to terrorism or torture will prompt people to respond in a primal way and increase support for torture. Furthermore, because depictions of torture and violence should increase support for the practice, we expect that showing participants the opposite—rapport-building—should decrease support for torture. Finally, as we saw in chapter 1, we expect that about a quarter of the participants will have fluid views of torture that shift with framing, whereas the other three-quarters will have fixed, immovable views.

METHODS

SAMPLE

In this chapter, we are interested in how mortality salience and media depictions of interrogations impact support for torture. We collected data from a sample of adults in the United States that approximates the national population. The sample was provided by YouGov, an online survey company that academic researchers often partner with to provide a panel of American adults to participate in research.[26] YouGov has a panel of potential participants that they invite to participate in studies via email. People who complete the survey are compensated with points that can be redeemed for gift cards through YouGov.

EXPERIMENTAL DESIGN AND PROCEDURE

Similar to chapter 1, we recruited participants to a study on "current event issues." Participation took place in a single online session. Participants who agreed to complete this survey were first asked a series of questions measuring how much they care about a handful of current event issues, included but not limited to the issues discussed later in the survey. Participants then answered blocks of questions about their news consumption, TV viewing, and support for three current event issues: legalization of marijuana, teaching intelligent design/creationism in public schools, and the use of torture in interrogations. Similar to the design in chapter 1, we included two filler issues to mask the true purpose of our study.

Next, we randomly assigned participants either to be primed on mortality or not primed, and we controlled the prime through random assignment. To accomplish this, we used the "mortality salience" prime that has been employed in a cross-disciplinary body of literature.[27] Here participants are randomly assigned to answer two open-ended questions either on their own death (mortality prime) or on dental pain (no mortality prime).[28]

After that, we randomly assigned participants to one of seven treatment videos. This creates fourteen possible conditions (2 mortality salience options × 7 video options), with each participant randomly assigned to only one of the fourteen combinations. Every participant saw the same clips for the two filler issues (legalization of marijuana and teaching creationism in public schools). After the treatment, we again ask participants about their level of support for the three current event issues (two filler issues and the use of torture in interrogations).

We are, of course, interested not just in what people say but what they will do. As we show in chapter 3, however, participants in online surveys are reluctant to indicate that they would sign a petition. For this study, we ask participants to imagine that they are in charge of allocating the federal budget on national security to five areas. The five areas included a soft response (relationship-building between law enforcement and the public) and a harsh response (research on enhanced interrogation and torture). We then compared budget allocations across conditions to see whether watching violence makes people more likely to fund aggressive policies.

DEPENDENT VARIABLES

We are interested in two things: what people say about torture and how they behave. Our first outcome of interest is stated support for torture posttreatment. We measure support for torture both pretreatment and posttreatment using a 4-point Likert scale in which response options are ordered from "completely disagree" to "completely agree" each time. This allows us to compare the average level of support for torture in each condition before and after participants watch one of the seven treatment videos.

For participants who changed their stated support from pretest to posttest, we also included questions to probe *why* they changed their mind. A person less supportive of torture posttest can select any of the following options or write in his or her own response:

> Torture is harmful to the person.
> Torture is illegal.
> Torture is ineffective.
> I am not sure.

In contrast, a person more supportive of torture posttest can select any of the following options or write in his or her own response:

> Torture needs to be more harmful to be useful.
> Torture is acceptable to prevent an attack.
> Torture is effective.
> I am not sure.

We are also interested in actions, and we presented participants with a scenario in which they are in charge of allocating the federal budget on national security (as well as public health and education, the filler issues). There are five areas under national security:

> Building relationship between law enforcement and the public.
> Research on enhanced interrogation and torture techniques.
> Building the nuclear arsenal.
> Military.
> Cybersecurity capabilities.

We can then compare budget allocations across treatment conditions.

MANIPULATED INDEPENDENT VARIABLES

There are two manipulations in this study: (1) whether or not participants are primed to think about their own mortality to create a threat environment, and (2) what video condition they watch. Participants are randomly assigned to answer a few questions either about their own death or about dental pain. The mortality salience prime was adopted from other studies that have also sought to instantiate thoughts of death.[29] This creates two conditions for mortality salience.

Participants were randomly assigned to see one of seven possible treatment videos. The video clips vary on the tactic used and the efficacy of the interrogation. We also include a control video in which an interrogation does not use torture or rapport-building, and the outcome is unclear. Finally, results from chapter 1 suggest that merely priming people on violence rather than on torture specifically makes people more supportive of aggression. To examine this further, we include a video clip that shows violence that is unrelated to an interrogation. Table 2.1 shows details on each treatment clip (see appendix for more details). In addition to the treatment video, every participant saw the same clips for the two filler issues.

TABLE 2.1 Treatment Video Details

Treatment	Source	Episode	Clip Length (minutes)
Torture, result effective	24	Season 2, episode 12	3:46
Torture, result ineffective	24	Season 2, episode 12	2:42
Torture, result ambiguous	24	Season 2, episode 12	2:39
No torture or rapport, result ambiguous	24	Season 2, episode 6	2:21
Rapport-building, result effective	*Criminal Minds*	Season 2, episode 10	4:07
Rapport-building, result ineffective	*Criminal Minds*	Season 2, episode 10	4:05
General violence	*Fighting*	Movie	1:48

In part, we replicated the study in chapter 1 with a national sample. Our torture treatments used the same torture scene that was shown to participants in the previous study. In this scene, Jack Bauer has a suspect in his custody and uses both psychological and physical torture to discover a bomb's location. In the effective condition, the clip ends with the suspect telling Bauer where to locate the bomb with enough time for Bauer's team to stop the planned attack on Los Angeles.

One concern from our design in chapter 1 is that our ineffective video did not make it clear that torture didn't work. To address this, we used the same clip from chapter 1 to create two conditions: *torture ambiguous* (same as ineffective in chapter 1) and *torture ineffective*. In what is now called the torture ambiguous condition, the clip ends with Bauer demanding the bomb's location and the suspect yelling, "I will never tell you." In our new torture ineffective condition, we add a scene that shows a bomb detonating on a bridge, causing massive damage. This makes it clear that torture did not yield information to prevent the attack.

We use the exact same *no torture* clip in both chapter 1 and this chapter. The no torture or control clip comes from a different episode of *24*. In this clip, Bauer interrogates a different suspect about the location of a different bomb. Bauer does not use torture, and it is unclear whether the interrogation yields any information that would prevent an imminent attack.

Our initial study in chapter 1 raised a few questions that we test here. First, one concern is that our videos were simply priming people to respond to violence in general rather than to torture specifically. To address this, we included a clip on *general violence*. In this clip, two male characters are engaged in a bare knuckles fight surrounded by a crowd. This fight is unrelated to terrorism or torture.

Second, if media depictions of torture can push people to support the practice, can showing people an alternative—rapport-building counter-terrorism interrogations—reduce support for torture? To test this, we included two additional conditions: *rapport-building effective* and *rapport-building ineffective*. The rapport-building clips both come from an episode of *Criminal Minds* in which the team travels to Guantanamo Bay Prison to interview a member of a group that is planning an imminent attack in the Washington, D.C. metro area. Special Agent Jason Gideon, a seasoned profiler, takes the lead in the interrogation. The Guantanamo guards have been abusive, but Gideon shows the suspect respect. Gideon and the suspect have many conversations about religion and prayer. Of particular note, Gideon insists that the suspect is allowed to pray. To control for racial primes, we chose a show in which the interrogator was also a white man, like Jack Bauer, and the suspect was also a Middle Eastern man, like in the clips from 24.

In the rapport-building ineffective clip, we spliced together scenes from the first half of the episode in which the suspect does not divulge that there is a wired decoy location, which results in a bomb detonating and killing members of federal law enforcement. In the rapport-building effective clip, we spliced together scenes from the second half of the episode in which the suspect is tricked into thinking that the bomb did detonate. He then tells Gideon about the plan, including the bomb's location. The FBI team is able to use this information in enough time to foil the plot and kill the would-be attackers.

MEASURED INDEPENDENT VARIABLES

Beyond our treatment conditions, views on torture are conditioned by a person's political views. We measured political ideology on a 5-point scale from very liberal to very conservative. We also created two dummy variables for liberal and conservative participants.

ANALYSES

We argue that people support torture in response to threat. In this chapter, we expect to replicate our findings from chapter 1; that is, people will be more supportive of torture when it works and will not change their support when torture either fails or is not shown. We also expect that seeing violence in general will elicit a similar aggressive response by increasing support for torture. In contrast, people should be less supportive of torture when they see an alternative, nonviolent interrogation approach. Finally, people who are primed to think about a threatening environment should respond more aggressively than those who were not primed to think about their own death.

We find support for some of our expectations and the opposite result for others. Our results in this chapter replicate findings from chapter 1. Contrary to our expectation, however, seeing general violence decreased support for torture, and seeing rapport-building—regardless of its efficacy—increased support for torture. Furthermore, priming people to think about their own mortality did not have a consistent impact on support for torture across video treatment conditions. We discuss our specific findings next and offer potential explanations for why some of our results contradict our expectations.

STATED SUPPORT FOR TORTURE

Similar to our analyses in chapter 1, here we also asked people about their support for torture before and after watching a treatment video. We again measured support for torture on a 4-point Likert scale. Also similar to chapter 1, in this national sample about one-quarter (25.15 percent) of people changed their level of support for torture from pretest to posttest. This further supports our argument that some people have fixed views on torture, and others have fluid views. Changes among those who have fluid views explain aggregate shifts over time and framing. Figure 2.1 shows the percentage change in support for torture from pretest to posttest for each of the seven video conditions.

Our results from chapter 1 demonstrate that media representations of torture influence support for the practice among the public. This raises two questions. First, would showing people violence in general—rather than torture specifically—drive support for the practice? Second, can media representations of an alternative to torture—rapport-building interrogations—similarly influence public support for torture?

We expected that media depictions of terrorism interrogations would impact support for torture and that seeing torture work would again increase support. We also expected that seeing general violence would similarly prime people to respond in emotional ways—with aggression. Because dramatic depictions of torture sway support, we expected that dramatic depictions of the opposite—rapport-building—would similarly impact views, particularly when rapport-building works. In short, we expected that people who saw rapport-building work would be less

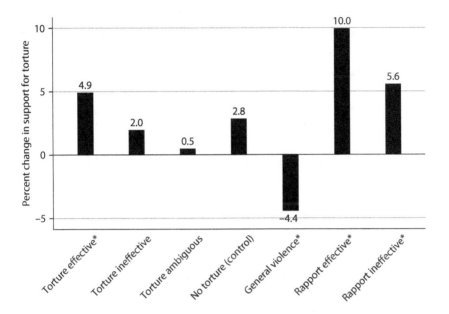

FIGURE 2.1 Change in support for torture pretest and posttest by video condition

Note: * Indicates significant change.

supportive of torture, whereas people who saw rapport-building fail may be more likely to support torture. To test these expectations, we compared support for torture before and after watching the treatment videos.

To test whether there are significant differences as a result of our experimental manipulations, we used *t*-tests to compare the mean level of support for torture in each condition pre- and posttreatment. We discuss the findings here and present the full statistical results in the appendix. Although there is some difference for all conditions from pretest to posttest, we are only interested in statistically meaningful differences (shown by asterisks next to the condition labels). If the percentage is positive, then average support for torture in that condition increased posttreatment, whereas a negative percentage indicates decreased support posttreatment. As shown in figure 2.1, participants in a national sample are more likely to support torture when they see a clip in which torture is effective. Seeing torture as ineffective, ambiguous, or not present has no impact on support for the practice.

Our two surprising findings come from the new treatment conditions. First, a common counterargument to the findings in chapter 1 is that our results are about priming people on violence generally, not torture specifically. Surprisingly, however, results here show that this is not the case. In fact, people were significantly less supportive of torture after seeing a clip showing general violence. This result suggests that the impact of entertainment media on support for torture is specific to the issue as opposed to a general prime to respond aggressively.

Perhaps empathy can help to explain why general violence reduced support for torture. Most people can imagine what it would be like to be punched, so they are able to empathize with the characters in the general violence condition. When people see violence that could impact them personally, they may be less supportive of violence generally, at least in the short term. Supporting this supposition, Norgren and colleagues found that people were more empathetic of pain when they themselves were experiencing it, like being exposed to extreme cold, and this decreased support for torture. In contrast, most people do not think they could ever be in the position to be tortured or interrogated as a terrorism suspect.[30] Therefore, people may empathize less with these characters and be more supportive of harsh practices against them.

Second, we expected that seeing rapport-building work would decrease support for torture, but our results show that this is not the case. In fact, whether rapport-building was effective or not, people were *more* supportive of torture after seeing a clip with this interrogation approach. As Mark Fallon noted in our interview with him, dramatic depictions of rapport-building counterterrorism interrogations are far less common than depictions of torture. Scott Edwards, senior advisor at Amnesty International, expanded on this point:

Certainly, it's always easier to convince segments of populations to be willing to dehumanize others than the reverse. That cost of relationship is very hard to reverse. Anytime there is perceived threat, whether it's real or not, you're going to have people who will naturally be more inclined to respond to threat in a way that violates international law. Torture's certainly an example of that.

It is possible that participants respond to seeing what amounts to "being nice to a terrorist" as an affront to their expectations. Rather than accept this new information, they doubled down on their prior knowledge about counterterrorism interrogations, which largely suggest that torture is at least a necessary evil. In short, being primed with counterterrorism interrogation prompts someone to respond with violence.

HOW PARTISANSHIP IMPACTS SUPPORT FOR TORTURE ACROSS VIDEO CONDITIONS

Regardless of video condition, we expect that participants' political views have a strong impact on support for torture. We first compared overall support for torture between conservative and liberal participants. Unsurprisingly, we see that conservative participants are significantly more supportive of torture both pre- and posttreatment.

As shown in figure 2.2, political ideology impacts how participants responded to some of the video treatments. For example, conservative participants increased support for torture after seeing a clip in which it

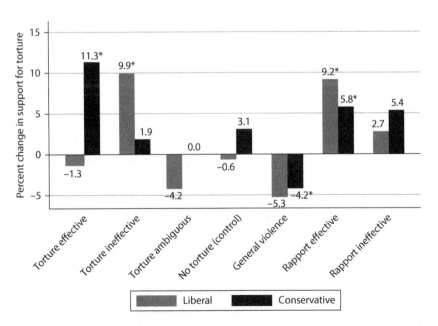

FIGURE 2.2 Change in support for torture pretest and posttest by video and participant political views

Note: * Indicates significant change.

was effective, but liberal participants' support is unchanged. In contrast—and surprisingly—liberal participants increased support for torture after seeing a clip in which it was ineffective, whereas conservative participants' support was unchanged. Furthermore, conservative participants decreased their support for torture after seeing a clip showing violence in general, but liberal participants didn't.

In other conditions, political views do not change the impact of the video clips. Both liberal and conservative participants are more supportive of torture after seeing a clip in which rapport-building is effective. This result is counterintuitive and may suggest that people think that if being nice works then being harsh will work better. Furthermore, neither liberal nor conservative participants changed their views on torture after seeing a clip in which torture is ambiguous, there is no torture, or rapport-building is ineffective. As we see in other experiments, partisanship is a strong factor that guides decision-making. Consistent with political scientists Donald Green, Bradley Palmquist, and Eric Schickler, partisanship in this context is not a rational cost-benefit calculation but potentially an expression of identity less subject to change or negotiation. In short, support for torture is influenced more strongly by partisan cues than by our experimental treatments.[31]

MORTALITY SALIENCE AND SUPPORT FOR TORTURE ACROSS VIDEO CONDITIONS

To further probe the impact of our treatments, we explored how both video condition and mortality salience impact support for torture. Across conditions, we expected that participants who were primed to think about their own mortality (as opposed to dental pain) would respond with more support for torture. As shown in figure 2.3, mortality salience—which creates a threat environment—does not have a clear impact on support for torture across video conditions. People who were both primed to think about their own death and saw torture work were more supportive of torture posttest. This supports our expectation that people will respond more aggressively in a threatening environment. In contrast, priming on mortality and seeing a video with general violence significantly decreased support for torture posttest.

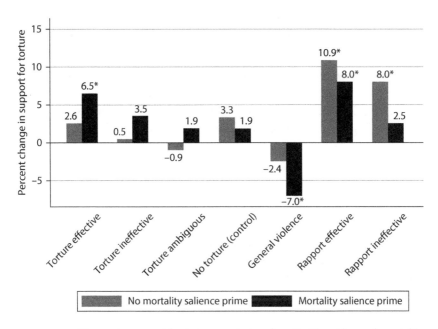

FIGURE 2.3 Change in support for torture pretest and posttest by video and mortality salience condition

Note: * Indicates significant change.

The adage "a picture is worth a thousand words" may be instructive here. It is possible that we swamped the effect of mortality salience with the video treatments. Visual primes from movies and television may be more influential than verbal primes. Simply seeing a threat and a response to it may have a stronger impact on opinion than asking someone to think about a threatening topic.

WHY DO PEOPLE CHANGE THEIR MINDS ON TORTURE?

Some people change their level of support for torture after seeing a dramatic depiction of a counterterrorism interrogation, and others don't. We are also interested in factors that people say impacted their decision.

To explore this, we asked what impacted this decision for people who changed their level of support for torture. Only participants who either increased or decreased their support for torture posttest were asked what impacted this decision. Each of these participants was presented with three possible reasons as well as the option to provide their own reason or indicate that they didn't know. The response options were not mutually exclusive, so people could select multiple reasons.

INCREASED SUPPORT

Across treatments, 15.1 percent of participants were more supportive of torture posttest. As shown in figure 2.4, the most common reason people stated they increased their support for torture was because it is "acceptable to prevent an attack." A smaller number of participants indicated that their increase in support for torture is either because "it needs to be more

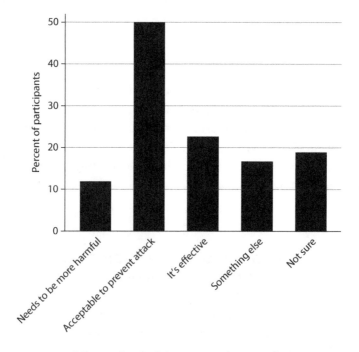

FIGURE 2.4 Why people stated they increased support for torture

harmful to work" or because "it is effective." Participants were also given the option to state that their reason was "something else" and were asked to write in the reason (these responses did not show a clear pattern). Finally, participants could indicate that they were not sure why they were more supportive of torture posttreatment.

Figure 2.5 shows the reasons people say they increased support for torture by video treatment conditions. People who saw a clip in which torture was ineffective were more than twice as likely as those who saw other clips to indicate that torture needs to cause more harm to be effective. This suggests that, for some, seeing a clip in which torture is ineffective does not suggest that the approach doesn't work; rather, it needs to be even more harsh to have the desired effect. Across conditions, people were similarly likely to indicate that torture is acceptable to prevent an attack, although this was a less common response for people who saw a clip of general violence as opposed to a counterterrorism interrogation.

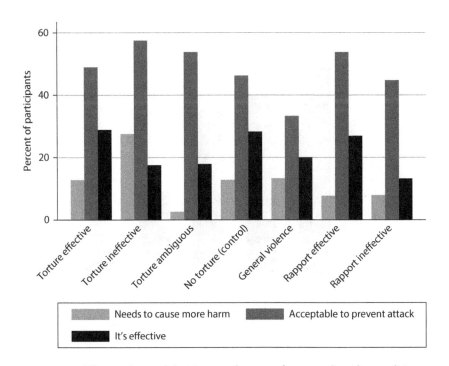

FIGURE 2.5 Why people stated they increased support for torture by video condition

Finally, people were somewhat more likely to say that torture is effective when they saw it work, saw the control in which there was no torture, or saw rapport-building work.

DECREASED SUPPORT

Across treatments, 10.1 percent of participants were less supportive of torture posttreatment. As figure 2.6 shows, the most common reason people said they were less supportive of torture posttest is because it is "harmful to the person." Approximately a third of participants who decreased their support for torture indicated it was either because torture is illegal or because torture is ineffective. A smaller proportion of these participants either indicated that they lowered their support for another reason (again, these open-ended responses did not show a clear pattern) or that they were not sure what changed their mind.

Next we break out why people say they are less supportive of torture posttest by video condition (figure 2.7). People tend to say that they

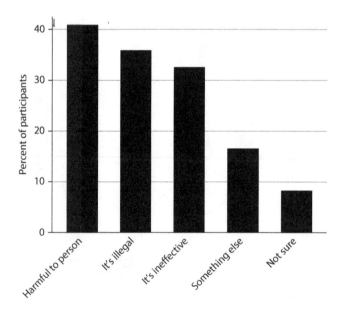

FIGURE 2.6 Why people stated they decreased support for torture

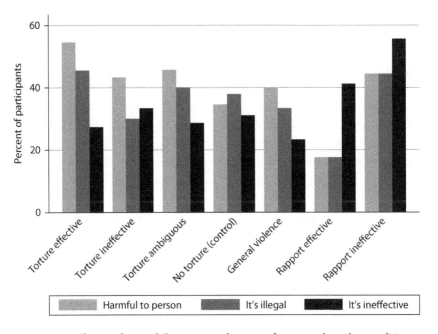

FIGURE 2.7 Why people stated they increased support for torture by video condition

are less supportive of torture either because it is harmful to the person or because it is illegal. However, in the rapport-building effective condition, neither of these explanations is as common. In contrast, participants in the rapport-building conditions were more likely to state that torture's inefficacy was a driving force in their reduced support for the practice.

ARE PARTICIPANTS WILLING TO TAKE ACTION?

So far we have presented results that explain changes in participants' stated views about torture. As in the previous chapter, we are also interested in how treatments impact actions. In chapter 1, we asked people to sign petitions, which was easily accomplished because data collection took place in person. As we show in chapter 3, we tried to replicate petition signing in an online survey, but the response rates were very low.

In this online survey, we presented participants with a hypothetical scenario in which they had to allocate part of the federal budget on national security issues across five areas: building the relationship between law enforcement and the public; research on enhanced interrogation and torture techniques; building the nuclear arsenal; the military; and cybersecurity capabilities. We compared budget allocations across treatment conditions (figure 2.8). People generally want to spend more of the national security budget on relationship building between law enforcement and the public, the military, and cybersecurity capabilities, and spend less on research on torture and the nuclear arsenal.

We compared these responses across video treatments (see appendix), but there are no meaningful differences in how people allocated the budget depending on which videos they watched. Political views do explain how people allocate the budget. In short, more conservative participants allocate significantly less money to relationship building between law enforcement and the public and cybersecurity capabilities. More conservative participants allocate significantly more money to research on enhanced interrogation and torture, the nuclear arsenal, and the military.

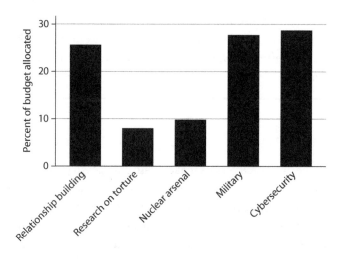

FIGURE 2.8 National security budget allocation

SUMMARY AND DISCUSSION OF THE FINDINGS

As we stated in the introduction to the book, some observers have suggested that support for torture is relatively static, and others suggest that support is more malleable. What we find is that both are right. As in chapter 1, here we also found that about 25 percent of our sample changed their level of support for torture posttreatment. Taken together, this suggests that most people have relatively fixed views on torture and that about a quarter of the population's views are fluid and can shift with relative ease. If one in four people can change their views on torture, that can have a potentially large effect on public policy outputs.

Our overarching argument is that people support torture as a response to violence with more violence but that this support can be influenced. Although some of our findings in this chapter are surprising and contrary to our expectations, they still support our overall view on support for torture. Findings in this chapter suggest a few key takeaway points, raise questions that we address in chapter 4, and suggest ideas for future research.

The first takeaway from this chapter is that seeing torture work does make people more supportive of the practice. We found the same thing in chapter 1, but the results here demonstrate that the findings hold with a nationally representative sample. Furthermore, support for torture does not change when torture either doesn't work or the result is ambiguous. Merely priming people on torture is not enough; it must also be effective for people to support it more. Similar results here show that our result from chapter 1 is not due to priming people on violence generally. Rather, torture is a thing apart. In fact, seeing general violence reduced support for torture. This may suggest a difference in empathy. People support torture when it is targeted at a perceived responsible "other" with whom people see little similarity to themselves. In contrast, people can empathize with someone who is punched and—at least temporarily—are less supportive of violence as a result.

The second takeaway from this chapter is that media depictions of counterterrorism can push people to support torture but cannot pull people away from supporting it. Steven Kleinman and Mark Fallon both suggested to us that television could show counterterrorism interrogations that more closely mirror reality. From this chapter, however, showing people using rapport-building interrogations increased support for torture regardless of whether it did or did not work. This suggests that support for torture is more punitive than instrumental. If people were mostly concerned with the outcome, seeing rapport-building work should have reduced support for torture. Perhaps people were instead focused on the suspect's guilt and deservedness, so they were more supportive of torture even if it would not help prevent an attack. In our interview, Steven Kleinman echoed this:

> People are fairly open in conflating an intelligence collection methodology—interrogation—with punishment. Prejudicial punishment, I might add, because even when you capture people in war, you have no right to punish. You have the right to detain and even the right to punish attempts to escape, or attacks on people. But if they're following your rules, you're responsible for their safety. You can't punish them. To do so is yet another breach of the rule of international law.

Media depictions of counterterrorism interrogations often show torture, and this is engrained in the public's mind. Showing rapport-building may have caused cognitive dissonance in participants because it contradicted the narrative most commonly told in media. In response, some people are more likely to double down on their prior view, even if it is incorrect. Building from this, Mark Fallon told us:

> If I knew where the bomb was planted, I wouldn't have to torture you to find out where the bomb was planted. But I'll just keep torturing you whether you know where it is or not, because I need to know where the bomb is planted. And so you get in that kind of loop in the public's mind. And I also think that there's a certain bit of revenge in people where they think they're bad guys and they immediately go back to retribution. On social media, the minute that someone argues against torture, someone will show a picture of someone jumping out of the Twin Towers. But they killed 3,000 people. I'm not sure who this they are, but in their minds, they try to justify that we'll match their tactic with our tactic. And as I always argue, we need to match a tactic with a strategy. Not an equal tactic.

As Fallon notes, many members of the public are predisposed to think that torture would work because it would work on them.

The third takeaway from this chapter is that mortality salience doesn't have a clear impact on support for torture across video treatments. The most plausible explanation for this is simply that the visual media treatments drowned out the effect of this treatment. Visual media has a powerful impact on perceptions across a range of topics. In contrast, reading a statement and thinking about it may not have the same deep or lasting impact on people. It is also possible that seeing threats elicits a different emotional response than thinking about threats. It is beyond the scope of this book to unpack our findings here further, although this is a possible direction for future research.

The fourth takeaway from this chapter is that general media violence may not always be bad. Here we see that general violence, which perhaps people can empathize with, constrains support for torture in a way that no other treatments do. For those who argue that violent video games change behavior, killing zombies may be different from torturing a suspect to get information. One is a release, whereas the other influences public policy. Probing the mechanisms at play here is beyond the scope of this book, though it is certainly worth future exploration.

The fifth takeaway from this chapter is that we have seen a consistent breakdown of participants with fixed versus fluid views on torture. Across the samples discussed so far, about 25 percent of each sample changed their views on torture after receiving our experimental manipulations. This suggests that roughly a quarter of the public can be influenced on torture. Shifts among this group may explain overall changes in public opinion polls' support for torture across time and framing. For roughly the other 75 percent, however, views on torture appear to be fixed and immune to framing effects. Among this group, it may not matter how torture is contextualized. We have seen a similar breakdown of people with fixed versus fluid views across multiple samples. To understand shifts in aggregate support for torture across time and framing, this suggests that we need to better understand these people whose views are fluid.

WHY IT MATTERS

Contrary to Finnegan's and many military interrogators' expectations, results here show that we cannot constrain support for torture by depicting counterterrorism interrogations that are more realistic and less violent. People are more supportive of torture when they see it work. When it fails, support does not decrease. When the interrogation uses rapport-building, support for torture increases whether the approach is effective or not. Rather than suggest that Hollywood present interrogations in a more realistic light, it would be better that they not show interrogations at all. Of course, we cannot and should not try to place restrictions on media. As past attempts have shown, many producers are simply uninterested in having conversations with counterterrorism experts. Entertainment media's job is to entertain and to make money. As long as shows and movies are doing that, producers are unlikely to alter their formula.

Media clearly influence people. As our findings suggest, visual primes such as television and movies have a stronger influence on people than other types of primes. Seeing threats may elicit emotional responses in a different, more intense way than would thinking or reading about threats. In effect, visual cues may enhance the salience of a topic, which connects back to our findings from chapter 1.

WHAT'S NEXT

Results from this chapter generate many additional questions, some of which we explore in chapters 3 and 4 and others we pose as future research directions beyond the scope of this book. If the counterintuitive impacts of both general violence and rapport-building can be explained, at least partially, by empathy, then we should see different levels of support for torture based on other measures of similarity. In chapter 3, we examine how ethnicity, location, type of harm, and the salience of torture influence views of interrogations. In chapter 4, we examine how nationality and partisanship influence support for torture.

Findings in this chapter also identify two processes that could be explored in future research. First, what impact do visual media have on views of terrorism and counterterrorism threats? And how does the impact of visual media differ from the impact of other types of primes, such as reading or thinking about threatening material? Second, if empathy for the victim can partially explain why seeing a fistfight reduced support for torture, what impact do other forms of violence have on different types of responses to that aggression specifically and to other forms of aggression more broadly?

3

CONTEXT MATTERS?

I don't think anybody thought about torturing Timothy McVeigh . . . Ted Kaczynski. . . . Post 9/11 . . . there were a couple of things at play. Number one, it was foreigners. Number two, it was Islamic foreigners . . . the archetypal concept of America as strong, virile, untouched sort of came crumbling down. But at the same time, I think it was just this massive storm that came together . . . people in the news started chest thumping and saying, well, we've got to torture people. . . . Somewhere between those things that are fictionalized, like a show like 24, and some news outlets that were pandering to ignorance and fear, you have a very sweet storm that came together.

—JOE NAVARRO, RETIRED FBI SPECIAL AGENT AND EXPERT
IN NONVERBAL COMMUNICATION

The 9/11 attacks horrified much of the world[1] and terrified citizens of the United States. In response, the United States pursued two large-scale conflicts in Iraq and Afghanistan that, at least initially, enjoyed wide public support.[2] As internal government memos suggest, there was a push to pursue actionable intelligence in both conflict zones.[3] Pressure came from within the highest levels of the executive branch of the United States to use whatever means necessary to gather intelligence.[4] In this milieu, it is unsurprising that torture was used in an attempt to extract actionable information.[5] Given the broad public support for the wars, a public debate over these tactics did not emerge until after the April 2004 shocking revelations that U.S. soldiers engaged in torture at Abu Ghraib prison in Iraq.[6]

Prior to the Abu Ghraib scandal and certainly before 9/11, torture was not a regular part of American political discourse. Tricia Bacon, a former member of the intelligence community and current professor at American University, told us, "it wasn't really something people thought about because it wasn't very relevant. It was just . . . accepted as a norm that we didn't do that, and there wasn't really that much thinking about it beyond that. And so it wasn't until . . . what had happened in that post-9/11 environment that people started to become even cognizant of the issue."

Torture had not been a salient part of American public discourse or consciousness before Abu Ghraib, but it was fiercely debated in the immediate aftermath of this scandal.[7] Despite this boom of attention in 2004, torture quickly fell out of the public's attention. However, legal battles were waged in the following years over U.S. treatment of detainees,[8] and scholars continued to study torture and public support for it. Although much of the public was disengaged from these events, opinion polls show that the public's views on torture are mixed and can vary based on how the question is framed.[9] For example, political scientists Paul Gronke, Darius Regali, Dustin Drenguis, James Hicks, Peter Miller, and Bryan Nakayama aggregated polls from 2001 to 2009,[10] and their results show that the majority of the American public supported torture between mid-2001 and mid-2008, although support began to drop around 2005 after the Abu Ghraib scandal was revealed. Public debate on torture largely dissipated after the shock of Abu Ghraib, and by the early 2010s, the majority of Americans no longer supported torture.[11]

Beyond the specific discussion of torture in counterterrorism, there has been a larger debate on law enforcement tactics more broadly in recent years. The killings of Michael Brown in Ferguson, Missouri, Eric Garner in New York City, Jamar Clark in Minneapolis, Minnesota, along with many others sparked protests and critical examinations of law enforcement's treatment of minority populations. This criticism of brutality was not related to harsh interrogations. Police in the United States have formally disallowed coercive physical techniques from interrogations for over seven decades.[12] However, in places like Chicago under

Police Commander Jon Burge, torture ran rampant in the interrogation room, particularly against minority suspects.[13] What these examples of police use of force may indicate is that certain communities are affected by police misconduct more than others.

Backlash has been more frequent and intense in places such as Baltimore, where Freddie Gray's spinal injury and death while in police custody led to riots and protests that only abated when charges were formally brought against the officers involved.[14] The protests revolved around Gray's death, but police transparency and larger issues of excessive use of force contributed to public discontent. In Baltimore, views on excessive force and police tactics were divided along racial lines, and this often was the case in other areas of the country.[15] Is that true of perceptions of harsh interrogations as well? Are people from the minority communities most likely to be affected by these policies more critical than members of the majority? If so, this would suggest varying levels of support for such policies. Perhaps proximity to mistreatment helps to explain why some people have fixed views on torture and others' views are more fluid. When these actions are psychological versus physical, will this change support? So-called torture lite, forms of harsh interrogation that do not leave scars, may be just as, if not more, damaging, but does this difference matter for support?

Of course, torture and harsh treatment do not occur in a vacuum. Whether trying to achieve a mission, reduce crime, or restore order, police and military are often in a threat environment that privileges results above process. In short, intelligence was prioritized above the need for proper oversight.[16] In this environment, we might expect that support for more intense tactics would grow.

As in chapters 1 and 2, part of our explanation for why members of the public often support violent state responses has in its roots in psychology and the 1960s canonical Bobo Doll experiments. As psychologist Albert Bandura and colleagues found, exposing toddlers to violent modeling increased the likelihood that the children would display similar behaviors.[17] In a follow-up study, they exposed toddlers to watching film depictions of aggression. In this study, children showed increased aggression, which suggests that films provide models of this behavior.[18]

Some of the criticisms of the Bobo Doll experiments relate to the feasibility of modeling aggression in a lab setting,[19] the conditional and mediating effects of other factors,[20] and how prior predisposition toward aggression may explain the outcomes.[21] With that in mind, the basic mechanism of violence leading to imitation seems supported under certain conditions and for certain people. In her work on citizen responses to terrorism, political scientist Carly Wayne found that citizens overwhelmingly support violent responses in retaliation in the wake of a terrorist attack,[22] and this support for military retaliation is greatest among citizens who are the *least* personally affected but the *most* personally outraged. Wayne did not ask about media consumption, but we would expect that this consumption influences outrage and support for military force. What is still unclear, however, is how some people's views on counterterrorism responses may be fixed and others' views are more fluid. We are interested in a less direct pathway that may be more difficult to measure. We have shown that support for torture increased with consumption of the TV show 24. That mechanism may be a function of imitation: I saw Jack Bauer do it, so I will support its use.

With this background of Abu Ghraib, police brutality, and other misuses of force, we wanted to examine how and why people support harsh interrogation. Building from scholarly research, the data discussed in this chapter come from an experimental study we conducted in mid-2014. Specifically, we were interested in how three factors impact support for torture: (1) the ethnicity of both interrogator and suspect, (2) whether the event took place domestically or internationally, and (3) whether the torture was psychological or physical.

In early December 2014, the Senate Select Committee on Intelligence released its report from the Committee Study of the Central Intelligence Agency's Detention and Interrogation Program. This report is informally known as the Senate Torture Report (STR). In the weeks following its release, coverage of the report dominated the U.S. news cycle, and public debate on torture resurfaced. In short, torture was *salient* in public memory for the first time in many years (arguably since the April 2004 release of photos from Abu Ghraib prison in Iraq). Release of the STR and the resulting swell of public debate on torture provided us with an opportunity to test how issue salience impacts support for torture in general and across our experimental conditions. We collected a second wave of data in the weeks following release of the STR. To put this in context, we did not know when the report would be issued. We fielded the first study without this knowledge. When the report was issued, we replicated the study because we saw an opportunity for a natural experiment. That is, the only difference in the results between these studies should be due to the release of the STR. We discuss this in more detail in the methods section.

In this chapter, we examine the following question: Why do people sometimes care about torture, whereas at others times they do not? Our overarching argument is that support for torture is an emotional psychological response to violence with more violence but that this can be tempered. In this case, we argue that people are more supportive of torture when it is used in response to violence against *our* kind by other kinds. In other words, this is an argument about in-groups and out-groups. People won't care so much about torture when it's being used against someone who isn't "like us," but we will care when it's being used against someone who is similar to us. Furthermore, we expect that some people have more fluid views on torture and thus will be influenced by our manipulations in framing, whereas others have more fixed views that will not be influenced by context or salience.

As shown in chapters 1 and 2, our responses to torture may be sharpened when the issue is more salient, that is, when it has greater resonance in public memory. Saliency influences perceptions on a range of issues. Most of the time people don't think about torture. When events such as Abu Ghraib or the Senate Torture Report happen, torture becomes a focusing event in media coverage and public discourse. When torture is a salient issue, people may have more sharpened views on it and should be more willing to take action in support of those views.

We asked Curt Goering, executive director of the Center for Victims of Torture, about the impact the STR had on public perceptions of torture.

> I think it had an important impact. Limited, but important impact. . . . The report was the most in-depth investigation about U.S. torture . . . up to that time and still today. And it helped I think to explain to the general public that things were actually a lot worse, and the U.S. had engaged in torture that was . . . far worse and more extensive, with fewer results than had previously been understood or talked about. It was very important to have that on the record, and yet I think it ultimately had limited impact, at least so far. It's an important document, it contains important factual material, some, for the first time, but where did it go at the end of the day? It became very quickly a partisan issue, and that doesn't help, in terms of

moving an issue forward when it's seen as politicized. And at the end of the day, zero accountability.

In much of the literature to date on support for torture, in-groups and out-groups are operationalized by nationality[23] or personal closeness,[24] although political scientists Courtenay Conrad, Sara Croco, Brad Gomez, and Will Moore recently cued participants to suspect ethnicity.[25] Thought of more broadly, however, in-groups and out-groups can mean many things ranging from sports team fan bases to racial or religious groups. Opinions on torture also may be contingent on location. Local news and actions may be more critical at shaping opinions than international news. In other words, torture done in Kansas may be more important at shaping public opinions (likely negatively) than torture in Kabul. When actions occur in far-away places, Americans may either care less because non-Americans are affected (social distance) or because of spatial differences (geographical distance). Although we do not evaluate all the possible options of what it means to be an in-group or an out-group, we expect that the conclusions from this chapter would generalize to other types of ways people create in-groups and out-groups.[26]

In this chapter, we focus on two types of social similarities: ethnicity and proximity. We also examine how support for torture varies by type of action: physical harm or psychological harm. Finally, as previously mentioned, the Senate Torture Report's release serves as a natural experiment. We collected data prior to its release and again following its release to test how issue salience impacts perceptions of and support for torture.

Scott Edwards, senior advisor at Amnesty International, echoed our thoughts on torture's salience among the public.

> Torture's not relevant for the . . . vast majority of Americans. I think those stories, those experiences are the most direct experience that any American has of torture and what it is like. Otherwise, it's easy to identify an out-group and not be concerned with a violation of their most fundamental rights. But easily looking at the state of prisons in the United States. The solitary confinement, the way it's used in the United States, for the durations it's used certainly constitutes torture by international standards, and those are quite pervasive. Those are instances of torture that occur very often in the United States.

Although some punitive practices in the United States could be considered torture, they are generally not framed in these terms in public discourse. Thus most Americans do not think about torture or deem it relevant to their lives much of the time.

Some of our results supported our expectations and some did not. We manipulated group similarities in two ways: ethnicity and proximity. Contrary to our expectation, suspect and interrogator ethnicity largely did not impact people's views of the interrogations. However, the location of the interrogation did have a consistent impact on perceptions. Specifically, participants' perceptions of the interrogation are generally more favorable when the interrogation takes place in Afghanistan versus in the United States. It is not surprising that people had the most positive views of interrogations that did not involve harm. When harm was involved, people had more negative views of physical versus psychological pain. We expected that people would respond differently to our study right after the Senate Torture Report was released when compared to responses prior to its release. Although we do see some differences in views of the interrogation pre- and post-STR, there are no clear shifts in attitudes. We do, however, see a clear impact of salience on behavior; specifically, people are more likely to sign a petition on torture when this issue is salient, which aligns with our findings in chapter 1.

In this chapter, we first discuss arguments for why people might be more supportive of torture in some situations than others, and we identify counterarguments to test. We next outline the design for our experiment and describe our methodological approach, sample, and analyses. We then present the results and discuss their implications for policy: how they tie into our overarching argument and what additional questions are raised that we explore in the next chapter.

WHY SUPPORT TORTURE?

One might argue that support for torture is relatively static. People either tend to support torture and harsh interrogation or they do not. This unwavering support or opposition might relate to partisanship or ideology, for example. A study by public policy scholars Jeremy Mayer and

David Armor in 2012 illustrates this alternative.[27] They argue that the public is largely stable in its views on interrogation tactics and cite a change in government policy after 2009 that supports this contention. What this argument cannot explain is why there were changes in beliefs about interrogation tactics after Abu Ghraib. As we found in chapters 1 and 2, some people seem to have fixed views of torture that are immovable regardless of framing, and others have more fluid views that explain aggregate change over time.

Our results and numerous public opinion polls[28] show that partisanship and ideology do matter in explaining support for these tactics, but they do not tell the whole story. As we discussed earlier, views on torture may be relatively static and difficult to sway. An individual's partisan leanings may be a good predictor of whether they favor harsher tactics.[29] If this is the case, the story is very easy and consistent because most studies on torture explicitly account for partisanship.[30] We certainly recognize partisan influences, but partisanship is a relatively slow-moving variable. That is, we have a variable that does not change much (partisanship) used to explain change in support (for torture) that, as we've noted, has fluctuated more. At the individual level, interrogators justified torture post-9/11 as the will of the American public.[31] By 2007, support for torture in the United States, according to some polls, had slipped to around 27 percent. By 2012, support was as high as 41 percent, a substantial rise for an opinion that some would call "sticky."[32] Our studies for this book show that individual beliefs can be modified based on different experimental treatments as well as on different social contexts. One alternative hypothesis is that partisanship or ideology explain the small variations we may see in views on torture or harsh interrogation.

Next, it might be that the salience of the issue drives support or lack of support. Issue salience may influence both what we think and what we think about.[33] The media can be a leader in agenda setting,[34] and as we've shown in chapters 1 and 2, media may influence policy beliefs. But political scientists Benjamin Page and Robert Shapiro find that public opinion is a fairly proximate cause of policy change in America and that politics influences opinion in many areas rather than the other way around.[35] In a review of what we know about public opinion and policy outcomes, many studies find that saliency of an issue only enhances the impact of public opinions on policy.[36] It stands to reason that the extent of torture's salience at any moment impacts opinions on torture policy. The STR is a great example of an event that would raise the importance of the issue in the public's mind. In a perfect world, we would be able to examine opinions immediately before and after Abu Ghraib—the moment when torture policy was, perhaps, the most salient. Unfortunately, we are not aware of any such public opinion data. The biggest limitation of social science is that we cannot rerun history, but the release of the STR and our ability to survey before and immediately after it is a next-best alternative.

Finally, contextual factors such as the identity of the suspect[37] and the interrogator or the ways that the interrogation is conducted might influence support. A YouGov poll taken right after the release of the STR suggested little change in people's overall perceptions of torture, but support for different tactics varied considerably. For example, people are much more supportive of sleep deprivation (55 percent found it acceptable) than to threats of sexual violence (31 percent found it acceptable).[38] This shows that general questions about support for torture miss the nuance. Support for torture varies across different forms of the practice. For example, we would expect people to be more supportive of waterboarding than of rectal feeding. These results highlight the importance of measuring support for torture in less abstract terms. Furthermore, people are more supportive of some tactics than others, so it stands to reason that other contextual factors can influence public support for torture.

In the analysis and conclusion, we return to these alternative explanations in light of evidence from the experiments. In short, we find that social identity largely doesn't matter for many of the outcomes of our interest. Contrary to our expectations, the saliency of torture has no effect on beliefs but does consistently influence behavior. This brings up an interesting conundrum that we discuss more in the conclusion. The closer the harsh interrogation occurs to Americans, the more critical views of coercive behavior increase. Although social identity is often discussed as a cause of torture support in public discussions, we find that it largely doesn't matter.

We argue that torture and aggressive interrogation policies are driven by more primal psychological motivations. As discussed in chapters 1 and 2, we think that aggression as a response to threat is plausible. What is puzzling is why torture is sometimes not used when we are under threat. In short, we need a story that can explain its use and nonuse. As discussed previously, we expect that the following may influence when we see support for torture: the ethnicity of both the interrogator and the suspect, whether the event took place domestically or internationally, and whether the torture was psychological or physical. When Americans see someone as different from "us" as the deserving recipient—whether this occurs domestically or abroad and whether this is scarring torture or torture lite—determines the variation in support. Furthermore, as we saw in chapters 1 and 2, some people have fixed views on torture, and others have more fluid views. Does this hold when we manipulate factors beyond torture's efficacy?

We expect that people will have more positive views of an interrogation when the target is an out-group. This means both that the suspect has a Middle Eastern name versus a Caucasian-sounding one and that the interrogation occurs in Afghanistan versus the United States. We also expect people will have the most favorable views of interrogations in which there is neither psychological nor physical harm. Furthermore, people will have more positive views on causing psychological harm than on causing physical harm. Finally, we expect people to be more likely to take action on torture when the issue itself is more salient in public discourse.

METHODS

SAMPLE

In this study, we are interested in the impact that identity, location, type of interrogation, and salience have on support for torture. We collected two waves of original survey data from adults in the United States using Amazon Mechanical Turk's (MTurk) interface. The MTurk platform allows requestors to pay workers to complete human intelligence tasks (HITs). The requestors (us) can place various restrictions on who is allowed to complete our HIT, and we specify the amount that workers (participants) will be paid upon completion of the HIT. Eligible workers can then choose to complete our HIT.

MTurk is a common way for academic researchers to recruit participants to our studies. The typical experiment in the social and psychological sciences is done on a classroom of college students, as we did in chapter 1. Using a college student sample for research is low cost, and participants are easy to recruit. The major downside to this approach is that undergraduate samples are not representative of the larger population of interest to most researchers (including us). In contrast, MTurkers (as their participants are known) are much more diverse on a number of dimensions than the typical undergraduate samples in the United States. MTurk samples are also a bit better than the average internet sample,[39] and using MTurk is relatively inexpensive. Studies have compared the results from MTurk samples to those from nationally representative samples, and the results tend to be overwhelmingly consistent among approaches across different disciplines.[40]

The first wave of data were collected from June 10–19, 2014, the summer before the Senate Torture Report was released. Data from 1,206 participants were used for Wave 1 of the survey. Because the STR had not yet been released and torture hadn't been a major news story recently, this group was not primed on the salience of torture. That is, the public was not thinking about torture or discussing it regularly in their daily lives when Wave 1 data were collected. To examine how salience impacts public support for torture, we fielded the study again immediately after the STR was released (Wave 2). Release of this report served as a natural experiment within our survey-experimental design. We did not control or manipulate release of the STR, but its release could impact public views of torture. Unlike the sample in Wave 1, the sample in Wave 2 was primed on the salience of torture through media coverage, political discussion, and public discourse immediately following release of the STR. An experiment has three main traits: (1) a group that will receive treatment is chosen at random; (2) there is a treatment and a control group; and (3) the application of the treatment is under the control of the researcher.

In a natural experiment, nature—not the experimenter—controls the treatment. For this to be more of an experimental study, we hope nature administers the treatment "as if" randomly and that a control group does not receive the treatment.[41] In our case, the release of the STR is the treatment that serves to raise the saliency of the public's assessment of torture. The control was the original fielding of the survey prior to the report. For this to be a true "natural" experiment, the treatment would be assigned randomly. Of course, the appearance of the STR was not completely random because the decision to release the report was political. The original report was approved in December of 2012. After votes to release parts of the report, the 525-page executive summary and key findings were released December 9, 2014.[42]

What is important from our perspective is that respondents in Wave 1 were not primed with the saliency of torture in the same way the respondents in Wave 2 were, and characteristics such as gender, ethnicity, or political ideology were not correlated with the treatment. Again, release of the report was a result of Washington politics, so it is difficult to imagine that the public was anticipating the release and that this influenced their perceptions.

The second wave of data were collected from December 17–18, 2014. In total, 1,212 participants completed Wave 2 of the survey. The average completion time was seven minutes and twenty-six seconds in Wave 1 and seven minutes and fifty-three seconds in Wave 2. Participants were paid $2 for their time, which translates to between $15.22 and $16.14 per hour.[43] We show a breakdown of participant demographics for each wave and compare them to national data in appendix table 3.A1.

EXPERIMENTAL DESIGN AND PROCEDURE

Participation in this study took place in a single online session. After agreeing to complete the HIT on MTurk, each participant completed the survey-embedded experiment. All participants answered a series of questions about their own attitudes and opinions about various harsh interrogations techniques and practices. We then randomly assigned each participant to read one interrogation scenario. Each scenario, or vignette, randomly varied on three factors: interrogator and suspect ethnicity (four conditions), location (two conditions), and type of treatment used in the interrogation (three conditions). This created twenty-four possible vignettes. Participants then answered questions about this interrogation—for example, do they consider it torture, it is legal, it is moral, etcetera. Participants then answered another series of questions on their general views of harsh interrogation practices. To control for order-effect bias (that the answer to a question may be influenced by what was asked before it), questions were presented in random order.[44]

Beyond these attitudinal measures, we are also interested in behaviors. After completing the survey, participants were asked if they would be willing to sign a petition about the interrogation procedure described in the study.[45] There were three petition options: (a) in support of the techniques in the vignette, (b) in opposition to the techniques in the vignette, or (c) skip this option without penalty. Participants were told that this petition would be sent to the White House. At the end of the survey, participants answered demographic questions.

DEPENDENT VARIABLES

Our main outcomes in this study measured how participants described the interrogation scenario in the vignette.[46] After reading the vignette, we asked participants to rate whether the interrogation was torture, justified, legal, or moral. We also asked participants to rate the extent to which the suspect deserved the treatment, the suspect was responsible for the treatment, or the interrogator was responsible for the treatment. Each of these seven questions was presented in random order. Responses for each question were measured using a 4-point Likert scale in an ordered ranking from "completely disagree" to "completely agree."[47] See the appendix for a full copy of the survey used in this chapter.

INDEPENDENT VARIABLES

We manipulated three pieces of information in each interrogation vignette: (1) the interrogator and suspect ethnic dyad, (2) where the interrogation took place, and (3) the type of treatment the suspect received. To cue on ethnicity, both interrogator and suspect were given either a Caucasian name or a Middle Eastern name. This created four possible dyads: Caucasian interrogator and Caucasian suspect (CC dyad); Caucasian interrogator and Middle Eastern suspect (CM dyad); Middle Eastern interrogator and Caucasian suspect (MC dyad); and, Middle Eastern interrogator and Middle Eastern suspect (MM dyad). Second, the interrogation either took place in the United States or in Afghanistan. Third, the interrogation tactics described in the vignette either constituted psychological torture, physical torture, or no torture. See the appendix for how we coded variables and conducted our analyses.

In summary, we have a 4 × 2 × 3 experiment with twenty-four possible conditions in which each participant is randomly assigned to read only one interrogation scenario. For example, one condition described an interrogation in the United States that used psychological torture in which the interrogator was Caucasian and the suspect was Middle Eastern. Another condition described an interrogation in Afghanistan that used physical tortures in which the interrogator is Middle Eastern and the suspect is Caucasian. See appendix table 3.A2 for a full list of the possible treatment conditions.

When we collected data for Wave 1, we were interested only in our three manipulated experimental variables. However, when we collected Wave 2 data, we were also interested in any differences in findings between the waves. We conducted all of our analyses on Wave 1 and Wave 2 separately. We were also interested in whether people viewed the scenarios differently in Wave 1 and Wave 2. To examine this, we compared the average rating for each outcome variable—for example, whether the interrogation is torture—for participants in Wave 1 and Wave 2 using a t-test, which allows comparison of the means for two groups to see whether or not they are significantly different from one another. We discuss these results in text and present the full statistical analyses in the appendix. Table 3.A3 provides descriptive statistics for all variables for Wave 1 and Wave 2.

ANALYSES

In this study, we are interested in how interrogator and suspect identity, location, and the type of tactics used impact how people describe the interrogation scenario. Release of the STR served as a natural experiment to see how issue salience influenced views of torture. Our first set of analyses focus on how participants described the interrogation scenario. We then briefly discuss the extent to which people support various harsh interrogation practices in general. Finally, we examine factors that influence whether or not a person is willing to essentially "put their money where their mouth is" by signing a petition on torture.

Although our main interest here is in how people describe the interrogation scenario, we also asked about support for torture before and after reading the vignette. Consistent with chapters 1 and 2, we found that approximately a quarter (22.5 percent) of participants changed their views on torture from pretest to posttest. This further supports our argument that support for torture is fixed for many, but fluid for some.

Both location and type of interrogation mattered for how people described situations. People are more critical of harsh practices when the interrogation takes place in the United States versus in Afghanistan. As expected, people are also more critical of interrogations that involve psychological or physical torture. To our surprise, the interrogator and suspect identity often did not impact how people perceived the interrogation. Salience in public discourse impacts some opinions but definitely influences action. Reading about an interrogation often decreases support for coercive practices, but the treatments (factors we manipulated) don't really matter—the scenario is more impactful when the issue is less salient. Finally, after the STR was released, people were more likely to sign a petition both in support of and in opposition to torture. Our findings suggest that saliency is more impactful on actions than on beliefs.

HOW DO PARTICIPANTS DESCRIBE THE SCENARIO?

After reading the interrogation vignette, participants rated the extent to which the interrogation was torture, justified, legal, and moral. Participants also indicated the extent to which they thought the suspect deserved the treatment, the suspect was responsible for the treatment, or the interrogator was responsible for the treatment. Across these seven outcomes, the main takeaway is that location almost always impacts how participants view the scenario and that the type of tactic often matters as well. Contrary to expectation, however, interrogator and suspect ethnicity generally did not impact how people perceived the interrogation.[48] Largely, our results for this portion of the study were consistent regardless of whether torture was salient in public debate at the time or not.

Table 3.1 offers an overview of the findings. The rows represent the different conditions from the experiment. The columns are the key dependent or outcome variables of interest (how the participant views the

TABLE 3.1 Summary of Results

	Is It Torture		Is It Justified		Is It Legal		Is It Moral		Suspect Deserved		Suspect Responsible		Interrogator Responsible	
	Pre-STR	Post-STR	Pre-STR	Post-STR	Pre-STR	Post-STR	Pre-STR	Post-STR	Pre-STR	Post-STR	Pre-STR	Post-STR	Pre-STR	Post-STR
CC dyad										+		+		+
CM dyad						+		+		+		+		
MM dyad	+							+		+		+		
Domestic	+	+	+	+	+	+	+	+	+	+	+	+	+	+
Psychological	+	+	+	+	+	+	+	+	+			+		
Physical	+	+	+	+	+	+	+	+	+			+		

interrogation and who is responsible for it) broken down by before release and after release of the Senate Torture Report. A plus sign indicates that the effect of the treatment we manipulated on the dependent variable was positive and statistically significant. A minus sign indicates that the effect was negative and significant. If the impact cannot be distinguished from zero, that cell of the table is left blank.

IS IT TORTURE?

Our first outcome of interest is whether or not people describe the interrogation scenario as torture. We expect that people will be more likely to call it torture when the suspect is someone like us, that is, when the suspect has a white, American-sounding name and when the interrogation takes place in the United States. We also expect that people will be more likely to call it torture when the interrogation involves either psychological or physical harm.

After the STR release, when torture was a more salient topic in public discourse, we expect that people would be more comfortable labeling the interrogation as torture. To test this, we compared the average rating for whether an interrogation is torture for Wave 1 to the average rating for Wave 2 and found that there was no difference between the groups. Salience does not impact whether or not people consider the interrogation to be torture.

Figure 3.1 illustrates the impact each manipulated factor had on whether or not participants in Wave 1 (black circle) and Wave 2 (gray diamond) consider the interrogation to be torture. Our next series of figures show results for how participants view the interrogation vignette. For each figure, we present results for the Caucasian interrogator/Caucasian suspect condition (CC dyad), the Caucasian interrogator/Middle Eastern suspect condition (CM dyad), the Middle Eastern interrogator/Caucasian suspect condition (MC dyad), if the interrogation happens in the United States (Domestic), and if the tactics used are either psychological harm (Psychological) or physical harm (Physical). See the appendix for more information about our analytic approach.

Full statistical results are presented in the appendix, but in this chapter we only show figures that represent our findings in the text. Each figure

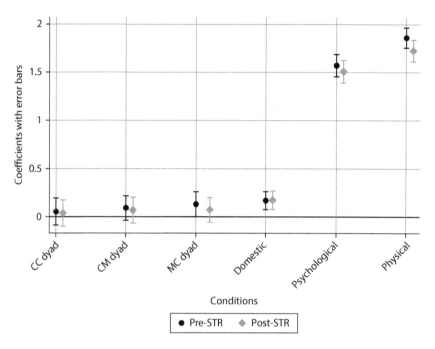

FIGURE 3.1 Is the interrogation torture?

includes the binary indicators, shown on the y-axis, and the estimate (represented by a dot) and confidence interval (represented by the bar through the dot) for each binary indicator interpreted relative to the reference category for that variable on the x-axis. Other figures can be interpreted in the same manner as the following explanation for figure 3.1.

Let's start with the three interrogator-suspect dyads shown in figure 3.1. The Middle Eastern interrogator/Middle Eastern suspect dyad was the reference category, so it is not included in the figure. Rather, we interpret each of the other dyads relative to it. Looking at the CC dyad, we see that the estimates for both Wave 1 (black) and Wave 2 (gray) are slightly to the right of the vertical line at 0. However, the confidence intervals for both estimates cross the 0 line, which tells us that there is no significant difference in calling the interrogation torture between the CC dyad and MM dyad in either Wave 1 or Wave 2. We see the same thing when looking at the CM dyad as well. However, when we compare the MC dyad to the MM dyad, the confidence interval line for Wave 1 does not cross the vertical line at 0.

This means that there is a significant difference. Simply stated, participants in Wave 1 were slightly more likely to call it torture when the interrogator is Middle Eastern and the suspect is Caucasian compared to the baseline Middle Eastern suspect/Middle Eastern interrogator condition.[49] The confidence interval for participants in Wave 2 does cross the vertical line at 0. So after release of the STR, there were no differences in how people described the interrogation based on the interrogator and suspect names.

Looking now at the location, we include a binary indicator for the Domestic condition and compare it to the reference category of International condition. In both waves, the estimates are positive (see the number on the x-axis), and the confidence intervals do not cross the vertical line at 0. This means that people were more likely to call it torture when the interrogation occurred in the United States versus when it occurred in Afghanistan. Findings partially support our expectation that people would be more likely to call the interrogation torture when the suspect is someone like us. Interrogator and suspect ethnicity sometimes impacts how people define the interrogation, but this does not show consistent in-group bias on the basis of ethnicity. Results show that people have higher standards for interrogations that occur on U.S. soil, which suggests in-group bias on the basis of nationality.

Finally, we turn to the two binary indicators for interrogation type—Psychological harm or Physical harm—which are compared against the reference category of No torture. In both waves, the estimates for Psychological and Physical are positive, and none of the confidence intervals cross the vertical line at 0. In both waves, people were more likely to call it torture when it involved psychological or physical harm to the suspect. We are also interested to see whether there is a difference in how people label psychological versus physical harm. We compared the estimates and found that people were more likely to consider physical harm versus psychological harm as torture both pre- and post-STR.

How people describe an interrogation depends on both the tactics used and the location where it took place. Physical harm is viewed as more torturous than psychological harm, even though evidence shows that both cause long-term damage.[50] The interrogator's and suspect's ethnicity do not have a clear impact on how the interrogation is defined. Furthermore, when torture is salient in public discourse, neither interrogator nor suspect ethnicity have any impact on whether the interrogation is defined as torture. Ethnicity often does not impact how the interrogation is described, but its location does. People are more likely to call it torture when the interrogation takes place in the United States than when it occurs halfway around the world.

Our overarching argument is that people support torture for emotional reasons but that this support can be tempered by context. Results here show that context impacts how people classify an interrogation. Views on what constitutes torture are not static, and they shift in predictable ways. When people define an interrogation as torture, we expect they should be less supportive of it. Our next analyses examine the contours of this support.

IS IT JUSTIFIED?

Our second outcome of interest is whether or not people describe the interrogation scenario as justified. We expect that people will think the interrogation is less justified when the suspect is someone like us and when the tactics involve psychological or physical harm. We also expect that people will think the interrogation is less justified after the STR release when torture is a salient topic. We found, however, that salience does not impact whether or not people consider the interrogation to be justified. When people are primed to think about torture, this does not make them think the interrogation is more justifiable.

Regardless of when a person was surveyed, figure 3.2 shows that people think the interrogation is less justified when it happens in the United States or involves psychological or physical harm. There are no differences in the magnitude of these effects pre- and post-STR. People think that the interrogation is less justified when it involved physical harm versus psychological harm both pre- and post-STR. In short, location and type of tactics impact the extent to which people think the interrogation was justified.

Results here also support our main argument that support for torture can be tempered in predictable ways by manipulating the context. Again, views are influenced by location but not ethnicity. People think the interrogation is less justified when it occurs in the United States versus Afghanistan. Similarly, causing psychological and physical harm are seen as less justified than an interrogation without harm. We again see no real differences based on the saliency of torture in public discourse.

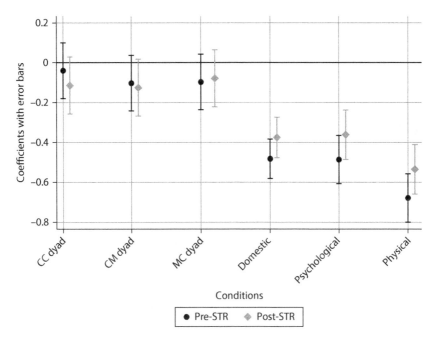

FIGURE 3.2 Is the interrogation justified?

IS IT LEGAL?

Our third outcome of interest is whether or not people describe the interrogation scenario as legal. We expect that people will be more likely to think the interrogation is legal when it occurs against "others"—meaning that it either occurs faraway or against a suspect with a foreign-sounding name. We also expect that people will think that psychological or physical harm is less legal. After the STR's release, we expected that people would be less likely to think that the interrogation is legal. However, salience does not impact whether or not people consider the interrogation to be legal.

Figure 3.3 shows that people think the interrogation is less legal when it happens in the United States or involves psychological or physical harm regardless of when they were surveyed. Interestingly, pre-STR people indicated that physical harm was less legal than psychological harm, but this is reversed after the STR's release. Post-STR, people also think that

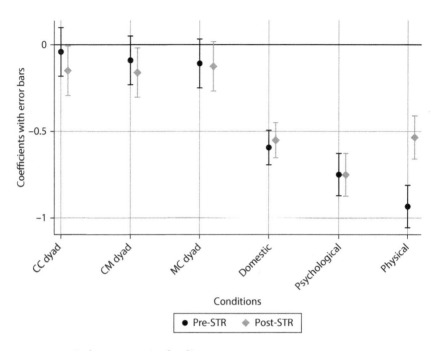

FIGURE 3.3 Is the interrogation legal?

interrogations when the interrogator is Caucasian are less legal than when both the interrogator and suspect are Middle Eastern.

Taken together, results here continue to support our overarching argument that support for torture can be shifted in expected ways. Location influences views on the act's legality, but identity does not. Torture is viewed as less legal when it occurs domestically versus abroad. We also see that people predictably view psychological and physical harm as less legal than a control scenario. Views of an interrogation's legality are largely not influenced by issue saliency.

IS IT MORAL?

Our fourth outcome of interest is whether or not people describe the interrogation scenario as moral. We expect that people will think the scenario is less moral when the suspect is a member of our in-group or

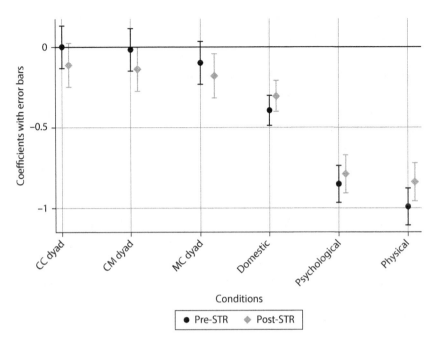

FIGURE 3.4 Is the interrogation moral?

involves psychological or physical harm. We also expected that people would view the interrogation as less moral after the STR release. However, in line with our other findings but contrary to expectation, salience does not impact whether or not people consider the interrogation to be moral.

Our findings here further support our main argument that support for torture can be manipulated in predictable ways. Results in figure 3.4 reflect what we have found for other outcome variables. People are less likely to think the interrogation is moral when it happens in the United States. Although we see slight differences in the impact of ethnicity pre- and post-STR, issue salience largely did not influence results.

DOES THE SUSPECT DESERVE IT?

Our fifth outcome of interest is whether or not people think the suspect deserved his treatment in the interrogation. We expect that people will think the suspect is more deserving when he is someone different from us. Our expectations about type of harm and issue salience are more complicated. On one hand, more harmful treatment and awareness of its real-world consequences may decrease the perception that the suspect deserves his treatment. On the other hand, the just world hypothesis suggests that people assume bad things happen to bad people, so people may think that the suspect deserves harm.

Figure 3.5 shows that people consistently think the suspect deserves his treatment less when the interrogation occurs in the United States. Salience does not impact whether or not people think the suspect deserves the treatment overall, but we do see that contextual factors have differing influence on views of deservedness pre- and post-STR. Supporting the just world hypothesis, people thought the suspect deserved physical harm more post-STR than pre-STR. Similarly, ethnicity impacted views of deservedness before the STR but not after. These results further support our argument that views of torture can be influenced in expected ways and also show that salience can influence views of torture in some contexts.

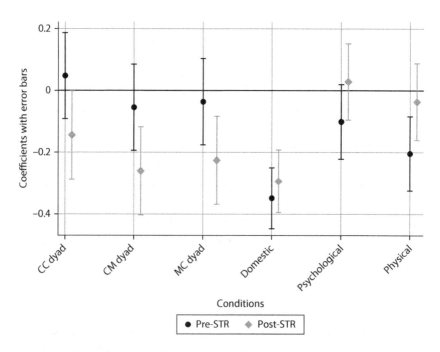

FIGURE 3.5 Does the suspect deserve treatment?

IS THE SUSPECT RESPONSIBLE?

Our sixth outcome of interest is whether or not people think the suspect is responsible for his treatment. We expected that people would think the suspect was less responsible when he is more like us. Again, there are reasons to expect that harm and issue salience would both increase and decrease views of suspect responsibility.

Results here show similar patterns to those for views of suspect's deservedness. As figure 3.6 shows, people think the suspect is less responsible for his treatment when the interrogation happens in the United States. Salience does not impact whether or not people think the suspect is responsible for his treatment. Before the STR's release, neither ethnicity nor type of interrogation influenced views of the suspect's culpability. However, after the STR's release, people think the suspect is most responsible when both suspect and interrogator are Muslim. Supporting the just world hypothesis, when torture is salient, people view the suspect as

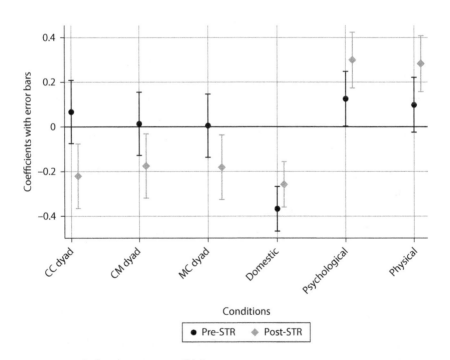

FIGURE 3.6 Is the suspect responsible?

more responsible when he is subjected to physical or psychological harm. Again, we see that views of torture can be meaningfully shifted by context and issue salience.

IS THE INTERROGATOR RESPONSIBLE?

Our seventh outcome of interest is whether or not people think the interrogator is responsible for the treatment he uses against the suspect. We expected that people would hold the interrogator less responsible when he is similar to us and more responsible when the issue is salient. We found, however, that salience does not impact whether or not people think the interrogator is responsible. It is worth noting that people rated the interrogator as more responsible than the suspect both before and after the STR's release.

Figure 3.7 shows that people think the interrogator is more responsible when the interrogation is domestic. Yet none of the other experimental variables impact views of the interrogator's responsibility, and the magnitude of the effects are not impacted by how salient torture is.

Overall, support for torture can be reduced in predictable ways. However, contextual factors influence some views on torture more than others. Location and type of harm systematically influence views of whether the interrogation is torture and how justified, legal, or moral the act is. Furthermore, issue salience does not impact these results. Perceptions of the suspect's deservedness and responsibility are less consistent pre- and post-STR, which suggests that these views are more "sticky." In addition, people view the interrogator as more responsible when the scenario occurs in the United States, but none of the other contextual factors matter, which suggests that this view is more fixed. Finally, we again see that some people have fixed views on torture, and others have more fluid views.

ARE PARTICIPANTS WILLING TO TAKE ACTION?

Beyond what people say about the scenario, we are also interested in whether or not people are willing to take action by signing a petition.

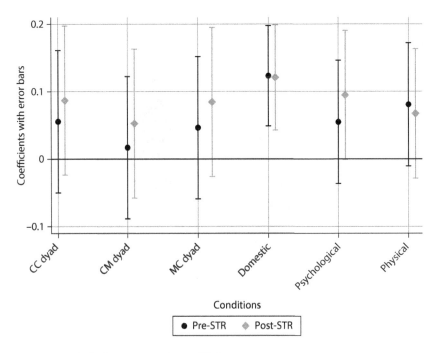

FIGURE 3.7 Is the interrogator responsible?

At the end of the survey, we asked participants if they would be willing to sign a petition either in support of or in opposition to harsh interrogation tactics. Contrary to our expectation, whether or not a person was willing to sign either petition was unrelated to any of our experimental manipulations. Issue salience, however, does impact willingness to act. After the STR's release, people were significantly more willing to sign a petition both in support of and in opposition to torture. This suggests that salience galvanized people to action across the spectrum. To probe this further, we compared results by participant ideology and found that this helped to explain *which* petition a person was willing to sign.

As figure 3.8 shows, participants were more willing to sign a petition both in support of and in opposition to torture after the STR was released. In short, people are more willing to take action when the issue has increased salience.

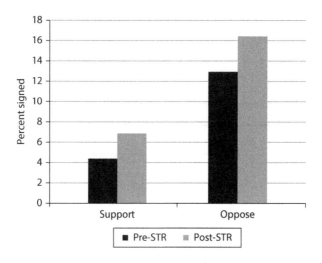

FIGURE 3.8 Willingness to sign a petition

It is clear that salience impacts the likelihood that a person will act on his or her views about torture. As Tom Parker, former MI5 officer, told us:

> people are very, very reluctant to change deeply held views, particularly if they're bound up in other issues of identity. I tend to think things more and more come down to identity than anything else. You know, and if you identify as a tough guy or you identify as being part of a particular party, information is not really why you are holding onto a particular point of view, right? It's much more about group membership.

Perhaps political views condition not just how a person views torture but also when and how that person is willing to change his or her mind on torture.

Building from our findings in chapters 1 and 2, here we also examine how participants' political views impact their willingness to sign either petition. Political ideology is measured on a 5-point scale ranging from very liberal to very conservative, and results are presented in the appendix. Similar to the interpretation of figures 3.1 through 3.7, figures 3.9 and 3.10 present estimates (dots) and confidence intervals (lines). When the confidence interval does not cross the 0 line, there is a significant impact of that variable on the outcome.

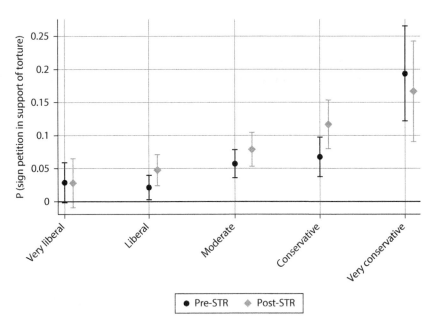

FIGURE 3.9 Willingness to sign petition in support of torture by political views and salience

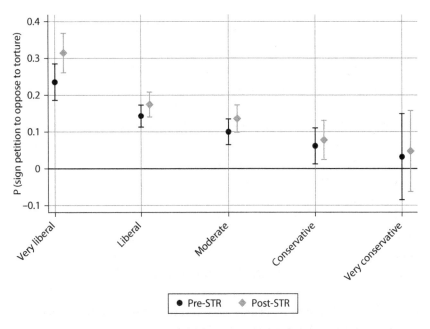

FIGURE 3.10 Willingness to sign petition to oppose torture by political views and salience

Figure 3.9 shows predicted probabilities for a participant's willingness to sign a petition in support of torture by both political views and issue salience. Here we see that the likelihood of signing a petition to support torture increases as the participant's political views are more conservative.

Political ideology had a predictable impact on likelihood to sign a petition in opposition to torture. As figure 3.10 shows, the predicted probabilities for a participant's willingness to sign a petition in opposition to torture is impacted by both political views and issue salience. Here we see that the likelihood of signing a petition in opposition to torture decreases as the participant's political views are more conservative.

SUMMARY AND DISCUSSION OF THE FINDINGS

Our broad argument for this book is that people support torture as a response to violence but that this support can be mediated in some situations. As in chapters 1 and 2, here we also see that some people have fixed views on torture, and others have more fluid views. This chapter provides a few takeaways to support our broad argument, and it also shows some scenarios in which support is less malleable. These results lead to additional questions that we address in the following chapters.

First, social similarities impact views of interrogation in some cases but not in others. Social identity theory[51] suggests that in-groups and out-groups should predictably impact views on violence and aggression. However, we did not find this. Proximity did impact views of the interrogation, with people generally being more critical of the incident if it occurred in the United States versus in Afghanistan. Surprisingly, interrogator and suspect ethnicity largely did not influence how the interrogation was defined or the views on how culpable people rated both actors. This contradicts political scientist Conrad and colleagues' finding that people were more supportive against a suspect with an Arabic name. Perhaps differences in results are a function of the dyad or other manipulated factors.[52]

Second, the type of harm impacts views of the interrogation. Unsurprisingly, people are more critical of the act itself when it involves either physical or psychological harm. In line with the just world hypothesis, however, harming a suspect has less impact on viewing the suspect as deserving treatment and assessments of both the suspect's and the interrogator's culpability.

Third, although we expected the saliency of torture to influence both the beliefs as well as the actions of respondents, only actions seemed to matter. This could be a form of social desirability bias in which respondents claimed their beliefs were more similar to perceived acceptable behavior (antitorture). Or it might be that the link between beliefs and actions is not as tidy as many social scientists think. Assuming that beliefs and actions are causally linked is critical to appropriate policy interventions. In a democratic society, we assume that if opinions change, policy will change in line with these views. For example, views on marijuana legalization have drastically changed since the 1960s when the issue became publicly salient. In 1969, for example, a poll found that about 12 percent supported legalization, whereas by 2017 that number had risen to 61 percent.[53] Since the late 1990s, decriminalization steadily increased in U.S. states, and now marijuana is legal in at least eight states and the District of Columbia for recreational use, and thirty states have legalized marijuana in some form. In this example, changing opinions are clearly connected to changing policies. In a study of consumer behavior that examines how product placement in movies influences purchasing behavior, advertising scholars Cynthia Morton and Meredith Friedman found that product placement can influence brand recognition attitudes about it.[54] In a related way, showing a policy such as harsh interrogation could influence the desire to use it. Although this advertising research and other policy research suggests a link between actions and beliefs, the difference between the two in our study suggests a need for ways to investigate this link further to determine whether it is merely lightly correlated or strongly connected and the mechanisms that would explain this.[55]

Fourth, here we again find that some people have fixed views on torture and that others have more fluid views. In chapters 1 and 2, about 25 percent of the sample changed their level of support for torture after seeing our experimental manipulation on torture's efficacy. In this chapter, we similarly see that about 25 percent of people changed their level of support for torture after reading a vignette in which we manipulate social similarity, geographic distance, and type of interrogation. Taken together, these findings suggest that only a small subset of individuals explain variance in aggregate support for torture.

WHY IT MATTERS

When we discuss torture, it is almost exclusively in the context of military or intelligence interrogations in faraway places. Harsh treatment by law enforcement more broadly, however, has been a main topic of public debate in recent years. What we see here is that people are more critical of harsh treatment that occurs in the United States compared to harsh treatment that takes place in Afghanistan. If this is the case, then people should care more about domestic police brutality when compared to torture abroad. As debates over appropriate police interactions with communities and appropriate ways to protest these interactions show, many Americans still view this as a nonissue. Taken to its logical conclusion, this can partially explain the apathy that many Americans show toward torture.

We see that salience does not impact what people say about the scenario, but similar to the results in chapter 1, we again see that issue salience does influence action. When people are primed to be thinking about the issue, they are more willing to sign a petition on torture. Perhaps issue salience increases willingness to take action because the topic seems more policy relevant in that moment. For example, we see upswings in donations to humanitarian NGOs in the immediate aftermath of natural disasters because people are primed to think about the issue and react to it.

WHAT'S NEXT

Results from this chapter also generate additional questions that we explore in the next experiments in this book. From a social identity perspective, we should see that people respond predictably to in-groups versus out-groups. However, one of the surprising findings here is that social similarities do not have the same impact on views of torture: proximity matters but ethnicity does not. This suggests that there is more nuance to the impact of in-groups and out-groups on support for violence. In chapter 4, we examine how two other types of social similarity—nationality and ideology—impact views on torture.

In both this chapter and chapters 1 and 2, we found that issue salience can influence actions. So far, we have examined only the salience of torture itself. However, torture is often discussed as a response to terrorism and framed as a necessary evil in counterterrorism. People fear that there will be another attack—and resulting loss of life—so torture becomes more acceptable to prevent this. In chapter 4, we examine how elite cues, suspect nationality and goals, and interrogation outcomes influence differences in support for torture both within and between participants.

4

ELITE CUES, IDENTITY, AND EFFICACY

I think it causes so much cognitive dissonance that they would rather just hang onto a false belief than to do the hard work to intellectually address it. I've seen that too many times. I have stood in front of huge groups where I say I'm the guy that's been there doing the interviews, that's taught the advanced counterterrorism interviewing course for the FBI, and I don't do it and it doesn't work. And they just ignore that, they want to hold onto some discredited individual's words or their belief that says it's OK. Well, it isn't OK, it doesn't work, and it is illegal.

—JOE NAVARRO, RETIRED FBI SPECIAL AGENT AND
EXPERT IN NONVERBAL COMMUNICATION

In the aftermath of the attacks on 9/11, the Bush administration initially pursued Al-Qaeda into its safe haven of Afghanistan and later into a misguided and ill-fated invasion of Iraq. Within two weeks of the 9/11 attacks, the United States had inserted special forces into Afghanistan, and within a month the United States launched a full-scale invasion. When the capital, Kabul, fell in November 2001, the United States began amassing detainees. These detainees included large numbers from the Taliban regime and other Afghani militants or suspected militants.

In December 2002, Secretary of Defense Donald Rumsfeld signed a memorandum authorizing harsh interrogation techniques against Afghan and suspected Al-Qaeda detainees. He famously wrote in the margins of the memo,[1] "I stand for 8–10 hours a day, Why is standing limited to four hours?"[2] In these and other memos written by White House personnel and lawyers, the Bush administration outlined and authorized what they termed *enhanced interrogation* techniques.

In a February 2002 memo, Attorney General John Ashcroft argued that the Geneva Conventions did not apply to Al-Qaeda and Taliban detainees because they were not a state entity nor a party to the treaty. Ashcroft determined that they were *unlawful* combatants who were not subject to Geneva Convention protections.[3] Senior officials in the Bush administration from Ashcroft to Rumsfeld to Vice President Dick Cheney signaled to both lower-level officials and troops that these enhanced interrogation techniques were allowed, lawful, and encouraged. Do these kinds of cues from superiors or elites influence public perceptions of these techniques?

As we show in chapter 1, media can influence both ideas about effective policy and whether a member of the public is willing to act in concert with these beliefs. Chapter 2 demonstrates that media depictions of counterterrorism interrogations can push people to be more supportive of the practice, but these depictions don't appear to be able to pull people away from support. Chapter 3 shows how situational factors and saliency can impact both beliefs about policy as well behaviors in support of those policies.

In this chapter, we investigate the effect of elite cues and consider how the identity of the suspect affects whether someone sees the harsh interrogation as worthy of support or not. We use a relatively new kind of experiment, a *conjoint experiment*, to examine how multiple factors simultaneously and iteratively influence support for torture, meaning that a person can evaluate multiple scenarios without prior scenarios influencing their responses. We manipulate four contextual factors: (1) the expert who is talking about torture, (2) the suspect's nationality, (3) the suspect's goal or ideology, and (4) the expected outcome.

We examine how the interaction of situational factors and a person's identity as well as elite opinions can sway beliefs about interrogation policies. In chapter 3, many factors rooted in the identity of the suspect and interrogator were found to have little effect on support for its use. We examine some similar contextual factors but also consider elite cues and more detailed identity options. In chapter 3's experiment, the number of questions we could ask a respondent were limited. Here we introduce a different experimental technique to examine more options. We ask similar sorts of questions related to support for torture against certain nationalities, such as Chinese or Syrians, and we suggest elites, such as Republican lawmakers or the Supreme Court Justices, support these actions. The results in chapter 3 suggested conditional support for torture, and in this chapter we examine many of these conditions.

We find that people are more supportive of torture when the suspect is a member of a group that poses a greater perceived threat and when the outcome is more likely to yield at least some actionable information. Generally, people are not influenced by the source of information about torture. The exception is that people are influenced by elites whose expertise relates to interrogations. Furthermore, suspect nationality did not have a strong influence on support for the practice. As we also found in chapter 3, some forms of identity matter, and others don't. Not all in-groups and out-groups yield the same responses to torture.

In this chapter, we first examine why people's support for torture can diverge. We discuss how elites and partisan cues can influence an individual's support for torture. We then discuss how group identity and the suspect's goal or ideology affect a person's support for the use of torture. Although elite cues and identity seem to matter, we conclude this section by explaining how the perceived efficacy of torture has an impact on public support. We then outline expectations and discuss the experimental design. Following that, we analyze and discuss these results in light of the previous experiments from chapters 1, 2, and 3.

WHY PEOPLE'S SUPPORT FOR TORTURE CAN DIFFER

To say that support for a policy is directly related to a single factor is unrealistic. Humans are complicated and rarely make decisions based on a single cause. With that said, in some of the previous chapters, we examined individual characteristics, exposure to media, and issue salience. In this chapter, we outline how cues from elites can affect public opinion. In a simple cost-benefit calculation, we might reject other forms of social influence. We know, however, that our decisions are often influenced by others, and prominent or well-regarded others may have an outsized influence. To better understand how we make decisions about complicated policies, we need to incorporate some understanding of social influence. Membership in a particular group might exert influence over our seemingly individual choice. Any fan of baseball's New York Yankees is likely to despise members and fans of the Boston Red Sox. Membership in these groups is very often determined by where one lives, where one grew up, possibly includes an ethnic component, and is often not necessarily a choice itself. One hates the other for membership in the out-group. Sometimes this hatred is generalized into most aspects of the out-group's existence, and at other times it is a source of discomfort that can be overcome. For example, one author of this book is an Ohio State football fan and the other is a Florida State football fan. We have chided each other about these choices for years, but we can overcome our biases against an out-group for a shared purpose, such as, say, writing this book.

The starkest example of this may be Hall of Fame National Football League wide-receiver Michael Irvin, who sustained a spinal cord injury in Philadelphia that ended his career. After the brutal hit, many Philadelphia fans cheered and a few continued after it became apparent that Irvin would need a stretcher. This is not to say that all Philadelphia fans are bloodthirsty. The point is that support for harming the other may translate into seemingly innocuous places such as professional sports. When threats to national and personal security come into play, this effect may be even more pronounced.

Being part of an in-group helps solidify a sense of identity. A component of this identity may be related to simple membership but could also include development and reinforcement of an ideology that helps draw stark lines between us and them. We also discuss how ideology may affect one's policy views.

Finally, we again discuss, in a condensed way, how the *efficacy* of a policy such as torture or enhanced interrogation might lead to support for it. One may be opposed to torture for ethical or moral reasons regardless of whether it works as a policy. In contrast, a supporter may question the morality of such a policy but could be persuaded to support it when the policy produces the desired results.[4] We discuss each of these options in turn.

ELITE CUES AND PUBLIC OPINION

To say we make decisions on our own without social influence is ignoring the multibillion dollar advertising that most large corporations use. The Nike shoe company pays athletes millions of dollars to endorse their products so people can "be like Mike" or LeBron James or Serena Williams[5] or even the controversial ex-49er quarterback Colin Kaepernick.

Product endorsements are a form of elite cue. As long as the person doing the endorsement has a moderate level of credibility, this form of endorsement should have influence on purchasing decisions.[6] Applying this to political decisions, how does a credible elite endorsement affect a policy? Credibility is often a function of partisanship, expertise, or ideology, and Americans take cues from politicians, policy experts, journalists, interest groups, and religious leaders, to name a few possible sources.[7]

Over the last few decades, Senator John McCain was one of the most outspoken opponents of torture, particularly among politicians. Curt Goering, executive director of the Center for Victims of Torture, discussed the impact of elite cues for public support of torture with us. He also saw the impact of these cues: "I think [cues] also matter. Whether it's a John McCain, in part because of his own experience, and he was a highly credible voice on that issue because of that. And he was outspoken and wasn't afraid to speak against torture."

Most other Republican elites, however, support torture. Goering continued:

> or you have a presidential candidate like Trump, who extolled the virtues of torture and said, "Not only would I bring back waterboarding and a hell of a lot worse. They deserve it anyhow." So he fed into this sense, amongst certain parts of his base, to get tough, be hard on terrorists. We're fighting for our national security. And that resonates with certain people.

When elite cues send conflicting signals, it is unclear how members of the public process this information. When asked about the impact elite cues have on the general public, Goering said:

> I think it goes to the point about what's the most effective message to which audience, and at which times. And I think in terms of building an

effective strategy, those are really important questions. Who is the messenger, who's the audience, what does the message consist of? It's one of the reasons why McCain's voice was so important on this issue. Secretary of Defense Mattis, who by all accounts is the person standing between Trump and the return to torture, if it were a human rights group saying what Mattis is saying, it might not matter very much.

The main takeaway from our discussion with Goering is that the message matters, but the source of that message is far more important. People may be more receptive to hearing a message they would otherwise disagree with if it comes from a credible elite from their own in-group.

Scott Edwards, senior advisor at Amnesty International, echoed Goering's comments with regard to President Trump and agenda setting and told us this:

> If you have a leader coming out saying, "If I get elected, I'll torture" . . . that's a piece of agenda setting. I don't think the average person consults experts when deciding how they feel about a particular government action that may constitute ill treatment. Of course, lawyers do. And, of course, judges and those of us who are involved in governance or advocacy obviously do. But how that impacts the average attitude on the street? I'm not sure it does. Because torture is not relevant to the lives of most people except the people who are being tortured and their loved ones.

So perhaps elite cues are less of a driver of support for torture among the general public.

In the context of the climate change debate, for example, sociologist Robert Brulle and colleagues found that along with structural economic factors elite cues have the largest effect on public opinion over time.[8] On top of this direct effect on citizen opinions, they also found a troubling indirect effect. Elite cues also influence media coverage of climate issues, which may lessen any impact of media in altering the debate.[9]

On a more hopeful note, political scientist John Bullock examined elite cues and support for more general policies.[10] Using experimental methods, he found that elite cues matter but so does how much information citizens possess. The upside is that prior information can outweigh elite cues in decision-making. The downside is that people rarely have a lot of information about policies. When this information vacuum exists, elite cues tend to fill it. Elites also may only persuade the public on issues that are discussed extensively and not on peripheral or unrelated topics.[11] In the context of torture, it is plausible to assume that many citizens do not have a great deal of information about the policy lending support to the more negative assessment.

Political scientists Bruce Jentleson and Rebecca Britton examined U.S. support for military force.[12] Although interrogation policy is different, it is a form of the use of more forceful methods. In their research, they found that elite cues are less important than the rational stated purpose of the use of force. In the context of torture, this might mean that support for the policy may be greater when it is clear what the purpose of the policy is and what the country hopes to gain.

Although elites may influence and guide decisions made by the public, as we noted previously, the type of elite matters. When a liberal Democratic senator warns the public about the dangers of climate change, we would expect that this message is not received in the same way by different audiences. It might be a function of credibility. That is, a registered Democrat may believe this Democratic senator more than a registered Republican would. Looking at elite cues and terrorism information, partisanship matters sometimes[13] but not others.[14] Stemming from this, Elizabeth Grimm Arsenault, former member of the intelligence community and current professor at Georgetown University, told us this: "I think the presidential campaign in 2016 devolved into an attempt among some GOP presidential candidates to outbid each other in their embrace of torture. The discourse from President Trump around the idea that torture works or that going 'farther than waterboarding' is allowed was increasingly impactful on public preferences."

With that said, political scientists Matthew Baum and Tim Grolling found that more costly communication is the most believable and able to move public opinion.[15] In short, when a Republican senator such as John McCain warns the public against using torture—a policy generally more favored among partisan Republicans—this has a larger effect than when a Democrat makes this case. The type of threat environment and hawkishness of the cue may also matter. As political scientist Shana Gadarian shows, threatening news stories matched with fear-inducing cues make people more supportive of hawkish stories than they would be without these cues.[16]

Much has been made recently about polarization and partisanship in American politics and the media. According to the Pew Research Center, which tracks public opinion, the number of people who consider themselves more extreme at both ends of the political spectrum has doubled since 1994, from around 10 percent of the public to over 20 percent. It is not surprising that with more people identifying with the extremes there are greater feelings on each side of animosity toward the other. In 2014, 27 percent of Democrats believed Republicans were a threat to the well-being of the United States, and 36 percent of Republicans had this same feeling about Democrats.[17] This was, of course, prior to what many observers see as the hyperpartisan environment that has developed during the Trump presidency and after the bitter 2018 midterm election. Political scientist James Druckman and colleagues show that this type of polarized environment leads to an increased influence of elite cues.[18]

In this chapter and experiment, we test the influence of elite cues and endorsements of policies. In typical experiments, as we have discussed in previous chapters, there are control conditions. These conditions serve as a baseline and are compared to the treatment conditions, in which the key causal variable is manipulated.

Based on the evidence and academic literature, we believe that endorsements by partisan figures will matter *for* partisans. For example, a Democratic senator such as Dianne Feinstein, typically considered one of the more partisan furthest left senators, may express opposition to torture.[19] Her opposition to torture may influence liberal Democrats but is unlikely to move conservative Republicans in the same direction.

News media provide a platform for elites to discuss relevant policy issues, but many of these elites are television personalities more than experts on a particular issue, as former MI5 officer Tom Parker told us.

> The media is more interested in putting on people who will give them a good sound bite then getting the right person and having the right conversation. . . . We don't have credible voices . . . you look at all the people that are interviewed on television, the national security experts, and it's mostly a bunch of colonels and generals you've never heard of, but who can be relied upon to turn up and play a part. But it's not insightful conversation.

In short, many of the talking heads on television are pandering to a partisan audience rather than imparting actual expertise on the topics they discuss.

The talking heads on MSNBC are generally different from those on Fox News. If people do hear information that contradicts their prior beliefs, they often do not change their views. As political scientist Brendan Nyhan and colleagues have shown, when a person's views are challenged, even when they are false, individuals may double down on those beliefs.[20] This suggests that an endorsement from a partisan may increase support among partisans and lead the opposing side to double down on the opposite perspective regardless of evidence.

We want to test these effects in our experiments. In a typical endorsement experiment, a question is asked of the respondent about support for a policy. In the treatment condition, that same question is asked but begins with "Senator A endorses this policy." The average of this answer is compared to the control condition, allowing the researcher to examine how much this endorsement influences support for the policy. For example, in the control condition, a researcher could ask a respondent, "Do you support tax cuts for the wealthy?" In the treatment condition, the respondent is asked, "Senator Dianne Feinstein (D) is opposed to tax breaks for wealthy Americans; do you support tax cuts for the wealthy?" Again, the difference in the average of the answer to these questions (average support for the policy) is due to Dianne Feinstein's hypothetical endorsement.

Endorsement experiments are often used to get honest answers to sensitive questions. It is a well-known effect in survey research that people often respond to researchers in ways they think the researchers want, which is sometimes called *social desirability bias*. This bias may be reduced by asking sensitive questions in ways that avoid or minimize this bias. In recent research on support for insurgencies and militants, for example, this approach is used to examine policy support for counterinsurgency or militants.[21]

We are less concerned about social desirability bias itself, but we do want to examine the influence of endorsements. Our experiment is a little different from a classic endorsement experiment because we want to look at a larger number of potential elites who may be influencing the process. To do this effectively, we need a slightly different tool, the conjoint experiment.

GROUP-BASED PREFERENCES

A long line of research demonstrates that people tend to have an affinity for members of their in-group over an out-group.[22] As we discussed, partisan cues—a type of group-based preference—can inform perception on many issues. In the context of contentious politics, people are more likely to mobilize to and justify both nonviolent and violent action on behalf of their in-group.[23]

In discussing support for torture and group-based preferences, Steven Kleinman, retired Air Force colonel with extensive experience in strategic interrogation, argues that

> it's like the death penalty. People often change their perspective when the case involves the murder of a loved one. And that's completely understandable. But we can't make policy based on personal connections. It has to be based on what is best for the safety and security of the nation and our alliances. And torture doesn't meet that standard. It doesn't even come close.

Basically, Kleinman suggests that people's support for harsh punishment would change if someone like them—their in-group member—is impacted by it. Building from his suppositions, we may see that people are less supportive of torture when the suspect is someone who shares their nationality or ideological views.

Looking at torture, specifically, people tend to be more supportive of torture when the suspect is an out-group member or the interrogator is an in-group member.[24] In previous chapters, in-groups and out-groups were generally operationalized as a shared nationality. In chapter 3, we examined the impact of interrogator's and suspect's ethnic identity on views of torture and found that these dyads largely had no impact. We also considered whether the interrogation took place in the United States or Afghanistan, which *did* influence views.

Group-based identity, however, can take many forms. In this chapter, we operationalize in-groups and out-groups in two ways. First, we consider nationality, but we do so beyond whether the suspect is either American or of another nationality. Here we compare four nationalities:

U.S. (purely an in-group); UK (similar to us but different nationality); Chinese (different from us but not generally viewed as a potential terrorism threat by media, politicians, and the public); and Syrian (different from us and associated with terrorism threats).

Second, psychologist J. Ian Norris and colleagues show that participants' political ideology impacts perceptions of torture.[25] Furthermore, political scientist James Piazza found that people were less likely to support torturing a domestic right-wing suspect than a Muslim suspect.[26] To probe this further, we also manipulated the suspect's cause. For example, we expect that people will generally be more supportive of using torture against a member of ISIS than a member of either an anti-abortion group or an animal rights group. In addition, we expect that participants' own partisanship will impact the extent to which they support torture against members of groups whose causes they may identify with more versus those they identify with less. For example, a conservative participant may be more supportive of using torture against an animal rights group (far left extremism) versus an anti-abortion group (far right extremism).

Looking at perceptions of terrorism threats broadly, a body of recent research shows biases in both media coverage and public views. In a ten-year examination of print media coverage in the United States, Kearns and colleagues found that terrorist attacks by Muslim perpetrators receive disproportionate attention from the media when compared to attacks by other actors from different religions.[27] Looking at post-9/11 terrorism coverage in the *New York Times*, criminologist Zackary Mitnik and colleagues found a similar trend.[28] Political scientist Bryan Arva and colleagues examined the content of terrorism media coverage and found that Muslim perpetrators are more likely to be labeled as "terrorists."[29] Similarly, political scientist Emily Gade and colleagues found that perpetrator ethnicity, religion, and immigrant status influenced whether or not mass shooters were portrayed as terrorists.[30] Turning to public perception, political scientists Connor Huff and Joshua Kertzer found that people are more willing to categorize an attack as terrorism if is attributed to a Muslim or left- or right-wing ideologues than if it is a Christian or someone with no ideology.[31] Similarly, political scientists Vito D'Orazio and Idean Salehyan found that Arab perpetrators were more likely to be considered terrorists by the public.[32] From this, we would expect that an alleged perpetrator from Syria would be seen as more dangerous and that respondents would be more likely to support torture against him or her.

There is ample evidence that the perpetrators goals or ideologies could impact whether someone supports torturing them. In fact, political scientist James Piazza used a survey experiment comparing specific harsh interrogation techniques, such as indefinite detention, and found greater support for their use on Muslims than on non-Muslims.[33] Overall, the results point to in-group support for their kind, and out-group negative affect toward Muslims. Political scientists Nazli Avdan and Clayton Webb found that people are more concerned about terrorist attacks close to home (proximity in terms of geography) or that happen to types or people similar to "us" (proximity in terms of social characteristics).[34] In terms of policy, they found respondents to be more supportive of policy measures when terrorists target close to home or to similar kinds of people. Certain features of attacks affect public perception of them. Using experimental evidence, they found more sophisticated, coordinated attacks were viewed by the public as more terrifying.[35] We test these impulses in our experiment.

THE EFFICACY OF TORTURE

Does torture work? That is the critical question for a subset of supporters. What does it mean for torture to work or to be effective? Many think it is related to a ticking time bomb scenario in which accurate information is needed to thwart an impending attack. James Mitchell, a psychologist involved in development of the CIA's enhanced interrogation program, certainly believes this to be the case, and he argued for the program based on its efficacy at attaining actionable intelligence.[36] As discussed in the introduction, another way torture could be effective is related to its deterrent value. If using harsh techniques makes adversaries reconsider challenging U.S. authority, then torture may be viewed as effective.[37]

Let's assume two primary reasons for supporting or opposing a policy that uses harsh interrogation are efficacy and morality.[38] The previous discussion only discussed the former reason. People may be opposed to harsh interrogation for moral reasons as well. Table 4.1 offers a 2 × 2 illustration

TABLE 4.1 Efficacy vs. Morality of Torture

		Morality	
		Moral	*Immoral*
Efficacy	*Effective*	Effective, moral	Effective, immoral
	Ineffective	Ineffective, moral	Ineffective, immoral

of the debate over torture. In the cells in the upper left (torture is viewed as effective and moral) and lower right (torture is ineffective and immoral), we might include the hard-core supporters and opponents of the policy. The other cell worthy of note is in the upper right, in which some may support the policy for cost-benefit reasons because they see it working. They have hesitations about the policy's morality, but they support it nonetheless. Logically, people would not support the policy if it were both ineffective and immoral. Much of the area in which support can swing is where torture is seen as effective but its morality is in question. Some may admit that torture is not an effective method of gathering information but still argue that it is a morally appropriate punishment for those who harm us. This is predicated on the assumption that the person being tortured is guilty of the offense, which can be disproven in some cases and thus sway support on a case-by-case basis. Factors such as the identity and ideology of the suspect, the endorsement and trusted partisan, and the efficacy of torture combine to help an individual support or oppose the policy.

Donald Rumsfeld, secretary of defense in the Bush administration during the attacks of 9/11 and in the aftermath, was extremely concerned about how effective various tactics were in winning the war on terrorism. In a leaked memo, Rumsfeld stated, "Today, we lack metrics to know if we are winning or losing the global war on terror. Are we capturing, killing or deterring and dissuading more terrorists every day than the madrassas and the radical clerics are recruiting, training and deploying against us?"[39] We think many Americans concur with Rumsfeld that policies should be judged at least in part by whether they achieve their goals. We think people are most likely to support torture when they see it as moral and effective. When people have questions about its efficacy, we expect decreases in levels of support.

In chapter 3, we examined questions about ethnicity, proximity, and saliency of torture by exploiting a natural experiment. Here we are able to bring in more identity and in-group factors and, similar to chapters 1 and 2, examine the efficacy of the policy using a novel experimental approach.

EXPECTATIONS

Before discussing the nuts and bolts of the experiments, we want to make our expectations clear. We expect that experts or elite cues will matter. The type of expert will matter. A partisan expert will matter to partisans. The suspect's identity will influence support for torture. The more the suspect is like us, the less likely it is that people will support the use of harsh interrogation. The suspect's ideology or goals will impact support for torture. Partisanship matters; liberals are less likely to support torture for a suspect with left-leaning goals, and conservatives are less likely to support torture for a suspect with right-leaning goals. Finally, the outcome or efficacy of the policy matters. Where torture was effective at eliciting actionable intelligence, people will support it more. In the next section, we discuss the experimental design and results.

METHODS

SAMPLE

In this chapter, we are interested in the impact that expert opinion, nationality and ideology of the suspect, and usefulness of information gathered have on support for torture. Our data are from an original survey of adults in the United States using Amazon's Mechanical Turk (MTurk) interface between May 31 and June 1, 2018. We provided a detailed explanation of the MTurk platform in chapter 3. As a brief refresher, the MTurk interface allows requesters (us) to pay workers (participants) for taking our survey. In recent years, MTurk has become a common way for academic researchers to collect data from the general public. On average, this study took ten minutes and forty-eight seconds to complete. We paid each participant $1.50 for their time, which translates to $8.33 per hour.

In total, 1,142 people completed the study. We discarded responses from another ten people for either speeding through the survey or straight-lining responses. It is common practice for survey researchers to discard and replace these kinds of responses. A breakdown of participant demographics for this project is shown in appendix table 4.A1. MTurk samples are not nationally representative across demographics, but research shows that results obtained from MTurk samples are fundamentally similar to those obtained from the same studies in which data were collected from a nationally representative sample.[40]

WHAT IS A CONJOINT EXPERIMENT, AND WHY DID WE USE ONE?

For this study, we used a conjoint experiment, an approach fairly common in market research but newer to social science applications.[41] Using a market research example, here's how the conjoint design works. Let's say a cell phone manufacturer wants to know what features people prefer on a cell phone and how much they're willing to pay. You could just ask people what features they prefer, but this doesn't measure latent preferences, that is, preferences people may not even be aware they have. A conjoint experiment is useful for presenting people with many options and asking for assessments of each combination of features. Using the cell phone example, the conjoint would vary a few key features, such as screen size, memory, and color. People would be presented with a pair of phone options that randomly vary in each feature and would be asked which of these two options they prefer and how likely they would be to purchase each option. Each person would then assess a number of pairs. This is one way market researchers can help cell phone manufacturers figure out what features to put on their next phone to increase its appeal to a broader market. Another virtue of these experiments is that many factors and combinations of factors can be evaluated in a relatively short time period.

Social scientists have recently begun to use conjoint designs to examine other aspects of human preferences and behaviors.[42] You may be familiar with more traditional experiments, such as those discussed in previous chapters. In those experiments, some people are randomly assigned to a treatment condition (i.e., get the medicine) and others are randomly assigned to a control condition (i.e., get the placebo). Although this design has many benefits, researchers are limited by the number of treatments they can give and the types of comparisons that can be done across subsets of the population, such as between men and women. One significant benefit of conjoint experiments is that researchers are able to examine many more relationships. For example, conjoint analyses allows researchers to identify how each combination is rated; how each feature impacts decisions; how each option for each feature impacts decisions; and how these assessments vary across subsets of the sample. In short, we can see many more relationships from a fixed number of participants with conjoint experiments than we can see with traditional vignette-based experiments.

PROCEDURE

We are interested in understanding and explaining two sets of causes: (1) how situational factors impact a person's support for torture, and (2) how individual factors (general views on torture and partisanship, in this case) interact with situational factors to change support for torture. We use a relatively brief survey that allows us to vary many of these factors randomly while avoiding fatigue in the person responding. During a ten-minute study, we asked participants about their news and television consumption, knowledge of political events, and demographics. We also presented participants with a series of interrogation scenarios.

DEPENDENT VARIABLE

We are interested in the extent to which people support the use of torture across incidents. To measure this, participants were asked to indicate their support for torture in each incident on a 4-point scale (1 = completely agree to 4 = completely disagree). We then collapsed these responses to create a simple variable in which 1 = some support for torture and 0 = some opposition to torture. Across the 11,420 incidents, participants indicated that they would completely support the use of torture in 7.5 percent of the incidents, somewhat support torture in 18.0 percent of the incidents, somewhat don't support torture for 23.8 percent of the incidents, and completely don't support torture for 50.7 percent of the incidents.

MANIPULATED INDEPENDENT VARIABLES IN THE CONJOINT DESIGN

We are interested in factors that impact support for torture in counterterrorism. Using the conjoint design, each interrogation scenario included four pieces of information, or attributes: the expert, the suspect's nationality, the suspect's ideology or group, and the expected outcome of using torture. Each piece of information had multiple possible values (table 4.2). There are six possible experts, four possible citizenships, six

TABLE 4.2 Factors and Possible Levels in each Conjoint Vignette

Factor	Possible Levels
Expert	Military interrogator
	Academic researcher
	Supreme Court
	Republican member of Congress
	Democratic member of Congress
	Friend
Suspect citizenship	U.S. citizen
	UK citizen
	Syrian citizen
	Chinese citizen
Suspect goal	Militia with stockpile of weapons
	ISIS
	Neo-Nazi group
	Antifa
	Animal rights group
	Anti-abortion group
Outcome	Accurate information that prevents an attack
	Mixed information and impact on attack prevention is unclear
	Inaccurate information that does not prevent an attack

possible goals, and three possible outcomes, for a total of 432 unique scenarios (6 × 4 × 6 × 3).

Interrogation scenarios were presented in pairs. For each pair, the participant was asked to pick the scenario in which they would be more supportive of torture and to indicate the extent that they would support torture in each scenario separately.[43] Figure 4.1 illustrates a pair of interrogation scenarios. Each participant evaluated a total of five interrogation pairs, for a total of ten interrogation scenarios.[44]

As previously stated, there are four attribute categories: (1) the kind of expert who is making the recommendation; (2) the citizenship of the suspect being interrogated; (3) the goal of the suspect; and (4) the outcome of

Please read the descriptions of 2 scenarios carefully. Indicate whether **you personally** are more likely to support the use of torture in the interrogation in Incident A or the interrogation in Incident B.

Incident A
A friend expects that using torture against **a U.S. citizen** who is a suspected member of **ISIS** will provide **mixed information and the impact it has on attack prevention is unclear.**

Incident B
A Republican member of Congress expects that using torture against **a Syrian citizen** who is a suspected member of **ISIS** will provide **mixed information and the impact it has on attack prevention is unclear.**

If you had to choose, in which of these two incidents are you more likely to support the use of torture?

Incident A	Incident B

I support the use of torture in INCIDENT A.

Completely agree	Somewhat agree	Somewhat disagree	Completely disagree

I support the use of torture in INCIDENT B.

Completely agree	Somewhat agree	Somewhat disagree	Completely disagree

FIGURE 4.1 Example of conjoint design question

the interrogation. We believe that varying these attributes will influence a person's preference for torturing the suspect.

We expect that, on average, experts who are seen as more informed and less partisan will be more influential than a friend or a partisan member of Congress. At the individual level, copartisans should be more influential than politicians from an opposing party. On average, however, this should balance out. We expect people will be more supportive of torture of non-U.S. citizens and citizens from countries associated with terrorism. Although we think suspect goals also matter, this is more complicated than the other categories. We expect respondents with contrary political views from the suspect will be more supportive of torturing these people. In short, a stronger self-identified liberal should be more supportive of torturing a member of a neo-Nazi group than, say, an animal rights group.[45] Finally, we expect that the outcome of the interrogation will influence support for torture. The more the outcome can aid in preventing an attack, the more we expect people to be supportive.

MEASURED INDEPENDENT VARIABLES

Beyond the factors we manipulated in the conjoint incidents, we are also interested in how characteristics of the participants—things we measure by asking questions about them—impact our results. The measured independent variables come from the survey. We asked participants if they would ever support torture and if they think torture is ever effective. From this, we can compare responses for people who respond "never" to each question to those who would either support it or think it is effective in rare circumstances. We also measured participants' political ideology to compare responses for liberals, moderates, and conservatives.

One of the benefits of conjoint designs is that researchers can also compare how the manipulated attributes impact decisions differently across subgroups of the sample.[46] In this project, we look at how subgroups exhibit different preferences for when to use or support torture in counterterrorism. We compare support for torture based on a few participant factors: general support for torture, general views of torture's efficacy, political views, military experience, and general political knowledge. Appendix table 4.A2 shows the breakdown of the dependent variable (support for torture) and the measured independent variables (characteristics of the participants) across the sample. We discuss each of these participant factors in more detail next.

Conjoint analyses do not compare absolute support for torture across these participant factors (i.e., whether conservatives or liberals are more supportive of torture overall). Rather, conjoint analyses show how subgroups of the sample differentially weight manipulated factors (i.e., do conservatives weight whether or not torture is effective more heavily than liberals). For each set of analyses, we compare the absolute differences across the subgroups first; then we report how subgroups differentially weight factors that we manipulated in the experiment.

ANALYSES

Despite the seeming complexity of conjoint designs and the number of unique profiles, analyses are quite straightforward. We compare the impact of multiple factors (the manipulated levels of each attribute) simultaneously to see how they influence support for torture.[47] As we did in chapter 3, the full results are presented in the appendix. We show figures that depict our findings here in the main text. Each attribute (source, suspect nationality, suspect ideology, outcome) can have one of a few values. For example, there are six possible sources: a friend, a Democratic member of Congress, a Republican member of Congress, academic researchers, the Supreme Court, and a military interrogator. Just as we did in chapter 3, we create a binary variable for each level of each attribute (friend = 1 when the source was a friend, and friend = 0 when the source was anyone else), and we repeat this for each of the other possible sources. In analyses, we then must leave one possible value as the reference category. In all figures, the reference category is the one that garnered the least support for torture. People were least likely to support torture when the source was a friend, so we use that as the baseline or reference category. All possible categories are shown on the y-axis in each figure. The x-axis of each graph then shows the average change in the likelihood that people support torture for each category of each attribute relative to the reference category for that attribute. On each graph, the dot represents the estimated change in probability and the line through the dot shows the 95 percent confidence interval.[48]

Figure 4.2 shows the influence of source on support for torture. Let's walk through how to interpret the results. The graph shows the difference in probability of supporting torture relative to a baseline option. Recall that the friend is the reference category, so it is included simply as a dot at 0 without a confidence interval. We then examine the estimated change in probability of supporting torture for the other five source categories to see which sources more strongly influence support for torture relative to the baseline category of a friend. If the confidence interval line for any source crosses the vertical line at 0, there is no statistically significant difference from the baseline category of friend. In figure 4.2, only one source has

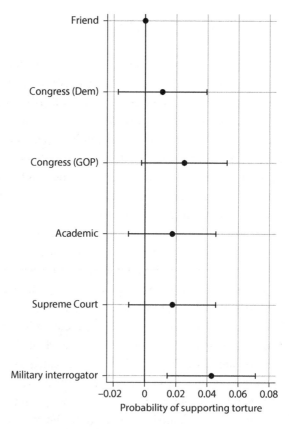

FIGURE 4.2 Effects of source on probability of supporting torture

a significantly different influence on support for torture relative to the reference source. We see that people are 4.3 percentage points more likely to support torture if the source is a military interrogator versus a friend. Throughout this chapter, we only discuss statistically significant differences from the baseline category in text.

The graph shows the change in probability for each level relative to that baseline category. What this does not tell us, however, is the actual probability of supporting torture in the baseline category and the other categories. We present the changes in probability in graphs, as is standard practice for conjoint experiments. In text, we discuss the probability of supporting torture for the baseline conditions and then how support changes for any other category that is significantly different from that baseline.

We are interested in how supportive people are of torture in each incident. Each of the 1,142 participants evaluated five pairs of incidents. Each pair involved two different incidents, of course, so each participant evaluated their support for a total of ten incidents. Across the sample of 1,142 participants, respondents evaluated their support for torture in a total of 11,420 scenarios. The unit of analysis in conjoint designs is the incident rather than the individual person, as was the case in previous chapters. Our first set of analyses include the whole sample with 11,420 observations. Our second set of analyses compare subsets of the sample, so the number of observations vary and are noted in text.[49]

We first present the graphs for each attribute separately and discuss the results. We then combine all attributes to show how each factor impacts support for torture relative to the other factors. Then we show graphs that demonstrate how situational factors have varying impacts on support for torture across subgroups.

SOURCE

We expect that people would be more supportive of torture when information comes from an expert source that is not partisan. Military interrogators by definition have real-world experience with interrogations. Thus these experts should have the strongest influence on participant views of torture. Results here support this expectation. The baseline likelihood of support for torture when the source is a friend is 23.6 percent. Partisan sources, academics, and the Supreme Court have the same impact on support for torture as a friend. However, when the source is a military interrogator, the likelihood of supporting torture increases to 27.9 percent. Military interrogators do have an impact on support for torture, but it is a minimal change.

As we see here, support for torture does not differ depending on whether the source of information is a friend, congressman, academic, or the Supreme Court.[50] This suggests that overall public support for torture is less swayed by partisan cues. Although this contradicts our expectation, it does seem to support political scientists Joshua Kertzer and Thomas Zeitzoff's findings that peer cues influence public opinion on policy at least as much as elite cues.[51] It is possible, however, that subsets of the sample respond to partisan cues differently. For example, Republican participants may be more influenced by a Republican member of Congress and vice versa for Democrats. We examine this in the subgroup analyses later in this chapter.

The former interrogators we spoke with largely echoed our finding with stories from their own experiences. When asked whether expert opinion can change minds on torture, Joe Navarro, retired FBI special agent and expert in nonverbal communication, told us the following:

> Sometimes you have to subscribe to Mark Twain's admonitions. . . . He said, don't try to teach a pig to sing, it annoys the pig, and it wastes your time. Because there's a world full of those that you can just tell them over and over when large swaths of generals and military intelligence people came forward and said no, we must not torture, and many did not want to listen.

The other former interrogators we spoke with offered a range of experiences when discussing the efficacy of torture with members of the public. For example, Tony Lagouranis, former Army interrogator, told us, "I'm thinking particularly like when I'm having a conversation with somebody at a dinner party. They'll listen to me . . . but they know I interrogated in war, and so they kind of have to listen to me as an authority. But whether they go home and that's processed or not, or they just throw it out . . . I don't know." He continued, "I certainly think that people who've had experience doing interrogation, especially at a high level, I think people will tend to listen to them. But I think I really can't overstate just how viscerally conditioned people are to believing it works. Because they've seen it happen so many times on television and movies." Steven Kleinman, retired Air Force colonel who spent a career in intelligence, also offered a range of experiences he's had discussing torture with members of the public. He told us this about his general experiences.

> I've had discussions with people, just spontaneous conversations at a party or on a plane. I've found it interesting—and often disturbing—that so many people maintain such a strong belief that torture works and that we need to employ it to keep the country safe. When I beg to differ, they'll often ask about my background. But even when I share my experience and expertise in the field of interrogation, they are undeterred and continue to argue in favor of torture. It's not unlike the experience of many physicians. Patients will present themselves and be told, for example, that they must have their gallbladder removed. Rather than accept the highly trained and experienced doctor's recommended treatment, they will context it with some pseudoscientific treatment they read about on the internet. Now, the average person has a right to ignorance—and when I say ignorant, I don't mean it in the pejorative, just the reality of not possessing relevant knowledge. I don't, however, cut that same slack to policymakers. They must operate from a place of knowledge, not from unfounded belief.

Kleinman did recount a time when he was invited to speak at Stanford University and changed someone's mind on torture.

> I was speaking at an event relating to national security, and each day all of the speakers were transported between our hotel and the conference site by van. One of the other speakers was a very politically conservative, pro-torture law professor who challenged my position against torture. He told me upfront that he didn't think torture was "nice" in any respect, but he did believe it was absolutely necessary. He also stated his conviction that I would not be able to change his mind. Every day, during the half-hour drive morning and afternoon, he would challenge me with question after question. By the end, I'd had the opportunity to refute every one of the myths that had informed his position. And to his credit, he finally offered on the final day, "You know, you've convinced me."

In the absence of time, expertise, and a willing listener, Kleinman's experiences suggest that it is difficult to change a person's views on torture.

Similarly, referring to national security professionals, Mark Fallon, former NCIS deputy assistant director for counterterrorism, recounted that "I change minds all the time. . . . And that's what drives me. So I'll speak out publicly on this, and I'll go to conferences and various platforms. . . . I've been on the networks, particularly when the torture report came out in 2014. I did a lot of public speaking about this area. And with national security professionals, I come out at conferences and I frequently change their minds because I give them a different perspective." Turning to members of the general public, however, Fallon was less optimistic.

> I can talk to my neighbors, and they'll tell me, "Yeah, but you don't understand. I'd give you whatever you wanted to hear if I was tortured." And I'd say I know you would. And that's exactly the point. It's whatever I wanted to hear. And so the public, I think they put themselves in that position, and they say, well, I'm a patriotic guy, if I'd give in and give up stuff under torture, well then so would the bad guy. But they don't understand that we're not just picking up the bad guys, we're picking up some people who aren't bad guys, that we just think are associated with bad guys and that we don't know when that information is valid, so we just keep torturing you because if we knew it we wouldn't have to torture you for it to start with.

We expect that experts would have the most credibility and be most impactful at changing minds. From these former interrogators' own experiences, they have been able to change some people's minds some of the time. But these are not the predominant responses from the public. Our results similarly support former interrogators' experiences; we find that military interrogators influence support for torture, but only slightly. To fully test some of the experienced interrogators' suppositions about persuading a reticent public, we would need a design that incorporated longer, more deliberate dialogue with an experienced interrogator. Given the expense, time, and challenge of such a design, we do not pursue that approach here. We would expect that what we do find is likely a conservative estimate of what would be a stronger effect if we were able to implement such a design.

NATIONALITY

Data for this project were collected from a sample of the U.S. public, so we expect that participants will view fellow Americans as part of their in-group. The other nationalities were chosen to be a group similar to ourselves (UK) and two groups different from ourselves (Chinese and Syrian). Furthermore, media coverage of China or Chinese citizens is rarely associated with terrorism. In recent years, however, much discussion of Syria and Syrian citizens has focused on terrorism and national security threats. From this, we expect participants to be most supportive of torture against Syrian, followed by Chinese, then UK and U.S. citizens.

Results, however, show that participants are no more supportive of torture against UK or Chinese citizens than they are toward U.S. citizens.[52] These differences in nationality do not seem to influence opinions (figure 4.3). The baseline likelihood of support for torture when the suspect

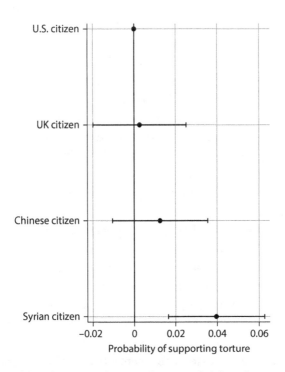

FIGURE 4.3 Effects of the suspect's nationality on probability of supporting torture

is a U.S. citizen is 24.1 percent. When the suspect is a Syrian citizen, the likelihood of supporting torture increases to 28.1 percent. As expected, when a suspect's nationality is associated with a group connected to terrorism in the public's mind, overall support for torture increases.

GOAL

Public perception of terrorism often does not match reality. In the United States, terrorist attacks receive 4.5 times more media coverage on average when the perpetrator is Muslim and that coverage is more likely to mention terrorism.[53] Although it is not clear how this impacts public opinion, research shows that people are more likely to call an attack terrorism when the perpetrator is Muslim.[54] Yet groups from ideologies spanning from far-left to far-right also use terrorism as a tactic to achieve their goals.[55]

In this project, we varied the suspect's goal on two dimensions: level of threat and ideology. Animal rights groups and anti-abortion groups use terrorism for extreme left- and extreme right-wing causes, respectively, but typically do not aim to kill. Antifa and neo-Nazis are both somewhat nebulous groups or movements on the far left and far right, respectively. These two movements can encompass a variety of actors who sometimes use tactics that could be considered terrorism. We expect that perceptions of these groups and support for torturing members of them will depend on the participant's political views. Finally, militias with stockpiles of weapons and ISIS both pose the greatest threat in terms of recent terrorism in the United States. Thus we expect people to be most supportive of torturing members of these groups.

The suspect's goal clearly impacts support for torture.[56] As expected, people are most supportive of using torture against members of ISIS or a militia with a stockpile of weapons (figure 4.4). The baseline likelihood of supporting torture when the suspect is a member of an animal rights group is 15.5 percent. When the suspect is an anti-abortion activist, likelihood of support for torture rises to 19.7 percent. The likelihood of supporting torture for a member of Antifa is 24.8 percent. The chances of supporting torture increase to 28.3 percent when the suspect is a member of a neo-Nazi group. People are most likely to support torture when

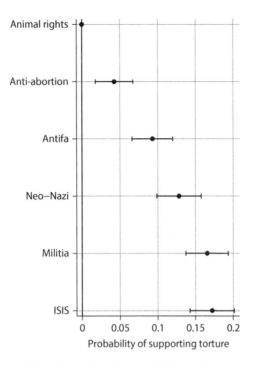

FIGURE 4.4 Effects of group's goal on probability of supporting torture

the suspect is either a member of a militia with a stockpile of weapons (32.0 percent) or a member of ISIS (32.7 percent).

OUTCOME

There is a common assumption that torture works. If the goal of torture is to cause pain or intimidate, torture does accomplish that end. However, as mentioned in previous chapters, those who support torture tend to claim that it works to extract actionable intelligence from a suspect. To check this claim, we varied the outcome with regard to the information acquired: ineffective/inaccurate, mixed, or effective/accurate (figure 4.5). Participants were significantly more supportive of torture when there was at least a chance that it could gather intelligence.[57] When torture would likely be ineffective and yield inaccurate information, the likelihood of

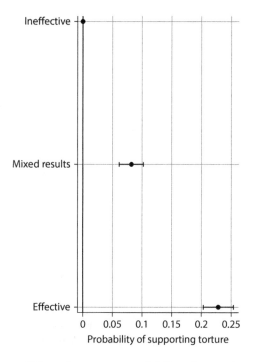

FIGURE 4.5 Effects of outcome on probability of supporting torture

supporting torture was 15.2 percent. When torture would likely yield mixed results, the likelihood of support increases to 23.4 percent. When support is effective and yields accurate information, the likelihood of support jumps to 38.0 percent. Torture is often justified on utilitarian grounds, which implies that people would not support it unless it works, but this study shows that some people support torture for another reason, such as deterrence or punishment.

OVERALL

Figure 4.6 combines the previous four figures to show how each factor impacts support for torture. Taken together, we see that source and suspect nationality have either no or only a slight impact on support for

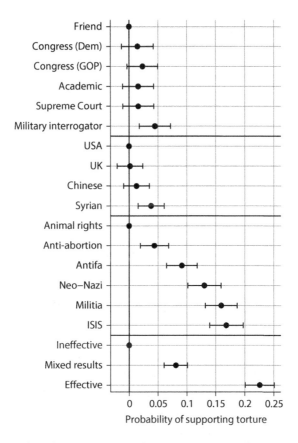

FIGURE 4.6 Effect of interrogation attributes on probability of supporting torture

torture. In contrast, support for torture is more strongly impacted by the suspect's group or cause and the likelihood that torture would provide useful information to prevent an attack.

Across all scenarios, participants are only supportive of torture in 25.5 percent of the cases. Of course, each scenario presents a combination of factors that vary the source, suspect nationality, goal or cause, and likely outcome. To better understand what impacts support for torture, table 4.3 presents the six scenarios in which torture is supported most and the six scenarios in which torture is supported least across the study. The top six scenarios have one thing in common—torture is expected to

TABLE 4.3 Scenarios in Which Torture is Most and Least Supported

Source	Nationality	Goal	Outcome	Supported (%)
Interrogator	Syrian	Neo-Nazi	Effective	63.64
Republican	Syrian	Militia	Effective	62.50
Democrat	U.S.	Militia	Effective	61.76
Democrat	U.S.	ISIS	Effective	58.62
Democrat	Chinese	Neo-Nazi	Effective	58.33
Interrogator	U.S.	Militia	Effective	58.33
Democrat	Chinese	Antifa	Ineffective	0.00
Republican	U.S.	Animal	Ineffective	0.00
Republican	Chinese	Animal	Ineffective	0.00
Republican	U.S.	Abortion	Ineffective	0.00
Republican	Syrian	Animal Rights	Mixed	0.00
Academic	UK	Neo-Nazi	Ineffective	0.00

produce accurate intelligence that would prevent an attack. In these scenarios, the suspect is a member of one of the more threatening groups as well. In contrast, none of the participants supported torture in six scenarios. Most of the scenarios involved inaccurate information and a suspect from a group that poses a lower general threat. In short, these results further support our overall finding that support for torture is more swayed by the suspect's group membership and the likely outcome from using torture. The source of information about torture and the suspect's nationality, in contrast, have less impact on opinions about torture.

SUBGROUP ANALYSES

One benefit of conjoint analyses is that they allow for comparison of results across subgroups. Returning to our cell phone example earlier in the chapter, our analyses so far show how the overall population weights various characteristics when making decisions. But suppose subgroups of the population place different weights on each factor. For example, younger people may want additional storage on their cell phones, whereas older people may want a larger screen that is easier to read. The overall conjoint analyses would not show these differences. We now turn to subgroup analyses to determine whether the results hold across subsets of the sample. Specifically, what if factors that impact support for torture differ based on personal characteristics such as political views, political knowledge, or experience in the military? The results of our analyses allow us to examine these potential differences.

To examine how participant demographics interact with the manipulated attributes, we split our overall sample into subsamples based on factors such as political views, conducted the analyses on each subsample separately, and compared the results.[58] Subgroup analyses do not show between-group differences in support for torture overall (i.e., from these analyses we cannot compare average support for torture between liberals and conservatives). Rather, these analyses show differences in the relative impact each attribute level has on support for torture between the two groups (i.e., are conservatives more influenced by the efficacy of torture than liberals).

GENERAL SUPPORT FOR TORTURE

As we know from public opinion polls, some Americans state that they do not approve of torture in any circumstance. We can assume, then, that people who never would support torture might respond differently in this study than people who may support torture in some cases. In the present study, 30.3 percent of participants stated that they would never support torture in counterterrorism. The remaining participants stated that they rarely (29.9 percent), sometimes (36.0 percent), or always (3.9 percent) support torture in counterterrorism.

In previous chapters, we saw that about 75 percent of the sample did not change their stated support for torture before and after being exposed to our experimental manipulations. This suggests that most people have fixed views on torture, and about 25 percent of people's views are fluid and movable. Here, though, when asked directly about general support for torture, only about 34 percent of people stated that they would either never or always support torture—fixed positions. Despite 34 percent of the sample stating that their opinions were fixed, when we look across the ten scenarios, only 26.7 percent of the sample indicated the same level of support for torture in each incident. Of the 305 people who stayed consistent across all ten scenarios, almost all of them (99.7 percent) completely disagreed with torture and one (0.3 percent) somewhat disagreed. This finding highlights the difference between what people say in abstract questions on torture and how they respond to various scenarios or primes.

People who indicated that they could support torture are significantly more supportive of torture in these scenarios than those who indicated that they would never support torture. For the first subgroup analyses, we compared responses for participants who said that they never support torture (black) to responses for those who at least support it in some cases (gray), as shown in figure 4.7. Among participants who indicated they would never support torture, few of the attributes impacted their support for torture in the presented scenarios. We do see, however, that even among torture opponents, some contextual factors can sway support. The baseline likelihood of supporting torture when the source is a friend is 2.5 percent. When the source is an interrogator, the likelihood of supporting torture increases to 4.4 percent. Similarly, although the baseline likelihood of supporting torture for a U.S. citizen is 3.7 percent, this decreases to 3.0 percent for a UK citizen. Otherwise, none of the factors impacted contextual support for torture among these participants.

Turning to participants who think torture can be acceptable in at least some circumstances, we see that situational factors impact support. For these participants, the baseline likelihood of supporting torture when the source is a friend is 32.7 percent. When the source of information is a military interrogator versus a friend, the likelihood of supporting torture increases to 37.5 percent. The likelihood of supporting the use of torture against a U.S. citizen is 33.3 percent, and support jumps to 39.6 percent when the suspect is a Syrian citizen. Among these participants, the likelihood of supporting torture against a member of an animal rights group is 21.3 percent. Support increases when the suspect is associated with an anti-abortion group (26.4 percent), Antifa (34.8 percent), neo-Nazis (38.5 percent), an armed militia (44.5 percent), or ISIS (46.3 percent). Even when torture is likely to be ineffective, the likelihood of support is 21.0 percent for this group. Support for torture increases when it would likely produce information of mixed value (32.2 percent) or yield information that would help prevent an attack (52.2 percent).

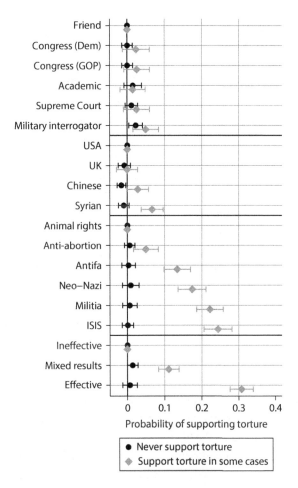

FIGURE 4.7 Effect of interrogation attributes on probability of supporting torture by whether or not the person would ever support torture

In short, some people indicate that there is no situation in which they would support the use of torture. Among this group, it does not matter who the suspect is or what the likely outcome would be. They won't support torture; their lack of support is fixed. Others, however, think torture can sometimes be acceptable. Among this group, support for torture is malleable.

GENERAL VIEWS OF TORTURE'S EFFICACY

How participants view the scenarios in our study could reasonably be impacted by how effective they generally think torture is in counterterrorism. Across our sample, participants were roughly split on whether they thought torture was never or rarely effective (48.9 percent) versus sometimes or always effective (51.1 percent). People who indicated that torture was sometimes or always effective were significantly more supportive of torture in these scenarios than those who indicated that it was rarely or never effective. We next tested whether incident-level factors have a differential impact on support for torture based on whether someone generally thinks torture works (gray) or not (black), as shown in figure 4.8.

First, we examined responses for participants who generally do not think torture works. Among this group, the baseline likelihood of supporting torture when the source is a friend is 7.8 percent. When information comes from a military interrogator, the likelihood of supporting torture increases to 12.0 percent. There are no differences in support for other sources. Similarly, the suspect's nationality does not impact results. The likelihood of supporting torture against an animal rights activist is 5.4 percent. Support for torture increases when the suspect is a member of an anti-abortion group (7.8 percent), Antifa (8.8 percent), ISIS (10.7 percent), an armed militia (11.0 percent), or neo-Nazis (11.4 percent). Similarly, among these participants the likelihood of supporting torture when the outcome is likely inaccurate information is 5.8 percent. The likelihood of supporting increases when it would produce either mixed results (8.6 percent) or effective information (13.3 percent).

We now look at results for people who think torture is more effective in general. Among this group, the baseline likelihood of supporting torture when the source is a friend is 38.9 percent. When the source is a military interrogator, the likelihood of support increases to 42.9 percent. Here nationality does matter. The baseline likelihood of supporting torture when the suspect is a U.S. citizen is 38.4 percent. The likelihood of support increases when the suspect is a UK (38.6 percent) or Syrian (46.1 percent) citizen. The baseline likelihood of support for torturing a member of an animal rights group is 25.5 percent. Support increases when the suspect is a member of an anti-abortion group (30.6 percent), Antifa (41.2 percent), neo-Nazi

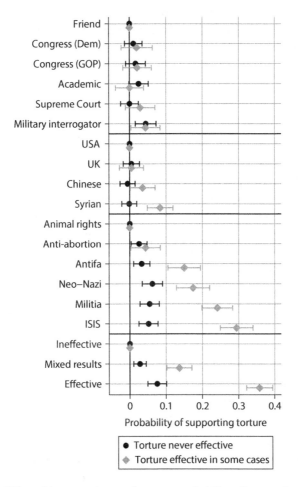

FIGURE 4.8 Effect of interrogation attributes on probability of supporting torture by views of torture's general efficacy

(43.2 percent), an armed militia (50.1 percent), or ISIS (55.4 percent). Finally, among this group, the likelihood of supporting torture even if it wouldn't work is 24.4 percent. Support increases when torture would produce mixed (37.9 percent) or accurate intelligence (60.5 percent).

In short, some people tend to think torture doesn't work, and others think that it does. Among those who think torture is ineffective, contextual factors have less influence on support for torture. Their lack of support is more fixed. Among those who think torture is more effective, however, contextual factors have a larger influence on support. Their support is more malleable.

POLITICAL VIEWS

Torture can be framed as a partisan issue. For this reason, we may expect that participants will have different views of torture in our scenarios depending on their political views. Liberals were overall less supportive of torture relative to both moderates and conservatives. Subgroup analyses allowed us to examine how incident-level factors impact support similarly or differently as a function of participants' political ideology. We expect that the partisan sources (Democrat and Republican) will have distinct impacts on support for torture based on the participant's views. For example, liberal participants should be more supportive of torture when their copartisan, a Democratic congressman, is the source and less supportive of torture when the source is a Republican. We expect the reverse to also hold for conservative participants. As shown in figure 4.9, we examined how liberal (black circles), moderate (dark gray diamonds), and conservatives (light gray squares) differentially weight contextual factors when deciding whether or not to support torture.

Regardless of participants' political views, sources only impact support for torture in a few cases and only for liberals and moderates. Among liberals, the baseline likelihood of supporting torture when the source is a friend is 16.2 percent. When the source is a military interrogator, the likelihood of supporting torture among liberals increases to 21.7 percent. Among moderates, the baseline likelihood of supporting torture when the source is a friend is 25.7 percent, and support increases to 32.1 percent when the source is a military interrogator. For moderates, the likelihood of supporting torture increases to 34.4 percent when the source is a Republican member of Congress. Source did not influence support for torture among conservatives.

The suspect's citizenship did not impact support for torture among liberal or moderate participants. Among conservatives, however, the baseline likelihood of supporting torture against a U.S. citizen of 32.5 percent increased to 41.1 percent when the suspect is a Syrian citizen.

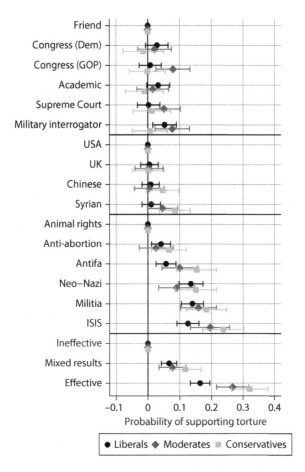

FIGURE 4.9 Effect of interrogation attributes on probability of supporting torture by political views

For the most part, the suspect's goal or ideology impacts support for torture regardless of participant political views. Among liberals, the baseline likelihood of supporting torture against an animal rights activist is 9.9 percent. The likelihood that a liberal supports torture increases when the suspect is a member of an anti-abortion group (13.9 percent), Antifa (15.8 percent), ISIS (22.9 percent), neo-Nazis (23.2 percent), and an armed militia (24.3 percent). Among moderates, the baseline likelihood of supporting torture against an animal rights activist is 20.4 percent, and these participants showed no difference in support for torture against animal rights versus anti-abortion activists. Still, the likelihood that a moderate supports torture increases when the suspect is a member of neo-Nazis (28.6 percent), Antifa (30.2 percent), an armed militia (36.3 percent), or ISIS (39.8 percent). Among conservatives, the baseline likelihood of supporting torture against an animal rights activist is 22.0 percent. The likelihood that a conservative supports torture increases when the suspect is associated with anti-abortion groups (28.6 percent), neo-Nazis (38.1 percent), Antifa (38.6 percent), an armed militia (42.6 percent), and ISIS (46.2 percent).

Regardless of political ideology, people are more supportive of torture when it is likely to produce either mixed results or yield accurate information. Among liberals, the likelihood of supporting torture that would be ineffective is 10.5 percent, and this increases when the outcome would produce mixed information (17.1 percent) or accurate intelligence (27.1 percent). For moderates, the likelihood of supporting torture even if it is ineffective is 18.4 percent. Support for torture increases when the outcome would be mixed results (26.0 percent) or accurate information (45.0 percent). Among conservatives, the likelihood of supporting torture that wouldn't be effective is 21.3 percent, and this increases when the outcome would be mixed information (33.6 percent) or accurate intelligence (54.2 percent). These results show that both efficacy and partisanship influence support for torture. Among liberals, the percent who support effective torture is somewhere between the percent of conservatives who support torture when it would be either ineffective or produce mixed results. If torture was merely justified on utilitarian grounds, as many claim, we would not see these differences among partisans.

A host of other individual-level factors may impact support for torture. We also compared responses based on participants' general political knowledge (low/high) and experience with the military (yes/no). Results were largely consistent across these models, so we report the figures in the appendix but do not discuss them in text.

SUMMARY AND DISCUSSION OF THE FINDINGS

We've shown that people tend to support torture as a justified response to violence with more violence but that this support can be tempered in some cases for some people. Results in this chapter support that argument. There are four main takeaways from this chapter, and we identify some additional avenues for future research.

The first main takeaway from this chapter, which is also supported by findings from chapters 1 and 2, is that efficacy matters. Resoundingly, people are most supportive of torture when it is expected to be effective at eliciting actionable intelligence. When torture would likely produce a mix of accurate and inaccurate information, people tend to support it to a lesser degree than when the results would be purely accurate. Finally, people are least supportive of torture when the results would be ineffective at gathering intelligence.

Even when torture would not be effective at gathering information, the probability of supporting it is about 15 percent. Torture is often justified as a necessary evil to keep us safe. However, even when it doesn't work, there is at least a subset of the population who still can support torture's use. This demonstrates that, for at least some, support for torture has a motivation beyond efficacy. As we discuss in previous chapters, punishment or deterrence may be reasons people support torture beyond efficacy. Although we do not specifically ask why someone would support torture if it doesn't gather intelligence, it is plausible to assume that punishment or deterrence may be reasons for this baseline support.

The second main takeaway from this chapter, which is also echoed in chapter 3, is that in-group bias sometimes matters more than others. In chapter 3, we saw that proximity (by country) mattered but ethnic cues for the actors did not. Here the suspect's ideology impacts support for torture but the suspect's nationality largely does not. Preferences for in-groups over out-groups is well documented in literatures on both social psychology and political violence. Yet our findings show more nuance in group-based preferences and support for torture.

The third main takeaway from this chapter is that elite cues do not have much influence on support for torture. Overall, people were slightly more influenced by military interrogators than by any other sources, but this effect was slight. We do see, however, that a person's partisan identification influences support for torture generally and across members of different groups. People tend to be more supportive of torturing members of a group that is less like them than one that may share some similar viewpoints. The lack of a stronger effect for elite cues could be due to a relatively weak treatment in our experiment as opposed to real life.

A partisan leader may be in the news constantly, essentially applying our treatment many times.

The fourth main takeaway from this chapter is that these results provide a more nuanced understanding of the fixed versus fluid nature on views of torture. Throughout the book, we have discussed how some argue that support for torture is fixed and others argue that support is more fluid. When we asked people about support for torture pretest and posttest in previous chapters, we found that about 25 percent of each sample had fluid views on torture—they responded differently after being exposed to various experimental manipulations. In this chapter, about 30 percent of the sample indicated that they would never support torture, and about 4 percent indicated that they would always support torture in a counterterrorism interrogation. For these groups, the source, the suspect, and the outcome had little or no influence on situation-specific support for torture. Among the other two-thirds of the public, however, we see that the contextual factors we manipulated do have an impact on average support for torture.

Taken together, these results suggest that views on torture are fixed for between 34 and 75 percent of the population, depending on how the questions are worded or the issues are framed. For the rest of the population, support for torture is fluid. It can and does move depending on framing. Although 34 to 75 percent is a wide range, results here do show that some subset of the populations' views on torture are fixed and others are fluid. Furthermore, one argument about the fluctuating public support for torture is that questions are asked in different ways. Here, however, participants responded iteratively to the exact same questions, and the only difference was the randomly assigned contextual factors. There is variation within how most (73.3 percent) people respond, which suggest that variance is more about the incident itself than about general support or opposition to torture or a function of question wording.

WHY IT MATTERS

Throughout this study, we have found that support for torture is mostly fixed for some people, but others can be swayed depending on context.

Here we see that elite cues are largely not influential. However, partisanship does influence support for torture. Taken together, this may suggest that people have been influenced by partisan elites to either support or not support torture. In the context of our experiment, this manipulation had little impact on support for torture. We have also found that group-based dynamics do not consistently impact support for torture. Here we see that people are more supportive of torturing someone whose ideology or goal is different from their own, but that nationality does not matter. This may be tapping into the increasingly polarized nature of U.S. society in recent years. Finally, the efficacy of torture is important for support. But even when torture is expected to yield no information, some people still support it. This lends more credence to the argument that torture is sometimes a punitive measure rather than a utilitarian one.

WHAT'S NEXT

Our findings in this chapter raise additional question about public support for torture. We see fairly clearly that some people have a fixed view on torture, whereas others can be swayed. Results show that partisanship influences whether and how people's support for torture can be shifted. What other factors may influence this? Perhaps media consumption plays a more central role. Furthermore, participant demographics beyond political ideology could help to explain when and why people change their views on torture. In the conclusion, we raise a number of questions related to how people's views may change. Using interviews and discussing our surveys, we examine the problem of persuasion from a half-empty or half-full perspective.

CONCLUSION

Torture, Terrorism, and the Future

Why do Americans support torture? Some portion of the answer is fairly direct. Citizens are often far removed from implementation of this policy. When nasty things are done to people in faraway places, it is easier for even a democratic polity to look the other way in the name of safety and security. As many scholars and experts we interviewed noted, the terrorist attacks on September 11, 2001, created a threat environment conducive to justifying or turning a blind eye to harsh interrogation techniques in an effort to quickly make America safe again. Other events, such as the Abu Ghraib prison scandal, also shifted opinion. But as former MI5 officer Tom Parker told us, opinions supporting torture are stickier than opposition to torture.

A portion of society, maybe the majority, are *fixed* in their views on torture and enhanced interrogation. When faced with different scenarios, suspects, threats, and endorsements, they remain steadfast in their support or opposition to torture. In contrast, a smaller, but still important, portion of society has more *fluid* views on torture. For this group, increased threat, the ethnicity of the subject, media depictions of torture as effective, and other manipulated factors can shift opinion. In our interviews, almost all of the professionals who worked in this area cited the role the TV show *24* had in providing a simple scenario and narrative in response to an impending threat.

In chapters 1 and 2, we examined media influences on support for torture. In multiple experiments, we found that 24's dramatic depictions of torture being effective increased support for torture and persuaded some people to act in accordance with this belief. We considered that showing torture as ineffective would persuade people in the opposite direction. This did not in fact occur. Whether torture worked or not, showing torture seemed to activate something in people to support its use in the future. When presenting versions of this experiment in public and academic settings, several people suggested that just showing people violence elicited calls for violent responses. To see if this mechanism was in operation, we also tested the effect of showing respondents a scene with nonpolitical violence (a fistfight with no reason for the pugilism). Seeing this general violence did not increase support for torture; to the contrary, it led to a decline in support for its use. We cannot be completely sure of any mechanism, but in conjunction with evidence from other experiments and interviews, we think this evidence suggests that there is something unique about torture. It is not just about seeing and being activated by violence.

Our experiments as well as political scientist Courtenay Conrad and colleagues' clearly show that when torture is viewed as effective some portion of society will support it.[1] Also, a nonnegligible segment of Americans will support using torture even when it is not effective at gaining actionable intelligence. As discussed in the introduction and in chapters 1 and 2, it might be that people think it is effective when torture punishes or deters. We intend to and hope others will investigate how these different reasons for torture lead to varying levels of support across different groups of people. As we developed in chapters 1 and 2, both punishment and deterrence may be evolutionary responses to aggression. Some combination of nature, nurture, and the environment may produce support for torture by otherwise pro-social members of the public. This would help explain why threatening environments such as the post-9/11 world activate support for torture of groups deemed responsible for horrific violence. Although we cannot definitively confirm that this is the reason people respond to terrorism with support for state violence, we can eliminate credible alternatives such as exposure to general violence.

Contrary to conventional wisdom, in chapter 3 many factors rooted in the identity of the suspect and interrogator were not found to affect support for its use. The interrogator's and suspect's ethnicity did not impact people's support. People were much more supportive of psychological torture than of physical pain. This result confirms much of what political scientist Darius Rejali describes in the rise of torture lite among democratic states.[2] When examining attitudes before and after release of the Senate Torture Report in 2014, the saliency of the topic did not seem to shift opinions, but it moved people toward action. Had we been able to do this experiment closer to the events of 9/11, we would expect stronger findings for ethnicity. This effect likely has faded over time.

In chapter 4, we examined similar contextual factors but also considered elite cues and more detailed identity options. In chapter 3's experiment, using traditional experimental methods, we were limited by the number of questions we could ask a respondent. In chapter 4, we introduced conjoint experiments, which are increasingly utilized in social and behavioral sciences because this tool allows researchers many more options. We asked similar questions in chapters 4 related to support for torture against certain nationalities (Chinese or Syrians) and suggested elites, such as Republican lawmakers or Supreme Court Justices. The results in chapter 3 suggested conditional support for torture, and in chapter 4 we examined many of these conditions. The most supported outcomes were that people tended to be influenced by military interrogators more than by other elites. Respondents were most supportive of torturing Syrians as opposed to people close to home (Americans) and there was no difference in support for torturing fellow Americans and either people similar in language and ethnicity (British) or people not normally associated with terrorism (Chinese). This tended to fit with our expectations for the experiments in chapter 3. If the suspect was a member of ISIS, a militia member, or a neo-Nazi, support for torturing them was much higher than for an animal rights activist, an anti-abortion activist, or a member of Antifa.

CAN PEOPLE BE PERSUADED?

At the heart of our experiments is the notion of persuasion. How can people be persuaded to change their views? As we found in our experiments, some individuals were *fixed* in their positions, and others were much more *fluid*. The focus of this book is on changing attitudes about torture—the folks who have fluid views. What we see across our experiments, however, is that there is a fairly consistent subset who indeed have fluid views, but the majority have fixed views on torture. Might there be differences between these two groups? We looked at the demographics of the fixed and fluid groups across each sample. The most consistent pattern is that Caucasians tend to have more fixed views and minorities have more fluid views on torture. Although we did not ask about political identification in most samples, when we did, Democrats had far more fixed views and Republicans had far more fluid views. Other demographic factors showed mixed results. In some samples, younger people had slightly more fluid views. Both men and low-income participants had more fluid views in some samples and more fixed views in others. Finally, we found no difference in views based on education or military experience. In short, it is clear that some people have fixed views of torture and others have fluid views. Beyond these few demographic factors, however, it is unclear why people fall into one category or the other. Recent research by political scientists Marc Hetherington and Jonathan Weiler uses these same terms to unlock partisan differences in beliefs. They claim that fixed types tend to identify as Republican and the fluid as Democrat.[3] However, we found the opposite to be true. This could be due to different samples of people or differences in the ways we use the terms. Hetherington and Weiler found that people who display a mixture of fixed and fluid beliefs will move toward fixed views under threatening conditions, which supports the evolutionary mechanism we discuss. Regardless, we think this a difference that matters for behavior and should warrant a good deal of future study.

The academic literature on persuasion is vast.[4] The empirical findings range from large effects to small or nonexistent effects. When people have weak prior beliefs about an issue and few elite cues about ways to think about the issue, they may be able to be swayed quite dramatically. How people feel about the rapper Kanye West may be very malleable, but when he expresses support for the Republican president, these effects are less fluid. When there are strong prior beliefs and partisan cues, such as trying to persuade a person to vote in a general election for a high-profile office such as governor or president, the effects of persuasion could be small or nonexistent.[5]

The strength of the person's attitude is also important. People who have strong beliefs or attitudes are hard to persuade. When attitudes are weaker or less informed, people can be moved. The irony is that once they are moved, the attitudes remain malleable and require repeated interventions to stay moved.[6]

In the context of torture policy, these attitudes are likely somewhere near the middle of completely fixed and completely fluid. Prior beliefs and information are likely limited. Few people actively gather information about the policy options and efficacy of each option. But as we have seen in public discourse and in our experiments, partisan cues matter, media matters, and messages are prevalent and likely are sent to provide shots of information to persuade people. On the flipside, views are more fixed on domestic issues such as abortion or tax policy than in foreign policy issues such as use of force.[7] Again, torture policy is likely a bit in between because it can have domestic or foreign implications. As we saw in our experiments, people were more supportive of the use of torture when it was done abroad than domestically. An important condition that can likely shift opinions is the threat environment.[8] As noted in many of our interviews, a high-threat environment shifts opinion toward actions such as torture. It is less clear whether those attitudes shift back in times of peace in the same amount and in an opposite direction. As Steven Kleinman, career military intelligence officer and interrogator, made clear in our interview with him, "regrettably, the pro-torture people have a better narrative than the anti-torture people. Theirs is quick and requires little understanding of an incredibly complex issue. Keep America safe. Torture works. If it doesn't, they deserve it anyway." If Kleinman's claim is accurate, the likelihood of shifting people away from torture as the threat abates is unlikely. Our experiments showed increased support for torture regardless of whether torture worked or not, which suggests support for Kleinman's insight. Even more unsettling, imagine that we could design a study that could definitively show whether torture was effective or not at eliciting actionable information. As political scientists D. J Flynn, Brendan Nyhan, and Jason Reiffler's work demonstrates, this likely would only make partisans double down on their incorrect beliefs.[9]

Many studies on persuasion in different contexts are one-shot between-subject experiments. These experiments measure differences in persuasion between groups or differences between people at one point in time. In contrast, many of our experiments have pre and post data on the same people. In studies like ours, we would typically expect that the pressure to maintain consistency reduces the effects of persuasion when compared to the between-subject experiments.[10]

LIMITATIONS

We are confident in the validity of our findings because they are based on having nationally representative samples in most cases and randomization in all cases. However, we are concerned about whether these results apply outside of the United States. All of our surveys and experiments were done within the United States, so we should be careful to avoid applying these findings to other countries in the world. We would be reticent to use our findings to explain support for torture in many other countries. We do agree with political scientist Darius Rejali that there are common patterns and trends among developed democracies, such as the United States and France, with regard to many aspects of torture.[11] In addition to the tactics, the mechanism through which citizens can provide institutional oversight is similar. Although different cultures and personalities may matter, we are more comfortable applying some of the results and expecting them to be consistent in the United Kingdom, Australia, etcetera. Wherever public opinion influences policy and the state is capable of both protecting citizens and harming them, we think our results would apply. Democratic institutions provide the mechanisms through which citizens can express their discontent. An effective judiciary can also limit the state's use of torture.[12]

In a more perfect set of studies, we might include the realism in either the population of people answering the questions or in terms of the experimental treatments. On the first point, we would like to extend these experiments to people working in the field and people charged with making and implementing these policies. The extent to which these people are nationally representative would not make a difference. If, however, there is something about them prior to service or factors of serving the country that lead to differences in their beliefs and actions, having this sample would be more realistic in terms of who is actually making the decisions and implementing harsh interrogation. In our current framework, we have a sense for national public opinion on these issues, but this assumes a process in which opinion translates into policy and action. We have begun pursuing such populations, but they are more difficult to reach and more expensive to survey.

As discussed in earlier chapters, the most realistic experiment when examining support for torture is a series of trials designed by psychologist Loran Nordgren and colleagues.[13] Like us, they repeated measures of support for torture before and after exposure to treatments. These interventions—extreme temperature, sleep deprivation, and others—are meant to more accurately simulate torture. None was as serious as what detainees in harsh interrogation often receive, but these treatments more closely approximate this exposure than a simple hypothetical or vignette or watching a video. The effects were fairly powerful, and they suggested that the *empathy gap* explained shifts in opinion. That is, harsh interrogation does not seem overly harsh until one is exposed to it, even mildly. When this gap is closed, people shift their opinions away from torture or harsh interrogation. Future experiments could build on what Nordgren and colleagues found and examine conditions that lead to large changes in opinion as well as to changes in opinion in targeted populations that are in charge of implementing and making policy. An interesting group to survey would be members of the military SERE training, who are exposed to harsh interrogation to see how this exposure influences their opinions on the practice.[14]

These suggestions apply to experimenting with why people support the use of torture. As we have seen in our experiments as well as others, such as political scientists Conrad and colleagues, perceived efficacy of torture has a large influence on support.[15] Experiments on whether or not torture is effective are extremely challenging to implement in a safe yet realistic way. Future work in this area could expand from other clever designs that mirror serious, real-world decision-making in a controlled laboratory setting. For example, as law professor Lucian Dervan and psychologist Vanessa Edkins's work on plea bargaining shows, coercive interrogations likely generate false confessions.[16] Applying this to the counterterrorism domain would suggest similar outcomes, but no study directly does this.

These experiments require greater financial support and access than we have had. Our experiments are not the final word on any of these issues, and we suggest future experiments increase realism, extend generalizability, and create greater scientific understanding in a research domain in great need of it.

ACADEMIC IMPLICATIONS

An important limitation of our work is that we are not introducing a grand new theory. For some, this may be a fatal limitation. Many academics make their careers on introducing a powerful new theory that can explain a lot more than previous theories. These academics then often spend a good deal of time and their careers defending this theory, sometimes even when mounting evidence casts serious doubt on the theory in relation to relevant alternatives.

In international relations, for example, the big three grand theories—realism, liberalism, and constructivism—remain prominent.[17] Over time, there have been extensive debates over which one is more powerful.[18] While all remain, as political scientist Daniel Maliniak and colleagues demonstrate, more recent work focuses on testing midrange theory and less on a new grand theory.[19] Some may mourn the loss of grand theorizing, but the trend seems to be toward validating and refining existing midrange theory rather than developing new grand ones.[20] Again, there are reasonable debates over this issue in many fields from international relations to sociology. We want to be transparent about our approach and its limitations. We are primarily focusing on an approach more rooted in individual psychology, with insights from criminology, economics, political science, and sociology. We hope our study provides some small steps toward better understanding individual choice in the context of counterterrorism policy.

We built in behavioral tests such as signing petitions in some of our experiments, but there is still much to learn about the link between attitudes and behaviors in this context. In the study of radicalization and terrorism, we know that many people have extreme thoughts and say extreme things, but we do not fully know the link between these ideas and taking extreme actions.[21] Some, like Dylann Roof, the Charleston Church shooter, say violent racist things online and then act, but many people who post on Storm Front or other white nationalist message boards never engage in violent action. In torture policy, some people state support for the practice but would never use harsh interrogation themselves. In a domain in which there is social and geographic distance between beliefs and actions, this may be less of a concern than in the radicalization field. However, knowing the links between beliefs and actions in this domain should be a priority in future research, especially regarding how this link influences policy and implementation.

We have consciously tried to remain neutral about what ought to be done in this policy domain, but we think future work should peel apart why state violence is often so acceptable to the public and rebel violence is not. Going back to the Weberian definition of the state as the group in society that exercises legitimate force, perhaps the answer is simply about how the state can use violence when it chooses. Future work, however, should explore why legitimacy for state violence varies and how public support for violence outside of institutional channels leads to its use and nonuse. From the Philippines to Brazil, we are currently witnessing a rise in extrajudicial killings and other state-sanctioned or state-allowed violence that is similar to torture and that is beyond the rule of law. What else explains this?

Our experiments used samples of people from the United States, and we stated that the argument and results easily travel to developed, Western-style democracies such as the UK, Australia, France, and Japan. We would expect slight cultural differences based on different histories, but we expect that the main mechanisms would be similar. What we are less confident in is how the results might travel to places like Brazil, Argentina, India, or other democracies in which public opinion matters but checks on the executive are less and judiciaries are more subject to political manipulation.[22] Similarly, in Russia, Turkey, and the Philippines, which are inching toward authoritarianism, and other places that are already there, such as Iran or Saudi Arabia, we would expect the link between opinion and policy to be much murkier. We do not think, however, that it is nonexistent. Even authoritarian states can be punished for unpopular policies. To be able to confidently claim how this might work would require new studies in places that are more authoritarian.

Findings from chapters 1 and 2 also identify two processes that could be explored in future research. First, what impact do visual media have on views of terrorism and counterterrorism threats, and how does the impact of visual media different from the impact of other types of primes, such as reading or thinking about threatening material? Second, if empathy for the victim can partially explain why seeing a fistfight reduced support for torture, what impact do other forms of violence have on different types of responses to that aggression specifically and to other forms of aggression more broadly? The empathy gap that Nordgren and colleagues identify suggests reducing this gap can help move opinion on violent action.[23] More work needs to be done to examine the conditions under which the empathy gap exists and whether fixed or fluid actors are most affected after reducing this empathy gap.

At some level, as social researchers, we believe that all people can be changed or influenced. It is often a question of probabilities and amounts. With that said, as political scientists Joshua Kalla and David Brockman find and most political campaigns know, trying to persuade more fixed types is at best an expensive endeavor and at worst a losing strategy.[24]

Finally, it is not clear how torture is an example of a larger phenomenon. In other words, do the same factors that explain disappearances, political imprisonment, and other state-sanctioned or supported personal integrity rights violations explain torture? In short, is support for torture a thing apart, or is it similar to support for other state policies that abuse the personal integrity rights of its citizens? Political scientists David Cingranelli and David Richards, among others, clearly believe torture should be considered in the same breath as forced disappearances, extrajudicial killings, and political imprisonment because these four factors make up their CIRI scale of state abuses of human rights.[25] In our experiments, there are hints that something is unique about torture. Whether we are prompting people with threats, mortality, or showing them violence, something about exposure to torture moves them differently. We cannot resolve this here. Across the study of political violence, the issue of whether to study types of violence by themselves or to come up with explanations across types remains. We think future work should try to disentangle whether torture is an example of a larger phenomenon or thing to explain in its own right.

POLICY IMPLICATIONS

Political scientists Conrad and colleagues note that elections are a mechanism that cannot provide accountability at the precise moment they should.[26] When the state was under threat was the moment in which discussions were made in the Bush administration about enhanced interrogations. This was also the moment when our experiments and Conrad and colleagues suggest people can be persuaded to support harsher interrogation.[27] If steps are taken to reduce the likelihood of using torture in interrogation of terrorism suspects, this suggests it needs to occur at a time of relative peace and security. During times of real or perceived heightened threat, most of the inertia in debates will lead to the use of torture. Again, the mechanism could be that individuals under threat have evolved to respond instinctively with violence to deter or survive. It may also be a little more complicated and indirect. People are influenced by elites and media that reinforce the perceived threat and suggest violent options in response. Regardless of which mechanism is prominent, real debate can only be fruitful outside of this threat environment.

Some of the policy implications of our findings are troubling. Exposure to pop-culture media depictions of torture working makes people more supportive of the practice in counterterrorism. One policy recommendation could be to limit media depictions of torture. Of course, constraining media would be an affront to our free and open society and its democratic values. Legal prohibitions on media depictions are out of the question in such a society if we are to remain free. But are requests from the public, academics, or political leaders appropriate? In the 2007 meeting in which military and interrogation professionals tried to convince the producers of 24 not to show torture working, one of the attendees, General Finnegan, is said to have asked that they "do a show where torture backfires . . . [because] the kids see it and say, 'If torture is wrong, what about 24'?" However, our findings here show that depicting torture as ineffective may backfire. Priming people with threat and torture may already suggest violence as the appropriate response. So what can be done to minimize the impact of media on public perception of torture?

For over a decade, public officials, scholars, and the general public have debated whether and when torture is acceptable in counterterrorism. Consensus among scholars and high-level military officials is clear. Torture does not lead to accurate, actionable intelligence. In fact, torture may be counterproductive in at least three ways: (1) inaccurate information wastes time and resources; (2) suspects who have information may have divulged it under a different interrogation approach but will not after they are tortured (Abu Zubaydah, for example); and (3) when the United

States uses torture, this can serve as a recruitment tool that leads to further violence (see Abu Ghraib).

As we've mentioned in previous chapters, it is difficult to precisely pinpoint the number of Americans that support the practice of torture. It is fair to say that this number changes, but a nontrivial percent—and depending on circumstance, potentially a majority—of the public supports its use.

Unfortunately, academic research is inaccessible to much of the public, whereas television, video games, and fiction are readily available. Our results here suggest that media depictions of torture help to drive public support for the practice. Recent experiments such as those by political scientists Calvert Jones and Celia Paris show that fiction can also shape political opinions.[28] Dystopian narratives, for example, increase the willingness of people to support violence.

To narrow the gap between expert and public opinion, we must change the narrative on torture. Finnegan's recommendation to show torture as ineffective at gathering information might be counterproductive. We need more complicated portrayals of torture and terrorism that move beyond the ticking time bomb scenario. For example, in the show 24, Jack Bauer does not face psychological or physical struggles based on his actions, nor does he have a long time to deliberate on the best course of action in a sixty-minute program. Real-life interrogators who have conducted or witnessed torture, however, do face long-lasting effects and often need time to build effective strategies.[29] Media also do not show the damage torture does to victims who face myriad long-term physical and psychological struggles.[30] Perhaps depicting torture's impact on both victims and perpetrators would be a step toward making the damage of this practice more real for the public. Humanizing torture can make it less abstract, which could erode public support for the practice and potentially reduce the empathy gap.

As results from chapters 1 and 3 show, saliency does matter when moving people to action. We should expect forward motion in an enhanced threat environment. Again, this is likely why we need deliberation and changes in attitude prior to an unforeseen terrorist event that threatens public safety.

Those in opposition to torture as a policy should likely push for detainees to be housed in the United States. As our experiments show, people are less supportive of the use of harsh interrogation when it is done close to home. We should expect also that it will be less likely used as a tool in counterterrorism when the alleged perpetrators are American, domestic, and do not have transnational or Islamist ideology.

Psychological torture can be just as destructive to the victim as physical torture, but we should expect it more often as Americans in our chapter 3 sample seem more supportive of it. France and the United States have been innovators in this nonscarring form of harsh interrogation. We would expect that it will be the most difficult for opponents to stop, especially during times of heightened threat of terrorism.

MORALITY AND SECOND-ORDER EFFECTS

We have deliberately, as detailed in the introduction, avoided the moral debate, but we believe this debate has value and should occur in the larger American marketplace of ideas. Our intention here, however, is to highlight evidence and academic research while attempting to be more apolitical. To some this may itself seem amoral. One may question the morality of harsh interrogation but decide to use the technique if it is deemed effective for any or all of the reasons we have discussed thus far. Another limitation of this discussion and how we framed it is that we are concerned with *direct* effects. That is, we examined in the experiments and academic literature how immediate stimuli led to changes in beliefs and behaviors. But what if these effects are not so immediate? What if these effects are mediated or moderated with substantial temporal delays? In an interview with the authors, Steven Kleinman suggested the following:

> Apart from the debate about its efficacy as a means of eliciting reliable information, torture generates undeniable consequences. I'd like to think we've learned from studying the impact of drone strikes. When a targeted individual is killed, and especially when members of that target's family are also killed—either accidentally or, as our president has recommended, as a direct objective—you eliminate a handful of people but simultaneously create the conditions that generate 100 new recruits. This same phenomenon unfolds when the knowledge that America is torturing reaches

the global public. From my vantage point as a senior intelligence officer, I would have grave reservations if information obtained from torture were used to drive operations, even if those operations resulted in the removal of ten high-value terrorists. My reservations would be based on the knowledge that torture has been used as a major recruiting theme for violent extremist groups, and the stories of torture have the potential to lead to hundreds of new extremists arrayed against us. So many interrogators have asked detainees about the reasons they joined an extremist movement, and so many detainees have stated it was their responsibility to do so when they heard their brothers had been tortured.

It is an extremely difficult task to assess how torture affects populations downstream. To the extent that Kleinman is accurate that torture may be a tool for future mobilization, next wave research should consider how to best measure this effect. Of course, deterrence arguments are the flipside of the coin to Kleinman's claim. If torture deters future involvement, then we would need to develop research designs that could accurately measure these demobilizing effects. As generations of scholars can attest, it may be the most difficult task to measure an outcome that does not occur.[31]

FINAL REMARKS

We have attempted to provide experimental and interview evidence relating to why Americans do or do not support torture. We have focused on the context of counterterrorism for many reasons. First, in the interviews, respondents all suggested that this is the moment when we need to have restraints on the use of torture. Ironically, this is also the time when many Americans will be more supportive of its use. One of the limitations of the interviews is that most of the people who responded to our requests were opposed to the use of torture for either moral or efficacy reasons. Proponents of the policy that we contacted rejected or did not reply to our requests. To the extent that they could have pointed us toward some insights into why people support torture, we missed these. If this were a book about efficacy, this would be a glaring omission. Given that our task is about support, this is an unfortunate fact but does not likely undermine what we found. In debates over policy in which partisans have intense feelings on all sides, it is likely that some piece of our work will be used to justify one policy or another. We hope that all sides will avoid confirmation bias or simply picking and choosing small pieces of evidence to support their preferred outcome regardless of all of the evidence. We would like to think that decent, reasonable people can disagree on the best path forward for making the United States secure from terrorism. In discussing these disagreements, we hope people seek out and evaluate evidence.

APPENDIX

Semistructured Interviews of Experts

APPENDIX TO THE INTRODUCTION

METHOD

Semistructured interviews on views of what has impacted public awareness and perceptions of torture across their careers. Interviews will last between forty-five and sixty minutes and will be recorded and transcribed. We also use snowball sampling to identify other stakeholders who can provide additional perspectives and insights on our research topic.

INTRODUCTION

We are academic researchers writing a book on public support for and opinions of torture. We are interested in factors that influence public support. Our book is mostly focused on public opinion surveys. We are also interested in what stakeholders in this field—members military, interrogators, politicians, and NGO employees—think impacts public opinion on torture. We would like to ask a few questions and have a conversation about your experiences and thoughts on this question. Our plan is to use quotes and stories from experts like you to motivate each chapter of the book and hopefully make it appeal to a broader audience. We will be recording this session for our records to ensure accuracy. Before using any quote or story, we will circle back with you to ensure that we are doing so accurately. We're interested in this being a conversation more than an interview, so please talk to us as if we're your friends.

EXPERTS INTERVIEWED

Elizabeth Grimm Arsenault, former member of the intelligence community and current professor at Georgetown University. Interviewed on November 19, 2018

Tricia Bacon, former member of the intelligence community and current professor at American University. Interviewed on November 14, 2018

Scott Edwards, senior advisor at Amnesty International. Interviewed on August 8, 2018

Mark Fallon, former NCIS deputy assistant director for counterterrorism and commander of the USS Cole Task Force, author of *Unjustifiable Means*. Interviewed on July 6, 2018

Curt Goering, executive director of the Center for Victims of Torture. Interviewed on September 19, 2018

Steven Kleinman, retired Air Force colonel and career military intelligence officer and interrogator with experience in human intelligence, special operations, and counterterrorism. Interviewed on July 16, 2018

Tony Lagouranis, former Army interrogator who served in the Iraq War and was stationed at Abu Ghraib prison in 2004. Interviewed on September 14, 2018

Joe Navarro, retired FBI special agent and expert in nonverbal communication. Interviewed on September 18, 2018.

Tom Parker, former MI5 officer. Interviewed on July 20, 2018

Leslie Parsons, commander of the Criminal Investigations Division of the Washington, D.C. Metropolitan Police Department. Interviewed on August 8, 2018

OUTLINE OF QUESTIONS

[Start with warm-up questions]

Can you please state your name and give us an overview of your professional background?

[probe about experiences]

Please tell us a little bit about your professional background as it relates to interrogations and counterterrorism.

[probe about experiences]

In your experience as X, what do you see has impacted public support for torture?

[probe on these views]

From what you've seen, how do you think people form their opinions about torture?

[probe on these views]

Can those opinions change? If so, how?

[probe on these views]

What role do you think media has on opinion about torture?

[probe on these views]

How does expert opinion impact views on torture among the public?

[probe on these views]

Is there anything else that we haven't discussed that you think is important for this topic?

[probe on these views]

APPENDIX TO CHAPTER 1

DETAILS OF THE SAMPLE

We conducted a prior power analyses to determine the necessary sample size for the experiment in this chapter. Our within-subject hypotheses required a sample size of at least 45 participants per condition, and we had at least 48 participants per condition. Our between-subject hypotheses required a sample size of at least 74 total participants, and we had 147. Across the three conditions, participants were balanced by demographic factors.

TABLE 1.A1 Participant Demographics

Demographic Factor	Percent
Race: White	66.9
Race: Hispanic or Latino	6.1
Race: Black or African American	6.1
Race: Asian	13.5
Race: Multiple	7.4
Gender: Male	43.3
Gender: Female	54.7
Freshman	16.8
Sophomore	16.1
Junior	16.8
Senior	22.2
Graduate Student	28.2
Christian	42.7
Jewish	10.7
Muslim	3.3
Buddhist	2.7
Hindu	2.0
Atheist/agnostic	36.0
Other religion	2.7
Very liberal	16.2
Liberal	43.4
Moderate	31.1
Conservative	8.8
Very conservative	0.7

DETAILS ON THE KEY VARIABLES

TABLE 1.A2 Dependent and Independent Variables Over Sample

Variable	Range	Effective %	Effective Mean (SD)	Ineffective %	Ineffective Mean (SD)	Control %	Control Mean (SD)
Dependent variables							
Pretest support	1–4	—	1.82 (0.90)	—	1.67 (0.83)	—	1.79 (0.74)
Posttest support	1–4	—	2.04 (0.92)	—	1.77 (0.82)	—	1.79 (0.74)
Sign any petition	—	66.0	—	60.0	—	42.0	—
Petition: Support torture	—	16.0	—	10.0	—	10.0	—
Petition: Oppose torture	—	50.0	—	60.0	—	32.0	—
Independent variable							
Political ideology	1–5	—	2.35 (0.86)	—	2.29 (0.91)	—	2.40 (0.88)
Politics: Very liberal	—	16.3	—	18.4	—	14.0	—
Politics: Liberal	—	40.8	—	44.9	—	44.0	—
Politics: Moderate	—	34.7	—	28.6	—	30.0	—
Politics: Conservative	—	8.2	—	6.1	—	12.0	—
Politics: Very conservative	—	0.0	—	2.0	—	0.0	—

TREATMENT EFFECTS ON SUPPORT FOR TORTURE

Here we present the t-test results comparing pretest to posttest support for torture in each of the three experimental conditions. People are more supportive of torture after watching a clip in which torture works, $t(49) = -2.76$, $p = 0.005$, but the effect size is small ($d = 0.24$). People who saw ineffective torture were slightly—but not significantly—more supportive of torture after watching the video clip, $t(47) = -0.89$, $p = 0.19$. There was no difference in pre- and posttest support for torture among participants in the control condition, $t(47) = 0.00$, $p = 0.50$.

PETITION SIGNING

To see if there are differences in petition signing across conditions, we estimated a logistic regression model to compare *if* any petition was signed and a multinomial logistic regression model to compare *which* petition was signed across conditions.

TABLE 1.A3 Differences in Petition Signing by Condition

Petition Signed	Condition	Coefficient	Standard Error
Any petition	Effective	1.09**	0.42
	Ineffective	0.80†	0.41
	Constant	−0.51†	0.30
Petition to oppose	Effective	0.98*	0.44
	Ineffective	0.83†	0.44
	Constant	−0.69*	0.32
Petition to support	Effective	1.49*	0.74
	Ineffective	0.64	0.82
	Constant	−2.30†	0.61

Note: Results for "any petition" estimated with a logit model. Results for "petition to oppose" and "petition to support" estimated with a multinomial logit model. For both models, "no petition signed" is the base category.

†$p < 0.10$. *$p < .05$. **$p < .01$.

TABLE 1.A4 Differences in Petition Signing by Condition and Political Ideology

Petition Signed	Condition	Coefficient	Standard Error
Any petition	Effective	1.16**	0.43
	Ineffective	0.75†	0.42
	Political ideology	−0.35†	0.20
	Constant	0.29	0.55
Petition to oppose	Effective	1.06*	0.47
	Ineffective	0.82†	0.46
	Political ideology	−0.81**	0.25
	Constant	1.10†	0.62
Petition to support	Effective	1.65*	0.79
	Ineffective	0.22	0.93
	Political ideology	1.33**	0.644
	Constant	−6.15**	1.54

Note: Results for "any petition" estimated with a logit model. Results for "petition to oppose" and "petition to support" estimated with a multinomial logit model. For both models, "no petition signed" is the base category. Political ideology is coded on a 5-point scale in which higher scores signify being more conservative.

†$p < 0.10$. *$p < .05$. **$p < .01$.

Participants who did not see torture were significantly less likely to sign a petition than those who saw it work ($p = 0.010$) and somewhat less likely to sign a petition than those who saw torture not work, although this is not quite significant ($p = 0.054$).

We then look at *which* petition participants are more likely to sign by condition. Participants who did not see torture were significantly less likely than those who saw it work to sign a petition either in support of ($p = 0.027$) or in opposition to ($p = 0.044$) torture. There were no differences in which petition was signed between those who saw torture not work and those who didn't see torture. As expected, people who are more conservative were less likely to sign a petition in opposition to torture ($p = 0.001$) and more likely to sign a petition in support of it ($p = 0.002$)

SURVEY

{Everyone gets Consent Form first}

OPINIONS ABOUT CURRENT EVENTS

IDENTIFICATION OF INVESTIGATORS AND PURPOSE OF STUDY

You are being asked to participate in a research study conducted by Dr. Joseph K. Young and Erin M. Kearns from American University. The purpose of this study is to assess opinions on current event issues. This study will contribute to the student's completion of one of her research projects and doctoral dissertation.

RESEARCH PROCEDURES

Should you decide to participate in this research study, you will be asked to sign this consent form once all your questions have been answered to your satisfaction. This study consists of a survey that will be administered to individual participants at American University. You will be asked to provide answers to a series of questions related to your opinions about current event issues. You will then have the option to sign petitions about the current event issues discussed in the study, which will be sent to the Chairman of the Senate Committee under which the issue falls.

TIME REQUIRED

Participation in this study will require roughly 45 minutes of your time.

RISKS

The investigator perceives the following are possible risks arising from your involvement with this study: some of the questions may be upsetting to some people. If you feel uncomfortable, you are free to skip any individual question, portions of surveys, or an entire survey without penalty.

The foreseeable risks involved with this study are minimal. However, if you are upset by or feel uncomfortable about the material, there is help. The American University Counseling Center, located at 214 Mary Graydon Center, can be reached at (202) 885–3500.

BENEFITS

There are no direct benefits to the participant for this study. However, this present study will benefit research as a whole by providing a more complete understanding of opinions about current event topics.

CONFIDENTIALITY

Your identity will remain completely anonymous unless you alone choose otherwise. The results of this research will be presented at the 2014 American Political Science Association conference. The results of this project will be coded in such a way that the respondent's identity will not be attached to the final form of this study. The researcher retains the right to use and publish non-identifiable data. While individual responses are confidential, aggregate data will be presented representing averages or generalizations about the responses as a whole. All data will be stored in a secure location accessible only to the researcher. Upon completion of the study, all information that matches up individual respondents with their answers will be destroyed.

PARTICIPATION AND WITHDRAWAL

Your participation is entirely voluntary. You are free to choose not to participate. Should you choose to participate, you can withdraw at any time without consequences of any kind. You may also refuse to answer any individual question without consequences. You will receive $10 for your time.

QUESTIONS ABOUT THE STUDY

If you have questions or concerns during the time of your participation in this study, or after its completion or you would like to receive a copy of the final aggregate results of this study, please contact:

Erin M. Kearns
School of Public Affairs
American University
erin.kearns@student.american.edu

Dr. Joseph K. Young
School of Public Affairs
American University
Telephone: (202) 885-2618
jyoung@american.edu

QUESTIONS ABOUT YOUR RIGHTS AS A RESEARCH SUBJECT

Anthony Ahrens
Chair, Institutional Review Board
American University
(202) 885-1714
ahrens@american.edu

Matt Zembrzuski
IRB Coordinator
American University
(202) 885-3447
irb@american.edu

GIVING OF CONSENT

I have read this consent form and I understand what is being requested of me as a participant in this study. I freely consent to participate. I have been given satisfactory answers to my questions. The investigator provided me with a copy of this form. I certify that I am at least 18 years of age.

_____
Name of Participant (Printed)

_____   _____
Name of Participant (Signed)   Date

_____   _____
Name of Researcher (Signed)   Date

Background Information

- **[gender]** What is your gender? _____{open-ended question}
- **[sex_orient]** What is your sexual orientation?_____ {open-ended question}
- **[age]** How old are you? _____{open-ended question}
- **[collegeyear]** What year are you in college? _____ {open-ended question}
- **[major]** What is your major? _____{open-ended question}
- **[race]** What is your race? _____{open-ended question}
- **[religion]** What is your religious affiliation? _____ {open-ended question}
- **[dadeducation]** What is your father (or primary guardian)'s highest completed level of education?

  | Less than High School | High School | Some College |
  | Associates | Bachelors | Graduate Degree |

- **[dadpolitics]** How would you describe your father (or primary guardian)'s political views?

  | Very Liberal | Liberal | Moderate | Conservative | Very Conservative |

- **[momeducation]** What is your mother (or primary guardian)'s highest completed level of education?

Less than High School	High School	Some College
Associates	Bachelors	Graduate Degree

- **[mompolitics]** How would you describe your mother (or primary guardian)'s political views?

  Very Liberal   Liberal   Moderate   Conservative   Very Conservative

- **[yourpolitics]** How would you describe your political views?

  Very Liberal   Liberal   Moderate   Conservative   Very Conservative

- **[residency]** Where do your parents (or primary guardians) live?

City	Suburbs	Rural Area

Opinions About Current Events

Listed below are a series of statements about current events.

Please remember that your answers are totally anonymous. We are interested in you honest attitudes about this topic. There are no "right" or "wrong" answers; there are only your opinions. We thank you in advance for your honesty.

Please indicate the degree to which you agree or disagree with each of the statements using the following scale:

1 = Completely disagree
2 = Disagree
3 = Agree
4 = Completely agree

{Question order & response options both presented in randomized order}

[preKeystone] I support building the Keystone pipeline.   _____

[preMarijuana] I do not support the legalization of marijuana.   _____

[preTorture] I support the use of torture in interrogations.   _____

[preMarriage] I support the legalization of same-sex marriage.   _____

[preIntelDesign] I do not support teaching intelligent design in   _____
public schools.

Video Treatments

**All participants watched five videos that were presented in a random-
ized order. Each participant was randomly assigned to watch only one
of the videos on torture.**

1. **Climate Change**
2. **Side Effects of Marijuana**
3. **Torture**
   a. **Torture Effective**
   b. **Torture Ineffective**
   c. **No Torture (control)**
4. **Gay Marriage**
5. **Teaching Intelligent Design in Public Schools**

Opinions About Current Events

Listed below are a series of statements about current events.

**Please remember that your answers are totally anonymous. We
are interested in your honest attitudes about this topic. There are no
"right" or "wrong" answers; there are only your opinions. We thank
you in advance for your honesty.**

Please indicate the degree to which you agree or disagree with each of
the statements using the following scale:

1 = Completely Disagree
2 = Disagree
3 = Agree
4 = Completely Agree

**Question order and response options both presented in randomized
order that matches presentation in the pretest.**

[**postKeystone**] I support building the Keystone pipeline.   _____

[**postMarijuana**] I do not support the legalization of marijuana.   _____

[**postTorture**] I support the use of torture in interrogations.   _____

[**postMarriage**] I support the legalization of same-sex marriage. _____

[**postIntelDesign**] I do not support teaching intelligent design _____
in public schools.

Opinions About Current Events

We are interested in how American University students view key current event issues. The issues discussed in this study are contentious, and can lead to strong feelings on both sides.

As you may be aware, citizens can petition the government regarding these issues. In addition to your stated levels of support or opposition, we would like to extend the opportunity to take action in support/opposition by signing a petition to your member of Congress. Please note that this is completely voluntary, but if you do choose to do so then your name will be identified.

Enclosed in this packet are petitions on the current event issues that we have discussed. The pages in BLUE are in SUPPORT of the issue in question. The pages in GREEN are in OPPOSITION to the issue in question. Please sign the petitions with which you agree. If you do not have a strong opinion on the issue or are not comfortable doing so, you are under no obligation to sign any of these petitions. You can sign petitions for none, some, or all six of the issues. This will have no impact on your compensation for the study.

We will send the signed petitions on both sides of each issue to the Chairman of the Senate Committee under which the issue falls.

[Opposition Letters – Green in the Original Version that Participants Saw]

Date:
The Honorable Barbara Boxer
Committee on Energy and Natural Resources
112 Hart Senate Office Building
Washington, DC 20510

Dear Senator Boxer,

The Keystone XL Pipeline is dangerous, dirty, and destructive—and the latest Environmental Impact Statement was both inaccurate and incomplete.

It ignores the pipeline's significant risk for toxic spills, ignores its catastrophic impacts on our climate, and ignores the clear consensus among financial analysts and oil executives who agree Keystone XL will make the difference in tar sands development.

For the National Interest and the future of our country and our planet, I urge you to reject this pipeline.

Sincerely,

_____

signature

Date:
The Honorable Patrick J. Leahy
Committee on the Judiciary
437 Russell Senate Office Building
Washington, DC 20510

Dear Senator Leahy,

Marijuana has been essentially illegal since 1937 and the prohibition of this plant should remain in place. While some argue that marijuana is relatively harmless, it has side effects that are as detrimental as those from alcohol or tobacco.

While the government could make money through taxation of marijuana if it were legalized, there are too many risks associated. The damage to society would be too great to justify the legalization of marijuana for profit purposes.

For the health and safety of our country, now and in the future, I urge you to reject calls for the legalization of marijuana.

Sincerely,

_____

signature

Date:

The Honorable Thomas R. Carper

Senate Committee on Homeland Security and Governmental Affairs

513 Hart Senate Office Building

Washington, DC 20510

Dear Senator Carper,

Several reports from international NGOs have confirmed the use of torture and cruel, inhuman and degrading treatment of prisoners in United States' custody. These revelations bring shame to our nation. As an advocate who believes in the humane treatment of prisoners and who relies on our laws to protect prisoners and citizen alike, this issue is of the utmost importance to me.

By participating in torture and improper treatment of prisoners, members of the United States law enforcement, intelligence, and military communities have committed grave violations of human rights and participated in crimes under U.S. and international law. Such violations are truly disturbing and cannot be tolerated.

I urge you to support a bill that prohibits the use of torture by all members of United States law enforcement, intelligence community, and military.

Sincerely,

_____

signature

Date:

The Honorable Dick Durbin

Subcommittee on the Constitution, Civil Rights and Human Rights

711 Hart Senate Office Building

Washington, DC 20510

Dear Senator Durbin,

Same-sex marriage should be banned. Homosexual behavior is environmentally influenced, and choosing to live a homosexual lifestyle should not come with special rights.

Equality demands that we treat in the same way things that are the same. But a same-sex relationship is fundamentally different from a marriage. No same-sex union can produce a child. Male and female were made for each other. Same-sex couples were not.

We must protect the laws set by nature and human design. I ask you to support a ban on the special right of homosexual marriage and protect us from ourselves.

Sincerely,

_____

signature

Date:
The Honorable Tom Harkin
Committee on Health, Education, Labor, and Pensions
731 Hart Senate Office Building
Washington, DC 20510

Dear Senator Harkin,

The United States was founded on the principle that there should be separation between church and state. Teaching Intelligent Design or Creationism in public schools violates this separation.

Intelligent Design as not [a] valid worldview in any scientific context and should not be taught within our public schools. Evolution is a scientific theory, supported by evidence, which has stood up to decades of empirical scrutiny. Intelligent Design is based in religious beliefs and has not withstood empirical examination. For this reason, evolution has a place in public schools whereas Intelligent Design does not.

I ask you to support a bill that would prohibit the discussion of Intelligent Design in public schools.

Sincerely,

_____

signature

[Support Letters – Blue in the Original Version that Participants Saw]

Date:
The Honorable Barbara Boxer
Committee on Energy and Natural Resources
112 Hart Senate Office Building
Washington, DC 20510

> *Dear Senator Boxer,*
>
> Keystone XL has undergone one of the most thorough environmental assessments ever conducted. I support TransCanada's proposed Keystone XL pipeline and urge you to swiftly finalize the draft SEIS.
>
> As our economy struggles to recover, Keystone XL will provide much-needed jobs to construction workers, manufacturers, and other laborers. As the draft SEIS outlines, the project will support over 42,100 jobs during the construction phase and will generate over $5 billion in economic activity, including $2.05 billion in worker salaries.
>
> Keystone XL will be critical to improving American energy security and boosting our economy, and I encourage its expeditious approval.
>
> Sincerely,
>
> _____
>
> signature

Date:
The Honorable Patrick J. Leahy
Committee on the Judiciary
437 Russell Senate Office Building
Washington, DC 20510

> *Dear Senator Leahy,*
>
> It is understood that while marijuana has been essentially illegal since 1937, the prohibition of this plant has not worked. There have been studies done that prove it has medical uses. It has also been proven that in recreational use it does less harm than alcohol.

Please look at how much our government spends on trying to fight something that is of no threat to our society. There are many other ways that money could be spent to make this a stronger country. The government could also make money through taxation, as it does with alcohol and tobacco.

Don't be afraid to stand up and say this to your fellow politicians. I am asking you to do this for us and for our country.

Sincerely,

_____

signature

Date:
The Honorable Thomas R. Carper
Senate Committee on Homeland Security and Governmental Affairs
513 Hart Senate Office Building
Washington, DC 20510

Dear Senator Carper,

The use of torture is essential to our national security. While these methods of interrogation are not always ideal, and should not be abused, they are also necessary in certain situations.

Torture is a helpful tool for extracting critical information about our enemies, their plans, and future targets. Furthermore, these tactics allow us to gather key details about the structure of enemy groups and how they recruit and communicate, which is critical to homeland security.

For safety and security of our country and its citizens, I urge you to support a bill that calls for the use of ill treatment and torture against enemy combatants when necessary.

Sincerely,

_____

signature

Date:

The Honorable Dick Durbin

Subcommittee on the Constitution, Civil Rights and Human Rights

711 Hart Senate Office Building

Washington, DC 20510

Dear Senator Durbin,

In America everyone is entitled to equal rights by the law. However, gay and lesbian couples still do not have the legal right to marriage throughout much of the United States. Gay and lesbians deserve the same respects and rights as heterosexuals. Still, in over 30 states, citizens in same-sex relationships are still being denied the equal opportunity of marriage.

In order for us to move forward as a nation, we need to set aside religious beliefs, realizing that the government is separated from the church for a reason, and legalize same-sex marriage. We are lucky enough to live in a country where we are ensured equal rights and liberties, but if we fail to protect them, we are in turn neglecting the very beliefs that America was founded upon.

This is a human right: all people should be treated equally. I urge you to support a bill to legalize same-sex marriage for everyone in the United States.

Sincerely,

---

signature

Date:

The Honorable Tom Harkin

Committee on Health, Education, Labor, and Pensions

731 Hart Senate Office Building

Washington, DC 20510

Dear Senator Harkin,

In the United States, we allow for differing views, cultures and ideologies of fellow citizens. We do this while maintaining the common values of peace, respect, and understanding. Sadly these values are being eroded when it comes to a belief in Almighty God as Creator of the earth and all life upon it.

Intelligent Design as a valid worldview is in danger of not being tolerated by our Government in any scientific context within our schools. Neither Intelligent Design nor The Theory of Evolution provides empirical evidence within a lab. They are differing interpretations of facts and are both accepted upon the basis of faith according to a person's chosen interpretation.

I ask you to support a bill that would allow any public school in the United States to discuss or teach Intelligent Design as a valid worldview should they desire to do so.

Sincerely,

_____

signature

OPINIONS ABOUT CURRENT EVENTS

Information Sheet/Debriefing

The overall purpose of this study is to examine how framing can impact public perceptions of current event issues, specifically the use of torture in interrogations. We are interested in how the perceived efficacy of torture impacts how an individual's attitudes toward the practice. Furthermore, we are interested in assessing behaviors in support of stated beliefs.

In the past decade, there has been increased scholarly attention on torture, especially in the context of counterterrorism. Research on torture has focused on perceptions of the practice, support of the practice, perceptions of what constitutes torture, why the use of torture persists despite arguments against it, and the efficacy of the practice. While many of these studies assess stated attitudes toward torture, research has not yet adequately addressed how media influences perceptions on torture or whether people take action that is in line with their stated beliefs on torture.

As a reminder, your responses in this study are completely anonymous unless you alone chose otherwise. The data will not be connected to any identifying information, and will only be used for research purposes.

We ask that you do not share the nature of this study with others, especially on campus, as that could damage the integrity of the data in this study.

The foreseeable risks involved with this study are minimal. However, if you are upset by or feel uncomfortable about the material, there is help. The American University Counseling Center, located at 214 Mary Graydon Center, can be reached at (202) 885-3500.

If you would like more information about the use of torture in interrogations, you may find the following article interesting or useful:

Carlsmith, Kevin M., & Sood, Avani Mehta. (2009). The fine line between interrogation and retribution. *Journal of Experimental Social Psychology*, 45, 191–196.

Gray, Kurt, & Wegner, Daniel M. (2010). Torture and judgments of guilt. *Journal of Experimental Social Psychology, 46*, 233–235.

Janoff-Bulman, Ronnie. (2007). Erroneous assumptions: Popular belief in the effectiveness of torture interrogation. *Peace and Conflict: Journal of Peace Psychology, 13*(4), 429–435.

For more information on this study, or if you would like the results when they are available, contact:

Dr. Joseph K. Young   Erin M. Kearns
jyoung@american.edu   erin.kearns@student.american.edu

APPENDIX TO CHAPTER 2

DETAILS OF THE SAMPLE

Data for this chapter were collected via YouGov, an international survey company, from September 18–25, 2018. To be eligible for participation, a person had to be located in the United States. In total, 1,945 participants completed the survey. Of these, 152 participants were excluded from analyses because they either sped through the survey or straightlined responses by giving the same answer to each question. Both of these behaviors indicate that these participants were not paying attention to the questions. Analyses were conducted for the remaining 1,793 participants, which approximates the national population on race, gender, age, income, and education.

TABLE 2.A1 Participant Demographics

Demographic Factor	Our Sample on YouGov (%)	U.S. Population (%)
Race: White	67.9	60.4
Race: Hispanic or Latino	12.8	18.3
Race: Black or African American	12.3	13.4
Race: Asian	3.3	5.9
Race: Native American	0.7	1.3
Race: Middle Eastern	0.2	—
Race: Other	1.3	—
Race: Multiple	1.6	2.7
Gender: Male	45.8	49.2
Gender: Female	53.8	50.8
Gender: Other	0.4	—
Age: 18–24	9.7	11.1
Age: 25–34	19.7	18.0
Age: 35–44	15.5	16.3
Age: 45–54	14.5	16.7

Age: 55–64	22.4	16.7
Age: 65+	18.2	20.5
Education: Less than HS	5.7	10.9
Education: HS/GED	33.6	28.6
Education: Some college	21.6	18.5
Education: Associate's degree	10.3	9.7
Education: Bachelor's degree	18.4	20.6
Education: Graduate degree	10.5	11.6
Income: Less than $25,000	23.6	20.1
Income: $25,000–$49,999	24.1	21.7
Income: $50,000–$79,999	21.1	19.6
Income: $80,000–$99,999	6.7	9.4
Income: More than $100,000	12.1	29.3
Prefer not to say	12.3	—
Party ID: Democrat	35.8	32
Party ID: Republican	23.9	23
Party ID: Independent	29.3	39
Party ID: Other	4.6	——
Party ID: Not sure	6.3	——
Political Ideology: Very liberal	13.9	——
Political Ideology: Liberal	16.8	——
Political Ideology: Moderate	29.6	——
Political Ideology: Conservative	19.0	——
Political Ideology: Very conservative	11.4	——
Political Ideology: Not sure	9.3	—
Military Veteran	12.9	7

PILOTING THE VIDEO TREATMENTS

Prior to data collection, we piloted the treatment videos with 169 participants on Amazon's Mechanical Turk. Each participant in the pilot was randomly assigned to watch one of the seven videos and answer questions about what took place. Results from the pilot study show that treatment videos have the desired effect.

Participants rated the interrogator as significantly higher on trust fostering in the rapport-building videos, $t(167) = 8.18$, $p < 0.001$, and this holds across each condition separately. Similarly, participants rated that there was more psychological harm in the three torture videos versus the other videos, but no difference between those videos, $t(167) = 11.54$, $p < 0.001$. Participants rated that there was lower physical pain in the rapport-building treatments relative to the others, $t(167) = -13.50$, $p < 0.001$. There is no difference in views of physical pain across the 24 clips, and people rated the general violence condition as more physically painful ($p = 0.10$). Finally, participants rated the two videos in which the interrogator got information to prevent the attack as being more effective than the condition in which the interrogation was unsuccessful, $t(144) = 12.61$, $p < 0.001$. Note: the general violence condition was omitted from these analyses because there was no possible effective outcome.

DETAILS ON THE KEY VARIABLES AND DIFFERENCES AMONG GROUPS

ANOVA indicates that there is no significant difference in pretest support for torture across treatment conditions, $F(6, 1786) = 1.43$, $p = 0.20$.

Participants in a national sample are more likely to support torture when they see a clip in which torture is effective ($t(242) = 2.05$, $p = 0.02$). Again, seeing torture as either ineffective ($t(260) = 1.06$, $p = 0.14$), ambiguous ($t(251) = 0.26$, $p = 0.40$), or not present ($t(254) = 1.30$, $p = 0.10$) has no impact on support for the practice. People were significantly less supportive of torture after seeing a clip showing general violence ($t(264) = -2.24$, $p = 0.008$). Regardless of whether rapport-building was effective or not, people were *more* supportive of torture after seeing a clip with this interrogation approach ($t(267) = 3.97$, $p < 0.001$), ($t(254) = 2.87$, $p = 0.002$).

People who were both primed to think about their own death and saw torture work were more supportive of torture posttest ($t(114) = 1.97$, $p = 0.03$). In contrast, priming on mortality and seeing a video with general violence significantly decreased support for torture posttest ($t(118) = -2.39$, $p = 0.009$).

TABLE 2.A2 Dependent and Independent Variables

Video Treatment	Overall			No Mortality Salience			Mortality Salience		
	Pre M (SD)	Post M (SD)	Change p (sign)	Pre M (SD)	Post M (SD)	Change p (sign)	Pre M (SD)	Post M (SD)	Change p (sign)
Torture effective	2.04 (1.00)	2.14 (1.06)	0.02 (+)	1.95 (0.99)	2.00 (1.01)	0.18 (ns)	2.15 (1.00)	2.29 (1.09)	0.03 (+)
Torture ineffective	2.05 (0.97)	2.09 (1.06)	0.14 (ns)	2.13 (1.03)	2.14 (1.09)	0.41 (ns)	1.98 (0.91)	2.05 (1.03)	0.09 (app +)
Torture ambiguous	2.11 (1.01)	2.12 (1.03)	0.40 (ns)	2.11 (1.05)	2.09 (1.08)	0.39 (ns)	2.11 (0.98)	2.15 (1.00)	0.29 (ns)
No torture	2.13 (1.00)	2.19 (1.04)	0.10 (app +)	2.10 (0.94)	2.17 (1.02)	0.08 (app +)	2.16 (1.06)	2.20 (1.06)	0.28 (ns)
General violence	2.03 (1.03)	1.94 (0.98)	0.008 (−)	2.05 (1.04)	2.00 (1.02)	0.15 (ns)	2.00 (1.02)	1.86 (0.94)	0.009 (−)
Rapport effective	1.91 (1.01)	2.10 (1.06)	<0.001 (+)	1.84 (0.93)	2.04 (1.02)	0.0002 (+)	1.99 (1.08)	2.15 (1.09)	0.01 (+)
Rapport ineffective	1.98 (0.93)	2.09 (1.01)	0.002 (+)	1.99 (0.92)	2.15 (1.03)	0.002 (+)	1.97 (0.95)	2.02 (0.98)	0.16 (ns)

Conservative participants are significantly more supportive of torture both pre- ($p < 0.001$) and post- ($p < 0.001$) treatment. Conservative participants increase support for torture after seeing a clip in which it is effective ($t(72) = 3.05$, $p = 0.002$), but liberal participants' support is unchanged ($t(73) = -0.34$, $p = 0.37$). In contrast, liberal participants increase support for torture after seeing a clip in which it was ineffective ($t(77) = 1.80$, $p = 0.04$), whereas conservative participants' support is unchanged ($t(71) = 0.70$, $p = 0.24$). Further, conservative participants decrease their support for torture after seeing a clip showing violence in general ($t(89) = -2.29$, $p = 0.01$), but liberal participants didn't ($t(81) = -1.10$, $p = 0.14$).

More conservative participants allocate significantly less money to relationship-building between law enforcement and the public ($p < 0.001$) and cybersecurity capabilities ($p < 0.001$). More conservative participants allocate significantly more money to research on enhanced interrogation and torture ($p < 0.001$), the nuclear arsenal ($p < 0.001$), and the military ($p < 0.001$).

TABLE 2.A3 Why People Increased Support for Torture Video Condition

Treatment	# ↑ Support	Needs to Be More Harmful	Acceptable to Prevent Attack	It's Effective	Not Sure	Something Else
Torture effective	47	6 (12.8%)	23 (48.9%)	14 (29.8%)	10 (21.3%)	9 (19.1%)
Torture ineffective	40	11 (27.5%)	23 (57.5%)	7 (17.5%)	3 (7.5%)	7 (17.5%)
Torture ambiguous	39	1 (2.6%)	21 (53.8%)	7 (17.9%)	8 (20.5%)	6 (15.4%)
No torture	39	5 (12.8%)	18 (46.2%)	11 (28.2%)	5 (12.8%)	9 (23.1%)
General violence	15	2 (13.3%)	5 (33.3%)	3 (20.0%)	7 (46.7%)	1 (6.7%)
Rapport effective	52	4 (7.7%)	28 (53.8%)	14 (26.9%)	11 (21.2%)	5 (9.6%)
Rapport ineffective	38	3 (7.9%)	17 (44.7%)	5 (13.2%)	7 (18.4%)	8 (21.2%)
Total	270	32 (11.9%)	135 (50.0%)	61 (22.6%)	51 (18.9%)	45 (16.7%)

TABLE 2.A4 Why People Decreased Support for Torture Video Condition

Treatment	# ↓ Support	Torture Is Harmful	Torture Is Illegal	Torture Is Ineffective	Not Sure	Something Else
Torture effective	22	12 (54.5%)	10 (45.5%)	6 (27.3%)	4 (18.2%)	0 (0%)
Torture ineffective	30	13 (43.3%)	9 (30.0%)	10 (33.3%)	6 (20.0%)	3 (10%)
Torture ambiguous	35	16 (45.7%)	14 (40.0%)	10 (28.6%)	3 (8.6%)	4 (11.4%)
No torture	29	10 (34.5%)	11 (37.9%)	9 (31.0%)	3 (10.3%)	4 (13.8%)
General violence	30	12 (40.0%)	10 (33.3%)	7 (23.3%)	6 (20.0%)	2 (6.7%)
Rapport effective	17	3 (17.6%)	3 (17.6%)	7 (41.2%)	6 (35.3%)	1 (5.9%)
Rapport ineffective	18	8 (44.4%)	8 (44.4%)	10 (55.6%)	2 (11.1%)	1 (5.6%)
Total	181	74 (40.9%)	65 (35.9%)	59 (32.6%)	30 (16.6%)	15 (8.3%)

BUDGET ALLOCATION

TABLE 2.A5 Budget Allocation by National Security issue and Video Condition

Treatment	Relationship-Building Between LE & Public	Research on Enhanced Interrogations & Torture	Building the Nuclear Arsenal	Military	Cybersecurity Capabilities
Torture effective	26.2 (19.4)	8.5 (11.2)	9.6 (11.6)	27.3 (18.2)	28.3 (16.1)
Torture ineffective	25.0 (19.4)	6.2 (9.2)	10.1 (13.5)	28.7 (20.0)	29.9 (19.5)
Torture ambiguous	26.0 (20.6)	9.7 (14.3)	11.3 (14.2)	27.7 (20.0)	25.4 (17.4)
No torture	24.6 (18.6)	7.9 (10.3)	9.6 (12.2)	28.3 (19.4)	29.6 (19.3)
General violence	26.9 (22.1)	7.3 (10.3)	9.5 (11.7)	28.1 (20.7)	28.2 (19.9)
Rapport effective	24.3 (18.6)	8.6 (11.6)	10.4 (13.3)	27.8 (19.2)	29.8 (17.8)
Rapport ineffective	26.6 (18.8)	8.1 (11.3)	8.1 (10.0)	27.4 (20.3)	29.8 (19.3)
Total	**25.6 (19.7)**	**8.0 (11.3)**	**9.8 (12.5)**	**27.7 (19.7)**	**28.7 (18.6)**

Note: Numbers in parentheses are the standard deviation.

SURVEY

CURRENT EVENTS AND ISSUES

IDENTIFICATION OF INVESTIGATORS AND PURPOSE OF STUDY

You are being asked to participate in a research study conducted by Dr. Joseph K. Young from American University and Dr. Erin Kearns from the University of Alabama. The purpose of this study is to assess opinions on current event issues. This study will contribute to the Investigators' book project.

RESEARCH PROCEDURES

This study consists of a survey that will be administered online to a sample of approximately 1,200 individuals from across the United States. You will be asked to provide answers to a series of questions related to your opinions about current event issues.

TIME REQUIRED

Participation in this study will require roughly 20 minutes of your time.

RISKS

The investigator perceives the following are possible risks arising from your involvement with this study: some of the questions may be upsetting to some people. If you feel uncomfortable, you are free to skip any individual question, portions of surveys, or an entire survey without penalty.

The foreseeable risks involved with this study are minimal. However, if you are upset by or feel uncomfortable about the material, there is help. The American University Counseling Center, located at 214 Mary Graydon Center, can be reached at (202) 885–3500.

BENEFITS

There are no direct benefits to the participant for this study. However, this present study will benefit research as a whole by providing a more complete understanding [of] opinions about current event topics.

CONFIDENTIALITY

Your identity will remain completely anonymous unless you alone choose otherwise. The results of this research will be presented at academic conferences, in reports to practitioners, and as part of the researcher's doctoral dissertation. The results of this project will be coded in such a way that the respondent's identity will not be attached to the final form of this study. The researcher retains the right to use and publish non-identifiable data. While individual responses are confidential, aggregate data will be presented representing averages or generalizations about the responses as a whole. All data will be stored in a secure location accessible only to the researcher. Upon completion of the study, all information that matches up individual respondents with their answers will be destroyed.

PARTICIPATION AND WITHDRAWAL

Your participation is entirely voluntary. You are free to choose not to participate. Should you choose to participate, you can withdraw at any time without consequences of any kind. You may also refuse to answer any individual question without consequences.

QUESTIONS ABOUT THE STUDY

If you have questions or concerns during the time of your participation in this study, or after its completion or you would like to receive a copy of the final aggregate results of this study, please contact:

Dr. Joseph K. Young
American University
jyoung@american.edu

———— ⊷∞⊶ ————

Dr. Erin M. Kearns
University of Alabama
emkearns@ua.edu

QUESTIONS ABOUT YOUR RIGHTS
AS A RESEARCH SUBJECT

Matt Zembrzuski
IRB Coordinator
American University
(202) 885-3447
irb@american.edu

GIVING OF CONSENT

I have read this consent form and I understand what is being requested of me as a participant in this study. I have been given satisfactory answers to my questions. The investigator provided me with a copy of this form. I certify that I am at least 18 years of age.

By clicking the "next" button, I freely consent to participate in this study.

{Survey Opens—everyone sees questions on this page first}

{Start INTRO questions}

[VideoTest] In this survey, we will ask you to watch a few video clips. To be sure that your audio and video are working, please click on the test clip below.

{Page break}

[Intro] We would like to start with a few questions about how things are going for you, your city, and the country.

[I1] In general, how satisfied are you with *your life*?
    <1> Very satisfied
    <2> Somewhat satisfied
    <3> Somewhat dissatisfied
    <4> Very dissatisfied

[I2] In general, how satisfied are you with how things are going *in your city*?
    <1> Very satisfied
    <2> Somewhat satisfied
    <3> Somewhat dissatisfied
    <4> Very dissatisfied

[I3] In general, how satisfied are you with how things are going *in the country*?
    <1> Very satisfied
    <2> Somewhat satisfied
    <3> Somewhat dissatisfied
    <4> Very dissatisfied

{End INTRO questions}
{Start ISSUE IMPORTANCE questions}
{Question order randomized within this section—dynamic grid}

[IssueImportance] Some people care a lot about public policy issues while others care little about them. Thinking about the following issues, how important is each one to you? (**reverse coded response options**)

[II1] Marijuana: legalization v. keeping it illegal
[II2] Terrorism Interrogations: debate over whether or not torture is acceptable
[II3] Public schools: teaching creationism v. evolution
[II4] Police interactions with minorities: significant problem or not
[II5] Voter fraud: significant issue or not
[II6] Climate change: significant issue or not
    <1> This issue is <u>very important</u> to me
    <2> This issue is <u>somewhat important</u> to me
    <3> This issue is <u>not too important</u> to me
    <4> This issue is <u>not important at all</u> to me

{End ISSUE IMPORTANCE questions}

{Present the following Modules in a randomized order:

- *News Consumption Module*
- *TV Consumption Module*
- *Experimental Materials Module}*

{Start NEWS CONSUMPTION MODULE}

Thinking about **the news,** please answer the following questions.

[NC1] Many people do not find news to be important in their daily life. How important is following the news to you?

(reverse coded in Stata so Very important =4)

<1> Very important

<2> Somewhat important

<3> Not too important

<4> Not important at all

[NC2] In the past 48 hours have you . . . (check all that apply) {**order randomized**}

<1> Watched local TV news

<2> Watched national TV news

<3> Read a print newspaper

<4> Read an online newspaper

<5> Read a blog

<6> Listened to a radio news program or talk radio

<7> Used social media (such as Facebook, YouTube or Twitter)

<8 fixed> None of these

{If NC2=7, then show to NC3}

[NC3] Did you do any of the following *on social media* (such as Facebook, YouTube or Twitter)? {**order randomized**}

<1> Posted a story, photo, video or link about politics

<2> Posted a comment about politics

<3> Read a story about politics

<4> Watched a video about politics

<5 fixed > None of these

{If NC2=!8, then show to NC4}

[NC4] In the past 48 hours, have you gotten news from any of the following sources? Check all that apply. **{order randomized}**

<1> ABC/ABC News
<2> AOL
<3> BBC
<4> Breitbart
<5> CBS
<6> CNN
<7> Drudge Report
<8> Economist
<9> ESPN
<10> Facebook/Twitter
<11> Fox/Fox News
<12> Google/Google News
<13> Huffington Post
<14> Infowars
<15> Local news source
<16> MSN
<17> MSNBC
<18> New York Times
<19> NBC
<20> NPR
<21> USA Today
<22> Wall Street Journal
<23> Washington Post
<24> Yahoo/Yahoo News
<25 fixed> Other {text}
<26 fixed> None

{End NEWS CONSUMPTION MODULE}

{Start TV CONSUMPTION MODULE}

Now thinking about the **TV shows that you watch . . .**

[TV1] Some people watch a lot of TV while others don't. Have you *ever* seen an episode of any of the following popular TV shows? Select all that apply. **{order randomized in clumps of 5}**

<1> 24

<2> Breaking Bad

<3> Community

<4> Designated Survivor

<5> Dexter

<6> Downton Abbey

<7> Friday Night Lights

<8> Game of Thrones

<9> Grey's Anatomy

<10> Hawaii Five o

<11> How I Met Your Mother

<12> Homeland

<13> Law & Order (any)

<14> Modern Family

<15> The Office

<16> Parks & Recreation

<17> Quantico

<18> Scandal

<19> The Sopranos

<20> The Wire

[**TV2**] How many episodes have you watched of each show? {**present as dynamic matrix w/random order**}

<1> Just one episode

<2> A few episodes

<2> Most episodes

<3> Every episode

{End TV CONSUMPTION MODULE}

{Start EXPERIMENTAL MATERIALS MODULE}
{PRE-questions}

We would like your views on various issues. There are no right or wrong answers—just your opinions. {**Question order randomized within this section**}

Please indicate how much you agree or disagree with each of these statements: {response order = reverse; set to a variable so you can reuse the same order in the post}

[PreMarijuana] I support legalization of marijuana.

[PreTorture] I support the use of torture in interrogations.

[PreCreationism] I support teaching creationism in public schools.

<1> Completely agree

<2> Somewhat agree

<3> Somewhat disagree

<4> Completely disagree

{Page break}
{Mortality Salience Priming}

We would like you to consider something difficult. It will help us understand how you make decisions.

{RANDOMIZE MORTALITY SALIENCE PRIMING:

- 1 = YES
- 0 = NO}

If MortalitySalience = 1, show:

[MS1] Briefly describe the emotions that the thought of your own death arouses in you. {open ended}

[MS2] Describe, as specifically as you can, what you think will happen to you physically as you die and once you are physically dead. {open ended}

If MortalitySalience = 0, show:

[NMS1] Briefly describe the emotions that the thought of dental pain arouses in you. {open ended}

[NMS2] Describe, as specifically as you can, what you think will happen to you physically as you experience dental pain. {open ended}

{Page break}
{Videos}

In this section, you will watch a series of 3 video clips, each lasting only a couple minutes.

Please be sure your speakers are turned on and the volume is at a proper level for you to hear.

(Videos) {Show video clips in a random order}

{RANDOMIZE INTERROGATION STORY—each person only sees one of these}

1. **torture effective**
2. **torture ineffective**
3. **torture ambiguous**
4. **no torture/no rapport-building & outcome unclear**
5. **general violence**
6. **rapport-building effective**
7. **rapport-building ineffective}**

{CONTROL VIDEOS}

{Everyone sees the same clip for creationism and marijuana legalization}

{End VIDEOS}

{End EXPERIMENTAL MATERIALS MODULE}

{Start POST questions}

We would like to get a sense of your views on various issues. There are no right or wrong answers—just your opinions. {Question order in the same order as PRE questions}

Please indicate how much you agree or disagree with each of these statements:

[PostMarijuana] I support legalization of marijuana.

[PostTorture] I support the use of torture in interrogations.

[PostCreationism] I support teaching creationism in public schools.

<1> Completely agree

<2> Somewhat agree

<3> Somewhat disagree

<4> Completely disagree

{End POST questions}

{Start BUDGET questions}

[BCMarijuana] Imagine that a portion of the federal budget on <u>drug issues and public health</u> has to be allocated to the following areas. Please indicate what percentage should be spent in each area:

<1> Drug treatment

<2> More prisons for drug users and drug dealers

<3> Public health programs

<4> Drug abuse education programs

<5> More police presence in places with high drug use

{choose, then rank if more than one selected}

[BCTorture] Imagine that a portion of the federal budget on <u>national security matters</u> has to be allocated to the following areas. Please indicate what percentage should be spent in each area:

<1> Building relationship between police and the public

<2> Research on enhanced interrogation and torture

<3> Building the nuclear arsenal

<4> Military

<5> Cyber security

{choose, then rank if more than one selected}

[BCCreationism] Imagine that a portion of the federal budget on <u>education</u> has to be allocated to the following areas. Please indicate what percentage should be spent in each area:

<1> Science-based curriculum

<2> Multiple views on human history

<3> Creation as discussed in the Bible

<4> Critiques of science

<5> Critiques of religious teachings

{choose, then rank if more than one selected}
{End BUDGET questions}

{Start ANSWER CHANGE questions}
{If PreMarijuana>PostMarijuana, then show MarijuanaChangeLess}

[**MarijuanaChangeLess**] After the videos, you said you were <u>less support-ive of legalizing marijuana</u>. Why? Choose all that apply. {**randomize options**}
<1> Marijuana is harmful
<2> Marijuana is illegal
<3> Marijuana is a gateway drug
<4 fixed> Something else {text}
<5 fixed > Not sure

{If PreMarijuana<PostMarijuana, then show MarijuanaChangeMore}

[**MarijuanaChangeMore**] After the videos, you said you were <u>more sup-portive of legalizing marijuana</u>. Why? Choose all that apply. {**randomize options**}
<1> Marijuana is helpful
<2> Marijuana is legal in many places
<3> Marijuana is not a gateway drug
<4 fixed> Something else {text}
<5 fixed> Not sure

{If PreTorture>PostTorture, then show TortureChangeLess}

[**TortureChangeLess**] After the videos, you said you were <u>less support-ive of torture in interrogations</u>. Why? Choose all that apply. {**randomize options**}
<1> Torture is harmful to the person
<2> Torture is illegal
<3> Torture is ineffective
<4 fixed> Something else {text}
<5 fixed> Not sure

{If PreTorture<PostTorture, then show TortureChangeMore}

[**TortureChangeMore**] After the videos, you were <u>more supportive of torture in interrogations</u>. Why? Choose all that apply. {**randomize options**}
<1> Torture needs to be more harmful to be useful
<2> Torture is acceptable to prevent an attack

<3> Torture is effective
<4 fixed> Something else {text}
<5 fixed> Not sure

{If PreCreationism>PostCreationism, then show CreationismChange Less}

[**CreationismChangeLess**] After the videos, you said you were <u>less support-</u>
<u>ive of teaching creationism in public schools</u>. Why? Choose all that apply.
{randomize options}
<1> Creationism is harmful
<2> The Constitution requires separation of Church and State
<3> Creationism is not scientific
<4 fixed> Something else {text}
<5 fixed> Not sure

{If PreCreationism<PostCreationism, then show CreationismChange More}

[**CreationismChangeMore**] After the videos, you said you were <u>more sup-</u>
<u>portive of teaching creationism in public schools</u>. Why? Choose all that
apply. **{randomize options}**
<1> Creationism helps students understand human history
<2> Creationism offers another perspective
<3> Creationism is religion-based
<4 fixed> Something else {text}
<5 fixed> Not sure

{Everyone sees questions on this page}
Finally we have a few questions for statistical purposes.
(<u>Low Sensitivity Demographics</u>)

[**LSD1**] What is your gender?
<1> Male
<2> Female
<3> Other {text}
[**LSD2**] In what year were you born?

{dropdown}

[**LSD3**] Please select the race/ethnicity with which you most strongly identify.

    <1> White

    <2> Black or African-American

    <3> Hispanic or Latino

    <4> Asian or Asian-American

    <5> Native American

    <6> Middle Eastern

    <7> Mixed Race

    <8> Other [txt] {open varlabel = "Race, other"}

[**LSD4**] What state do you live in?

<STATE> {dropdown}

[**zip**] What is your zip code?

{open ended}

[**PSD1**] What is your present religion, if any?

    <1> Protestant

    <2> Roman Catholic

    <3> Mormon

    <4> Eastern or Greek Orthodox

    <5> Jewish

    <6> Muslim

    <7> Buddhist

    <8> Hindu

    <9> Atheist

    <10> Agnostic

    <11> Nothing in particular

    <12> Something else {open}

[**PSD2**] How often do you attend formal religious services?

    <1> Once a week or more

    <2> A few times a month

    <3> Less than once a month

    <4> Almost never or never

    <5 fixed> Not sure

[**PSD3**] What is the highest level of education you have completed?

    <1> Did not graduate from high school

    <2> High school graduate

<3> Some college, but no degree (yet)

<4> 2-year college degree

<5> 4-year college degree

<6> Postgraduate degree (MA, MBA, MD, JD, PhD, etc.)

[PSD4] Were you born in the United States?

<1> Yes

<2>No

{If PSD4=2, then continue to 4a and 4b. If not, skip to PSD5}

[PSD4a] What country were you born in? {text}

[PSD4b] Which country do you identify with more strongly?

<1> Country of Birth

<2> United States

<3> Both equally

[PSD5] We'd like to know whether you or someone in your immediate family is currently serving or has ever served in the U.S. military. Immediate family is defined as your parents, siblings, spouse, and children. Please check all boxes that apply.

<1> I am currently serving in the U.S. military

<2> I have immediate family members currently serving in the U.S. military

<3> I previously served in the U.S. military but I am no longer active

<4> Members of my immediate family have served in the U.S. military but are no longer active

<5> Neither myself nor any members of my immediate family have ever served in the U.S. military

[PSD6] Thinking back over the last year, what was your family's annual income?

<1> Less than $10,000

<2> $10,000–$14,999

<3> $15,000–$19,999

<4> $20,000–$24,999

<5> $25,000–$29,999

<6> $30,000–$39,999

<7> $40,000–$49,999

<8> $50,000–$59,999

<9> $60,000–$69,999

<10> $70,000–$79,999

<11> $80,000–$99,999

<12> $100,000–$119,999

<13> $120,000–$149,999

<14> $150,000 or more

<15> Prefer not to say

[PSD7] What is your marital status?

<1> Married

<2> Separated

<3> Divorced

<4> Widowed

<5> Never married

<6> Domestic / civil partnership

[PSD8] In general, how would you describe your own political viewpoint?

<1> Very liberal

<2> Liberal

<3> Moderate

<4> Conservative

<5> Very conservative

<6 fixed> Not sure

[PSD9] Generally speaking, do you think of yourself as a. . . .?

<1> Democrat

<2> Republican

<3 fixed> Independent

<4 fixed> Other [pid] {open}

<5 fixed> Not sure

[PSD10] Political Party Identification

<1> Strong Democrat

<2> Weak Democrat

<3> Lean Democrat

<4> Independent

<5> Lean Republican

<6> Weak Republican

<7> Strong Republican

<8> Not sure

<9> Don't know

[**PSD11**] Many people weren't able to vote in the 2016 presidential election. How about you?

    <1> Yes, I voted

    <2> No, I was not registered to vote in 2016

    <3> No, I was too young or otherwise ineligible to vote

    <4> No, I just didn't vote

{If PSD11=1, then continue to 11a and 11b}

[**PSD11a**] Who did you vote for in the election for President?

    <1> Hillary Clinton

    <2> Donald Trump

    <3 fixed> Gary Johnson

    <4 fixed> Jill Stein

    <5 fixed> Evan McMullin

    <6 fixed> Other [presvote16post_t] {open}

    <7 fixed> Did not vote for President

[**PSD11b**] To what extent did you support the candidate for whom you voted?

    <1> Strongly supported

    <2> Somewhat supported

    <3> Somewhat did not support

    <4> Strongly did not support

APPENDIX TO CHAPTER 3

DETAILS OF THE SAMPLE

Both waves of data for this chapter were collected via Amazon's Mechanical Turk (MTurk) platform. We collected the first wave of data from June 10–19, 2014, and the second wave from December 17–18, 2014. To be eligible for participation in both waves, a person had to be located in the United States, have completed at least 1,000 tasks (HITs) on MTurk, and have an approval rating greater than 98 percent for those tasks. People who participated in the first wave of data collection were not eligible to participate in the second wave.

In Wave 1, 1,229 people completed the survey but 23 were dropped from analyses for either speeding through the survey, straight-lining answers, or failing the attention check. In sum, 1,206 participants were used for analyses in Wave 1 of the study. In Wave 2, 1,363 people completed the survey, but 151 were dropped from analyses for speeding, straight-lining, or failing the attention check. In total, 1,212 participants were used for analyses in Wave 2.

Table 3.A1 shows a breakdown of participant demographics for both waves of this project and compares our samples to what would be nationally representative.

TABLE 3.A1 Participant Demographics

Demographic Factor	June 2014 MTurk Sample (%)	December 2014 MTurk Sample (%)	U.S. Population (%)
Race: White	77.3	75.6	62.8
Race: Hispanic or Latino	3.8	5.4	16.9
Race: Black or African American	6.7	6.7	12.6
Race: Asian	6.9	7.2	5.0
Race: Middle Eastern	0.3	0.2	not listed
Race: Other	0.5	0.2	5.2
Race: Multiple	4.5	4.9	2.9

Gender: Male	54.7	57.3	49.2
Gender: Female	45.3	42.7	50.8
Age: 18–24	18.0	17.5	12.8
Age: 25–34	43.2	45.6	17.7
Age: 35–44	20.4	20.5	16.5
Age: 45–54	11.5	9.0	17.7
Age: 55–64	5.5	6.1	16.3
Age: 65+	1.5	1.4	18.9
Education: Less than HS	0.4	0.4	13.6
Education: HS/GED	13.4	10.5	28.0
Education: Some college	29.3	29.9	21.2
Education: Associate's degree	10.7	12.9	7.9
Education: Bachelor's degree	36.8	36.4	18.3
Education: Graduate degree	9.3	9.9	11.0
Income: Less than $20,000	17.3	17.2	18.0
Income: $20,000–$39,999	28.8	29.5	20.3
Income: $40,000–$59,999	23.2	24.7	15.9
Income: 60,000–$79,999	15.4	12.6	12.4
Income: $80,000–$99,999	7.4	8.2	8.8
Income: More than $100,000	7.9	7.7	24.7
Live In[1]: City	34.9	36.2	31
Live In: Suburbs	47.8	44.5	55
Live In: Rural area	17.3	19.3	14
Political Views[2]: Liberal	53.5	51.2	23
Political Views: Moderate	29.1	30.4	34
Political Views: Conservative	17.4	18.4	39

1. https://www.pewsocialtrends.org/2018/05/22/demographic-and-economic-trends-in-urban-suburban-and-rural-communities/

2. https://news.gallup.com/poll/245813/leans-conservative-liberals-keep-recent-gains.aspx

DETAILS OF THE MODELING APPROACH

Our $4 \times 2 \times 3$ experimental design creates a total of 24 possible conditions, and each participant is randomly assigned to one. Here we manipulate the interrogator-suspect dyad, the location, and the interrogation tactic. The interrogator-suspect dyad can be one of four possible categories, location takes one of two possible categories, and interrogation tactic takes one of three possible categories. For analyses, we must create a series of binary variables for each possible category. For example, for each interrogator-suspect dyad, we created a binary variable for each dyad in which the variable equals 1 if the participant was assigned to that condition and 0 if not. We then created a binary variable for domestic location that equals 1 if the participant was assigned to the United States condition and 0 if they were assigned to the Afghanistan condition. Finally, we created a binary variable for each type of treatment in which the variable equals 1 if the participant was assigned to that treatment and 0 if not.

Each participant was assigned to one and only one condition, so each of the binary variables we created is exhaustive and mutually exclusive. For example, every participant read a vignette that was based in either the United States or Afghanistan, but not both. If a person read about the vignette in the United States, the domestic location binary variable would score a 1 and, by definition, that means that the participant did not read a vignette based in Afghanistan. Although we could also create an international location binary variable, this is not necessary because a 0 on the domestic binary variable has the same meaning.

To examine the impact that each factor has on the outcomes, we estimated a series of regression models. Regression allows researchers to simultaneously examine the impact of multiple independent variables—here each treatment option—on the outcome or dependent variable. Because every person falls into one and only one category for each manipulated factor, regression analyses require that we exclude at least one binary variable indicator for each of the three manipulated factors. For example, it is impossible to include the binary variables for the CC, CM, MC, and MM dyads in the same regression model because they are exhaustive, so there is no other group to compare these groups against. For this reason, we must exclude at least one of these binary variables for each manipulated factor from our regression models.

Because we expect that there may be differences in support for torture across all of the dyads, there is no theoretical reason to exclude a particular dyad, but for our analyses we must use one category as the reference category. We use the MM dyad as the reference category and compare results for the other dyads against the MM dyad. As a robustness check, models are also estimated with separate dummies for the interrogator ethnicity and the suspect ethnicity. Results are reported in the appendix and are fundamentally the same. There are only two options for location, so it does not matter which one we exclude because they are being directly compared to one another. Here we include the domestic binary variable and interpret it relative to the international condition. Finally, we are interested in differences between each treatment group and the control group, so we leave the no torture condition as the reference category.

In the survey, we also asked participants about demographic factors that could impact our results. Our main analyses do not include these variables because random assignment should mean that demographics are evenly distributed across the treatment conditions.

AVERAGE DIFFERENCES IN OUTCOME VARIABLE SCORES FROM WAVE 1 TO WAVE 2

Here we present the t-test results comparing the mean score on each outcome variable between Wave 1 and Wave 2. Salience does not impact whether people consider the interrogation torture ($t(2410) = 0.77$, $p = 0.44$); consider the interrogation justified ($t(2405) = -1.31$, $p = 0.19$); consider the interrogation to be legal ($t(2294) = 0.12$, $p = 0.91$); think that the suspect deserves the treatment overall ($t(2398) = -0.50$, $p = 0.62$); think that the suspect is responsible for his treatment ($t(2411) = -1.12$, $p = 0.23$); think that the interrogator is responsible ($t(2398) = 0.29$, $p = 0.78$).

Participants were more willing to sign a petition both in support of ($t(2416) = 2.62$, $p = 0.004$) and in opposition to ($t(2416) = 2.62$, $p = 0.004$) torture after the Senate Torture Report was released.

EQUALITY OF COEFFICIENTS

There are four possible conditions for dyad and three possible conditions for interrogation type, and sometimes we want to know if there is a significant difference among the binary variables included in the model. Regression allows up to compare each binary indicator to the reference category only, and equality of coefficients tests allow us to compare the estimates between two binary indicators to see if they are significantly different from one another. When multiple binary indicators for the same manipulated factor (for example, psychological and physical harm) are significant, we conduct these equality of coefficients tests. We discuss the findings in text and present the p-values here in the appendix.

- People were more likely to consider physical harm v. psychological harm as torture both pre-STR ($p < 0.0001$) and post-STR ($p = 0.0003$).
- People think the interrogation is less justified when it involves physical harm versus psychological harm both pre-STR ($p = 0.002$) and post-STR ($p = 0.006$).
- People rate the interrogator as more responsible than the suspect both before ($p < 0.001$) and after ($p < 0.001$) release of the STR.

TABLE 3.A2 Experimental Conditions

Condition	Interrogator	Suspect	Location	Interrogation Tactic
1	Caucasian	Caucasian	U.S.	Psychological torture
2	Caucasian	Middle Eastern	U.S.	Psychological torture
3	Middle Eastern	Caucasian	U.S.	Psychological torture
4	Middle Eastern	Middle Eastern	U.S.	Psychological torture
5	Caucasian	Caucasian	Afghanistan	Psychological torture
6	Caucasian	Middle Eastern	Afghanistan	Psychological torture
7	Middle Eastern	Caucasian	Afghanistan	Psychological torture
8	Middle Eastern	Middle Eastern	Afghanistan	Psychological torture
9	Caucasian	Caucasian	U.S.	Physical torture
10	Caucasian	Middle Eastern	U.S.	Physical torture
11	Middle Eastern	Caucasian	U.S.	Physical torture
12	Middle Eastern	Middle Eastern	U.S.	Physical torture
13	Caucasian	Caucasian	Afghanistan	Physical torture
14	Caucasian	Middle Eastern	Afghanistan	Physical torture
15	Middle Eastern	Caucasian	Afghanistan	Physical torture
16	Middle Eastern	Middle Eastern	Afghanistan	Physical torture
17	Caucasian	Caucasian	U.S.	No torture (control)
18	Caucasian	Middle Eastern	U.S.	No torture (control)

19	Middle Eastern	Caucasian	U.S.	No torture (control)
20	Middle Eastern	Middle Eastern	U.S.	No torture (control)
21	Caucasian	Caucasian	Afghanistan	No torture (control)
22	Caucasian	Middle Eastern	Afghanistan	No torture (control)
23	Middle Eastern	Caucasian	Afghanistan	No torture (control)
24	Middle Eastern	Middle Eastern	Afghanistan	No torture (control)

DETAILS ON THE KEY VARIABLES

TABLE 3.A3 Dependent and Independent Variables

		Wave 1		Wave 2	
Variable	Range	Frequency (%)	Mean (SD)	Frequency (%)	Mean (SD)
Dependent Variables					
It is torture	1–4	—	2.66 (1.16)	—	2.62 (1.14)
It is justified	1–4	—	2.36 (0.95)	—	2.41 (0.94)
It is legal	1–4	—	2.15 (1.01)	—	2.14 (1.00)
It is moral	1–4	—	2.16 (0.95)	—	2.18 (0.95)
Suspect deserves it	1–4	—	2.20 (0.89)	—	2.22 (0.91)
Interrogator responsible	1–4	—	3.39 (0.66)	—	3.38 (0.69)
Suspect responsible	1–4	—	2.19 (0.90)	—	2.24 (0.93)
Sign petition—Support	—	4.4	—	6.9	—
Sign petition—Oppose	—	12.9	—	16.4	—
Don't sign petition	—	82.7	—	76.73	—

GENERAL VIEWS ON HARSH INTERROGATION TACTICS

We also asked participants about their general support for eleven interrogation practices. Participants answered these questions before and after reading the experimental vignette. All responses were measured on 4-point Likert scales. We conducted a series of within-subject t-tests to compare views on each of these eleven interrogation practices pretest and posttest for each participant.

As shown on table 3.A4, reading a vignette about an interrogation decreased general support for physical pain and enhanced interrogation techniques in both Waves 1 and 2. Similarly, in both waves, participants were significantly less likely to say that the United States uses torture after reading the vignette. In Wave 1 only, participants were less supportive of psychological pain, subjecting suspects to cold temperatures, beatings, and waterboarding after reading the interrogation vignette.

We also conducted a series of between-subjects t-tests to compare the average views on each practice before and after the STR release. Table 3.A5

TABLE 3.A4 Views of General Harsh Interrogation Practices: Within-subject Comparisons

	Psychological Pain		Physical Pain		Torture		Enhanced Interrogation Techniques		Does U.S. Torture	
	Before STR	*After STR*	*Before STR*	*After STR*	*Before STR*	*After STR*	*Before STR*	*After STR*	*Before STR*	*After STR*
Direction	Less posttest	ns	Less posttest	Less posttest	ns	ns	Less posttest	Less posttest	Less posttest	Less posttest
P-value	0.004	0.11	0.004	0.003	0.25	0.06	0.003	0.01	0.006	0.03
Effect size (d)	−0.05		−0.05	−0.05			−0.05	−0.03	−0.09	−0.06
N	1160	1194	1162	1196	1163	1202	1165	1193	1173	1202

	Sleep Deprivation		Cold Temperatures		Lie About Evidence		Beatings		Water boarding		Starvation	
	Before STR	*After STR*	*Before STR*	*After STR*	*Before STR*	*Before STR*	*Before STR*	*After STR*	*Before STR*	*After STR*	*Before STR*	*After STR*
Direction	Less posttest	Less posttest	Less posttest	ns	ns	ns	Less posttest	ns	Less posttest	ns	ns	ns
P-value	<0.001	<0.001	0.03	0.28	0.23	0.31	0.02	0.59	0.0498	0.54	0.57	0.23
Effect size (d)	−0.07	−0.07	−0.05				−0.03		−0.03			
N	1162	1193	1164	1198	1170	1197	1169	1195	1161	1191	1163	1193

shows only one difference in either pretest or posttest support for any of these eleven issues as a function of issue salience. After the STR's release, people were significantly less supportive of using psychological pain at the beginning of our study, although this difference disappeared after reading the vignette.

TABLE 3.A5 Views of General Harsh Interrogation Practices: Between-subject Comparisons

	Psychological Pain		Physical Pain		Torture		Enhanced Interrogation Techniques		Does U.S. Torture	
	Before STR	*After STR*	*Before STR*	*After STR*	*Before STR*	*After STR*	*Before STR*	*After STR*	*Before STR*	*After STR*
Direction	Less posttest	ns	ns	ns	ns	ns	ns	Ns	ns	Ns
P-value	0.016	0.07	0.18	0.21	0.33	0.24	0.08	0.15	0.41	0.63
Effect size (d)	0.09									
N	2366	2375	2367	2378	2372	2380	2370	2375	2380	2381

	Sleep Deprivation		Cold Temperatures		Lie About Evidence		Beatings		Waterboarding		Starvation	
	Pretest	*Posttest*	*Pretest*	*Posttest*	*Pretest*	*Posttest*	*Pretest*	*Posttest*	*Pretest*	*Posttest*	*Pretest*	*Posttest*
Direction	ns	ns	ns	ns	ns	ns	ns	ns	ns	ns	ns	ns
P-value	0.10	0.07	0.06	0.27	0.20	0.20	0.33	0.53	0.09	0.23	0.09	0.22
Effect size (d)												
N	2370	2372	2372	2376	2378	2376	2372	2379	2370	2369	2370	2373

It is also possible that our experimental treatments impact how participants views these eleven practices. We estimated a series of models to test this and found that our manipulated treatment variables (dyad, location, and type of tactic) did not impact participants' views on these eleven general questions about interrogations. In short, these results show that reading about an interrogation often decreases support for coercive practices. This effect is more impactful when the issue is less salient.

PETITION SIGNING

We conducted a series of multinomial logistic regression models to examine whether our experimental treatment conditions had an impact on participants' likelihood of signing a petition either in support of or in opposition to torture.

As tables 3.A6 and 3.A7 show, our experimental variables are largely unrelated to whether or not a person is willing to sign a petition about torture. None of the treatment variables impact likelihood to sign a petition in support of torture. In Wave 1, participants in the physical harm

TABLE 3.A6 Willingness to Sign a Petition Supporting Torture by Experimental Treatments

	Overall		White		Minority		Before STR		After STR	
CC dyad	1.07		1.25		0.51		1.54		0.86	
	(0.26)		(0.33)		(0.29)		(0.62)		(0.26)	
CM dyad	0.85		0.76		1.23		1.41		0.61	
	(0.21)		(0.23)		(0.60)		(0.57)		(0.20)	
MC dyad	0.82		0.81		0.83		1.00		0.74	
	(0.21)		(0.24)		(0.32)		(0.44)		(0.24)	
Muslim interrogator		0.95		0.91		1.11		0.68		1.19
		(0.17)		(0.18)		(0.42)		(0.19)		(0.27)
Muslim suspect		0.98		0.86		1.61		0.95		1.01
		(0.18)		(0.18)		(0.62)		(0.27)		(0.23)
Domestic	1.06	1.06	1.15	1.13	1.62	0.82	1.18	1.18	0.98	0.98
	(0.19)	(0.19)	(0.23)	(0.23)	(0.77)	(0.32)	(0.33)	(0.33)	(0.22)	(0.22)
Psychological torture	1.10	1.09	1.01	1.00	1.39	1.56	1.36	1.35	0.95	0.95
	(0.19)	(0.23)	(0.24)	(0.24)	(0.69)	(0.72)	(0.46)	(0.46)	(0.26)	(0.26)
Physical torture	0.87	0.86	0.78	0.77	0.98	1.03	1.08	1.07	0.74	0.73
	(0.19)	(0.19)	(0.20)	(0.20)	(0.36)	(0.38)	(0.39)	(0.39)	(0.21)	(0.21)
Post STR	1.68**	1.68**	1.92**	1.94**						
	(0.31)	(0.30)	(0.40)	(0.41)						

Note: Multinomial logits w/RRR present & robust SE in parentheses.

*p < 0.05, **p < 0.01, ***p< 0.001, †p < 0.10.

TABLE 3.A7 Willingness to Sign a Petition Opposing Torture by Experimental Treatments

	Overall		White		Minority		Before STR		After STR	
CC dyad	1.19		1.04		1.89†		1.36		1.06	
	(0.20)		(0.20)		(0.68)		(0.33)		(0.24)	
CM dyad	1.13		0.99		1.71		1.12		1.13	
	(0.19)		(0.19)		(0.72)		(0.28)		(0.25)	
MC dyad	1.08		0.94		1.75		0.97		1.17	
	(0.18)		(0.18)		(0.64)		(0.25)		(0.26)	
Muslim interrogator		0.90		0.96		0.76		0.80		1.00
		(0.10)		(0.13)		(0.18)		(0.14)		(0.16)
Muslim suspect		0.94		1.00		0.74		0.92		0.96
		(0.11)		(0.13)		(0.18)		(0.16)		(0.15)
Domestic	1.01	1.01	1.04	1.04	0.94	0.93	1.40†	1.40†	0.77	0.77†
	(0.12)	(0.12)	(0.14)	(0.14)	(0.23)	(0.22)	(0.24)	(0.24)	(0.12)	(0.12)
Psychological torture	0.93	0.93	1.01	1.00	0.75	0.73	1.15	1.15	0.79	0.79
	(0.14)	(0.14)	(0.17)	(0.17)	(0.21)	(0.21)	(0.26)	(0.26)	(0.15)	(0.15)
Physical torture	1.20	1.20	1.34†	1.34†	0.88	0.86	1.72*	1.71**	0.90	0.90
	(0.17)	(0.17)	(0.22)	(0.22)	(0.25)	(0.25)	(0.36)	(0.36)	(0.17)	(0.17)
Post STR	1.37**	1.37**	1.35***	1.35*	1.44	1.46				
	(0.16)	(0.16)	(0.03)	(0.18)	(0.34)	(0.35)				

Note: Multinomial logits w/RRR present & robust SE in parentheses.

*p < 0.05, **p <0.01, ***p< 0.001, †p < 0.10.

condition were significantly more likely to sign a petition in opposition to torture, but this effect disappeared for Wave 2. Results here suggest that our treatments largely did not impact willingness to take action vis-à-vis signing a petition on torture. However, as discussed in the main text of chapter 3, issue salience and participant's political views are both significantly related to one's willingness to sign a petition.

Table 3.A8 shows the results of logistic regression models for likelihood to sign each petition by issue salience and participant's political ideology. As shown in the main text of chapter 3, people were significantly more likely to sign a petition after the STR. Political ideology explains which petition people are likely to sign: conservatives are more likely to support torture and liberals are more likely to oppose it.

TABLE 3.A8 Willingness to Sign a Petition as Expected and Regardless of Condition, Conservative Participants were more Willing to Sign a Petition in Support of Torture and Liberal Participants were more Willing to Sign a Petition in Opposition to Torture.

Petition Signed	Wave	Coefficient	SE
Any petition	Post STR	1.47***	0.15
	Political Ideology	0.82***	0.05
Petition to oppose	Post STR	1.40**	0.16
	Political Ideology	0.61***	0.04
Petition to support	Post STR	1.64**	0.30
	Political Ideology	1.57***	0.14

Note: Logit w/OR and Multinomial logits w/RRR present & robust SE.

*p < 0.05, **p < 0.01, ***p< 0.001, †p < 0.10.

SURVEY

{Everyone gets Consent Form first.}

OPINIONS ABOUT INTERROGATION PRACTICES

IDENTIFICATION OF INVESTIGATORS AND PURPOSE OF STUDY

You are being asked to participate in a research study conducted by Dr. Joseph K. Young and Erin M. Kearns from American University. The purpose of this study is to assess opinions on interrogation practices. This study will contribute to the student's completion of one of her research projects and doctoral dissertation.

RESEARCH PROCEDURES

Should you decide to participate in this research study, you will be asked to give your consent once all your questions have been answered to your satisfaction. This study consists of a survey that will be administered to individual participants via Mechanical Turk. You will be asked to provide answers to a series of questions related to your opinions about interrogation practices.

TIME REQUIRED

Participation in this study will require roughly 15 to 20 minutes of your time.

RISKS

The investigator perceives the following are possible risks arising from your involvement with this study: some of the questions may be upsetting to some people. If you feel uncomfortable, you are free to skip any individual question, portions of surveys, or an entire survey without penalty.

BENEFITS

There are no direct benefits to the participant for this study. However, this present study will benefit research as a whole by providing a more complete understanding of opinions about current event topics.

CONFIDENTIALITY

Your identity will remain completely anonymous. The results of this research will be presented at the 2015 American Political Science Association conference. Since all Human Intelligence Tasks (HITs) completed on MTurk are not connected with the participant's identity, there is no way to connect your identity with your responses. The researcher retains the right to use and publish non-identifiable data. While individual responses are confidential, aggregate data will be presented representing averages or generalizations about the responses as a whole. All data will be stored in a secure location accessible only to the researcher.

PARTICIPATION AND WITHDRAWAL

Your participation is entirely voluntary. You are free to choose not to participate. Should you choose to participate, you can withdraw at any time without consequences of any kind. You may also refuse to answer any individual question without consequences. You will receive $2 for your time.

QUESTIONS ABOUT THE STUDY

If you have questions or concerns during the time of your participation in this study, or after its completion or you would like to receive a copy of the final aggregate results of this study, please contact:

Erin M. Kearns
School of Public Affairs
American University
erin.kearns@student.american.edu

Dr. Joseph K. Young
School of Public Affairs
American University
jyoung@american.edu

QUESTIONS ABOUT YOUR RIGHTS AS A RESEARCH SUBJECT

Anthony Ahrens
Chair, Institutional Review Board
American University
(202) 885–1714
ahrens@american.edu

Matt Zembrzuski
IRB Coordinator
American University
(202) 885–3447
irb@american.edu

GIVING OF CONSENT

By clicking "continue" I acknowledge that I have read this consent form and I understand what is being requested of me as a participant in this study. I freely consent to participate. I have been given satisfactory answers to my questions. The investigator provided me with a copy of this form. I certify that I am at least 18 years of age.

{Start PRE OPINION ABOUT INTERROGATIONS MODULE}

Listed below are a series of statements about interrogation practices against terrorism suspects.

Please remember that your answers are totally anonymous. We are interested in you honest attitudes about this topic. There are no "right" or "wrong" answers; there are only your opinions. We thank you in advance for your honesty.

Please indicate the degree to which you agree or disagree with each of the statements using the following scale:

1 = Completely Disagree
2 = Disagree
3 = Agree
4 = Completely Agree

{Question order and response options both presented in randomized order}

[**preSleepDep**] I do not support the use of sleep deprivation in interrogations.
[**preColdTemp**] I support exposure to cold temperatures in interrogations.
[**preLieEvidence**] I support lying about evidence against the accused in interrogations.
[**preBeating**] I do not support the use of beatings in interrogations.
[**preTorture**] I support the use of torture in interrogations.
[**preEIT**] I do not support the use of enhanced interrogations techniques.
[**preWaterBoard**] I support the use of waterboarding in interrogations.
[**preStarve**] I do not support the use of starvation in interrogations.
[**prePsychPain**] I support causing psychological pain in interrogations.
[**prePhysicalPain**] I do not support causing physical pain in interrogations when necessary.
[**preUSTorture**] The United States does engage in torture.

{End PRE OPINION ABOUT INTERROGATIONS MODULE}

{Start TREATMENT VIGNETTES}
{Participants are assigned to one of twenty-four experimental conditions. The sample vignette below highlights changes in test across the twenty-four vignettes. There are four possible dyads (bold) and two possible locations (italics). The three possible types of treatment appear as separate paragraphs that are identified with underlined text.}

Below is a hypothetical interrogation scenario. Please read this scenario carefully. Once you are finished reading it, please click the button to be taken to a series of questions.

During a [*street patrol in the downtown area of a large East Coast city in the United States // routine patrol in the area near Bagram Airfield in Afghanistan*], [**Jake // Abdul**] and his [*partner // unit*] found [**Connor // Hassan**] on their route. There were a number of [*small explosive attacks // improvised explosive device (IED) attacks on U.S. convoys*] in this city in recent weeks, so tensions were high among [**Jake // Abdul**] and his [*partner // unit*]. [**Connor // Hassan**] was acting suspiciously, so [**Jake // Abdul**] and his [*partner // unit*] detained him for interrogation.

[**Jake // Abdul**] and his partner took [**Connor // Hassan**] to an abandoned [*warehouse /// farmhouse*] that they used occasionally [*on their beat // as a patrol base*]. Once at the [*warehouse /// farmhouse*], [**Jake // Abdul**] took [**Connor // Hassan**] to a small room to ask him questions. [**Jake // Abdul**] asked [**Connor // Hassan**] what he was doing in the area and if he knew anything about the recent attacks [*in the city // against U.S. troops*]. [**Connor // Hassan**] stated that [he] did not have any information about the attacks, and repeatedly asked to be released. [**Jake // Abdul**] was not convinced by [**Connor // Hassan**]'s claim that he did not have information and grew angry as [**Connor // Hassan**] refused to say anything about the attacks and who was responsible for them.

Psychological Harm

[**Jake // Abdul**] grabbed [**Connor // Hassan**] and blindfolded him with a piece of fabric in the room. [**Jake // Abdul**] continued to yell at [**Connor // Hassan**] and demand information about the attacks. [**Jake // Abdul**] told [**Connor // Hassan**] that he would be shot if he didn't give the information. [**Jake // Abdul**] held a gun to [**Connor // Hassan**]'s head while [**Connor // Hassan**] was in tears. [**Jake // Abdul**] pulled the trigger, but there is a blank. [**Jake // Abdul**] told [**Connor // Hassan**] that this was his last chance to give information. Moments later, [**Connor // Hassan**] finally told [**Jake // Abdul**] the names of three men in a nearby neighborhood who were responsible for the attack. [**Jake // Abdul**] then removed [**Connor // Hassan**]'s blindfold.

Physical Harm

[**Jake // Abdul**] tied [**Connor // Hassan**]'s hands behind his back using a rope in the room. [**Jake // Abdul**] used a metal hook to raise [**Connor // Hassan**]'s arms up, forcing him to try to balance on his toes with his arms raised behind his back. [**Jake // Abdul**] continued to yell at [**Connor // Hassan**] and demand information about the attacks. [**Jake // Abdul**] told [**Connor // Hassan**] that he would be shot if he didn't give the information. [**Jake // Abdul**] pulled on the hook to raise [**Connor // Hassan**]'s arms up further until [**Connor // Hassan**] could no longer touch the ground. [**Jake // Abdul**] told [**Connor // Hassan**] that this was his last chance to give information. Moments later, [**Connor // Hassan**] finally told [**Jake // Abdul**] the names of three men in a nearby neighborhood who were responsible for the attack. [**Jake // Abdul**] then loosened the hook and removed [**Connor // Hassan**]'s bindings.

Control Condition

[no additional text]

{page break}

{Questions presented in a randomized order}

[IsItTorture] Would you call this incident torture?
　　<1> Definitely
　　<2> Probably
　　<3> Probably Not
　　<4> Definitely Not

[IsItJustified] How justified is the interrogator [name]'s behavior in this situation?
　　<1> Completely Unjustified
　　<2> Somewhat Unjustified
　　<3> Somewhat Justified
　　<4> Completely Justified

[IsItLegal] How legal is the interrogator [name]'s behavior in this situation?
　　<1> Completely Illegal
　　<2> Somewhat Illegal
　　<3> Somewhat Legal
　　<4> Completely Legal

[IsItMoral] How moral is the interrogator [name]'s behavior in this situation?

<1> Completely Immoral

<2> Somewhat Immoral

<3> Somewhat Moral

<4> Completely Moral

[DoesSuspectDeserve] How much does the victim, [name], deserve the behavior he experiences in this situation?

<1> Completely Does Not Deserve

<2> Somewhat Does Not Deserve

<3> Somewhat Deserves

<4> Completely Deserves

[InterrogatorResponsible] How responsible is the interrogator, [name], for the outcome of this situation?

<1> Completely Not Responsible

<2> Somewhat Not Responsible

<3> Somewhat Responsible

<4> Completely Responsible

[SuspectResponsible] How responsible is the victim, [name], for the outcome of this situation?

<1> Completely Not Responsible

<2> Somewhat Not Responsible

<3> Somewhat Responsible

<4> Completely Responsible

{Start POST OPINION ABOUT INTERROGATIONS MODULE}

Listed below are a series of statements about interrogation practices against terrorism suspects.

Please remember that your answers are totally anonymous. We are interested in you honest attitudes about this topic. There are no "right" or "wrong" answers; there are only your opinions. We thank you in advance for your honesty.

Please indicate the degree to which you agree or disagree with each of the statements using the following scale:

1 = Completely Disagree

2 = Disagree

3 = Agree

4 = Completely Agree

{Question order and response options both presented in randomized order}

[**postSleepDep**] I do not support the use of sleep deprivation in interrogations.

[**postColdTemp**] I support exposure to cold temperatures in interrogations.

[**postLieEvidence**] I support lying about evidence against the accused in interrogations.

[**postBeating**] I do not support the use of beatings in interrogations.

[**postTorture**] I support the use of torture in interrogations.

[**postEIT**] I do not support the use of enhanced interrogations techniques.

[**postWaterBoard**] I support the use of waterboarding in interrogations.

[**postStarve**] I do not support the use of starvation in interrogations.

[**postPsychPain**] I support causing psychological pain in interrogations.

[**postPhysicalPain**] I do not support causing physical pain in interrogations when necessary.

[**postUSTorture**] The United States does engage in torture.

{End POST OPINION ABOUT INTERROGATIONS MODULE}

{Petitions}

We are interested in how the public views interrogation practices. The issues discussed in this study are contentious, and can lead to strong feelings on both sides.

As you may be aware, citizens can petition the government regarding these issues. In addition to your stated levels of support or opposition, we would like to extend the opportunity to take action in support or opposition by signing a petition to the White House. Please note that this is completely voluntary. Your decision to sign either petition or to skip this option will not impact your standing in the study or your compensation.

We will send the signed petitions on both sides of each issue to the White House.

Please take a moment to think about these options and select which you would like to make. Keep in mind that you cannot go back once you have selected.

<1> I would like to sign a petition in SUPPORT of the interrogation tactics in this study.

<2> I would like to sign a petition in OPPOSITION to the interrogation tactics in this study.

<3> I would like to skip this option and not sign either petition.

Petition Page

Thank you for taking a moment to consider the petition options. We are not actually providing a petition for you to sign, as doing so would violate MTurk's policies. Instead, the previous question will be used to measure willingness to sign a petition.

Please click "continue" to proceed to the final page of this HIT, the debriefing form.

{Demographics}

[gender] What is your gender?   _____

[age] How old are you?   _____

[race] What is your race? (circle all that apply)

Caucasian/White   African-American/Black

Asian/Asian   American Hispanic

Native American   Middle Eastern

Other_____

[religion] What is your religious affiliation?

Christian   Jewish

Muslim   Buddhist

Hindu   Atheist/Agnostic

Other_____

[education] What is the highest level of education that you have completed?

Less than High School   High School   Some College

Associates   Bachelors   Graduate Degree

[income] What is your estimated annual household income?

Less than $20,000 $20,000 to $39,999 $40,000 to $59,999

$60,000 to $79,999 $80,000 to $99,999   More than $100,000

[politics] How would you describe your political views?

Very Liberal   Liberal   Moderate   Conservative   Very Conservative [**live**] Which best describes where you live?

City   Suburbs   Rural Area

[**zip**] What is your zip code? {text}

[**travel**] Have you ever traveled outside of the United States? If so, please circle the continents to which you have been:

Africa   Asia   Australia   Europe   N. America   S. America

OPINIONS ABOUT INTERROGATION PRACTICES

Information Sheet/Debriefing

The overall purpose of this study is to examine how framing can impact public perceptions of interrogation practices. We are interested in how the perpetrator-victim dyad, proximity to the event, and type of interrogation tactic used impact an individual's attitudes toward the practice. Furthermore, we are interested in assessing behaviors in support of stated beliefs.

At the end of the study, you were led to believe that you had the option to sign a petition in support of the interrogation tactic, in opposition to that tactic, or to skip this option. However, in accordance with Amazon Mechanical Turk's policies, we are not able to ask participants for any identifying information. This deception was necessary to assess this behavioral information without violating MTurk's policy.

In the past decade, there has been increased scholarly attention on torture, especially in the context of counterterrorism. Research on torture has focused on perceptions of the practice, support of the practice, perceptions of what constitutes torture, why the use of torture persists despite arguments against it, and the efficacy of the practice. While many of these studies assess stated attitudes toward torture, research has not yet adequately addressed how the perpetrator-victim dyad and proximity to the event influence perceptions on interrogations practices or whether people take action that is in line with their stated beliefs on these practices.

As a reminder, your responses in this study are completely anonymous. The data will not be connected to any identifying information, and will only be used for research purposes.

The foreseeable risks involved with this study are minimal.

If you would like more information about the use of torture in interrogations, you may find the following articles interesting or useful:

Moghaddam, F. M. (2007). Interrogation policy and American psychology in the global context. *Peace and Conflict: Journal of Peace Psychology*, 13(4), 437–443.

Norris, J. I., Larsen, J. T., & Stastny, B. J. (2010). Social perceptions of torture: Genuine disagreement, subtle malleability, and in-group bias. *Peace and Conflict*, 16(3), 275–294.

Tarrant, M., Branscombe, N. R., Warner, R. H., & Weston, D. (2012). Social identity and perceptions of torture: It's moral when we do it. *Journal of Experimental Social Psychology*, 48(2), 513–518.

For more information on this study, or if you would like the results when they are available, contact:

Erin M. Kearns
School of Public Affairs
American University
erin.kearns@student.american.edu

Dr. Joseph K. Young
School of Public Affairs
American University
jyoung@american.edu

APPENDIX TO CHAPTER 4

DETAILS OF THE SAMPLE

Data for this chapter were collected via Amazon's Mechanical Turk (MTurk) platform from May 31 to June 1, 2018. To be eligible for participation, a person had to be located in the United States and have already completed at least 100 tasks (HITs) on MTurk with an approval rating of greater than 98 percent. In total, 1,152 participants completed the survey. Of these, 10 participants were excluded from analyses because they either sped through the survey or straight-lined responses by giving the same answer to each question. Both of these behaviors indicate that these participants were not paying attention to the questions. Analyses were conducted for the remaining 1,142 participants.

MTurk samples are not representative of the U.S. adult population, but studies have compared the results from MTurk samples to those from nationally representative samples. Overwhelmingly, the results tend to be consistent between samples, as discussed in chapter 4. Table 4.A1 shows a breakdown of participant demographics for this project and compares our sample to what would be nationally representative.

TABLE 4.A1 Participant Demographics

Demographic Factor	Our Sample on MTurk (%)	U.S. Population (%)
Race: White	79.0	60.4
Race: Hispanic or Latino	3.7	18.3
Race: Black or African American	6.5	13.4
Race: Asian	5.0	5.9
Race: Native American	1.2	1.3
Race: Middle Eastern	0.2	—
Race: Other	0.6	—
Race: Multiple	3.9	2.7
Gender: Male	54.1	49.2
Gender: Female	45.6	50.8
Gender: Other	0.3	—

Age: 18–24	8.4	11.1
Age: 25–34	43.3	18.0
Age: 35–44	24.3	16.3
Age: 45–54	13.0	16.7
Age: 55–64	8.5	16.7
Age: 65+	2.6	20.5
Education: Less than HS	0.4	10.9
Education: HS/GED	13.9	28.6
Education: Some college	24.1	18.5
Education: Associate's degree	11.1	9.7
Education: Bachelor's degree	36.1	20.6
Education: Graduate degree	14.4	11.6
Income: Less than $25,000	17.5	20.1
Income: $25,000–$49,999	33.4	21.7
Income: $50,000–$74,999	23.2	16.7
Income: $75,000–$99,999	13.5	12.3
Income: More than $100,000	12.4	29.3
Region: Northeast	17.3	21.6
Region: Midwest	20.9	23.4
Region: South	37.1	38.2
Region: West	23.8	16.8
Party ID:[1] Democrat	41.7	32
Party ID: Republican	20.6	23
Party ID: Independent	31.8	39
Party ID: Other	1.8	——
Party ID: None	4.0	——
Military Veteran[2]	4.9	7

1. http://www.people-press.org/interactives/party-id-trend/

2. http://www.pewresearch.org/fact-tank/2017/11/10/the-changing-face-of-americas-veteran-population/

DETAILS ON CONJOINT EXPERIMENTAL DESIGN

Traditional vignette-based experiments are limited in the number of treatments researchers can manipulate due to concerns with statistical power. In contrast, conjoint designs allow researchers to manipulate more variables, have more possible options within each variable, identify the relative weights participants put on each variable, and examine how these weights vary across subgroups.

Diagnostic analyses show that researchers can manipulate up to four variables in a conjoint design before participants show an increase in satisficing.[1] Further, Bansak, Hainmueller, Hopkins, and Yamamoto presented participants with thirty conjoints to see when they show evidence of tiring. Even at thirty scenarios, participant responses were largely consistent, which allows researchers to examine within-subject variation. In addition, Hainmueller, Hangartner, and Yamamoto found that results from a conjoint experiment showed stronger external validity than those from a vignette experiment and were largely consistent with behavioral data from a natural experiment.[2]

DETAILS ON THE KEY VARIABLES

In all analyses for this chapter, the dependent variable is whether or not torture is supported in the incident. Conjoint analyses traditionally use a binary outcome variable, so we collapsed support into some support (25.5 percent) and some opposition (84.5 percent).

The four manipulated variables—source, nationality, goal, and expected outcome—were randomly assigned across the incidents and were evenly distributed. For example, there were four possible nationalities, each of which occurred in 25 percent of the incidents.

We then measured five participant factors that we expected would impact the relative weight people put on each attribute. These factors are general support for torture, general view on torture's efficacy, political ideology, experience with military, and general political knowledge. For example, we would expect that people who said they would never support torture in general would not be swayed by attributes of the incident, whereas people who may support torture should be influenced by our manipulated factors.

TABLE 4.A2 Dependent and Independent Variables

Variable	Response Options	Frequency (%)
Dependent Variable		
Support torture in the incident	Completely disagree	50.7
	Somewhat disagree	23.8
	Somewhat agree	18.0
	Completely agree	7.5
Independent Variables		
General support for torture	Never	30.3
	Rarely	29.9
	Sometimes	36.0
	Always	3.9
General view of torture's efficacy	Never	9.7
	Rarely	39.1
	Sometimes	48.2
	Always	3.0
Political ideology	Liberal	50.0
	Moderate	26.4
	Conservative	23.6
Self or close family/friend is a veteran	Yes	53.4
General political knowledge	0 out of 4 correct	0.4
	1 out of 4 correct	2.6
	2 out of 4 correct	10.7
	3 out of 4 correct	29.4
	4 out of 4 correct	56.9

ADDITIONAL STATISTICAL DETAILS ON RESULTS REPORTED IN THE MAIN TEXT

People who indicated that they could support torture ($M = 0.35$ $SD = 0.005$) are significantly more supportive of torture in these scenarios than those who indicated that they would never support torture ($M = 0.03$, $SD = 0.003$), ($t(11,418) = 38,79$, $p < 0.0001$). This is, of course, unsurprising. People who indicated that torture was sometimes or always effective

(M = 0.41 SD = 0.006) are significantly more supportive of torture in these scenarios than those who indicated that torture was rarely or never effective (M = 0.09, SD = 0.004), ($t(11,418)$ = 42.11, p <0.0001). Again, this is not surprising. Liberals (M = 0.18, SD = 0.005) were overall less supportive of torture relative to both moderates (M = 0.30, SD = 0.008) and conservatives (M = 0.36, SD = 0.008), ($F(2,11397)$ = 176.49, p <0.0001).

ADDITIONAL ANALYSES

MILITARY EXPERIENCE AND SUPPORT FOR TORTURE

Military experience may condition how people view torture in counter-terrorism. Few participants (4.9 percent) in our sample were themselves veterans, which precludes our ability to conduct sound analyses on this small group. We did, however, compare results for participants who either are veterans themselves or have a close friend or family member who is or has served in the armed forces. Overall, about half of our sample had a direct tie to the military (52.4 percent).

Participants with a direct military connection were more likely to support torture across scenarios (M = 0.29, SD = 0.006) than those without a direct military connection (M = 0.22, SD = 0.006), ($t(11,418)$ = 9.17, p <0.001). Despite differences in overall support for torture, the results in figure 4.A3 show that these two groups do not differentially weight any of the manipulated factors when deciding whether or not to support torture in a given incident.

GENERAL POLITICAL KNOWLEDGE
SUPPORT FOR TORTURE

People who are more politically informed in general may have different views of torture than people who are less informed. On a host of topics, highly informed people process information more deeply, whereas less informed people rely more on heuristics.[3] As such, we may assume that more informed people rely less on stereotypical information about threats and the efficacy of torture.

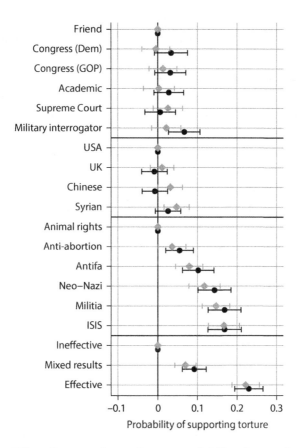

FIGURE 4.A3 Effect of interrogation attributes on probability of supporting torture by direct personal connection to military

Black circles represent response from participants who do not have a direct personal connection to the military (self, close family, or close friend is or has served) (N = 5,440). Gray diamonds represent responses from participants who do have a close personal connection to member(s) of the military (N = 5,980).

We asked participants four questions from a Pew poll to measure general political knowledge.[4] Participants were asked two open ended questions: "Who is the current vice president of the United States?" and "How many justices are on the Supreme Court of the United States?" Participants were asked two multiple choice questions: "In 2015, the U.S. reestablished diplomatic relations with which of the following countries?" and "To comply with the health care law, most Americans need to indicate they have health insurance coverage when they . . . "

In our sample, 56.9 percent of participants answered all four questions correctly, 29.4 percent answered three, 10.7 percent answered two, 2.6 percent answered one, and 0.4 percent missed all four questions. First, we examine the relationships between support for torture in our scenarios and general political knowledge. Results show that people are less supportive of torture as their general political knowledge increases ($F(4, 11,415) = 52.11$, $p < 0.0001$).[5]

Conditional AMCEs require two categories, so we compared results for participants who answered all four questions correctly to those who answered two or fewer correctly. As the results on figure 4.A4 show, there is more variance in how incident-level factors impact support for torture among participants with less political knowledge. Across attributes, only support for torturing anti-abortion activists showed different result by political knowledge ($p = 0.04$).

SURVEY

{Everyone gets Consent Form first.}

VIEWS ON COUNTERTERRORISM

IDENTIFICATION OF INVESTIGATORS AND PURPOSE OF STUDY

You are being asked to participate in a research study conducted by Dr. Joseph K. Young from American University and Dr. Erin Kearns from the University of Alabama. The purpose of this study is to assess opinions on counterterrorism. This study will contribute to the Investigators' book project.

RESEARCH PROCEDURES

This study consists of a survey that will be administered online to a sample of approximately 1,200 individuals from across the United States. You will be asked to provide answers to a series of questions related to your opinions about current event issues.

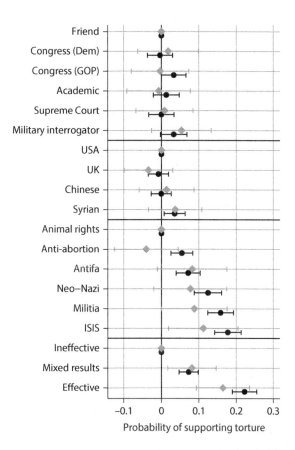

FIGURE 4.A4 Effect of interrogation attributes on probability of supporting torture by general political knowledge

Black circles represent response from participants who answered all four of the general political knowledge questions correctly (N = 6,500). Gray diamonds represent responses from participants who missed two or more of the four general political knowledge questions (N = 1,560).

TIME REQUIRED

Participation in this study will require roughly 10 minutes of your time.

RISKS

The investigator perceives the following are possible risks arising from your involvement with this study: some of the questions may be upsetting to some people. If you feel uncomfortable, you are free to skip any individual question, portions of surveys, or an entire survey without penalty.

The foreseeable risks involved with this study are minimal. However, if you are upset by or feel uncomfortable about the material, there is help. The American University Counseling Center, located at 214 Mary Graydon Center, can be reached at (202) 885–3500.

BENEFITS

There are no direct benefits to the participant for this study. However, this present study will benefit research as a whole by providing a more complete understanding opinions about current event topics.

CONFIDENTIALITY

Your identity will remain completely anonymous unless you alone choose otherwise. The results of this research will be presented at academic conferences, in reports to practitioners, and as part of the researcher's doctoral dissertation. The results of this project will be coded in such a way that the respondent's identity will not be attached to the final form of this study. The researcher retains the right to use and publish non-identifiable data. While individual responses are confidential, aggregate data will be presented representing averages or generalizations about the responses as a whole. All data will be stored in a secure location accessible only to the researcher. Upon completion of the study, all information that matches up individual respondents with their answers will be destroyed.

PARTICIPATION AND WITHDRAWAL

Your participation is entirely voluntary. You are free to choose not to participate. Should you choose to participate, you can withdraw at any time without consequences of any kind. You may also refuse to answer any individual question without consequences.

QUESTIONS ABOUT THE STUDY

If you have questions or concerns during the time of your participation in this study, or after its completion or you would like to receive a copy of the final aggregate results of this study, please contact:

Dr. Joseph K. Young
American University
jyoung@american.edu

Dr. Erin M. Kearns
University of Alabama
emkearns@ua.edu

QUESTIONS ABOUT YOUR RIGHTS AS A RESEARCH SUBJECT

Matt Zembrzuski
IRB Coordinator
American University
(202) 885-3447
irb@american.edu

GIVING OF CONSENT

I have read this consent form and I understand what is being requested of me as a participant in this study. I have been given satisfactory answers to my questions. The investigator provided me with a copy of this form. I certify that I am at least 18 years of age.

By clicking the "next" button, I freely consent to participate in this study. {**Survey Opens—everyone sees questions on this page first**} (<u>Low Sensitivity Demographics</u>)

[**LSD1**] What is your gender?
    <1> Male

<2> Female

<3> Other {text}

[LSD2] How old are you?

{dropdown}

[LSD3] Please select the race/ethnicity with which you most strongly identify.

<1> Caucasian/White

<2> African-American/Black

<3> Hispanic/Latino

<4> Asian/Asian American

<5> Native American

<6> Middle Eastern

<7> Other {text}

[LSD4] What state do you live in?

<STATE> {dropdown}

[Honesty] For the questions that follow, we are interested in your honest attitudes about topics related to current event issues. ALL OF YOUR ANSWERS ARE ANONYMOUS. There are no "right" or "wrong" answers; there are only your opinions. We thank you in advance for your honesty.

<1> Yes, I understand and agree.

<2> No, I am not comfortable providing honest answers. **TERMINATE**

{Randomize to Order 1 or Order 2.
Order 1 sees modules first—these modules are presented in a randomized order. Then sees conjoint experiments.
Order 2 sees conjoint experiments first. Then sees modules—these modules are presented in a randomized order.}

{Start NEWS CONSUMPTION MODULE}

Thinking about **your news consumption**, please answer the following questions.

[NC1] Many people do not find news to be important in their daily life. How important is following the news to you?

(reverse coded in Stata so Very important==4)

<1> Very important

<2> Somewhat important

<3> Not too important

<4> Not important at all

[NC2] In the past 48 hours have you . . . (check all that apply) {**order randomized**}

<1> Watched TV news

{**If NC1=1, then continue to NC2.1a & NC2.1b**}

[NC2.1a] Did you watch local news, national news, or both?

<1> Local news

<2> National news

<3> Both

[NC2.1b] How much time did you spend watching TV news in the last 48 hours?

<1> Less than 30 minutes

<2> 30–60 minutes

<3> More than an hour

<2> Read a newspaper in print or online

{**If NC2=2, then continue to NC2.2a & NC2.2b**}

[NC2.2a] Did you read a print newspaper, an online newspaper, or both?

<1> Print newspaper

<2> Online newspaper

<3> Both

[NC2.2b] How much time did you spend reading either print or online newspapers in the last 48 hours?

<1> Less than 30 minutes

<2> 30–60 minutes

<3> More than an hour

<3> Listened to a radio news program or talk radio

{**If NC2=3, then continue to NC2.3**}

[NC2.3] How much time did you spend listing to radio news programs or talk radio in the last 48 hours?

<1> Less than 30 minutes

<2> 30–60 minutes

<3> More than an hour

<4> Used social media (such as Facebook or YouTube)

{If NC2=4, then continue to NC2.4}

[NC2.4] How much time did you spend on social media in the last 48 hours?

    <1> Less than 30 minutes

    <2> 30–60 minutes

    <3> More than an hour

    <4> None of these

[NC3] Did you do any of the following on social media (such as Facebook, YouTube or Twitter)?

    <1> Posted a story, photo, video or link about politics

    <2> Posted a comment about politics

    <3> Read a story or watched a video about politics

    <4> Followed a political event

    <5> Forwarded a story, photo, video or link about politics to friends

    <6> None of these

{If NC2=5, then show to NC4}

[NC4] In the past 48 hours have you gotten news from the following source . . . (check all that apply)

    <1> ABC/ABC News

    <2> AOL

    <3> BBC

    <4> Breitbart

    <5> CBS

    <6> CNN

    <7> Drudge Report

    <8> Economist

    <9> ESPN

    <10> Facebook/Twitter

    <11> Fox/Fox News

    <12> Google/Google News

    <13> Huffington Post

    <14> Infowars

    <15> Local news source

    <16> MSN

    <17> MSNBC

    <18> New York Times

    <19> NBC

    <20> NPR

    <21> USA Today

<22> Wall Street Journal

<23> Washington Post

<24> Yahoo/Yahoo News

<25> Other {text}

<26> None

{End NEWS CONSUMPTION MODULE}
{Start TV CONSUMPTION MODULE}

Thinking about the **TV shows that you watch**, please answer the following questions.

[**TV1**] Some people watch a lot of TV, others don't. Please let us know if you have watched some of these popular TV shows. {**present as matrix w/ random order**}

<1> 24

<2> Breaking Bad

<3> Community

<4> Designated Survivor

<5> Dexter

<6> Downton Abbey

<7> Friday Night Lights

<8> Game of Thrones

<9> Grey's Anatomy

<10> Hawaii Five o

<11> How I Met Your Mother

<12> Homeland

<13> Law & Order (any)

<14> Modern Family

<15> The Office

<16> Parks & Recreation

<17> Quantico

<18> Scandal

<19> The Sopranos

<20> The Wire

    <1> I have never seen an episode

    <2> I have seen a few episodes

    <3> I have seen most episodes

    <4> I have seen every episode

{End TV CONSUMPTION MODULE}
(General Political Knowledge) **{Question order randomized within this section}**

[**GPK1**] Who is the current Vice President of the United States?
　　{text}
[**GPK2**] How many justices are on the Supreme Court of the United States?
　　{text}
[**GPK3**] In 2015, the U.S. re-established diplomatic relations with which of the following countries?
　　<1> Cuba
　　<2> Russia
　　<3> North Korea
　　<4> Yemen
[**GPK4**] To comply with the health care law, most Americans need to indicate they have health insurance coverage when they . . .
　　<1> Change their address
　　<2> Receive a driver's license
　　<3> File their taxes
　　<4> Vote in an election

{Start CONJOINT}
(Support for Torture) {Each participant sees ten of these—the different factors are randomly assigned each time with forty-five possible options}
　　Please read the descriptions of two scenarios carefully. Indicate whether **you personally** are more likely to support the use of torture in the interrogation in Incident A or the interrogation in Incident B.

	Incident A	Incident B
Expert		
Suspect		
Goal		
Outcome		

EXPERT

A military interrogator
An academic researcher
The Supreme Court
A Republican member of Congress
A Democratic member of Congress
A friend

SUSPECT

a U.S. citizen
a UK citizen
a Syrian citizen
a Chinese citizen

GOAL

Militia w/stockpile of weapons
ISIS
a Neo-nazi group
Antifa
an animal rights group
an anti-abortion group

OUTCOME

accurate information that prevents an attack
mixed information and the impact it has on attack prevention is unclear
inaccurate information that does not prevent an attack

[C1Choice] If you had to choose, in which of these two incidents are you *more likely* to support the use of torture?

<1> Incident A
<2> Incident B

[**C1ReportA**] I support the use of torture in <u>INCIDENT A</u>.

<1> Completely agree
<2> Somewhat agree
<3> Somewhat disagree
<4> Completely disagree

[**C1ReportB**] I support the use of torture in <u>INCIDENT B</u>.

<1> Completely agree
<2> Somewhat agree
<3> Somewhat disagree
<4> Completely disagree

Thanks for evaluating the interrogation scenarios.
[page break]
[Torture 1] **Some people always oppose torture in counterterrorism, some people always support it, and others' views vary depending on the situation.**
Please let us know where you stand on this.
I _____ support the use of torture in counterterrorism.

<1> always
<2> sometimes
<3> rarely
<4> never

[Torture 2] When torture is used in counterterrorism, I think it _____ works to gain accurate information from the suspect.

<1> always
<2> sometimes
<3> rarely
<4> never

{End CONJOINT}
{Everyone sees questions on this page}
(Potentially Sensitive Demographics)

[**PSD1**] What is your religious affiliation? {dropdown}
   <1> Catholic
   <2> Protestant, Mainline Protestant or Protestant non-Evangelical
   <3> Evangelical and Pentecostal
   <4> LDS (Mormon)
   <5> Jehovah's Witness
   <6> Traditional Religions or Native Religions
   <7> Jewish (Orthodox; Conservative; Reform)
   <8> Muslim
   <9> Buddhist
   <10> Hinduism
   <11> Atheist (Does not believe in God)
   <12> Agnostic (Unsure about existence of God)
   <13> None (Believes in a Supreme Entity but does not belong to any religion)
   <14> Other
[**PSD2**] If you have a religious affiliation, how often to you practice/attend services?
   <1> More than once a week
   <2> Weekly
   <3> Monthly
   <4> Yearly
   <5> I don't attend
   <6> Not applicable, no affiliation
[**PSD3**] What is the last year of schooling that you have completed?
   <1> Less than high school graduate
   <2> High school degree/GED
   <3> Some college, no degree
   <4> Associate's Degree (2-year degree)
   <5> Bachelor's Degree
   <6> Master's Degree
   <7> PhD or other Doctorate

[PSD4] Were you born in the United States?

    <1> Yes

    <1>No

{If PSD5=No, then continue to 5a and 5b. If not, skip to PSD6}

[PSD4a] What country were you born in? {text}

[PSD4b] Which country do you identify with more strongly?

    <1> Country of Birth

    <2> United States

    <3> Both equally

[PSD5] Are you or any close family members or friends members of the armed forces? **(select all the apply)**

    <1> I am currently a member of the armed forces.

    <2> I was previously a member of the armed forces.

    <3> A close family member or friend is currently a member of the armed forces.

    <4> A close family member or friend was previously a member of the armed forces.

    <5> None

[PSD7] What is your annual household income?

    <1> Less than $25,000

    <2> $25,000–$49,999

    <3> $50,000–$74,999

    <4> $75,000–$99,999

    <5> More than $100,000

[PSD8] What is your marital status?

    <1> Married

    <2> Single, never married

    <3> Divorced/Separated/Widowed

    <4> Civil union or domestic partnership

[PSD9] Thinking in political terms, would you say that you are . . .

    <1> Very Liberal

    <2> Liberal

    <3> Moderate

    <4> Conservative

    <5> Very Conservative

[PSD10] What is your political party?

<1> Democrat

<2> Republican

<3> Independent

<4> Other {text—please specify}

<5> None

[**PSD11**] Many people weren't able to vote in the 2016 presidential election between Hillary Clinton and Donald Trump. How about you?

<1> Yes, I voted.

<2> No, I was not registered to vote in 2016.

<3> No, I was too young or otherwise ineligible to vote.

<4> No, I just didn't vote.

{**If PSD11=1, then continue to 11a. If not, skip to PSD12**}

[**PSD11a**] In the 2016 presidential election, for whom did you vote?

<1> Hillary Clinton (Democrat)

<2> Donald Trump (Republican)

<3> Gary Johnson (Libertarian)

<4> Jill Stein (Green)

<5> Someone else (please specify){text}

[**PSD11b**] To what extent did you support the candidate for whom you voted?

<1> Strongly supported

<2> Somewhat supported

<3> Somewhat did not support

<4> Strongly did not support

[**PSD12**] In the last five years, have you:

[**PSD12a**] lived outside of the country?

<1> Yes

<2> No

[**PSD12b**] worked outside of the country?

<1> Yes

<2> No

[**PSD12c**] traveled to the moon?

<1> Yes

<2> No

NOTES

INTRODUCTION

1. 18 U.S.C. § 2340—the "Torture Act."
2. Shareen Hertel, Lyle Scruggs, and C. Patrick Heidkamp. "Human Rights and Public Opinion: From Attitudes to Action." *Political Science Quarterly* 124, no. 3 (2009): 443–59.
3. Darren W. Davis and Brian D. Silver, "Civil Liberties vs. Security: Public Opinion in the Context of the Terrorist Attacks on America," *American Journal of Political Science* 48, no. 1 (2004): 28–46.
4. Shannon C. Houck and Lucian Gideon Conway III, "What People Think About Torture: Torture Is Inherently Bad . . . Unless It Can Save Someone I Love," *Journal of Applied Security Research* 8, no. 4 (2013): 429–54; Shannon C. Houck and Meredith A. Repke, "When and Why We Torture: A Review of Psychology Research," *Translational Issues in Psychological Science* 3, no. 3 (2017): 272.
5. Alec Tyson, "Americans Divided in Views of Use of Torture in U.S. Anti-Terror Efforts," *Pew Research Center*, January 26, 2017, http://www.pewresearch.org/fact-tank/2017/01/26/americans-divided-in-views-of-use-of-torture-in-u-s-anti-terror-efforts/Tyson 2017.
6. Paul Gronke, Darius Rejali, Dustin Drenguis, James Hicks, Peter Miller, and Bryan Nakayama, "US Public Opinion on Torture, 2001–2009," *PS: Political Science and Politics* 43, no. 3 (2010): 437–44.
7. William Jordan, "Americans Find Some Tortures More Acceptable Than Others," YouGov, December 12, 2014, https://today.yougov.com/topics/politics/articles-reports/2014/12/12/torture-report.
8. Pew Research Center, "Global Publics Back U.S. on Fighting ISIS, but Are Critical of Post-9/11 Torture," June 23, 2015, https://www.pewresearch.org/global/2015/06/23/global-publics-back-u-s-on-fighting-isis-but-are-critical-of-post-911-torture/.

9. Throughout the book, we use the terms *enhanced interrogation* and *torture* as synonyms. Later in the chapter, we define each more extensively.

10. Tyson, "Americans Divided in Views."

11. Darren Clarkson, "Public Believes U.S. Government Has Tortured Prisoners," Gallup, November 29, 2005, https://news.gallup.com/poll/20170/public-believes-us-government -has-tortured-prisoners.aspx.

12. International Committee of the Red Cross, "People on War 2016," December 5, 2016, https://www.icrc.org/en/document/people-on-war.

13. Gronke et al., "US Public Opinion on Torture."

14. Joan M. Blauwkamp, Charles M. Rowling, and William Pettit, "Are Americans Really Okay with Torture? The Effects of Message Framing on Public Opinion," *Media, War and Conflict* 11, no. 4 (2018): 446–75.

15. Bruce Hoffman, *Inside Terrorism* (New York: Columbia University Press, 2006); Joseph K. Young and Michael G. Findley, "Promise and Pitfalls of Terrorism Research," *International Studies Review* 13, no. 3 (2011): 411–31.

16. UN General Assembly, *Convention Against Torture and Other Cruel, Inhuman or Degrading Treatment or Punishment* (UN-CAT), December 10, 1984, Article 1, United Nations, Treaty Series, vol. 1465, p. 85, https://www.refworld.org/docid/3ae6b3a94.html.

17. Darius Rejali, *Torture and Democracy* (Princeton, N.J.: Princeton University Press, 2009).

18. UN General Assembly, *Convention Against Torture*, Article 16.

19. Courtenay R. Conrad, Jillienne Haglund, and Will H. Moore provide data on torture and ill-treatment allegations across countries and disaggregated by alleged perpetrators within states. Courtenay R. Conrad, Jillienne Haglund, and Will H. Moore, "Disaggregating Torture Allegations: Introducing the Ill-Treatment and Torture (ITT) Country-Year Data," *International Studies Perspectives* 14, no. 2 (2013): 199–220.

20. Avery F. Gordon, "Abu Ghraib: Imprisonment and the War on Terror," *Race and Class* 48, no. 1 (2006): 42–59.

21. James Mitchell, one of the architects of the CIA interrogation program, describes the full range of approved techniques in James E. Mitchell, with Bill Harlow, *Enhanced Interrogation: Inside the Minds and Motives of the Islamic Terrorists Trying to Destroy America* (New York: Crown Forum, 2016).

22. Rebecca Gordon, "Torture Comes Out of the Closet," *Peace Review: A Journal of Social Justice* 18, no. 4 (2006): 447–54.

23. For full text, see Office of Legal Counsel, U.S. Department of Justice, "Memorandum for Alberto R. Gonzales, Counsel to the President," August 1, 2002, https://nsarchive2.gwu.edu/NSAEBB/NSAEBB127/02.08.01.pdf.

24. Kevin M. Carlsmith and Avani Mehta Sood, "The Fine Line Between Interrogation and Retribution," *Journal of Experimental Social Psychology* 45, no. 1 (2009): 191–96; Kenneth Roth, "Justifying Torture," in *Torture: Does It Make Us Safer?*, ed. Kenneth Roth, Minky Worden, and Amy D. Bernstein (New York: New Press, 2005), 184–202.

25. Richard E. Nisbett and Dov Cohen, *Culture of Honor: The Psychology of Violence in the South* (Boulder, Colo.: Westview Press, 1996).

26. Lisa M. Hepburn and David Hemenway, "Firearm Availability and Homicide: A Review of the Literature," *Aggression and Violent Behavior* 9, no. 4 (2004): 417–40; David Hemenway and Matthew Miller, "Firearm Availability and Homicide Rates Across 26 High-Income Countries," *Journal of Trauma and Acute Care Surgery* 49, no. 6 (2000): 985–88; Matthew Miller, Deborah Azrael, and David Hemenway, "Household Firearm Ownership and Suicide Rates in the United States," *Epidemiology* (2002): 517–24; Matthew Miller, David Hemenway, and Deborah Azrael, "State-Level Homicide Victimization Rates in the US in Relation to Survey Measures of Household Firearm Ownership, 2001–2003," *Social Science and Medicine* 64, no. 3 (2007): 656–64.

27. Gary Kleck, *Point Blank: Guns and Violence in America* (London: Routledge, 2017).

28. Dee Brown provides the most comprehensive look at some of the violence perpetrated by Americans against Native populations during the late 1800s. Dee Brown, *Bury My Heart at Wounded Knee: An Indian History of the American West* (New York: Henry Holt, 2007).

29. Samuel C. Gwynne, *Empire of the Summer Moon: Quanah Parker and the Rise and Fall of the Comanches, the Most Powerful Indian Tribe in American History* (New York: Simon and Schuster, 2010).

30. Wayne E. Lee, *Barbarians and Brothers: Anglo-American Warfare, 1500–1865* (New York: Oxford University Press, 2011).

31. See, for example, Robert William Fogel, *Without Consent or Contract: The Rise and Fall of American Slavery* (New York: Norton, 1994); John Hope Franklin and Loren Schweninger, *Runaway Slaves: Rebels on the Plantation* (Oxford: Oxford University Press, 2000); and Stephanie M. H. Camp, *Closer to Freedom: Enslaved Women and Everyday Resistance in the Plantation South* (Chapel Hill: University of North Carolina Press, 2005).

32. Franklin and Schweninger, *Runaway Slaves.*

33. This tactic usually involves forcing the subject to drink large amounts of water until the stomach is close to bursting. It is often coupled with beatings until the subject vomits, and then it is repeated.

34. "The Water Cure Described: Discharged Soldier Tells Senate Committee How and Why the Torture Was Inflicted," *New York Times*, May 4, 1902.

35. Philip K. Lundeberg, "Operation Teardrop Revisited," in *To Die Gallantly: The Battle of the Atlantic*, ed. Timothy J. Runyan and Jan M. Copes (Boulder, Colo.: Westview Press, 1994), 210–30.

36. Ronald D. Crelinsten, "The World of Torture: A Constructed Reality," *Theoretical Criminology* 7, no. 3 (2003): 293–318.

37. Darius Rejali, "Ice Water and Sweatboxes: The Long and Sadistic History Behind the CIA's Torture Techniques," *Slate*, March 17, 2009, https://slate.com/news-and-politics/2009/03/the-history-of-cia-torture.html.

38. Rejali, *Torture and Democracy.*

39. Mark Fallon, *Unjustifiable Means: The Inside Story of How the CIA, Pentagon, and US Government Conspired to Torture* (New York: Regan Arts, 2017).

40. Bruce Arrigo, "Punishment, Freedom, and the Culture of Control: A Review of Torture—America's Brutal Prisons," *Contemporary Justice Review* 9, no. 2 (2006): 229–33.

41. Erin M. Kearns and Joseph K. Young, "Military Tactics in Civil War," in *Routledge Handbook of Civil Wars*, ed. Edward Newman and Kal DeRouen Jr. (New York: Routledge, 2014), 257–67.

42. Rebecca Leung, "Abuse of Iraqi POWs by GIS Probed," *60 Minutes*, April 27, 2004, https://www.cbsnews.com/news/abuse-of-iraqi-pows-by-gis-probed/.

43. Seymour Hersh, "Torture at Abu Ghraib: American Soldiers Brutalized Iraqis. How Far Up Does the Responsibility Go?," *New Yorker*, May 10, 2004, https://www.newyorker.com/magazine/2004/05/10/torture-at-abu-ghraib.

44. R. Gordon, "Torture Comes Out of the Closet."

45. Christian S. Crandall, Scott Eidelman, Linda J. Skitka, and G. Scott Morgan, "Status Quo Framing Increases Support for Torture," *Social Influence* 4, no. 1 (2009): 1–10; Gronke et al., "US Public Opinion on Torture."

46. Amnesty International, Amnesty International 1996 Report, (London: Amnesty International, 1996), https://www.amnesty.org/en/documents/pol10/0002/1996/en/.

47. Amnesty International, Amnesty International 2000 Report (London: Amnesty International, 2000), https://www.amnesty.org/en/documents/pol10/0001/2000/en/.

48. Amnesty International, Amnesty International 2010 Report (London: Amnesty International, 2010), https://www.amnesty.org/en/documents/pol10/001/2010/en/.

49. Rejali, *Torture and Democracy*.

50. Crelinsten, "The World of Torture."

51. Courtenay R. Conrad, Justin Conrad, James Igoe Walsh, and James A. Piazza, "Who Tortures the Terrorists? Transnational Terrorism and Military Torture," *Foreign Policy Analysis* 13, no. 4 (2016): 761–86; Amos N. Guiora and Erin M. Page, "The Unholy Trinity: Intelligence, Interrogation and Torture," *Case Western Reserve Journal of International Law* 37, no. 2 (2005): 427–47; Joe Santucci, "A Question of Identity: The Use of Torture in Asymmetric War," *Journal of Military Ethics* 7, no. 1 (2008): 23–40; Christopher W. Tindale, "The Logic of Torture: A Critical Examination," *Social Theory and Practice* 22, no. 3 (1996): 349–74.

52. Conrad et al., "Who Tortures the Terrorists?"; Tindale, "The Logic of Torture."

53. Tindale, "The Logic of Torture."

54. Leonard Wantchekon and Andrew Healy, "The 'Game' of Torture," *Journal of Conflict Resolution* 43, no. 5 (1999): 596–609.

55. Derek B. Cornish and Ronald V. Clarke, "Understanding Crime Displacement: An Application of Rational Choice Theory," *Criminology* 25, no. 4 (1987): 933–48.

56. Conrad, Haglund, and Moore, "Disaggregating Torture Allegations."

57. Laura Dugan and Erica Chenoweth, "Moving Beyond Deterrence: The Effectiveness of Raising the Expected Utility of Abstaining From Terrorism in Israel," *American Sociological Review* 77, no. 4 (2012): 597–624.

58. Tindale, "The Logic of Torture."

59. Martha Crenshaw, "Counterterrorism Policy and the Political Process," *Studies in Conflict and Terrorism* 24, no. 5 (2001): 329–37.

60. Laura Dugan, Gary LaFree, and Alex R. Piquero, "Testing a Rational Choice Model of Airline Hijackings," in *International Conference on Intelligence and Security Informatics*, ed. Paul Kantor, Gheorghe Muresan, Fred Roberts, Daniel D. Zeng, Fei-Yue Wang, Hsinchun Chen, and Ralph C. Merkle (Berlin: Springer, 2005), 340–61.

61.   Dugan and Chenoweth, "Moving Beyond Deterrence."

62.   Gary LaFree, Laura Dugan, and Raven Korte, "The Impact of British Counterterrorist Strategies on Political Violence in Northern Ireland: Comparing Deterrence and Backlash Models," *Criminology* 47, no. 1 (2009): 17–45.

63.   James I. Walsh and James A. Piazza, "Why Respecting Physical Integrity Rights Reduces Terrorism," *Comparative Political Studies* 43, no. 5 (2010): 551–77.

64.   Gary Kleck, Brion Sever, Spencer Li, and Marc Gertz, "The Missing Link in General Deterrence Research," *Criminology* 43, no. 3 (2005): 623–60.

65.   Michael Tonry, "Learning from the Limitations of Deterrence Research," *Crime and Justice* 37, no. 1 (2008): 279–311.

66.   James A. Piazza and James Igoe Walsh, "Physical Integrity Rights and Terrorism," *PS: Political Science and Politics* 43, no. 3 (2010): 411–14.

67.   Mitchell, *Enhanced Interrogation*.

68.   Jon Gould, Julia Carrano, Richard Leo, and Joseph Young, "Predicting Erroneous Convictions: A Social Science Approach to Miscarriages of Justice," Department of Justice Document 241389, February 2013, https://www.ncjrs.gov/pdffiles1/nij/grants/241389.pdf; Gisli H. Gudjonsson, *The Psychology of Interrogations, Confessions, and Testimony* (Newark, N.J.: Wiley, 1992); Saul M. Kassin and Katherine L. Kiechel, "The Social Psychology of False Confessions: Compliance, Internalization, and Confabulation," *Psychological Science* 7, no. 3 (1996): 125–28; G. Daniel Lassiter and Christian A. Meissner, *Police Interrogations and False Confessions: Current Research, Practice, and Policy Recommendations* (Washington, D.C.: American Psychological Association, 2010); Richard J. Ofshe and Richard A. Leo, "The Social Psychology of Police Interrogation: The Theory and Classification of True and False Confessions," *Studies in Law, Politics and Society* 16 (1997): 189–254; Allison D. Redlich, "False Confessions, False Guilty Pleas: Similarities and Differences," in *Police Interrogations and False Confessions: Current Research, Practice, and Policy Recommendations*, ed. G. Daniel Lassiter and Christian A. Meissner (Washington, D.C.: American Psychological Association, 2010), 49–66.

69.   Melissa B. Russano, Christian A. Meissner, Fadia M. Narchet, and Saul M. Kassin, "Investigating True and False Confessions Within a Novel Experimental Paradigm," *Psychological Science* 16, no. 6 (2005): 481–86.

70.   Lucian E. Dervan and Vanessa A. Edkins, "The Innocent Defendant's Dilemma: An Innovative Empirical Study of Plea Bargaining's Innocence Problem," *Journal of Criminal Law and Criminology* 103, no. 1 (2013): 1–48.

71.   Roth, "Justifying Torture."

72.   See, for example, James N. Druckman, Erik Peterson, and Rune Slothuus, "How Elite Partisan Polarization Affects Public Opinion Formation," *American Political Science Review* 107, no. 1 (2013): 57–79; Alex Mintz, Steven B. Redd, and Arnold Vedlitz, "Can We Generalize from Student Experiments to the Real World in Political Science, Military Affairs, and International Relations?," *Journal of Conflict Resolution* 50, no. 5 (2006): 757–76; Alan S. Gerber and Donald P. Green, *Field Experiments: Design, Analysis, and Interpretation* (New York: Norton, 2012); Joshua D. Kertzer and Kathleen M. McGraw, "Folk Realism: Testing the Microfoundations of Realism in Ordinary Citizens," *International Studies Quarterly* 56, no. 2 (2012): 245–58; Thomas Zeitzoff, "Anger, Exposure to

Violence, and Intragroup Conflict: A 'Lab in the Field' Experiment in Southern Israel," *Political Psychology* 35, no. 3 (2014): 309–35; Anthony F. Lemieux, Erin M. Kearns, Victor Asal, and James Igoe Walsh, "Support for Political Mobilization and Protest in Egypt and Morocco: An Online Experimental Study," *Dynamics of Asymmetric Conflict* 10, no. 2–3 (2017): 124–42.

73. See Gerber and Green, *Field Experiments*, for an overview and details on conducting field experiments.

74. Erin M. Kearns, "If You See Something, Do You Say Something? The Role of Legitimacy and Trust in Policing Minority Communities in Counterterrorism" (PhD diss., American University, 2016); Erin M. Kearns, Victor Asal, James Igoe Walsh, Christopher Federico, and Anthony F. Lemieux, "Political Action as a Function of Grievances, Risk, and Social Identity: An Experimental Approach," *Studies in Conflict and Terrorism* (2018): 1–18; Erin M. Kearns, Allison E. Betus, and Anthony F. Lemieux, "When Data Don't Matter: Exploring Public Perceptions of Terrorism," *Studies in Conflict and Terrorism* (2019); Erin M. Kearns and Joseph K. Young, "If Torture Is Wrong, What About *24*? Torture and the Hollywood Effect," *Crime and Delinquency* 64, no. 12 (2018): 1568–89; Lemieux et al., "Support for Political Mobilization."

75. Hannah Arendt, *Eichmann in Jerusalem: A Report on the Banality of Evil*, rev. and enlarged (New York: Viking, 1964), xv.

76. Larry Christensen, "Deception in Psychological Research: When Is Its Use Justified?," *Personality and Social Psychology Bulletin* 14, no. 4 (1988): 664–75; Ian Nicholson, "'Torture at Yale': Experimental Subjects, Laboratory Torment, and the 'Rehabilitation' of Milgram's 'Obedience to Authority,' " *Theory and Psychology* 21, no. 6 (2011): 737–61.

77. Field experiments when studying torture are difficult, but they are not impossible. Nordgren et al. had subjects, among other interventions, place their hands in freezing water and then asked people whether exposure to extreme temperatures constitutes torture. Loran F. Nordgren, Mary-Hunter Morris McDonnell, and George Loewenstein, "What Constitutes Torture? Psychological Impediments to an Objective Evaluation of Enhanced Interrogation Tactics," *Psychological Science* 22, no. 5 (2011): 689–94.

78. We use the "pundit" label for commentators on the topic with subject knowledge. An expert may be a pundit when making more mass media appeals as some of the experts we interviewed have.

79. Michael Walzer, "Political Action: The Problem of Dirty Hands," *Philosophy and Public Affairs* 2, no. 2 (1973): 160–80.

80. Andrew Dugan, "A Retrospective Look at How Americans View Torture," Gallup, December 10, 2014, https://news.gallup.com/opinion/polling-matters/180008/retrospective-look-americans-view-torture.aspx.

81. Richard Wike, "Global Opinion Varies Widely on Use of Torture Against Suspected Terrorists," Pew Research Center, February 9, 2016, http://www.pewresearch.org/fact-tank/2016/02/09/global-opinion-use-of-torture/.

1. MEDIA AND PERCEPTIONS OF TORTURE

1. Parents Television Council, "24 Advertiser Campaign," February 12, 2007, http://www.parentstv.org/PTC/campaigns/24/main.asp.

2. For a detailed discussion, see Stephen Prince, *Firestorm: American Film in the Age of Terrorism* (New York: Columbia University Press, 2009); Michael Flynn and Fabiola F. Salek, eds., *Screening Torture: Media Representations of State Terror and Political Domination* (New York: Columbia University Press, 2012).

3. Casey Delehanty and Erin M. Kearns, "Wait, There's Torture in Zootopia? Examining the Prevalence of Torture in Popular Movies," *Perspectives on Politics* (2020): 1–16.

4. Asawin Suebsaeng, "Torture-Heavy '24' Was Actually a Pretty Damn Liberal TV Show," Mother Jones, May 2, 2014, http://www.motherjones.com/media/2014/05/24-live-another-day-jack-bauer-politics-torture-muslims-liberal-tv-show.

5. Troy Patterson, "Senator, We're Ready for Your Cameo," *Slate*, February 7, 2006, https://slate.com/culture/2006/02/john-mccain-on-24.html.

6. Hanna Adoni and Sherrill Mane, "Media and the Social Construction of Reality: Toward an Integration of Theory and Research," *Communication Research* 11, no. 3 (1984): 323–40; George Gerbner, "Cultivation Analysis: An Overview," Mass Communication and Society 1, no. 3–4 (1998): 175–94; Maxwell McCombs, "The Agenda-Setting Role of the Mass Media in the Shaping of Public Opinion," Mass Media Economics Conference, London School of Economics, 2003, https://www.infoamerica.org/documentos_pdf/mccombs01.

7. Andrew Buncombe, "US Military Tells Jack Bauer: Cut Out the Torture Scenes . . . or Else," *The Independent*, February 13, 2007, http://www.independent.co.uk/news/world/americas/us-military-tells-jack-bauer-cut-out-the-torture-scenes—or-else-436143.html.

8. Jim Sidanius, Michael Mitchell, Hillary Haley, and Carlos David Navarrete, "Support for Harsh Criminal Sanctions and Criminal Justice Beliefs: A Social Dominance Perspective," *Social Justice Research* 19, no. 4 (2006): 433–49; Kevin M. Carlsmith, "On Justifying Punishment: The Discrepancy Between Words and Actions," *Social Justice Research* 21, no. 2 (2008): 119–37; Christian S. Crandall, Scott Eidelman, Linda J. Skitka, and G. Scott Morgan, "Status Quo Framing Increases Support for Torture," *Social Influence* 4, no. 1 (2009): 1–10; Paul Gronke, Darius Rejali, Dustin Drenguis, James Hicks, Peter Miller, and Bryan Nakayama, "US Public Opinion on Torture, 2001–2009," *PS: Political Science and Politics* 43, no. 3 (2010): 437–44; David L. Richards, Mandy M. Morrill, and Mary R. Anderson, "Some Psycho-Social Correlates of US Citizen Support for Torture," *Nordic Journal of Human Rights* 30, no. 1 (2012): 63–95; Peter Liberman, "Retributive Support for International Punishment and Torture," *Journal of Conflict Resolution* 57, no. 2 (2013): 285–306; Peter Liberman, "War and Torture as 'Just Deserts,' " *Public Opinion Quarterly* 78, no. 1 (2014): 47–70; Bernhard Leidner, Peter Kardos, and Emanuele Castano, "The Effects of Moral and Pragmatic Arguments Against Torture on Demands for Judicial Reform," *Political Psychology* 39, no. 1 (2018): 143–62; Kimberly Rios and Dominik Mischkowski, "Shaping Responses to Torture: What You Call It Matters," *Personality and Social Psychology Bulletin* 45, no. 6 (2019): 934–46.

9. Michaël Dambrun, Johan Lepage, and Stéphanie Fayolle, "Victims' Dehumanization and the Alteration of Other-Oriented Empathy Within the Immersive Video Milgram Obedience Experiment," *Psychology* 5, no. 17 (2014): 1941–56; James A. Piazza, "Terrorist Suspect Religious Identity and Public Support for Harsh Interrogation and Detention Practices," *Political Psychology* 36, no. 6 (2015): 667–90; Courtenay R. Conrad, Sarah E. Croco, Brad T. Gomez, and Will H. Moore, "Threat Perception and American Support for Torture," *Political Behavior* 40, no. 4 (2018): 1–21.

10. Mary R. Anderson and David L. Richards, "Beyond the Media's Explanation: Examining the Determinants of Attitudes Toward Torture," *Journal of Human Rights* 17, no. 3 (2018): 1–14; J. Ian Norris, Jeff T. Larsen, and Bradley J. Stastny, "Social Perceptions of Torture: Genuine Disagreement, Subtle Malleability, and In-Group Bias," *Peace and Conflict* 16, no. 3 (2010): 275–94; Loran F. Nordgren, Mary-Hunter Morris McDonnell, and George Loewenstein, "What Constitutes Torture? Psychological Impediments to an Objective Evaluation of Enhanced Interrogation Tactics," *Psychological Science* 22, no. 5 (2011): 689–94.

11. Jean Maria Arrigo and Ray Bennett, "Organizational Supports for Abusive Interrogations in the 'War on Terror,' " *Peace and Conflict: Journal of Peace Psychology* 13, no. 4 (2007): 411–21.

12. Ronnie Janoff-Bulman, "Erroneous Assumptions: Popular Belief in the Effectiveness of Torture Interrogation," *Peace and Conflict: Journal of Peace Psychology* 13, no. 4 (2007): 429–35; Joe Santucci, "A Question of Identity: The Use of Torture in Asymmetric War," *Journal of Military Ethics* 7, no. 1 (2008): 23–40; Kevin M. Carlsmith and Avani Mehta Sood, "The Fine Line Between Interrogation and Retribution," *Journal of Experimental Social Psychology* 45, no. 1 (2009): 191–96; Kurt Gray and Daniel M. Wegner, "Torture and Judgments of Guilt," *Journal of Experimental Social Psychology* 46, no. 1 (2010): 233–35; Jared Piazza, Paulo Sousa, and Colin Holbrook, "Authority Dependence and Judgments of Utilitarian Harm," *Cognition* 128, no. 3 (2013): 261–70; Joseph Spino and Denise Dellarosa Cummins, "The Ticking Time Bomb: When the Use of Torture Is and Is Not Endorsed," *Review of Philosophy and Psychology* 5, no. 4 (2014): 543–63.

13. Geoffrey P. R. Wallace, "Martial Law? Military Experience, International Law, and Support for Torture," *International Studies Quarterly* 58, no. 3 (2014): 501–14; Adam S. Chilton and Mila Versteeg, "International Law, Constitutional Law, and Public Support for Torture," *Research and Politics* 3, no. 1 (2016): 1–9.

14. Darius Rejali, *Torture and Democracy* (Princeton, N.J.: Princeton University Press, 2009).

15. Courtenay R. Conrad, Daniel W. Hill Jr., and Will H. Moore, "Torture and the Limits of Democratic Institutions," *Journal of Peace Research* 55, no. 1 (2018): 3–17.

16. Hans Toch, *Violent Men: An Inquiry Into the Psychology of Violence* (Washington, D.C.: American Psychological Association, 1969).

17. David M. Buss and Todd K. Shackelford, "Susceptibility to Infidelity in the First Year of Marriage," *Journal of Research in Personality* 31, no. 2 (1997): 193–221; Grant S. McCall, and Nancy Shields, "Examining the Evidence from Small-Scale Societies and Early Prehistory and Implications for Modern Theories of Aggression and Violence," *Aggression*

and Violent Behavior 13, no. 1 (2008): 1–9; Joseph E. McEllistrem, "Affective and Predatory Violence: A Bimodal Classification System of Human Aggression and Violence," *Aggression and Violent Behavior* 10, no. 1 (2004): 1–30.

18. Richard E. Nisbett and Dov Cohen, *Culture of Honor: The Psychology of Violence in the South* (Boulder, Colo.: Westview Press, 1996).

19. Henri Tajfel and John C. Turner, "An Integrative Theory of Intergroup Conflict," in *Social Psychology of Intergroup Relations*, ed. William G. Austin and Stephen Worchel (Monterey, Calif.: Brooks/Cole, 1979), 33–47.

20. Anca M. Miron, Nyla R. Branscombe, and Monica Biernat, "Motivated Shifting of Justice Standards," *Personality and Social Psychology Bulletin* 36, no. 6 (2010): 768–79.

21. Ed O'Brien and Phoebe C. Ellsworth, "More Than Skin Deep: Visceral States Are Not Projected Onto Dissimilar Others," *Psychological Science* 23, no. 4 (2012): 391–96.

22. Norris, Larsen, and Stastny, "Social Perceptions of Torture"; Mark Tarrant, Nyla R. Branscombe, Ruth H. Warner, and Dale Weston, "Social Identity and Perceptions of Torture: It's Moral When We Do It," *Journal of Experimental Social Psychology* 48, no. 2 (2012): 513–18.

23. Carlsmith and Sood, "The Fine Line Between Interrogation and Retribution."

24. Deirdre Golash, *The Case Against Punishment: Retribution, Crime Prevention, and the Law* (New York: NYU Press, 2005).

25. Spino and Cummins, "The Ticking Time Bomb"; Conrad et al., "Threat Perception and American Support for Torture."

26. Gray and Wegner, "Torture and Judgments of Guilt."

27. Miroslav Nincic and Jennifer Ramos, "Torture in the Public Mind," *International Studies Perspectives* 12, no. 3 (2011): 231–49; Paolo Riva and Luca Andrighetto, " 'Everybody Feels a Broken Bone, but Only We Can Feel a Broken Heart': Group Membership Influences the Perception of Targets' Suffering," *European Journal of Social Psychology* 42, no. 7 (2012): 801–6.

28. Linda Piwowarczyk, Alejandro Moreno, and Michael Grodin, "Health Care of Torture Survivors." *JAMA* 284, no. 5 (2000): 539–41; Robin R. Vallacher, "Local Acts, Global Consequences: A Dynamic Systems Perspective on Torture," *Peace and Conflict: Journal of Peace Psychology* 13, no. 4 (2007): 445–50; James Sanders, Melissa Wagner Schuman, and Anne M. Marbella, "The Epidemiology of Torture: A Case Series of 58 Survivors of Torture," *Forensic Science International* 189, no. 1–3 (2009): e1–e7.

29. Carlsmith and Sood, "The Fine Line Between Interrogation and Retribution."

30. Richards, Morrill, and Anderson, "Some Psycho-Social Correlates of US Citizen Support for Torture."

31. Liberman, "Retributive Support for International Punishment and Torture."

32. Conor Gearty, "Terrorism and Human Rights," *Government and Opposition* 42, no. 3 (2007): 340–62.

33. Janoff-Bulman, "Erroneous Assumptions."

34. Donald Canestraro, "Experienced Interrogator: Torture Doesn't Work," *The Hill*, December 13, 2014, http://thehill.com/blogs/congress-blog/homeland-security/226866 -experienced-interrogator-torture-doesnt-work.

35. Janoff-Bulman, "Erroneous Assumptions"; Santucci, "A Question of Identity"; Carlsmith and Sood, "The Fine Line Between Interrogation and Retribution"; Douglas A. Johnson, Alberto Mora, and Averell Schmidt, "The Strategic Costs of Torture: How Enhanced Interrogation Hurt America," *Foreign Affairs* 95 (2016); Ursula Daxecker, "Dirty Hands: Government Torture and Terrorism," *Journal of Conflict Resolution* 61, no. 6 (2017): 1261–89.

36. Ali Soufan, "My Tortured Decision," *New York Times*, https://www.nytimes.com/2009 /04/23/opinion/23soufan.html

37. Paul Szoldra, "Marine General 'Mad Dog' Mattis Got Trump to Rethink His Position on Torture in Under an Hour," *Business Insider*, November 22, 2016, http://www.businessinsider.com/james-mattis-trump-torture-2016-11.

38. Jacqueline R. Evans, Christian A. Meissner, Amy B. Ross, Kate A. Houston, Melissa B. Russano, and Allyson J. Horgan, "Obtaining Guilty Knowledge in Human Intelligence Interrogations: Comparing Accusatorial and Information-Gathering Approaches with a Novel Experimental Paradigm," *Journal of Applied Research in Memory and Cognition* 2, no. 2 (2013): 83–88; Christian A. Meissner, Allison D. Redlich, Stephen W. Michael, Jacqueline R. Evans, Catherine R. Camilletti, Sujeeta Bhatt, and Susan Brandon, "Accusatorial and Information-Gathering Interrogation Methods and Their Effects on True and False Confessions: A Meta-Analytic Review," *Journal of Experimental Criminology* 10, no. 4 (2014): 459–86.

39. Shannon C. Houck and Lucian Gideon Conway III, "What People Think About Torture: Torture Is Inherently Bad . . . Unless It Can Save Someone I Love," *Journal of Applied Security Research* 8, no. 4 (2013): 429–54.

40. Allison D. Redlich, "Military Versus Police Interrogations: Similarities and Differences," *Peace and Conflict: Journal of Peace Psychology* 13, no. 4 (2007): 423–28.

41. James I. Walsh and James A. Piazza, "Why Respecting Physical Integrity Rights Reduces Terrorism," *Comparative Political Studies* 43, no. 5 (2010): 551–77.

42. Alec Tyson, "Americans Divided in Views of Use of Torture in U.S. Anti-Terror Efforts," Pew Research Center, January 26, 2017, http://www.pewresearch.org/fact-tank/2017/01/26 /americans-divided-in-views-of-use-of-torture-in-u-s-anti-terror-efforts/.

43. McCombs, "The Agenda-Setting Role of the Mass Media."

44. Adoni and Mane, "Media and the Social Construction of Reality."

45. Gerbner, "Cultivation Analysis."

46. Daniel Kahneman and Amos Tversky, "On the Study of Statistical Intuitions," *Cognition* 11, no. 2 (1982): 123–41.

47. John Koblin, "How Much Do We Love TV?," *New York Times*, June 30, 2016, https://www. nytimes.com/2016/07/01/business/media/nielsen-survey-media-viewing.html?_r=0.

48. Bryan Arva, Muhammed Idris, and Fouad Pervez, "Almost All News Coverage of the Barcelona Attack Mentioned Terrorism. Very Little Coverage of Charlottesville Did," *Washington Post*, August 31, 2017, https://www.washingtonpost.com/news/monkey-cage /wp/2017/08/31/almost-all-news-coverage-of-the-barcelona-attack-mentioned-terrorism -very-little-coverage-of-charlottesville-did/; Scott W. Duxbury, Laura C. Frizzell, and Sadé L. Lindsay, "Mental Illness, the Media, and the Moral Politics of Mass Violence:

The Role of Race in Mass Shootings Coverage," *Journal of Research in Crime and Delinquency* 55, no. 6 (2018): 766–97; Erin M. Kearns, Allison E. Betus, and Anthony F. Lemieux, "When Data Don't Matter: Exploring Public Perceptions of Terrorism," *Studies in Conflict and Terrorism* (2019); Zachary S. Mitnik, Joshua D. Freilich, and Steven M. Chermak, "Post-9/11 Coverage of Terrorism in the *New York Times*," *Justice Quarterly* (October 2018): 1–25.

49. Ashley Marie Nellis and Joanne Savage, "Does Watching the News Affect Fear of Terrorism? The Importance of Media Exposure in Terrorism Fear," *Crime and Delinquency* 58, no. 5 (2012): 748–68; Pew Research Center, "Public Perceptions of Crime Rate at Odds with Reality," April 16, 2015, http://www.pewresearch.org/fact-tank/2015/04/17/despite-lower-crime-rates-support-for-gun-rights-increases/ft_15-04-01_guns_crimerate/.

50. Shawna M. Brandle, *Television News and Human Rights in the US and UK: The Violations Will Not Be Televised* (New York: Routledge, 2016).

51. Delehanty and Kearns, "Wait, There's Torture in Zootopia?"

52. Janoff-Bulman, "Erroneous Assumptions," 431.

53. Kahneman and Tversky, "On the Study of Statistical Intuitions."

54. Delehanty and Kearns, "Wait, There's Torture in Zootopia?"

55. Valerie J. Callanan and Jared S. Rosenberger, "Media and Public Perceptions of the Police: Examining the Impact of Race and Personal Experience," *Policing and Society* 21, no. 2 (2011): 167–89; Amy K. Donahue and Joanne M. Miller, "Experience, Attitudes, and Willingness to Pay for Public Safety," *American Review of Public Administration* 36, no. 4 (2006): 395–418; Kenneth Dowler, "Media Influence on Citizen Attitudes Toward Police Effectiveness," *Policing and Society* 12, no. 3 (2002): 227–38; Kenneth Dowler and Valerie Zawilski, "Public Perceptions of Police Misconduct and Discrimination: Examining the Impact of Media Consumption," *Journal of Criminal Justice* 35, no. 2 (2007): 193–203.

56. Kenneth Dowler, "Media Consumption and Public Attitudes Toward Crime and Justice: The Relationship Between Fear of Crime, Punitive Attitudes, and Perceived Police Effectiveness," *Journal of Criminal Justice and Popular Culture* 10, no. 2 (2003): 109–26.

57. Connie McNeely, "Perceptions of the Criminal Justice System: Television Imagery and Public Knowledge in the United States," *Journal of Criminal Justice and Popular Culture* 3, no. 1 (1995): 1–12; Sarah Eschholz, Brenda Sims Blackwell, Marc Gertz, and Ted Chiricos, "Race and Attitudes Toward the Police: Assessing the Effects of Watching 'Reality' Police Programs," *Journal of Criminal Justice* 30, no. 4 (2002): 327–41; Ronald Weitzer and Steven A. Tuch, "Determinants of Public Satisfaction with the Police," *Police Quarterly* 8, no. 3 (2005): 279–97; Donahue and Miller, "Experience, Attitudes, and Willingness to Pay for Public Safety"; Joel Miller and Robert C. Davis, "Unpacking Public Attitudes to the Police: Contrasting Perceptions of Misconduct with Traditional Measures of Satisfaction," *International Journal of Police Science and Management* 10, no. 1 (2008): 9–22; Lisa Graziano, Amie Schuck, and Christine Martin, "Police Misconduct, Media Coverage, and Public Perceptions of Racial Profiling: An Experiment," *Justice Quarterly* 27, no. 1 (2010): 52–76; Diana C. Mutz and Lilach Nir, "Not Necessarily the News: Does Fictional Television Influence Real-World Policy Preferences?," *Mass Communication and Society*

13, no. 2 (2010): 196–217; Yuning Wu, "College Students' Evaluation of Police Performance: A Comparison of Chinese and Americans," *Journal of Criminal Justice* 38, no. 4 (2010): 773–80; Majid Yar, "Screening Crime: Cultural Criminology Goes to the Movies," in *Framing Crime: Cultural Criminology and the Image*, ed. Keith J. Hayward and Mike Presdee (Abingdon, UK: Routledge-Cavendish, 2010), 80–94; Callanan and Rosenberger, "Media and Public Perceptions"; Kathleen M. Donovan and Charles F. Klahm IV, "The Role of Entertainment Media in Perceptions of Police Use of Force," *Criminal Justice and Behavior* 42, no. 12 (2015): 1261–81.

58.   Jeffrey M. Glas and J. Benjamin Taylor, "The Silver Screen and Authoritarianism: How Popular Films Activate Latent Personality Dispositions and Affect American Political Attitudes," *American Politics Research* 46, no. 2 (2018): 246–75.

59.   Matthew J. Dolliver, Jennifer L. Kenney, Lesley Williams Reid, and Ariane Prohaska, "Examining the Relationship Between Media Consumption, Fear of Crime, and Support for Controversial Criminal Justice Policies Using a Nationally Representative Sample," *Journal of Contemporary Criminal Justice* 34, no. 4 (2018): 399–420.

60.   Ronald Weitzer, "Incidents of Police Misconduct and Public Opinion," *Journal of Criminal Justice* 30, no. 5 (2002): 397–408.

61.   Adoni and Mane, "Media and the Social Construction of Reality."

62.   Eytan Gilboa, "The CNN Effect: The Search for a Communication Theory of International Relations," *Political Communication* 22, no. 1 (2005): 27–44.

63.   Piers Robinson, "The Policy-Media Interaction Model: Measuring Media Power During Humanitarian Crisis," *Journal of Peace Research* 37, no. 5 (2000): 613–33.

64.   Ronald D. Crelinsten, "The World of Torture: A Constructed Reality," *Theoretical Criminology* 7, no. 3 (2003): 293–318.

65.   Conor Gearty, "Terrorism and Human Rights," *Government and Opposition* 42, no. 3 (2007): 340–62; Susan Opotow, "Moral Exclusion and Torture: The Ticking Bomb Scenario and the Slippery Ethical Slope," *Peace and Conflict: Journal of Peace Psychology* 13, no. 4 (2007): 457–61.

66.   Janoff-Bulman, "Erroneous Assumptions"; Alexander Horne, "Torture: A Short History of Its Prohibition and Re-emergence," *Judicial Review* 14, no. 2 (2009): 155–69.

67.   Joanne Savage and Christina Yancey, "The Effects of Media Violence Exposure on Criminal Aggression: A Meta-Analysis," *Criminal Justice and Behavior* 35, no. 6 (2008): 772–91.

68.   Craig A. Anderson, Brad J. Bushman, Edward Donnerstein, Tom A. Hummer, and Wayne Warburton, "SPSSI Research Summary on Media Violence," *Analyses of Social Issues and Public Policy* 15, no. 1 (2015): 4–19; Craig A. Anderson, Brad J. Bushman, Bruce D. Bartholow, et al., "Screen Violence and Youth Behavior," *Pediatrics* 140, supp. 2 (2017): S142–S147; Brad J. Bushman and Craig A. Anderson, "Understanding Causality in the Effects of Media Violence," *American Behavioral Scientist* 59, no. 14 (2015): 1807–21.

69.   Christopher J. Ferguson, "Does Media Violence Predict Societal Violence? It Depends on What You Look At and When," *Journal of Communication* 65, no. 1 (2014): E1–E22.

70.   Alexandra Merritt, Rachel LaQuea, Rachel Cromwell, and Christopher J. Ferguson, "Media Managing Mood: A Look at the Possible Effects of Violent Media on Affect," *Child and Youth Care Forum* 45, no. 2 (2016): 241–58; Raul A. Ramos, Christopher J.

Ferguson, and Kelly Frailing, "Violent Entertainment and Cooperative Behavior: Examining Media Violence Effects on Cooperation in a Primarily Hispanic Sample," *Psychology of Popular Media Culture* 5, no. 2 (2016): 119.

71. Douglas A. Gentile, Dongdong Li, Angeline Khoo, Sara Prot, and Craig A. Anderson, "Mediators and Moderators of Long-Term Effects of Violent Video Games on Aggressive Behavior: Practice, Thinking, and Action," *JAMA Pediatrics* 168, no. 5 (2014): 450–57; Erin Glackin and Sarah A. O. Gray, "Violence in Context: Embracing an Ecological Approach to Violent Media Exposure," *Analyses of Social Issues and Public Policy* 16, no. 1 (2016): 425–28; Lelia Samson and Robert F. Potter, "Empathizing and Systemizing (Un) Justified Mediated Violence: Psychophysiological Indicators of Emotional Response," *Media Psychology* 19, no. 1 (2016): 156–80; Edward L. Swing and Craig A. Anderson, "The Role of Attention Problems and Impulsiveness in Media Violence Effects on Aggression," *Aggressive Behavior* 40, no. 3 (2014): 197–203.

72. Christopher J. Ferguson and Eugene Beresin, "Social Science's Curious War with Pop Culture and How It Was Lost: The Media Violence Debate and the Risks It Holds for Social Science," *Preventive Medicine* 99 (2017): 69–76; Karin M. Fikkers, Jessica Taylor Piotrowski, Peter Lugtig, and Patti M. Valkenburg, "The Role of Perceived Peer Norms in the Relationship Between Media Violence Exposure and Adolescents' Aggression," *Media Psychology* 19, no. 1 (2016): 4–26; Douglas A. Gentile, "The Evolution of Scientific Skepticism in the Media Violence 'Debate,' " *Analyses of Social Issues and Public Policy* 16, no. 1 (2016): 429–34.

73. In this article, Justice Scalia refers, with reverence, to the specific clip from *24* that we use in the treatment conditions. "Scalia and Torture," *The Atlantic*, June 19, 2007, http://www.theatlantic.com/daily-dish/archive/2007/06/scalia-and-torture/227548/.

74. Justice Scalia is referring to the very clip from *24* that we use in the treatment conditions for this chapter. "Scalia and Torture."

75. Dahlia Lithwick, "How Jack Bauer Shaped U.S. Torture Policy," *Newsweek*, June 25, 2008, http://www.newsweek.com/lithwick-how-jack-bauer-shaped-ustorture-policy-93159.

76. Joshua Hill, Willard M. Oliver, and Nancy E. Marion, " 'Shaping History' or 'Riding the Wave'? President Bush's Influence on the Public Opinion of Terrorism, Homeland Security, and Crime," *Journal of Criminal Justice* 38, no. 5 (2010): 896–902.

77. Anthony M. Yezer, Robert S. Goldfarb, and Paul J. Poppen, "Does Studying Economics Discourage Cooperation? Watch What We Do, Not What We Say or How We Play," *Journal of Economic Perspectives* 10, no. 1 (1996): 177–86; Sara L. Rynes, Barry Gerhart, and Kathleen A. Minette, "The Importance of Pay in Employee Motivation: Discrepancies Between What People Say and What They Do," *Human Resource Management* 43, no. 4 (2004): 381–94.

78. Paul Collier and Pedro C. Vicente, "Votes and Violence: Evidence from a Field Experiment in Nigeria," *Economic Journal* 124, no. 574 (2014): F327–55.

79. Online survey companies that we contacted were not able to ask participants to sign petitions. We weighed the pros and cons of each option and decided that the benefits of the behavioral commitment outweighed the drawbacks of the convenience sample with this experimental study. The major drawback of the convenience sample is related to

generalizability, but the randomization in even this convenience sample allows for strong internal validity. The study in chapter 3 tests the same mechanisms discussed in this chapter with a more representative sample. No approach is perfect, each has its drawbacks, but we feel using both gets us closer to unpacking what is happening.

80. "Enhanced interrogation techniques" is a commonly used euphemism for torture. To see whether differences in phrasing influenced responses, we piloted the survey using both versions and did not find a significant difference in support for enhanced interrogation techniques versus torture. Our findings here contrast with findings by Rios and Mischkowski, "Shaping Responses to Torture."

81. Participants were asked questions and shown videos in a randomized order to control for order effects bias. See William D. Perreault, "Controlling Order-Effect Bias," *Public Opinion Quarterly* 39, no. 4 (1975): 544–51.

82. The five video clips together ranged from 10:23 to 11:26 in length.

83. It is likely that our study underestimated the effect of this media on people's perceptions. In our study, participants only receive one short treatment. In the real world, however, media exposure is more constant, and people receive messages from multiple sources.

84. In accordance with institutional review board guidelines, we sent the signed petitions, a draft of our paper, and an explanation of the project to the chairperson of the congressional committee for each policy area.

85. There is some debate regarding the optimal number of response options to use for a Likert scale. We removed the neutral option to reduce central tendency bias. See Ron Garland, "The Mid-Point on a Rating Scale: Is It Desirable," *Marketing Bulletin* 2, no. 1 (1991): 66–70.

86. In reality, this is a ruse, but neither the suspect nor the viewer is aware of that at the time.

87. Random assignment to treatment can sometimes lead to imbalanced groups; it is important that the process not be correlated or directly related to the concerning variable. For example, if we used an ad from the *Washington Post* to recruit subjects and more readers of the *Post* lean Democratic, we are creating bias in our sample and results related to partisanship.

88. Tyson, "Americans Divided in Views of Use of Torture."

89. Across the other policy areas, we generally do not see an impact of the video clips on support for each issue. After watching a clip about its negative effects, however, participants were slightly less supportive of legalizing marijuana.

90. Although the pretest levels of support for torture are not identical across treatments, the differences are not statistically significant ($F(2, 143) = 0.47$, $p = 0.625$).

91. We also conducted an ANCOVA (analysis of covariance) in which we included pretest support for torture as well as dummies for each treatment variable to predict posttest support for torture. The results were the same as what we have reported here; that is, participants who saw torture work were more supportive of it, and there was no difference in support across the other two conditions.

92. Descriptive information about the dependent and independent variables is broken out by condition and reported in the appendix.

93. One participant signed both petitions for and against the Keystone Pipeline, and these were dropped from analyses.

94. Three participants—one in each condition—indicated posttreatment support for torture but signed a petition in opposition to the practice. Two participants indicated posttreatment opposition for torture—one in the ineffective condition and one in the no torture condition—but signed a petition in support of the practice. The mismatch between what people say and what they do could be a result of social desirability bias, that is, people say what they think people want to hear, or it may result from inattention to detail.

95. Additional details from these models appear in the appendix. We also compared differences in petition signing between the two treatment conditions only. These results were not significant, so we do not report them.

96. Albert Bandura, Dorothea Ross, and Sheila A. Ross, "Transmission of Aggression Through Imitation of Aggressive Models," *Journal of Abnormal and Social Psychology* 63, no. 3 (1961): 575–82; David Eitle and R. Jay Turner, "Exposure to Community Violence and Young Adult Crime: The Effects of Witnessing Violence, Traumatic Victimization, and Other Stressful Life Events," *Journal of Research in Crime and Delinquency* 39, no. 2 (2002): 214–37.

97. L. Rowell Huesmann, "The Impact of Electronic Media Violence: Scientific Theory and Research," *Journal of Adolescent Health* 41, no. 6 (2007): S6–S13.

98. Tony Lagouranis and Allen Mikaelian, *Fear Up Harsh: An Army Interrogator's Dark Journey Through Iraq* (New York: Penguin, 2007).

99. Darius Rejali, *Torture and Democracy* (Princeton, N.J.: Princeton University Press, 2009); Sanders, Schuman, and Marbella, "The Epidemiology of Torture."

2. FEAR, DEATH, AND TV

1. Pär Anders Granhag, Steven M. Kleinman, and Simon Oleszkiewicz, "The Scharff Technique: On How to Effectively Elicit Intelligence from Human Sources," *International Journal of Intelligence and Counterintelligence* 29, no. 1 (2016): 132–50.

2. Jane Goodman-Delahunty, Natalie Martschuk, and Mandeep K. Dhami, "Interviewing High Value Detainees: Securing Cooperation and Disclosures," *Applied Cognitive Psychology* 28, no. 6 (2014): 883–97.

3. Amos Tversky and Daniel Kahneman, "The Framing of Decisions and the Psychology of Choice," *Science* 211, no. 4481 (1981): 453–58; Daniel Kahneman and Amos Tversky, "On the Study of Statistical Intuitions," *Cognition* 11, no. 2 (1982): 123–41; Daniel Kahneman and Amos Tversky, "Choices, Values, and Frames," *American Psychologist* 39, no. 4 (1984): 341–50; Maxwell McCombs, "The Agenda-Setting Role of the Mass Media in the Shaping of Public Opinion," Mass Media Economics Conference, London School of Economics, 2003, https://www.infoamerica.org/documentos_pdf/mccombs01.

4. Hanna Adoni and Sherrill Mane, "Media and the Social Construction of Reality: Toward an Integration of Theory and Research," *Communication Research* 11, no. 3 (1984): 323–40; George Gerbner, "Cultivation Analysis: An Overview," *Mass Communication and Society* 1, no. 3–4 (1998): 175–94.

5. Connie McNeely, "Perceptions of the Criminal Justice System: Television Imagery and Public Knowledge in the United States," *Journal of Criminal Justice and Popular Culture*

3, no. 1 (1995): 1–12; Sarah Eschholz, Brenda Sims Blackwell, Marc Gertz, and Ted Chiricos, "Race and Attitudes Toward the Police: Assessing the Effects of Watching 'Reality' Police Programs," *Journal of Criminal Justice* 30, no. 4 (2002): 327–41; Ronald Weitzer and Steven A. Tuch, "Determinants of Public Satisfaction with the Police," *Police Quarterly* 8, no. 3 (2005): 279–97; Amy K. Donahue and Joanne M. Miller, "Experience, Attitudes, and Willingness to Pay for Public Safety," *American Review of Public Administration* 36, no. 4 (2006): 395–418; Joel Miller and Robert C. Davis, "Unpacking Public Attitudes to the Police: Contrasting Perceptions of Misconduct with Traditional Measures of Satisfaction," *International Journal of Police Science and Management* 10, no. 1 (2008): 9–22; Lisa Graziano, Amie Schuck, and Christine Martin, "Police Misconduct, Media Coverage, and Public Perceptions of Racial Profiling: An Experiment," *Justice Quarterly* 27, no. 1 (2010): 52–76; Diana C. Mutz and Lilach Nir, "Not Necessarily the News: Does Fictional Television Influence Real-World Policy Preferences?," *Mass Communication and Society* 13, no. 2 (2010): 196–217; Yuning Wu, "College Students' Evaluation of Police Performance: A Comparison of Chinese and Americans," *Journal of Criminal Justice* 38, no. 4 (2010): 773–80; Majid Yar, "Screening Crime: Cultural Criminology Goes to the Movies," in *Framing Crime: Cultural Criminology and the Image*, ed. Keith J. Hayward and Mike Presdee (Abingdon, UK: Routledge-Cavendish, 2010), 80–94; Valerie J. Callanan and Jared S. Rosenberger, "Media and Public Perceptions of the Police: Examining the Impact of Race and Personal Experience," *Policing and Society* 21, no. 2 (2011): 167–89; Kathleen M. Donovan and Charles F. Klahm IV, "The Role of Entertainment Media in Perceptions of Police Use of Force," *Criminal Justice and Behavior* 42, no. 12 (2015): 1261–81.

6.   Allison D. Redlich, "Military Versus Police Interrogations: Similarities and Differences," *Peace and Conflict: Journal of Peace Psychology* 13, no. 4 (2007): 423–28; Laurence Alison and Emily Alison, "Revenge Versus Rapport: Interrogation, Terrorism, and Torture," *American Psychologist* 72, no. 3 (2017): 266–77.

7.   Stanley Milgram, "Behavioral Study of Obedience," *Journal of Abnormal and Social Psychology* 67, no. 4 (1963): 371–78.

8.   Craig Haney, Curtis Banks, and Philip Zimbardo, "Interpersonal Dynamics in a Simulated Prison," *International Journal of Criminology and Penology* 1 (1973): 69–97.

9.   Darrin Brown, Sharon Lauricella, Aziz Douai, and Arshia Zaidi, "Consuming Television Crime Drama: A Uses and Gratifications Approach," *American Communication Journal* 14, no. 1 (2012): 47–60; Christopher J. Ferguson, "Evidence for Publication Bias in Video Game Violence Effects Literature: A Meta-Analytic Review," *Aggression and Violent Behavior* 12, no. 4 (2007): 470–82.

10.   Kenneth Dowler, "Media Consumption and Public Attitudes Toward Crime and Justice: The Relationship Between Fear of Crime, Punitive Attitudes, and Perceived Police Effectiveness," *Journal of Criminal Justice and Popular Culture* 10, no. 2 (2003): 109–26; Lisa A. Kort-Butler and Kelley J. Sittner Hartshorn, "Watching the Detectives: Crime Programming, Fear of Crime, and Attitudes About the Criminal Justice System," *Sociological Quarterly* 52, no. 1 (2011): 36–55; Mutz and Nir, "Not Necessarily the News."

11.   Matthew J. Dolliver, Jennifer L. Kenney, Lesley Williams Reid, and Ariane Prohaska, "Examining the Relationship Between Media Consumption, Fear of Crime, and Support

for Controversial Criminal Justice Policies Using a Nationally Representative Sample," *Journal of Contemporary Criminal Justice* 34, no. 4 (2018): 399–420.

12. Jennifer S. Lerner, Roxana M. Gonzalez, Deborah A. Small, and Baruch Fischhoff, "Effects of Fear and Anger on Perceived Risks of Terrorism: A National Field Experiment," *Psychological Science* 14, no. 2 (2003): 144–50.

13. Leonie Huddy, Stanley Feldman, Charles Taber, and Gallya Lahav, "Threat, Anxiety, and Support of Antiterrorism Policies," *American Journal of Political Science* 49, no. 3 (2005): 593–608; Bethany Albertson and Shana Kushner Gadarian, *Anxious Politics: Democratic Citizenship in a Threatening World* (Cambridge: Cambridge University Press, 2015).

14. Ruth Horry and Daniel B. Wright, "Anxiety and Terrorism: Automatic Stereotypes Affect Visual Attention and Recognition Memory for White and Middle Eastern Faces," *Applied Cognitive Psychology* 23, no. 3 (2009): 345–57.

15. Steven J. Stroessner, Abigail A. Scholer, David M. Marx, and Bradley M. Weisz, "When Threat Matters: Self-Regulation, Threat Salience, and Stereotyping," *Journal of Experimental Social Psychology* 59 (2015): 77–89.

16. Daphna Canetti-Nisim, Eran Halperin, Keren Sharvit, and Stevan E. Hobfoll, "A New Stress-Based Model of Political Extremism: Personal Exposure to Terrorism, Psychological Distress, and Exclusionist Political Attitudes," *Journal of Conflict Resolution* 53, no. 3 (2009): 363–89.

17. Connor Huff and Joshua D. Kertzer, "How the Public Defines Terrorism," *American Journal of Political Science* 62, no. 1 (2018): 55–71; Erin M. Kearns, Allison Betus, and Anthony Lemieux, "Why Do Some Terrorist Attacks Receive More Media Attention Than Others?" *Justice Quarterly* 36, no. 6 (2019): 985–1022; Allison Betus, Erin Kearns, and Anthony Lemieux," 'Terrorism' or 'Mental Illness'? Factors That Impact How Media Label Terrorist Attacks," *Washington Post*, August 7, 2019. http://dx.doi.org/10.2139/ssrn.3433933; Jack G. Shaheen, *Reel Bad Arabs: How Hollywood Vilifies a People* (Northampton, Mass: Olive Branch Press, 2012).

18. Emily Pronin, Kathleen Kennedy, and Sarah Butsch, "Bombing Versus Negotiating: How Preferences for Combating Terrorism Are Affected by Perceived Terrorist Rationality," *Basic and Applied Social Psychology* 28, no. 4 (2006): 385–92.

19. Shana Kushner Gadarian, "The Politics of Threat: How Terrorism News Shapes Foreign Policy Attitudes," *Journal of Politics* 72, no. 2 (2010): 469–83.

20. Neil Malhotra and Elizabeth Popp, "Bridging Partisan Divisions Over Antiterrorism Policies: The Role of Threat Perceptions," *Political Research Quarterly* 65, no. 1 (2012): 34–47.

21. Jamie Arndt, Jeff Greenberg, and Alison Cook, "Mortality Salience and the Spreading Activation of Worldview-Relevant Constructs: Exploring the Cognitive Architecture of Terror Management," *Journal of Experimental Psychology: General* 131, no. 3 (2002): 307–24.

22. Jeff Greenberg, Tom Pyszczynski, Sheldon Solomon, Abram Rosenblatt, Mitchell Veeder, Shari Kirkland, and Deborah Lyon, "Evidence for Terror Management Theory II: The Effects of Mortality Salience on Reactions to Those Who Threaten or Bolster the Cultural Worldview," *Journal of Personality and Social Psychology* 58, no. 2 (1990): 308–18; Michael J. Halloran and Emiko S. Kashima, "Social Identity and Worldview Validation:

The Effects of Ingroup Identity Primes and Mortality Salience on Value Endorsement," *Personality and Social Psychology Bulletin* 30, no. 7 (2004): 915–25.

23. Jeff Greenberg, Linda Simon, Tom Pyszczynski, Sheldon Solomon, and Dan Chatel, "Terror Management and Tolerance: Does Mortality Salience Always Intensify Negative Reactions to Others Who Threaten One's Worldview?," *Journal of Personality and Social Psychology* 63, no. 2 (1992): 212–20.

24. Mark J. Landau, Sheldon Solomon, Jeff Greenberg, Florette Cohen, Tom Pyszczynski, Jamie Arndt, Claude H. Miller, Daniel M. Ogilvie, and Alison Cook, "Deliver Us from Evil: The Effects of Mortality Salience and Reminders of 9/11 on Support for President George W. Bush," *Personality and Social Psychology Bulletin* 30, no. 9 (2004): 1136–50.

25. Abram Rosenblatt, Jeff Greenberg, Sheldon Solomon, Tom Pyszczynski, and Deborah Lyon, "Evidence for Terror Management Theory: I. The Effects of Mortality Salience on Reactions to Those Who Violate or Uphold Cultural Values," *Journal of Personality and Social Psychology* 57, no. 4 (1989): 681–90.

26. See, e.g., Albertson and Kushner Gadarian, *Anxious Politics*; Dolliver, Kenney, Reid and Prohaska, "Examining the Relationship"; Brendan Nyhan and Thomas Zeitzoff, "Conspiracy and Misperception Belief in the Middle East and North Africa," *Journal of Politics* 80, no. 4 (2018): 1400–1404; Matthew Wright, Morris Levy, and Jack Citrin, "Public Attitudes Toward Immigration Policy Across the Legal/Illegal Divide: The Role of Categorical and Attribute-Based Decision-Making," *Political Behavior* 38, no. 1 (2016): 229–53.

27. Rosenblatt et al., "Evidence for Terror Management Theory"; Greenberg et al., "Evidence for Terror Management Theory II"; Greenberg et al., "Terror Management and Tolerance"; Arndt, Greenberg, and Cook, "Mortality Salience and the Spreading Activation of Worldview-Relevant Constructs"; Halloran and Kashima, "Social Identity and Worldview Validation"; Landau et al., "Deliver Us from Evil"; Clay Routledge and Jacob Juhl, "When Death Thoughts Lead to Death Fears: Mortality Salience Increases Death Anxiety for Individuals Who Lack Meaning in Life," *Cognition and Emotion* 24, no. 5 (2010): 848–54.

28. Dental pain or intense pain has been used as a control prime in other studies where mortality salience is the experimental prime. Arndt, Greenberg and Cook, "Mortality Salience and the Spreading Activation of Worldview-Relevant Constructs"; Landau et al., "Deliver Us from Evil."

29. Arndt, Greenberg, and Cook, "Mortality Salience and the Spreading Activation of Worldview-Relevant Constructs"; Greenberg et al., "Evidence for Terror Management Theory II"; Greenberg et al., "Terror Management and Tolerance"; Halloran and Kashima, "Social Identity and Worldview Validation"; Landau et al., "Deliver Us from Evil"; Routledge and Juhl, "When Death Thoughts Lead to Death Fears."

30. Loran F. Nordgren, Mary-Hunter Morris McDonnell, and George Loewenstein, "What Constitutes Torture? Psychological Impediments to an Objective Evaluation of Enhanced Interrogation Tactics," *Psychological Science* 22, no. 5 (2011): 689–94.

31. Donald P. Green, Bradley Palmquist, and Eric Schickler, *Partisan Hearts and Minds: Political Parties and the Social Identities of Voters* (New Haven, Conn.: Yale University Press, 2004).

3. CONTEXT MATTERS?

1. In France, for example, the headline of *Le Monde* on September 12, 2001, claimed, "We are all Americans."

2. According to a Gallup/CNN/USA Today poll, 88 percent of Americans supported a military assault on Afghanistan. In March 2003, right after the beginning of the war, a Gallup/CNN/USA Today poll found that 62 percent of Americans supported the Iraq decision: http://www.pollingreport.com/iraq.htm.

3. See, for example, Donald. H. Rumsfeld, "Memorandum to President George W. Bush," September 23, 2001, http://library.rumsfeld.com/doclib/sp/1495/2001-09-23%20to%20 President%20George%20W%20Bush%20re%20(no%20subject).pdf.

4. Jonathan S. Landay, "Report: Abusive Tactics Used to Seek Iraq–al Qaida Link," *McClatchy DC*, April 21, 2009, https://www.mcclatchydc.com/news/nation-world/world /article24535114.html.

5. Craig Haney and Philip G. Zimbardo, "Persistent Dispositionalism in Interactionist Clothing: Fundamental Attribution Error in Explaining Prison Abuse," *Personality and Social Psychology Bulletin* 35, no. 6 (2009): 807–14.

6. See, for example, Seymour Hersh, "Torture at Abu Ghraib: American Soldiers Brutalized Iraqis. How Far Up Does the Responsibility Go?," *New Yorker*, May 10, 2004, https:// www.newyorker.com/magazine/2004/05/10/torture-at-abu-ghraib.

7. Nick Childs, "Abu Ghraib Reports Re-Ignite Debate," BBC News, August 26, 2004, http:// news.bbc.co.uk/2/hi/americas/3600112.stm.

8. Hamdan v. Rumsfeld 2006, https://supreme.justia.com/cases/federal/us/548/557 /; Boumediene v. Bush 2008, https://supreme.justia.com/cases/federal/us/553/723/.

9. Joan M. Blauwkamp, Charles M. Rowling, and William Pettit, "Are Americans Really Okay with Torture? The Effects of Message Framing on Public Opinion," *Media, War and Conflict* 11, no. 4 (2018): 446–75.

   Public opinion polls also show that support for torture increases when it is framed as a means to gain information about terrorist activities. Chris Kahn, "Exclusive: Most Americans Support Torture Against Terror Suspects," Reuters, March 30, 2016, https:// www.reuters.com/article/us-usa-election-torture-exclusive/exclusive-most-americans -support-torture-against-terror-suspects-reuters-ipsos-poll-idUSKCN0WW0Y3.

10. Paul Gronke, Darius Rejali, Dustin Drenguis, James Hicks, Peter Miller, and Bryan Nakayama, "US Public Opinion on Torture, 2001–2009," *PS: Political Science and Politics* 43, no. 3 (2010): 437–44.

11. Bruce Drake, "Americans' View on Use of Torture in Fighting Terrorism Have Been Mixed," Pew Research Center, December 9, 2014, http://www.pewresearch.org/fact-tank/2014/12/09 /americans-views-on-use-of-torture-in-fighting-terrorism-have-been-mixed/.

12. Mark Costanzo and Allison Redlich, "Use of Physical and Psychological Force in Criminal and Military Interrogations," in *Policing Around the World: Police Use of Force*, ed. J. Knuttson and J. Kuhns, 43–51 (Santa Barbara, Calif.: Praeger, 2010).

13. Noah Berlatsky, "When Chicago Tortured," *The Atlantic*, December 17, 2014, https://www .theatlantic.com/national/archive/2014/12/chicago-police-torture-jon-burge/383839/.

14. These charges were eventually dropped. German Lopez, "The Baltimore Protests Over Freddie Gray's Death, Explained," *Vox*, August 18, 2016, https://www.vox.com/cards /freddie-gray-baltimore-riots-police-violence/baltimore-protests-freddie-gray.

15. Brentin Mock, "The Persistent, Wide Racial Gap in Attitudes Toward the Police," Citylab. com, September 21, 2017, https://www.citylab.com/equity/2017/09/the-wide-racial-gap-in -attitudes-toward-police/540456/.

16. Ann Scott Tyson, "What Went Wrong in Abu Ghraib," *Christian Science Monitor*, June 10, 2004, https://www.csmonitor.com/2004/0610/p02s01-usmi.html.

17. Albert Bandura, Dorothea Ross, and Sheila A. Ross, "Transmission of Aggression Through Imitation of Aggressive Models," *Journal of Abnormal and Social Psychology* 63, no. 3 (1961): 575–82.

18. Albert Bandura, "The Role of Imitation in Personality Development," in *Dimensions of Psychology*, ed. Glenn T. Morris (New York: MSS Educational Publications, 1971), 16–23.

19. James T. Tedeschi and Brian M. Quigley, "Limitations of Laboratory Paradigms for Studying Aggression," *Aggression and Violent Behavior* 1, no. 2 (1996): 163–77.

20. Linda Heath, Candace Kruttschnitt, and David Ward, "Television and Violent Criminal Behavior: Beyond the Bobo Doll," *Violence and Victims* 1, no. 3 (1986): 177–90; Linda Heath, Linda B. Bresolin, and Robert C. Rinaldi, "Effects of Media Violence on Children: A Review of the Literature," *Archives of General Psychiatry* 46, no. 4 (1989): 376–79.

21. Amanda E. Pennell and Kevin D. Browne, "Film Violence and Young Offenders," *Aggression and Violent Behavior* 4, no. 1 (1999): 13–28.

22. Carly N. Wayne, "Risk or Retribution: How Citizens Respond to Terrorism," paper presented at the American Political Science Association Annual Meeting (2018).

23. J. Ian Norris, Jeff T. Larsen, and Bradley J. Stastny, "Social Perceptions of Torture: Genuine Disagreement, Subtle Malleability, and In-Group Bias," *Peace and Conflict* 16, no. 3 (2010): 275–94; Mark Tarrant, Nyla R. Branscombe, Ruth H. Warner, and Dale Weston, "Social Identity and Perceptions of Torture: It's Moral When We Do It," *Journal of Experimental Social Psychology* 48, no. 2 (2012): 513–18.

24. Shannon C. Houck, Lucian Gideon Conway III, and Meredith A. Repke, "Personal Closeness and Perceived Torture Efficacy: If Torture Will Save Someone I'm Close To, Then It Must Work," *Peace and Conflict: Journal of Peace Psychology* 20, no. 4 (2014): 590–92.

25. Courtenay R. Conrad, Sarah E. Croco, Brad T. Gomez, and Will H. Moore, "Threat Perception and American Support for Torture," *Political Behavior* 40, no. 4 (2018): 1–21.

26. For a theory about how in-group/out-group dynamics leads to terrorism, see Jeff Goodwin, "A Theory of Categorical Terrorism," *Social Forces* 84, no. 4 (2006): 2027–46.

27. Jeremy Meyer and David J. Armor, "Support for Torture Over Time: Interrogating the American Public About Coercive Tactics," *Social Science Journal* 49, no. 4 (2012): 439–46.

28. See, for example, Jessica Schulberg, "It's Depressing How Many Americans Still Support Torture," *New Republic*, December 12, 2014, https://newrepublic.com/article/120548 /yougov-study-finds-republicans-approve-cia-torture; or more recently, see Ariel Edwards-Levy, "Just a Third of Americans Think Trump's CIA Pick Should Be Blocked for Overseeing Torture," *Huffington Post*, March 27, 2018, https://www.huffingtonpost .com/entry/just-a-third-of-americans-think-trumps-cia-pick-should-be-disqualified -for-overseeing-torture_us_5aba87f2e4b03e2a5c76dcd0.

29. Richard C. Eichenberg, "When Gender (Sometimes) Trumps Party: Citizen Attitudes Toward Torture in the War Against Terror," 2014, https://papers.ssrn.com/sol3/papers .cfm?abstract_id=2480104.

30. Peter Liberman, "Retributive Support for International Punishment and Torture," *Journal of Conflict Resolution* 57, no. 2 (2013): 285–306.

31. Shankar Vedantam, "The Psychology of Torture: Past Incidents Show Abusers Think Ends Justify the Means," *Washington Post*, May 11, 2004.

32. Amy Zegart, "Torture Creep," *Foreign Policy*, September 25, 2012, https://foreignpolicy .com/2012/09/25/torture-creep/.

33. David Weaver, "Issue Salience and Public Opinion: Are There Consequences of Agenda-Setting?," *International Journal of Public Opinion Research* 3, no. 1 (1991): 53–68.

34. Shanto Iyengar and Adam Simon, "News Coverage of the Gulf Crisis and Public Opinion: A Study of Agenda-Setting, Priming, and Framing," *Communication Research* 20, no. 3 (1993): 365–83.

35. Benjamin I. Page and Robert Y. Shapiro, "Effects of Public Opinion on Policy," *American Political Science Review* 77, no. 1 (1983): 175–90.

36. Paul Burstein, "The Impact of Public Opinion on Public Policy: A Review and an Agenda," *Political Research Quarterly* 56, no. 1 (2003): 29–40.

37. James A. Piazza, "Terrorist Suspect Religious Identity and Public Support for Harsh Interrogation and Detention Practices," *Political Psychology* 36, no. 6 (2015): 667–90.

38. William Jordan, "Americans Find Some Tortures More Acceptable Than Others," YouGov, December 12, 2014, https://today.yougov.com/topics/politics/articles-reports/2014/12/12 /torture-report.

39. Michael Buhrmester, Tracy Kwang, and Samuel D. Gosling, "Amazon's Mechanical Turk: A New Source of Inexpensive, Yet High-Quality, Data?," *Perspectives on Psychological Science* 6, no. 1 (2011): 3–5.

40. Adam J. Berinsky, Gregory A. Huber, and Gabriel S. Lenz, "Evaluating Online Labor Markets for Experimental Research: Amazon.com's Mechanical Turk," *Political Analysis* 20, no. 3 (2012): 351–68; Scott Clifford, Ryan M. Jewell, and Philip D. Waggoner, "Are Samples Drawn from Mechanical Turk Valid for Research on Political Ideology?," *Research and Politics* 2, no. 4 (2015): 1–12; Hyoun S. Kim and David C. Hodgins, "Reliability and Validity of Data Obtained from Alcohol, Cannabis, and Gambling Populations on Amazon's Mechanical Turk," *Psychology of Addictive Behaviors* 31, no. 1 (2017): 85–94.

41. Thad Dunning, "Improving Causal Inference: Strengths and Limitations of Natural Experiments," *Political Research Quarterly* 61, no. 2 (2008): 282–93.

42. For a timeline, see "Timeline: The History of the CIA Detention and Interrogation Program," *Los Angeles Times*, December 9, 2014, http://www.latimes.com/nation/la-na -timeline-of-cia-interrogation-program-20141209-story.html.

43. Critics argue that low compensation might affect responses made by MTurk respondents. Buhrmester et al., "Amazon's Mechanical Turk," refute that low compensation affects respondents. However, others suggest that low compensation may impact attention. Joseph K. Goodman, Cynthia E. Cryder, and Amar Cheema, "Data Collection in a Flat World: The Strengths and Weaknesses of Mechanical Turk Samples," *Journal of*

Behavioral Decision Making 26, no. 3 (2013): 213–24. Given the short length of time to completion, we are less concerned with this criticism.

44. William D. Perreault, "Controlling Order-Effect Bias," *Public Opinion Quarterly* 39, no. 4 (1975): 544–51.

45. Online survey platforms like MTurk do not allow participants to provide identifying information. Thus there was not an actual petition for participants to sign if they indicated a willingness to do so. Regardless of which option participants clicked, the next screen informed all participants that there was not actually a petition.

46. We also asked participants about their views on a host of specific harsh practices, but this was not central to this chapter, so we do not present these results in the main text. However, we do compare these views between Waves 1 and 2 and present them in tables 4.A4 and 4.A5 in the appendix.

47. There is still some debate about the optimal number of options to use for a Likert scale. The neutral option promotes central tendency bias, especially for more controversial subject matter, so we did not include a neutral option. Participants could skip questions for any reason. Ron Garland, "The Mid-Point on a Rating Scale: Is It Desirable," *Marketing Bulletin* 2, no. 1 (1991): 66–70.

48. Equality of coefficients tests show that there are no significant differences between coefficients before and after the Senate Torture Report.

49. Of course, our analyses presume that everyone in our sample has the same in-group and out-group vis-à-vis the interrogator and suspect names. To tease this out, we also estimated the models separately for white participants and minority participants. The results are the same.

50. Linda Piwowarczyk, Alejandro Moreno, and Michael Grodin, "Health Care of Torture Survivors," *JAMA* 284, no. 5 (2000): 539–41; Pauline Oosterhoff, Prisca Zwanikken, and Evert Ketting, "Sexual Torture of Men in Croatia and Other Conflict Situations: An Open Secret," *Reproductive Health Matters* 12, no. 23 (2004): 68–77; Robin R. Vallacher, "Local Acts, Global Consequences: A Dynamic Systems Perspective on Torture," *Peace and Conflict: Journal of Peace Psychology* 13, no. 4 (2007): 445–50.

51. Henri Tajfel and John C. Turner, "The Social Identity Theory of Intergroup Behaviour," in *Psychology of Intergroup Relations*, ed. William G. Austin and Stephen Worchel (Chicago: Nelson Hall, 1986), 7–24.

52. Courtenay R. Conrad, Daniel W. Hill Jr., and Will H. Moore, "Torture and the Limits of Democratic Institutions," *Journal of Peace Research* 55, no. 1 (2018): 3–17.

53. Hannah Hartig and Abigail Geiger, "About Six-in-Ten Americans Support Marijuana Legalization," Pew Research Center, October 8, 2018, http://www.pewresearch.org/fact-tank/2018/01/05/americans-support-marijuana-legalization/.

54. Cynthia R. Morton and Meredith Friedman, " 'I Saw It in the Movies': Exploring the Link Between Product Placement Beliefs and Reported Usage Behavior," *Journal of Current Issues and Research in Advertising* 24, no. 2 (2002): 33–40.

55. Miguel A. Costa-Gomes, Steffen Huck, and Georg Weizsäcker, "Beliefs and Actions in the Trust Game: Creating Instrumental Variables to Estimate the Causal Effect," *Games and Economic Behavior* 88 (2014): 298–309.

4. ELITE CUES, IDENTITY, AND EFFICACY

1. This memo along with others written by White House lawyers during this time in the Bush administration are often collectively called the torture memos.

2. For the memo, along with the note written by Rumsfeld in the margins, see the National Security Archive at George Washington University: https://nsarchive2.gwu.edu/NSAEBB /NSAEBB127/02.12.02.pdf.

3. Attorney General Ashcroft's memo is also available at the National Security Archive: https://nsarchive2.gwu.edu/torturingdemocracy/documents/20020201.pdf.

4. Joseph K. Young, "Morality, Efficacy, and Targeted Assassination as a Policy Tool," *Criminology and Public Policy* 16, no. 1 (2017): 225–30.

5. We do not know what Colin Kaepernick makes, but it is reported to be millions a year in Nike endorsements. Serena Williams signed a five-year $50 million deal with Nike in 2003.

6. Amanda Spry, Ravi Pappu, and T. Bettina Cornwell, "Celebrity Endorsement, Brand Credibility, and Brand Equity," *European Journal of Marketing* 45, no. 6 (2011): 882–909.

7. Martin Gilens and Naomi Murakawa, "Elite Cues and Political Decision Making," in *Political Decision-Making, Deliberation, and Participation*, ed. Michael X. Delli Carpini, Leonie Huddy, and Robert Shapiro (Bingley, UK: Emerald Group, 2002), 15–49. This is not to say that taking cues from elites is the *best* way to make a decision. In this chapter, we are interested in whether individuals take cues from elites and what kinds of elites influence them. Some others argue that taking cues from elites leads to worse decision-making and that there is no substitute for developing knowledge on a policy. See David Darmofal, "Elite Cues and Citizen Disagreement with Expert Opinion," *Political Research Quarterly* 58, no. 3 (2005): 381–95.

8. Robert J. Brulle, Jason Carmichael, and J. Craig Jenkins, "Shifting Public Opinion on Climate Change: An Empirical Assessment of Factors Influencing Concern Over Climate Change in the US, 2002–2010," *Climatic Change* 114, no. 2 (2012): 169–88.

9. Perhaps not surprising for some skeptical observers, technical and scientific information does not seem to alter opinions and is overshadowed by elite cues.

10. John G. Bullock, "Elite Influence on Public Opinion in an Informed Electorate," *American Political Science Review* 105, no. 3 (2011): 496–515.

11. William Minozzi, Michael A. Neblo, Kevin M. Esterling, and David M. J. Lazer, "Field Experiment Evidence of Substantive, Attributional, and Behavioral Persuasion by Members of Congress in Online Town Halls," *Proceedings of the National Academy of Sciences* 112, no. 13 (2015): 3937–42.

12. Bruce W. Jentleson and Rebecca L. Britton, "Still Pretty Prudent: Post-Cold War American Public Opinion on the Use of Military Force," *Journal of Conflict Resolution* 42, no. 4 (1998): 395–417.

13. Daniel Silverman, Daniel Kent, and Christopher Gelpi, "Public Fears of Terrorism, Partisan Rhetoric, and the Foundations of American Interventionism," Presentation at the International Studies Association Annual Meeting in San Francisco, CA, 2018.

14. Erin M. Kearns, Allison E. Betus, and Anthony F. Lemieux, "When Data Don't Matter: Exploring Public Perceptions of Terrorism," *Studies in Conflict and Terrorism* (2019).

15. Matthew A. Baum and Tim Groeling, "Shot by the Messenger: Partisan Cues and Public Opinion Regarding National Security and War," *Political Behavior* 31, no. 2 (2009): 157–86.

16. Shana Kushner Gadarian, "The Politics of Threat: How Terrorism News Shapes Foreign Policy Attitudes," *Journal of Politics* 72, no. 2 (2010): 469–83.

17. Caroll Doherty, "7 Things to Know About Polarization in America," Pew Research Center, June 12, 2014, http://www.pewresearch.org/fact-tank/2014/06/12/7-things-to-know -about-polarization-in-america/.

18. James N. Druckman, Donald P. Green, James H. Kuklinski, and Arthur Lupia, "The Growth and Development of Experimental Research in Political Science," *American Political Science Review* 100, no. 4 (2006): 627–35.

19. The DW Nominate score is a widely accepted scholarly approach to classifying the degree of liberalism or conservatism among members of the U.S. Congress. It is based on the actual voting behavior of each member. For an overview, see "Parties: Parties Overview—Congress at a Glance: Major Party Ideology," Voteview.com, https://voteview .com/parties/all.

20. Brendan Nyhan, "Why the 'Death Panel' Myth Wouldn't Die: Misinformation in the Health Care Reform Debate," *The Forum* 8, no. 1 (2010). doi: 10.2202/1540-8884.1354; Brendan Nyhan and Jason Reifler, "When Corrections Fail: The Persistence of Political Misperceptions," *Political Behavior* 32, no. 2 (2010): 303–30; Brendan Nyhan, Ethan Porter, Jason Reifler, and Thomas Wood, "Taking Corrections Literally but Not Seriously? The Effects of Information on Factual Beliefs and Candidate Favorability," *SSRN Electronic Journal*, January 2017, doi: 10.2139/ssrn.2995128.

21. C. Christine Fair, Neil Malhotra, and Jacob N. Shapiro, "Faith or Doctrine? Religion and Support for Political Violence in Pakistan," *Public Opinion Quarterly* 76, no. 4 (2012): 688–720; Jason Lyall, Graeme Blair, and Kosuke Imai, "Explaining Support for Combatants During Wartime: A Survey Experiment in Afghanistan," *American Political Science Review* 107, no. 4 (2013): 679–705.

22. Henri Tajfel and John C. Turner, "The Social Identity Theory of Intergroup Behaviour," in *Psychology of Intergroup Relations*, ed. William G. Austin and Stephen Worchel (Chicago: Nelson Hall, 1986); Bernd Simon and Bert Klandermans, "Politicized Collective Identity: A Social Psychological Analysis," *American Psychologist* 56, no. 4 (2001): 319–31; Martijn van Zomeren, Tom Postmes, and Russell Spears, "Toward an Integrative Social Identity Model of Collective Action: A Quantitative Research Synthesis of Three Socio-Psychological Perspectives," *Psychological Bulletin* 134, no. 4 (2008): 504–35.

23. Marga De Weerd and Bert Klandermans, "Group Identification and Political Protest: Farmers' Protest in the Netherlands," *European Journal of Social Psychology* 29, no. 8 (1999): 1073–95; Jeff Goodwin, "A Theory of Categorical Terrorism," *Social Forces* 84, no. 4 (2006): 2027–46; Erin M. Kearns, Victor Asal, James Igoe Walsh, Christopher Federico, and Anthony F. Lemieux, "Political Action as a Function of Grievances, Risk, and Social Identity: An Experimental Approach," *Studies in Conflict and Terrorism* (2018): 1–18.

24. J. Ian Norris, Jeff T. Larsen, and Bradley J. Stastny, "Social Perceptions of Torture: Genuine Disagreement, Subtle Malleability, and In-Group Bias," *Peace and Conflict* 16, no. 3

(2010): 275–94; Mark Tarrant, Nyla R. Branscombe, Ruth H. Warner, and Dale Weston, "Social Identity and Perceptions of Torture: It's Moral When We Do It," *Journal of Experimental Social Psychology* 48, no. 2 (2012): 513–18; James A. Piazza, "Terrorist Suspect Religious Identity and Public Support for Harsh Interrogation and Detention Practices," *Political Psychology* 36, no. 6 (2015): 667–90.

25. Norris, Larsen, and Stastny, "Social Perceptions of Torture."

26. Piazza, "Terrorist Suspect Religious Identity."

27. Erin M. Kearns, Allison Betus, and Anthony Lemieux, "Why Do Some Terrorist Attacks Receive More Media Attention Than Others?," *Justice Quarterly* 36, no. 6 (2019): 985–1022.

28. Zachary S. Mitnik, Joshua D. Freilich, and Steven M. Chermak, "Post-9/11 Coverage of Terrorism in the *New York Times*," *Justice Quarterly* (October 2018): 1–25.

29. Bryan Arva, Muhammed Idris, and Fouad Pervez, "Almost All News Coverage of the Barcelona Attack Mentioned Terrorism. Very Little Coverage of Charlottesville Did," *Washington Post*, August 31, 2017, https://www.washingtonpost.com/news/monkey-cage /wp/2017/08/31/almost-all-news-coverage-of-the-barcelona-attack-mentioned-terrorism -very-little-coverage-of-charlottesville-did/.

30. Emily K. Gade, Dallas Card, Sarah K. Dreier, and Noah A. Smith, "What Counts as Terrorism? An Examination of Terrorist Designations Among U.S. Mass Shootings," paper presented at Political Methodology Conference, Salt Lake City, Ut., 2018.

31. Connor Huff and Joshua D. Kertzer, "How the Public Defines Terrorism," *American Journal of Political Science* 62, no. 1 (2018): 55–71.

32. Vito D'Orazio and Idean Salehyan, "Who Is a Terrorist? Ethnicity, Group Affiliation, and Understandings of Political Violence," *International Interactions* 44, no. 6 (2018): 1017–39.

33. Piazza, "Terrorist Suspect Religious Identity."

34. Nazli Avdan and Clayton Webb, "Not in My Back Yard: Public Perceptions and Terrorism," *Political Research Quarterly* 72, no. 1 (2018): 90–103.

35. Nazli Avdan and Clayton Webb, "The Big, the Bad, and the Dangerous: Public Perceptions and Terrorism," *Dynamics of Asymmetric Conflict* 11, no. 1 (2018): 3–25.

36. James E. Mitchell, with Bill Harlow, *Enhanced Interrogation: Inside the Minds and Motives of the Islamic Terrorists Trying to Destroy America* (New York: Crown Forum, 2016).

37. This is a more indirect and difficult outcome to test. Deterrence is notoriously difficult to test because success often leads to a nonaction. For examples in international conflict, see Paul Huth and Bruce Russett, "General Deterrence Between Enduring Rivals: Testing Three Competing Models," *American Political Science Review* 87, no. 1 (1993): 61–73; Paul K. Huth, "Deterrence and International Conflict: Empirical Findings and Theoretical Debates," *Annual Review of Political Science* 2, no. 1 (1999): 25–48. For an example in crime, see Raymond Paternoster and Alex Piquero, "Reconceptualizing Deterrence: An Empirical Test of Personal and Vicarious Experiences," *Journal of Research in Crime and Delinquency* 32, no. 3 (1995): 251–86.

38. One of the authors made a related set of arguments when evaluating support for drone strikes in counterterrorism. See Young, "Morality, Efficacy, and Targeted Assassination."

39. Donald Rumsfeld's now infamous memo from October 16, 2003 is available at https://fas .org/irp/news/2003/10/rumsfeld101603.pdf

40.   Adam J. Berinsky, Gregory A. Huber, and Gabriel S. Lenz, "Evaluating Online Labor Markets for Experimental Research: Amazon.com's Mechanical Turk," *Political Analysis* 20, no. 3 (2012): 351–68; Scott Clifford, Ryan M. Jewell, and Philip D. Waggoner, "Are Samples Drawn from Mechanical Turk Valid for Research on Political Ideology?," *Research and Politics* 2, no. 4 (2015): 1–12; Hyoun S. Kim and David C. Hodgins, "Reliability and Validity of Data Obtained from Alcohol, Cannabis, and Gambling Populations on Amazon's Mechanical Turk," *Psychology of Addictive Behaviors* 31, no. 1 (2017): 85–94.

41.   Examples include Jens Hainmueller and Daniel J. Hopkins, "Public Attitudes Toward Immigration," *Annual Review of Political Science* 17 (2014): 225–49; Jens Hainmueller, Daniel J. Hopkins, and Teppei Yamamoto, "Causal Inference in Conjoint Analysis: Understanding Multidimensional Choices via Stated Preference Experiments," *Political Analysis* 22, no. 1 (2014): 1–30; Huff and Kertzer, "How the Public Defines Terrorism"; Matthew Wright, Morris Levy, and Jack Citrin, "Public Attitudes Toward Immigration Policy Across the Legal/Illegal Divide: The Role of Categorical and Attribute-Based Decision-Making," *Political Behavior* 38, no. 1 (2016): 229–53. Erin M. Kearns, *If You See Something, Do You Say Something? The Role of Legitimacy and Trust in Policing Minority Communities in Counterterrorism*, PhD diss., American University, 2016.

42.   Hainmueller and Hopkins, "Public Attitudes Toward Immigration"; Jens Hainmueller and Daniel J. Hopkins, "The Hidden American Immigration Consensus: A Conjoint Analysis of Attitudes Toward Immigrants," *American Journal of Political Science* 59, no. 3 (2015): 529–48; Hainmueller, Hopkins, and Yamamoto, "Causal Inference in Conjoint Analysis"; Huff and Kertzer, "How the Public Defines Terrorism"; Kearns, "If You See Something, Do You Say Something?"; Wright, Levy, and Citrin, "Public Attitudes Toward Immigration Policy."

43.   There is some debate on the optimal number of response options to give for a Likert scale; we removed the neutral option to reduce central tendency bias. Ron Garland, "The Mid-Point on a Rating Scale: Is It Desirable," *Marketing Bulletin* 2, no. 1 (1991): 66–70.

44.   Some combinations, such as someone being of Asian descent and also a neo-Nazi, are rare, but they do exist in the real world. Anntoinette Moore, " 'Asian Nazi' Says Lawyer Trying to Get Him Convicted, Seeks Release from Gregg County Jail," *Longview News-Journal*, July 12, 2018, https://www.news-journal.com/news/police/asian-nazi-says -lawyer-trying-to-get-him-convicted-seeks/article_7942e916-861f-11e8-ba34-cba7f9ee2968 .html.

45.   Richard Spencer, a white nationalist leader, was punched by a protester after President Trump's inauguration. This event spurred a debate, particularly among those on the left, about the acceptability of punching a Nazi. Some argued that this was an acceptable action, but others opposed this violence. Andrew Buncombe, "White Supremacist Richard Spencer Asked 'How Did It Feel to Get Punched in the Face?' by Egyptian-Puerto Rican Woman," *The Independent*, October 20, 2017, https://www.independent.co.uk /news/world/americas/us-politics/richard-spencer-punched-face-what-was-it-like -speech-neo-nazi-question-woman-a8012071.html; Jesse Singal, "The Careful, Pragmatic Case Against Punching Nazis," *New York Magazine*, August 19, 2017, http://nymag .com/intelligencer/2017/08/the-careful-pragmatic-case-against-punching-nazis.html.

46. Jens Hainmueller, Dominik Hangartner, and Teppei Yamamoto. "Validating Vignette and Conjoint Survey Experiments Against Real-World Behavior." *Proceedings of the National Academy of Sciences* 112 (2015): 2395-400. doi: 0.1073/pnas.1416587112.

47. See Hainmueller, Hopkins, and Yamamoto, "Causal Inference in Conjoint Analysis," for a full discussion of this approach with relevant proofs and sensitivity checks. Given the binary outcome, some prefer to estimate logit or probit regression models. Ordinary least squares (OLS), however, is standard practice for conjoint analyses. OLS produces unbiased and consistent estimates that are substantively unchanged from, but easier to interpret than, logit or probit models. See Alan S. Gerber and Donald P. Green, *Field Experiments: Design, Analysis, and Interpretation* (New York: Norton, 2012), 34–35. We use simple ordinary least squares (OLS) regression to estimate the average marginal component effects (AMCEs) for each attribute value.

48. Hainmueller, Hopkins, and Yamamoto, "Causal Inference in Conjoint Analysis."

49. Each participant evaluates multiple scenarios, so conjoint analyses are estimated with standard errors and are clustered by participant to capture any within-participant variation, as is standard practice. Hainmueller, Hopkins, and Yamamoto, "Causal Inference in Conjoint Analysis"; Huff and Kertzer, "How the Public Defines Terrorism."

50. We also conduct equality of coefficients tests to compare the relative change across the five possible sources. People are significantly more influenced by a military interrogator than by a Democratic member of Congress ($p = 0.03$). There are no significant differences in the influence of the other sources relative to one another.

51. Joshua D. Kertzer and Thomas Zeitzoff, "A Bottom-Up Theory of Public Opinion About Foreign Policy," *American Journal of Political Science* 61, no. 3 (2017): 543–58.

52. Equality of coefficients tests show that people are significantly more supportive of torture against Syrian citizens than both UK ($p = 0.002$) or Chinese citizens ($p = 0.02$). There are no differences in support for torture against UK versus Chinese citizens.

53. Allison Betus, Erin Kearns, and Anthony Lemieux, " 'Terrorism' or 'Mental Illness'? Factors That Impact How Media Label Terrorist Attacks," *Washington Post*, August 7, 2019, http://dx.doi.org/10.2139/ssrn.3433933. Kearns, Betus, and Lemieux, "Why Do Some Terrorist Attacks Receive More Media Attention Than Others?"

54. Huff and Kertzer, "How the Public Defines Terrorism."

55. Bruce Hoffman, *Inside Terrorism* (New York: Columbia University Press, 2006).

56. We also conduct equality of coefficients tests to compare the relative change across the five possible goals. Relative to an anti-abortion activist, people are significantly more supportive of torturing a member of Antifa ($p = 0.0004$), a neo-Nazi ($p < 0.0001$), a member of an armed militia ($p < 0.0001$), or a member of ISIS ($p < 0.0001$). Relative to a member of Antifa, people are significantly more supportive of torturing a neo-Nazi ($p = 0.02$), a member of an armed militia ($p < 0.0001$), or a member of ISIS ($p < 0.0001$). Relative to a neo-Nazi, people are significantly more supportive of torturing a member of an armed militia ($p = 0.02$) or a member of ISIS ($p = 0.002$). There is no difference in support for torturing a member of an armed militia versus a member of ISIS.

57.   An equality of coefficients test shows that people are significantly more supportive of torture when it would likely be effective than when it would likely yield mixed results (p <0.0001).

58.   Hainmueller, Hopkins, and Yamamoto, "Causal Inference in Conjoint Analysis," call these "conditional AMCEs."

CONCLUSION

1.   Courtenay R. Conrad, Daniel W. Hill Jr., and Will H. Moore, "Torture and the Limits of Democratic Institutions," *Journal of Peace Research* 55, no. 1 (2018): 3–17.

2.   Darius Rejali, *Torture and Democracy* (Princeton, N.J.: Princeton University Press, 2009).

3.   Marc Heatherington and Jonathan Weiler, *Prius or Pickup? How the Answers to Four Simple Questions Explain America's Great Divide* (Boston: Houghton Mifflin, 2018).

4.   For example, see Diana Carole Mutz, Paul M. Sniderman, and Richard A. Brody, eds., *Political Persuasion and Attitude Change* (Ann Arbor: University of Michigan Press, 1996).

5.   We are grateful to Brendan Nyhan for help and advice on this point. Joshua L. Kalla and David E. Brockman, "The Minimal Persuasive Effects of Campaign Contact in General Elections: Evidence from 49 Field Experiments," *American Political Science Review* 112, no. 1 (2018): 148–66.

6.   Lauren C. Howe and Jon A. Krosnick, "Attitude Strength," *Annual Review of Psychology* 68 (2017): 327–51.

7.   Joshua D. Kertzer and Thomas Zeitzoff, "A Bottom-Up Theory of Public Opinion About Foreign Policy," *American Journal of Political Science* 61, no. 3 (2017): 543–58.

8.   Ted Brader, Nicholas A. Valentino, and Elizabeth Suhay, "What Triggers Public Opposition to Immigration? Anxiety, Group Cues, and Immigration Threat," *American Journal of Political Science* 52, no. 4 (2008): 959–78.

9.   D. J. Flynn, Brendan Nyhan, and Jason Reifler, "The Nature and Origins of Misperceptions: Understanding False and Unsupported Beliefs About Politics," *Political Psychology* 38 (2017): 127–50; Brendan Nyhan and Jason Reifler, "When Corrections Fail: The Persistence of Political Misperceptions," *Political Behavior* 32, no. 2 (2010): 303–30.

10.   Thanks to Thomas Zeitzoff for making these points.

11.   Rejali, *Torture and Democracy*.

12.   Courtenay R. Conrad, "Divergent Incentives for Dictators: Domestic Institutions and (International Promises Not to) Torture," *Journal of Conflict Resolution* 58, no. 1 (2014): 34–67; Conrad, Hill, and Moore, "Torture and the Limits of Democratic Institutions."

13.   Loran F. Nordgren, Mary-Hunter Morris McDonnell, and George Loewenstein, "What Constitutes Torture? Psychological Impediments to an Objective Evaluation of Enhanced Interrogation Tactics," *Psychological Science* 22, no. 5 (2011): 689–94.

14.   Marcus K. Taylor, Katherine E. Stanfill, Genieleah A. Padilla, Amanda E. Markham, Michael D. Ward, Matthew M. Koehler, Antonio Anglero, and Barry D. Adams, "Effect of Psychological Skills Training During Military Survival School: A Randomized, Controlled Field Study," *Military Medicine* 176, no. 12 (2011): 1362–68.

15. Conrad, Hill, and Moore, "Torture and the Limits of Democratic Institutions."

16. Lucian E. Dervan and Vanessa A. Edkins, "The Innocent Defendant's Dilemma: An Innovative Empirical Study of Plea Bargaining's Innocence Problem," *Journal of Criminal Law and Criminology* 103, no. 1 (2013): 1–48.

17. Some also consider Marxism, feminism, and a form of postmodernism as on par with the big three.

18. David Allen Baldwin, *Neorealism and Neoliberalism: The Contemporary Debate* (New York: Columbia University Press, 1993); Robert Powell, "Anarchy in International Relations Theory: The Neorealist-Neoliberal Debate," *International Organization* 48, no. 2 (1994): 313–44; Alexander Wendt, *Social Theory of International Politics* (Cambridge: Cambridge University Press, 1999).

19. Daniel Maliniak, Amy Oakes, Susan Peterson, and Michael J. Tierney, "International Relations in the US Academy," *International Studies Quarterly* 55, no. 2 (2011): 437–64.

20. John J. Mearsheimer and Stephen M. Walt, "Leaving Theory Behind: Why Simplistic Hypothesis Testing Is Bad for International Relations," *European Journal of International Relations* 19, no. 3 (2013): 427–57.

21. Clark McCauley and Sophia Moskalenko, "Mechanisms of Political Radicalization: Pathways Toward Terrorism," *Terrorism and Political Violence* 20, no. 3 (2008): 415–33.

22. To be fair, we are using terms such as *less* and *more*. No state is perfect. All have corruption, issues with rule of law, and other assorted social ills.

23. Nordgren, McDonnell, and Loewenstein, "What Constitutes Torture?"

24. Kalla and Brockman, "The Minimal Persuasive Effects of Campaign Contact."

25. David L. Cingranelli and David L. Richards, "The Cingranelli and Richads (CIRI) Human Rights Data Project," *Human Rights Quarterly* 32, no. 2 (2010): 401–24.

26. Conrad, Hill, and Moore, "Torture and the Limits of Democratic Institutions."

27. Conrad, Hill, and Moore.

28. Calvert W. Jones and Celia Paris, "It's the End of the World and They Know It: How Dystopian Fiction Shapes Political Attitudes," *Perspectives on Politics* 16, no. 4 (2018): 969–89.

29. Tony Lagouranis and Allen Mikaelian, *Fear Up Harsh: An Army Interrogator's Dark Journey Through Iraq* (New York: Penguin, 2007).

30. Rejali, *Torture and Democracy*; James Sanders, Melissa Wagner Schuman, and Anne M. Marbella, "The Epidemiology of Torture: A Case Series of 58 Survivors of Torture," *Forensic Science International* 189, no. 1–3 (2009): e1–e7.

31. The most famous literary example is from Sir Arthur Conan Doyle's Sherlock Holmes short story, "The Adventures of Silver Blaze." The famed detective, Sherlock Holmes, is able to solve a perplexing case through the use of nonevidence—dogs *not* barking.

APPENDIX

1. Jens Hainmueller, Daniel J. Hopkins, and Teppei Yamamoto, "Optimizing Survey Designs in Conjoint Analysis" (Working paper shared with the authors of this book, nd). H. A. Simon introduced the term "satisficing"—a portmanteau of satisfy and suffice—to

explain a decision-making process in which no solution is optimal, so people simplify the problem to find either an optimal solution or an acceptable solution. In this context, satisficing means that participants discount some of the randomly varied attributes when making their decisions. H. A. Simon, "Rational Choice and the Structure of the Environment," *Psychological Review* 63 (1956): 129–38, doi:10.1037/h0042769.

2.   Kirk Bansak, Jens Hainmueller, Daniel J. Hopkins, and Teppei Yamamoto, "The Number of Choice Tasks and Survey Satisficing in Conjoint Experiments," *Political Analysis* 26 (2017): 112–19, doi: 10.1017/pan.2017.40; Jens Hainmueller, Dominik Hangartner, and Teppei Yamamoto, "Validating Vignette and Conjoint Survey Experiments Against Real-World Behavior." *Proceedings of the National Academy of Sciences* 112, no. 8 (2015): 2395–2400.

3.   John Zaller, *The Nature and Origins of Mass Opinion* (Cambridge: Cambridge University Press, 1992.

4.   Questions from the July 2017 version are available at http://www.pewresearch.org/quiz /the-news-iq-quiz/results/.

5.   Results by number of questions correct: 0 correct (M = 0.70, SD = 0.07), 1 correct (M = 0.43, SD = 0.02), 2 correct (M = 0.34, SD = 0.01), 3 correct (M = 0.28, SD = 0.007), and 4 correct (M = 0.21, SD = 0.005).

BIBLIOGRAPHY

Adoni, Hanna, and Sherrill Mane. "Media and the Social Construction of Reality: Toward an Integration of Theory and Research." *Communication Research* 11, no. 3 (1984): 323–40.

Albertson, Bethany, and Shana Kushner Gadarian. *Anxious Politics: Democratic Citizenship in a Threatening World.* Cambridge: Cambridge University Press, 2015.

Alison, Laurence, and Emily Alison. "Revenge Versus Rapport: Interrogation, Terrorism, and Torture." *American Psychologist* 72, no. 3 (2017): 266–77.

Amnesty International. *Amnesty International 1996 Report.* London: Amnesty International, 1996.

Amnesty International. *Stopping the Torture Trade.* New York: Amnesty International, 2000.

Amnesty International. *Amnesty International Report 2010: The State of the World's Human Rights.* New York: Amnesty International Publications, 2010. http://report2010.amnesty.org /facts-and-figures.

Anderson, Craig A., Brad J. Bushman, Bruce D. Bartholow, Joanne Cantor, Dimitri Christakis, Sarah M. Coyne, Edward Donnerstein, et al. "Screen Violence and Youth Behavior." *Pediatrics* 140, supp. 2 (2017): S142–S147.

Anderson, Craig A., Brad J. Bushman, Edward Donnerstein, Tom A. Hummer, and Wayne Warburton. "SPSSI Research Summary on Media Violence." *Analyses of Social Issues and Public Policy* 15, no. 1 (2015): 4–19.

Anderson, Mary R., and David L. Richards. "Beyond the Media's Explanation: Examining the Determinants of Attitudes Toward Torture." *Journal of Human Rights* 17, no. 3 (2018): 1–14.

Arendt, Hannah. *Eichmann in Jerusalem: A Report on the Banality of Evil.* rev. ed. New York: Viking, 1964.

Arndt, Jamie, Jeff Greenberg, and Alison Cook. "Mortality Salience and the Spreading Activation of Worldview-Relevant Constructs: Exploring the Cognitive Architecture of Terror Management." *Journal of Experimental Psychology: General* 131, no. 3 (2002): 307–24.

Arrigo, Bruce. "Punishment, Freedom, and the Culture of Control: A Review of Torture—America's Brutal Prisons." *Contemporary Justice Review* 9, no. 2 (2006): 229–33.

Arrigo, Jean Maria, and Ray Bennett. "Organizational Supports for Abusive Interrogations in the 'War on Terror.'" *Peace and Conflict: Journal of Peace Psychology* 13, no. 4 (2007): 411–21.

Ashcroft, John. Memo to the President. February 1, 2002. https://nsarchive2.gwu.edu/NSAEBB /NSAEBB127/020201.pdf

Arva, Bryan, Muhammed Idris, and Fouad Pervez. "Almost All News Coverage of the Barcelona Attack Mentioned Terrorism. Very Little Coverage of Charlottesville Did." *Washington Post*, August 31, 2017. https://www.washingtonpost.com/news/monkey-cage/wp/2017/08/31 /almost-all-news-coverage-of-the-barcelona-attack-mentioned-terrorism-very-little-coverage -of-charlottesville-did/.

Avdan, Nazli, and Clayton Webb. "The Big, the Bad, and the Dangerous: Public Perceptions and Terrorism." *Dynamics of Asymmetric Conflict* 11, no. 1 (2018): 3–25.

——. "Not in My Back Yard: Public Perceptions and Terrorism." *Political Research Quarterly* 72, no. 1 (2018): 90–103.

Baldwin, David Allen. *Neorealism and Neoliberalism: The Contemporary Debate*. New York: Columbia University Press, 1993.

Bandura, Albert. "The Role of Imitation in Personality Development." In *Dimensions of Psychology*, ed. Glenn T. Morris, 16–23. New York: MSS Educational Publications, 1971.–.

Bandura, Albert, Dorothea Ross, and Sheila A. Ross. "Transmission of Aggression Through Imitation of Aggressive Models." *Journal of Abnormal and Social Psychology* 63, no. 3 (1961): 575–82.

Bansak, Kirk, Jens Hainmueller, Daniel J. Hopkins, and Teppei Yamamoto. "The Number of Choice Tasks and Survey Satisficing in Conjoint Experiments." *Political Analysis* 26 (2017): 112–19. doi: 10.1017/pan.2017.40

Bartsch, Anne, Marie-Louise Mares, Sebastian Scherr, Andrea Kloß, Johanna Keppeler, and Lone Posthumus. "More Than Shoot-Em-Up and Torture Porn: Reflective Appropriation and Meaning-Making of Violent Media Content." *Journal of Communication* 66, no. 5 (2016): 741–65.

Baum, Matthew A., and Tim Groeling. "Shot by the Messenger: Partisan Cues and Public Opinion Regarding National Security and War." *Political Behavior* 31, no. 2 (2009): 157–86.

Berinsky, Adam J., Gregory A. Huber, and Gabriel S. Lenz. "Evaluating Online Labor Markets for Experimental Research: Amazon.com's Mechanical Turk." *Political Analysis* 20, no. 3 (2012): 351–68.

Berlatsky, Noah. "When Chicago Tortured." *The Atlantic*, December 17, 2014. https://www.theatlantic .com/national/archive/2014/12/chicago-police-torture-jon-burge/383839/.

Betus, Allison, Erin Kearns, and Anthony Lemieux. "'Terrorism' or 'Mental Illness'? Factors That Impact How Media Label Terrorist Attacks." *Washington Post*, August 7, 2019. http://dx.doi .org/10.2139/ssrn.3433933.

Blauwkamp, Joan M., Charles M. Rowling, and William Pettit. "Are Americans Really Okay with Torture? The Effects of Message Framing on Public Opinion." *Media, War and Conflict* 11, no. 4 (2018): 446–75.

Boumediene v. Bush (Nos. 06–1195 and 06–1196), 2008. https://supreme.justia.com/cases /federal/us/553/723/.

Bowman, Karlyn. "U.S. Public Opinion and the Terrorist Threat." American Enterprise Institute, November 1, 2005. http://www.aei.org/publication/u-s-public-opinion-and-the-terrorist-threat/.

Brader, Ted, Nicholas A. Valentino, and Elizabeth Suhay. "What Triggers Public Opposition to Immigration? Anxiety, Group Cues, and Immigration Threat." *American Journal of Political Science* 52, no. 4 (2008): 959–78.

Brandle, Shawna M. *Television News and Human Rights in the US and UK: The Violations Will Not Be Televised*. New York: Routledge, 2016.

Brown, Darrin, Sharon Lauricella, Aziz Douai, and Arshia Zaidi. "Consuming Television Crime Drama: A Uses and Gratifications Approach." *American Communication Journal* 14, no. 1 (2012): 47–60.

Brown, Dee. *Bury My Heart at Wounded Knee: An Indian History of the American West*. New York: Henry Holt, 2007.

Brulle, Robert J., Jason Carmichael, and J. Craig Jenkins. "Shifting Public Opinion on Climate Change: An Empirical Assessment of Factors Influencing Concern Over Climate Change in the US, 2002–2010." *Climatic Change* 114, no. 2 (2012): 169–88.

Buhrmester, Michael, Tracy Kwang, and Samuel D. Gosling. "Amazon's Mechanical Turk: A New Source of Inexpensive, Yet High-Quality, Data?" *Perspectives on Psychological Science* 6, no. 1 (2011): 3–5.

Bullock, John G. "Elite Influence on Public Opinion in an Informed Electorate." *American Political Science Review* 105, no. 3 (2011): 496–515.

Buncombe, Andrew. "US Military Tells Jack Bauer: Cut Out the Torture Scenes . . . or Else." *The Independent*, February 13, 2007. http://www.independent.co.uk/news/world/americas /us-military-tells-jack-bauer-cut-out-the-torture-scenes—or-else-436143.html.

——. "White Supremacist Richard Spencer Asked 'How Did It Feel to Get Punched in the Face?' by Egyptian-Puerto Rican Woman." *The Independent*, October 20, 2017. https://www .independent.co.uk/news/world/americas/us-politics/richard-spencer-punched-face-what -was-it-like-speech-neo-nazi-question-woman-a8012071.html.

Burstein, Paul. "The Impact of Public Opinion on Public Policy: A Review and an Agenda." *Political Research Quarterly* 56, no. 1 (2003): 29–40.

Bushman, Brad J., and Craig A. Anderson. "Understanding Causality in the Effects of Media Violence." *American Behavioral Scientist* 59, no. 14 (2015): 1807–21.

Buss, David M., and Todd K. Shackelford. "From Vigilance to Violence: Mate Retention Tactics in Married Couples." *Journal of Personality and Social Psychology* 72, no. 2 (1997): 346.

Callanan, Valerie J., and Jared S. Rosenberger. "Media and Public Perceptions of the Police: Examining the Impact of Race and Personal Experience." *Policing and Society* 21, no. 2 (2011): 167–89.

Camp, Stephanie M. H. *Closer to Freedom: Enslaved Women and Everyday Resistance in the Plantation South*. Chapel Hill: University of North Carolina Press, 2005.

Canestraro, Donald. "Experienced Interrogator: Torture Doesn't Work." *The Hill*, December 13, 2014. http://thehill.com/blogs/congress-blog/homeland-security/226866-experienced-interrogator -torture-doesnt-work.

Canetti-Nisim, Daphna, Eran Halperin, Keren Sharvit, and Stevan E. Hobfoll. "A New Stress-Based Model of Political Extremism: Personal Exposure to Terrorism, Psychological Distress, and Exclusionist Political Attitudes." *Journal of Conflict Resolution* 53, no. 3 (2009): 363–89.

Carlsmith, Kevin M. "On Justifying Punishment: The Discrepancy Between Words and Actions." *Social Justice Research* 21, no. 2 (2008): 119–37.

Carlsmith, Kevin M., and Avani Mehta Sood. "The Fine Line Between Interrogation and Retribution." *Journal of Experimental Social Psychology* 45, no. 1 (2009): 191–96.

Childs, Nick. "Abu Ghraib Reports Re-Ignite Debate." BBC News, August 26, 2004. http://news.bbc.co.uk/2/hi/americas/3600112.stm.

Chilton, Adam S., and Mila Versteeg. "International Law, Constitutional Law, and Public Support for Torture." *Research and Politics* 3, no. 1 (2016): 1–9.

Christensen, Larry. "Deception in Psychological Research: When Is Its Use Justified?" *Personality and Social Psychology Bulletin* 14, no. 4 (1988): 664–75.

Cingranelli, David L., and David L. Richards. "The Cingranelli and Richads (CIRI) Human Rights Data Project." *Human Rights Quarterly* 32, no. 2 (2010): 401–24.

Clarkson, Darren. "Public Believes U.S. Government Has Tortured Prisoners." Gallup, November 29, 2005. https://news.gallup.com/poll/20170/public-believes-us-government-has-tortured-prisoners.aspx.

Clifford, Scott, Ryan M. Jewell, and Philip D. Waggoner. "Are Samples Drawn from Mechanical Turk Valid for Research on Political Ideology?" *Research and Politics* 2, no. 4 (2015): 1–12.

Collier, Paul, and Pedro C. Vicente. "Votes and Violence: Evidence from a Field Experiment in Nigeria." *Economic Journal* 124, no. 574 (2014): F327–55.

Conrad, Courtenay R. "Divergent Incentives for Dictators: Domestic Institutions and (International Promises Not to) Torture." *Journal of Conflict Resolution* 58, no. 1 (2014): 34–67.

Conrad, Courtenay R., Justin Conrad, James Igoe Walsh, and James A. Piazza. "Who Tortures the Terrorists? Transnational Terrorism and Military Torture." *Foreign Policy Analysis* 13, no. 4 (2016): 761–86.

Conrad, Courtenay R., Sarah E. Croco, Brad T. Gomez, and Will H. Moore. "Threat Perception and American Support for Torture." *Political Behavior* 40, no. 4 (2018): 1–21.

Conrad, Courtenay R., Jillienne Haglund, and Will H. Moore. "Disaggregating Torture Allegations: Introducing the Ill-Treatment and Torture (ITT) Country-Year Data." *International Studies Perspectives* 14, no. 2 (2013): 199–220.

Conrad, Courtenay R., Daniel W. Hill Jr., and Will H. Moore. "Torture and the Limits of Democratic Institutions." *Journal of Peace Research* 55, no. 1 (2018): 3–17.

Cornish, Derek B., and Ronald V. Clarke. "Understanding Crime Displacement: An Application of Rational Choice Theory." *Criminology* 25, no. 4 (1987): 933–48.

Costa-Gomes, Miguel A., Steffen Huck, and Georg Weizsäcker. "Beliefs and Actions in the Trust Game: Creating Instrumental Variables to Estimate the Causal Effect." *Games and Economic Behavior* 88 (2014): 298–309.

Costanzo, Mark, and Allison Redlich. "Use of Physical and Psychological Force in Criminal and Military Interrogations." In *Policing Around the World: Police Use of Force*, ed. J. Knuttsson and J. Kuhns, 43–51. Santa Barbara, CA: Praeger Security International, 2010.

Coyne, Sarah M., Mark A. Callister, Douglas A. Gentile, and Emily Howard. "Media Violence and Judgments of Offensiveness: A Quantitative and Qualitative Analysis." *Psychology of Popular Media Culture* 5, no. 4 (2016): 372–89.

Crandall, Christian S., Scott Eidelman, Linda J. Skitka, and G. Scott Morgan. "Status Quo Framing Increases Support for Torture." *Social Influence* 4, no. 1 (2009): 1–10.

Crelinsten, Ronald D. "The World of Torture: A Constructed Reality." *Theoretical Criminology* 7, no. 3 (2003): 293–318.

Crenshaw, Martha. "Counterterrorism Policy and the Political Process." *Studies in Conflict and Terrorism* 24, no. 5 (2001): 329–37.

Dambrun, Michaël, Johan Lepage, and Stéphanie Fayolle. "Victims' Dehumanization and the Alteration of Other-Oriented Empathy Within the Immersive Video Milgram Obedience Experiment." *Psychology* 5, no. 17 (2014): 1941–56.

Darmofal, David. "Elite Cues and Citizen Disagreement with Expert Opinion." *Political Research Quarterly* 58, no. 3 (2005): 381–95.

Davis, Darren W., and Brian D. Silver. "Civil Liberties vs. Security: Public Opinion in the Context of the Terrorist Attacks on America." *American Journal of Political Science* 48, no. 1 (2004): 28–46.

Daxecker, Ursula. "Dirty Hands: Government Torture and Terrorism." *Journal of Conflict Resolution* 61, no. 6 (2017): 1261–89.

Delehanty, Casey, and Erin M. Kearns. "Wait, There's Torture in *Zootopia*? Examining the Prevalence of Torture in Popular Movies." *Perspectives on Politics* (2020): 1–16.

Department of Defense, U.S. "The Interrogation Documents: Debating U.S. Policy and Methods," December 2, 2002. https://nsarchive2.gwu.edu/NSAEBB/NSAEBB127/index.htm

Dervan, Lucian E., and Vanessa A. Edkins. "The Innocent Defendant's Dilemma: An Innovative Empirical Study of Plea Bargaining's Innocence Problem." *Journal of Criminal Law and Criminology* 103, no. 1 (2013): 1–48.

De Weerd, Marga, and Bert Klandermans. "Group Identification and Political Protest: Farmers' Protest in the Netherlands." *European Journal of Social Psychology* 29, no. 8 (1999): 1073–95.

Doherty, Caroll. "7 Things to Know About Polarization in America." Pew Research Center, June 12, 2014. http://www.pewresearch.org/fact-tank/2014/06/12/7-things-to-know-about -polarization-in-america/.

Dolliver, Matthew J., Jennifer L. Kenney, Lesley Williams Reid, and Ariane Prohaska. "Examining the Relationship Between Media Consumption, Fear of Crime, and Support for Controversial Criminal Justice Policies Using a Nationally Representative Sample." *Journal of Contemporary Criminal Justice* 34, no. 4 (2018): 399–420.

Donahue, Amy K., and Joanne M. Miller. "Experience, Attitudes, and Willingness to Pay for Public Safety." *American Review of Public Administration* 36, no. 4 (2006): 395–418.

Donovan, Kathleen M., and Charles F. Klahm IV. "The Role of Entertainment Media in Perceptions of Police Use of Force." *Criminal Justice and Behavior* 42, no. 12 (2015): 1261–81.

D'Orazio, Vito, and Idean Salehyan. "Who Is a Terrorist? Ethnicity, Group Affiliation, and Understandings of Political Violence." *International Interactions* 44, no. 6 (2018): 1017–39.

Dowler, Kenneth. "Media Consumption and Public Attitudes Toward Crime and Justice: The Relationship Between Fear of Crime, Punitive Attitudes, and Perceived Police Effectiveness." *Journal of Criminal Justice and Popular Culture* 10, no. 2 (2003): 109–26.

——. "Media Influence on Citizen Attitudes Toward Police Effectiveness." *Policing and Society* 12, no. 3 (2002): 227–38.

Dowler, Kenneth, and Valerie Zawilski. "Public Perceptions of Police Misconduct and Discrimination: Examining the Impact of Media Consumption." *Journal of Criminal Justice* 35, no. 2 (2007): 193–203.

Drake, Bruce. "Americans' View on Use of Torture in Fighting Terrorism Have Been Mixed." Pew Research Center, December 9, 2014. http://www.pewresearch.org/fact-tank/2014/12/09 /americans-views-on-use-of-torture-in-fighting-terrorism-have-been-mixed/.

Druckman, James N., Donald P. Green, James H. Kuklinski, and Arthur Lupia. "The Growth and Development of Experimental Research in Political Science." *American Political Science Review* 100, no. 4 (2006): 627–35.

Druckman, James N., Erik Peterson, and Rune Slothuus. "How Elite Partisan Polarization Affects Public Opinion Formation." *American Political Science Review* 107, no. 1 (2013): 57–79.

Dugan, Andrew. "A Retrospective Look at How Americans View Torture." Gallup, December 10, 2014. https://news.gallup.com/opinion/polling-matters/180008/retrospective-look-americans -view-torture.aspx.

Dugan, Laura, and Erica Chenoweth. "Moving Beyond Deterrence: The Effectiveness of Raising the Expected Utility of Abstaining from Terrorism in Israel." *American Sociological Review* 77, no. 4 (2012): 597–624.

Dugan, Laura, Gary LaFree, and Alex R. Piquero. "Testing a Rational Choice Model of Air-line Hijackings." In *International Conference on Intelligence and Security Informatics*, ed. Paul Kantor, Gheorghe Muresan, Fred Roberts, Daniel D. Zeng, Fei-Yue Wang, Hsin-chun Chen, and Ralph C. Merkle, 340–61. Berlin: Springer, 2005.

Dunning, Thad. "Improving Causal Inference: Strengths and Limitations of Natural Experi-ments." *Political Research Quarterly* 61, no. 2 (2008): 282–93.

Duxbury, Scott W., Laura C. Frizzell, and Sadé L. Lindsay. "Mental Illness, the Media, and the Moral Politics of Mass Violence: The Role of Race in Mass Shootings Coverage." *Journal of Research in Crime and Delinquency* 55, no. 6 (2018): 766–97.

Edwards-Levy, Ariel. "Just a Third of Americans Think Trump's CIA Pick Should Be Blocked for Overseeing Torture." *Huffington Post*, March 27, 2018. https://www.huffingtonpost .com/entry/just-a-third-of-americans-think-trumps-cia-pick-should-be-disqualified-for -overseeing-torture_us_5aba87f2e4b03e2a5c76dcd0.

Eichenberg, Richard C. "When Gender (Sometimes) Trumps Party: Citizen Attitudes Toward Torture in the War Against Terror." 2014. https://papers.ssrn.com/sol3/papers.cfm?abstract _id=2480104.

Eitle, David, and R. Jay Turner. "Exposure to Community Violence and Young Adult Crime: The Effects of Witnessing Violence, Traumatic Victimization, and Other Stressful Life Events." *Journal of Research in Crime and Delinquency* 39, no. 2 (2002): 214–37.

Eschholz, Sarah, Brenda Sims Blackwell, Marc Gertz, and Ted Chiricos. "Race and Attitudes Toward the Police: Assessing the Effects of Watching 'Reality' Police Programs." *Journal of Criminal Justice* 30, no. 4 (2002): 327–41.

Evans, Jacqueline R., Christian A. Meissner, Amy B. Ross, Kate A. Houston, Melissa B. Russano, and Allyson J. Horgan. "Obtaining Guilty Knowledge in Human Intelligence Interrogations: Comparing Accusatorial and Information-Gathering Approaches with a Novel Experimen-tal Paradigm." *Journal of Applied Research in Memory and Cognition* 2, no. 2 (2013): 83–88.

Fair, C. Christine, Neil Malhotra, and Jacob N. Shapiro. "Faith or Doctrine? Religion and Sup-port for Political Violence in Pakistan." *Public Opinion Quarterly* 76, no. 4 (2012): 688–720.

Fallon, Mark. *Unjustifiable Means: The Inside Story of How the CIA, Pentagon, and US Govern-ment Conspired to Torture.* New York: Regan Arts, 2017.

Ferguson, Christopher J. "Does Media Violence Predict Societal Violence? It Depends on What You Look At and When." *Journal of Communication* 65, no. 1 (2014): E1–E22.

——. "Evidence for Publication Bias in Video Game Violence Effects Literature: A Meta-Analytic Review." *Aggression and Violent Behavior* 12, no. 4 (2007): 470–82.

Ferguson, Christopher J., and Eugene Beresin. "Social Science's Curious War with Pop Culture and How It Was Lost: The Media Violence Debate and the Risks It Holds for Social Science." *Preventive Medicine* 99 (2017): 69–76.

Fikkers, Karin M., Jessica Taylor Piotrowski, Peter Lugtig, and Patti M. Valkenburg. "The Role of Perceived Peer Norms in the Relationship Between Media Violence Exposure and Adolescents' Aggression." *Media Psychology* 19, no. 1 (2016): 4–26.

Flynn, D. J., Brendan Nyhan, and Jason Reifler. "The Nature and Origins of Misperceptions: Understanding False and Unsupported Beliefs About Politics." *Political Psychology* 38 (2017): 127–50.

Flynn, Michael, and Fabiola F. Salek, eds. *Screening Torture: Media Representations of State Terror and Political Domination*. New York: Columbia University Press, 2012.

Fogel, Robert William. *Without Consent or Contract: The Rise and Fall of American Slavery*. New York: Norton, 1994.

Franklin, John Hope, and Loren Schweninger. *Runaway Slaves: Rebels on the Plantation*. Oxford: Oxford University Press, 2000.

Gadarian, Shana Kushner. "The Politics of Threat: How Terrorism News Shapes Foreign Policy Attitudes." *Journal of Politics* 72, no. 2 (2010): 469–83.

Gade, Emily, Dallas Card, Sarah Dreier, and Noah Smith. "What Counts as Terrorism?" Paper presented at the 2018 Society for Political Methodology annual meeting, Salt Lake City, UT.

Garland, Ron. "The Mid-Point on a Rating Scale: Is It Desirable." *Marketing Bulletin* 2, no. 1 (1991): 66–70.

Gearty, Conor. "Terrorism and Human Rights." *Government and Opposition* 42, no. 3 (2007): 340–62.

Geiger, Abigail. "About Six-in-Ten Americans Support Marijuana Legalization." Pew Research Center, January 5, 2018. http://www.pewresearch.org/fact-tank/2018/01/05/americans-support-marijuana-legalization/.

Gentile, Douglas A. "The Evolution of Scientific Skepticism in the Media Violence 'Debate.'" *Analyses of Social Issues and Public Policy* 16, no. 1 (2016): 429–34.

Gentile, Douglas A., Dongdong Li, Angeline Khoo, Sara Prot, and Craig A. Anderson. "Mediators and Moderators of Long-Term Effects of Violent Video Games on Aggressive Behavior: Practice, Thinking, and Action." *JAMA Pediatrics* 168, no. 5 (2014): 450–57.

Gerber, Alan S., and Donald P. Green. *Field Experiments: Design, Analysis, and Interpretation*. New York: Norton, 2012.

Gerbner, George. "Cultivation Analysis: An Overview." *Mass Communication and Society* 1, no. 3–4 (1998): 175–94.

Gilboa, Eytan. "The CNN Effect: The Search for a Communication Theory of International Relations." *Political Communication* 22, no. 1 (2005): 27–44.

Gilens, Martin, and Naomi Murakawa. "Elite Cues and Political Decision Making." In *Political Decision-Making, Deliberation, and Participation*, ed. Michael X. Delli Carpini, Leonie Huddy, and Robert Shapiro, 15–49. Bingley, UK: Emerald Group, 2002.

Glackin, Erin, and Sarah A. O. Gray. "Violence in Context: Embracing an Ecological Approach to Violent Media Exposure." *Analyses of Social Issues and Public Policy* 16, no. 1 (2016): 425–28.

Glas, Jeffrey M., and J. Benjamin Taylor. "The Silver Screen and Authoritarianism: How Popular Films Activate Latent Personality Dispositions and Affect American Political Attitudes." *American Politics Research* 46, no. 2 (2018): 246–75.

Golash, Deirdre. *The Case Against Punishment: Retribution, Crime Prevention, and the Law.* New York: NYU Press, 2005.

Goodman, Joseph K., Cynthia E. Cryder, and Amar Cheema. "Data Collection in a Flat World: The Strengths and Weaknesses of Mechanical Turk Samples." *Journal of Behavioral Decision Making* 26, no. 3 (2013): 213–24.

Goodman-Delahunty, Jane, Natalie Martschuk, and Mandeep K. Dhami. "Interviewing High Value Detainees: Securing Cooperation and Disclosures." *Applied Cognitive Psychology* 28, no. 6 (2014): 883–97.

Goodwin, Jeff. "A Theory of Categorical Terrorism." *Social Forces* 84, no. 4 (2006): 2027–46.

Gordon, Avery F. "Abu Ghraib: Imprisonment and the War on Terror." *Race and Class* 48, no. 1 (2006): 42–59.

Gordon, Rebecca. "Torture Comes Out of the Closet." *Peace Review: A Journal of Social Justice* 18, no. 4 (2006): 447–54.

Gould, Jon, Julia Carrano, Richard Leo, and Joseph Young. "Predicting Erroneous Convictions: A Social Science Approach to Miscarriages of Justice." Department of Justice Document 241389, February 2013. https://www.ncjrs.gov/pdffiles1/nij/grants/241389.pdf.

Granhag, Pär Anders, Steven M. Kleinman, and Simon Oleszkiewicz. "The Scharff Technique: On How to Effectively Elicit Intelligence from Human Sources." *International Journal of Intelligence and Counterintelligence* 29, no. 1 (2016): 132–50.

Graziano, Lisa, Amie Schuck, and Christine Martin. "Police Misconduct, Media Coverage, and Public Perceptions of Racial Profiling: An Experiment." *Justice Quarterly* 27, no. 1 (2010): 52–76.

Gray, Kurt, and Daniel M. Wegner. "Torture and Judgments of Guilt." *Journal of Experimental Social Psychology* 46, no. 1 (2010): 233–35.

Green, Donald P., Bradley Palmquist, and Eric Schickler. *Partisan Hearts and Minds: Political Parties and the Social Identities of Voters.* New Haven, Conn.: Yale University Press, 2004.

Greenberg, Jeff, Tom Pyszczynski, Sheldon Solomon, Abram Rosenblatt, Mitchell Veeder, Shari Kirkland, and Deborah Lyon. "Evidence for Terror Management Theory II: The Effects of Mortality Salience on Reactions to Those Who Threaten or Bolster the Cultural Worldview." *Journal of Personality and Social Psychology* 58, no. 2 (1990): 308–18.

Greenberg, Jeff, Linda Simon, Tom Pyszczynski, Sheldon Solomon, and Dan Chatel. "Terror Management and Tolerance: Does Mortality Salience Always Intensify Negative Reactions to Others Who Threaten One's Worldview?" *Journal of Personality and Social Psychology* 63, no. 2 (1992): 212–20.

Gronke, Paul, Darius Rejali, Dustin Drenguis, James Hicks, Peter Miller, and Bryan Nakayama. "US Public Opinion on Torture, 2001–2009." *PS: Political Science and Politics* 43, no. 3 (2010): 437–44.

Gudjonsson, Gisli H. *The Psychology of Interrogations, Confessions, and Testimony.* Newark, N.J.: Wiley, 1992.

Guiora, Amos N., and Erin M. Page. "The Unholy Trinity: Intelligence, Interrogation and Torture." *Case Western Reserve Journal of International Law* 37, no. 2 (2005): 427–47.

Gwynne, Samuel C. *Empire of the Summer Moon: Quanah Parker and the Rise and Fall of the Comanches, the Most Powerful Indian Tribe in American History.* New York: Simon and Schuster, 2010.

Hainmueller, Jens, Dominik Hangartner and Teppei Yamamoto. "Validating Vignette and Conjoint Survey Experiments Against Real-World Behavior." *Proceedings of the National Academy of Sciences* 112 (2015): 2395–2400.

Hainmueller, Jens, and Daniel J. Hopkins. "The Hidden American Immigration Consensus: A Conjoint Analysis of Attitudes Toward Immigrants." *American Journal of Political Science* 59, no. 3 (2015): 529–48.

——. "Public Attitudes Toward Immigration." *Annual Review of Political Science* 17 (2014): 225–49.

Hainmueller, Jens, Daniel J. Hopkins, and Teppei Yamamoto. "Causal Inference in Conjoint Analysis: Understanding Multidimensional Choices via Stated Preference Experiments." *Political Analysis* 22, no. 1 (2014): 1–30.

Halloran, Michael J., and Emiko S. Kashima. "Social Identity and Worldview Validation: The Effects of Ingroup Identity Primes and Mortality Salience on Value Endorsement." *Personality and Social Psychology Bulletin* 30, no. 7 (2004): 915–25.

Hamdan v. Rumsfeld 548 U.S. 557. 2006. https://supreme.justia.com/cases/federal/us/548/557/.

Haney, Craig, Curtis Banks, and Philip Zimbardo. "Interpersonal Dynamics in a Simulated Prison." *International Journal of Criminology and Penology* 1 (1973): 69–97.

Haney, Craig, and Philip G. Zimbardo. "Persistent Dispositionalism in Interactionist Clothing: Fundamental Attribution Error in Explaining Prison Abuse." *Personality and Social Psychology Bulletin* 35, no. 6 (2009): 807–14.

Hartig, Hannah, and Abigail Geiger. "About Six-in-Ten Americans Support Marijuana Legalization." Pew Research Center, October 8, 2018. http://www.pewresearch.org/fact-tank/2018/01/05/americans-support-marijuana-legalization/.

Hartwig, Maria, Christian A. Meissner, and Matthew D. Semel. "Human Intelligence Interviewing and Interrogation: Assessing the Challenges of Developing an Ethical, Evidence-Based Approach." In *Investigative interviewing*, 209–28. New York: Springer, 2014.

Heath, Linda, Linda B. Bresolin, and Robert C. Rinaldi. "Effects of Media Violence on Children: A Review of the Literature." *Archives of General Psychiatry* 46, no. 4 (1989): 376–79.

Heath, Linda, Candace Kruttschnitt, and David Ward. "Television and Violent Criminal Behavior: Beyond the Bobo Doll." *Violence and Victims* 1, no. 3 (1986): 177–90.

Hemenway, David, and Matthew Miller. "Firearm Availability and Homicide Rates Across 26 High-Income Countries." *Journal of Trauma and Acute Care Surgery* 49, no. 6 (2000): 985–88.

Hepburn, Lisa M., and David Hemenway. "Firearm Availability and Homicide: A Review of the Literature." *Aggression and Violent Behavior* 9, no. 4 (2004): 417–40.

Hersh, Seymour. "Torture at Abu Ghraib: American Soldiers Brutalized Iraqis. How Far Up Does the Responsibility Go?" *New Yorker*, May 10, 2004. https://www.newyorker.com/magazine/2004/05/10/torture-at-abu-ghraib.

Hertel, Shareen, Lyle Scruggs, and C. Patrick Heidkamp. "Human Rights and Public Opinion: From Attitudes to Action." *Political Science Quarterly* 124, no. 3 (2009): 443–59.

Hetherington, Marc, and Jonathan Weiler. *Prius or Pickup? How the Answers to Four Simple Questions Explain America's Great Divide*. Boston: Houghton Mifflin, 2018.

Hill, Joshua, Willard M. Oliver, and Nancy E. Marion. "'Shaping History' or 'Riding the Wave'? President Bush's Influence on the Public Opinion of Terrorism, Homeland Security, and Crime." *Journal of Criminal Justice* 38, no. 5 (2010): 896–902.

Hoffman, Bruce. *Inside Terrorism*. New York: Columbia University Press, 2006.

Horne, Alexander. "Torture: A Short History of Its Prohibition and Re-emergence." *Judicial Review* 14, no. 2 (2009): 155–69.

Horry, Ruth, and Daniel B. Wright. "Anxiety and Terrorism: Automatic Stereotypes Affect Visual Attention and Recognition Memory for White and Middle Eastern Faces." *Applied Cognitive Psychology* 23, no. 3 (2009): 345–57.

Houck, Shannon C., and Lucian Gideon Conway III. "What People Think About Torture: Torture Is Inherently Bad . . . Unless It Can Save Someone I Love." *Journal of Applied Security Research* 8, no. 4 (2013): 429–54.

Houck, Shannon C., Lucian Gideon Conway III, and Meredith A. Repke. "Personal Closeness and Perceived Torture Efficacy: If Torture Will Save Someone I'm Close to, Then It Must Work." *Peace and Conflict: Journal of Peace Psychology* 20, no. 4 (2014): 590–92.

Houck, Shannon C., and Meredith A. Repke. "When and Why We Torture: A Review of Psychology Research." *Translational Issues in Psychological Science* 3, no. 3 (2017): 272–83.

Howe, Lauren C., and Jon A. Krosnick. "Attitude Strength." *Annual Review of Psychology* 68 (2017): 327–51.

Huddy, Leonie, Stanley Feldman, Charles Taber, and Gallya Lahav. "Threat, Anxiety, and Support of Antiterrorism Policies." *American Journal of Political Science* 49, no. 3 (2005): 593–608.

Huesmann, L. Rowell. "The Impact of Electronic Media Violence: Scientific Theory and Research." *Journal of Adolescent Health* 41, no. 6 (2007): S6-S13.

Huff, Connor, and Joshua D. Kertzer. "How the Public Defines Terrorism." *American Journal of Political Science* 62, no. 1 (2018): 55–71.

Huth, Paul K. "Deterrence and International Conflict: Empirical Findings and Theoretical Debates." *Annual Review of Political Science* 2, no. 1 (1999): 25–48.

Huth, Paul, and Bruce Russett. "General Deterrence Between Enduring Rivals: Testing Three Competing Models." *American Political Science Review* 87, no. 1 (1993): 61–73.

Iyengar, Shanto, and Adam Simon. "News Coverage of the Gulf Crisis and Public Opinion: A Study of Agenda-Setting, Priming, and Framing." *Communication Research* 20, no. 3 (1993): 365–83.

Janoff-Bulman, Ronnie. "Erroneous Assumptions: Popular Belief in the Effectiveness of Torture Interrogation." *Peace and Conflict: Journal of Peace Psychology* 13, no. 4 (2007): 429–35.

Jentleson, Bruce W., and Rebecca L. Britton. "Still Pretty Prudent: Post-Cold War American Public Opinion on the Use of Military Force." *Journal of Conflict Resolution* 42, no. 4 (1998): 395–417.

Johnson, Douglas A., Alberto Mora, and Averell Schmidt. "The Strategic Costs of Torture: How Enhanced Interrogation Hurt America." *Foreign Affairs* 95 (2016).

Jones, Calvert W., and Celia Paris. "It's the End of the World and They Know It: How Dystopian Fiction Shapes Political Attitudes." *Perspectives on Politics* 16, no. 4 (2018): 969–89.

Jordan, William. "Americans Find Some Tortures More Acceptable Than Others." YouGov, December 12, 2014. https://today.yougov.com/topics/politics/articles-reports/2014/12/12/torture-report.

Kahn, Chris. "Exclusive: Most Americans Support Torture Against Terror Suspects." Reuters, March 30, 2016. https://www.reuters.com/article/us-usa-election-torture-exclusive/exclusive-most-americans-support-torture-against-terror-suspects-reuters-ipsos-poll-idUSKCN-0WW0Y3.

Kahneman, Daniel, and Amos Tversky. "Choices, Values, and Frames." *American Psychologist* 39, no. 4 (1984): 341–50.

——. "On the Study of Statistical Intuitions." *Cognition* 11, no. 2 (1982): 123–41.

Kalla, Joshua L., and David E. Brockman. "The Minimal Persuasive Effects of Campaign Contact in General Elections: Evidence from 49 Field Experiments." *American Political Science Review* 112, no. 1 (2018): 148–66.

Kassin, Saul M., and Katherine L. Kiechel. "The Social Psychology of False Confessions: Compliance, Internalization, and Confabulation." *Psychological Science* 7, no. 3 (1996): 125–28.

Kearns, Erin M. "If You See Something, Do You Say Something? The Role of Legitimacy and Trust in Policing Minority Communities in Counterterrorism." PhD diss., American University, 2016.

Kearns, Erin M. "When to Take Credit for Terrorism? A Cross-National Examination of Claims and Attributions. *Terrorism and Political Violence* (2019): 1–30.

Kearns, Erin M., Victor Asal, James Igoe Walsh, Christopher Federico, and Anthony F. Lemieux. "Political Action as a Function of Grievances, Risk, and Social Identity: An Experimental Approach." *Studies in Conflict and Terrorism* (2018): 1–18.

Kearns, Erin M., Allison E. Betus, and Anthony F. Lemieux. "When Data Don't Matter: Exploring Public Perceptions of Terrorism." *Studies in Conflict and Terrorism* (2019).

Kearns, Erin M., Allison Betus, and Anthony Lemieux. "Why Do Some Terrorist Attacks Receive More Media Attention Than Others?" *Justice Quarterly* 36, no. 6 (2019): 985–1022.

Kearns, Erin M., and Joseph K. Young. "If Torture Is Wrong, What About 24? Torture and the Hollywood Effect." *Crime and Delinquency* 64, no. 12 (2018): 1568–89.

——. "Military Tactics in Civil War." In *Routledge Handbook of Civil Wars*, ed. Edward Newman and Kal DeRouen Jr., 257–67. New York: Routledge, 2014.

Kertzer, Joshua D., and Kathleen M. McGraw. "Folk Realism: Testing the Microfoundations of Realism in Ordinary Citizens." *International Studies Quarterly* 56, no. 2 (2012): 245–58.

Kertzer, Joshua D., and Thomas Zeitzoff. "A Bottom-Up Theory of Public Opinion About Foreign Policy." *American Journal of Political Science* 61, no. 3 (2017): 543–58.

Kim, Hyoun S., and David C. Hodgins. "Reliability and Validity of Data Obtained from Alcohol, Cannabis, and Gambling Populations on Amazon's Mechanical Turk." *Psychology of Addictive Behaviors* 31, no. 1 (2017): 85–94.

Kleck, Gary. *Point Blank: Guns and Violence in America*. London: Routledge, 2017.

Kleck, Gary, Brion Sever, Spencer Li, and Marc Gertz. "The Missing Link in General Deterrence Research." *Criminology* 43, no. 3 (2005): 623–60.

Knetsch, Jack L., and John A. Sinden. "Willingness to Pay and Compensation Demanded: Experimental Evidence of an Unexpected Disparity in Measures of Value." *Quarterly Journal of Economics* 99, no. 3 (1984): 507–21.

Koblin, John. "How Much Do We Love TV?" *New York Times*, June 30, 2016. https://www
.nytimes.com/2016/07/01/business/media/nielsen-survey-media-viewing.html?_r=0.

Kort-Butler, Lisa A., and Kelley J. Sittner Hartshorn. "Watching the Detectives: Crime Programming, Fear of Crime, and Attitudes About the Criminal Justice System." *Sociological Quarterly* 52, no. 1 (2011): 36–55.

LaFree, Gary, Laura Dugan, and Raven Korte. "The Impact of British Counterterrorist Strategies
on Political Violence in Northern Ireland: Comparing Deterrence and Backlash Models."
Criminology 47, no. 1 (2009): 17–45.

Lagouranis, Tony, and Allen Mikaelian. *Fear Up Harsh: An Army Interrogator's Dark Journey
Through Iraq*. New York: Penguin, 2007.

Landau, Mark J., Sheldon Solomon, Jeff Greenberg, Florette Cohen, Tom Pyszczynski, Jamie
Arndt, Claude H. Miller, Daniel M. Ogilvie, and Alison Cook. "Deliver Us from Evil: The
Effects of Mortality Salience and Reminders of 9/11 on Support for President George W.
Bush." *Personality and Social Psychology Bulletin* 30, no. 9 (2004): 1136–50.

Landay, Jonathan S. "Report: Abusive Tactics Used to Seek Iraq–al Qaida Link." *McClatchy DC*,
April 21, 2009. https://www.mcclatchydc.com/news/nation-world/world/article24535114.html.

Lassiter, G. Daniel, and Christian A. Meissner. *Police Interrogations and False Confessions: Current Research, Practice, and Policy Recommendations*. Washington, D.C.: American Psychological Association, 2010.

Lee, Wayne E. *Barbarians and Brothers: Anglo-American Warfare, 1500–1865*. New York: Oxford
University Press, 2011.

Leidner, Bernhard, Peter Kardos, and Emanuele Castano. "The Effects of Moral and Pragmatic
Arguments Against Torture on Demands for Judicial Reform." *Political Psychology* 39, no. 1
(2018): 143–62.

Lemieux, Anthony F., Erin M. Kearns, Victor Asal, and James Igoe Walsh. "Support for Political
Mobilization and Protest in Egypt and Morocco: An Online Experimental Study." *Dynamics
of Asymmetric Conflict* 10, no. 2–3 (2017): 124–42.

Lerner, Jennifer S., Roxana M. Gonzalez, Deborah A. Small, and Baruch Fischhoff. "Effects of
Fear and Anger on Perceived Risks of Terrorism: A National Field Experiment." *Psychological Science* 14, no. 2 (2003): 144–50.

Leung, Rebecca. "Abuse of Iraqi POWs by GIS Probed." *60 Minutes*, April 27, 2004. https://www
.cbsnews.com/news/abuse-of-iraqi-pows-by-gis-probed/.

Liberman, Peter. "Retributive Support for International Punishment and Torture." *Journal of
Conflict Resolution* 57, no. 2 (2013): 285–306.

——. "War and Torture as 'Just Deserts.'" *Public Opinion Quarterly* 78, no. 1 (2014): 47–70.

Lithwick, Dahlia. "How Jack Bauer Shaped U.S. Torture Policy." *Newsweek*, June 25, 2008. http://
www.newsweek.com/lithwick-how-jack-bauer-shaped-ustorture-policy-93159.

Lopez, German. "The Baltimore Protests Over Freddie Gray's Death, Explained." *Vox*, August 18,
2016. https://www.vox.com/cards/freddie-gray-baltimore-riots-police-violence/baltimore
-protests-freddie-gray.

Lundeberg, Philip K. "Operation Teardrop Revisited." In *To Die Gallantly: The Battle of the Atlantic*, ed. Timothy J. Runyan and Jan M. Copes, 210–30. Boulder, Colo.: Westview Press, 1994.

Lyall, Jason, Graeme Blair, and Kosuke Imai. "Explaining Support for Combatants During Wartime: A Survey Experiment in Afghanistan." *American Political Science Review* 107, no. 4 (2013): 679–705.

Malhotra, Neil, and Elizabeth Popp. "Bridging Partisan Divisions Over Antiterrorism Policies: The Role of Threat Perceptions." *Political Research Quarterly* 65, no. 1 (2012): 34–47.

Maliniak, Daniel, Amy Oakes, Susan Peterson, and Michael J. Tierney. "International Relations in the US Academy." *International Studies Quarterly* 55, no. 2 (2011): 437–64.

Mayer, Jeremy D., and David J. Armor. "Support for Torture Over Time: Interrogating the American Public About Coercive Tactics." *The Social Science Journal* 49, no. 4 (2012): 439–46.

McCall, Grant S., and Nancy Shields. "Examining the Evidence from Small-Scale Societies and Early Prehistory and Implications for Modern Theories of Aggression and Violence." *Aggression and Violent Behavior* 13, no. 1 (2008): 1–9.

McCauley, Clark, and Sophia Moskalenko. "Mechanisms of Political Radicalization: Pathways Toward Terrorism." *Terrorism and Political Violence* 20, no. 3 (2008): 415–33.

McCombs, Maxwell. *The Agenda-Setting Role of the Mass Media in the Shaping of Public Opinion.* In Mass Media Economics Conference, London School of Economics, 2003.

McEllistrem, Joseph E. "Affective and Predatory Violence: A Bimodal Classification System of Human Aggression and Violence." *Aggression and Violent Behavior* 10, no. 1 (2004): 1–30.

McNeely, Connie. "Perceptions of the Criminal Justice System: Television Imagery and Public Knowledge in the United States." *Journal of Criminal Justice and Popular Culture* 3, no. 1 (1995): 1–12.

Mearsheimer, John J., and Stephen M. Walt. "Leaving Theory Behind: Why Simplistic Hypothesis Testing Is Bad for International Relations." *European Journal of International Relations* 19, no. 3 (2013): 427–57.

Meissner, Christian A., Allison D. Redlich, Stephen W. Michael, Jacqueline R. Evans, Catherine R. Camilletti, Sujeeta Bhatt, and Susan Brandon. "Accusatorial and Information-Gathering Interrogation Methods and Their Effects on True and False Confessions: A Meta-Analytic Review." *Journal of Experimental Criminology* 10, no. 4 (2014): 459–86.

Meissner, Christian A., Frances Surmon-Böhr, Simon Oleszkiewicz, and Laurence J. Alison. "Developing an Evidence-Based Perspective on Interrogation: A Review of the US Government's High-Value Detainee Interrogation Group Research Program." *Psychology, Public Policy, and Law* 23, no. 4 (2017): 438–57.

Merritt, Alexandra, Rachel LaQuea, Rachel Cromwell, and Christopher J. Ferguson. "Media Managing Mood: A Look at the Possible Effects of Violent Media on Affect." *Child and Youth Care Forum* 45, no. 2 (2016): 241–58.

Milgram, Stanley. "Behavioral Study of Obedience." *Journal of Abnormal and Social Psychology* 67, no. 4 (1963): 371–78.

Miller, Joel, and Robert C. Davis. "Unpacking Public Attitudes to the Police: Contrasting Perceptions of Misconduct with Traditional Measures of Satisfaction." *International Journal of Police Science and Management* 10, no. 1 (2008): 9–22.

Miller, Matthew, Deborah Azrael, and David Hemenway. "Household Firearm Ownership and Suicide Rates in the United States." *Epidemiology* (2002): 517–24.

Miller, Matthew, David Hemenway, and Deborah Azrael. "State-Level Homicide Victimization Rates in the US in Relation to Survey Measures of Household Firearm Ownership, 2001–2003." *Social Science and Medicine* 64, no. 3 (2007): 656–64.

Minozzi, William, Michael A. Neblo, Kevin M. Esterling, and David M. J. Lazer. "Field Experiment Evidence of Substantive, Attributional, and Behavioral Persuasion by Members of Congress in Online Town Halls." *Proceedings of the National Academy of Sciences* 112, no. 13 (2015): 3937–42.

Mintz, Alex, Steven B. Redd, and Arnold Vedlitz. "Can We Generalize from Student Experiments to the Real World in Political Science, Military Affairs, and International Relations?" *Journal of Conflict Resolution* 50, no. 5 (2006): 757–76.

Miron, Anca M., Nyla R. Branscombe, and Monica Biernat. "Motivated Shifting of Justice Standards." *Personality and Social Psychology Bulletin* 36, no. 6 (2010): 768–79.

Mitchell, James E. "Sorry, Mad Dog, Waterboarding Works." *Wall Street Journal*, December 9, 2016. https://www.wsj.com/articles/sorry-mad-dog-waterboarding-works-1481242339.

Mitchell, James E., with Bill Harlow. *Enhanced Interrogation: Inside the Minds and Motives of the Islamic Terrorists Trying to Destroy America*. New York: Crown Forum, 2016.

Mitnik, Zachary S., Joshua D. Freilich, and Steven M. Chermak. "Post-9/11 Coverage of Terrorism in the *New York Times*." *Justice Quarterly* (October 2018): 1–25.

Mock, Brentin. "The Persistent, Wide Racial Gap in Attitudes Toward the Police." Citylab.com, September 21, 2017. https://www.citylab.com/equity/2017/09/the-wide-racial-gap-in-attitudes-toward-police/540456/.

Moore, Anntoinette. "'Asian Nazi' Says Lawyer Trying to Get Him Convicted, Seeks Release from Gregg County Jail." *Longview News-Journal*, July 12, 2018. https://www.news-journal.com/news/police/asian-nazi-says-lawyer-trying-to-get-him-convicted-seeks/article_7942e916-861f-11e8-ba34-cba7f9ee2968.html.

Morton, Cynthia R., and Meredith Friedman. "'I Saw It in the Movies': Exploring the Link Between Product Placement Beliefs and Reported Usage Behavior." *Journal of Current Issues and Research in Advertising* 24, no. 2 (2002): 33–40.

Mutz, Diana C., and Lilach Nir. "Not Necessarily the News: Does Fictional Television Influence Real-World Policy Preferences?" *Mass Communication and Society* 13, no. 2 (2010): 196–217.

Mutz, Diana Carole, Paul M. Sniderman, and Richard A. Brody, eds. *Political Persuasion and Attitude Change*. Ann Arbor: University of Michigan Press, 1996.

Nacos, Brigitte L., and Yaeli Bloch-Elkon. "US Media and Post-9/11 Human Rights Violations in the Name of Counterterrorism." *Human Rights Review* 19, no. 2 (2018): 193–210.

Nellis, Ashley Marie, and Joanne Savage. "Does Watching the News Affect Fear of Terrorism? The Importance of Media Exposure in Terrorism Fear." *Crime and Delinquency* 58, no. 5 (2012): 748–68.

Nicholson, Ian. "'Torture at Yale': Experimental Subjects, Laboratory Torment, and the 'Rehabilitation' of Milgram's 'Obedience to Authority.'" *Theory and Psychology* 21, no. 6 (2011): 737–61.

Nincic, Miroslav, and Jennifer Ramos. "Torture in the Public Mind." *International Studies Perspectives* 12, no. 3 (2011): 231–49.

Nisbett, Richard E., and Dov Cohen. *Culture of Honor: The Psychology of Violence in the South.* Boulder, Colo.: Westview Press, 1996.

Nordgren, Loran F., Mary-Hunter Morris McDonnell, and George Loewenstein. "What Constitutes Torture? Psychological Impediments to an Objective Evaluation of Enhanced Interrogation Tactics." *Psychological Science* 22, no. 5 (2011): 689–94.

Norris, J. Ian, Jeff T. Larsen, and Bradley J. Stastny. "Social Perceptions of Torture: Genuine Disagreement, Subtle Malleability, and In-Group Bias." *Peace and Conflict* 16, no. 3 (2010): 275–94.

Nyhan, Brendan. "Why the 'Death Panel' Myth Wouldn't Die: Misinformation in the Health Care Reform Debate." *The Forum* 8, no. 1 (2010). doi: 10.2202/1540-8884.1354.

Nyhan, Brendan, Ethan Porter, Jason Reifler, and Thomas Wood. "Taking Corrections Literally but Not Seriously? The Effects of Information on Factual Beliefs and Candidate Favorability." *SSRN Electronic Journal* (January 2017). doi: 10.2139/ssrn.2995128.

Nyhan, Brendan, and Jason Reifler. "When Corrections Fail: The Persistence of Political Misperceptions." *Political Behavior* 32, no. 2 (2010): 303–30.

Nyhan, Brendan, and Thomas Zeitzoff. "Conspiracy and Misperception Belief in the Middle East and North Africa." *Journal of Politics* 80, no. 4 (2018): 1400–1404.

O'Brien, Ed, and Phoebe C. Ellsworth. "More Than Skin Deep: Visceral States Are Not Projected Onto Dissimilar Others." *Psychological Science* 23, no. 4 (2012): 391–96.

Ofshe, Richard J., and Richard A. Leo. "The Social Psychology of Police Interrogation: The Theory and Classification of True and False Confessions." *Studies in Law Politics and Society* 16 (1997): 189–254.

Office of Legal Counsel. U.S. Department of Justice. "Memorandum for Alberto R. Gonzales, Counsel to the President." August 1, 2002. https://nsarchive2.gwu.edu/NSAEBB/NSAEBB127/02.08.01.pdf.

Oosterhoff, Pauline, Prisca Zwanikken, and Evert Ketting. "Sexual Torture of Men in Croatia and Other Conflict Situations: An Open Secret." *Reproductive Health Matters* 12, no. 23 (2004): 68–77.

Opotow, Susan. "Moral Exclusion and Torture: The Ticking Bomb Scenario and the Slippery Ethical Slope." *Peace and Conflict: Journal of Peace Psychology* 13 no. 4 (2007): 457–61.

Page, Benjamin I., and Robert Y. Shapiro. "Effects of Public Opinion on Policy." *American Political Science Review* 77, no. 1 (1983): 175–90.

Parents Television Council. "24 Advertiser Campaign." February 12, 2007. http://www.parentstv.org/PTC/campaigns/24/main.asp.

"Parties: Parties Overview—Congress at a Glance: Major Party Ideology." Voteview.com. https://voteview.com/parties/all.

Paternoster, Raymond, and Alex Piquero. "Reconceptualizing Deterrence: An Empirical Test of Personal and Vicarious Experiences." *Journal of Research in Crime and Delinquency* 32, no. 3 (1995): 251–86.

Patterson, Troy. "Senator, We're Ready for Your Cameo." *Slate*, February 7, 2006. https://slate.com/culture/2006/02/john-mccain-on-24.html.

Pennell, Amanda E., and Kevin D. Browne. "Film Violence and Young Offenders." *Aggression and Violent Behavior* 4, no. 1 (1999): 13–28.

Perreault, William D. "Controlling Order-Effect Bias." *Public Opinion Quarterly* 39, no. 4 (1975): 544–51.

Pew Research Center. "Global Publics Back U.S. on Fighting ISIS, but Are Critical of Post-9/11 Torture." June 23, 2015. https://www.pewresearch.org/global/2015/06/23/global-publics-back -u-s-on-fighting-isis-but-are-critical-of-post-911-torture/.

Pew Research Center. "Public Perceptions of Crime Rate at Odds with Reality." April 16, 2015. http:// www.pewresearch.org/fact-tank/2015/04/17/despite-lower-crime-rates-support-for-gun -rights-increases/ft_15-04-01_guns_crimerate/.

Piazza, James A. "Terrorist Suspect Religious Identity and Public Support for Harsh Interroga-tion and Detention Practices." *Political Psychology* 36, no. 6 (2015): 667–90.

Piazza, James A., and James Igoe Walsh. "Physical Integrity Rights and Terrorism." *PS: Political Science and Politics* 43, no. 3 (2010): 411–14.

Piazza, Jared, Paulo Sousa, and Colin Holbrook. "Authority Dependence and Judgments of Util-itarian Harm." *Cognition* 128, no. 3 (2013): 261–70.

Piwowarczyk, Linda, Alejandro Moreno, and Michael Grodin. "Health Care of Torture Survi-vors." *JAMA* 284, no. 5 (2000): 539–41.

The Polling Report. http://www.pollingreport.com/iraq.htm

Powell, Robert. "Anarchy in International Relations Theory: The Neorealist-Neoliberal Debate." *International Organization* 48, no. 2 (1994): 313–44.

Prince, Stephen. *Firestorm: American Film in the Age of Terrorism*. New York: Columbia Uni-versity Press, 2009.

Pronin, Emily, Kathleen Kennedy, and Sarah Butsch. "Bombing Versus Negotiating: How Pref-erences for Combating Terrorism Are Affected by Perceived Terrorist Rationality." *Basic and Applied Social Psychology* 28, no. 4 (2006): 385–92.

Ramos, Raul A., Christopher J. Ferguson, and Kelly Frailing. "Violent Entertainment and Coop-erative Behavior: Examining Media Violence Effects on Cooperation in a Primarily Hispanic Sample." *Psychology of Popular Media Culture* 5, no. 2 (2016): 119–32.

Redlich, Allison D. "False Confessions, False Guilty Pleas: Similarities and Differences." In *Police Interrogations and False Confessions: Current Research, Practice, and Policy Recommenda-tions*, ed. G. Daniel Lassiter and Christian A. Meissner, 49–66. Washington, D.C.: American Psychological Association, 2010.

Redlich, Allison D. "Military Versus Police Interrogations: Similarities and Differences." *Peace and Conflict: Journal of Peace Psychology* 13, no. 4 (2007): 423–28.

Rejali, Darius. "Ice Water and Sweatboxes: The Long and Sadistic History Behind the CIA's Torture Techniques." *Slate*, March 17, 2009. https://slate.com/news-and-politics/2009/03 /the-history-of-cia-torture.html.

Rejali, Darius. *Torture and Democracy*. Princeton, N.J.: Princeton University Press, 2009.

Richards, David L., Mandy M. Morrill, and Mary R. Anderson. "Some Psycho-Social Cor-relates of US Citizen Support for Torture." *Nordic Journal of Human Rights* 30, no. 1 (2012): 63–95.

Rios, Kimberly, and Dominik Mischkowski. "Shaping Responses to Torture: What You Call It Matters." *Personality and Social Psychology Bulletin* 45, no. 6 (2019): 934–46.

Riva, Paolo, and Luca Andrighetto. "'Everybody Feels a Broken Bone, but Only We Can Feel a Broken Heart': Group Membership Influences the Perception of Targets' Suffering." *European Journal of Social Psychology* 42, no. 7 (2012): 801–6.

Robinson, Piers. "The Policy-Media Interaction Model: Measuring Media Power During Humanitarian Crisis." *Journal of Peace Research* 37, no. 5 (2000): 613–33.

Rosenblatt, Abram, Jeff Greenberg, Sheldon Solomon, Tom Pyszczynski, and Deborah Lyon. "Evidence for Terror Management Theory: I. The Effects of Mortality Salience on Reactions to Those Who Violate or Uphold Cultural Values." *Journal of Personality and Social Psychology* 57, no. 4 (1989): 681–90.

Roth, Kenneth. "Justifying Torture." In *Torture: Does It Make Us Safer*, ed. Kenneth Roth, Minky Worden, and Amy D. Bernstein, 184–202. New York: New Press, 2005.

Routledge, Clay, and Jacob Juhl. "When Death Thoughts Lead to Death Fears: Mortality Salience Increases Death Anxiety for Individuals Who Lack Meaning in Life." *Cognition and Emotion* 24, no. 5 (2010): 848–54.

Rumsfeld, Donald. H. "Memorandum to President George W. Bush." September 23, 2001. http://library.rumsfeld.com/doclib/sp/1495/2001-09-23%20to%20President%20George%20W%20Bush%20re%20(no%20subject).pdf.

Rumsfeld, Donald. H. "Global War on Terror." *Memorandum*, October 16, 2003. https://usatoday30.usatoday.com/news/washington/executive/rumsfeld-memo.htm.

Russano, Melissa B., Christian A. Meissner, Fadia M. Narchet, and Saul M. Kassin. "Investigating True and False Confessions Within a Novel Experimental Paradigm." *Psychological Science* 16, no. 6 (2005): 481–86.

Rynes, Sara L., Barry Gerhart, and Kathleen A. Minette. "The Importance of Pay in Employee Motivation: Discrepancies Between What People Say and What They Do." *Human Resource Management* 43, no. 4 (2004): 381–94.

Samson, Lelia, and Robert F. Potter. "Empathizing and Systemizing (Un) Justified Mediated Violence: Psychophysiological Indicators of Emotional Response." *Media Psychology* 19, no. 1 (2016): 156–80.

Sanders, James, Melissa Wagner Schuman, and Anne M. Marbella. "The Epidemiology of Torture: A Case Series of 58 Survivors of Torture." *Forensic Science International* 189, no. 1–3 (2009): e1–e7.

Santucci, Joe. "A Question of Identity: The Use of Torture in Asymmetric War." *Journal of Military Ethics* 7, no. 1 (2008): 23–40.

Savage, Joanne, and Christina Yancey. "The Effects of Media Violence Exposure on Criminal Aggression: A Meta-Analysis." *Criminal Justice and Behavior* 35, no. 6 (2008): 772–91.

"Scalia and Torture." *The Atlantic*, June 19, 2007. http://www.theatlantic.com/daily-dish/archive/2007/06/scalia-and-torture/227548/.

Schulberg, Jessica. "It's Depressing How Many Americans Still Support Torture." *New Republic*, December 12, 2014. https://newrepublic.com/article/120548/yougov-study-finds-republicans-approve-cia-torture.

Senate, U. S. "Senate Select Committee on Intelligence (2014) Committee Study of the Central Intelligence Agency's Detention and Interrogation Program." https://www.intelligence.senate.gov/sites/default/files/documents/CRPT-113srpt288.pdf

Shaheen, Jack G. *Reel Bad Arabs: How Hollywood Vilifies a People*. Northampton, Mass: Olive Branch Press, 2012.

Sidanius, Jim, Michael Mitchell, Hillary Haley, and Carlos David Navarrete. "Support for Harsh Criminal Sanctions and Criminal Justice Beliefs: A Social Dominance Perspective." *Social Justice Research* 19, no. 4 (2006): 433–49.

Silverman, Daniel, Daniel Kent, and Christopher Gelpi. 2018. "Public Fears of Terrorism, Partisan Rhetoric, and the Foundations of American Interventionism," Presentation at the International Studies Association Annual Meeting in San Francisco, CA.

Simon, Herbert A. "Rational Choice and the Structure of the Environment." *Psychological Review* 63, no. 2 (1956): 129–38.

Simon, Bernd, and Bert Klandermans. "Politicized Collective Identity: A Social Psychological Analysis." *American Psychologist* 56, no. 4 (2001): 319–31.

Singal, Jesse. "The Careful, Pragmatic Case Against Punching Nazis." *New York Magazine*, August 19, 2017. http://nymag.com/intelligencer/2017/08/the-careful-pragmatic-case-against-punching-nazis.html.

Spino, Joseph, and Denise Dellarosa Cummins. "The Ticking Time Bomb: When the Use of Torture Is and Is Not Endorsed." *Review of Philosophy and Psychology* 5, no. 4 (2014): 543–63.

Spry, Amanda, Ravi Pappu, and T. Bettina Cornwell. "Celebrity Endorsement, Brand Credibility, and Brand Equity." *European Journal of Marketing* 45, no. 6 (2011): 882–909.

Stroessner, Steven J., Abigail A. Scholer, David M. Marx, and Bradley M. Weisz. "When Threat Matters: Self-Regulation, Threat Salience, and Stereotyping." *Journal of Experimental Social Psychology* 59 (2015): 77–89.

Suebsaeng, Asawin. "Torture-Heavy '24' Was Actually a Pretty Damn Liberal TV Show." *Mother Jones*, May 2, 2014. http://www.motherjones.com/media/2014/05/24-live-another-day-jack-bauer-politics-torture-muslims-liberal-tv-show.

Swing, Edward L., and Craig A. Anderson. "The Role of Attention Problems and Impulsiveness in Media Violence Effects on Aggression." *Aggressive Behavior* 40, no. 3 (2014): 197–203.

Szoldra, Paul. "Marine General 'Mad Dog' Mattis Got Trump to Rethink His Position on Torture in Under an Hour." *Business Insider*, November 22, 2016. http://www.businessinsider.com/james-mattis-trump-torture-2016-11.

Tajfel, Henri, and John C. Turner. "An Integrative Theory of Intergroup Conflict." In *Social Psychology of Intergroup Relations*, ed. William G. Austin and Stephen Worchel, 33–47. Monterey, Calif.: Brooks/Cole, 1979.

Tajfel, Henri, and John C. Turner. "The Social Identity Theory of Intergroup Behaviour." In *Psychology of Intergroup Relations*, ed. William G. Austin and Stephen Worchel. Chicago: Nelson Hall, 1986.

Tarrant, Mark, Nyla R. Branscombe, Ruth H. Warner, and Dale Weston. "Social Identity and Perceptions of Torture: It's Moral When We Do It." *Journal of Experimental Social Psychology* 48, no. 2 (2012): 513–18.

Taylor, Marcus K., Amanda E. Markham, Jared P. Reis, Genieleah A. Padilla, Eric G. Potterat, Sean P. A. Drummond, and Lilianne R. Mujica-Parodi. "Physical Fitness Influences Stress Reactions to Extreme Military Training." *Military Medicine* 173, no. 8 (2008): 738–42.

Taylor, Marcus K., Katherine E. Stanfill, Genieleah A. Padilla, Amanda E. Markham, Michael D. Ward, Matthew M. Koehler, Antonio Anglero, and Barry D. Adams. "Effect of Psychological Skills Training During Military Survival School: A Randomized, Controlled Field Study." *Military Medicine* 176, no. 12 (2011): 1362–68.

Tedeschi, James T., and Brian M. Quigley. "Limitations of Laboratory Paradigms for Studying Aggression." *Aggression and Violent Behavior* 1, no. 2 (1996): 163–77.

"Timeline: The History of the CIA Detention and Interrogation Program." *Los Angeles Times*, December 9, 2014. http://www.latimes.com/nation/la-na-timeline-of-cia-interrogation -program-20141209-story.html.

Tindale, Christopher W. "The Logic of Torture: A Critical Examination." *Social Theory and Practice* 22, no. 3 (1996): 349–74.

Toch, Hans. *Violent Men: An Inquiry Into the Psychology of Violence*, rev. ed. Washington, D.C.: American Psychological Association, 1969.

Tonry, Michael. "Learning from the Limitations of Deterrence Research." *Crime and Justice* 37, no. 1 (2008): 279–311.

The Torture Act. 18 U.S.C. § 2340. https://www.justice.gov/archives/jm/criminal-resource -manual-20-torture-18-usc-2340a.

Tversky, Amos, and Daniel Kahneman. "The Framing of Decisions and the Psychology of Choice." *Science* 211, no. 4481 (1981): 453–58.

Tyson, Alec. "Americans Divided in Views of Use of Torture in U.S. Anti-Terror Efforts." Pew Research Center, January 26, 2017. http://www.pewresearch.org/fact-tank/2017/01/26/americans -divided-in-views-of-use-of-torture-in-u-s-anti-terror-efforts/.

Tyson, Ann Scott. "What Went Wrong in Abu Ghraib." *Christian Science Monitor*, June 10, 2004. https://www.csmonitor.com/2004/0610/p02s01-usmi.html.

UN General Assembly. *Convention Against Torture and Other Cruel, Inhuman or Degrading Treatment or Punishment*. United Nations, vol. 1465, p. 85, December 10, 1984. https://www .refworld.org/docid/3ae6b3a94.html.

Vallacher, Robin R. "Local Acts, Global Consequences: A Dynamic Systems Perspective on Torture." *Peace and Conflict: Journal of Peace Psychology* 13, no. 4 (2007): 445–50.

Van Zomeren, Martijn, Tom Postmes, and Russell Spears. "Toward an Integrative Social Identity Model of Collective Action: A Quantitative Research Synthesis of Three Socio-Psychological Perspectives." *Psychological Bulletin* 134, no. 4 (2008): 504–35.

Vedantam, Shankar. "The Psychology of Torture: Past Incidents Show Abusers Think Ends Justify the Means." *Washington Post*, May 11, 2004.

Vrij, Aldert, Christian A. Meissner, Ronald P. Fisher, Saul M. Kassin, Charles A. Morgan III, and Steven M. Kleinman. "Psychological Perspectives on Interrogation." *Perspectives on Psychological Science* 12, no. 6 (2017): 927–55.

Wallace, Geoffrey P. R. "Martial Law? Military Experience, International Law, and Support for Torture." *International Studies Quarterly* 58, no. 3 (2014): 501–14.

Walsh, James I., and James A. Piazza. "Why Respecting Physical Integrity Rights Reduces Terrorism." *Comparative Political Studies* 43, no. 5 (2010): 551–77.

Walzer, Michael. "Political Action: The Problem of Dirty Hands." *Philosophy and Public Affairs* 2, no. 2 (1973): 160–80.

Wantchekon, Leonard, and Andrew Healy. "The 'Game' of Torture." *Journal of Conflict Resolution* 43, no. 5 (1999): 596–609.

"The Water Cure Described: Discharged Soldier Tells Senate Committee How and Why the Torture Was Inflicted." *New York Times*. May 4, 1902.

Weaver, David. "Issue Salience and Public Opinion: Are There Consequences of Agenda-Setting?" *International Journal of Public Opinion Research* 3, no. 1 (1991): 53–68.

Weitzer, Ronald. "Incidents of Police Misconduct and Public Opinion." *Journal of Criminal Justice* 30, no. 5 (2002): 397–408.

Weitzer, Ronald, and Steven A. Tuch. "Determinants of Public Satisfaction with the Police." *Police Quarterly* 8, no. 3 (2005): 279–97.

Wendt, Alexander. *Social Theory of International Politics*. Cambridge: Cambridge University Press, 1999.

Wike, Richard. "Global Opinion Varies Widely on Use of Torture Against Suspected Terrorists." Pew Research Center, February 9, 2016. http://www.pewresearch.org/fact-tank/2016/02/09/global-opinion-use-of-torture/.

Wright, Matthew, Morris Levy, and Jack Citrin. "Public Attitudes Toward Immigration Policy Across the Legal/Illegal Divide: The Role of Categorical and Attribute-Based Decision-Making." *Political Behavior* 38, no. 1 (2016): 229–53.

Wu, Yuning. "College Students' Evaluation of Police Performance: A Comparison of Chinese and Americans." *Journal of Criminal Justice* 38, no. 4 (2010): 773–80.

Yar, Majid. "Screening Crime: Cultural Criminology Goes to the Movies." In *Framing Crime: Cultural Criminology and the Image*, ed. Keith J. Hayward and Mike Presdee, 80–94. Abingdon, UK: Routledge-Cavendish, 2010.

Yezer, Anthony M., Robert S. Goldfarb, and Paul J. Poppen. "Does Studying Economics Discourage Cooperation? Watch What We Do, Not What We Say or How We Play." *Journal of Economic Perspectives* 10, no. 1 (1996): 177–86.

Young, Joseph K., and Michael G. Findley. "Promise and Pitfalls of Terrorism Research." *International Studies Review* 13, no. 3 (2011): 411–31.

Zaller, John. *The Nature and Origins of Mass Opinion*. Cambridge: Cambridge University Press, 1992.

Zegart, Amy. "Torture Creep." *Foreign Policy*, September 25, 2012. https://foreignpolicy.com/2012/09/25/torture-creep/.

Zeitzoff, Thomas. "Anger, Exposure to Violence, and Intragroup Conflict: A 'Lab in the Field' Experiment in Southern Israel." *Political Psychology* 35, no. 3 (2014): 309–35.

INDEX

Page numbers in *italics* indicate tables or figures.

COLUMBIA STUDIES IN TERRORISM
AND IRREGULAR WARFARE

Bruce Hoffman, Series Editor

Ami Pedahzur, *The Israeli Secret Services and the Struggle Against Terrorism*

Ami Pedahzur and Arie Perliger, *Jewish Terrorism in Israel*

Lorenzo Vidino, *The New Muslim Brotherhood in the West*

Erica Chenoweth and Maria J. Stephan, *Why Civil Resistance Works: The Strategic Logic of Nonviolent Conflict*

William C. Banks, editor, *New Battlefields/Old Laws: Critical Debates on Asymmetric Warfare*

Blake W. Mobley, *Terrorism and Counterintelligence: How Terrorist Groups Elude Detection*

Jennifer Morrison Taw, *Mission Revolution: The U.S. Military and Stability Operations*

Guido W. Steinberg, *German Jihad: On the Internationalization of Islamist Terrorism*

Michael W. S. Ryan, *Decoding Al-Qaeda's Strategy: The Deep Battle Against America*

David H. Ucko and Robert Egnell, *Counterinsurgency in Crisis: Britain and the Challenges of Modern Warfare*

Bruce Hoffman and Fernando Reinares, editors, *The Evolution of the Global Terrorist Threat: From 9/11 to Osama bin Laden's Death*

Boaz Ganor, *Global Alert: The Rationality of Modern Islamist Terrorism and the Challenge to the Liberal Democratic World*

M. L. R. Smith and David Martin Jones, *The Political Impossibility of Modern Counterinsurgency: Strategic Problems, Puzzles, and Paradoxes*

Elizabeth Grimm Arsenault, *How the Gloves Came Off: Lawyers, Policy Makers, and Norms in the Debate on Torture*

Assaf Moghadam, *Nexus of Global Jihad: Understanding Cooperation Among Terrorist Actor*

Bruce Hoffman, *Inside Terrorism*, 3rd edition

Stephen Tankel, *With Us and Against Us: How America's Partners Help and Hinder the War on Terror*

Wendy Pearlman and Boaz Atzili, *Triadic Coercion: Israel's Targeting of States That Host Nonstate Actors*

Bryan C. Price, *Targeting Top Terrorists: Understanding Leadership Removal in Counterterrorism Strategy*

Mariya Y. Omelicheva and Lawrence P. Markowitz, *Webs of Corruption: Trafficking and Terrorism in Central Asia*

Aaron Y. Zelin, *Your Sons Are at Your Service: Tunisia's Missionaries of Jihad*

Lorenzo Vidino, *The Closed Circle: Joining and Leaving the Muslim Brotherhood in the West*

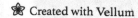

THE MECHANIC

A JOHN TYLER ACTION THRILLER (#1)

TOM FOWLER

For Lisa and Isabel.

"There you go. Line it up and squeeze the trigger."

John Tyler directed his daughter Lexi using the power screwdriver to tighten a bolt. They both lay under a decade-old Honda Accord coupe in desperate need of a new exhaust system. The old one showed more rust than unmarred metal. Tyler found a replacement which would sound better, add more horsepower through enhanced efficiency, and check in at ten pounds lighter.

Lexi took her free hand off of the muffler. "I think I got it, Dad."

Tyler scooted closer to check their work. All the connections proved solid as he grabbed and tested them. He brought the knowledge and experience to the project, but Lexi did at least half the work. "Looks good. We might make a mechanic out of you yet."

Lexi squirmed out from under the Honda and stood. Despite the summer heat in the garage, she wore jeans and a long-sleeved shirt. "I think that's more your skill set than mine."

Tyler crawled out and lowered the powerful jacks holding the coupe up at each corner. "You did well, though."

"I had a good teacher," she said with a smile. It was an expression Tyler missed seeing a lot of while Lexi grew up.

"Most of this work isn't hard," he said. "We tackled the difficult bits when we were under the hood."

They both walked into the house and changed into clothes more befitting the weather. At the kitchen counter, Tyler drank from a bottle of water, and he pushed one toward Lexi when she sat beside him. "Thanks, Dad. It was a lot of work, but I'm glad I have a car."

She'd chosen it herself. Like both her parents, Lexi loved driving fast. She and Tyler scoured online listings—he'd also looked in the newspaper classifieds, though he didn't confess the low-tech hunt to Lexi—before she selected the right car. Other than the exhaust and the normal wear and tear coming from age, the coupe was in good shape. The combination of the V6 and manual transmission would allow for some fun behind the wheel. "I figured you'd be driving it to college," Tyler said. "I'm glad you're going online."

Lexi unscrewed the cap and downed half the water in a single gulp. "I don't feel comfortable going on campus."

"I know. It's nice to have you here." Lexi had lived with Tyler a little more than a year now. Between deployments and moving around, he'd missed a lot of time during her formative years. A couple months ago, he quit his job with a private security company. With Lexi's mother in jail, Tyler wanted to be a reliable parent. His daughter was too polite to call him out on being absent, but she'd been ecstatic when he resigned.

"Don't get all sentimental on me, old man. Aren't you supposed to look for a job?"

Tyler nodded. "I need to. It's just ..."

"Weird?"

"Yeah," he said. "I don't think I've ever applied for a job before." Lexi shot him a funny look. "Enlisting isn't the same thing. Then, when I left the service, I knew I had a gig waiting for me." He shrugged. "I don't even have a résumé."

"If you want to make one," Lexi said, "I can help you. I think you should start with the listings, though. See what's out there. You have a lot of experience."

"I don't think many tanks or Hum-Vees pull into civilian repair shops."

She grinned. "Well, if they do, you'll be very qualified to work on them." Lexi drained the rest of her water and stood. "I have a virtual visit with school soon. Let me know if you need a hand putting a résumé together."

"I will," Tyler said.

Lexi stood beside Tyler, wrapped her left arm around him, and kissed him on the cheek. At five-eight, she stood only two inches shorter than him. "Thanks again, Dad."

"You might want to shower before you get online with your college."

"I'll have to do it after," she said, walking upstairs. "Good thing they can't smell me on the call."

Tyler sat at the counter staring at his water bottle. After years of not being a great parent, he'd adjusted to being a full-time father. Lexi finished high school, made the honor roll, and earned a partial scholarship to the University of Maryland. She inherited her smarts from both parents, her looks from her mother—thank goodness—and her attitude from both. After an interesting year, Tyler liked having his daughter live with him.

He finally had a chance to make it right, and he meant to take it.

∼

LEXI CHECKED her hair in the mirror. She'd tied her dark brown locks back into a ponytail. Sweating in the garage made any other style impossible. The college encouraged people to turn their video on, and she would. She'd even chosen a virtual background for the occasion. Lexi clicked on the link in her email invitation. WebEx launched, and she connected to the online conference call.

Once it got underway, her advisor walked her and a dozen other students through course selection, picking a major, and accessing online materials. All her fellow freshmen said they originally planned to attend in person. The advisor hoped the spring semester would allow for it. Lexi did, too. She enjoyed living with her father, but she also wanted a chance to be on her own. Her dad got to leave home for the army, and her mother moved most of the way across the country for college almost thirty years ago.

Toward the end of the session, everyone shared what they'd been working on for the first few weeks of summer. A couple guys who dressed like they lived in the gym boasted about shredding their workouts. Lexi rolled her eyes. The worst part about going to school on campus would be the frat boys who lived down to every stereotype. When it came around to her, Lexi said she'd worked on fixing a car with her dad.

No one said anything until the advisor asked, "Is it his car?"

"No," Lexi said. "It's mine. I figured I'd be commuting in it every day, but at least I'll have something to drive now."

A screen full of neutral expressions staring back at her told Lexi no one shared her enthusiasm for cars. If she revealed she'd be working a stick shift, the reactions probably would've been worse. Her dad remarked it was a great anti-theft device. It also made driving a lot more fun. "Well, we hope to see you in it when the campus fully reopens," the advisor said politely.

Lexi disconnected a few minutes later and perused the course catalog. She hadn't decided on a major, but first-year requirements chewed up all her selections. Some courses still listed building and room numbers even though they'd be

offered virtually. Lexi made a few selections and submitted
them to her academic counselor.

Then, she kicked her sweaty clothes off, turned the water
on full blast, and took a badly-needed shower.

A JOB. It seemed like such a simple concept. Most people
worked. The last time Tyler thought about what he wanted to
do, he was eighteen. He enlisted, then toured the world for the
next twenty-four years, sometimes choosing where he went and
others going where the army sent him. When he retired, he
already had the gig at Patriot Security lined up. Now, thirty-two
years since he made a meaningful decision about his future
employment, Tyler pondered what to do next.

When Tyler quit Patriot, he envisioned working on classic
cars. He owned one, after all, and he'd restored it and even
modernized it a little himself. In the army, he originally went in
as a mechanic, keeping tanks and Hummers running in some
of the worst conditions on earth. Scavenging parts and rigging
temporary repairs were daily acts of necessity. Fixing someone's
forty-year-old Camaro would be easy by comparison.

Job listings online proved depressing. Every posting wanted
someone to work on modern cars. Tyler could stumble his way
through the computer on his desk, but he didn't care for ever-
growing systems in current vehicles. Besides, the shops wanted
certifications he didn't possess and practical experience he'd
never had the chance to acquire.

Tyler shut down his laptop. If the cars he wanted to work on
didn't run on computers, why should he find the job in such a
way? He walked to the kitchen, snagged the *Baltimore Sun* off
the counter, and took it back to his desk. The classifieds beck-
oned—did they even call them the want ads anymore? Tyler
remembered when job listings were the thickest part of the

paper. Now, they were down to a few pages, having grown even thinner since spring.

He discovered two listings for a classic car mechanic. Smitty and Son—by far the closer of the two—was the winner by default. Tyler wanted to check out the shop at his interview . . . if he got one. Reconnaissance was important. Wandering into a situation blind increased the odds of things not ending well. The location was easy enough to find, and the business sat in a good area. Tyler circled the ad and committed the address to memory. He hoped the owner would be amenable to hiring someone without much of a documented history.

Since leaving his security gig, Tyler chafed for steady work. Lexi wouldn't admit it, but he thought she got tired of having him around all the time. Multiple deployments for special operations interrupted his work as a mechanic, but Tyler always enjoyed fixing things. He understood cars, trucks, and tanks. People—daughters in particular—were another story altogether.

Maybe after more than three decades of following orders, he could have a normal life.

~

KENT MAXWELL LOOKED up as the email chime on his laptop dinged. He glanced at the sender's name: Arthur Bell. "Dammit," he grumbled as he opened the message.

MAXWELL,

Your company's review is due tomorrow. Please contact me at once.

Arthur Bell

. . .

THE DATE in the taskbar confirmed what Bell said. Maxwell logged into his company's bank account and frowned. He could cover Bell's blood money, but they'd need to make some headway soon. Maxwell setup the transfer and clicked yes when the site prompted him to confirm. Then, he logged off and closed his laptop lid with much more force than the manufacturer recommended.

Maxwell picked up the phone and made a call. Arthur Bell picked up. "Good morning."

"We secure?"

"We are," Bell said.

"I submitted the review paperwork." Maxwell kept his language in line with Bell's like they'd agreed to when they first made the arrangement.

"Excellent. I'm sure things will go smoothly."

"You going to confirm receipt?" Maxwell said.

"I'll let you know if there's an issue." Bell paused. "How goes the work?"

"It's going."

"You're not going to tell me anything else?"

Maxwell leaned back in his chair and sighed. "Fine. I think we're close."

"How close?"

"Hard to know for sure." Maxwell recalled the encrypted memo he read last night. War changed the landscape of Afghanistan, and the easy markers of the past were gone. A knowledgeable local put them on to a possible location. It took three hours of torture, but he complied, and a bullet to the head after an additional hour of agony ensured his silence. "We have a good lead on the location."

"Good," Bell said. "What about the potential complication you mentioned last time?"

Maxwell smiled, even though he was alone in his office. "He'll be dealt with soon."

2

It took until the next day for someone to answer at Smitty and Son. Based on the qualities of the voice, Tyler presumed he spoke to the former. Whoever answered was willing to talk about the open position in person. Tyler cold-called two other shops he knew and got swiftly rejected each time. Smitty won by default again. Tyler put on a pair of black chinos and a red button-down shirt. While Tyler inhaled a mug of coffee, Lexi came downstairs and poured herself a cup.

She looked at him and raised an eyebrow. "You're looking fancy . . . for you at least."

"I'm going to see a man about working as a classic car mechanic."

"That's great, Dad." Lexi smiled and clinked her mug against his. "I'm so glad you're getting to use what you know."

"Me, too," Tyler said.

"You've always told me you were a mechanic. Now, you're getting another chance."

"I doubt I'll get pulled away this time."

"Enjoy it, Dad. Go do what you're meant to."

"You sound like your grandfather, now," Tyler said.

Lexi nodded. "He's a smart guy. 'A man's got to be who he is.' One of these days, I need to ask him if it extends to women, too."

Tyler grinned. "I'm sure it does . . . even if it may take him a little while to admit it."

His daughter took her coffee upstairs, and Tyler climbed into his 1972 Oldsmobile 442. Even if he owned a different car, Smitty might want to see this one as a sort of audition. Tyler left the Mount Washington area of Baltimore, picked up Northern Parkway, and took it east. Architecture morphed with the neighborhoods, starting out fancy at Roland Park but growing older and more rundown as he passed Mercy High School. As he made a left onto Belair Road and headed toward Overlea, he realized the area changed a lot since the last time he drove through. Some of the restaurants and businesses he remembered had shut their doors, and new ones sprang up in the same locations.

After cresting a hill, Tyler saw the shop on the right and pulled into the lot. A sign mounted above the asphalt flickered on the word *Son*. Side streets surrounded the property, and a church sat immediately past it. Maybe people whose cars were beyond fixing could go there and pray about it.

Tyler walked around the building, which wasn't much to look at. There were three garage bays, and the windows in two were broken and covered in plastic. The bottom glass panel of the main door had received the same treatment. Tyler paused at the door. Was this random vandalism? Bad weather? What was he walking into? It took a few seconds of pondering, but Tyler opened the door.

A quiet electronic chime rang when he walked in. The front area of the interior held a coffee pot, medium-sized TV, and four chairs for the waiting room. Despite the brew station, the place smelled of metal shavings and oil. The linoleum floor had seen better days. Wood paneling clung to the walls like it was still the 'eighties, and it begged for someone to give it a good cleaning. A laptop sat on the counter, and behind it were three desks, all set with one short edge against the wall. In the middle of the wall, a door led to the repair bays. A man of about sixty emerged from there. His appearance could be a good sign. The two guys who rejected him over the phone sounded young, like new enlisted men. Here was a seasoned sergeant major. He wiped his hands on a towel. "Help you?"

"I called earlier about your ad."

"Ah, right. Tom Smith. They call me Smitty." He nodded.

Tyler bobbed his head in return. He imagined every large neighborhood in an eastern city like Baltimore held a Smitty and a Sully. "John Tyler. I go by Tyler."

Smitty eyed Tyler like he knew him but moved on to business. "You got a résumé or anything?"

"Haven't made one of those in . . . ever."

"No shit?" Smitty said with wide eyes.

Tyler shrugged. "I enlisted in the army at eighteen. Spent twenty-four years there. Then, I went into private security. I left a few months ago."

"I thought I recognized you."

"You're one up on me, then," Tyler said.

Smitty pointed to a picture mounted on the paneled wall behind the largest desk. "My son, Jake. He's a reservist now, but several years ago, you talked to him about special operations."

Tyler looked at the photo. Bits of the conversation played in his memory. It happened after his third tour in Afghanistan. "It must have been a decade or so by now."

"Probably," Smitty said. "My boy did well."

"Where is he now?"

"Taking some time off. His name's on the sign, but he ain't here too much. It's why I'm trying to hire someone."

"Conveniently enough, I'm here to apply."

"You were special forces?" Smitty asked.

Tyler nodded. "For a while. Four tours of Afghanistan. The rest of the time, I was a Ninety-One Bravo . . . wheeled vehicle mechanic."

"Now, you want to work on classic cars?"

"Better than computerized ones. I fixed Jeeps and Hummers in the service."

Smitty walked behind the counter and retrieved a dingy mug. He poured himself a cup of coffee whose consistency reminded Tyler of motor oil. "Want any?"

"I already had two," Tyler said.

"A third ain't gonna hurt."

Based on what Smitty poured out of the pot, it probably would. "Maybe later."

Smitty added some powdered creamer, stirred the dull brown liquid, and took a sip. "So you split your time between working on vehicles and special operations." Tyler nodded. "You better at fixing cars or shooting people?"

"I'd like to think I'm good at both."

"Anything else?"

"You can check out my car." Tyler tossed him the key. "I've done all the work myself."

"What are you driving?"

"The Four-Four-Two out there."

"I'll take a look." Smitty walked outside. Tyler didn't watch him, instead looking at the desks. He presumed the largest one belonged to Smitty himself. When your name was first on the sign, you got the biggest workspace. The second looked like the larger model at three-quarters scale. The third desk was basically shoved into the corner. It looked straight out of a middle school surplus store.

A minute later, the chime dinged again. "What year is she?" Smitty said.

"Seventy-two."

"Rocket V8?"

"You looked at it," said Tyler. "All four hundred fifty-five cubic inches worth."

"Didn't want the three-fifty?" Smitty asked.

"Why would you ever get the smaller engine?"

"The automatic, though?"

"Needed one," Tyler said. "Lots of wear and tear on my legs. I couldn't handle stop-and-go with a stick anymore."

"Original parts?"

"Is this a quiz?"

"Maybe," Smitty said with a smile. "Hell, I like the fact you called it a Four-Four-Two instead of a Four-Forty-Two. Young people get it wrong."

"They get a lot wrong," Tyler said.

The comment drew a knowing smirk. "Original parts?"

"Mostly. I've gotten a little more power out of the engine. It's about four hundred now. And I just put a new titanium exhaust on."

"You said you were looking for a job?"

If this constituted a job interview, it was easy. "I am."

"Good. Can you start at nine o'clock tomorrow morning?"

"I'll be here," Tyler said.

"See you then," said Smitty. They bumped elbows.

Tyler walked out and got back in his car. He smiled and pounded the steering wheel. Lexi would be pleased. No more bureaucracy. No more petty bosses. No more shooting and killing.

He could finally move on with his life.

～

JAKE SMITH LOOKED at his phone.

It was the second burner he bought this week. They learned the number of the first one. A few threatening texts later, and

Jake tossed it off a bridge and purchased a different model. So far, no one reached out to him. He'd maintained radio silence on his end.

The contact listed as *Tom's Pizza* was really his father. Jake wanted to call him and let him know things were all right . . . for large values of "all right" at least. Sure, he was hiding out in a hotel he'd never set foot in otherwise, keeping a constant watch on his surroundings, and doing his best to sleep with one eye open.

It all beat the alternative.

The army taught Jake a few things about tech, and he used what he learned now to help himself stay a step ahead of his pursuers. This hotel didn't have much in the way of security. It made sneaking downstairs and installing a wide-angle webcam above the door easy. Jake also set one up in the hallway leading to his room. He could monitor the stairs and elevator at the same time.

Both devices fed their data into an app on his phone. Motion activated them, and they could last a couple days on a single charge. Jake's mobile would buzz once when the front-door camera picked something up and twice for the hallway. He figured the second one going off gave him a minute to get out of the room. It would be enough time. He'd done it before.

Jake sat on the bed. His father always taught him to be honest. Tell the truth. Do the right thing. He did, and it landed him squarely in the soup. The army talked a good game about wanting soldiers to report bad behavior. They didn't do a lot to protect those who came forward, however. Once Jake learned he vaulted to enemy number one on his former commander's list, he hit the road, and he'd been there for the last week. He wanted to get out of the city, but he also needed to make sure nothing happened to his dad. It was a delicate and tiring balance.

One day soon, he hoped he could go back to a normal life.

T yler woke up early. He'd been doing it since he was eighteen, and no matter the day or occasion, his brain kicked into gear around six o'clock. He trudged downstairs, started a pot of coffee, and brought the newspaper in. The delivery guy kept it in the same ZIP code as his front porch this time.

After a hot cup of caffeine and a quick perusal of depressing headlines, Tyler walked back upstairs. He sat in an old wooden chair his grandfather made by hand. A fresh sheet of cold-pressed watercolor paper stared back at him. Despite never being a talented artist, Tyler had been painting for about six years. A psychiatrist at the VA diagnosed him with PTSD. She offered a couple of possible alternative therapeutic suggestions, because Tyler loathed the idea of a support group. He chose painting.

It sounded like bunk at first, but he could track his moods in his outputs. When he first took it up, his work was dark and gloomy. Over time—and with semi-regular visits to the shrink—the colors brightened, and the gloominess left. Recently, Tyler took to drawing classic cars he liked. His most recent effort—a Corvette—waited for a frame. He didn't display much of his work out of concerns for the quality of the output and his own privacy. The 'Vette looked good, though. It deserved a spot on the wall.

A short while into his new hobby, Tyler upgraded his supplies. He bought a proper easel, better paper, and high-quality watercolors. They helped elevate the quality of his compositions. His father's voice reminded him only a poor craftsman would blame his tools, but Tyler saw the results. Practice helped, but so did working with better materials.

Tyler started with the blue sky, choosing a color to represent the early morning. He would let it dry before adding the sun. He'd rushed this on some of his initial projects and paid for it with a dismal circle of green on the horizon. White fluffy clouds would come next. Early on, Tyler blitzed through paintings as quickly as he could. Over time, he grew to appreciate what he did, and each now took many hours longer than they did then.

After filling in the sky and drawing a ribbon of black stretching into the distance, Tyler packed up his supplies. He threw on a pair of jeans and a plain black T-shirt. Lexi's bedroom door remained closed. Like most teenagers, she could sleep for twelve hours and still manage to be tired at night. When he got downstairs, Tyler left her a quick note on the dining room table.

He climbed into the 442 and drove to Smitty and Son. Twenty-five minutes later, Tyler parked in the lot and walked into the shop. The chime went off when the door opened, and Smitty's head whipped around. His shoulders loosened, and his grip on the desk relaxed. Tyler frowned. "Everything all right?"

"Sure." Smitty waved a hand. "Didn't sleep well last night. I guess I'm a little jumpy is all."

It made Tyler wonder. The outside of the shop still showed damage. It could have been bad weather or maybe a few local punks wreaking havoc. Then, there was the matter of Smitty's son. Missing in action . . . allegedly taking some time off. The whole situation added up to something dangerous, and Tyler didn't care for the math. He was finished playing hero. "Nothing else is wrong?"

"Nope," Smitty said. "You here to be a shrink or work on cars? I don't pay to sit on your couch."

"All right. What do we have today?"

Smitty jerked his head to the side. "Oil change on the Camaro in bay one."

Tyler smiled. "Starting me off easy?"

"Pretty much."

A locker inside the repair area held work shirts, and Tyler slipped one on. It was a little long, but it fit pretty well. He raised the Camaro and inspected the undercarriage. The exhaust was aftermarket and recent, but most of the engine looked original. Changing the oil would be quick and easy. Tyler wondered why someone who drove such a classic car wouldn't also do at least the basic maintenance on it.

While old sludge drained into a pan, Tyler looked through the window. Smitty sat behind the desk. He glanced around often and nearly jumped out of his seat when the phone rang. A growing unease gripped Tyler as he wondered what Smitty was involved in.

JAKE TOSSED and turned throughout the night. He hadn't gotten any real sleep in at least two weeks. The price he paid for what he did. *It's worth it*, he told himself. He repeated the mini-mantra every morning. Some days, belief came easier than others.

When he rolled out of bed, Jake checked his phone first. No activity anywhere. He was safe for now. He got in the shower, and the hot water helped him wake up. He'd need to figure out washing his clothes soon. Jake put on his last clean ones and stuffed what he wore the previous day into his rucksack. He checked his app again.

Still good.

When Jake dropped out of sight, he knew he'd be missing out on things like eating in restaurants and going to bars. He popped into convenience stores or supermarkets at odd hours, making sure to hide his face while he bought snacks and water for a couple days. He'd need to pop in to some place again soon.

With the coast still clear, Jake dropped to the hotel floor. In sets, he performed a hundred crunches, a hundred pushups, planked for four minutes, and did sixty body-weight squats. When he finished, he ripped open a bland protein bar and ate it, washing it down with his second-to-last bottle of water. He'd refill it in the bathroom sink before he left in case he couldn't hit up a store today.

Jake's phone buzzed, and a feeling of dread gripped him. He checked his security app first, but it still showed no alerts. Next, he went into texts. One new message.

Good morning, Jake. How much longer can you stay on the run?

"Shit," Jake said to the empty room. He packed his rucksack again, collected his cameras, and left the hotel. As he crossed the street, he scanned the area. No one he recognized. No car or SUV casing the place. They found his burner number again, but they still didn't have his location.

Not yet at least.

Jake would need another new phone soon. He tried to puzzle out how they found his present number and came up empty. As he walked away from the hotel, Jake wondered how much longer he could stay on the lam.

∼

A LITTLE WHILE LATER, the Camaro owner walked in. Smitty took care of printing the receipt. Tyler was fine to let him handle the customers. He'd rather work on cars than deal with people. No sooner did he finish the thought than Smitty brought the guy around to the work bays. His face and hair made him look about Tyler's age, though he was much taller and thinner. "She ready?"

"She is," Tyler said. He thought he'd be pulling the car out into the lot. Instead, he handed the owner the keys. He found the whole situation irregular, but Smitty didn't seem to care.

"You new?"

Tyler didn't want to engage the man in conversation. Another car waited for him. Smitty stood there watching them, an awkward third wheel to a chat Tyler now felt compelled to engage in. "First day here."

The customer nodded. "Smitty and his boy put the exhaust on for me. I love looking at these cars and driving them, but I don't know how to fix them."

"Good thing we're here, then," Tyler said.

"It is." The man clapped him on the shoulder and got into the Camaro. He fired it up and drove it out of the bay.

"You let all of them come back here?" Tyler asked once the classic muscle car pulled out of the lot with a roar.

"No," he said. "Frank there lost his wife a year or so ago. I think he needs the company. He's a good guy, so I indulge him."

Tyler couldn't find fault with the reasoning. "What's the newer Camaro need?" He inclined his head toward the red IROC edition awaiting his care.

"Oil and brakes."

"Trusting me with two jobs now?" Tyler said. "I must be moving up in the world."

"Figured I'd wait a few days before I give you an engine rebuild," Smitty said with a chuckle.

"It's been a while since I've done one."

A dark gray SUV pulled into the lot. Its windows were closer to black than clear, obscuring the view of the people in the front seats. Tyler could see the outlines of a driver and passenger. The vehicle stopped in the lot and idled. Smitty wiped his hand over his mouth and paced back and forth. Tyler glanced between his new boss and the Yukon. Did Smitty know these guys, whoever they were? Were they responsible for the damage to the shop?

Tyler didn't want to get involved in someone else's mess. He left his crusading ways behind when he walked away from Patriot Security. Working on cars was a less stressful job which allowed him to be a better father to Lexi. Still, Smitty's demeanor made him curious. "Everything all right?" he asked when the other man walked past.

"Sure." Smitty turned around and began another loop of the shop floor. Whoever sat in the SUV hadn't gotten out yet. Whoever they were, they upset Smitty by pulling into the lot and sitting there. Tyler looked at the vehicle and committed the license plate to memory.

Then, he got to work on the IROC.

4

Tyler got the car on the lift and tried to ignore the SUV but couldn't stand with his back to the open bay knowing two men sat out there. Once he stood under the vehicle, he gave it the once-over. It was a mid-'eighties IROC Camaro. Tyler remembered when they came out. He liked them but preferred the similar Pontiac Trans Am. The pop-up headlights made it much cooler—this was the 'eighties, after all—and *Knight Rider* chose the Trans Am over its Chevy cousin. Tyler, who was twelve when the show debuted, would have made the same decision.

He drained the old oil and inspected the chassis. The brakes were worn; the owner brought the car in just in time. The front CV joints would need to be replaced soon. The shocks were also coming to the end of their useful life. The owner should have noticed the diminished ride quality. Maybe the sound of the V8 covered the multitude of suspension sins.

With the old oil safely in a container, Tyler put the cap back on and lowered the car. He added new oil and checked the other engine fluids. All good. If he needed to leave Smitty's, Jiffy lube would want him. Tyler smirked at the thought and shook his head. Classic car people liked and appreciated their vehicles. They were a tolerable subset of the general public. Jiffy Lube invited all sorts. Soccer moms who drove massive SUVs to take their kids to practice. Stuffed shirts who drove German luxury cars for the badges and kept their hipster beards neatly groomed.

They were the kind of people Tyler could live without.

After Tyler lowered the hood back into place, he heard voices coming from the office. Not just Smitty's. The silhouettes no longer appeared in the black Yukon. Tyler couldn't make out anything being said. He moved closer to the door separating the work area from the office and peeked through the small window. Two guys talked to Smitty, who leaned away from them and stared down at the desk. The wiry member of the duo did the talking. His larger compatriot stood there and looked menacing, and he was very good at it. Both their jackets showed telltale bulges at the hip. Their posture and short hair suggested military pasts. Tyler was close enough now to hear what they said. "You expect me to believe you don't know where your son is?" the more slender one asked.

"I don't," Smitty said in a defeated tone.

"You don't what? Don't know where he is or don't expect me to believe it?"

"He left. He didn't tell me where or for what." Whatever the reason, if these two assholes were asking around about him, it couldn't be good. The confrontation—probably not the first— explained the damage to the shop and Smitty's nervousness. Now Tyler understood what he got himself into. He should have trusted his instincts when he saw the broken windows.

He opened the door, and everyone looked at him. "Everything all right, Smitty?"

"We're good, friend," the mouthpiece of the pair said.

"I'm fine," Smitty said to Tyler. His wide eyes conveyed the opposite.

"We need a few minutes. You mind?"

The problem was Smitty's. Actually, it sounded like his son's problem, and these guys were making it the father's. Probably over money or drugs. It would be a shame. Tyler remembered Jake as a promising soldier, but substance abuse after leaving the service was an unfortunately common issue. *I'm a mechanic,* Tyler said to himself. He finally got his chance to work on cars and put the past behind him. The war. The killings. *I'm a mechanic.*

"No problem," Tyler said. He left the door open and went back into the shop. The IROC still needed its brakes replaced. He picked up a large wrench and wiped it with a rag.

Things soon got worse for Smitty. The talkative goon yelled at him. Then, Tyler heard the unmistakable sound of someone being punched. He gripped the wrench harder. *I'm a mechanic.* Another punch. Tyler wiped the tool again even though it didn't need it. Smitty apologized and got yelled at some more.

He took another wallop and crashed to the floor. Tyler didn't need to see it to know what happened. Smitty was a good guy in a bad situation, dealing with a pair of experts at intimidating and beating guys like him. Sometimes, they did worse things. Tyler saw behavior like theirs many times in his deployments overseas. He drew in a deep breath and held it. *What am I doing? I can't let this happen to Smitty.* He relaxed his white-knuckle grip on the wrench.

He tried to be a simple mechanic. Not a soldier. Not a killer. It didn't work out, and he didn't think he'd get another opportunity.

Tyler strode back to the door.

～

THE OLD GUY was an easy mark, Rick Rust thought. He was so worried about his son he'd do anything. Agree to anything.

Probably pay anything, too, if money were the object. He hadn't learned from getting his shop vandalized, and Jake quickly went into hiding. Now Rick and Bobby had to come and follow up. Rick was realistic—the old man probably didn't have any knowledge of his son's whereabouts. He liked it better this way. He loved to intimidate people, and Bobby loved to hurt them.

Then, the other guy opened the door. When the hell did he start? No matter. The previous one got scared off in one day. The newest fellow lasted a minute before he went back into the shop. He left the door open, but it didn't matter. He knew his place. They all did. Now Rick and Bobby could get back to work. The part they enjoyed would be coming up. "Your boy is still in the wind," Rick said. Bobby stood to his left. Rick glanced at him. He fixed the old man with a menacing stare.

Smitty looked once at Bobby, then looked away. "I told you . . . I don't know where he is," he said.

"Neither do we," Rick said. "And it's a problem, especially for you. You're his father. You should be able to find him. How do we know he didn't talk to you? Maybe he told you everything."

"If he did," Bobby said, "we're gonna hurt you." He didn't say much, but when he did, it promised pain.

"I don't know anything," the old man said. His eyes were wide, but his gaze was steady. "Jake left. He didn't tell me why. He didn't tell me where he was going."

"Why don't I believe you?" Rick said.

"You guys have to realize I don't know anything. You're costing me business. I still need to fix the damage you did."

"Blame your son." Rick drew his fist back and socked the owner in the stomach. He doubled over in his chair and nearly hit his head on the desk. His ragged breaths made Rick and Bobby smile. "Now . . . how about the truth?"

"I've been telling you the truth."

"You think we believe you all of a sudden?" Rick hit the

older man again, now targeting the face. It didn't knock him out of the chair, but it would leave a mark. He'd look in the mirror and remember.

"Please," Smitty said. "I don't know where he went. Tell your boss—"

"You don't get to tell us what to do," Bobby broke in. The second punch to the face sent Smitty toppling from the chair like a rag doll tossed to the floor. Rick loved it when Bobby hit people. Even if they stayed conscious, they didn't make the mistake of getting up again. Smitty looked woozy, but he didn't pass out.

Smitty continued to plead ignorance. He lied even when it was apparent Rick and Bobby knew better. For an insult like this, Rick would enjoy watching Bobby pummel the old man into unconsciousness. Or worse.

Silver flashed in Rick's sight as something flew through the air and whacked Bobby full in the face. He dropped like he'd been shot. The guy who went back into the shop now bolted from the door. Rick reached for the gun holstered on his left hip. His hand shook a little. No one took out Bobby. He swung the pistol around when the new guy surged forward and kicked Rick in the chest. It didn't knock him down, but it did stagger him.

Worst of all, it made him drop the gun.

The new guy picked it up, pulled the hammer back, and buried the gun under Rick's chin as he shoved him into a nearby wall. Rick glanced at Bobby. He wasn't moving. The old man sat on the floor looking stunned.

Rick looked at the guy with the gun. During his time in the National Guard, he'd locked eyes with a few people who wanted to kill him. He saw no pity in the dark brown, almost black eyes staring back at him. The new hire—whoever he was —was a killer, and for the first time in a long time, Rick Rust worried he might die.

5

Tyler pushed the muzzle of the Glock 19 hard under the skinny one's chin. It bent his neck back until his head thudded into the wall. "Give me a reason not to blow your brains all over this paneling," he said.

"Piss off," the guy said.

"Eloquent." Tyler pulled the gun back and jabbed the wiry guy in the solar plexus with its snout. He gasped for air and bent over, then got straightened up by the pistol under his jaw again. "Take a second. Breathe. When you can, you're going to tell me your names."

"Rust. I'm Rick Rust . . . he's Bobby."

"Wasn't so hard, was it?" Tyler said. "Now, I want to know who sent you here."

"Tyler, I don't want any trouble," Smitty croaked.

"You already had trouble, Smitty. It wasn't going to resolve itself."

"Don't shoot him."

"I won't. As long as he answers me." Tyler pressed the Glock hard enough under Rust's chin to bend his neck back again. He saw the fear wash over him as his eyes went wide and the reality of the situation set in.

"OK, OK," he said.

"Who sent you?" Tyler said through gritted teeth.

"We're looking for the kid."

"You see him here?"

"No," Rust admitted.

"Then, you're going to collect your friend and piss off. *After* you tell me the name of the asshole who gave you your orders."

"I don't know. He goes by Max."

"Just Max?"

"It's all I know," Rust said. "He sent us. Can I go now?"

"No," Tyler said. "You're going to tell him Smitty doesn't know anything. His son is missing. It's the son's problem. Stop coming here and harassing a man who has nothing to do with whatever's going on."

"Max ain't patient."

"He'd better be. If he sends you two assholes again, I'll send you back with a few pounds of lead in you."

Tyler pulled the gun back, elbowed Rust in the face, then shoved him toward his larger partner. Bobby still hadn't moved, though he groaned and looked to be coming to. Tyler walked to him, opened his jacket, and took his gun. "Get him out of here," Tyler said.

"I can't carry him," the slender Rust said.

Tyler pointed the gun at Bobby. "You can either man up and help him out the door or drag his body out. I don't care which one you pick, but he might."

Rust glared at Tyler for a second and then nodded. He jostled his large friend to wake him up. Tyler moved back to the desks. He kept the gun trained on the two goons as Bobby rose to unsteady feet. His eyes couldn't focus on anything and he nearly capsized a couple times. It was all Rust could do to keep his partner on his feet and help him wobble in the direction of the door.

"I guess I'm not getting the gun back?" Rust asked, Bobby's meaty arm draped across his shoulders.

"You can have a couple of the bullets," Tyler said. "Express delivery."

The smaller enforcer shook his head and helped the shaky Bobby to the door. Once outside, they climbed back into the Yukon. Bobby still needed help, and Tyler laughed when he hit his head on the door frame and almost fell over again. After a minute, Rust got him situated, then climbed in the driver's side. Tyler double-checked the plate as the SUV drove away.

He tucked the larger gun into the back of his jeans. Smitty sat behind his desk and stared ahead. It had been a rough day for him. Now, Tyler had a clearer picture of what happened to the *and Son* part of the business, at least. He still didn't understand the circumstances of Jake's disappearance, and he wondered if Smitty knew anything or just snowed his tormentors to protect his boy.

"Anything you want to tell me, Smitty?" he asked.

"Jesus Christ. How about something you might want to tell me!"

"You know I spent some time in special operations. Your story's the important one now."

Smitty looked like a balloon someone had let half the helium out of. "Hell, you can probably figure it out," he said. He sat behind his desk and rubbed his face.

"You'll have a couple nice bruises."

"Good thing no one comes here for my looks."

At least he maintained a sense of humor. Tyler showed Smitty the smaller Glock. "You know how to use one of these?"

"I don't like guns."

"They probably don't like you, either," Tyler said. "But

you'll be a fan if these two shitheads come back. Can you shoot?"

"Of course I can shoot."

"Good." Tyler cracked the slide of the Glock 19 to see a brass 9 MM cartridge in the chamber. He handed it to Smitty. "Be careful. It's ready to shoot. There's no conventional safety to click off. It's in the trigger, so just point, squeeze, and *bang!* Keep it out of sight in a desk drawer or something. Don't hesitate to use it if those two assholes pay you another visit."

"I'm no killer," Smitty said.

"Everyone can be a killer," Tyler said. "It just takes the right motivation." He retrieved the wrench which sent Bobby crashing to the floor. It had been a hell of a toss.

"You've killed men before," Smitty said. He didn't intone it as a question.

"I have," Tyler said. "All things being equal, I'd prefer not to do it again. We'll see if it holds."

Smitty fell silent behind the desk. Some color returned to his face. He stared at the gun for a few seconds before hurrying it into the upper right desk drawer. "I'm . . . I'm glad you were here," he said.

"I'd like to know what's going on."

"You probably heard most of it."

Tyler nodded. "I'd like you to explain it to me. I think you owe me as much."

"All right." Smitty took a deep breath to collect himself and then launched into the story. "Jake took off a while ago. Didn't tell me where he was going. He just said he needed some time. I asked for what? He didn't say."

"Drugs?"

Smitty frowned and shook his head. "No. He's clean. My guess is he knows something he shouldn't."

It made sense. If Jake made it into special ops, it would open all kinds of doors for him. Some were worth walking through, and others were only trouble. Not everyone could tell the difference. The lure of intelligence work and easy money ensnared many a soldier over the years. "At least one of those two looked like former military. They the same ones who damaged the shop?"

"Yeah. Bastards."

"Smitty, what are you going to do about this?"

"Hell, I don't know." He leaned back in his chair and rubbed his face again.

"This Max or whoever they work for will probably send someone else if he's convinced you know something. I'd guess more men, and they won't waste as much time bantering."

"I feel bad asking, but . . . can you stick around?"

Tyler already blew being just a mechanic. Might as well see this through. Lexi always wanted him to do the right thing. She would understand. "I can," he said, "but I think we're going to need to find Jake before these assholes do."

"Can you do it?"

He was better at storming buildings and shooting people. Finding a former soldier in the wind to protect the man and his secrets would be stretching the skill set. Still, Smitty and Jake needed his help. "I'll see what I can do," Tyler said.

6

Once Jake realized no one followed him from the hotel, he allowed himself to relax a little. Despite the summer heat, he wore a lightweight hoodie and kept his head covered. An Orioles cap and sunglasses helped hide the rest of his face. It all earned him a few funny looks, but he ignored them.

After about twenty minutes of walking the streets in a haphazard pattern, Jake came upon the Central Diner. His stomach immediately rumbled. After subsisting on protein bars and packaged food for so long, he wanted a real meal. Jake checked around and saw no one to give him cause for alarm. He crossed the road and walked inside.

The restaurant was small, though the owners would probably prefer to call it cozy. With the breakfast rush long over and lunch not quite here yet, about half the chairs and booths sat empty. Jake slid into a booth, careful to sit facing the door. A middle-aged waitress approached, and he ordered coffee.

When she dropped off his hot beverage, Jake went with two fried eggs, toast, bacon, and fruit. Might as well live it up a little. He didn't know when he'd get another chance to sit and indulge even if for a few minutes. At some point, he needed to get out of Maryland and put some distance between himself and his pursuers. How to do this without access to most of his resources was the challenge. Jake considered calling some friends and asking for favors.

Whatever he needed to do to get away.

The price of principles, he thought, and not for the first time, he wondered if doing the right thing was worth all the trouble. His answer came in the form of a glorious plate of greasy breakfast food. Jake thanked the waitress and dove in. The eggs were cooked just right, the bacon came out crispy, and even the toast held the right amount of butter. Jake wolfed down the food faster than he expected. He nursed his coffee. When the waitress came to take his plate, he asked for a refill.

Then, he saw the SUV pull in.

The hairs on his arm stood up. They were common enough vehicles as a class these days. No one bought sedans anymore. Still, the vehicle was a dark late-model Yukon, exactly the kind his pursuers would drive. Favored by governments across the country. The windows were just dark enough to prevent anyone from seeing inside.

Jake's pulse increased. He fumbled out his wallet, threw enough cash down to cover his meal plus a tip, and stood. Going out the front door wasn't an option. The small diner featured no other visible exit, but there had to be one in the kitchen. Jake walked down the hallway toward the restrooms and turned into the kitchen. He got a few more funny looks, but he saw the door at the back.

One of the cooks told him he wasn't supposed to be here. Jake ignored him. He pushed the door open, strode into the alley, and was on the run again.

~

BOBBY HAD LOOKED BETTER, Rick Rust realized. Still, considering he recently took a wrench to the mug, he looked pretty good. A large bruise dominated the left side of his face. The doctor at the urgent care place said Bobby had a fractured cheekbone and a concussion. There wasn't much they could do for either except have him stay in a hospital for observation. With some prodding from Rick, Bobby declined, and after a few hours, he sounded more coherent but his eyes still looked a little foggy.

They would both need to be coherent. Their boss summoned them to the site near the airport. Sally, the pretty daytime receptionist, didn't work evenings, and the office looked stark and bleak like anyone barely spent time here. Even her desk was mostly bare. A single door was behind her workstation.

It opened a moment later. A voice told them to come in. Bobby went first and had a little trouble moving in a straight line. He got it sorted out after a few seconds and then he and Rick walked into the office and slouched into chairs before the desk. A familiar man of about forty stared back at them.

Rick looked around the room. Whoever owned the place had inexpensive tastes. The desk was a plain, medium brown, matching the single, mostly-empty bookcase. A few stacks of paper covered the top, alone save for an old clock. The desk, three chairs, and the bookcase were the only furniture in the room. The walls were covered in wood paneling looking straight out of the 'seventies.

"Talk to me, gentlemen," the man sitting across from them said. "What the hell happened?"

"You told us before you ain't the boss," Rick said.

"No, I'm not. When you screw up like this, you don't get to talk to the man. You can call me Max."

"We want to see the boss."

"He doesn't deal with losers," Max said.

"Hey, we're no losers! What the hell were we supposed to do?"

"You were supposed to locate the kid."

"We tried," Bobby said. It was about time he joined the conversation. "We did. It started off good. The old man knows something. I think we coulda gotten him to talk."

"Yet here we are discussing his lack of cooperation," Max said.

Bobby waved a large hand. "Whatever. Me and Rick cuffed the old man around a bit. Then, there was . . . another guy."

"Another guy?" Max turned to Rick. "He looks like his brains are scrambled. What's he saying?"

"Bobby's a little foggy," Rick said, "but he's right. The old man had someone else there."

"So what?" Max said. "He probably needed a new mechanic with his son missing."

Rick shook his head. "This guy ain't just a mechanic," he said. "He threw a wrench and damn near took Bobby's head off. Dropped him like he'd been shot. Next thing I know, he's on me before I could get my gun. I saw his eyes." Rick paused and shuddered. "He has a killer's eyes."

Max steepled his fingers under his chin and sat in silence for a moment. Then, he said, "Describe this man."

Rick shrugged. "Not too tall . . . five-ten, I guess. Average build but pretty solid. He's older than us. Maybe late forties or fifty?"

"White?" Max asked. Rick nodded. Max took his phone out of his pocket. Rick and Bobby sat quietly while he tapped on the screen. A minute later, he turned the screen around. "Is this him?"

Rick shook his head. "No. The eyes are too light."

"They were dark?"

"Yeah."

"Like . . . black?"

"Pretty much," Rick said. He tried not to think about the stare.

Max tapped on his phone some more. He swiped a few times, then turned the device around. "Age him up a few years."

Rick focused on the photo, and the eyes grabbed him right away. A chill crawled down his back. The picture must have been several years old. The man in it wore an army uniform with warrant officer insignia. His head moved up and down. "It's him." Max frowned and put the mobile away. "Who is he?"

"A problem."

"The kind me and Bobby get to solve?"

"You had a chance already," Max said.

"You know this guy," Bobby said. "Tell us about him."

"He serve with you guys?" Rick added.

"Yeah," Max said. "We were in the same special ops unit for a while."

"What happened?"

Max took a few seconds to answer. "You know how the colonel ended up in hot water?"

"Yeah."

"This son of a bitch is the reason."

"Jesus," Rick said. "You think he knows what the kid knows?"

Max shook his head. "They didn't really overlap."

No one said anything for at least a minute. Bobby broke the silence. "What are we gonna do about him?"

"If he continues to be a problem," Max said, "we'll kill him."

7

I t was after closing time, but Tyler wanted to finish the car. Following earlier events, Smitty stayed out of the shop, confining himself to his desk. He looked to be in a haze when Tyler tried to talk to him. Rather than deal with his frazzled boss, Tyler found the list of vehicles waiting to be serviced. He wrapped up the day by buffing out a dent on a classic Mustang. Body work had never been his strong suit, but the sheet metal looked unmarred, and no signs of the prior damage would remain once the paint dried.

"Why don't you call it a night, Tyler?" Smitty said from the door to the work bays.

"Just finishing this one car."

"You certainly had a productive day."

"You don't pay me to stand around," Tyler said.

Smitty grabbed a nearby task chair and lowered himself onto it. "I also don't pay you to deal with hostile intruders."

Tyler wiped his hands on a rag. "Taking out the trash is part of the job."

Smitty smiled, though Tyler didn't see any humor in the older man's eyes. "You really think you can find my boy?"

"Like I said, it's not my specialty." Tyler found another chair, wheeled it near Smitty, and sat. "I'd be a better fit if you needed me to kick in doors and shoot people . . . but I'll try."

"Why?"

"You and Jake are in a bad way." Tyler shrugged. "I won't say I know your son. It took me a minute to remember talking to him. If he's in trouble, though, I'd like to see what I can do."

"He make an impression on you?" Smitty asked.

Tyler recalled the encounter. He was about to deploy overseas with special operations again. They would hunt the Taliban. Jake was young, newly promoted to corporal, and eager to fight the nation's battles. He wanted to move into special ops, and Tyler encouraged him with some practical advice and pointers. He even gave him a name. It seemed like a good idea at the time, though he regretted it now.

What if I never told Jake to look up Leo Braxton? Tyler thought. He realized Smitty asked him a question. "He did."

"Jake was a good soldier."

"Smitty, if I'm going to look for him, I need to know what happened. Who he's running from would be a good place to start."

Smitty slapped his hands on his knees. "You want a beer?"

"We're off the clock, right?" Tyler asked.

"Yeah."

"Sure, I'd love one."

"Me, too." Smitty walked to an old refrigerator in the corner of the bay and opened the door. He pulled out two longneck bottles and carried them to where the two men sat. Before handing one to Tyler, Smitty used an opener on his keychain to pop the tops.

Tyler accepted the bottle with a nod. "Thanks." He took a long pull of it. It was a Belgian beer he'd never heard of. Tyler preferred whiskey, Scotch, and American lager. This brew had a light crisp flavor to it, and drinking it felt good after a long day in the shop.

"Where were we?" Smitty said.

"You were going to tell me who Jake's hiding from."

Silence served as Smitty's reply for a moment. He took a few drinks of beer as if it really were liquid courage. When the bottle was mostly empty, he said, "He's never come out and told me. For my safety, he says . . . but I know."

"You think it's some of the guys from special ops," Tyler said.

"Yeah. Why else would he refuse to tell me?"

All manners of questions sprang to Tyler's mind. He'd mentioned Braxton and the unit to Jake, but he didn't know who the younger soldier served under. A Braxton connection made sense. The man was dirty. Tyler hated the fact it took him so many years to realize it. In the end, the former colonel got what he deserved, but he racked up a lot of collateral damage along the way. Tyler suspected this now included Jake. Rather than bring up his former commanding officer directly, Tyler tried an indirect approach. "Do you know what he did overseas?"

"A little," Smitty said. He stared at the beer bottle when he talked. "He couldn't tell me most of it, of course. I understood."

"Where was he deployed?"

"Afghanistan."

"Did his mission involve the Taliban?"

Smitty nodded. "He didn't tell me much about it, but he did say he was hunting those bastards."

"None of this seems unusual," Tyler said. "I went over there a bunch of times and killed a lot of Taliban soldiers. I'm not in hiding."

"Something changed," Smitty said after a moment. "It wasn't long into his last tour." The older man lapsed into silence again.

"Do you know anything about what happened?"

"He mentioned they were looking for something. I don't know what it was . . . Jake never gave me those details. I figured it had something to do with the Taliban, though, and it must've been valuable."

Now it was Tyler's turn to sip his beer and contemplate. The timeline worked. After Tyler left the unit, Braxton remained overseas with most of the same men. Maybe he even had a new recruit in eager Corporal Jake Smith. Within a few months, Braxton's career unraveled, and he landed in Leavenworth where he'd remain for many years to come. He knew a lot of secrets, however. Tyler never made the list of his personal favorites. He missed out on a lot of conversations, even though he heard the rumors. "I think Jake could be in real trouble."

"I was hoping you'd tell me something else."

"I wish I could," Tyler said. He played it close to the vest with his boss. Jake had been careful not to drop Braxton's name. It was probably a good call, so Tyler respected the decision. "I can't say I know for certain what he's involved in, but based on the two assholes who paid us a visit earlier, I'd guess his old unit is pissed at him—and you, by extension."

"What could he have done?" Smitty said. "Jake's a good kid. He wouldn't be involved in anything illegal."

"I suspect his good nature is part of his problem." Tyler didn't offer any further explanation, and Smitty didn't ask for clarification.

"You think you can find him? Or at least get him out from under with these guys?"

Tyler's dream of working as a mechanic was gone. His old life maintained its hooks in him no matter how much he tried to distance himself from it. How would he explain this to Lexi? She'd been after him to quit Patriot Security since before she moved in. After a couple short months of freedom, Tyler got sucked right back in. He couldn't walk away from Jake, however, especially if he hid from Leo Braxton's men. Lexi would just have to understand. "I'm pretty sure I could find him."

"Can you get him off their radar?" Smitty asked.

"Maybe, but it'll probably get bloody."

"I don't want to put you in a bad spot, Tyler. Asking for help makes me feel like a heel, but he's my boy. I know you said you didn't want to kill anyone again."

Tyler shrugged. "Some people have it coming."

KENT MAXWELL STARED at the image on his screen. He'd hoped never to see John Tyler again. The end of their lucrative special forces platoon had been entirely his fault. Here he was again sticking his nose and his principles in something which didn't concern him. Maxwell couldn't allow Tyler to threaten the business. The nascent company worked its first few contracts, and getting it to this point proved hard enough.

He debated telling Braxton. The man would probably want to know. He was probably the only man in America who hated Tyler more than Maxwell did. The boss had enough on his plate with the company up and running, however. Maxwell would handle the Tyler situation. Personally if he needed to, but they employed enough men who should be able to deal with him.

Maxwell perused Tyler's army file. He retired as a Chief Warrant Officer 3. He listed a Baltimore address, and Maxwell confirmed he still lived there. Tyler would be fifty now, a decade older than Maxwell and twice the age of some of their operatives. Putting a middle-aged man down wouldn't be difficult. Rick Rust and Bobby didn't expect to encounter resistance when they went to Smitty's shop to cuff the old man around. They'd be prepared next time, and Maxwell knew they'd want another crack at Tyler.

He drafted an email to every recipient in the company and attached Tyler's picture.

This man is an enemy of our operation. If you remember serving with him, you're already aware. If you think the name is familiar, it probably is—John Tyler is the man who ruined Leo Braxton's career and took the rest of us down with him.

He's recently come up in one of our domestic operations. For now, I don't want anyone to seek him out. I'm working on a plan to deal with him once and for all. Once he's greenlit, he'll no longer be a problem.

Maxwell sent the message. He figured the two who failed would want the first crack at killing Tyler, and he planned to offer it to them.

8

The next morning, Tyler woke up early as usual. He slipped on a pair of athletic shorts, an old T-shirt, and his running shoes, and he ventured outside. Humidity hung in the air already. Tyler walked a couple blocks to warm up before starting his run. In his last fitness test with Patriot Security, Tyler's two-mile time matched what he did at age forty in the army. He'd never been especially fast, which helped, but he also worked hard to maintain his fitness as he turned fifty.

About three miles later, Tyler returned home and picked up the morning paper. After a shower, he walked downstairs and made a pot of coffee. While he ate a bowl of yogurt and perused the local section, Lexi joined him in the kitchen. "Morning, Dad," she mumbled in a sleepy haze on her way to the freshly-brewed java.

"You're up early."

Lexi sat at the small table a moment later. "I don't want to sleep the summer away. Too many bad habits, especially once I have to go to class."

"It's a couple months off," Tyler said. "You're eighteen. You're supposed to sleep until noon."

She grinned. "Maybe tomorrow, I'll try for nine. What are you up to today? Going back to the shop?"

Tyler shook his head. "No. I'm . . . looking into something for Smitty. He's the owner."

A stern look quickly replaced the mirth on Lexi's face. "Dad . . . what did you get yourself into?"

"Nothing." Tyler sipped some coffee, which had grown lukewarm while he ate and chatted. "His son is having a problem, and he asked me if I could help."

"Why do I think there's more to it than that?"

Tyler stood and added a fresh jolt of hot caffeine to his mug. "Maybe it's my knack for simple storytelling."

Lexi crossed her arms under her chest. "Is someone Smitty knows in trouble?"

"Yes."

"Are you going to break out your Patriot laptop?"

"Yes," Tyler said.

"You're going to need my help, then."

"Probably."

"Fine," Lexi said. "I want to know what's going on."

"Let's do a little research first. This could end up being easy."

"OK. I want a little breakfast. I'll join you in a few minutes."

In his office, Tyler took out the laptop Patriot Security issued to all its field agents. It was one of those rugged models you could drop off a dresser and kick around, and it would still work. When Tyler quit the company, he figured he would need to return it. Danny was the type who would make a show of demanding it. However, Cliff, the more silent of the two partners, told him to keep it. They'd enjoyed a good chat about Danny's management style—or lack thereof—and Tyler hoped some changes would be coming to the company.

For now, he was glad to have the computer. He only used it when he needed its capabilities. Tyler never became fluent with technology. He could do most of the basics, but complex tasks eluded him, and he had no idea how the blasted machines did what they did. Especially this laptop, which ran something called Linux and provided intimate details of people with a few mouse clicks.

Tyler logged in and refamiliarized himself with the home screen. It looked and operated sort of like Windows. He brought up the *Target Details* app, keyed in Jake's information, and waited. A few seconds later, the program assembled a dossier. If Jake really were a target, there would be plenty of information here to find him or to use against him. Tyler started with the basics.

Jake rented a studio apartment in the Rosedale area of Baltimore County. He worked for his father part-time, put in an occasional shift at the garage on Fort Meade, and served as an army reservist. Jake earned promotions to sergeant first class almost two years ago after first cycling into special operations as a corporal, then deploying for a year to Afghanistan before returning to his regular post. It told Tyler Jake's immediate superiors liked the soldier's performance enough for rapid promotion. Tyler found little other information on this period of his service history which meant much of it was classified.

Leo Braxton's career would have come to its abrupt and fitting end during Jake's time in Afghanistan . . . about two-thirds of the way into it if Tyler did his math correctly. It meant Jake served under the disgraced former colonel for about eight months. If he were now on the run from men formerly under Braxton's command, what did Jake learn or do in those eight months to put him on the hit list?

Tyler knew he wouldn't learn those answers today. He'd probably need to find Jake to hear the truth. Lexi walked into the office, grabbed the second chair, and sat next to Tyler. "This is the guy you're trying to find?" Tyler nodded. "What did he do?"

"Part of the mystery," Tyler said. "The answer's almost certainly classified."

Lexi pointed to a tab on the screen. "This thing shows you his social media?"

"Yeah. A couple red team guys developed it. I don't understand everything it does."

"You want me to look it over?"

Tyler handed her the laptop. "You know those sites a lot better than I do."

"They're not complicated, Dad."

"Is MySpace still around?"

Lexi rolled her eyes and smiled. Tyler watched her click onto the program's social media tab. Profiles for Facebook, Twitter, and Instagram popped up on the screen. Tyler was familiar with those, at least. Things like Snapchat and Pinterest always threw him for a loop. Lexi perused the data, focusing on the friends and close acquaintances the app identified. Tyler couldn't wrap his head around the concept of a friend being someone you never met.

"I think I found a few people," Lexi said.

"These are his friends?"

"Your program picked them as close ones, yeah."

"Good," Tyler said. "I have a place to start." He reached for the laptop.

Lexi held onto it. "Now you're going to tell me what's going on."

~

TYLER READ the resolve in his daughter's eyes. She was at least as much his child as Rachel's. Trying to take the device from her would be futile. Even if he got it away, Lexi would be pissed, and it would damage their relationship. She deserved an explanation, and Tyler debated how much to tell her. "I'm waiting," she prompted.

"All right. Smitty's son is in trouble."

"What kind of trouble?"

"I'm still figuring all the details out," Tyler said. "He was in the army. I met him briefly years ago . . . probably about a decade. He wanted to go into special ops, and I encouraged him. Smitty thinks he's on the run from some of the guys he used to serve with."

"Goddamn, Dad." Lexi handed him the laptop. "Why would they be after him?"

"I don't know. By the time he would have made the leap, I'd already gone back to finishing my time as a mechanic and teacher."

"But you feel responsible." It wasn't a question. Tyler nodded. "You didn't get him in trouble, Dad. Maybe he did something awful."

"Maybe," Tyler said, though he didn't believe it. "He seemed like a good kid, though. His immediate superiors liked him well enough, too. I think he got caught up in something too big for him."

"Seems like a long time," Lexi said. "If he landed in trouble almost ten years ago, why would people go after him now?"

"I don't know."

"Shouldn't you?"

"I'm working on it," Tyler said. "I just found all this out. Smitty didn't have a detailed feel of the case to give me. He's just worried about his son." Tyler pointed at the screen. "Can you tell me what all this means?"

"I don't know the ins and outs of how your app works, either," Lexi said. "It scours social media. I saw it scraping posts and photos. It makes some calculations about who people's close friends are based on what it finds."

"I guess these would be the folks to start with." Tyler perused the names, none of which were familiar to him. Based on the information displayed, Jake's identified contacts never served in the military.

"What are you going to do?"

"For now, I want to know where Jake went," Tyler said. He picked up a small notebook and jotted down the relevant details for the people the app selected.

"You could print the screen, you know," Lexi said, the corner of her mouth turned up in amusement.

"You spend twenty-four years in the army, and you forget how to write. I need the practice."

"Dad." Lexi stared at Tyler. "I still want to know what you're going to do. These guys could tell you anything. What if one of them knows where Jake is?"

"It's a good question." Tyler closed the laptop and set it aside. "I'm not sure. This isn't an investigation, and I'm probably not qualified to be doing whatever I'm doing. If someone tells me where Jake is, I'll check it out."

"Be careful. I know you feel responsible in some way, but still. I don't want my only parent to be a jailbird."

"You could go live with your grandfather."

Lexi wrinkled her nose. "Aren't you supposed to meet him for lunch today?"

"Shit," Tyler said. "I already postponed on him once. I guess I need to suck it up and go."

"He'll probably understand."

Tyler tore off the notebook paper and slipped it into his pocket. "Probably . . . but he wouldn't let me live it down for a month. Besides, every now and then the old man says something useful."

"That's funny," Lexi said. "I feel the same way about you."

All Tyler could do was smile.

9

Tyler's father moved into a retirement community when he turned seventy-five a couple months ago. He didn't need the extra support many residents did, but the place was nice, and his dad had the money. Tyler was supposed to help him move and didn't as he was busy with his last case for Patriot Security. Ever since, his father seemed salty when they talked. Bailing on lunch today would only make it worse.

His father called Tyler while he was en route. "You're coming this time, right?"

"Nice to talk to you, too, Dad."

"Yeah, yeah. You blowing me off again?"

"I'm headed your way now. Am I meeting you at your apartment?"

"Sure. We'll just stay here. They opened the restaurant again. Food is good. And you'll finally get to see the place."

It was a minor guilt trip, but they counted, too. "All right. See you soon."

The 442 lapped up the miles from Baltimore to Bel Air, the seat of Harford County. Farmland surrounded pockets of civilization, and Bel Air formed one of the largest—and the most expensive—such pocket. Zeke Tyler sold his house in Pasadena without telling anyone. The old man remained sharp, so Tyler couldn't question his mental fitness. Maybe his father finally got lonely. If so, it took him long enough.

Tyler arrived at the retirement community a few minutes early. Zeke would be pleased. Being on time equaled being late in his world, something Tyler never understood. Evergreen Acres comprised five identical apartment buildings, a sixth for administration and medical facilities, and a few smaller places for activities, including a dining hall. Judging by signage, only the eatery remained open. Every time Tyler heard something called a dining hall, it conjured images of an army mess. He hoped this one would be better. Being worse would prove difficult.

Tyler's father lived in the outermost building, farthest away from the dining hall and the auxiliary structures. It suited him. The old man was still active. Leave the closer residences for people who couldn't walk as far or as well. Why his dad decided such a facility was the way to go when he needed—or wanted—very little assistance remained a mystery.

The plain brown door to apartment 417 boasted of only a plain brass knocker. No other decorations. Other residents had flowers on the door, or trinkets on little tables nearby. Not Zeke Tyler. Spartan all the way. If Tyler's dad could get away with stringing only a handful of lights and hang one ball on the Christmas tree, he'd be happy. A Santa in the lawn was a bridge too far.

Tyler rapped the knocker onto the door four times. Never five. Zeke answered quickly. No doubt he'd been waiting in the small foyer, watching the second hand advance on his watch. "Dad," Tyler said.

"You're early," he said.

"I figured you'd appreciate the change." Zeke shrank a little over the years, now standing an inch shorter than Tyler at five-nine. He never gained weight in his life. Tyler would be surprised if he'd added five pounds since retiring from the navy some eighteen years prior. Other than silver hair, wire-rimmed glasses, and a slight stoop in his posture, no one would guess Zeke for seventy-five. For his part, he tried not to act his age.

They walked across the campus. Zeke had an anecdote ready for every building. One had ants in the spring. A bunch of pretty women lived in another one. A third saw more residents die than any other, and Zeke's voice went from chipper to somber as he talked about it. They passed a few people along the way, all of whom greeted Zeke as Mister Tyler.

The quarter-full dining hall saw more of the same. Tyler's father may as well have been a celebrity. People older and younger knew who he was and called out to him by name. He was like Norm on *Cheers*. Even the staff treated him like a visiting monarch, exchanging greetings and fully extended fist bumps. Now, Tyler understood why his dad came here. Living by himself, he lacked an audience. Here, he could still be Chief Tyler, but the old, beloved version rather than the naval taskmaster. How many men reinvented themselves in their seventies? Hell, Tyler couldn't even do it at fifty.

They sat at a table for two. Tyler noticed all the seating options were about six feet apart, which reduced the usable capacity of the hall below half. Evergreen Acres decorated the place like a generic American restaurant. Maroon tablecloths. White plates. Square chandeliers overhead. If the hall hadn't been the eatery in a retirement community, it could have occupied a spot in a strip mall.

"You pay to eat here?" Tyler said.

Zeke shook his head. "Part of the monthly dues. You get to bring a few guests."

A waiter who could have been dressed for a shift at Chili's dropped off two menus. Tyler looked it over. Simple and classic

American fare with a few staples borrowed from other countries. The waiter returned a minute later. Zeke ordered prime rib with mashed potatoes. Tyler opted for a burger and fries. It was hard to go wrong with the classics.

"What are you up to?" Zeke asked when the server left.

"I just took a job as a classic car mechanic."

"Really? You turning over a new leaf or something?"

Tyler said, "I'm trying to. Or I was at least."

"What do you mean?" his father said.

He relayed the story about Jake being gone and the two goons coming in to rough Smitty up. "I tried to be a mechanic. Even got a few days out of it, but I couldn't stand there while they beat up Smitty. A couple of assholes like those could've killed him."

"Listen to me," Zeke said. "I know I always gave you shit for choosing the army over the navy." This marked the first time he'd acknowledged it. "Truth is, I admire anyone who serves their country, and you did it better than most."

"Thanks, Dad, but what's your point?"

"My point is you're no goddamn mechanic."

"Sure I am," Tyler said. "It was my original MOS."

"Only because killer isn't an MOS. The army knew what you were. Sure, you were good at fixing Jeeps, Hummers, and all those. They knew you'd be better at shooting terrorists, though. It's who you are."

"And a man's gotta be who he is," said Tyler, repeating a maxim he heard his father use many times over the years.

Zeke smiled. He didn't do it often. "You remembered."

"You said it often enough."

"Had to, as stubborn as you were."

Tyler chuckled. He didn't doubt he was stubborn, and he knew he inherited it from the man across the table. "So I should give up being a mechanic?"

The waiter dropped off their food before his father could

respond. After the server walked away, they ate in silence for a few minutes. Then Zeke said, "Do what you want. You're going to, anyway. I just don't want you to get your head wrapped up in being something you're not."

"There aren't many job openings for killer, Dad."

"I know. Look, fix cars all you want. Don't forget the other things you're good at. Act decisively when you feel you need to, like when those two shitheads started cuffing your boss around. You know they'll probably come back, right?"

Tyler nodded. "I gave one of their guns to Smitty."

Zeke waved his hand. "Smitty ain't gonna shoot anybody. If you're there when they come back, what are you gonna do?"

After a bite of his burger, Tyler said, "Act decisively."

Zeke spread his hands. "There you go."

They went back to eating. Tyler watched his father cut his prime rib. He trimmed the fat like a surgeon making an incision near an artery. Then, he cut the meat in precise rows, slicing each piece to be as close to the same size as possible. Other people just took a knife and fork to their meat. Zeke Tyler made it into an operating room theater.

"I'm working on finding Jake," Tyler said when they had eaten most of their food.

"Any leads?"

"Found a couple of his friends. They're on my agenda after I leave here."

"You packing?" Zeke said.

Tyler rolled his eyes. "Really, Dad? If guns resisted water better, I'd carry in the shower."

"That's my boy," his dad said.

～

IN HER OFFICE at the Pentagon, Sara Morrison performed a periodic review of active contracts. Her predecessor always delegated such tasks to his deputy—her at the time—but Sara preferred doing it herself. Her title as the Assistant Secretary of Defense for Special Operations and Low-Intensity Conflict meant she didn't need to spend time reviewing line items. Sara felt too many people punted routine matters to their seconds-in-command. She didn't mind working long hours. Once you broke into the boys' club, you needed to stay there.

As she usually did, Sara worked alphabetically. Specifically, she focused on the country of conflict. Afghanistan topped the list and featured several active operations outside the normal military channels. The United States' interest in curbing terrorism and neutering the influence of the Taliban took many forms. Sara and her team supported most of the ones the American public heard little or nothing about.

A bit over an hour into her review, she came across the name of a new organization: Hexagon Security. Businesses came into the space with some regularity. The story was usually the same: a few retired military guys missed the life and formed an LLC. Sara couldn't complain—these private military companies helped the country with important and sometimes unsavory work. Considering what they did and where they did it, however, someone needed to vet them well.

It was another area in which Sara rarely delegated.

She realized Hexagon must have been one of the rare times she did. The company's file showed it to be a nascent business still in its first year of operation. Despite being new, Hexagon earned an important—and potentially lucrative—contract in Afghanistan. They went there to subvert and dismantle the Taliban's intelligence network. Sara's deputy Arthur Bell signed off on the organization's background work and approved them getting the job. She kept reading the file and came to the people in charge: co-founders Victor White and Kent Maxwell.

Neither hailed from an intelligence background, which made their selection for the contract unusual. Something else nagged at her. Maxwell's name was familiar. She'd heard it before, and she didn't think it came up in a good context. Sara hit the intercom button on her phone, and her assistant Ellen answered a moment later. "Yes, Miss Morrison?"

"I need a service file on someone . . . Kent Maxwell. I think he was army."

"I'll get right on it."

"Thanks, Ellen." Sara stared at the screen. Hexagon Security. Kent Maxwell. She couldn't help feeling he and his company were the wrong choices for the work. The file would tell her for certain. If her suspicions were correct, she'd need to have a long talk with Arthur Bell and then rescind the contract he approved.

10

Tyler left about a half-hour later. It was a good visit with the old man. They didn't always get along over the years, and Tyler being deployed halfway around the world only added strain to the relationship. Maybe they could interact now like most elderly fathers and middle-aged sons. Tyler chuckled to himself at thinking of Zeke as elderly. By age, he was, but by fitness, mental sharpness, and skills like shooting a gun, he could pass as Tyler's older brother.

While still in the parking lot, Tyler checked his notes. He wanted to look into two contacts his laptop identified as Jake's close friends. First, he tried Mike Watson. No answer on his home number or cell. Next, Tyler called Sam Fisher, who answered his landline. Tyler hung up right away. The info he jotted down told him Fisher found himself in legal trouble several times. If Jake went to him, he probably received bad advice, which could have compounded his situation and led to him being on the run. Tyler plotted a course to the house on his GPS and drove off.

The navigation system guided him to a neighborhood in Perry Hall. It was in the county and only a couple miles from

Smitty's shop. Close enough for Jake to pop over there before or after work and get his head filled with a bunch of bullshit. Tyler parked in a vistor's spot. Fisher owned an end unit. All the houses looked more or less the same. A couple had ugly dormer windows on their top floors, and a smattering of brick fronts broke up the white siding monotony, but these homes obviously got punched out of the same cookie cutter. Even though townhouses were a more modern take on Baltimore rowhouses, Tyler preferred the original. They held much more character.

Lights were on upstairs and downstairs in Fisher's house. From the information Tyler reviewed, he lived alone. Fisher's car, a late-model BMW 3-series coupe, sat in its assigned spot. Tyler was about to get out of the car when his phone rang. He glanced at the number. What the hell did Danny want? "I don't work for you anymore."

"You have my property." Danny's voice hadn't changed. Still too much of a whiny undertone to command respect. Tyler wondered if it contributed to his former boss being terminal at Specialist E-4.

"What are you talking about?"

"The laptop, Tyler. I know you turned it on."

"I did," Tyler said. "There was a competition for biggest asshole boss. I wanted to make sure someone nominated you."

Danny sighed into the phone. He did it often even when Tyler worked there. Pushing the man's buttons was one of the few things Tyler liked about interacting with Danny. "You should return it."

"Talk to Cliff. He said I could keep it."

"He didn't tell me."

"Sorry," Tyler said. "You needed to at least make corporal to attend the meeting."

"I don't need to listen to your cheap shots anymore." If Danny weren't so sensitive about his rank, Tyler wouldn't needle him so much about it. The reality was he'd never been a good soldier, and the army recognized the fact before he moved up too far. They didn't always get it right, but they did in his case. Seeing the writing on the wall, Danny didn't re-enlist. Everyone who worked for him at Patriot outranked him in their active duty days, and it always bothered him.

"Yet you still are." Tyler watched a light wink out on the second level of Fisher's house. "You want the laptop back?"

"I do," Danny said. "I don't care what Cliff told you."

"You know where I live. Come and take it." Tyler broke the connection. He pictured Danny cursing and slamming his phone down. He wouldn't show up. His type never did.

Despite the pleasant thought of Danny fuming in his office, the conversation left Tyler on edge. He wanted to cool off before confronting Sam Fisher. Tyler shifted in the 442's seat and kept an eye on the house.

JAKE VERIFIED his setup at the new hotel. The two cameras were charged and rolling. The footage—which consisted of an empty parking lot at the moment—displayed in the app. No new calls or texts to his burner. For now at least, things were good.

His time lying low wore on Jake. The face in the mirror looked a little more thin and drawn, and the unkempt beard made him appear homeless. If his appearance gave his pursuers pause, he would accept the reproachful stares of people he encountered on the streets. Jake checked his M11 pistol, found everything to be in order, and set it beside himself on the bed. He stretched out and tried to relax.

This is what I get for trying to do the right thing, he thought not for the first time. When he heard about the formation of Hexagon a few months ago, he'd been happy for his former special operations colleagues. When he learned what they were going back to Afghanistan to do, he felt horrified. Still, they were a new company, and contracts like the one they bid on went to businesses with proven track records.

Then, Maxwell told him they'd won.

Jake knew what he needed to do. He declined the offer. Unlike the rest of the guys, he was still in the reserves. He couldn't afford the hit to his reputation and the likely loss of freedom which would follow if someone discovered what the company was really up to. Jake couldn't believe they'd even won the contract, so he did the right thing and reported what he knew and suspected to the Pentagon.

Since then, his life had gone off the rails. Jake wanted to check on his father, but he also didn't want to risk putting anyone onto him. They'd know about the shop, of course, but why draw attention to his dad? He didn't know anything. Jake told him almost nothing about what happened overseas, and both men were happy with the arrangement.

He'd recently closed his eyes when his phone threw an alert. Jake checked the feed. A familiar dark SUV entered the lot. "Shit." Jake shot out of bed, threw on his shoes, and repacked his bag. He tucked the M11 into his waistband. The SUV drove to the other side of the building. Jake watched the video but didn't see anyone moving around. He opened his door as little as he could and grabbed the camera and mount. He'd try to come back later for the other one.

For now, he shut and locked the door and walked into the bathroom. The window didn't cooperate at first, but Jake got it open. He stuck his head out, looked in both directions, and then tossed his bag through. He climbed out after it. A quick check of his phone showed the SUV circling back. Jake slung the bag over his shoulder, hopped a short fence at the rear of the property, and was in the wind again.

MAXWELL REVIEWED the latest reports in his office. The door remained open only a crack. All the men knew to knock before coming in. When the door swung into the room, Maxwell looked up and prepared to chew out whoever violated protocol. His words died in his throat when Leo Braxton entered. "Something you want to tell me, Maxwell?"

"No, sir."

Braxton sat in the little-used guest chair. He was a fair bit older than Maxwell, probably in his mid-fifties, though he maintained his fitness. Only a head full of gray hair betrayed the man's age. Despite everything which transpired at the end of his tenure in the army, Braxton still carried himself like a colonel. "Are you sure?"

"Everything looks like it's going well overseas," Maxwell said. "The crew expects a breakthrough soon."

Braxton steepled his fingers under his chin. "Do I need to spell it out for you? When were you going to tell me some of our men encountered John Tyler?"

Maxwell stared ahead for a few seconds. He'd hoped his boss wouldn't find out. Tyler had been instrumental in everything coming apart the first time, and the company didn't need Braxton distracted by revenge—however justified it might be. "I figured you wouldn't want to be preoccupied."

"Do you think Tyler consumes my every waking thought?"

"If I were you?" Maxwell said. "After what he did, I doubt I could think of much else besides getting even."

"Good thing you're not me, then," Braxton said. "I knew Tyler lived in Maryland. I'd hoped our paths wouldn't cross, but it seems inevitable."

"Are you going to kill him?"

"Normally, I would say we have plenty of men on the payroll who could do it." Braxton frowned. "A couple have already seen Tyler is not someone to take lightly. We'll see what happens."

"You're going to handle him?" Maxwell said.

"Yes, Kent. If Tyler continues causing problems, I have a plan to deal with him."

11

After an hour, nothing happened in the house. With his head clearer, Tyler walked up the steps and knocked on the door. A few seconds later, a man answered. He was tall, probably about six-three, and paunchy. An unkempt mop of brown hair sat atop his head. His short sleeves revealed at least a dozen tattoos and arms showing he knew how to do bicep curls. Tyler noticed a tattoo peeking above the T-shirt onto Sam Fisher's neck. He fancied himself a tough guy. The ink, biceps, and attempted menacing stare confirmed it. "Who the hell are you?"

"I work with Jake Smith," Tyler said. "I hear he's a friend of yours."

"Yeah? Where from?"

"Around. I'd like to talk to you about him."

"What makes you think I got anything to say?"

"You don't seem to lack for words," Tyler said. "Jake's been gone a couple days. We're trying to find him."

"You a cop?" Fisher said. He narrowed his eyes, probably thinking it added more malice to his glare. It didn't. He looked like a squinting constipated man.

"I told you I work with Jake."

"Jake works with his old man," Fisher said. "Why don't you piss off?" He went to close the door. Tyler blocked it with his foot.

"I think we need to talk, Sam. Better for you if we just have a conversation."

"I said piss off!" Fisher thrust his arm out to push Tyler away, but it didn't work. Tyler leaned back, reducing the shove to a minor annoyance, moved his foot to the rear, grabbed Fisher's arm, and slammed the door on it. Fisher yelped, pulled his wounded wing back, and retreated into the house.

Tyler followed him. "I'm just here to talk," he said. "Don't make it worse."

They stood in a small entryway. Fisher withdrew onto a carpeted landing at the bottom of the stairs. "I'm a lot bigger than you, now," he snarled.

"You were a few seconds ago, too," Tyler said. "Didn't seem to help you much then."

Fisher launched a kick at Tyler's head. With his height advantage plus being on the steps, he didn't have to raise his leg much past his waist. But he didn't even try to defend himself when he did it. Tyler was never a fan of kicks; even with a good defense, he felt they often left him too exposed. Fisher made it easy. Tyler swayed to the side to avoid the kick and punched Fisher hard in the groin. He folded in half and almost tumbled down the steps.

Tyler grabbed him by the belt and rolled him into the living room. Fisher coughed and flopped onto his back. "Don't throw up on me, Sam," Tyler said. "This carpet is pretty nice. You don't want to ruin it."

Fisher rose to his knees. His face was bright red. "I should call the cops."

"Go ahead. I'm sure they'd love to talk to you. Maybe I can tell them some of the things you've been up to recently."

"Go to hell." Fisher dragged himself into a recliner. Tyler sat in the neighboring one. A matching sofa was nearby. The living room had a cohesive look, which made Tyler wonder if Fisher contributed anything to its design. He didn't seem the type to care about carpet colors, let alone getting everything to come together.

"Jake Smith."

"What about him?"

"He's been gone a while," Tyler said. "His dad is concerned."

Fisher let out a dry chuckle. His coloring returned to normal. "What makes you think I know where he is?" Fisher said.

"Because I looked at his friends," Tyler said. "You seem exactly the type to give him some bad advice." No reaction. "So what was it?"

"Nothing."

Tyler looked around. A large TV hung on the wall. A small bookcase sat in a corner. On the top shelf, a bookend separated three books from the rest.

Be a Day Trading Millionaire.

How to Short the Stock Market.

Day Trade Your Way to Millions!

"Day trading? Did you get Jake into your risky shit?"

"It works," Fisher said. "Jake wasn't interested, though. Said he didn't need money."

"He's probably right," Tyler said. "Where is he?"

"I don't know."

"Not good enough."

Before Tyler could get up, Fisher snatched a gun out of the table between them. He stood and pointed it at Tyler. It was a black Glock semiauto, a 9 MM or .380 by the size of its bore. Fisher, showing his ignorance, held it sideways. He stared at Tyler, who stared back. "Get out of my house," he said.

"Or what?"

"Or I'll shoot you."

Tyler laughed. "You think holding a pistol makes you a tough guy?"

"You think slamming my arm in a door makes *you* one?" Fisher said.

"I'm not scared of you. I'm not scared of the gun. What do you think it says about the combo of you *plus* the gun?" Fisher frowned. "Eight years in Afghanistan. Much bigger weapons got pointed at me by far worse people than you. And you think holding a pistol like an idiot is going to get me to run in terror? You little pissant. You can't even turn the safety off."

Fisher canted the weapon to check the smooth, unbroken slide, and Tyler sprang forward. He braced Fisher's forearm and got the gun away from him, and then whacked him in the head with it. Fisher crumpled to the floor. Tyler leveled the pistol at him, sights uppermost. "This is how you hold a gun. Glocks don't have safeties by the way."

"Don't shoot," Fisher said. He propped himself up on one elbow while he rubbed his head. Tyler popped the magazine, then ejected the cartridge from the chamber. He put both in his pocket and tossed the pistol—now an expensive paperweight— across the room. "Hey! Give me those."

"You're the one making so much money day trading," Tyler said. "Buy a new mag. Now, tell me where Jake is."

"He's switching locations. Last I heard, he was at the Downtown Arms near Greektown."

"You in contact with him?"

"He's going through burners, but yeah . . . we talk."

"I'll need the number," Tyler said.

"I don't know if I should—"

"Give me your damn phone, Sam." Fisher complied. Tyler found the contact and entered the information in his mobile. Jake moving from place to place made sense, especially given

the people pursuing him. Dodging them so far showed his skill
—and maybe a little bit of luck, too. It always helped to have
both. "Don't tell him about this little chat," Tyler said. "If this
number stops working, we're going to have another talk."

Fisher grunted. Tyler left.

JAKE DUCKED into a store selling tacky clothes. Most were Balti-
more-themed with the Orioles, Ravens, and the city's love for
crabs serving as popular designs. He picked a couple ugly T-
shirts, some new shorts, and a hat. Jake paid with his dwindling
reserve of cash. He needed it to last a while longer. Using something like a debit card would only give away his location.

Down the block, Jake slipped into a drugstore. He bought a
razor and shaving cream and added them to his rucksack. A
check of his surroundings showed no pursuers. Jake wormed
his way back to the hotel. The SUV was gone. He fetched his
second camera and left the way he came. Another place to stay
waited a half-mile away.

After checking into the motel and setting up a camera
outside his door, Jake worked on his appearance. Everyone
would be searching for him based on what he looked like. He
couldn't do much about his height and weight, but hair was an
easy fix. Jake applied the cream and used the razor to shave his
head bald. He wouldn't win any comparisons to Patrick Stewart,
but it should help eyes pass over him.

Jake ditched some old clothes in the motel's dumpster.
While outside, he capitalized on the lack of activity and rigged
his second camera. The app displayed both feeds. Jake sat on
the bed and let out a deep breath. Weariness hung over him all
the time. He'd never been a heavy sleeper, but this situation
made it much worse. If he rested for too long, nightmares about
Afghanistan and his pursuers dogged him.

"How much longer can I keep this up?" Jake asked the empty room. It offered no reply. He checked his phone. All clear. Might as well take advantage of the calm—the storm would return at some point. Jake lay flat and put his head on the mediocre pillow. Despite the middling quality of the bed, he was asleep within seconds.

Tyler curbed the 442 on a side street near the Downtown Arms Hotel. Considering most people thought downtown Baltimore comprised the Inner Harbor area, the stadiums, Fells Point, and maybe Federal Hill, the hotel was not aptly named. It sat miles away on Eastern Avenue just before Greektown.

Tyler entered the lobby, which was mostly a carpeted area to wait in front of the desk. A hallway on his right led to guest rooms. A door on the left opened to a paved walkway to the other side of the hotel. Three exits in close proximity. It would be easy for a small team to take this place down.

The woman staffing the desk looked tired, probably of working here as much from lack of sleep. She didn't smile when Tyler approached. He didn't take it personally. Few people smiled at him, anyway.

"I'm wondering if my friend is still staying here," he said.

"Name?" she said, popping a bubble in her gum. The sound of her chewing reminded Tyler of horses noshing from their feed bags.

"Here's his picture." He showed her a good picture of Jake on his phone. "Sometimes, he checks in under different names because he thinks he's funny."

She blew a new bubble and typed a few keystrokes. Tyler wondered how often the bubbles got tangled in her wild hair. "I seen him. He left a while ago, though."

Damn. "Did he happen to say where he was going?"

"He didn't check out," she said. "Just split at some point."

"Did you run into him at any point during his stay?" Tyler said. "Did he seem nervous?"

"Actually, yeah," she said. "Like he didn't want to give no one a close look."

Tyler figured many people staying here didn't want to be seen at the place. "He didn't come this way, then. Is there a way out of the rooms?"

"I guess he coulda squeezed out the bathroom window," the girl said while looking at her phone. "He insisted on the first floor."

Jake probably saw something out front to spook him. Probably a couple of goons like Rust and Bobby. "You have a gift shop?" Tyler said. The girl snickered. "Vending machines?"

She inclined her head to the main hotel corridor. "Down there."

Tyler bought a bottle of water and two bags of trail mix whose freshness he doubted. He got a paper bag from the girl at the desk and walked outside, pretending to be talking on his phone. His eyes swept the street. They soon landed on a gray SUV. Past the tinted windows, Tyler discerned two silhouettes inside.

He walked back to his car. Their position left them outside his vision. Tyler pulled forward until he could see the Yukon. He turned the engine off again and waited.

He wouldn't need to wait long. About a half-hour into his vigil, the gray SUV finally pulled away from the curb. Tyler made the turn and slipped into traffic three cars behind them. Despite the preponderance of crossovers on the roads, Tyler felt confident in his ability to follow the large GMC. He tailed it up Eastern Avenue to I-95 North. Shadowing these guys was easy. They didn't employ any countermeasures. Tyler still hung back, but he probably could have tailgated them the whole way without being noticed.

The SUV took the exit for the Baltimore Beltway headed toward Towson. Tyler stayed behind it. They continued a few miles before taking the ramp for Loch Raven Boulevard. The SUV drove through a traffic light which went yellow as they cleared the intersection. Tyler stomped on the gas. The Rocket V8 roared as the transmission dropped a gear, and the 442 powered past the signal as it flickered to red.

This part of Parkville featured apartments, houses, plus all kinds of shops and eateries. To say nothing of the network of side streets wide and narrow. Tyler followed the SUV directly now; he couldn't afford to lose them if they made a quick turn while he hung back three hundred feet.

A few minutes later, they turned into an apartment complex, parking in front of a building in the second group to the left off the main road. Tyler didn't press his luck. He went to the right and pulled into the first space he saw. He eyed the nearby street sign. Little Flower Terrace. The name struck Tyler as familiar. He took out his notes and frowned.

Jake's friend Mike Watson lived here, and Tyler doubted the guys in the SUV were making a social call.

12

T wo burly men got out of the Yukon and entered the building. They didn't seem the types to ask nicely. Mike Watson was about to be in the soup way over his head. Tyler took a deep breath. Helping Smitty deal with two goons in the shop was one thing. He wouldn't give up his son. Watson constituted an unknown. If he talked, the pair from the SUV would know Jake's location.

If he didn't talk, they'd probably beat him to death. Hell, they might do it for the sport. Tyler got out of the car, dashed across the complex's main road, and ran into Watson's building. His apartment was 3A. Tyler took the stairs two at a time. As he came around the corner to the last flight, he noticed one enforcer standing outside the open door to the unit in question. Inside, someone got punched and grunted in pain.

"Move along, pal," the big guy said when Tyler came up the steps. He stood about six-two, was built like a football player, and wore his blond hair in a buzz cut. Tyler put up his hands and pointed to the last door on the right. The guy shook his head. "Doing some maintenance work."

"Where are your tools, then?" Tyler asked.

The guy took a knife out of his coat. "How's this?"

"Looks pretty inefficient for most maintenance work."

The guy waved the blade at Tyler before lunging toward him. Tyler stepped to the side the instant he recognized the telegraphed attack. Knife fights needed to end quickly. One lucky nick of an artery, and it was all over. Untrained opponents were less skilled but also less predictable. Tyler grabbed his attacker's forearm with one hand and his fingers with the other.

He twisted. Something in the guy's wrist snapped. He managed a brief cry of pain before Tyler swatted the knife from his grip, then gave his foe a chop to the throat, staggering him. Tyler let go of the man's arm and slammed his head into the railing. His skull bounced off it with a satisfying *bong*, but the lights were still on. Tyler kicked the guy's head into the metal again, and it put him out.

The partner appeared in Watson's apartment door. Like his coworker, he was over six feet, but this man carried a lot more weight on his frame. He frowned at the sight of his fellow goon unconscious on the landing. "What the hell?"

"He started it," Tyler said with a shrug. "Be smarter and hit the road."

The new assailant didn't listen—they never did—and led with a couple of wild punches. They were long and slow, and Tyler dodged them easily. Here was a large fellow used to one punch ending a fight. By his fourth haymaker, the guy's breath resounded off the nearby walls and doors. Following another swing, Tyler waded in, striking the unsurprisingly soft solar plexus. The man's breath now came in a ragged gasp. Tyler walloped him twice in the face, then led him to the stairs and tossed him down. He bounced off the brick wall at the bottom and lay still.

"Mike Watson?" Tyler called from the doorway to apartment 3A. "Are you all right?"

"I'll live," a voice croaked from somewhere inside.

"I'm coming in," Tyler said. "Those two assholes won't bother you anymore."

Inside, a pair of dining room chairs lay toppled over, a few framed pictures lay in ruins of kindling and glass, and the living room coffee table had been knocked flat. Watson sat against the wall near his TV. Blood seeped from some cuts on his face, and he held his arms loosely around his torso. "Small comfort right now," he said. Watson was a wiry black man, a little taller than Tyler, and looked to be an age peer of Jake. A pair of glasses lay smashed beside him.

"I work for Jake's father," Tyler said. "We're trying to find him."

"Lots of people looking for Jake right now, it seems." Watson held his hand out, and Tyler pulled him upright. "Who the hell were they?"

"I'm not certain, but I'm pretty sure I know who they work for."

"Let me guess," Watson said, wiping a hand at his facial cuts. "Someone in the military?"

Tyler nodded. "Former, but yeah. You know what Jake did?"

"Not really. He told me some bad shit went down overseas. I know he told somebody, but I didn't press him too much about it."

"Probably for the best," Tyler said. He wondered who Jake unburdened himself to and if it contributed to his current dire circumstances. "You have anywhere you can go?"

He bobbed his head. "Got a brother down near DC."

Tyler frowned. "I'd avoid family. The men looking for Jake seem good at finding people."

"Fine," Watson said. "I'll get a hotel a little ways away, then."

"Good. Pay in cash."

They walked out together after Watson spent a few minutes packing a bag and shaking his head at the damage to his apartment, mostly the destroyed pictures. "I'll need to call the management company," he said.

At the top of the stairs, Tyler inclined his head toward the two goons—one still unconscious and the one down the stairs starting to shake off the cobwebs. "And an ambulance. I'd appreciate it if you'd leave me out of it, though."

Watson grimaced as he regarded the two men who'd been abusing him mere minutes before. "Sure, I'll think of something."

Tyler wished him good luck and walked down the stairs. The guy he'd tossed down worked himself onto all fours. As he moved past, Tyler kicked him hard in the head, bouncing his dome off the wall and sending him to dreamland again. Tyler patted the unconscious man down and found his wallet. The name didn't mean anything, but he carried a company ID for Hexagon Security. Tyler left the cash for Watson, who pocketed it as he walked by.

Once outside, Tyler got back into his car. He looked at his hands, clenched and unclenched his fists. It was amazing how easily he fell back into the old mindset. The old habits. *A man's got to be who he is.* "Dammit, Dad," Tyler muttered. He grounded his thoughts on the current situation. Today's assault showed Maxwell or his minions were upping the ante on finding Jake and didn't care about collateral damage.

Tyler fired up the 442. He needed to find Jake before another goon squad did.

~

SARA MORRISON CALLED her deputy Arther Bell. They were both working from home today. Each went into the office at the Pentagon two different days a week to deal with classified matters, but most of their duties could be done from their houses. Sara was surprised how much she liked dodging the hellish commute and working from her spare bedroom. It needed some work before it could be considered a proper office, but it would do for now.

Bell answered the video call request. As usual, he didn't turn on his video, so Sara kept hers dark, too. "How are you, Arthur?"

"I'm all right," he said in his deep voice.

"I wanted to ask you about Hexagon Security," Sara said. "It's a private military contractor you signed off on. You remember?"

"Hexagon . . ." Sara heard the telltale sign of Bell flipping through papers. She hoped he only took unclassified documents out of the building. "OK, yeah. I remember. What's going on?"

"Did you vet the executives?"

"Sure," Bell said.

"Victor White and Kent Maxwell?"

Bell paused a beat or two and said, "Those sound like the right names. Why?"

"They seemed familiar to me, so I did a little digging. Turns out both served with a man named Leo Braxton. Do you recognize the name?"

"Not offhand, no."

"Braxton was a colonel until he got busted for a couple war crimes in Afghanistan. One of the men in his unit reported him. Maxwell and White were his chief toadies."

"He's in jail, though," Bell said.

Sara sighed. "He *was.* The old boys club strikes again. Turns out they released him a few weeks ago . . . five years early."

"Wow. I didn't discover those details."

"Apparently not," Sara said. "Braxton's barred from having anything to do with the government besides paying his taxes. I want to be sure he's not involved with Hexagon."

"What do you want me to do?" Bell asked.

"I want you to look into it. Be thorough. If he *is* involved, we're canceling their contract right away." Bell didn't reply at first. "Arthur, you there?"

"I'm here. I'll get right on it."

"Good," Sara said. "Let me know as soon as you can as long as it's no later than the middle of next week." She broke the connection. Bell normally ran down things like Braxton, but it's possible he could have missed the man's release. It wasn't widely disseminated, almost as if the army were embarrassed about it.

Sara typed a memo about the phone call, saved it, and moved a copy to cloud storage. Whatever the outcome of Bell's inquiry, there would be an official government record about its beginning.

SARA SCROLLED through an old personnel file for her next call. She found John Tyler's cell number, hoped it was still correct, and dialed. "Hello?" a man's voice said.

"Is this Mister Tyler?"

"Yes."

"You don't know me. My name is Sara Morrison, and I work at the Pentagon."

"I'm sorry," Tyler said.

"I said—"

"I heard you, Miss Morrison. I was offering condolences."

Sara smiled. "It's not so bad. The reason I'm calling is about a couple of men you served with. Kent Maxwell and Victor White."

Tyler sighed into the phone, and the hiss forced Sara to move the phone away from her ear. "What about them? If you're asking for a letter of recommendation, I can only provide whatever its opposite would be."

"Are you aware they started a private security company?"

"Let me guess. Hexagon Security?"

"Yes," Sara said. "How did you know?"

"I ran into a couple of their recruiters earlier. They . . . weren't successful."

"So you don't know anything about what the company might be doing?"

"What's your job at the Pentagon?" Tyler asked.

"I have a long and boring title. Let's just say I deal with things like special operations and private military contractors."

"Then, it sounds like you should know what they might be doing."

"I'll cut to the chase, Mister Tyler." Sara found a lot of former longtime service members terse on the phone. Tyler could certainly be counted among their number. "I know about your history with Leo Braxton."

"So?"

"Did you know he recently got out of Leavenworth?"

Tyler didn't say anything for a few seconds. Finally, he asked, "Are you shitting me?"

"I'm afraid not."

"After what he ord . . . after what he did? How does this happen?"

"I wish I could give you a good answer. He had years left to go. Someone commuted his sentence. He was popular in his day."

"I'm aware," Tyler said in a flat tone.

"Have you heard from Braxton?" Sara said.

"No, and I don't expect to. He hates me because he thinks I put him in prison. I guess it's true from a deluded point of view, but his own actions and orders landed him there."

"You're surprised he's out?"

"Of course," Tyler said. "When they threw him in there,

they should have melted the key and buried the slag a hundred feet underground."

"Looking at his file, I'm inclined to agree." Tyler remained silent. "All right. I was checking into their company and figured I'd give you a heads-up."

"Thanks, Miss Morrison." Tyler broke the connection.

Sara set her phone down. She perused Tyler's file. After reporting Braxton, he left special operations and finished his final year of service as a wheeled vehicle mechanic. Since then, he'd had nothing to do with the armed forces or any of his former army colleagues. Sara couldn't ignore the connection between Maxwell, White, and Braxton, and she wondered if the two lackeys only kept the seat warm for their former commander. John Tyler had good reason to hate all three men.

Maybe he could solve the Hexagon problem for her.

13

J ake looked at his burner phone. It was time for a new one. He changed devices any time he got a threatening text, but he also swapped them out every few days as a precaution. Tech-savvy red teamers could be among the people after him, and Jake didn't intend to provide an easy target. His dwindling funds complicated the issue. Jake couldn't risk going to an ATM, and he wouldn't resort to things like robbery to raise some cash.

He needed the whole sordid mess to wrap up soon. Maybe it was time to stop playing defense and go on the offense. It was something to stew on later. Jake survived so far, and he didn't know how well going after his former service mates would go. He didn't want his father to stand over his grave wondering what went wrong.

After checking his cameras and seeing the coast was clear, Jake slipped out onto the streets. It was a muggy July evening. He pulled his baseball cap low on his head and scrutinized everyone who came near him. After about a five-minute walk, Jake ducked into a random convenience store which advertised phones on its window.

The guy ahead of him in line berated the cashier over not having change for large bills. He waved a couple of them around like it would alter the outcome. From the rear, Jake thought the guy wore a mediocre suit. If he had a large enough bankroll to flaunt a few hundred-dollar bills, he could have put them toward some nicer threads. When the rude fellow continued his tirade, Jake broke in. "Move along, pal. It's not all about you."

The man spun on him, red-faced. He looked to be about forty, sported a dad bod, and probably suffered from self-inflicted high blood pressure. The guy was about to say something, but he stared at Jake, and his mouth hung open. So it went for bullies. They lost their bluster when they ran into someone who wouldn't knuckle under. "Something you want to say?" Jake asked. The belligerent man frowned and stuffed his money back into his pocket with shaky hands and stormed out.

Jake looked down and saw a fresh hundred-dollar bill on the floor. He covered it with his shoe and waited a moment, even when the cashier prompted him. When he saw a Lexus sedan leave the parking lot, Jake crouched, picked up the money, and held it in his fist. If he ran into enough self-impressed assholes, maybe he could get past his temporary money problem.

A burner wouldn't cost enough to use the large bill, so Jake paid with his existing cash. He could get change somewhere else. Jake carried his new purchase out of the store. He'd wiped the old phone back at his hotel room. He crossed the street, walked behind a pickup truck, and slipped the old mobile into the bed. If his pursuers managed to track it, they'd wind up disappointed. Jake maintained a constant vigil on the way back to his hotel. He chose a longer route for the return trip, even doubling back on himself once, but no one followed.

Several minutes later, Jake duplicated his setup. The surveillance app displayed the camera feeds on his new phone.

The few numbers he stored populated his contact list. He looked at the aliases for Sam and Mike and hoped they'd avoided being dragged into his mess. Jake held his thumb over the pizza shop disguised as his father's phone number. Hearing his voice would be good for Jake. Telling him things were OK— relatively speaking, at least—would be good for the old man. This was a new phone. No association to him.

Jake took a deep breath and decided against it. If his old crew tapped his dad's phones—something easily within their wheelhouse—he'd be handing over his new number. It would then be easier to find him. It wasn't worth the risk. Jake pondered taking the bus a few miles away and using a pay phone . . . if he could still find one.

It was something to think about another day.

MAXWELL LOOKED up to find two men in his office doorway. Judging by the shiner on Blake's face, things didn't go well. "Come in," he said. He heard the exasperation in his own tone, and he knew they would, too.

Blake and Stanton sat in his guest chairs. Both looked like they'd gone a couple unproductive rounds with a heavyweight. Maxwell hired both of them without serving with them. They came recommended. Now, he wondered if he'd need to clear out some dead weight and recruit better men. The company's best were in the Middle East, but even they'd been unsuccessful in their quest.

"We went to see Watson," Blake said.

"He's Jake's friend," Stanton added.

Maxwell slapped his desktop, and both men straightened in their chairs. "I know who he is. I want you to tell me what happened."

"We got there all right," Blake said. He was the younger and smaller of the two. Less experienced. Maxwell heard he was a diligent soldier and good shooter, and so far, he'd seen neither of those in action. "Watson was home. Stanton went in to talk to him, and I stayed by the door."

Maxwell's eyes flicked to Stanton, who nodded. "The guy said he didn't know anything. I beat on him a little, but he didn't talk."

"Did you escalate from there?" Maxwell said.

"Didn't really have a chance," Stanton said. His face was a mess of bruises, and dried blood remained caked in his hair. Whoever took him out would be a skilled operative. A thought burned in Maxwell's mind, and he didn't like it.

Blake shifted in his seat. "Some guy came up the stairs. I told him to buzz off. He started asking questions, so I went after him with a knife. He ... uh ... got it away from me and took me out quick."

"I came out, then," Stanton said. "Blake was lying on the carpet like his head got bounced off the railing. I went after the guy but couldn't connect. Next thing I know, I'm going down the stairs. I hit the wall and ..." He spread his hands.

"One guy did this?" Maxwell asked. They both bobbed their heads. "Describe him."

"Middle-aged," Stanton said. "A few years older than you, I'd guess. Not too tall ... under six feet. Pretty average build, though I could tell he kept in shape. Not a weightlifter or anything. Dark eyes."

For a big meathead, Stanton turned out to be pretty observant. Maybe he could stay on the payroll. Maxwell called up another photo of John Tyler from the end of his military career and showed it to both of them. "This the guy?"

"Yeah," they both said in unison.

"Don't worry about who he is," Maxwell said, preempting the question he knew would be coming. "We're going to deal with him. You're dismissed."

They both shuffled out of the office. Once they were down the hall and out of earshot, Maxwell picked up his phone and dialed Braxton. "It's Tyler, sir. He's continuing to be a pain in the ass."

"It's all he knows, Maxwell."

"I think we need to escalate against him."

"Do what you need to do," Braxton said.

14

T yler arrived home and tossed his keys onto the small table in the entryway like normal. He needed normality now, even if it came in small gestures and tiny bits. Lexi didn't appear to be anywhere on the main level. Tyler grabbed a beer from the fridge, plopped onto the couch, and took a long pull.

There wasn't enough booze in the house to make up for Leo Braxton being out of prison. How could it happen? During their time serving together, Tyler always knew Braxton was popular with the brass. He got results. His unit killed terrorists. They repelled the Taliban. When Tyler discovered the real horrors of Braxton's leadership, he reported what he knew. It was his duty to the army and the rest of the men he served with. Every flag officer should've been happy to be rid of the former colonel who tainted the service.

Yet here he was walking around. According to Sara Morrison, Braxton's freedom came because he still retained a couple friends in high places. Considering her position, she would know. Tyler drank some more beer. His father's words from lunch echoed in his head. *Killer isn't an MOS. They knew you'd be better at shooting terrorists. It's who you are.* So far, Tyler encountered four men he now knew worked for Braxton, and he'd killed none of them.

It would need to change.

"Dad!" Lexi waved her hand in front of Tyler's face. "What the hell? You were zoned out there. You almost spilled your beer."

Tyler looked down. He held the bottle cock-eyed, and the amber liquid threatened to tumble from the opening. He held it upright and set it on the end table. "Sorry."

"You all right?"

It was such an easy question. Tyler wished he could provide an easy answer. "Sit down, Lexi." He patted the cushion beside him.

"Oh, god." She dropped onto the sofa. "Is something wrong with Grandpa?"

Tyler scoffed. "Not at all. Hell, he'll probably outlive us both." He paused, unsure of how to proceed. Lexi never heard the full story of Leo Braxton, and Tyler wasn't too keen to provide it now. Still, she deserved to know something was amiss. The Braxton playbook could include Lexi at some point, and while Tyler would do everything he could to prevent it, his daughter deserved to know she could soon be in a maniac's sights.

"Dad, you're worrying me."

"All right," Tyler said. "Do you remember me telling you about a man I served under named Leo Braxton?"

Lexi frowned and closed her eyes. A few seconds later, she said, "Is he the war crimes guy?"

The attribution made Tyler smile. Considering she would've been about eight when the whole mess went down, it served as quite a fitting moniker. "The same."

"Isn't he rotting in jail?"

"He was in Leavenworth. Somehow, he got released."

"What the hell?" Lexi shook her head. "I don't know a lot about what he did, but it sounded serious at the time. You and mom didn't tell me much, though."

"In our defense," Tyler said, "you were pretty young. Besides, I didn't exactly give your mother all the details. She wouldn't have been able to provide a lot."

"I'm not young anymore." Lexi stared at Tyler defiantly to emphasize her point.

"I know. What he did a decade ago isn't important right now, though. I wanted you to know he's out."

Lexi crossed her arms under her chest. "Dad, is he going to come after us?"

Tyler turned up his hands. "I don't know. I'm pretty sure Smitty's son Jake is on the run from Braxton and whoever he pulled into his organization." Tyler paused and thought about the timing. His former commander sat behind bars until recently, according to Sara Morrison. It meant someone like Kent Maxwell must've started the company. It would allow them to dodge an obvious association with a war criminal. "Anyway, I've run into a few of his men. It . . . hasn't gone well for them, but they're still alive."

"You might need to start killing them, though."

"Yeah." Tyler nodded. He heard his father's words again but ignored them this time. "It's possible Braxton doesn't know I'm involved. It's not like any of these assholes saw my ID. They could describe me, though, and anyone I served with could put two and two together."

Lexi took a deep breath and sat on her hands. "Am I in danger?"

"We both might be. I won't lie to you. Coming after you to get to me is something Braxton might try. I don't think he'll go for it first, though. He'll probably keep coming after me . . . if he knows I'm involved."

"Let's assume he does," Lexi said. "Does he hate you?"

"Of course," Tyler said. "He blamed me for the end of his military career. Never mind he brought it all on himself. The truly guilty and deluded never think they're to blame for their own misfortune."

Lexi's head bobbed slowly as she took it all in. Tyler felt bad for dropping it all on her. She probably should've learned all this in stages over the years. "What should I do?"

"Go to the range and practice with your Walther. If anyone but me comes through the door, aim for center mass. When in doubt, empty the magazine."

Despite the dire tone of the conversation, Lexi grinned. "I'd pretty much decided the same thing."

"That's my girl," Tyler said.

THE LARGE BLACK phone on Maxwell's desk rang. The secure line. He'd paid extra to get it installed over Victor White's objections. Bean counters often stood in the way of what needed to be done in Maxwell's experience. Having the options for private communication already helped the company in its legitimate contracting work. Maxwell picked up the receiver. "It's Bell," the man on the other end said.

A direct call from Arthur Bell was unusual. Maxwell wondered what was wrong but kept his voice composed like an officer should. "What can I do for you?"

"I think it's what I might be doing for you ... again."

"I'm afraid you'll have to be more specific," Maxwell said.

Bell's voice dropped even though the line prevented eavesdropping. "Sara just signed off for the day. Finally. Earlier, she asked me to look into your company."

"And?"

"She's going to expect something," Bell said. "She was

looking over stuff recently, came across Hexagon, and asked me if I'd vetted you. I—"

"You said yes, of course."

"Sure. The thing is Sara usually does it herself. She doesn't like delegating certain tasks. It makes working for her a little boring, honestly."

"If only I'd learned to play the violin," Maxwell said.

Bell sighed into the phone. "Look . . . I can probably stall her a little and say I'm working on gathering some info. She knows things move at government speed. I can't keep her in the dark forever, though."

Maxwell leaned back in his chair and stared at the drop ceiling. "What are you suggesting we do, Mister Bell?"

"I'm not suggesting anything. You handle your own shit. I just tell you what I hear. I let you know about Jake reaching out to me, and now I'm telling you Sara Morrison is interested in your company. You decide what to do about it."

"I presume we'll work something out in this instance," Maxwell said, "like we did in the first?"

"A new company has a lot of expenses," Bell said, "especially in such a competitive industry."

"Thanks for the heads-up, Mister Bell." Maxwell broke the call. Sara Morrison poking around was inevitable. Her reputation preceded her. Arthur Bell was starting to get expensive, however. The information about Jake was worth paying for. He knew too much to walk around freely. This bit about Morrison didn't constitute a revelation.

Still, Maxwell would tell Braxton. Sara Morrison would need to be dealt with just like Jake Smith.

15

C olumbia was close enough to DC for Kent Maxwell to dislike it. Despite being a couple Maryland counties away, it was an auxiliary to the swamp and equally as fetid. If Braxton hadn't requested him personally on this job, he would have gladly stayed far away. They sat outside a house, which Maxwell would admit was a nice one. He would even live in it if it weren't in hoity-toity Columbia.

All the houses featured garages, plus all the bells and whistles a rich suburbanite could want. It was a community made for defense contractors, consultants, and government executives. Tonight, he and Braxton surveilled the latter. They were spying on Sara Morrison, the Assistant Secretary of Defense for Special Operations and Low-Intensity Conflict. A fancy title . . . especially for a woman.

"You were right to come to me, Maxwell," Braxton said from the passenger's seat.

"I hope so, sir."

Braxton shifted so he could stare Maxwell down. "You doubt me?"

Maxwell understood the woman's position at the Pentagon

and what it meant for Braxton's nascent company. She potentially stood in the way of them all becoming wealthy. Still, she was a DoD civilian. Maxwell didn't harbor a lot of love for them —especially the ones who'd been in their jobs too long—but ultimately, they were on the same side. He didn't want to hurt her, either. "I know how you favor resolving things. A dead body here doesn't help our cause even if her deputy would be easier to deal with."

"I'm sure she's a reasonable woman," Braxton said. "Maybe she just needs the proper motivation to drop her little investigation."

Maxwell frowned. "We're here to get dirt on her?"

"You call it dirt," Braxton said. "I prefer to think of it as motivational material."

"What makes you think tonight is the time for your blackmail plan?" Maxwell heard the frustration in his own tone.

Braxton must have, too, but if he did, he never showed it. "She's been on a date."

"How do you know?" Maxwell asked.

"You really need to work with our cyber guys sometimes. They did similar work on the red team." He shrugged. "Social media, mostly. We figured out who she's seeing. He checked in from a place called Clyde's not far from here."

"What if they go back to his place?"

Braxton grinned. It always made him look like a predator, and his graying hair accentuated the look. "He lives much farther away. Their nightcap will be here."

"Just because she's on a date doesn't mean we're going to get anything good." Maxwell fidgeted in the driver's seat. As usual, they parked their butts in a gray SUV. Braxton favored the look, and he liked the horsepower and American-made factor of the GMC Yukon. In many areas, SUVs blended in. Even the larger ones in darker colors looked like many other vehicles on the road or in a lot. In this neighborhood, however, they stood out.

Most of the cars parked on the street belonged to luxury brands like Lexus or Audi. Their domestic beast could get them noticed.

"I understand it's at least their sixth," Braxton said. "We should expect . . . fireworks. It's why we brought the camera, Kent."

Maxwell blinked hard. "Wait . . . we're going to take pictures of her fucking some dude?"

"Yes."

"Why?"

"Because she's a professional woman."

"So?" Maxwell said. "It's the twenty-first century."

"By the calendar," Braxton said, "yes. But by attitude . . . well, I don't think we're quite there yet. 'Me too' or not. She's a woman in a position of power in a male-dominated arena. And a bunch of old white men will be horrified if compromising pictures of her turn up."

"Unbelievable," Maxwell muttered, shaking his head.

"You're only looking at the prurient angle," said Braxton. "Photos like these are an old spy tactic. People will wonder if she's under surveillance by a foreign intelligence service. They might even think she's been compromised."

A car drove down the road. Both Maxwell and Braxton shifted lower in their seats. Headlights washed over them and moved on as the car kept going. "Are we really going to need this?" Maxwell said, straightening back up.

"I hope not. But we must be prepared for all outcomes and have a plan for each."

It was among Braxton's favorite things to say. Maxwell found it perfectly sensible in general, but he didn't like applying it here. It fell somewhat lightly under the category of hurting Sara Morrison. It wouldn't wound her physically, but it could damage her career and her psyche. Maxwell hoped they didn't wind up with anything to photograph. "What's the endgame for the company?" he wanted to know after a moment of silence.

"We do the work we're good at," Braxton said. "There are always terrorists to kill."

"I mean, why focus on working in the Middle East once we get what we're after? There are plenty of opportunities in other parts of the world. Domestically, even."

"The Middle East is a wasteland. I don't just mean the desert. It's largely ungoverned. Many of the governments there are openly hostile to the west and western values. Terror thrives because no one over there will put it down, and our politicians have the same problem. They don't have the spine or the balls or whatever you want to call it. They won't do what needs to be done. Companies like ours fill the gap. We can solve the problem other governments, including our own, refuse to."

Maxwell stewed on Braxton's words. On a basic level, he agreed. Most of the rulers in the Middle East were worthless. The people, however, were solid. Maxwell met many of them during his time there. A few turned out to be terrorists or sympathizers, but by and large, they were simply people who didn't want to die. There was definitely a gap to be filled, but he and Braxton would disagree on how wide it was.

Another vehicle approached from behind. It slowed as it neared Sara Morrison's house and turned into her driveway. The garage door went up, revealing a tidy interior and late-model Infiniti sedan. The BMW pulling in would look right at home beside it. The German car's engine cut off, and the garage door descended.

"Ready the camera and directional microphone," Braxton said.

Maxwell tried not to feel insulted. He prepared them ninety seconds after arrival. The only remaining step was recording. They wouldn't get any useful video unless Sara Morrison and her date approached an open window, but the mic had enough

power to pick up a conversation from inside the house.
Maxwell wondered if a round of dirty talk would mean as much
for Braxton's agenda as a high-res image of Morrison's tits.

They engaged in post-date small talk for a few minutes. It
was a lovely dinner, the wine was exquisite, yada yada. "Make
sure we're getting video," Braxton said. "We can always get stills
from it."

"I'm rolling, sir. So far, we have a lovely shot of the exterior
of her house."

"Just keep shooting. She has a first-floor master suite. I'm
sure you were wondering about climbing a tree."

The thought crossed Maxwell's mind, but he didn't mention
it. A few minutes later, Sara Morrison and her date walked
farther into the house. It seemed the gentleman was spending
the night. He mentioned it in passing, and she didn't object.
They both expected it. Maxwell noticed a window with the
blinds up. If it were Morrison's bedroom, they had a chance to
get some usable footage.

"*You have anything early in the morning?*" the man said.

"*My calendar is clear until nine-thirty,*" Sara Morrison said.
Maxwell could hear them well enough. The recording wouldn't
be perfect because they sat across the street and captured
sound through the walls, but he could clean it up.

"*Good. You're mine until at least two, then.*"

"*Well, we'd better get started.*"

Maxwell heard them kissing, then the rustling of clothes. A
minute later, they appeared in the window. He centered it in the
camera. Sara Morrison faced out, the man behind her. She
wore a black bra and matching panties; he was naked above the
waist. He wrapped his arms around her and kissed her neck.
She angled her head, her dark hair spilled to the side, and her
sigh came through clearly on the audio. A few seconds later,
her date's hands moved, and her bra fell away. Maxwell realized

they now had the dirty talk and a shot of Morrison's tits. He found them quite nice for whatever it was worth.

As soon as the bra tumbled away, the man behind Maxwell cupped her breasts. He trailed kisses up and down her neck. Then he took a step back, and she pivoted and followed him. Another couple feet and they were out of sight again. The audio continued recording, however. Maxwell frowned and fidgeted as he listened to the sounds of Morrison and her date having sex. Braxton stared ahead. He didn't mention getting out of the car for a better shot. It would've been a bridge too far for Maxwell.

When the lovebirds finished, Braxton told Maxwell to keep recording. "They agreed they'd be at this for a while," he said.

"They're both over forty," Maxwell pointed out.

"Aren't you over forty, Kent?"

"By a year, sir."

"Are you telling me you couldn't plow your girlfriend until at least two, like the man inside promised?"

"I don't like to boast."

Braxton smirked. "Bullshit. You see my point, though. They could very well be at it again. The more we have to use against Miss Morrison should it come to it, the better."

They remained in the SUV. Sure enough, Morrison and her lover took a brief respite and then went back for round two. Maxwell made sure they recorded pictures and sound.

He still didn't like it, and he hoped they wouldn't need any of this.

But he would follow orders.

axwell extracted some choice still images from the video and provided them to Braxton. He scrutinized them. As he rose through the ranks, some of his compatriots loved offloading work onto the enlisted men. Braxton never minded reviewing his subordinates' work, however. It was necessary to make sure they did things right, of course, but they also needed to know their commander was involved and invested. Leaders always were, and soldiers recognized leadership.

Braxton had to admit Sara Morrison was attractive. For a woman in her mid-forties who prioritized rising through the ranks of the DoD, she turned out more than OK. The photos of her bra coming off before her boyfriend cupped her breasts were terrific. Back in the day, he would have shared them with his fellow colonels.

Now, he was going to send them to Sara Morrison.

Getting her personal email was easy. Even people who do good jobs protecting their privacy share their information with companies who don't care. Braxton setup a temporary email account, untraceable to him. A former soldier under his command helped him with computer security, and all the traffic his laptop generated was anonymized. Even if Sara Morrison sicced her DoD IT security people on the problem—and she wouldn't—they'd all die of old age before they unraveled everything.

Braxton sent the email with a high importance flag. Then, he waited. He thought about his organization. They'd earned two contracts so far. One essentially served as a cover, and the other was their real goal. Progress moved slowly, but what Braxton lost years ago would be found soon enough. He focused on the bigger picture, which began with Sara Morrison.

After about twenty minutes, he called her. It was a burner phone, equally as untraceable as the email account, and it would disguise his voice. When Sara Morrison answered, Braxton swore he heard a little quiver in her tone. "Hello?"

"Good morning, Miss Morrison."

"Who is this?" The quivering vanished, and a hard edge replaced it. It was a shame Braxton needed to target Morrison and wear her down. He might have liked her under different circumstances.

"An interested party."

"What exactly are you interested in?" she said.

"More than just your . . . sleeping habits."

"I figured you were the asshole who sent me these pictures. Did you like sitting outside my house watching me? Did you beat off to these pictures?"

"Miss Morrison," Braxton said, "there's no need to be crass. I have a concern, and I wanted to make sure I got your attention."

"What do you want?" Morrison said, icicles hanging from each word.

"I want you to drop your investigation into Hexagon."

"Why?"

"Because the government no longer has the spine to do what needs to be done over there. Companies like theirs can solve a lot of problems for you."

"Men like you disgust me."

Braxton leaned back in his chair. He didn't think she'd be receptive, and he kind of enjoyed the back and forth. "The problem is . . . you need men like me. The country does, too. The men we've elected, along with the ones appointed above you, are a bunch of cowards. They want to fight a war with two hands tied behind their backs, and then they wonder why we're not winning." He took a breath to calm himself.

"Let me guess," said Morrison in a tone suggesting she did not in fact need to speculate. "I either bend to your wishes, or you send those pictures to someone above me. Someone you think would care a lot about how it looks and broom me out of here."

"I hope it doesn't get so far," Braxton said. "But if I need to, I'll do just what you said."

"Here you are on a blocked phone number, disguising your voice, and sending me this message from some bullshit email account. You're a coward, Braxton."

"I'm not who you think I am. I want you to consider what we talked about."

"Here's your consideration," Morrison said. "Stick your blackmail up your ass . . . if anything still fits up there after Leavenworth." She hung up.

Braxton slammed his phone down. He didn't expect an official like Sara Morrison to knuckle under right away. A woman didn't make it in a male-dominated industry by being the shy, retiring type. Her open defiance and antagonism angered him, however.

Maybe Braxton needed to take more drastic steps regarding Sara Morrison.

TYLER AND SMITTY worked together on the engine replacement. They'd dropped the old one and moved it aside and were now taking a brief break. Smitty handed Tyler a cold bottle of water, which he accepted with a nod of gratitude. "I wanted to do this yesterday," Smitty said, "but I know you were doing other stuff for me. How did it go?"

"I haven't found Jake yet," Tyler said.

"I figured you woulda told me."

"Yes. I discovered a hotel where he was staying, but he'd just checked out."

"You think you could find him again?"

"Probably," Tyler said. "I also tracked down a friend of his. Two, actually, but one's an asshole. Anyway, it turns out the people looking for Jake found one of them, too. I saved him from a beating."

"Anyone get hurt?" Smitty said.

"Yes."

"Jesus," Smitty said, letting out a slow breath. "This is serious."

"It's been serious," Tyler said. "I'm sure Jake did what he did to protect you, but he's in the sights of some very dangerous men."

Smitty blanched and drank some water with an unsteady hand. "What are you going to do next?"

"Keep looking for Jake. Try to stay one step ahead of everyone else." Tyler again wondered how much to tell Smitty. Jake kept him in the dark, but Braxton's men paid several visits to the shop. He deserved to know who he was up against. "I guess Jake hasn't told you very much."

"Still ain't heard from him since he took off," Smitty said. His shoulders slumped, and he dropped onto a chair.

"He's hiding from men he served with," Tyler said. "I'm sure you've figured it out by now. I haven't uncovered why yet, but he must know something . . . maybe details about black ops gone south. I'm not sure. What I am sure about is a bunch of men want to kill him to keep him quiet."

"I think I liked not knowing better." Smitty rubbed his forehead.

"I'm sure you did." Tyler sat in a task chair and wheeled it beside his boss. "I wasn't sure how much I should tell you, but if it were me, I'd want to know."

"Thanks." Smitty offered a fractional nod. "Doesn't make me feel any better, but I've felt like shit about this mess since it began."

"If it's any help, I'm sort of in the same boat."

"You?"

"Me," Tyler said. "I've . . . been trying to put what I did in the past behind me. Just fix some old cars. Then, those two assholes paid you a visit. I got involved again and saved Mike Watson from two different assholes. My father likes to say a man can't run from who he is." Tyler shrugged. "I guess I'm a killer. I think I need to be, all things considered." He fell silent and let his words hang in the air. Smitty didn't answer. "I'd like to think I'm a pretty good mechanic, too. Once this is wrapped up, if you'll keep me around, I'd like to stay."

"You gonna try not to shoot anybody?"

"No promises."

Smitty grinned. "Stay as long as you like. Let's get my boy back home first before we start talking about which desk you want."

"Deal," Tyler said. He hoped he could deliver on his end.

～

TYLER LEFT the shop right after six. It was a long day. Changing out the engine, plus making sure the new one worked, consumed most of it. It took a few attempts for Tyler to wash all the grease from his hands and forearms. Sweat dampened his T-shirt, and fluid stains marred the rest of it. Still, he drove away with a feeling of satisfaction. Getting his hands dirty with oil rather than blood made for a refreshing change.

The portable GPS showed traffic was better going through the city for a while, so Tyler cruised down Belair Road. He noticed the tail after a mile or so. It was a different vehicle with a silver sedan taking the place of the usual SUV. A smart swap —the make, model, and color were popular enough to blend in anywhere. When the car changed lanes to follow him, Tyler saw a Honda badge. An Accord, judging by its size. The most popular car in America up until its CR-V cousin overtook it. Even more invisible.

Tyler drove like he didn't know anyone tailed him. The guy back there picked a good car and didn't give away his position. Most people, probably even the majority of those with training, wouldn't have noticed. Sometimes, the paranoia others accused Tyler of harboring turned out to be a good thing.

Belair Road was three lanes wide but had a speed limit of only thirty through this stretch. Businesses dotted the sides. Houses were relegated to the side streets, of which there were many. Tyler drove past a cluster of three gas stations and stopped at a light. More shops and eateries lay ahead. He pondered how to use the landscape to his advantage. The Accord sat two cars behind him—a little brazen, perhaps, but the driver seemed competent.

In the present situation, having a distinctive car constituted a drawback. Tyler couldn't blend in on the road. His 442 would stand out for its shape and vintage, never mind its telltale dark green paint. If he were going to turn the tables on his pursuer, he needed to do it off the road. The light turned green. Tyler scouted the left side. If he could make the turn before the guy following him, it would give him an advantage.

The Gardenville Shopping Center lay ahead, just before a green light at Frankford Avenue. Traffic came the other direction. Tyler saw a gap, didn't signal for a turn, and swung a hard left with screeching tires. The Japanese SUV coming toward him honked its wimpy horn. At least ten cars trailed it. The silver Accord wouldn't get to turn for at least twenty seconds. Maybe the driver would figure he got made and simply keep going.

Tyler looked for a place to park and get out. He drove past a church, wondering why someone would put a place of worship in a shopping center. An Aldi and some other stores lay ahead. Tyler pulled into a spot next to a van, got out, and sprinted toward the shops. He ducked behind a thick post as the Accord finally made the turn.

The driver took it slowly, scanning left and right. The van would block his view of the 442 until he got closer. As the car approached, Tyler leaned out from behind the pillar, his phone at the ready. The driver's head swiveled toward him, and he snapped three photos in rapid succession. The man sported the short hair many former service members favored. His features were hard and unfriendly. He scowled when he realized he'd been photographed. The silver sedan sped up and drove away.

Tyler watched it leave before strolling back to his car. He drove home, transferred the photos to his laptop, and connected to the State Police database. It was one of the functions he didn't need Lexi to help him with. A minute later, his search spat out a result: Lawrence Shah, formerly of the US Army, given a bad conduct discharge from his rank as lieutenant six years ago. His file read like a horror show of American foreign policy missteps: physical and sexual assault, robbery, and a suspicion of murder. He was the kind of soldier who made the rest look bad. His eviction came after a court martial and a very light sentence of three years in prison. It must have been a deal to avoid the dreaded dishonorable discharge.

Lieutenants were officers but sat at the lowest rung. Sometimes, they commanded small platoons. Other times, they fetched coffee for captains and majors. Shah's record showed he saw combat and made some positive contributions in Iraq before his career crashed and burned. The file was absent anything about leadership or commendations. Not a commander.

He sounded like the perfect subordinate for Leo Braxton.

17

In the interests of due diligence, Tyler used the former Patriot laptop to take a deeper look into Shah. He'd ask Lexi about the social media stuff if he needed to, but he'd worked in the investigative toolkit before. Besides the bad conduct discharge, no crimes dotted Shah's record. He possessed a spotty credit history since getting the boot. Shah rented an apartment in Essex, and the silver Accord he pursued Tyler with was his own.

He worked for a small company called Former Military Partners LLC. Tyler had never heard of the outfit. The company maintained a very basic website which didn't even list a way of contacting them. The laptop could look up domain registration information, and Tyler selected the option once he remembered where it was. The company itself was listed as the owner, but a familiar name filled the *Technical Contact* entry.

Victor White. A sharp guy, formerly in the special forces unit, good with money and numbers, and a total toady for Braxton. If White owned a company, he did it on paper only, and it must have served to hide his former commander's involvement. A random Pentagon official poking around wouldn't see the name Leo Braxton, which might jump out. Even if it didn't, two seconds searching army records would reveal the horror show. White, on the other hand, was clean. He'd done his time and left with no charges or controversy.

Coupled with the news Braxton managed an early release from Leavenworth, it meant the man was up to something. Sara Morrison asked about Hexagon. Tyler checked their domain registration first. The technical point of contact showed as Former Military Partners LLC. Hexagon's website boasted about the military service and experience of its founders Kent Maxwell and Victor White. Despite being Braxton's chief bootlicker, Maxwell managed to land himself a general discharge—probably keeping his benefits in the arrangement. No red flags would pop out of his service file other than all the times he deployed with Braxton.

White and Maxwell just kept the seat warm. Braxton would be running Hexagon. He couldn't take a position which wasn't in command. The man's ego wouldn't allow for it. Without the disgraced colonel's involvement, Tyler might have figured Hexagon to be just another private military company started by guys who missed the fight. Something more sinister must have been at work, however. Whatever it was, Braxton knew about Tyler and ordered Shah to follow him.

Tyler heard his father's words again. *Killer wasn't an MOS. A man's got to be who he is.* "Fine, Leo," he said to the empty room. "I'll bury you and all your men. I should have done it a decade ago."

～

IT WAS worth the risk to talk to his dad.

Jake sat on a city bus. Few people shared it with him, so he got to spread out in the seat. Normally, he would have found it cramped and uncomfortable. He rode the CityLink yellow route, which terminated at the University of Maryland's Balti-more County campus. Jake got off before the final destination. A pay phone sat outside a Rite Aid, and he would use it to call his dad. Two bus routes and about a mile of walking got him here, but it would be worth it.

Street lights pierced the descending dusk. Smitty should have left the shop by now. Jake hoped the old man wasn't working too hard without him there. Maybe he finally followed through on his threat and hired some help. Jake dropped two quarters into the phone and called his dad's home number. He picked up on the second ring. "Jake?"

"It's me, Dad." Jake closed his eyes and took a deep breath. Relief washed over him at the sound of his father's voice after two weeks on the run.

"Jesus, boy, it's good to hear from you. You all right?"

"I'm surviving. I don't want to talk long because I don't know if anyone has tapped your phone."

"I want to talk to you more often than this," his father said. Jake swore he heard the old man's voice crack.

"Get a burner, Dad. Post the number in the place we talked about . . . which you haven't been using."

"I will. I hired someone to help me in the shop. I think he'll be able to help me with a couple other things, too."

Did his dad find someone who could get Jake out from under? If so, he'd welcome the help. His time on the run wore on him, and he didn't know how much longer he'd be able to keep going without someone finding him. So long as he stayed in Maryland, the odds were against him long-term. "Glad to hear it. I need to go. Do what we discussed."

"Right."

Jake hung up. He held on to the receiver a few seconds longer before turning and walking away.

～

JAKE WAITED for the bus on the opposite side of the road. It was due in about fifteen minutes. A ride halfway across the city, then a transfer, and then a mile on foot would put him back at his hotel. It took a long time and was well out of the way, but it was all worth it to talk to his dad, even for a minute. Jake wished he'd done it sooner. He felt bad about letting his dad stew in his worry for so long.

The potential helper could be a good or bad thing. Jake wondered if someone from his old unit posed as a mechanic to land the job. Once installed, he would pump Smitty for intel about Jake. His dad was an exacting worker, though. Someone would need the skill set to impress him enough to earn a job offer. Unless the gig came by force at the business end of a gun barrel. Jake shook his head. He felt terrible about leaving his father to his own devices. He was great at working on cars, but the kind of people looking for Jake operated in a separate world. A world his father wasn't a part of.

Screeching tires snapped Jake out of his reverie. An SUV skidded to a stop across the street. Jake didn't wait for anyone to get out; he took off from the bus stop. Behind him, automatic gunfire roared, and bullets peppered the vehicles in front of Jake. He kept low, crouching behind the front end of a Cadillac Escalade.

It had been years since Jake found himself pinned down by gunfire. He remembered the lessons he learned then. First among them: don't panic. Many people stood up and ran, which only served as an easy way to get shot. Jake stayed in place. The engine and wheels should soak up the bullets. Deep breaths helped manage his racing heartbeat. When pinned down in Afghanistan, Jake had a dozen of his closest friends around to help. Tonight, he was alone. The idea of his former unit mates now raining hot lead at him turned his stomach. Jake raised his head just enough to peer through the windshield. Two men fired on him. A few people on the opposite side of the street sprinted away.

The guns clicked empty. Jake glanced down the road. If he stayed out of sight, he could make the alley two houses down and try to lose his pursuers there. He maintained his crouch and moved down the row of vehicles. Thank goodness they were all pickup trucks or their sport-utility relatives. If the people who lived on this block owned Mini Coopers, he'd be spotted.

Jake made the alley and hugged the right-hand fence as he moved down. He took his hat off and tossed it as far as he could. If the men chasing him came here, they would see it and presume it flew off his head as he ran. Jake hopped the fence behind him and padded through someone's yard. He stopped at a bush, didn't see anyone, and inched his way behind a car in the driveway.

He saw two men walk down the alley. They stopped past where he'd come into the yard. "He must've come down here," one of the men said. The poor lighting in the alley prevented Jake from getting a good look at either of them.

"Risky to call the old man," the other said.

"Risky and stupid." At the moment, Jake agreed.

"Hey, wasn't he wearing a hat?" They moved farther down, confirmed Jake had in fact been wearing a cap, and came to the logical conclusion. They walked along. Jake stayed low and padded to the side street. He dashed across, moved through someone else's yard, crossed Oregon Avenue, and kept going. He could find another bus or get a taxi from Route One. Right now, putting distance between himself and his pursuers was the first priority.

18

"Y ou're grumpy, Dad. Even for you."

Tyler looked up from the dinner he'd picked at. Lexi stared at him, concern pulling her brows into a frown. "What are you talking about?"

"You've never been chatty, but you've barely grunted at me since we sat down to eat. At least you normally tell me I did a good job in the kitchen."

"Of course you did." Lexi insisted on cooking a few nights a week. When she set some unrecognizable meal in front of Tyler a few weeks ago, he asked her what it was. The answer didn't clarify the contents of the plate. Instagram and Youtube inspired her, she claimed, and she wanted to replicate what she saw there. Tonight's attempt was chicken marsala with home-made sauce, spinach, and a pile of mushrooms. "I can even tell what this one is."

"Mmm," Lexi said, still regarding Tyler with a skeptical look. "What's going on?"

"I'm fine, Lexi."

"Bullshit. You're in extra surly mode tonight, and I want to know why?" She waited for Tyler to say something, and he filled the gap with silence. The tactic saw diminishing returns as Lexi grew older and more headstrong—a trait she inherited from both her parents. "Does it have something to do with Braxton?"

Tyler nodded. "I did a little digging earlier . . . found a couple of companies and their domain records. Once I heard Braxton was out, I figured he'd be involved in something shady. Seeing it on the screen really drove it home, I guess."

"I want the whole story."

"What do you mean?" Tyler said.

Lexi set her fork down hard enough to make it rattle against her plate. "The truth about Braxton. What happened? You've never told me." She held up her hand when Tyler's mouth opened. "Don't give me some line about wanting to protect me. I'm eighteen, and I'm as good a shot as you are. I'll decide what I need protection from."

Tyler looked across the kitchen table at his daughter. The fire blazing in her eyes came from her mother. Her take-no-prisoners attitude was a gift from her father, though. Tyler felt proud his daughter grew into a strong and confident young woman, even if he currently sat on the wrong end of one of her tirades. He wished he'd been more present along the way, but nothing could change the past. All he could do was be here for her now. "Fine."

"That's it? 'Fine?'"

"I'll tell you the story after we eat," Tyler said. "I'll need a beer . . . maybe two. You might want one, too."

Lexi picked up her fork again. She'd eaten much more of the meal than Tyler. "You're going to let me drink a beer?"

"Would you listen to me if I said you couldn't?"

"No," she said.

Tyler spread his hands. "I know when things are pointless."

Once they'd finished eating and cleared the table, Tyler adjourned to the living room. He sat in his favorite recliner which occupied a prominent place in his living room for a decade. It looked a little old and rough around the edges. *Kind of like me*, Tyler thought. Lexi carried two longnecks in from the kitchen. She set a bottle of lager before Tyler and plopped onto the couch, curling her legs up beneath her. "Ready when you are."

Tyler took a long pull of the brew. "Never doubt the power of liquid courage," he said as he set the bottle down. Lexi remained silent. Tyler turned the story over in his head. She deserved to hear all of it, no matter what she thought of him for the telling. "It was my fourth deployment. My last one as it turned out."

"Braxton was your commander?" Lexi asked.

"Yeah. He was in charge of the unit. He'd been doing it for a while, and he delivered the kinds of results the brass liked. The military talked a good game about winning hearts and minds in the Middle East, but it's tough to quantify. You can count dead terrorists." Lexi grimaced, but Tyler continued. "A bunch of us had been in Afghanistan before. We knew the terrain, some of the locals. I guess you could think of it as an all-star crew.

"About seven months in, Braxton's behavior got a little erratic. He'd be gone more than usual. At random times, too. He was the commander, so we couldn't really grill him about it. If someone brought it up, he'd say he was checking out something nearby." Tyler shook his head. "Colonels don't go and check things out. They ask the grunts to do it."

"No one questioned it?" Lexi asked.

Tyler shook his head. "It's easy to say we should've in hindsight, but we were a well-oiled machine. If we raided a compound, we took people out and didn't sustain a casualty. We always got good intel, and we drew up solid plans."

"So what happened?"

After another long draught of the amber liquid, Tyler continued. "Braxton handed me orders one afternoon. Told me they were eyes only, and it would be a one-man job. A local family was making IEDs. They'd been linked to five deaths and three times as many injuries. The father was the actual bomb maker, but his wife and kids helped and supported him. Because they were direct enablers of terrorism, we could take them out."

Now, Lexi drank some beer, draining about a third of the bottle. "I'm guessing you did," she said as she set it back down on the coaster.

"I'll get to it." Tyler paused. He let the unpleasant memories come. "I waited until dusk. It was a little cooler by then, and twilight always helped. Most people didn't turn on the lights in their houses until it got darker . . . if their electricity even worked. I scoped out the house and property, went in through the front door, and took out all four of them."

"The kids, too?" Tyler offered a slight bob of his head. "How old were they?"

"The daughter was sixteen, and the son was fourteen."

"Jesus, Dad." Lexi turned away and ran a hand through her long hair. "When do we get to the part of the story where Braxton is the asshole?" Tyler winced. Lexi's expression softened right away. "Sorry. I didn't mean—"

Tyler held up a hand. "It's fine. It's a fair question . . . and one I've asked myself plenty of times over the years."

Lexi blew out a breath and shifted on the sofa, tucking her knees under her chin. "What happened next?"

"I wanted to gather some proof," Tyler said. "It's one thing to say you killed a bomb maker, but then some prick in Congress gets a bug up his ass and hauls you in to testify. They're not inclined to take anyone's word for anything. I'm the guy kicking the door in, so I'm probably not going to be the one staring down the committee . . . but still." He paused for a beat. "Anyway, I wanted evidence. IEDs, the ingredients to make them . . . something. I didn't find anything."

"They weren't making bombs?"

Tyler shook his head. "I went over the whole place. Every room of their house. The hut behind it. I looked everywhere for a hidden door or panel. Nothing. The father was about as old as I am now. He looked healthy. No scars, no burns, no signs of injury. Pretty unusual for someone who's supposed to be a notorious bomb maker."

"What did you do?" Lexi asked.

"I went back to base. Braxton asked me how it went, and I told him fine. It was the end of it as far as he was concerned. The whole thing didn't sit right with me. After Braxton turned in, I went to the XO, a major. I told him what happened, what I didn't find, and how I thought the whole thing stunk. He was a good officer and not a Braxton crony. We went back. He searched the place and agreed with me. Something was amiss. We sent for a medic. One of the first things she did was tell us the girl was pregnant."

Lexi recoiled on the couch. "Wasn't she sixteen?"

"Yeah." Tyler drained the last of his beer while Lexi shook her head. "Remember when I said Braxton had been randomly disappearing for a couple months?"

She grimaced. "He didn't."

"He did. We put it all together in the house and on the way back. I showed the major the orders Braxton gave me. He radioed someone in the J6 . . . intelligence. They confirmed they'd never issued the report."

"Let me make sure I have this straight." Lexi rubbed her forehead. "Braxton knocked up a teenaged girl in Afghanistan. I'm going to guess it wasn't consensual. To cover it up, he faked an intelligence report and sent you there to take out the family under the guise of eliminating terrorist enablers."

"You have it right," Tyler said.

"Oh, my god." Lexi stared at Tyler. Her expression was

unreadable. Too many emotions played out on her face. "What did you do once you knew?"

"I went with the XO and a few other soldiers to confront Braxton. As soon as I walked into his tent, I punched him in the face. It took three men to pull me off him. I wish they hadn't. I would've beaten him to death then and there, and the world would be a better place." Tyler sighed. "Braxton shouted I was done, but then we told him what we knew. He clammed up pretty quick. A couple MPs the major called kept everyone in line. A CID unit turned up to get to the bottom of the whole mess." Tyler paused. "Criminal Investigation Division."

"Figured it was something like that," Lexi said.

"They found it all. Braxton was defiant at first, but once they built a case, he knew the jig was up. I put in to leave the unit. Within a few days, I was on a plane to Germany, and then I was back stateside. Braxton kept command a while. He knew how to stall, and he had friends in high places. At some point, it stopped mattering, and his command crumbled. Once I got home, I was down under a year in my tour, so I filed the paperwork to leave. A few months later, I went on terminal leave. I think Braxton got bounced around the same time."

"You couldn't stand to be in the army anymore?"

"No," Tyler said. "It was a strange feeling after twenty-four years, but I knew it was right. They did a good job investigating Braxton and court-martialing him, but it never should've happened in the first place. Men like him stayed in positions of power too often."

"They're probably better about it now," Lexi said.

Tyler shrugged. "They couldn't be much worse." He frowned at his empty lager bottle. "There you have it . . . the Leo Braxton story. He blames me for the end to his career because I'm the one who fetched the major."

"I'm sorry you had to go through all that." Lexi wiped at her eyes. "I can't even imagine."

"I shot a lot a people over there," Tyler said. "Those four civilians are the only ones I regret, and I think about them every day."

Lexi stood. "Get up."

"What?"

"Get up, Dad."

Tyler stood, and his daughter wrapped him in a tight hug. He put his arms around her and held on tight. He'd told the story before but never to Lexi, and it felt like a weight came off his shoulders. "I'm sorry," she whispered.

"Me, too," Tyler said. They maintained their embrace. At this moment, it was the only bright spot in the world.

19

T yler watched the ten-o'clock local news. Lexi went upstairs shortly after their conversation. She looked drained, and Tyler felt it. He worked on his third lager of the evening when his phone rang. He didn't recognize the number, so he ignored it. It showed up again a moment later. He muted the TV and answered. "Mister Tyler?"

He was surprised to hear a woman's voice. It took a second or two to place it as belonging to Sara Morrison. "I figured you'd be some goon calling to issue a threat."

"I thought I might be warning you of one, though it sounds like you might've put the Braxton and Hexagon connection together on your own."

"They didn't hide it well from anyone in the know," Tyler said. "Maxwell and White inevitably lead to Braxton. He would've still been in Leavenworth when the company started, though. I guess they've been planning this for a while."

"Probably. My deputy and I are going to investigate the company as discreetly as we can. I was wondering if you knew what they might be doing."

"I haven't talked to anyone from the unit since I left. By design."

"I believe you," Sara said. "In your place, I'd probably do the same."

"They have at least one contract with the Pentagon, right?" Tyler asked.

"Yes."

He swirled his beer around in the bottle, watching the amber crawl back down the interior of the glass. "Then, you should already know what they're doing. You hired them for it."

"They're doing the work in the contract. Hell, we even get reports when we're supposed to. Braxton's a red flag, though, and it makes me question whether the company is referring to things which could be considered . . . off the books."

"In a Braxton company," Tyler said, "there's probably a lot of it going on. What work are they supposed to be doing?"

"You know I can't tell you that," Sara said. "If you'd like to come to the Pentagon and go into a SCIF, we can talk all about it."

Tyler turned the TV off. With the conversation focused on Braxton, he didn't feel like watching the news anymore. Like his former commander, it only served to remind him of everything going wrong in the world. "My days of visiting there are over." He paused, wondering the best way to approach the topic. Sara was right not to discuss classified details over the phone, of course. Tyler needed to find what she could discuss. "Maybe you could tell me where they are."

Sara blew a deep breath into the phone. "They're near Bagram Air Base." She paused. "I can tell you a few generalities."

"I'm listening," Tyler said.

"You know our government's official position on the Taliban has evolved over time. Even as we try to negotiate some things with them, we still recognize they're a cabal of assholes. So we're trying to do a few covert things to hit them in the wallet. Stuff they wouldn't be able to attribute to us directly."

Hence the use of a company like Hexagon. Even with American operatives, they weren't the government. Calling the operation covert probably meant the CIA had a piece of whatever went on. The Hexagon team could have cover identities painting them as being from somewhere else. Plausible deniability. Tyler pondered what could be of interest outside the gates of Bagram. The incident he detailed to Lexi took place in the town of Torkman about a mile and a half north of the air base. Tyler heard persistent fighting over the years ruined many of the buildings. Old landmarks were no more. He couldn't think of anything Braxton would want from there, anyway. "Braxton and I did a few tours together. We were never really tight, though. If he had something going back then, I didn't know about it."

"Something going?" Sara said.

"Money. A pile of heroin. Whatever. The army hauled him out of there, and I never heard about them finding a secret stash. If Hexagon is over there looking for something, I'm afraid I can't be much help."

"All right. Be careful, Mister Tyler."

"You, too," Tyler said. "If you keep poking around, you're going to land on Hexagon's radar, too."

"I already have," Sara said.

Tyler polished off the remainder of his beer. "Then, it sounds like we both need to be careful."

~

"MISTER SHAH," Braxton said, easing into his leather executive chair. He sat behind a large desk. A single chair awaited someone on the other side. He always set his offices up this way as a colonel. Make sure people sitting before you know their place and try to put them on edge. If more than one person waited, standing would make the others nervous. It was a great arrangement. Lawrence Shah fidgeted in the task chair, and Braxton never knew him as a man given to fidgeting.

Shah was in his mid-thirties, putting him about twenty years Braxton's junior. He'd been a good solider and unafraid to get his hands dirty even if Army regulations advised doing the opposite. Braxton valued flexibility highly; he found regulations and treaties too rigid. A bunch of guys sat around a table and came up with the supposed rules for combat. It was war. Imposing outside restrictions had no place. Men like Braxton and Shah understood this, even if they paid a price for it.

"Sir," Shah said after a moment, "I'm sorry."

"Tell me what happened."

"I followed the guy. Picked him up along Belair Road coming from the old man's shop. I didn't think he made me."

"Of course he made you," Braxton said.

"I'm good," Shah protested.

"Not good enough. Not this time." Before Shah could say anything else, Braxton raised his hand. "You were up against an experienced professional. Maybe I should've made the details clearer. Anyway, proceed."

"Yes, sir. I tailed him down the road, hanging two or three cars back, sometimes in a different lane. He must've seen me because he made a sudden left just ahead of oncoming cars. I couldn't turn for a good twenty seconds. When I did, it took me some time to reacquire the car."

"And he saw you." It wasn't a question.

Shah nodded. "He'd parked his vehicle and hidden behind a pole. When I drove up, he leaned out. I turned to look, and he snapped my picture."

"So you left."

"Yes, sir. I followed him, but he got the better of me. I figured it was best to abort."

"I think it was, Mister Shah." Braxton leaned back in the chair and kicked his feet up onto the desk. Another show of power. Shah noticed. "Did you ever serve with Mister Tyler?"

"I don't think so, sir. What rank was he?"

"A warrant officer. Warrant Three by the time he left."

"Doesn't sound familiar."

"You remind me of him in some ways," Braxton said. "It's a compliment. Tyler was a hell of a soldier. Great at planning, seeing the possibilities, then kicking the door in and shooting about a dozen people. He was a blunt instrument, but he was a smart one. We cleared a lot of buildings and secured a few towns because of what he did. Afghanistan might still be a shit-hole, but he helped make it safer for every person while he was there."

Shah said, "Yes, sir."

"Tyler and I have . . . history. You probably heard about it. He's dangerous. We can't have people getting spotted following him. I'm not going to give you the detail again."

"Probably for the best, sir."

"Don't screw up again, though," Braxton said. He opened the left-hand drawer and set a military-issue M11 semiautomatic pistol atop his desk. He left it on its side but pivoted it so the barrel pointed toward his subordinate. Shah's eyes followed the movements. "We're down one man because Tyler gave him a concussion. I don't want to have to replace another." Braxton fell silent a few seconds, letting the situation sink in. Make them sweat. "We clear, Mister Shah?"

Shah nodded like a bobblehead. "Crystal, sir."

"Good. Now get out of here."

He left. Braxton took his feet off the desk. He picked up the pistol and looked at it. He recently considered more aggressive measures when it came to Sara Morrison. Tyler posed a more immediate threat. He deserved a more immediate response.

T he next morning, Tyler parked in the lot and surveyed the shop. No new damage. No shadowy figures lurking in the area. When he walked into the garage, Smitty was already on his back under an old Trans Am. "The Bandit drop this off?" Tyler said as he washed his hands.

"Christ almighty!" Smitty said, flailing about under the car. "Don't scare me like that." Smitty wheeled himself out. His eyes retained a little wildness. "Just started. Owner says there's some noise in the engine."

"You find it yet?"

"Nope. He couldn't describe it really well. Someone who bought an older car without knowing anything about them."

"Or cars in general," Tyler added.

"Yeah."

They fired up the engine. Smitty revved it from inside while Tyler listened from the front of the car. Then, they switched. Neither heard anything unusual. The Trans Am featured a thirty-five-year-old V8. It was down on power in Tyler's opinion, but so were a lot of engines from the era. The specter of the 'seventies and the fuel crisis lingered well into the 'eighties and beyond. Tyler felt horsepower remained depressed until the early Aughts.

Next, Tyler listened by the exhaust while Smitty worked the engine. They switched places again and still heard nothing out of the ordinary. Smitty was right: someone bought a cool older car without knowing important things about it—like how it sounded. Someone had to operate a YouTube channel about the sonorous qualities of old Trans Ams. Self-education before buying the car should have been easy.

With the engine blasting, hearing anything else in the shop was impossible. Tyler was startled when Bobby the goon and his slender friend Rust appeared behind him. He had barely any time to react to Bobby's hard right cross. Tyler turned his head a fraction before the blow thundered in. It still took him square in the jaw. Bobby was a large, meaty guy, and he packed a piston-like punch. It drove Tyler back and sent him sprawling to the concrete floor.

"Remember me, asswipe?" he said. His voice sounded loud and rough past the ringing in Tyler's ears. Rust led Smitty back into the office at gunpoint, leaving Tyler alone with Bobby. He didn't have a wrench this time. No tools lay around him. His best shot was grabbing for his gun. Waiting for the right opening may not be an option. "I remember you," Bobby continued. He touched his face where bruising remained.

Bobby stood over Tyler and leaned down. "Where's your wrench now, tough guy?" Tyler went for the pistol, but Bobby swatted it out of his hand and across the floor. He grabbed Tyler by the collar and belt buckle, hoisted him, and flung him into the stacks of tires near the back of the shop. Tyler managed to protect his head with an upraised arm, but the rest of him took a battering. He grunted as vulcanized rubber crashed all around him. Tyler rolled off a tire and slumped to the floor. He wondered if waiting for the gun would have been better.

Tyler got himself up to all fours as Bobby strolled over like he owned the place. His casual demeanor gave Tyler time; he only needed to recover and be able to counter Bobby's attacks. The man was strong but unsophisticated, like someone accustomed to ending a fight in the first ten seconds. Most of the people he beat up were unskilled, and Tyler figured many of them would be cowering in the corner by now.

He was on his knees when his massive adversary stood in front of him. Bobby had something to prove. Tyler shamed him by knocking him out so quickly. He came here for revenge. It meant he wouldn't try to end this right away. He wanted to drag it out . . . savor the beating. The smart play was to knock your opponent out when you held the advantage.

Instead of going for the knockout, Bobby fired off a jab. Tyler turned it aside with his forearm. For the first time, concern darkened Bobby's expression. Another jab. Tyler blocked the second and got to his feet. When Bobby loaded up a haymaker, Tyler threw a short punch into the big man's solar plexus. It staggered him and left him gasping for air. He was smart enough to backtrack as Tyler advanced.

Even sucking wind, Bobby's size posed a problem. Men pushing three hundred pounds rarely toppled from a single blow. Tyler fired off a strong right jab, then a left cross. Bobby rocked backwards but didn't fall. He blocked Tyler's next punch and grabbed his arm. Tyler tried to jerk free, but Bobby shoved him away and spun him across the room. Tyler's feet got tangled, and he crashed to the concrete again. His MII lay too far away to matter.

Bobby stomped to him and leaned down again. "Not so tough without your tools, are you?" he said. Tyler saw the butt of a pistol peeking out of the denim just past the large man's hip. He could make a play for it if Bobby were distracted enough . . . or saw him as an insignificant threat. Tyler blinked rapidly as if trying to both focus on something and stay conscious at the same time. He let his head loll from side to side. "Giving up so soon? I haven't even started on you yet. And now I owe you for the punch."

He bent down farther, so his face was only inches from Tyler's. "I got a lot of pain coming your way, you son of a bitch." Tyler reached up with his left arm and flailed weakly at Bobby's face. As expected, he raised his arms to deflect.

It left the gun at his waist exposed.

Tyler grabbed it, sliding it out of the waistband. Bobby realized what was happening, his eyes went wide, and he used his left arm to try and block Tyler.

It didn't work. Tyler rolled his wrist, leaving the barrel of the gun pressed into Bobby's side above the hip. He pulled the trigger. Contact with flesh damped the report, yet it seemed to thunder in Tyler's ears, the empty space in the repair bay amplifying the sound. Bobby screamed and sagged down atop Tyler. He rolled the larger man off, shoving him onto his back. Before Bobby could say anything else or scream again, Tyler shot him in the head.

"Bobby?" came a voice from the office after the louder gunshot. Tyler scrambled to his feet and put his back to the shop wall. "Bobby?" Rust. Tyler crept along the wall toward the door connecting the shop to the office. "Everything all right in there?" Bobby lay on the left half of the bay. Anyone coming to the door would see the body.

Sure enough, Rust saw it when he poked his head through the door. He was about to say something when Tyler pressed the barrel of the pistol to his head. "We need to have a chat."

~

Tyler shoved Rust into Smitty's chair. Smitty sported a busted lip but otherwise looked none the worse for wear. "Close the shop," Tyler told his boss. "Lock the doors. Draw the blinds." Smitty walked across the office and busied himself with shutting things down and making sure no one could see in. "The bay door, too," Tyler added after a second. Smitty walked into the rear part of the building.

"You killed Bobby," Rust said as he slumped in his seat. His wide eyes darted around the room. Tyler heard a tremble in his voice.

"Yes. Which means I have no qualms about killing you, too."

"I'm not a threat to you."

"My comment stands."

Smitty re-entered the office, closing the connecting door to the work bay behind himself. "All done," he said.

"Good." Tyler sat on the edge of the desk. The first punch from Bobby rang his bell quite hard, and having something to put his weight on felt good. With the adrenaline wearing off, Tyler felt a little woozy. "We run a classic car shop, so I don't like calling you Rust. Let's start with your first name."

"Rick."

"OK, Rick. I think you know Smitty. You can call me Tyler, though I suspect you knew who I was before you came here today." Rick said nothing. "Why don't you tell me who sent you here?"

"I think you know," Rick muttered.

"Tell me, anyway. I'm fifty; I forget things."

"Max."

"Good," said Tyler. "See how easy this is, Rick? We're just having a conversation."

Rick offered a half-hearted nod. "Yeah . . . sure."

"Tell me about the man you know as Max."

"What do you mean?"

"You work for him," Tyler said. "You must know some things about him."

"I don't think he's the boss, but he's the guy we always deal with."

"We?"

"Me and Bobby."

"I guess now you'll have those conversations alone," Tyler said.

"Yeah," Rick said with a sigh.

Even though Tyler figured Max to be Kent Maxwell, he wanted to hear it from Rust. "Tell me what Max looks like."

"A little taller than you, I guess. Maybe six feet. Same kind of hair, though. Short, dark. Acted like he was used to being in charge."

"How old would you guess he was?"

"Younger than you," Rick said. "Maybe forty?"

It fit Maxwell's description. He'd avoided most of the stench and fallout surrounding Braxton at the end. Rather than distance himself from his former commander, however, Maxwell apparently decided to double down on working for him. Tyler didn't understand some people's decision-making abilities. "All right, Rick. Here's what we're going to do. You're going to load Bobby into the trunk of your car, and you're going to drive out of here. You won't tell anyone what really happened here. We clear?"

"Bobby's dead." Rick stared at Tyler, then his eyes flickered to the shop door. Where the body lay. "He's dead."

"Yes, he is," Tyler said.

"You think I can lift his body in my trunk?"

Tyler patted the pistol at his side. "You got him going last time. I think you'd better try."

Ten minutes later, Rick struggled to heft Bobby's corpse into his trunk. Covered in sweat, he climbed into the front seat and drove away. Tyler sank into a chair, and Smitty did the same. "Holy shit," Smitty said. "You killed a man in my shop."

"Yes," Tyler said with a nod, "and if I hadn't, they may have just finished loading *our* bodies into the trunk."

"I know . . . I know." Smitty waved his hands. "It's . . . a lot to take in is all."

"There's more."

"What the hell now?"

"Now, we have to tidy this up. You'll need strong cleaning supplies, bleach, trash bags, and lots of paper towels. Pay cash and split the list between at least two places."

"Sounds like you've done this before," Smitty said. Tyler remained silent. "What are you going to do?"

"The big asshole rang my bell. I'm going to sit here, turn the lights off, and put my head on the desk."

Smitty frowned in concern as he looked at Tyler. "Yeah, maybe you'd better. Wait here. I'll be back."

Tyler envisioned shooting Maxwell and Braxton as he drifted into a fitful rest.

21

After Smitty returned with a bunch of supplies, he closed the shop for the rest of the day. Tyler helped him clean up Bobby's blood and other bits from the bay. It took a few hours to do a thorough job. While everything dried, Tyler popped some acetaminophen. Moving around and breathing in the cleaning solution fumes only served to exacerbate his headache.

Once the floor and equipment were dry, Tyler suggested they leave for the day. Only two cars waited for service, and Smitty was good enough with customers to explain away a minor delay. Tyler pointed to the two large trash bags. "Let's take one each. Drop them in dumpsters at least a couple miles from here. Try not to be seen if you can help it."

Smitty concurred, and they both got in their cars and drove away. Tyler pulled into a small strip mall on Northern Parkway, stopped behind the slapdash building, and tossed the bag into the dumpster. He drove the rest of the way home, popped more pills for his headache, and lay down to rest.

A few hours later, Tyler sat up in bed and rubbed his face. He walked past Lexi's closed bedroom door, heard faint music, and kept going. On the kitchen counter, a pizza box with five slices remaining waited for him. Tyler smiled, put two on a plate, and ate them lukewarm. Getting concussed made him work up an appetite, so he went back and ate another two. He left the final one inside the fridge wrapped in foil.

Tyler settled in to paint. The last couple days ramped up his stress. Just hearing Braxton no longer rotted inside the walls of Leavenworth was bad enough. Piled onto the shit sandwich were getting followed by Lawrence Shah, being on Hexagon's radar, Rick Rust and Bobby coming back, and the latter's grisly —though deserved—demise. Tyler set a new piece of paper on his easel. He started this program to cope with the effects of the PTSD he'd always denied having. Maybe getting out in front of the stress of the last couple days would be better than letting it simmer.

As usual, Tyler didn't sit down to paint any specific thing. He let the creativity take him, as his therapist used to say. It sounded like hokum the first few times she suggested it, but it worked. Tyler picked up a brush, chose some color, and got to work. He lost track of time as the art flowed out of him. His thoughts coalesced on the task before him. When he set his tools down at the end, Tyler felt spent.

He stared at his creation. The ruins of a simple house broke a sun-baked desert landscape. Storm clouds gathered on the horizon, darkening the distant sky. Blood dotted the stones of the former structure. Tyler nodded in appreciation at what he'd created. Between pouring himself into his art and the lingering effects of getting his bell rung, he felt tired. Tyler left the painting where it was and climbed back into bed.

LEXI WALKED DOWNSTAIRS and refilled her water bottle. Her dad must've eaten the rest of the pizza. When she'd checked on him a few hours ago, he was sacked out hard. She opened the fridge, saw the single remaining slice, and grinned. Only her dad would leave one piece of pizza. She walked back upstairs. His bedroom door was closed again, but sounds of snoring still came through. Lexi was about to go back into her room when she noticed the other door open.

He always closed this room behind himself. Her dad didn't like showing off his art . . . even the good pieces. Lexi remembered when he first took up the brushes. He dismissed painting as some cockamamie therapy thought up by a hippie who'd never lived through real stress. In fact, he only did it because he found the idea of a support group repellent. Over time, though, her dad embraced what he created in this room. She never pushed for him to share his output with her. His art was more personal than most.

Her eyes fell on the paper still resting on the easel. It looked like a desert. He hadn't produced a desert piece in years. Worse, the bright sky on the right side of the painting yielded to a dark and ominous one on the left. Lexi counted three yellow lightning bolts set against the inky blackness. The remains of what must have been a house dominated the foreground. The blood on the stones was easy to see.

"Dad, what's going on?" Lexi whispered to the emptiness. In the few months before quitting Patriot Security, he'd produced darker works. Most of the time, though, her dad's watercolors captured bright and hopeful moods. On the crossbar of the tripod was the first bleak one in a while. Lexi sighed. She knew her dad dealt with a lot right now, especially the reemergence of Leo Braxton. A shiver crawled down her spine as she remembered the story.

Lexi stared at the painting. She hoped it wasn't the start of a trend.

∽

JAKE FELT lucky to survive the incident yesterday. Once he got away from the two men looking for him, he hailed a taxi to leave the immediate area. Then, he rode the bus back to where he was staying, conducted a thorough sweep of the area, and finally allowed himself to breathe. It took a few minutes for his hands to stop shaking. After steadying himself and taking down his cameras, Jake slipped out of the hotel.

A thought gnawed at him as he stuck to shadows and side streets. What if he somehow got spotted again? Calling his dad brought the goon squad down on him. They must've tapped his father's phone. Their conversation had been brief but apparently not brief enough. Jake wondered if anyone paid his father a visit afterward. He wished he could do more to help, but he'd only end up getting his dad killed.

Jake ventured into the seedier parts of Baltimore. These were the neighborhoods everyone thought about when they said they didn't like coming into the city. On a normal day, Jake would've avoided them, too, but they were useful for certain things. He needed to be able to protect himself—and his father, if it came down to it. Some things simply couldn't be acquired in the nice and shiny parts of the city.

Ten minutes later, Jake was the not-so-proud and definitely illegitimate owner of a gun. Finding someone to buy from proved easy. Selecting a model in his limited budget provided a bigger challenge. In the end, Jake went a little over what he wanted to spend. He purchased a .357 Ruger revolver, six rounds already in it and twelve more in two speed-loaders. It wouldn't be as much firepower as a semiautomatic, but Jake bought a lot of stopping power for the money he spent.

He needed to get out of Maryland. Under normal circumstances, it would be easy. However, he didn't have his car and felt he couldn't safely retrieve it. He also couldn't use a credit card to buy a bus, plane, or train ticket. It was risky, but he doubled back on himself, got cash from a convenience store ATM, and used different streets to return the way he'd come.

Jake managed to slug his way out of the city, catching a ride into Harford County. He was in Aberdeen, about forty minutes northeast of Baltimore by car. It was home to a large proving ground, and getting a hotel near the installation would chew up too much of his money. Instead, Jake found a place just off Route 40 which took cash and didn't ask questions. The best kind.

His door opened directly to the outside, so Jake mounted a camera above it and another one at the end of the building facing the parking lot and main road. For one night, it would have to do. Tomorrow, he'd work on getting north. He knew Philly pretty well and could probably lean on a non-military friend for some support once he got there. For now, Jake used his phone to make sure he got a clear picture of the outside. All good.

He checked his dad's business Yelp page. They'd established it as a way to get messages to one another in difficult times like past deployments. Nothing new for a while. Jake chose to leave a new review, selected five stars, and entered some text. *The owner is very responsive.* It was generic enough to sound like it came from someone who just wanted to fire off a quick comment. His father would read it, however, and know he needed to reach out.

Jake looked at the contact entry on his phone. His thumb hovered over the entry for his dad's cell phone, but he didn't tap it. Braxton knew red teamers, so he could have access to calls and texts. The indirect Yelp method would need to work for now.

One of the cameras showed an SUV pull into the parking lot. This one was white rather than gray or black, but the hairs on Jake's arms stood at attention. He grabbed the .357, held it at the ready, and crouched behind the bed. The app on his phone showed a man get out of the vehicle and walk toward the main office. Jake thumbed the hammer back. He'd never fired this gun, which was an unfortunate side effect of buying it where he did. If it came down to it, he hoped its good condition meant it worked.

A moment later, the man left the office and headed for the side of the building. All the doors ran down here. A bead of sweat rolled from Jake's temple as footsteps approached. He got a little lower, ensuring only his head stuck up above the mattress. The barrel of the .357 pointed at the door. Anyone walking through would get a nice hole right through his center.

The footfalls moved on. Jake maintained his vigilance. Maybe whoever it was would double back. Perhaps he met another enforcer behind the building. Two muted voices talked from a couple doors down, and two people drew closer. They passed the door. Only when Jake couldn't hear them anymore did he check the phone. Two men climbed back into the SUV and drove away.

Jake set the gun down atop the bed and inhaled a deep breath.

22

B raxton chose some more images from the collection Maxwell took of Sara Morrison. He would give her one more chance to listen to reason. If she remained defiant, there were plenty of other ways to solve the problem of an uppity woman with a fancy title. He attached two more to a new email message and sent it.

As before, he waited about twenty minutes before following up. Executives like Sara Morrison were glued to their government-issued laptops or mobile phones even after sundown. The expectation of eternal email vigilance came with the senior executive jobs. Flag officer, too. Had Braxton's career not been derailed, he would've delayed a promotion to brigadier general as long as he could.

The burner phone was new. Braxton insisted on it. She wouldn't recognize the number. Maybe it would put her back on her heels, make her think two people were coming after her. Her phone rang four times before she picked it up.

"Hello, Miss Morrison," Braxton said when she answered.

"Hello, Colonel Braxton," she said. Her words almost made him drop the phone. How did she know? Did he put something in the emails to give himself away? Maxwell insisted his messages would be anonymous. The burner couldn't be traced to him or the company. What if someone got to her? "Are you still there?"

"Yes," Braxton said.

"Surprised I know who you are?"

"I'll admit I am."

"Pricks like you love power plays," Morrison said. "Your record is full of bullshit like that. You're trying to do it now. Too bad for you I know who you are. I suppose I misspoke by addressing you as a colonel. The army didn't let you keep your rank when they banished you to Leavenworth."

"The army decided to fight the war with both hands tied behind their back," said Braxton. "I only wanted to make it even, make it fair. People like your bosses couldn't stand it. So they drummed me out for not being politically correct enough."

"You know I've read your file, right? I know what they charged you with. Rape of a teenaged Afghan girl, murdering her and her family, a bunch of other crimes . . . I'm surprised you got out when you did."

"A few people still like me," Braxton said. "People with spines. Men who know how wars are supposed to be fought."

"I could probably make some guesses who you're talking about." Braxton didn't say anything. "We just encouraged one to hang it up. They're dinosaurs exactly like you."

"You know who I am. Good job—someone tipped you off, and you can read a file." Now Morrison fell silent. She didn't deny someone told her about Braxton. He pondered who it could be. No one in Hexagon Security would be so disloyal. It had to be someone who disliked him and wanted to stop him. Maybe a person with a grudge. Someone like Tyler. It would fit his meddlesome pattern. "You can still make things easier for yourself, Miss Morrison. Call me a dinosaur all you want, but men like me know how to solve problems in the Middle East. No one else does."

"Go to hell, Braxton," said Morrison. "I'll never work with you or anyone like you."

"You're forcing my hand."

"No, I'm not. You're an asshole, and you're going to do what you want. Your record is the best example of that."

Braxton hung up. The hell with Sara Morrison. If she wouldn't play ball, Arthur Bell would be more than willing to accept a promotion.

MAXWELL ENDED the call with Braxton. His boss spent the prior ten minutes yelling at him about Sara Morrison. She refused to play ball and drop her investigation into Hexagon. Maxwell didn't think she'd find anything—even the connection to Braxton constituted a bit of a leap. He wasn't mentioned anywhere in the company's documentation. It would be an inconvenience, but nothing immediate would happen. They could still find what they were looking for in Afghanistan.

Braxton preferred a more immediate resolution. He was convinced Sara Morrison was a bulldog who wouldn't let the bone go, and she'd march up and down the halls of the Pentagon telling everyone to put their company on the blacklist. During their days serving together, Maxwell often found himself dulling the harder edges of Braxton's persona.

The former colonel wouldn't be restrained anymore, however. He wanted Sara Morrison dealt with. Maxwell sent a text to Arthur Bell inviting him to a Skype call. The company encrypted all communications end to end. Maxwell opened the app on his tablet, joined the conference, and Arthur Bell appeared a moment later. "It's late, Maxwell."

"I didn't know you could only get promoted to SES during daylight hours."

Bell frowned. "What are you talking about?"

"I think your boss is going to be . . . reassigned. It's logical to presume her deputy would take over . . . on an acting basis if not permanent."

"Usually how it works," Bell said.

"I presume investigations into the company would stop after this happened," Maxwell said. "You conducted a thorough background check, of course, and we don't need to waste any more time dealing with one woman's witch hunt."

"I think we're on the same page here."

"Good. Treat everything as normal for now. If you hear your boss has taken another position, don't be surprised."

"It's a competitive world out there," Bell said. "Hard to get ahead and stay there."

"Sometimes," Maxwell said, "the rat race can be murder."

TYLER WOKE up and felt like a fog lifted sometime in the night. If he suffered a concussion in the fight with Bobby yesterday, it had been a mild one. His last came more than a decade ago courtesy of a grenade tossed by a Taliban fighter. Tyler sat up and rubbed his face. He looked at the alarm clock on his night-stand. Not quite nine. Sleeping so late felt like a luxury. Tyler climbed out of bed, got in the shower, and put clean clothes on.

He walked downstairs to find half a pot of coffee still hot and waiting for him. In her morning sweep of the kitchen, Lexi also left a few slices of bacon on a plate. Tyler smiled. He never expected Lexi to come and live with him, but now, he wouldn't have it any other way. If she left for college in the spring after going online for the upcoming semester, the house would feel empty. Doubly so when she inevitably moved out. Not for the first time, Tyler wished he could rewind several years to do things differently.

After making some toast to go with his bacon, Tyler took a few minutes to eat breakfast. He felt like he'd neglected the search for Jake in all the hullaballoo over Braxton and Hexagon. Sorting out the whole mess would only help Jake, as he'd gotten entangled with the same men. Leo Braxton's pernicious influence served as one of the few constants in life. If Tyler could footprint the organization, he'd be better armed to deal with them, get Jake out from under, and shut Braxton and his cronies down for good.

He started by calling his boss. "You have a camera in the work bay?" Tyler said when Smitty answered the phone.

"Sure. Gotta make sure you really know how to do a brake job."

At least Smitty tried to stay in good spirits despite the shit piling up around him. "Can you send me some screen captures of Rust and Bobby? I want to run facial recognition on them."

"You still think you can find Jake?" Smitty asked.

"I know I haven't made a lot of progress there," Tyler admitted. "Knowing who's looking for him can help. If I learn as much as I can about their company, I'll know who we're up against, and we can figure some things out from there."

Smitty blew out a deep breath before answering. "Hell, I gotta figure out how to do it, but I think I can. I'll send something to you soon." Tyler confirmed Smitty had his email address—he didn't at first—before hanging up. The downtime waiting for the message proved an excellent excuse to get more coffee. A few minutes later, Smitty's email came in. Two photos stared back at Tyler.

Richard Rust served eight years in the national guard without distinguishment or demerit. He spent at least half his time in supply, eventually reaching staff sergeant before leaving the service. Robert Adamski never enlisted. Instead of a service record, he had a rap sheet. The late Bobby used his size to earn his money, garnering three charges for assault—convicted once—and another for attempted murder, which was dropped. Hiring a person like him would be out of character for Braxton. He favored a list of morally questionable attributes Bobby certainly possessed but also the self-discipline he appeared to lack.

These two plus Kent Maxwell, Lawrence Shah, Victor White, and Braxton himself were a good start. Tyler needed to connect the dots. He stared at the menu of options the laptop presented him. He'd seen these devices do a lot of frightening things in the hands of skilled operators. Tyler resided somewhere toward the end of the unskilled spectrum. Just when he was thinking about summoning some reinforcements, Lexi came downstairs. "Can you help me with something?"

"You need to turn the printer on," she said with her head in the fridge.

Tyler grinned. "I'm not a complete idiot when it comes to these things. I need to connect a few people. Social media and all. Much more up your alley than mine."

Lexi ripped the plastic top off a small yogurt. "All right." She grabbed a spoon and sat beside Tyler. "Let me see what you have."

He handed her the laptop. "What does this thing run?" Lexi said as she poked around a couple of the options.

"I don't know." Tyler shrugged. "Linus or something."

Lexi looked at her dad and rolled her eyes. "Linux. And it's a short 'i' sound. I learned some in high school."

"I learned woodworking and repair from a man with three fingers on one hand," Tyler said.

"Gross. I guess you win." Lexi opened a few applications. Tyler recognized one from her earlier help. She dragged their pictures into a folder. A circle in the center of the screen changed colors and rotated. When everything finished, several more faces filled the screen. Tyler spotted a few familiar ones, including Braxton, Maxwell, and White. Lexi clicked another button, and the laptop generated a report.

"I didn't know it could assemble and print it for me," Tyler admitted.

Lexi looked askance at him. "How did you use it?"

"Got the information I wanted, wrote it down, and turned the thing off."

"At least you didn't chisel out a stone tablet," Lexi said.

"It's hard to find a hammer sometimes, smartass," Tyler said.

"I learned from the best. You need anything else?"

"You've found all these people on social media, right?" Lexi nodded. "Does the laptop or the app keep track of what they post?"

"I think it can." She clicked on a menu of options. "Yeah, here." She pointed at one of the choices. "This can send you a text if they post something."

"Wow," Tyler said. "I guess I should've paid more attention to those red team guys. Go ahead and set it up."

"I did." Lexi leaned over, kissed Tyler on the cheek, and stood. "See you later, Dad."

"Yeah." Tyler looked at the output he wasn't aware the laptop could assemble. Danny giving one of these machines to every Patriot employee was a little frightening considering all the things they could do. It would be easy for someone to stalk an ex, for instance. These computers were tools, and any tool could be misused by a bad actor.

The names and connections between them helped Tyler footprint the organization. Some of the men—all the employees were male, which didn't surprise him—shared contacts outside their military pasts. Tyler wondered if these people were part of the organization or soon would be. A lot of names populated the list. Tyler had seen things like it before.

Taking out one Taliban commander or terrorist cell leader plunged their units into death spirals. The same would happen here. If Tyler took Braxton down—and maybe Maxwell, too, for good measure—Hexagon would unravel. The threats to him and Jake would cease.

It all started from the top.

23

Rick Rust owned a small detached home in Laurel. Beige siding covered the outside. A large porch allowed for seating outside the front door. The driveway led to a one-car garage. All the place needed was a white picket fence, and it could get listed in an Americana catalog. For a man of questionable ethics who worked for a war criminal, Rust chose a nice house in a good neighborhood.

Tyler sat in the 442. He curbed it across the street two homes up from Rust's. There had been little activity in the half-hour he sat and waited. Most people here were either in their offices or working from home. One man in a car didn't merit a lot of attention. Rust's house was dark. The garage made it difficult to know if he was home, but Tyler figured the man was out. He wondered what Rust was up to. Who was he strong-arming or harassing for the benefit of Leo Braxton today?

It made him wonder if Smitty's shop was still on the radar. Tyler fired off a text to his boss. *I'm outside someone's house. Keep your eyes open and remember what I gave you a few days ago.* He hoped Smitty would realize the last part referred to the gun Tyler took from Rust. Smitty insisted he knew how to shoot.

Tyler hoped he did, and he doubly hoped it wouldn't be necessary.

A return message came in. *I got it. All quiet so far. Good luck.*

Tyler looked at his stack of papers. He was glad the laptop would track things for him, especially on social media. In the meantime, he needed raw data, so he printed out the report Lexi helped him prepare. It produced a hefty output, and he split it up into a couple different folders. Rust still kept a land-line phone . . . an odd quirk for a millennial. In Tyler's limited experience, most of them dismissed the quaint technology while eating avocado toast. He called the number. It rang five times before clicking over to a generic voicemail greeting. Tyler hung up without leaving a message.

He shifted in the seat and kept his vigil. He'd done similar tasks in Afghanistan. Terrorist targets weren't always home when the army came calling. Recon was important. Tyler got out of the car, walked across the street with his hands in his pockets, and moved past Rust's house. After the next dwelling, he cut across a yard. Homes on the next street lay across a short stretch of trees. Tyler padded through the thicket and surveyed the back of Rust's place. No lights in the rear, either. A short chain-link fence would be easy to hop. The small yard led to another door.

Breaching the rear entrance would be easier. Tyler pondered how long to wait for Rust as he walked back to his car. What if the man was out all day? Maybe he could use the Patriot laptop to keep tabs on him. As Tyler considered the gaps in his understanding of technology, his phone vibrated in his pocket.

Sara Morrison.

～

Sara Morrison enjoyed working from home. She got to do it more in recent months but didn't expect this perk to last long-term. Not being in the office limited her to unclassified work only, but plenty still heaped her plate. Just catching up on email and routine tasks would make her next day in the office smoother.

It had been a productive morning. Were she in the office, Sara would have gone to lunch by now, but since she was already home, she kept working. There were always contracts and proposals to look over, not to dwell on ever-shifting rules and regulations to remain on top of. None of the work could be called exciting, but Sara spent years cultivating expertise. She could draft a scathing rebuke of a proposal before most people finished reviewing the particulars.

A major in the next office talked to Sara about working from home in trying times. He mentioned a gun, which she owned, and proficiency in using it, which she possessed from concealed carry classes and live fire. The tradeoff was not having the safety measures built in to working at the Pentagon. Getting past the gates would prove a challenge for most people. Gaining access to the building was almost impossible without the required ID and documentation. Moving around meant someone would encounter security frequently. Plenty of ways to stop a bad actor.

At home, Sara counted on a security system and a gun.

It would need to be enough. She'd practiced the scenarios since Braxton's initial contact and implied threat. Her office featured a metal door and industrial locks which would be a challenge to breach. She knew how to activate them quickly. The exterior wall of the second-story room was brick, and she brought in a contractor to reinforce the floor under her. The window represented a vulnerability, but Sara installed a metal cage behind it to help until she could upgrade it. She considered making more coffee when her system showed a dark gray

SUV pulling up near her house. She used the camera and zoomed in as much as it would allow. Two figures sat inside. They looked large and male.

She'd never seen a vehicle like this sitting in the neighborhood before. It couldn't be good. Braxton must have decided to take more aggressive action. Sara grabbed her phone. The police would take time to get here, and they might not recognize the threat even with her explanation. Anyone she knew in security at the Pentagon was too far away. Down on options, Sara dialed John Tyler and hoped for the best. "I think some men are here for me," she said when he picked up.

"How many?"

"Two so far."

"I'm in my car," he said. She heard a throaty engine fire up in the background. "Tell me what they're doing."

"Sitting there for now. I can't make out much more. They could be waiting for someone else."

"All right. Stay on the line for now. I'm heading your way."

"Please hurry, Mister Tyler," Sara said.

24

Tyler stomped on the accelerator, and the 442 surged around yet another Prius. Montgomery County was lousy with them for some reason. In his younger days, he would have relished snapping off a quick downshift. Now, he appreciated the automatic doing it for him. He didn't know if he'd ever come to like it, but he could live with it.

"I'm five minutes out," he said to Sara Morrison. "What's going on?"

"Another SUV pulled up," she said. "One of them just got out." Her voice trembled a bit. "He's big."

"Braxton attracts that type. If they can't make it in football, they'll find other ways to push people around."

"I'm securing my office door," Sara said. Tyler heard a slam, then a series of locks engaging. "It's solid. If they get past it, it won't be quickly. I had it specially added to the house."

"You anticipated an asshole former colonel would send a couple goons to shoot you?" Tyler said. "With your foresight, they should make you SECDEF."

Sara let out a light chuckle. Under different circumstances, Tyler would have liked the sound of it. "If I survive this, maybe

I'll have a chance." She paused. "Shit. Two others got out, too. They're headed toward the house."

"How long will your door hold them out?"

"It's designed to stop people breaking it down . . . small arms fire, those sorts of things. It should buy me a few minutes. It's supposed to keep me safe until the cops come."

"Have you called them?"

"Should I?" Sara said.

"It can't hurt. I think I'm pretty damn good, but you might want a plan B . . . especially if they have one."

"OK. I'll call them now. Hurry, Mister Tyler."

"I'm on it." He hung up and let Sara call the police. Three minutes remained, according to his GPS. It would take the two guys a minute to get into the house. Tyler knew from Google Sara's house was a two-story model. It would take them at least another minute to clear the first floor, presuming they were competent. It didn't leave them much time to try and breach the door.

A good security door could hold out for a minute.

Tyler got off the highway. He hit the ramp and sped down the road. Maybe two minutes. He needed to make a right in four blocks. Two lights stood in the way. The first flashed to red as he approached. Tyler saw only one car waiting to go on the cross street. He didn't slow down, and once the car passed, he blasted the 442 through the intersection. The next light remained green. It changed to yellow as Tyler approached. He was ready to go through it.

The minivan in front of him, however, hit its brakes.

Tyler jerked the wheel to the right. The 442's rear danced out, but he kept it in line and got around the van while the light still showed yellow. Two blocks later, he swung a hard right, working with the oversteer and getting back on the gas to pull out of the turn. Sara lived on a narrower street, and parked cars dotted both sides of it, so Tyler tempered his speed.

He saw two gray SUVs as he approached. Braxton must have gotten a volume discount on the damn things. The GPS's pseudo-friendly mechanical voice told Tyler he arrived. Three guys. Braxton was old-school enough and sexist enough to figure a trio of lummoxes could take out a woman. The residential neighborhood posed another problem. Tyler didn't bring heavy hardware for fear of collateral damage. Sara's single-family home was about thirty feet from her neighbors on either side. A stray round from a large-caliber rifle could take out someone next door.

Tyler slid his car into a spot across the street. He brought his trusty M11 with two spare magazines for offense and wore a bullet-resistant vest for defense. He could go in the front door. More direct. Also more likely to be heard or seen. Going in the back would increase his chances of being undetected. The tradeoff was time. It would take longer to get to the rear of the house, and then still longer to move throughout the house.

Sara may not have an abundance of time.

In the final analysis, it was familiar territory. In Afghanistan, Tyler kicked down lots of front doors and faced more than three assholes. He ducked and sprinted across the street, then up Sara's walkway. He put his back to the door and looked to the right. A large window. He peered into it and saw Sara's living room. Furniture but no people. Tyler tried the door —locked. He popped it with the snap gun and went inside.

Voices came from somewhere above. "Open up, bitch!"

"Eloquent," Tyler muttered to himself. Stairs leading to the second story were immediately inside the front door. Tyler turned to the side, led with his pistol, and climbed one carpeted step at a time. Braxton's goons yelled more curses and threats at Sara. They pounded the door but made no progress. Tyler reached the top of the stairs and walked onto the landing. A bathroom sat dead ahead, and 180-degree right led to the hall. From there, Sara's office was down another carpeted corridor to the left.

Tyler peeked around the junction. Three men stood outside the door. The largest tried kicking it to no avail. Another pulled a gun and fired a shot into the lock. They all covered their ears at the noise. Tyler took the opportunity to shoot the closest one twice in the back. His body slumped forward into the door and slid to the floor. The other two ducked into a crouch right away. Smart. As he turned, though, Tyler had ample opportunity to shoot one in the head right away. His body fell beside his teammate's.

The third scampered through a nearby door on the right before Tyler could draw a bead on him. He needed to end this quickly. No calls for reinforcements. Tyler put his back against the right-hand wall and moved down. He reached the door and popped his hand in the opening before retracting it. Sure enough, the guy inside opened fire. Tyler dropped to a crouch, spun into the doorway, and took the surprised gunman with two bullets in the chest. In case the man wore a vest, Tyler entered the room and finished him off with a round to the head.

With all three men down, Tyler knocked on the office door. "It's Tyler," he said. "The men here are dead." A moment later, locks disengaged from inside the room. Sara Morrison flashed a nervous smile. She was tall, probably five-eight in tennis shoes, and a full head of auburn hair framed her pretty face. Based on her position with the department, she must have been around her mid-forties but looked about a decade younger.

"Thanks for coming," she said.

"We shouldn't stick around," said Tyler. "Braxton might send more men. You should go somewhere."

Sara crossed her arms under her breasts, emphasizing

them. "I am not going into hiding, Mister Tyler. An asshole like Leo Braxton won't hold that kind of sway over me."

"I admire your spirit, Miss Morrison, but I want to keep you alive."

"Why?"

"Leo Braxton wants you dead," Tyler said, "and I hate him. For now, it's reason enough."

"I appreciate your honesty," she said.

"I can probably find someone to stay with you. How quickly can you pack a few things?"

"Already did just in case. I'll get it." While she did, Tyler collected phones from the three corpses. A moment later, Sara followed him downstairs with a leather overnighter slung over her left shoulder. "You have a gun in there?" Tyler said.

"Of course."

"Good. I hope you won't need it." One of the cell phones rang in Tyler's pocket. "We should go," he said.

25

Another cell phone rang as they walked to the car. Tyler let it go to voicemail. He and Sara got into the 442. "Nice car," she said while buckling her seatbelt.

"Thanks," Tyler said. "I put a lot of work into it." The engine rumbled as he pulled away from the curb. "You're sure you won't opt to get out of town for a while?"

"Absolutely not," Sara said. "Would you let Braxton drive you away?"

"Of course not. But I'm—"

"A man?"

Tyler smirked. "I was going to go with an experienced special forces operative. Seems more relevant than my sex." He took out his phone once they were on a wider street. "Man or woman, I don't think you should stay anywhere by yourself right now. I need to call someone who can help you."

"A babysitter?"

"Call it what you want, but you need one after tonight."

Sara nodded and took a deep breath. For a woman who recently hosted three uninvited killers in her house—and heard them shot outside her office door—Tyler thought she was holding up well. "You're right," she said after a moment. "I hate feeling like I'm being looked after, but you're right. Who are you calling?"

"Think you might know him?"

"I *have* read your file, Mister Tyler."

"I'm sure you did. His name is Rollins." Tyler dialed the number. The sound of ringing from the speakers filled the car.

"I'm guessing your Bluetooth setup isn't an Oldsmobile original," said Sara.

"The car's fifty years old," Tyler said. "I didn't see the need to keep it stock."

"Hello?" came through the audio systems.

"Rollins, it's Tyler."

Silence served as the only reply for a few seconds. Then, Rollins said, "What do you need?"

"Why do you assume I need something?"

"You're not the type to make social calls."

It was certainly a fair point. "Fine. I have someone I'd like you to look after."

"Look after?"

"Three men just came to her house to kill her," Tyler said. "I know who's responsible, but I can't go after them and see her safe."

"Who is she?" Rollins asked.

"Sara Morrison. She's—"

"She's tired of being talked about like she's not in the car," Sara broke in. "Hello, Mister Rollins. I work for the Department of Defense. My exact title isn't important, but apparently, a certain former colonel doesn't care for my investigation into his private military company."

The speakers gave Rollins' sigh a bigger hiss than it may have otherwise enjoyed. "I'm gonna guess we're talking about Braxton."

"We are," Tyler said.

"Shit. His company . . . did he get out of jail?"

"Unfortunately, yes. Many years too soon. Can you help us?"

"Sure," Rollins said. "Where are you?"

"Just leaving Columbia. I'm headed your way."

"Meet me on Fort Meade. The USO building."

"Done. Thanks." Tyler hung up.

They'd already left the area, so Tyler took the next ramp and got the car back on I-95, this time heading south. The exit he needed was six miles away, and the Fort wasn't far from there. Fifteen minutes, tops. He would have preferred to make the trip in silence, but Sara had other plans. "When did you become a knight-errant?" she said.

"I'll need to remember the title," Tyler said. "They always ask you when you file your taxes."

"I'm serious. You spent almost twenty-five years in the army. Then, you went on to some kind of executive protection thing."

"I did more than simply protect rich assholes."

"You did?"

"Sure," Tyler said. "I protected plenty of middle-class assholes, too."

Sara chuckled. It was good to see her retain a sense of humor after the day's events. "You left as a Warrant Three."

"Yep. Didn't try for four, and no one makes Warrant Five."

"True. But I'm guessing you left over the Braxton incident." Tyler remained silent. "Is that it?"

"You're oversimplifying it," he said after several seconds.

"Then, complicate it for me."

Tyler fought a grin. He liked Sara Morrison. She'd survived and thrived in a workplace dominated by men. A trio of murderous goons couldn't quell her spirit. "I've always felt I should've known the orders he gave me were fake."

"You needn't blame yourself," Sara said. "Braxton made sure everything looked legit."

"I know. Some part of me gets it. But I watched their house for a couple hours before. . . . None of the signs were there. We knew who a lot of people trafficking IEDs were. I didn't see any of them. Didn't hear from any on the comms. No signs of equipment." Tyler shook his head. "In the end, I thought maybe they were keeping things on the down-low, figuring we were onto them or something."

"It's a reasonable conclusion."

"Maybe it is." Tyler took his right hand off the wheel and waved it. "Anyway, I'm not trying to recount my tale of woe. Braxton ended up going down for it."

"So you moved on because it left you disillusioned," said Sara. "That's understandable."

"It wasn't just what Braxton did," Tyler said after a few seconds. "It was the support he got. The son of a bitch raped a teenaged girl and ordered her family killed to cover it up. Any rational person would want to shoot him or toss him into a hole and fill it with napalm. But a bunch of people came out in support for him. Other colonels. Flag officers. It was disgusting. Braxton delivered a lot of dead terrorists, and it was all they cared about. They were willing to paper over the rest if he could keep bringing in results."

Sara let out a long, slow breath. "Jesus. The good ol' boys really stand up for one another, don't they?" She shrugged. "Truth is, a lot of women are taking pages from the same sad playbook."

"The army still seems to prefer the male kind. You know a lot of them are still around, right? Some of the older ones retired or died, but the colonels and one-stars back then have two or three stars now. And they're the ones who want to see companies like Braxton's given free rein to shoot as many people as possible."

"You'll take him down," Sara said. "I'll give you what help I can."

Before Tyler could say anything else, one of the stolen phones rang again.

A FEELING of dread clawing at Leo Braxton's gut told him things went south. It should have been an easy mission. Three operatives against one middle-aged woman. How could it go off the rails? After another call went to voicemail, Braxton slammed his phone down. Sara Morrison worked around enough military men. She probably slept with some. Maybe one of them taught her to shoot. Her odds of taking out all three enforcers were nonexistent, however.

Braxton picked up his phone again and tried the first number. Finally, someone answered. "Sitrep."

"Hi, Leo," said a voice Braxton couldn't place at first. "I don't know if this is asshole one, two, or three's phone. I didn't have much time to assign them numbers. Whoever it is can't talk right now, though. Want to know why?"

He recognized the voice. "Tyler," Braxton said through clenched teeth.

"It's me. You didn't answer my question, though. Want to guess why your goons can't answer their phones?"

"They're dead."

"Very much so," Tyler said. "I stripped their comms, but I left their wallets. If they carried company IDs, I'm sure you and your toadies will have some questions to answer."

"I'm not worried," Braxton said.

"You should be. You were safe in Leavenworth. Out here, you're on my radar. Fold your company, stop all this bullshit, and we'll call it a day."

Braxton rolled his eyes to the empty room. "You'd really let me go?"

"Maybe," Tyler said. "You'd be looking over your shoulder regardless."

"I'm a man of many interests, *John*. You'd do well to stay away from my operation."

"Can't do it. Tell you what, Leo—walk away from Jake Smith and Sara Morrison. Then, you and I can hash out the rest with less collateral damage."

"I figured it was a matter of time before you got involved," Braxton said. "You always turn up where you're not welcome. What option could a do-gooder with so much blood on his hands have?" Tyler didn't reply. "You're always going to oppose me because you know we're so much alike . . . and you hate it."

"No," Tyler said, "I just hate you." He broke the connection. Braxton scowled at his phone before setting it back down. Tyler's prior involvement in all this had been peripheral. An annoyance. Now he killed three men and presumably rescued Sara Morrison.

His greater involvement deserved a swift and brutal response.

26

"**T**hat went well," Sara Morrison said after allowing Tyler a couple minutes to cool off.

"Considering I never wanted to talk to him again, I think it went better than I could've expected."

"I didn't know it was possible to blast so much testosterone through a cellular connection."

Tyler grinned in spite of himself. "You wouldn't let me talk about you like you weren't here. I needed another outlet."

One more exit remained on I-95. They would reach Fort Meade in under ten minutes. Tyler enjoyed the silence, though he also thought of some questions for Sara. It had been at least a decade since he set foot in the Pentagon and probably about as long since he talked to a high-ranking civilian. In her position, she knew more about Hexagon than anyone outside the company. "What do you think Braxton is after?"

"What do you mean?" she asked.

"We both know he didn't start a company so he could be a nice guy to the government. Even if his name isn't on the deed, he's been involved from the start. It means he wants something, and he's promised a piece of whatever it is to Kent Maxwell and Victor White."

"You served with the man . . . you'd probably have a better idea than I would."

Tyler was about to answer when he spied a gray SUV in the rearview. The phones. Braxton could be tracking them. He eased the 442 into the far right lane and backed off the throttle a bit. The car coasted along at the speed limit of 65. For most Maryland drivers, obeying the posted speed meant standing still. Sure enough, vehicles drove by on the left, some of them swinging out from behind Tyler to pass him. The SUV moved closer on the driver's side.

Sara ducked in her seat as Tyler moved his right hand to his gun and pulled it from the holster. He kept it hidden under his left arm as the gray vehicle approached. When it did, Tyler saw it was a Chevy Suburban, not the similar GMC Yukon. A man and woman cruised past him. Tyler holstered the pistol and handed Sara the phones. "Toss them out the window. I should've thought of it sooner."

"You were concerned the SUV was another Braxton crew?" She cranked the window down by hand. It amazed Tyler how many people didn't know what to do when no power switch was available.

"Yes." He sped up as Sara heaved each of the phones into the trees lining the highway. Once she'd discarded them all, Tyler moved a couple lanes to the left and gave the car more gas. "You mentioned I'd know more about what Braxton's looking for in Afghanistan. I'm afraid I don't. If you read our files, you know I had my issues with him, but I never knew him to be a thief."

"You think it's money?" Sara said.

Tyler shrugged. "It makes the most sense. He might have some hidden opium stash over there, I guess. Maybe even gold. Cash makes the most sense. We disrupted a lot of shady operations. MPs and CID took money and contraband when we found it. Braxton could've been skimming the till, and I never would've known."

"Any idea where he might hide it?"

"None," Tyler said. "When I left, the writing was on the wall for him. He ended up with more time than I thought, but I don't know if he could hide something major. There were a lot of eyes on him then." Tyler paused. "You must see the reports the company files."

"They come in to my office, yes," Sara said.

"Nothing you can glean from there?"

She shook her head as Tyler took the exit onto Route 32. The back gate of Fort Meade lay only a few minutes away. "It's all pretty vague. As far as we can tell, they're doing what we're paying them to. Considering the men involved with the company, though, I'm concerned about off-the-books stuff."

"I would have the same worries." A couple minutes later, Tyler and Sara showed their IDs and entered the installation. They drove a few blocks before Tyler pulled into a small parking lot outside a nondescript one-story building. A large pickup truck waited. As Tyler turned off the ignition, Rollins climbed down to meet them.

He was about ten years younger than Tyler. They'd overlapped a few times in the service, including once on a deployment to Bagram Air Base. Rollins stood a little taller than Tyler, though they probably weighed about the same. He was black and wore his hair very short. Tyler recalled his ability to sneak around virtually anywhere undetected. He also remembered Rollins as quiet and private; he didn't even know the man's first name. The two bumped fists. "Thanks for meeting us," Tyler said.

Rollins nodded. "Miss Morrison, I presume?"

"Mister Rollins," she said. "You're my designated bodyguard?"

"Not the term I'd use, but I'll keep you safe."

Sara collected her bag from the backseat. "I hope you're not expecting any Whitney Houston and Kevin Costner moments."

"You're not my type," Rollins said with the shadow of a grin playing on his face.

"Thank you, Mister Tyler," Sara said. She gave him a brief hug before walking around to the passenger's side of the pickup.

"I hope this doesn't last more than a few days," Tyler said.

"It takes as long as it takes," Rollins told him. "I don't hate Braxton like you do, but I get it. You need me to be more than a babysitter, call me."

"I will. Thanks." They bumped fists again, and Rollins returned to his pickup. Tyler watched them drive away before he got back into his car.

TYLER PULLED the 442 into his driveway. Despite helping Sara, he felt conflicted. He hadn't found Jake yet. How could he tell Smitty he saved a woman who works at the Pentagon while the man's own son still ran for his life? Killing three of Braxton's men would help from a numbers perspective, but it also put Tyler in the crosshairs. Finding new psychos to replace the deceased trio—not to mention Bobby—wouldn't be hard for a man like Braxton.

He turned the car off and walked into the house. Lexi stretched out on the couch, watching some TV show Tyler couldn't identify. She paused it when he came in. Her smile of greeting turned to a frown of concern. "What happened?"

Tyler realized he must have worn the stress of the past few hours on his face. "I left this morning to watch someone's house. Should have been easy . . . if a little boring." Thirst twisted his stomach, and Tyler grabbed a bottle of water from the fridge. He guzzled most of it before continuing. "It turned into a hell of a lot more."

Lexi sat up and glared at her dad. "Explain."

"I was sitting on someone's house," Tyler said. "I'd just gone to check the perimeter when I got a phone call. Sara Morrison . . . she works at the Pentagon. We've talked a little about Braxton and his company. She was concerned some men were coming to her house to attack her. Turns out she was right."

"And you dealt with them."

"Yes."

"They're Braxton's men?" Lexi asked.

"They are. He kept calling them after everything went down. I'd taken their phones, so I answered. We had a brief conversation."

Lexi smirked. "I'm going to guess it didn't go well."

"Depends on how you want to interpret it," Tyler said. "I pissed him off, which I always enjoy. It put me on his radar, though. I don't know if he suspected my involvement before, but he knows it for sure now."

"All right." Lexi's head bobbed slowly as she took it all in. Tyler understood it was a lot to unpack. "What happened to this Sara Morrison person?"

"I dropped her off with an old army buddy. He'll keep an eye on her."

"You're sure Braxton won't be able to get to her?"

"Positive," Tyler said. He downed the rest of his water and grabbed another. "Want one?"

"I'm good."

Tyler carried the bottle to the couch and sat beside his daughter. Worry still pulled her brows into a frown. "I'm not going to tell you not to be concerned. You're an adult. I'd like to avoid bullshitting you."

"Good," she said. "I wouldn't believe you."

"Braxton's probably going to come after me at some point.

I'm getting in the way of him going after Jake and getting whatever he's after in Afghanistan. I'll be smart, though. I'll wear a
vest, and you know I don't go anywhere without a gun."

Lexi didn't respond for a few seconds. Then, she blew out a
deep breath and said, "When you left Patriot, I kind of hoped
you'd settle into a normal life." She held up her hand when
Tyler started to answer. "I've realized it's not who you are. You
can fix old cars all you want, but you'll never be just a
mechanic."

Tyler smiled. "I wish you would've told me a few days ago."

"A man's gotta be who he is," she said, with no mimic of her
grandfather's voice like last time.

"Anyone ever tell you you're wise beyond your years?"

"I've had a couple pretty good teachers," Lexi said.

As soon as Braxton got off the phone with Tyler, he ordered a
full dossier on the man. Persistence was normally a virtue he
admired. Not in the case of John Tyler. He questioned orders,
couldn't let things go, and got way too attached to a few dispos-
able civilians. His tenacity brought the end of Braxton's career.
He'd been angry and bitter at first, and thinking about Tyler
still stirred those emotions. Working with Maxwell and White
to form Hexagon offered a reprieve, especially in the financial
sense.

Then, Tyler cropped up again.

Dealing with Jake Smith turning into a rat had been bad
enough. Braxton thought the young soldier possessed a good
deal of potential. Like Tyler, however, he saw the world in black
and white. Both his antagonists lacked a certain moral flexibility. Now, both needed to be dealt with. His men were close to
finding Jake. They'd almost nabbed him once. Catching him
was inevitable.

Tyler, however, proved a thornier problem.

He was smart and experienced. While he didn't dwell in the shades of gray Braxton favored, Tyler never had any problem killing the enemy. He was a blunt instrument and a damn good one. Sending a couple operatives to round him up wouldn't be enough. Braxton needed a plan, and he required information to make a good one.

John Tyler lived in Baltimore. He'd bought the house from his father during his active-duty years and settled there once he retired from the service. For the last year or so, his daughter Alexis lived with him. Braxton remembered meeting the girl a few times when she was young. Now, she was eighteen and about to begin her freshman year at the University of Maryland. Tyler's ex Rachel—the two never married—sat in prison for a litany of crimes.

Ezekiel Tyler, retired naval master chief, lived in an active adult community. The place featured manned gates at each entrance and a full-time security staff. Assaulting it would be possible but would also attract attention. Family constituted a vulnerability, but Zeke would be difficult to reach.

If Tyler wouldn't play ball, Braxton decided he would go after Lexi. He wondered how the man's idealism would play out with his daughter's life on the line, and the thought made him smile.

KENT MAXWELL KNOCKED on the door and rubbed his eyes. He couldn't remember the last time a phone call roused him in the middle of the night. He thought about blowing it off, but it required his attention. He knocked on the door again when no answer came. A light near the front of the house went on. Footsteps neared the door, locks disengaged, and it swung open.

"What the hell is going on?" Arthur Bell demanded.

"It's three AM," Maxwell said, "and you got me out of bed. You tell me."

"Get in here." Bell turned and walked toward his living room. "Close the door behind you."

Go to hell, Maxwell thought, but he shut and locked the door. Bell owned a nice house. Maxwell's shoes sank into the plush beige carpet. The walls were freshly painted. The granite counters in the kitchen gleamed in the light. In the main room, leather furniture dominated the floor space, and a large TV hung on the wall. "What's so important I had to drive to goddamn Potomac?" Maxwell demanded. Bell handed Maxwell a Blackberry. "You need a phone upgrade? Call your IT department."

"Read the email."

Maxwell opened the message. It was from Sara Morrison and time-stamped two hours earlier. A chill crawled up his spine.

STAFF,

I WILL NOT BE in the office over the weekend and probably next week. You can reach me on my cell phone, so I'll be around, and I can WebEx into any important meetings.

Keep this to yourselves, but there was an attack at my house tonight. I have an idea who's responsible, but I'm not naming names here. Our work is important, and the man who sent three killers to my house is trying to undermine it.

Don't worry about me. I'm safe, and I'll continue to be. Let's carry on our mission and make sure force and threats hold no sway in our organization.

. . .

V/R,

"THE HELL IS THIS?" Bell said. He snatched the phone back from Maxwell and threw it onto the couch. "The bitch is still alive."

Maxwell never heard anything from Braxton about the raid at Sara Morrison's house. This meant it went poorly. Had things gone according to plan, Braxton would have called him to gloat and go over the next steps. Silence meant failure, which he would stew over and process alone. "First I've heard of it," Maxwell said.

"I don't care. What are you doing to fix it?"

"Did you call me because you're pissed at not getting a promotion?"

Bell's mouth opened, then his jaw clicked shut. "No," he said to try and recover. Maxwell wasn't buying it. "This is about our plan. We both benefit from it."

"The plan hit a snag," Maxwell said. "It happens. We dealt with it overseas, and we'll deal with it now."

"You'd better," Bell said, settling onto the sofa.

"It really sounds like you're looking after yourself."

"Sure, I am. So are you, Mister Maxwell."

"I'm looking after a company."

"Same difference," Bell said, waving a dismissive hand. "You're motivated by money and power just like I am. Get it right next time. I'm not waiting forever."

Maxwell glared at Bell. "Meaning what?"

"Meaning other people are in the same boat as you. You think you're the only guy who has money and a squad of ex-soldiers? Guys like you are a dime a dozen around here. If you can't manage to get rid of Sara Morrison, I'm sure someone else can."

"Someone else?" Maxwell smirked. Then, he drew his pistol and shot Arthur Bell in the head.

Blood and brain bits dripped down the white wall behind Bell's body. The house sat in a posh neighborhood. Expensive price tags, lots of land. An area where meeting neighbors would never be a priority. Still, someone could have heard the report. In the ritzy suburbs in the middle of the night, no one would mistake it for an old car backfiring.

Maxwell wiped down anything he may have touched in Bell's house. He slipped out the door. Other houses remained dark. He strode to his car and drove away.

27

T yler left the house early the next morning. He didn't want to miss Rick Rust being home. The guy was probably still bitter over Bobby, but his service record suggested he wasn't one of Braxton's typical black-hearted minions. Tyler caffeinated himself before sunrise and hit the road while the first rays broke through the clouds.

Rust's Laurel street was lifeless. Other than a man walking a dog on the next road, no one so much as milled about. Tyler got out and checked his surroundings. All quiet. No curious eyes. Rust's house was dark. Tyler hopped the three-foot chain-link fence. He padded across the backyard and up the porch steps. Tyler crouched at the rear door and peeked in the back window. It was an unoccupied kitchen.

Among the tools he kept from his days at Patriot Security was a snap gun. It made picking locks quick and easy, especially for someone like Tyler, who never showed any aptitude for the old way. He popped the door open, drew a real gun to replace the lock picking one, and padded into the house.

Rust kept a kitchen so neat he could work in a restaurant.

Everything was put away to the point only a coffee machine and large hand mixer sat atop the counter. The sink held no dishes or utensils. A narrow closed door, probably leading to the basement, was to the right of the stainless steel refrigerator. An open doorway led to a dining room.

Tyler stepped off the tiled kitchen floor and onto the carpet. A large table with seating for six dominated the room though Tyler had yet to see signs anyone but Rust lived here. However many people occupied the place, they kept the dining room as clean as the kitchen. A buffet sat against the long wall past the table. A china cabinet, empty save for a few dishes and glasses, was against the house's back wall.

A pair of feet hit the floor upstairs. Tyler looked around past his current room. A large living area consumed the front of the house, leading to the stairs to the upper floor. The footsteps headed toward the front. A minute later, a toilet flushed, and water ran. Tyler backed onto the tiled floor. He half-opened the door to the basement and stood to the side of the fridge. Someone came down the stairs to the main level.

Tyler waited. The steps moved across the living and dining rooms and into the kitchen. The refrigerator door swung open. A moment later, Rick Rust placed a pitcher of cold water on the counter beside his coffee maker. He opened the top and extracted the old filter. When he turned, he faced Tyler, who put the barrel of an M11 to his head. "Hi, Rick."

Rick, for his part, didn't say anything. To his credit, he also didn't piss himself. He stood there holding the filter, which dripped brown water onto the kitchen floor. "Don't shoot me," he squeaked.

"I just want to talk. Why don't you finish making the coffee? I like mine strong."

"O . . . OK." Rick dropped the old filter in the trash, got a new one, and put it into the machine. He took a can of coffee from a cupboard. Folgers Black Silk. A perfectly acceptable dark roast in Tyler's opinion. He drank a lot of java and had thoughts on most of the ones sold or brewed in the area. Rick's hand shook as he spooned fresh grounds into the basket. A few tumbled onto the floor. He added water, turned the brewer on, and put the pitcher back in the fridge.

"I'd like to put my gun away, Rick. You're not going to try anything, are you?"

"I don't know," he said. At least he was honest. Most people would have offered a trembling negative.

"I'll do it as a sign of good faith," Tyler said. He slid the M11 into the holster on his left hip.

The smell of coffee filled the kitchen. Tyler gestured toward the dining room. Rust walked into it, and Tyler followed. Rust stopped, half-turned, and fired an elbow at Tyler's head. He blocked it with his forearm, pain cascading into his fingertips. Rust completed his pivot and threw a hard punch, which Tyler also turned aside. He gave Rust a short chop to the throat, which staggered him and left him gasping. Tyler took a step forward, punched Rust in the stomach, then straightened him up and clobbered him in the face.

Rust coughed and wheezed from the floor. Tyler stepped past him and sat on the couch in the living room. "Whenever you're ready, we can talk." After another bout of hacking, Rust dragged himself to a seated position. A series of quiet beeps came from the brew machine. "You might want to bring some coffee first. I take mine black."

It took a minute, but Rust got to his feet and trudged into the kitchen. He emerged soon after carrying two mugs of steaming coffee. He set one on the table in front of Tyler and took the other to a recliner. "Why should I talk to you?" he wanted to know. "You shot Bobby."

"Your friend would've beaten me to death," Tyler said.

"Besides, he should have taken better care to keep me from grabbing his gun."

Rust frowned and didn't say anything. He probably didn't know Bobby died by his own pistol. "You think you're tough?"

Tyler nodded. "If you'd survived what I did, you'd think you were tough, too."

They lapsed into silence. Rust drank his coffee. Tyler did the same. He smelled it first and took a small sip. Nothing seemed amiss. "What do you want to know?" Rust said, slumping in the chair.

"Braxton."

"Never met him."

It seemed plausible. Maxwell or White would've hired Rust while Braxton remained in prison. Even though he'd been out for a while, he'd never been a personable commander. It was possible some of the men wouldn't know him or only saw him in passing. "You've talked to other people, though. What about Maxwell?"

Rust nodded. "He was the boss, but I didn't think he was in charge." His somber face brightened for a wistful grin. "Just like the national guard sometimes."

Tyler understood, and he bobbed his head to show some empathy with Rust's plight. Winning people's trust had never been among Tyler's best attributes. He didn't excel at any of the soft skills. "I'm trying to figure out what they're after."

"What do you mean?" Rust said.

"Hexagon has some men in Afghanistan, yes?" Rust nodded in assent. "I'm sure the paperwork says they're over there for a specific mission. I think there's more to it, and I think Jake Smith knew it." It only happened for an instant, but Rust frowned at the name. "He must've told someone, and now Hexagon is after him."

"And you're trying to find him."

"I didn't know what was going on when I started working

for his father," Tyler said. "Now, I'm in the soup as much as they are."

Rust shrugged. "You made your choices."

Tyler let him stew for a moment while he enjoyed another couple sips of coffee. "You say you've never met Braxton. Know much about him?"

"Not really."

"I'm going to tell you a story, Rick. Braxton was my last commanding officer before I retired. He . . . got a little carried away in Afghanistan. I'm surprised he's out of prison. Let's say he's the kind of guy you probably don't want to work for in general. I'm going to try and take him down."

Rust remained quiet for a minute. "What do you mean by 'carried away'?"

"He raped a teenaged Afghan girl, got her pregnant, then ordered her and her family killed to cover it up."

"Jesus Christ," Rust whispered and let out a long, slow breath. 'No shit?"

"No shit. He's bad news. I'd get out if I were you."

"It's never so simple."

"It can be," Tyler said. "You seem pretty capable. I'm sure you could work against them without cluing anyone in. It's easier to topple an empire when you have some help on the inside."

Rust hung his head and fell silent. A moment later, he said, "All right. I'll be your confederate."

Tyler didn't think Rust would agree to lend a hand. He'd be glad to have the assistance, and he'd also keep an eye on Rust. It would be just like a Braxton employee to set Tyler up for a double-cross. By now, everyone at Hexagon must've been aware of the vendetta. "I'm happy to have your help."

"Count me in, then," Rust confirmed. "I'm no saint, but I can't stand for the kind of stuff he did."

"Me, either," Tyler said. "It's just one reason he needs to go down."

TYLER DROVE HOME from Laurel when his phone rang. He didn't recognize the number. Despite usually ignoring these calls, Tyler answered it. Braxton's voice came over the 442's speakers. "Hello, John."

Braxton employed enough people. Figuring out Tyler's information would only be a matter of time. Still, he bristled at his disgraced former commander calling on his personal cell. "What do you want, Leo?"

"We seem to be on a collision course."

"You can swerve at any time. Bonus points if you go off a cliff."

Braxton fell silent. Tyler made no effort to engage in the conversation. It was a farce. Braxton probably felt he was being magnanimous. The man always saw himself in a much better light than he deserved. It was the worst part of dealing with a sociopath—they never pictured themselves as the villain, and in fact tended to turn things around and paint themselves as victims. Braxton did it when he got court-martialed. Tyler didn't need to hear it again. "Nice chatting with you, Leo," he said. "Feel free never to call me again."

"We need to meet."

"What?"

"You and me," Braxton said. "There's some air to clear between us."

"I'm fine with it being murky and smoky," Tyler said.

"I'm sure you are after what you did. You probably expected me to die in Leavenworth."

"If I knew some idiot would let you out early, I would've paid one of your fellow inmates to shank you in the shower."

Braxton again lapsed into silence, but Tyler could hear his deep breathing. He grinned. If the universe forced him to deal with Leo Braxton again, he would spend as much time as he could riling the man. Eventually, the blessed quiet ended. "Tyler. We need to meet."

"Why?"

"Jake," Braxton said.

28

The one-syllable name twisted Tyler's stomach. Did Braxton's men catch up to Jake? Between dealing with Rust and Bobby, saving Sara Morrison, and now talking to his former commander, Tyler found little time he could devote to finding Smitty's son. If the Hexagon crew killed or captured Jake, Tyler would feel miserable. He'd never be able to look Smitty in the eye and tell him what happened. "What about him?"

"You recommended him to me," Braxton said. "Remember?"

"Yes. It was before I realized you were a monster."

"Labels, John," Braxton said. "One man's monster is another's terrorist hunter."

Tyler didn't want to venture down the semantic rabbit hole. He tried to refocus the conversation. "I thought we were talking about Jake."

"He was a good soldier. You had a keen eye for talent."

"Why are you trying to kill him, then?" Tyler asked.

"Jake disappointed me in the end. Maybe you recommended him because he was so much like you. Seeing the world in black and white. No consideration for nuance or shades of gray. A moralizer."

"Sounds like the kind of man who belonged in your unit. I wish you'd had a dozen more like him."

"One was enough," Braxton said, and it sounded like he spoke through clenched teeth.

Tyler exited the highway. He didn't want to keep the conversation going any longer than necessary, but he hoped Braxton might tell him something about Jake. "What's your obsession with the kid, anyway? He couldn't have served under you for very long."

"He let me down . . . much like you did."

"I think there's more to it," Tyler said. "You went overseas a bunch of times. Plenty of men and women under your command over the years. Hell, you blame me for what happened at the end, and I'm not the one hiding from the goon squad. Jake must be different. He knows something." Braxton didn't answer. "Maybe he knows what your company's really after in Afghanistan."

"I know what you're doing. It won't work."

"You're the one who brought him up, Leo."

"I know you're interested in saving him," Braxton said. "Another character flaw. You want to protect people who don't matter." Tyler didn't take the bait even though he wanted to strangle Braxton through the phone. "I want a face-to-face. We'll talk about Jake. Maybe you can help him, after all."

It could be a trap. Knowing Braxton and Maxwell, it *would* be. Tyler needed the meeting to be in public. He couldn't get talked into going to some Hexagon facility. Or could he? His old laptop would tell him all the places the company, Maxwell, or White leased. What if they drove him to a place off the books? It could be important intel to possess. After turning it over in his head, Tyler said, "Fine."

"I'll send someone to pick you up. Don't worry . . . I know where you live."

"I'm not getting into one of your SUVs if I'm still vertical. I'll drive myself."

"You'll get in the SUV and like it. Be ready at eighteen hundred."

Tyler didn't like it, but he didn't seem to have an alternative. "I will be." He hung up.

WHEN TYLER ARRIVED HOME, the first thing he did was sate his hunger with lunch. Fridge options were limited. Lexi had been ordering grocery deliveries, so he texted to remind her their situation would soon be dire. After polishing off his sandwich, Tyler guzzled one water, then another. He bounced on the balls of his feet in the kitchen. To calm himself, he walked into the living room but paced the carpet rather than sitting down.

Braxton was sending an SUV to collect him. It would involve two guys, minimum. Both armed. Tyler checked his weapons. He could bring the M11 and a spare magazine. They'd pat him down before going anyplace important, so he also slipped a small ceramic knife—invisible to wands and metal detectors—into the waistband of his jeans. Despite the bulk it added—and the high odds of it being spotted—Tyler slipped off his shirt to strap on a bullet-resistant vest before buttoning again.

A couple hours still remained before the pickup crew arrived. Tyler felt way too hopped up to rest. He walked upstairs. Lexi's door was closed, and he heard her voice as she conversed with someone. After a glance at his bed, Tyler walked into his spare room and painting studio. He already had a new piece of paper ready to go on the easel. Now, he just needed some inspiration.

Tyler selected some colors and picked up a brush. He closed his eyes, inhaled and exhaled deeply, and let the memories come. He'd talked about them enough with his VA shrink and recently with Lexi. It had been a few years since he put color to page when thinking about them, though. Tyler started with large strokes on the bottom of the paper.

He remembered setting out to scout the family's house. It was nothing special. His first thought was an IED maker should have been rewarded and purchased a larger dwelling. If he'd followed his gut, so much would've turned out differently. The recon was easy. The military maintained a presence in the area, so locals seeing a soldier wouldn't be alarmed. No one hassled him or even asked what he was doing. He wished someone had. It might have let him realize the mistake he would make.

Tyler reached for a different color. He cased the simple structure for hours. No one in or out. No phone calls—also curious for someone reputed to be a favored bomb maker. Another warning sign Tyler should've seen. His brush strokes grew quick and sharp. He chided himself and took his time. In his memory, the sun set on the town of Torkman. Unlike an American city, most activity stopped when daylight was lost.

The door yielded easily to his boot. One kick. Four surprised faces. Eight bullets. Nine seconds from initial breach until the time the final corpse hit the floor. Tyler cleared the house, found none of the paraphernalia he expected to, and searched again. Even including the small shed, he came up empty. The recollection made him reach for another brush.

Two sets of eyes remained open. Staring at Tyler. Accusing him of being a killer. For the first time since he put the uniform on, he doubted what he'd done. He dashed out of the house, ran to the Jeep, and drove back to base at speeds neither Chrysler nor the army would recommend. Tyler set his brush down. He took a deep breath. While he felt wired before, weariness settled in on him now.

He looked at his creation. A sandy landscape. Overhead, the moon hung in a dusky sky. A few black rocks broke the tan monotony. Pools of blood clung to the rocks and marred the sand. Tyler stared at it. He hadn't been aware of what he painted. As the scene played out in his mind, he must have captured it with his watercolors. Creativity was a funny process.

And a tiring one. Tyler glanced at his watch. Ten after five. Fifty minutes remained. Braxton's men would be on time. He would demand it. Tyler walked into his bedroom and lay down. He concentrated on waking up five minutes before the goon squad would knock on his door. A few seconds after his head hit the pillow, he drifted off.

GETTING out of Aberdeen proved harder than Jake expected. He was glad to lie low and not have so many eyes on him. The main strip of road passing for downtown was quieter than just about any area of Baltimore. Jake didn't feel like he needed to look over his shoulder all the time, though he maintained his vigilance. Braxton and his men were dangerous adversaries, and he couldn't afford to drop his guard just because he put some distance between them and himself.

He walked to a Wawa convenience store up the road. A fresh sub beat the processed crap which composed most of his diet since going on the run. Jake ordered the hoagie, and he ate it along with a bag of pretzels on a small bench outside the shop. It was his best meal in a week. Restlessness gnawed at him, though. Aberdeen wasn't far from the city in the grand scheme of things. Jake wanted to go farther north.

After striking out a couple times on hitching a ride, a trucker who also served in the army agreed to give Jake a lift north. Thankfully, the conversation proved light. They chatted about their military days for a couple minutes, but the other man didn't press him on anything. His ride came to an end at a warehouse in Elkton. Jake climbed out of the rig. He was closer to Pennsylvania or Delaware here. If he could get farther north, some friends in Philadephia could help him.

Jake walked to a large gas station. He bought a snack and a couple bottles of water. The first driver he approached about a ride was agreeable but headed south. It took another hour—and earned him a series of glares from the employees—for Jake to give up. It grew darker out. Most of the vehicles coming in were cars, and the drivers tended to look at Jake like he was homeless. His own reflection in a window compelled him to agree. "There's no way I'd give me a ride," he said under his breath.

Using his phone to guide him, Jake made his way to a park about a mile away. A few parents and children lingered on the nearby playground. Jake sat on a bench and ate a portion of his snack. The other people left a short while later. He had the place to himself. Jake found a flat area not easily seen from the road or parking lot. The playground equipment would make it hard to spot him.

Jake used a spare shirt as a pillow. He took the gun out of his bag, slipped it under his body, and lay on his stomach to get some badly-needed rest. Sleep came for him quickly. Some unknown time later, he awoke to nearby noises. A man stood over him. Jake slipped his right hand underneath his body and craned his neck.

A county sheriff's deputy stared back at him.

29

Without rolling over, Jake took in the deputy standing over him. He looked to be under six feet tall and middle-aged. He was out of shape enough to strain the bottom two buttons of his navy blue shirt. The flashlight beam made Jake squint when it shined in his face. "No place to go?" the deputy said. His voice hinted at a southern accent.

"Headed into Pennsylvania tomorrow." Jake rubbed his eyes. "My ride fell through for today."

"Can you get up?"

"What's the harm in letting me sleep here?"

"I'm asking politely," the cop said.

"All right." Jake pulled the gun toward his right side. He propped himself up on his left elbow. When he knew the cop was looking at him, he stared into the distance. The other man's eyes narrowed, but then he turned his head. With the deputy distracted, Jake shoved the pistol into his T-shirt pillow. By the time the older man's head pivoted back around, Jake sat up and held the shirt in his hand. "Thought I saw something."

"You're the only one here."

"Guess so." Jake stood and stuffed the shirt into his rucksack.

"Military?" the deputy asked.

Jake nodded. "Army."

"I hear a lot of soldiers have trouble once they're back home. Seen it a few times, myself."

"I don't think my problems are typical," Jake said.

"When's the last time you had a drink?" the cop said.

"I'm not drunk." Jake rolled his eyes. "I'm just dealing with a delay getting north."

"Not what I asked." The deputy focused the flashlight beam in Jake's face again, and he squinted against it. "You ever take a field sobriety test?"

"Once or twice."

"Ever fail one?"

"Nope," Jake said.

"Let's see how you do, then."

Jake knew resisting would be pointless. The deputy probably could have run him in on some vagrancy charge. His reflection earlier told Jake he looked like a homeless person, and sleeping in a park only added to the image. Dealing with this indignity would be a small price to pay in the grand scheme of things. So long as the deputy let him go at the end of it, of course. If the man decided he really needed to search Jake's bag or bring him to the station, they would have a problem.

Instructed not to move his head, Jake's eyes followed the cop's finger as he moved it side to side. Jake then stood on one leg, walked a straight line, and recited the alphabet both forwards and backwards. By the end, the deputy gave him a nod. "All right, you're not drunk. Still gonna need you to move along."

"You got an idea where I might go?"

The man shook his head. "I could drop you at a motel. Best I can do other than the station."

"I'll make my way," Jake said. "Thanks."

He slung the rucksack over his shoulder. Then, the deputy asked, "Can I look in your bag?"

Jake couldn't say yes. The gun would be way too easy to find, and it would bring a much more unpleasant set of questions with it. "Seriously?" Jake summoned his indignity. "I'm leaving your park. You already made me take a sobriety test when I haven't had a drink in weeks. You want to search my bag, get a warrant."

"You think I need one?"

"I think the Constitution I swore an oath to defend says you do."

The two stared at each other for several seconds. Jake took in the deputy's stance. His legs were straight. Tense. His right hand inched closer to his belt where a taser sat ready. Jake wouldn't let him finish the move, though he hoped he didn't need to take action. The deputy blinked. "Fine. Move along."

Jake walked away without another word.

TYLER STEPPED OUTSIDE at the appointed hour. He walked past the neighbor's house to make himself easier to spot. Sure enough, a gray Tahoe rolled up the street a few seconds later. The driver looked like Shah, the guy he gave the slip to in the parking lot a few days ago. Tyler didn't recognize the passenger. The man leaned out the open window and leveled an M9 at Tyler. "Get in."

"You don't need the gun," Tyler said.

"You packing?"

"Sure. But there are two of you, and you're both younger and dumber than I am. I need every advantage I can get."

"Get in," the man repeated. His beady eyes narrowed. He wore his brown hair short in the classic military haircut. His trigger discipline was terrible, though—he actually held his finger on it as if ready to fire. Braxton's standards were slipping. Maybe he needed to hire Hair-trigger Harry because Tyler killed a few of his men already.

"Guys, really?" Tyler said. "A gun in a residential neighborhood when people are home? When did Braxton start sponsoring amateur hour?"

"I'll shoot you."

"I'm sure it would make your boss real happy. He sent you here to pick me up, right?" The passenger spent a few seconds practicing his stare—it needed more work—but he finally nodded. "I'm sure he didn't mean for you to carry me in with a bullet in my head."

"Maybe he wants you dead."

"No doubt, but he wouldn't want a lackey like you to do it." Tyler considered his options. He couldn't reach for his own gun without drawing fire, and he stood on a street full of houses. The knife would only be useful if either of these idiots climbed out of the SUV. A late-model Toyota pickup sat at the curb behind Tyler and to his left. If the bullets flew, he would try to take cover there.

"You getting in . . . or what?" the guy yelled.

"You putting the gun away?"

"No."

"There's your answer, then."

"Braxton still wants to talk to you."

"Tell him to send higher quality men next time," Tyler said. "Better yet, he should come in person."

"Screw you, old man," the passenger said. He drew his arm back into the cabin and put the window up. The SUV sped off. Tyler watched it drive down his street and make the turn before he took himself back inside.

~

AFTER A RESTLESS NIGHT, Tyler put a plan together. Sometimes, walking into the lion's den turned out to be the best strategy. He'd used it a few times overseas. When the terrorists reacted in alarm and surprise at the small American contingent storming their building and killing their men, it always gave him a feeling of immense satisfaction. In his homeland setting, he wouldn't be visiting the lion's den, but rather standing near it and shouting over the fence.

Braxton answered the phone quickly. "I was wondering when you'd call."

"Glad I could solve the mystery for you. We need to talk. Leo."

A pause. "I don't like this first-name shit. You used to call me Colonel."

"You used to *be* a colonel."

"I guess I should've expected you to rub it in." Tyler heard annoyance in Braxton's voice, and it made him smile. "You could've come with my men last night."

"Those clowns?" Tyler scoffed. "Send better men next time. I want to talk to you, not a pair of idiot lackeys."

"We're already talking, aren't we? Say what you have to say."

"Not over the phone," Tyler said. "I want to meet. Just you. Any of your goons come with you, and you can take them back in a hearse."

"No need for any violence. I'll meet you. Where?"

Tyler didn't know where Braxton lived anymore. His ex-wife divorced him after the army court-martialed him. Were Maxwell or White big enough toadies to put him up in a guest room? The only address he could find for Hexagon was near BWI Airport. "Catonsville. Should be nice and convenient for you."

"Great. You know where the Double T is?"

"I'll find it."

"One hour." Braxton hung up. Tyler performed some body-weight exercises, showered, and made coffee. After downing a mug, he drove to Catonsville. The Double T Diner sat on a small side road not far from the main drag where a historic part of the town exuded a lot of old-time charm. Small places like coffee shops and art studios occupied large houses on both sides of the street. Tyler curbed the 442 about a block from the restaurant and walked inside.

Even considering the spacing of the tables, the diner wasn't busy. A young waitress seated him right away, and Tyler asked for coffee before she could depart. When she returned with the steaming cup, he ordered waffles, bacon, and hash browns. The girl walked into the kitchen. Braxton strode in a moment later. He'd aged more than ten years in the decade since Tyler saw him last. His hair had turned completely gray, and he wore it short to try and hide it. Despite his self-inflicted indignities, Braxton still carried himself like a man used to giving orders and having his subordinates follow them without delay or question. He slid into the booth across from Tyler.

"Leo."

"John."

Tyler took in the smells of the place while Braxton looked over the menu. With the dining area so empty, he could hear meat sizzling from the kitchen. The aromas of bacon and coffee dominated his nostrils, and Tyler figured it couldn't get much better. Braxton, of course, ruined it all by speaking. "What do you want to talk about?"

"Jake Smith," Tyler answered.

"Who?" Tyler repeated the name. Too quickly, Braxton replied, "Never heard of him."

"Let's not waste time on bullshit. Every second I sit with you taints me a little more. Besides, you mentioned him to me." The waitress dropped off Tyler's breakfast. She asked what Braxton wanted, and he said he would take the same thing. The former colonel craned his neck to watch her walk away. "She's a little too old and American for you, isn't she?"

"And here I thought we could have a pleasant chat." Braxton kept his tone civil, though the wrinkle between his brows told Tyler his barb found the mark. "Why do you always bring up the past?"

"We don't have any future to talk about," Tyler said. "If you prefer, though, we can stick to the present. Jake Smith."

"Fine. Jake joined the unit after your third tour. He came back for a while toward . . . the end of my tenure." Tyler grimaced. "You probably think they turfed me out right away." Braxton's head moved slightly from side to side. "It took a while. I knew people. Still do. You wouldn't know, of course . . . you left the second you could."

"Couldn't stand to be around you anymore. Let's focus on Jake, though. I know how you feel about me."

"He seemed like a good soldier," Braxton said. "I thought he would be a little more flexible than you."

"I guess you were wrong." Tyler buttered his waffle and cut into it. For his long list of faults, Braxton had always been a well-mannered man. He liked to insist everyone eat together. Tyler enjoying his meal out of turn would needle his former commander. It would make the waffles taste at least twenty percent better.

"You know by now I'm still acquainted with Maxwell and White."

"Once a toady," Tyler said.

Braxton didn't take the bait. "They tried to recruit Jake for the company. People who deployed with us—at least those we were still on good terms with—were the first priority. Maxwell told me Jake was interested at first but later balked."

"He knew what you were really after in Afghanistan."

"It's something you could've had a piece of," Braxton said.

He must've known the futility of denying Tyler's accusation. "Too bad your precious principles got in the way."

"Sounds like Jake's did, too."

A shrug served as Braxton's reply. Tyler followed his eyes as they panned from the kitchen. The waitress dropped off his identical breakfast and coffee a few seconds later. When she walked away again, Braxton said, "Disappointing, really. I thought he was better."

"He's better than the lot of you."

Braxton applied butter to his waffles meticulously. The same amount with every pass of his knife. Always exactly to the edge. Every doughy nook received the same treatment. When he finished, he cut them into precise bites. Tyler would need an electron microscope to spot any difference in size. After taking a forkful, Braxton said, "Thankfully, he reported his suspicions to someone we knew."

"Who?"

"Don't know everything, do you?" Braxton smiled. As usual, he looked like a predator when he did. "Tell you what, John. I'll forget all about Jake. We'll stop looking for him, and we'll leave his old man alone. I just have one condition."

"What?" Tyler asked.

"You come work for Hexagon."

Tyler laughed. "Really? Why in the world would I ever work for you again? Why would you want me in the fold?"

"You're damn good at what you do," Braxton said. "I hate you, John . . . I won't deny it. I'd like nothing more than to stab you in your smug face with this butter knife. You could be a big help to Hexagon, though. In the end, I like making money more than I dislike you."

"Another area where we differ," Tyler said.

"It's no, then?"

Tyler picked up a slice of bacon and ate it while staring at Braxton. "Of course it's no. Always and forever."

Braxton shrugged. "Then, I'm afraid it's still open season on Jake. I'll be nice and ease off the old man, though."

Considering the personnel Hexagon lost in the last few days, Tyler understood the real reason for Braxton's faux magnanimity but let him take his little victory lap. "It's something, at least."

"You might try being grateful," Braxton said.

"I'll never thank you for anything." Tyler finished his breakfast, swigged the rest of his coffee, and set a twenty on the table.

"Leaving so soon?"

"Enjoy the rest of your breakfast, Leo."

Braxton grabbed Tyler's wrist as he walked past. The two glared at each other for a moment. "Just remember, John. I offered you a way out."

Tyler jerked his arm free and left.

30

M axwell stopped the car at Rodney Standish's apartment building. The trail to Sara Morrison went cold after the attempt on her life failed. Tyler must have stashed her somewhere. Maxwell burned to do something about the meddlesome Tyler, but Braxton gave assurances he would handle it. He needed to hurry up. In the meantime, Maxwell would see if Rodney knew anything. He hoped the man didn't want to talk.

It was always more fun when they resisted.

He strode to the door. The label for 4C showed *STANDISH, R.* beside it on a separate label. Maxwell pushed a bunch of the other buttons. A moment later, a random resident buzzed him in. Someone always did. Maxwell dashed up the stairs in case whoever let him enter got curious about who walked in. He didn't see anyone on the short jaunt to the top level.

Apartment 4C was the third of three on the left. Maxwell put his ear to the door. He heard a muffled man's voice but nothing else. A soft knock didn't lead to any barking from within the apartment. Maxwell rapped harder. No response. He did it again. Footsteps approached, and a man opened the door.

He matched the fellow in the photos Maxwell took at Sara Morrison's house a few nights ago. "I'm busy," Standish said, frowning at Maxwell.

Despite working from home, Standish wore a pressed button-down shirt, dress pants, and a tie. The color of his brown hair must have come from a bottle, and the painstaking style required many minutes in front of a mirror. Maxwell kept his military haircut for a litany of reasons, one of which was the time he saved not having to do anything but dry it. This guy at the door with his middle-aged dad bod seemed like some kind of financial dweeb. Morrison could have done better a thousand different ways at the Pentagon. "You're Rodney Standish?"

"I am, but I told you I'm busy." He closed the door a few inches before Maxwell inserted his boot.

"It's about Sara Morrison."

Standish pursed his lips. "Is she in trouble?"

"I don't think we should talk in the hallway."

"Oh. Right." Standish moved to the side, and Maxwell walked in. The apartment was immaculate. It could have passed any military inspection Maxwell ever witnessed or conducted. The dark hardwood floors gleamed with reflected fluorescent light. Nary a speck of dust lay on any surface. Area rugs showed tracks from recent vacuuming. Standish could afford hiring it out, but he struck Maxwell as the type to put a lot of effort into appearances. Hence, the professional attire despite teleworking. "Is Sara in trouble?"

"You mind hanging up?" Maxwell pointed to Standish's earbuds.

"I'm not on a call at the moment," he said. "You interrupted me. I might need to take another one soon, though."

"What is it you do, Mister Standish?"

"I'm a financial manager, Mister . . .?"

"Max." The other man's profession didn't surprise Maxwell at all.

"Your first name?"

Maxwell shrugged. "Sure. We're not here to talk about me. When's the last time you heard from your girlfriend?"

Standish snorted. "Look, Sara and I are dating, but I'd hardly call her my girlfriend."

"How many times have you been out?"

"I don't know," Standish said. "Five . . . maybe six."

"You sleeping with her?"

"I don't see what this has to do with Sara being in trouble." Standish crossed his arms and did his best to look like he'd suffered some great indignity at Maxwell's question. He pulled it off. Probably thanks to lots of practice in the office.

Maxwell put up his hands in mock surrender. "You're right. We're concerned about her is all."

"You work with Sara?" Standish sat on a small sofa and gestured to the recliner opposite him.

"In a manner of speaking," Maxwell said. He sat on the edge of the chair, teetering it forward under him. "There are things we can't disclose publicly."

"I hear it a lot."

"I imagine you need to say it, too, from time to time."

"Sure," Standish said.

The guy was an easy mark to build rapport with. "I need to know if you've heard from Sara recently," Maxwell said.

"No . . . not for a couple days now."

"You don't seem overly concerned."

Standish shrugged. "We don't talk every day. Like I said, Sara's not my girlfriend." He glanced at his watch—an expensive model judging from the quick peek Maxwell got. "I'll need to get on a call in a moment. Was there anything else?"

"Just one thing," Maxwell said. "Has Sara ever mentioned a company called Hexagon?"

"No. Did they name themselves after the Pentagon?"

"I wouldn't know."

"Maybe they think they're better," Standish said with a dry chuckle.

"Maybe they are," Maxwell said.

"I wish I could be of more help, Mister . . . uh, Max." Standish stood. "The markets don't wait, though."

"I understand. I'll see myself out."

Standish walked from his living room and down a short hallway. Maxwell sprang from the recliner, unlatched his belt, and wrapped an end around each of his hands. Before Standish could enter his office, Maxwell looped the belt around the man's neck. Standish's protest died in his throat. His hands shot there and clawed at Maxwell's. He tried to move backward toward the open front area of the apartment. Maxwell kicked Standish in the back of the knee, and he went down. Leverage was easy from there. His quarry didn't have any, and Maxwell drew his arms back to tighten the hold. Of the many methods he'd employed to strangle someone, the belt garrote was his favorite. Standish's final breath rattled in his throat. After several more seconds to be certain, Maxwell released him.

He slipped his belt back on, buckled it, and left the corpse lying in the hallway.

JAKE WISHED he still carried his regular phone. The burner didn't hold his contacts. He knew people up here who could help him, but he lacked a way to reach them. Or did he? Since leaving active duty and joining the reserves, Jake exchanged numbers with most of the people in his unit. One of them—Vince, he thought—had an easy number with lots of repetition. He just needed to remember it.

It took three tries, but Jake guessed right. Vince couldn't help him directly, but he could put him in touch with someone who could. Carl lived nearby in North East. Jake didn't share his entire tale of woe, but his service buddy said he'd help. After walking a mile or so before lucking into a county bus to cover the bulk of the distance, the trip set Jake back two dollars and forty minutes. Worth it, he figured.

He found the house easily enough. North East, like many cities in Harford and Cecil Counties, stood in opposition to itself. New construction popped up in many places. All the houses looked alike. The asking prices didn't include any character. Not far away—across the street in some cases—homes a century or more old stood tall and proud. Carl possessed the good sense to live in a building which predated his grandparents.

The two men shook hands in the driveway. Despite being the same rank as Jake, Carl was four years older and twenty pounds heavier. "You look like hell, Jake."

"Feel like it, too."

"Want a beer?"

"Won't turn it down," Jake said.

A minute later, Carl returned with two Miller High Life longnecks. Jake sipped his and regarded his friend's neighborhood. The houses here had character. They'd witnessed a lot of stories unfolding. No two looked alike. A Nissan Sentra of recent vintage sat in the driveway. "Want to tell me what's going on?" Carl prompted.

"My old unit." Jake took a longer draught of the beer. "Special operations. Some of the guys . . . did some things they shouldn't have. The colonel even got the boot for a bunch of it." He sighed. "Fast forward years later, and the gang's getting back together again. They left a stash of money behind." Carl's eyes widened as Jake elaborated. "We busted up a lot of Taliban shit. Before I got there, too."

"How much we talking?"

"Millions," Jake said. "Problem is in the years since, war's changed the landscape. It's not so easy to find anymore."

"They try to recruit you?" Carl said.

Jake nodded. "I kept silent before. Figured the colonel going down would be the end of it. This time, I told what I knew . . . and I've been on the run ever since."

"Jesus Christ." Carl downed the brew until he grimaced and pulled the bottle away. "What do you need?"

"A car," Jake said. "I've been trying to get out of town."

"Where you gonna go?"

"North." Jake looked at the beer bottle, pondered another swig, and then set it down. He needed to travel with as few complications as possible. Guzzling a brew before leaving—presuming Carl lent him a car—would run counter to the goal. "I know some people in Philly."

Carl jutted his chin toward the Sentra. "My son's car. He's with his mom for a couple weeks. It's yours if you need it."

"I owe you one," Jake said.

"Repay me by getting away from the people chasing you." Carl went inside for a moment to get the keys and tossed them to Jake. "You know how to drive a stick?"

Jake grinned. "My dad's a mechanic. I knew before I was ten."

He drove the Sentra out of North East and onto I-95 North. Besides knowing a few people in Philly, he'd gone to college there. He could get around the city and even evade pursuit if he needed to. If circumstances forced him to avoid hotels, he could stay with his acquaintances up there. In the back of his mind, he also knew it was close enough to drive back if his dad landed in the soup.

The Sentra wasn't fast, but it maintained highway speed well. Jake stayed in the middle lane. He let the swifter drivers zoom around him. Behind him, a dark SUV merged from the right to get behind him. The hair on Jake's neck stood up. Was he being followed? If so, he didn't have the horsepower to get away. Jake could only hope his small car could outmaneuver the large SUV in traffic.

For now, he drove toward Philly. The headlights in his rearview served as a constant reminder he couldn't outrun his problems.

31

The SUV stayed behind Jake. It was like they didn't care if he saw them. If he changed lanes, the large vehicle would mirror him eventually. Not right away. Maybe they tried to be a little less obvious. Jake went from the middle lane to the right, then all the way to the left about five miles later. Each time, the SUV waited a minute or so, then did the same.

He wasn't paranoid—they really were after him.

It must have been Braxton's men. How did they pick him up well north of Baltimore? He'd changed phones, slugged rides, avoided contacting anyone, and stayed as much off the grid as possible. The familiar outline of Lincoln Financial Field appeared in the distance. On the highway, Jake couldn't escape his pursuers. The borrowed Sentra was easy to spot in light traffic, and he didn't have the power to outrun them. He knew the streets of Philadelphia, though. Many of them ran one way. Someone unfamiliar with the roads wouldn't be able to keep up with him.

Jake jerked the wheel, steered his car across all the traffic lanes, and ignored the angry honks of protest as he took the

Broad Street exit. The Tahoe did the same thing behind him, so they would know he was onto them. Let them. Jake drove north on Broad. All three major pro sports venues sat nearby. A little past them was Marconi Plaza, and then the side streets took over. There, Jake could use his knowledge of Philly's roads to evade the men chasing him.

After passing the ramp for I-76, Jake drove through the Plaza. Tires squealed as he swung a full-speed left onto Shunk Street, then an immediate right onto Rosewood. The SUV missed the first turn. Their next chance to make a left was two blocks up. One block before, Porter Street came one way toward Jake. He saw no cars or cops coming.

He made the illegal left. A car came toward him in the distance. Jake sped up and made another left to go the correct direction on Carlisle Street. He snaked his way back to Broad Street headed south, then picked up I-95 again. The big dark vehicle didn't reappear behind him. Jake released a deep breath. He'd probably have to avoid Philly altogether now, but he'd figure something out.

Jake got off the highway and drove until he found a parking garage. He pulled into it and left the Sentra amid a collection of other cars. Braxton hired meticulous men. They'd be searching downtown Philly for him. Probably the parking venues near the stadiums and arena. It would take them a while to make it to where he dumped his ride. Jake needed to use his time productively.

He left the garage and walked until he found signs of urban life. People congregated outside a movie theater. A man with a smug look on his face talked into a cell phone. As Jake closed the gap, he heard chatter about investments and markets. His planned grab would be easy. Jake bumped into the man and snatched his phone. With his other hand, he took his baseball cap off. A cry of "Hey!" went up behind him, but Jake already blended with the crowd. He waited a minute while the phone's former owner scanned the people near him.

When the guy turned to search behind him, Jake walked away. He made an immediate left and hurried to a jog to get some distance between himself and the scene of the crime. The phone was still unlocked and on the same call. Jake hung up. He walked another two blocks before he used the cell to call his father. "Hello?" his dad said. Jake smiled at hearing the old man's voice again. "Hello?"

"Hi, Dad."

"Jake! Where are you?"

"I'm all right. Listen, Dad . . . I'm sorry for everything. I know I put you in a bad spot."

"Don't worry about me," his father said. "Where are you?"

"I'd rather not tell you," Jake said. "Someone might be listening. I'm using a borrowed phone. I'll come back when I can."

"Jake, I know someone who can help you. A guy started working for me after you left. He's ex-Army. Special Ops. Pretty scary when he gets to work."

"I'm fine, Dad."

"I think he can help get you out of this," his dad said, voice threatening to break. "He can bring you home."

"I'll think about it," Jake said after a moment. He wasn't used to hearing emotion creep into his dad's words. "Take care. I'll call you when I can." Jake hung up as his father replied. He walked another few blocks away from where he left the car, wiped the phone off with his shirt, and tossed it down a sewer grate. Jake crossed the street and doubled back on himself, taking care to avoid the spot where he snagged the mobile a few minutes ago.

Once back in the garage, Jake opened the Sentra. He rooted around in his bag until he found a screwdriver. Even at one-third capacity, the garage still held a lot of cars. The bottom two levels were reserved for residents of the adjoining apartments. Jake wandered into their rows of vehicles. He didn't see anyone milling about, so he got to work. He popped the Pennsylvania tags off a Hyundai compact, carried them back to the Sentra, and replaced the Maryland plates. Jake presumed Braxton's men noted his license number. If they somehow traced him here, they'd pass by the Sentra.

On his way back to street level, Jake thought about what his father said. Someone might be able to help him out of this mess. But how? Braxton seemed to have a lot of men. What could one ex-soldier do for him? Jake thought about some of the men he'd served with over the years. Many were very capable. The best of the best, both in special operations and other branches. Some assistance was enticing. Jake didn't want to worry about someone else's survival, though. Enough people were already entangled in his mess, Carl being the most recent addition to the sad list.

No, he needed to get out of this on his own.

LEXI WATCHED her dad drive away. She told him she could simply order groceries through an app. Several apps, really. He insisted on going to the store. She knew the futility of arguing with him. Besides, with everything going on, maybe getting out of the house and not thinking about Braxton or anyone else from the army would be good for him.

Ever since she saw what he painted a few days ago, she'd been concerned. Lexi remembered when Tyler first told her about his therapeutic program years ago. He sat her down and explained what post-traumatic stress disorder was and how art was going to help him manage it. She already knew about PTSD from books. Her dad had never been the jumpy type, but he'd been constantly vigilant and suspicious of everyone. Over time, he dialed those back. He still liked to sit facing an exit, but his leg didn't bob up and down constantly, and he stopped staring and scrutinizing everyone.

She was proud of his progress and didn't want to see him lose ground. Especially not over someone like Braxton. The man sounded like a monster. Lexi understood what her dad did when he went overseas. She always wanted him to come home, but she also hoped he wouldn't have to kill anyone. At the moment, she very much wanted him to kill Leo Braxton. It would make the world a better place, and it would let her dad stop brooding and be normal again.

Lexi was about to go upstairs when she heard a knock at the door. She glanced out the front window. A plain blue van idled in the driveway. Through the peephole in the front door, Lexi saw a man holding a box and clipboard. She opened the door. "Delivery. Need a signature."

"Sure," Lexi said. She took the pen and clipboard. The paper was very basic. Just name, address, and signature columns. Nothing from the driver. Nothing indicating what the package was. She held the pen in place and looked up at the man standing on the porch. Her best guess put him in his thirties, a little taller than her dad, and built like someone who exercised. His uniform bore no company marking, and he wore the hat down far enough to hide much of his face. "Where's the package from?"

"I just deliver them," the guy said. Before Lexi could respond, he dashed into the house. The box tumbled to the floor as his left hand went over her mouth. Something in his right hand caught the light. Lexi bit down on one of his fingers. His grip loosened, and she kneed him in the groin. The fake delivery guy stepped back while she ran farther into the house.

It didn't buy her much of an opening, though. He chased her into the living room. She spun around and threw a kick at his midsection, but he blocked it with his forearm. Lexi now saw he held a needle in his right hand. She tried to back away but bumped into the sofa. He shoved her onto it and clamped his hand over her neck. Lexi struggled, pounding on his lower arm, but it did no good. The guy avoided a frantic kick and came up alongside her.

Something sharp bit into her neck, and Lexi watched the room grow black.

Tyler RAN A FEW ERRANDS, including a much-needed trip to the grocery store. He wanted to get out and clear his head. Too many thoughts of Braxton, the old unit, and what they'd all done. Seeing his former commander darkened Tyler's mood. Lexi liked getting stuff delivered, and Tyler was normally happy to let her handle the order. This afternoon, however, he craved fresh air and a setting other than his four walls.

As was typical with his shopping trips, Tyler spent more than he'd expected on fewer items than he thought he'd buy. He drove home, unlocked the door, and carried the bags inside. "Lexi? You here?" Silence served as the only reply. She was probably in her room either listening to music or chatting with someone. Either option required headphones. The girl was great at shutting the world off for a while. Tyler envied her. He could only do it if he felt inspired sitting at his easel.

Tyler unpacked the bags, putting everything in the fridge or pantry as appropriate. Still no Lexi. Even with music in her ears, she should've heard him come home. Never mind the fact he couldn't do any household task quietly. The living room sat empty, though the cushions on the couch were a mess. Lexi liked reading there, but she usually fixed the sofa when she finished. Tyler walked upstairs and rapped quietly on her bedroom door. No response. He knocked louder. Same result. Tyler nudged the door open.

No sign of Lexi.

It was a nice day. Not too hot for the summer. She could've gone for a run. One thing she frequently complained about with finishing her senior year of high school online was the lack of sports. It wasn't possible to simulate a cross-country competition on a jogging trail. Tyler joined her occasionally, but he usually held her back. He'd never been a fast runner, though his stamina let him maintain a steady pace for quite a while. Still, Lexi could win races, and such a feat was beyond Tyler's abilities.

After about a half-hour, he grew concerned. After confirming she wasn't in any other room of the house, Tyler sent Lexi a text. He waited a couple minutes, but no reply came. He called her. A pop-rock ringtone emanated from the kitchen. On the counter, Lexi's mobile displayed *Dad* on its caller ID. She would never leave the house without her phone.

Tyler's heart sank, and he bolted for the front door.

32

T he first thing Lexi noticed was the sensation of moving.

Grogginess lifted slowly. Based on the speed she felt, she must be in a car. Lexi let one eye flutter open. A black leather seatback eight inches past her nose blocked her view. The leather smelled faintly of polish or cleaner. Her lips were stuck together, and as the lights fully came on upstairs, she realized tape covered her mouth. Something rough like rope bound her hands behind her back.

"I think she's awake," a male voice said.

"It was a mild dose." The second man's voice sounded much more nasal . . . almost like John Lennon with an unidentifiable American accent. Lexi felt her pulse quicken and soon heard the rush of blood in her ears. She was tied up in a vehicle headed to parts unknown with two strangers who'd already abducted her in the front seat. The country music playing at low volume somehow made the situation worse.

"We ain't been told where to take her yet," the first man said. Based on where his voice came from in the vehicle, Lexi presumed him to be the driver.

"So?"

"So maybe we have some fun with her while we wait."

Lexi ran through scenarios in her head. Her legs weren't tied, so she could kick. She could headbutt. Both her parents insisted—separately, of course, because they rarely did anything together—she learn to defend herself from the time she started school. Her dad was the only one who tried to teach her. "Don't start a fight," he told her, "but make sure you can end one." She'd do her damnedest.

"What kind of asshole are you?" the Lennon-sounding guy said.

"What? We got a girl tied up in the backseat."

"For Christ's sake. She's here to draw out her old man."

"Be quiet," the driver said. "You want her to hear?"

"I doubt she's stupid. She must know what's going on."

A ringing cell phone interrupted their argument. "Sitrep," a new voice said a few seconds later. Whoever it was projected authority even through a Bluetooth setup. Braxton.

"We got her," the passenger said. "Just need to know where to take her before Anderson here gets any ideas."

"You dick," Anderson said.

"Listen to me," Braxton barked, "both of you. You'll bring her to facility three. Is she currently unharmed?"

"Yes, sir," Anderson said.

"Then, she is to remain that way. Am I clear?"

"Absolutely," the other man said.

"I'll expect you soon." Braxton hung up, and the quiet country song she heard before resumed.

"You know where facility three is?" the passenger asked.

"Sure," Anderson said. "Been there a few times." The vehicle turned suddenly. Lexi slid across the seat, and her head banged into the armrest on the door. "You?"

"Once or twice. I didn't know we were gonna use it for anything."

"You never know with Braxton."

The men fell into silence. Even though Braxton instructed them not to harm her, Lexi's pulse didn't slow. She struggled against the rope to no avail. Braxton was going to use her as bait for her father. He'd be walking into a building outnumbered and outgunned. If she could get free, maybe she could help him.

Lexi didn't want him to face down Braxton and all his men alone.

DRIVING AROUND PROVED FRUITLESS. Tyler didn't see Braxton or even a sign of activity at either of the sites he knew about. He got back on the highway and passed a couple of slower-moving cars. A quick glance at the speedometer showed him he'd crossed 85. Tyler took a deep breath and eased off the gas. Getting pulled over wouldn't help anyone, least of all Lexi.

He steered the 442 onto the shoulder. His right hand shook with adrenaline as he put the transmission into park. Tyler ran himself through the exercises he employed to slow his heart rate and calm himself before a big shot. Breathe in. Hold. Breathe out. He'd never been the best sniper, but he always fired with his lungs empty and his pulse as slow as he could get it.

Breathe in. Hold. Breathe out.

This was just like taking a shot at 200 yards. No—no, it wasn't. Lexi's life was never on the line in Afghanistan.

Breathe in. Hold. Breathe out.

Being amped up wouldn't get his daughter back.

A minute later, the tremble in his hand disappeared. Tyler thought about his next course of action. Braxton would call at some point and probably demand something in exchange for Lexi's safe return. Tyler harbored an idea what it would be. He wanted to get things moving before then. Don't let the enemy dictate the terms of battle. An idea popped into his mind, and he input an address into the GPS.

Tyler pulled back onto I-95 North. He stayed on it long enough to pick up the Baltimore Beltway headed toward Towson. Traffic was typically light for a Saturday afternoon. Tyler took the exit for I-83 North and soon got off the highway, ending up on York Road headed into Cockeysville. It was a nice area of Baltimore County, set between the more pedestrian Lutherville and the more upscale Hunt Valley. Tyler turned off York Road after about a mile and drove into a townhouse community.

Like most similar developments, its houses all looked alike in some way. A few had dormer windows, and some were larger or smaller than others, but anyone who lived here did so for comfort and convenience rather than individual expression. Tyler pulled into a guest parking spot near his destination. A few people milled about. He killed the engine, sat in the car, and waited for them to pass.

When they did, he got out of the car and skulked around to the rear of a group of houses. He'd seen the address from the front, and his target sat one from the far end. Tyler found it from the back and checked his surroundings. No one walking about. No one on a deck grilling. A wooden fence with a gate stared back at him. It was five feet tall. He could get over it but not quickly, and the process could attract attention.

Instead, Tyler took out a lock-blade knife and slid it between the planks of wood. He found the catch for the gate, steered it open with the blade, and moved into the backyard. Tyler pushed the gate closed behind himself. The grounds would be of sufficient size for the tiniest of dogs. It might have been twenty feet from gate to back door, and the yard was deeper than its width.

The rear door was not a slider, making it easier. A rear door on glides, especially one with the bar down, would take time to bypass. Time was the enemy. A glass door with a white frame and conventional lock provided entry to the house. Tyler opened it quickly with the snap gun, moved the plastic blinds aside, and snuck into the house. He closed up behind himself and padded across the basement. A finished living room yielded to a hallway with a bathroom and laundry area. Tyler took the stairs to the main level.

He checked the house thoroughly. No one was home. Tyler chose a seat at the kitchen hidden by a wall from the front of the house. He waited. He'd always been good at waiting. It seemed like a silly thing to claim proficiency in, but younger soldiers in particular showed no aptitude for a hurry-up-and-wait environment. They were too impatient, too used to instant gratification. Even ten years ago, many of them were too used to their phones or tablets to sit in silence for hours at a time with no outside distractions.

A half-hour into his vigil, a key turned in the front door. Footsteps entered. The door swung shut. Someone moved into the family room. The lightness of the steps confirmed it was a woman. She set something down, then walked into the kitchen. "Hello, Maggie."

"Jesus Christ!" She jumped as much as the heels of her shoes would allow. Maggie Braxton, ex-wife of Leo, bought this house once the allegations against her husband became public and credible. Braxton lost all his benefits, and his former wife reaped the rewards—diminished as they were by a reduction in rank from Colonel to Captain for his crimes. It still represented a tidy sum. Maggie was a year older than Tyler and three years younger than Braxton. Her wavy brown hair had gone gray, but she still wore it in the same shoulder-length style. The color looked good on her. In a different situation, Tyler would have called her pretty.

"Sorry to scare you."

"For Christ's sake, Tyler. What are you doing here?" She paused. "Is this about Leo? I haven't talked to him since he got out of prison." She blew out a snort. "Why they let him out is a mystery to me . . . but whatever. What do you want?"

"Nice to see you, too."

Maggie offered a small smile. "You were one of the good ones," she said. "Leo surrounded himself with a lot of people who loved to shoot first and skip the questions later. I always appreciated your influence on him." She leaned on a counter and removed her high heels. Maggie's jeans fit her very well.

"I don't know how much of an influence I was," Tyler said, "all things considered. How's Hannah?"

"She's good," Maggie replied. "Like you said, all things considered. She knows her dad went to jail. I haven't told her the exact circumstances yet."

"What is she now, seventeen?"

"Sixteen. Got her license a couple months ago."

"I'll be sure to stay off the sidewalks, then."

Maggie chuckled. "She's actually a good driver." Silence lingered between them for a couple minutes. Maggie left the counter and sat at the table in a chair to Tyler's right. "Why are you here?"

"Leo took Lexi."

"What?" Maggie's eyes widened, and her mouth hung open. After a moment of surprise, she said, "I knew Leo was a monster, but I never thought . . ."

"Me, neither."

"What do you need from me?"

"Honestly?" Tyler said. "I thought about taking Hannah in exchange." Maggie's eyes narrowed, but Tyler continued. "I'm not going to. I don't think Leo cares enough about her for it to matter."

"I wouldn't let you take her."

"I wouldn't let you stop me."

Silence returned. Maggie shook her head, got up, and walked to the fridge. She opened a beer and remained across the kitchen. "So you're not taking my daughter," she said. "What did you come here for, then?"

"Information," Tyler said. "I've been to every place I know Leo is using. No one's there. I have a feeling what he's going to want in exchange for Lexi. I'd rather cut things off before we get there."

"You think I know where he is?"

"Yes."

"And you think I'm going to tell you?" Maggie said, her eyes throwing daggers. "You break into my house, tell me you considered kidnapping my daughter, and now you want my help? Maybe I was wrong. Maybe you were just like the rest of the assholes Leo surrounded himself with."

"You know I'm not," Tyler said, not raising his voice to match hers.

"Do I?"

"And you know Lexi. She's a good kid. She's starting college in a few months." Tyler paused to let out a breath at the thought of it. "Unlike Leo, I love my daughter, and I care what happens to her. He has her somewhere. I want her back." Maggie didn't say anything. "I've been to Columbia and a place near the airport. Oh-for-two."

"You're a piece of work, you know that?" Maggie took a long pull of the beer.

"I'm well aware."

Maggie downed the rest of the beer and spiked the bottle into a trash can. "Are you going to kill Leo?"

Tyler pondered his reply a moment. "I'm not sure what to say here. I—"

"The truth, dammit. Tell me the truth. Leo never could. Show me you're better than him."

"Yes," Tyler said with a nod. "He's not getting out of this

alive, even if it means I go with him, but I'm getting Lexi to safety."

Maggie looked at Tyler for a long moment. She turned away, opened the fridge, and carried another beer to the table. "There might be a place," she said after taking her seat again. "Toward the end of his career, before the last deployment, Leo bought something." Maggie twisted the cap off the beer and drained a third of the bottle in a single swig. "That son of a bitch. Years after the fact, he still drives me to drink."

Tyler gave her a minute before following up. "The place you mentioned?"

"He and White did it. Something about setting up a base of operations for the future company they were planning. It's in the city . . . somewhere near the Port of Baltimore."

"You know the name they bought it under?"

"I think Leo's grandfather. Alphonse Braxton."

"I hope you're right," Tyler said.

"It's all I know." Maggie shrugged. "How many places can there be over there?" She drank some more beer. "Any other questions?"

"No." Tyler stood. "Keep an eye on the obituaries."

"I already do every day," Maggie said.

33

Anderson opened the back door. He was huge and imposing, standing at least six-five and built like he enjoyed tackling people—or worse. His wide eyes glaring down at her were very disconcerting. He flashed Lexi a wolfish grin. "Lights out, princess." He slipped a sack over her head and hoisted her from the car. Lexi tried to shout for help, but the tape on her mouth reduced her cries to mumbles.

The large man must have carried her over his shoulder. He made sure to rest his hand on her butt and not move it. By the sound of it, someone opened a door for them, and they entered through it. Lexi wished she could see where they were. In the car, Anderson snatched her before she could reposition herself to get her bearings. Now, she'd never know. The odds of getting a message to her dad were slim, but he needed to know her location.

"Set her down here," the guy with the Lennon voice said. Anderson squeezed Lexi's butt so hard it hurt before he tossed her down onto a hard chair. The other man took the bag from her head. He was tall like Anderson but thin, and his face lacked both the mania and cruelty of his compatriot's.

"Please, let me go," Lexi said. The tape muffled it.

"Shut up!" Anderson roared before the other man could answer. He got in Lexi's face and jabbed a meaty finger at her. "You sit here and be quiet. Hope your old man shows up while you're at it."

"He will." Despite her mouth being covered, she didn't sound too bad. These two could probably guess what she said, anyway. "When he does, he'll kill you all."

"I told you to be quiet." Anderson backhanded Lexi across the face. It spun her head around and sent her crashing to the floor.

"For Christ's sake," the other guy said. "You heard Braxton. Get out of here, Anderson."

"I'm gonna—"

"Out. Now. If anyone asks why the girl has a bruise on her face, I'll tell them you did it."

"It'd be a mistake," Anderson said.

The slender man hit him with a short jab in the solar plexus. Anderson stepped back and sucked wind. "Piss off and go somewhere else. I'll deal with her." Anderson's baleful stare made Lexi's pulse race anew, but the other guy didn't seem to care. After a few seconds of staring and posturing, Anderson stomped out of the room. "Sorry about him." He picked Lexi up gently and set her on the chair. "About the whole thing, really. I didn't sign up to kidnap girls."

Lexi tried to reply, but the tape made it unintelligible. Her captor grabbed one end of it. "If I pull this back, do you swear you won't scream?" She nodded. "All right. It'll hurt." He ripped it off, and fire blazed along Lexi's lips and cheeks.

"Holy shit," she said in a breathless voice. "What's your name?"

"Call me Rust."

"All right, Rust. Where are we?"

"I doubt I can tell you," he said. "I probably shouldn't have

taken the tape off. You start yelling, and I'll have to put it back."
He picked up another length of rope from a small shelf in the
corner.

"What are you doing with that?" Lexi wanted to know.
Blood rushed in her ears again.

"Gotta make sure you can't go anywhere." Rust walked
behind her. He took care to stay out of kicking range as he
bound her left ankle to the chair leg, then her right. "I'm going
to untie your arms. Lean forward." She did, and Rust undid the
knot. Circulation returned to Lexi's hands. "Enjoy it for a
minute." He bobbed his head toward the arms of the chair.

"What's going on? What does Braxton want with my dad?"

"He hates him."

Lexi narrowed her eyes. "It's mutual."

"I don't doubt it."

"Why do you work for such an asshole, then?"

Rust shrugged. "Needed a job, and I knew a couple guys
who served under Braxton years ago. Once this mess is done
with, I think we'll get back to what the company's supposed to
be doing."

"You could do better," Lexi said. "You're not like the other
guy."

"Being nicer than a monster doesn't make me a good guy,"
Rust said. "Hold out your arms." Lexi glared at him for a
moment but did what he asked. He bound her forearms to the
chair. The knots felt looser than last time, and Lexi watched
him tie both. "We'll check on you periodically. Stay quiet, and I
won't need to put the tape back on."

"Yeah, yeah." Rust walked out of the room, closed the door,
and locked it from the outside. One more obstacle. Lexi looked
at her restraints. Rust did a pretty good job with them. He'd
probably learned to tie a few hitches in the army. Lexi's grandfather, however, came from the navy, and he taught her all
kinds of knots. She never met her great-grandfather, but she'd

heard stories of his exploits on the Underwater Demolition Team, the precursor to the Navy SEALs.

She could undo these bonds.

TYLER DROVE from Maggie's house. He could go home, gear up, and be at the port to scout the location within an hour. As he neared the city, his phone rang. Braxton. "She'd better be alive."

"Tyler, please. I'm not a monster."

"The hell you're not."

"A matter of perspective," Braxton said.

"I went to Maggie's house, Leo." Braxton remained quiet. "Nothing to say, now? She's fine by the way. Thinks you're a miserable prick. She was always too smart for you."

"What were you doing there?"

"I considered returning the favor," Tyler said. "If I thought you gave a shit about Hannah, I would have. Then, we could have made a trade."

"You leave my daughter alone," Braxton said through clenched teeth.

"Careful, Leo. You came dangerously close to caring about another person there."

Braxton sighed. "I wonder why I bother with you some-times. Listen, dammit. You know I have Lexi. She's safe. She's fine. How long she remains this way is up to you."

Tyler pulled the 442 against a curb and killed the engine. The Bluetooth died when the stereo winked out, so he held his phone against his ear. "Leo," Tyler said. "If anything happens to her, I will kill everyone who works for you and everyone in your family. I'll murder Maggie and Hannah on camera and make you watch it before you die."

"No need for such theatrics," Braxton said. On some level, Tyler knew he cared about his ex-wife and daughter. It was buried beneath a lot of layers, however, most of them involving the desires to slaughter, pillage, and profit. Everyone had their priorities. "I want something from you."

"I know. You want me to ignore you and your men while you kill Jake Smith."

"Two things, then."

"What's the other?"

"I want you to kill Sara Morrison," Braxton said.

Tyler didn't know what to say. He should have anticipated this. Braxton came gunning for Morrison with a trio of armed men, and Tyler taunted him from one of their phones after killing all three. Sara was safe with Rollins, which Braxton couldn't know. When Tyler didn't say anything, Braxton took advantage of his silence. "Don't pretend you don't know who I'm talking about. You killed three of my men saving the bitch."

"What makes you think I have any idea where she is now?" Tyler said.

"You'd better find her, then."

"You're serious."

"Of course I am. She's standing in the way of my company not only making millions but doing work this country desperately needs going forward."

"But mostly making millions."

"The money is nice," Braxton admitted.

"You're not interested in helping the country," Tyler said. "There are plenty of ways to do it, even for a serial piece of shit like you. You just want to make money and kill a bunch of brown people."

"What's wrong with either of those?"

"You're insane."

"On the contrary," Braxton said, "I see clearly what needs to be done. And it starts with Sara Morrison's death."

"So I kill her, and Lexi goes free?"

"I'll need proof, Tyler. I'm not just going to take your word for it. You were always a good liar. Bring me what I need, and your daughter is free to leave."

"What kind of proof are we talking about?" Tyler said.

"How about her head on a silver platter?"

"Who is she, John the Baptist? This isn't the first century."

"Fine," Braxton said. "I'll settle for a photo or video. My people will need to authenticate it, of course. Once they do, Lexi can go. You have my word."

Tyler trusted Braxton about as far as he could dropkick him. Notions like honor mattered to him, though. It was all tied up in his identity as a colonel. However maniacal he was, Braxton had a core of old-school values he wouldn't betray. If he offered his word, he would keep it. "Your word?"

"Yes."

"All right," Tyler said. "I'll do it."

SOME THINGS NEEDED to be discussed in person.

Tyler stopped his drive toward the city and got back on the road. He dialed Rollins. "I'm headed your way."

"Why? What's going on?"

"An interesting development. Not unexpected, just . . . interesting."

"All right," Rollins said. "You know where I live."

He resided on the other side of Baltimore in Rosedale. Tyler drove around the city rather than through it and approached Rollins' area about fifteen minutes later. Rollins owned a house on Chivalry Court, which Tyler always found appropriate for him. The street featured a mix of architectural styles, but the plurality of homes were ranchers. Rollins' was at the end of the cul-de-sac, a brick-fronted single-story model with dark shutters and three thin white columns on the outside. Tyler wondered why Rollins never took advantage of his good taste to knock them down.

He pulled the 442 to the curb. Rollins' large black pickup sat in the driveway pointing toward the street. Always park like you need to make an escape. Tyler remembered learning it in the Army and passing it onto young Rollins at some point. As he got out of the car, the front door of the house swung open, and Rollins walked out. He waited on the small front stoop while Tyler approached. "What's going on?"

"How's Sara?" asked Tyler.

Rollins shrugged. "As well as she can be, I guess."

"She know you're out here talking to me?"

"No . . . she's in the shower."

Tyler nodded. "Something came up with Braxton."

"I figured. What's going on?"

"He took Lexi."

Rollins blew out a long breath through. "Damn. She OK?"

"He tells me she is for now."

"For now?"

"If I want to guarantee her safe return," Tyler said, "I need to kill Sara Morrison." Rollins stiffened, like he expected Tyler to try and charge past him into the house. His hands clenched. "At ease."

"You ask me to look after a woman, and now you tell me you need to kill her? How the hell is this supposed to put me at ease?"

"Braxton wants proof of death," Tyler said, avoiding the question. "I need to show him she's dead before he'll let Lexi go."

Rollins stared at Tyler for a few seconds before he said anything. "You'd do anything to get Lexi back, right?"

"I would."

"And you intend to provide proof you killed Sara Morrison?"

"I do."

"How do you plan on killing her?"

"With your help," Tyler said.

"What?"

"You spent some time in the theater, right?"

"I'm confused," Rollins said. He frowned at Tyler. "What does this have to do with killing a woman?"

"Answer the question," Tyler insisted.

"Fine. Sure, I did some stage work." He let out a dry chuckle. "You probably think all the gays spend time doing theater."

"I've heard you sing," Tyler said. "They weren't putting you on stage for your vocals."

Rollins grinned in spite of himself. "Fair enough."

"What did you do in the productions you worked on?"

"Little acting here and there. But I also did some behind-the-scenes work. Set building, a little makeup . . ." Rollins paused and smirked. "Now, I get it."

"Still have any of the stuff you used?" Tyler said.

"Sure. I did a community play a few weeks ago."

"I figured you'd keep it up."

"Why?"

Tyler smiled. "Because all the gays spend time doing theater."

"We *do* love it," Rollins said.

"How long would you need to get something ready?"

Rollins shrugged. "Depends on what I have. If I've got it all on hand, maybe an hour. If I need to borrow some supplies, make it two."

"All right," Tyler said. "Let's talk to Sara. It's only fair she knows what's going on."

They walked inside. Soft footsteps padded around down the hall. "Miss Morrison," Rollins called, "can we talk to you when you're decent?"

"Sure." She came out a couple minutes later in a T-shirt and sweats. Her wet hair hung loose and unkempt around her shoulders. With no makeup or time getting ready, she still looked stunning. Sara smiled at Tyler. It took him a few seconds to find the power of speech.

"Uh . . . Braxton took my daughter."

"That son of a bitch." They all sat in Rollins' spartan living room. The TV was mounted in the exact center of the wall. The furniture arrangement, while basic, fit the room well and allowed people to converse. No dust bunnies hopped around the laminate floor. Tyler sat in a recliner while Sara and Rollins took opposite ends of a couch.

"He offered me a way to get her back," Tyler said.

"Why are you telling me?"

"It involves you."

"It's your daughter," Sara said. "I'm sure you'd do anything to get her back. What do I need to do?"

"You need to die, Miss Morrison," Tyler said.

34

After lying low in Philly for a while, Jake needed to go back for the Sentra. He'd been vigilant but hadn't seen any of Braxton's men. A few SUVs gave him pause, but the damn things were all too common nowadays. He stuck to sidewalks, used alleys when he found them, and doubled back on himself a couple times. No tail.

A half-mile from the garage, he turned down an alley. A homeless man slept against the back wall of an unidentified building. A box held most of the man's worldly possessions. He left a cell phone lying beside him on the concrete. Jake looked both ways but didn't see anyone. He grabbed the phone and tucked three twenties under the man's arm.

On his walk, Jake texted his father. *Borrowing a phone for a few minutes. Can you give me the number of the guy you said could help?* He cut across the street, walked a block out of the way, and then got back on the path. A moment later, a reply came in. *Sure. He goes by Tyler. 410-555-4791.*

Jake stopped, ducked into a small coffee shop, and ordered an iced tea. Only one other table was occupied, so sitting far apart from other customers proved to be the easiest thing he'd done in a while. While he sipped his drink, he thought about his dad's message. Jake recalled meeting someone in special forces . . . Tyler. A warrant officer who encouraged him to go for the gold. He wondered if it was the same man. He fired off an encrypted message. *This is Jake. My dad gave me your #. Hope you can help us both.*

After a few more sips of tea, Jake's phone buzzed. He looked at the reply. *Working on it. Stay where you are.* Simple and direct. Here was a man who took army communication to heart. Jake composed a reply. *Do you know anyone I can talk to about what I know? Has to be trustworthy.*

It took a minute again, but Tyler sent a response. *Sara. Defense official. 240-555-6077. You can trust her.*

Could he trust her? Jake thought he could trust Arthur Bell, but the genesis of his problems traced back to his conversation with the Pentagon worker. Was this Sara any different? Jake didn't want to sign into any of his own accounts and create a trail for Braxton to follow. Reaching out to his father was far enough. He used Protonmail to send a secure message. In it, Jake laid out what he knew about Braxton, Hexagon, and what they were after in Afghanistan. It felt good to tell someone, even if he tapped the email with his thumbs using a phone lifted from a homeless guy.

Once the message sent, Jake finished his tea. He dropped the phone in the trash along with the cup. The garage lay about a third of a mile from his location, but it took him fifteen minutes to complete the circuitous route. No one followed.

FOR A MAN who often touted patience to those serving under him, Braxton possessed it in short supply. After an hour, Tyler's phone rang. He ignored it. Ten minutes later, Braxton called back, and Tyler answered.

"Sitrep." Tyler fought the urge to throw his phone out the window.

"I don't work for you anymore, Leo. I'm done giving you sitreps."

"It's a simple request. You used to be good at answering simple requests, John."

Tyler let the comment pass. "What do you want?"

"Is it done?"

"Not yet," Tyler said.

"Why not?"

"Because these things take time, especially if it's something you don't want turning up later."

"Fine," Braxton said. "You have a half-hour." He hung up before Tyler could say anything else.

"Prick," Tyler muttered to the empty line.

By now, Rollins should be almost finished. He said he would need to borrow some makeup from someone else he knew in the theater circle and to give him a little over an hour. Tyler passed the time driving back to Columbia. He surveilled Hexagon's main location. They rented the first floor of a brick two-story building in a complex not far from Fort Meade, nestled amid a bunch of defense and NSA contractors. Most of the structures sat empty, which Tyler would expect on a weekend. A few cars were parked outside one of the businesses, however. No signage indicated its name or what it did, which told people in the know all they needed.

The cars didn't move. The front door was mostly glass, and what Tyler could see inside past it remained dark. If anyone stirred inside, they were past the entry area. If they held his daughter captive in there, she must be somewhere toward the back. It made more sense, anyway. Fewer people gathered at the loading area. A lack of prying eyes made getting a kidnapping victim out of an SUV a lot easier.

Tyler knew this from his time in Special Forces. He figured most of the men working for Braxton did, too.

The 442's engine would give him away at some point. Tyler drove around to the rear of the row of buildings. He stopped short of the nameless enterprise's back entrance. A conventional metal door along with a loading dock and sliding receiving door comprised the entirety of the place's features. No windows. No lights. The best Tyler could hope for right now was some guy in a buzz cut to wander out for a smoke.

Before it could happen, Rollins sent a message via an encrypted app. It carried a photo attachment. Tyler looked at the picture. If he didn't know better, he would've assumed Sara Morrison was dead. She lay in the grass, a realistic bullet hole at her temple, and what looked an awful lot like blood spread on and around her. Rollins did a hell of a job, which Tyler told him via the app.

He waited until twenty-nine minutes went by before calling Braxton. Let the asshole twist in the wind. "It's done," Tyler said when his former CO answered and asked for another sitrep.

"Send proof." Tyler recommended the app he and Rollins used. Braxton said he'd never heard of it, but he would download and use it. He told Tyler to wait ten minutes, then send his evidence.

So he did. Tyler attached the photo to a basic message. *Taken care of. Lexi?*

A couple minutes later, Braxton replied.

Well done. Meet me tomorrow morning, 0600, new housing development. In lieu of an address, Braxton sent coordinates. Tyler punched them into Google Maps. The new development sat in the middle of a forest bordering Odenton—again not far from the Fort. Another community full of cookie-cutter homes. Tyler replied with his concurrence.

Six AM. Braxton used to make a point to tell his men to scout locations three hours early.

Tyler would need to be earlier.

MAXWELL ENTERED Braxton's office without knocking. His boss noticed the breach of protocol, of course, but an arched eyebrow served as his only reply. "You're really going to give Tyler his daughter back?" Maxwell asked as he sat uninvited in a guest chair.

"I'm not the monster he thinks I am." Braxton frowned as he regarded Maxwell. "Why?"

"Just wondering if you'd consider another idea."

"I'm not killing the girl."

Maxwell put his hands up. "Wasn't going to suggest you should. You should absolutely kill Tyler tomorrow, though."

"He's upheld his end of the bargain," Braxton said. "Sara Morrison is dead. We can deal with Arthur Bell from now on." When Braxton paused, Maxwell didn't fill in the gap with news of Bell's untimely demise. "I hate Tyler, but he's a man of his word. He'll leave us alone."

"I want to kill him," Maxwell said.

"You want to kill *everyone*."

Maxwell couldn't deny the charge. He grinned and shrugged. "I'm usually right about it, too. I know I am in this case. Tyler will keep being a thorn in our side."

Braxton leaned back in his chair. He narrowed his eyes at his longtime lieutenant. Maxwell met his gaze. Eventually, the former colonel said, "Tell me what you have in mind."

"I'll go tomorrow morning. One man with me in an SUV, and two more in houses at the far end of the street. The girl stays here. We catch Tyler in a crossfire, and the problem's solved. Do what you want with the girl afterward. I'd like to see her cry when we put her dad's corpse in front of her."

"Damn, you're bloodthirsty."

"You used to appreciate it."

"I still do," Braxton said. "The differences in our approaches have always led to our success." He paused and took a deep breath. "Fine. Do it your way. Take some of the new guys, though. If Tyler gets a few good shots off, I don't want to lose anyone important."

"He won't," Maxwell said.

"Don't underestimate him, Kent. For a blunt instrument, he's pretty smart. Make sure you get there early."

"We'll be there by four. Tyler will be dead by six."

"He'd better be," Braxton said.

Maxwell stood. "He will."

35

Tyler prepared for the early morning meeting. He expected Braxton would betray him somehow—if he even showed. Ensuring Lexi's safety was the priority. Braxton and his men were expendable. In his basement, Tyler pushed a heavy bookcase to the side, exposing a four-foot door. The secret room was his first project when he bought the house. Tyler entered the combination and dragged the cumbersome panel open.

He walked into a room ten feet wide, fifteen feet long, and with six-foot ceilings. Metal racks lined the walls. Many held rifles, shotguns, and other weapons, but Tyler also kept most of his memorabilia from his time in the army here. His final dress uniform hung near two sets of BDUs, a shelf full of medals and commendations, all above two foot lockers.

Tyler ejected the magazine from a Vietnam-era Colt .45. He turned it upside down, and a key slid into his waiting hand. He unlatched one of the foot lockers and scrutinized the contents. Braxton wouldn't come alone. It wouldn't be a simple meeting because nothing was ever simple when Leo Braxton stuck his nose into it. Before coming downstairs, Tyler used Google

Earth to look at the site. Two houses under construction represented great spots for snipers. Tyler didn't want to pull Rollins
away from Sara Morrison. He was on his own.

Plastique was a great equalizer.

Tyler grabbed two bricks plus two wireless blasting caps
and a detonator. Hiding the explosives in a work zone would be
easy. Their coloring would allow them to blend in with wood.
He put everything into a rucksack, secured his hidden room,
and dragged the bookcase back into place. A few hours
remained before he needed to leave. Tyler caught a nap on the
first-floor couch and woke up a few ticks past midnight.

After a quick convenience store stop for coffee and a muffin,
Tyler arrived at the new development close to one AM. The
Eagle's Landing promised luxurious single-family homes from
the mid $600s. So far, they'd cleared a lot of ground but done
little construction. A model home greeted visitors to the
community. It showed exterior options like a porch and brick
front which would add to the already-steep asking price. At the
end of a dirt road sat a mostly-completed house. Another one
in a similar state of construction sat on the opposite side of
what would eventually be a street. Both were about three
hundred yards from the showpiece.

Tyler walked down the hastily-graded avenue to confirm his
suspicion: it ran downhill toward the model. Not much, but
enough for the two dwellings at the other end to occupy higher
ground. Thus, they would make better spots for snipers.
Braxton would want to meet near the finished house, and he'd
station a man in each of the other two, ready to fire in case
things went awry.

Things would definitely go awry.

Tyler noticed a streetlight glinting off something mounted
onto the model. He took a wide arc in approaching. It was a
camera. Based on its position, it couldn't see anyone entering
the main house, but it had a great view of the rest of the

complex, including the two unfinished buildings at the end. Tyler drove away from the model, turning down the next street and leaving his car near the trees.

He approached the two houses from the rear and got to work. The model was a finished, pristine home. Its opposite numbers still contained some construction boxes and supplies. The interior walls required windows and needed to be finished and painted. Tyler busied himself setting everything up. The plastique bricks hid nicely among random supplies. He knew where the snipers would setup. They needed clear lines of sight. At about two-forty-five, he finished everything to his satisfaction. Braxton's men would be rolling in for recon soon.

They would find nothing amiss. They weren't smart enough.

Tyler left the development, drove about a mile away, parked the 442, and caught some more rest. It would be go time soon enough.

AT FIVE MINUTES TO SIX, Tyler navigated the 442 into the future Eagle's Landing. He drove to the model and saw no other cars. No signs of activity. The first rays of sunlight provided faint illumination. No lights on in any of the three houses. He parked near the finished home and got out. Tyler carried an M11 under his jacket and wore a bullet-resistant vest. He knew the men in the houses would have powerful rifles. The distance to the end of the street was about three hundred yards. Any competent sniper could hit someone in the nose from such a distance.

Tyler waited. The small wireless detonator in his hand would activate both blasting caps. Despite its tiny size, it weighed on his palm. He felt eyes on him, even though no one was visible when he turned. Neither of the other houses with cutouts instead of windows showed anyone inside. Braxton sent two capable men ahead. Tyler would expect nothing less. He waited for a minute, and then he heard another vehicle.

Of course, it was a gray SUV. It turned into the development and drove past him without acknowledgement. Tyler stood in place as the Tahoe swung a U-turn past the model and stopped. The driver's maneuver allowed for a quick exit. Rather than Braxton, Kent Maxwell got out of the front passenger's door. He stood in front of the building. The driver remained in the vehicle. Tyler saw no one else inside. He scowled at Maxwell. "Where is she?"

"We kept our word. She's alive."

"There's no 'our' here, Maxwell. I didn't talk to you. Your boss and I have an arrangement. Why don't you have your driver take you away so the grownups can talk?"

"Go to hell, Tyler." Maxwell took in a deep breath and made a show of surveying his surroundings. Tyler noticed his eyes pause for a beat at each of the other dwellings. "I'm here. You can deal with me."

"I'll wait for Leo," Tyler said. "When you talk to him, tell him to hurry. I know he hates being late."

"He's not coming," Maxwell said. "I gotta hand it to you, though. I didn't think you'd kill an innocent woman. Not again at least."

Tyler let the barb pass, but he filed it away in case he saw Maxwell again. "I did what your boss asked. Give me my daughter."

"You're not in a position to make demands. Do you think I came here alone?"

Tyler shook his head. "No. I figured you sent a couple guys ahead. The official Leo Braxton recon window is still three hours, right?" Maxwell frowned. "I got here five hours early, and you didn't bring the sharpest knives in the drawer." Tyler held up the small device in his hand. Before Maxwell could say anything, Tyler pushed the button.

Two explosions rang out from the other end of the dirt road. Tyler watched the dawning horror in Maxwell's eyes with satisfaction. He refused to take his gaze from the man, however, as much as he wanted to see the results of his handiwork. "Your reputation precedes you, Kent. You and your boss are predictable." Tyler shrugged. "You should tell me where Lexi is now." Free of the detonator, his hand inched toward the M11.

Maxwell reached for a weapon. Tyler pulled his pistol as he spun away from Maxwell and came up in a crouch. A bullet whizzed past him. Tyler returned fire, but Maxwell was already climbing back into the SUV. Bullets thudded into the door and body. The Yukon took off with screeching tires. Maxwell and the driver got as low in their seats as they could. Tyler squeezed the trigger until the slide locked back, but his small moving targets eluded him. "Dammit!" he shouted to the empty development.

Tyler traded a full mag for the empty. After pressing the slide release, he safetied his gun, put it away, and ran back toward his car. It was early on a Sunday morning, but the sounds of two explosions and gunfire would carry. Someone would be up and call 9-1-1. Tyler got in the 442, fired it up, and pulled away from the curb with screeching tires. He drove away from Eagle's Landing. About a mile down the main road, he passed a police car and a fire engine.

He needed to take this fight to Braxton. Today. Lexi couldn't wait.

When the emergency vehicles passed, Tyler mashed the accelerator to the floorboard and sped toward Baltimore.

~

MAXWELL STARED AT HIS PHONE. Braxton already called once. He didn't want the man to call again. Better to get out in front of the situation and own his mistakes. They still held the girl, and

Tyler didn't know where they were. Hexagon enjoyed all the advantages. If Braxton wasn't smart enough to see it, Maxwell would point it out for him.

He made the call. Braxton answered before the first ring even finished. "Not like you to let it go to voicemail, Kent." Maxwell frowned at the hard edge in his boss' voice.

"It didn't go as planned, sir."

"I kind of figured it didn't when you refused to answer." Braxton paused, and his deep breath hissed in Maxwell's ear. "What happened?"

"Tyler got there ahead of us. He . . . rigged some explosives and—"

"I warned you not to underestimate him," Braxton said.

"Yes, sir."

"You did it anyway."

"It would appear so," Maxwell said.

"Anyone besides you survive?"

"Shah is still driving me. The two new men . . . didn't make it."

"We can't afford to keep losing people, Maxwell. It's one thing if Tyler takes them out. It's another for you to squander them with some plan I never should've approved."

"Sir, we still have the girl," Maxwell said. "Tyler doesn't know where we are. The advantage is ours."

"You might be right," Braxton said. "I'm just not sure I can trust your judgment right now. Hurry back." He broke the connection.

Maxwell spiked his phone into the footwell. Tyler cost Hexagon a bunch of men, and now he'd cost Maxwell the trust of his commander. One more entry on a long list of reasons John Tyler needed to die.

36

L exi slept sitting in the chair. When she awoke in the morning, her arms were stiff, and she could barely feel her hands. Some anonymous goon untied her long enough to allow her to use the bathroom, drink some water, and eat a granola bar. He didn't strike her as military. The hair was too long and the belly a little too big. If he served, he'd let himself go in the time since. When Lexi complained about her arms and hands, he rolled his eyes and lashed her to the chair again.

Whoever he was, this guy couldn't tie a good knot. His rope work probably would have kept the average person tied down. Lexi used her fingers while the feeling and circulation remained in them. She felt around the knot, learned its shape, and began working on one of the ropes. A shouted curse startled her, and the door opened a moment later. "Your father just cost me two more men." This man was middle-aged, probably a few years older than her dad, and definitely presented himself like he still put a uniform on every day. "You must be Braxton."

Instead of answering, he leaned down and got in her face. "Did you hear me?"

"Maybe you should hire better men."

Braxton's lip curled, and his hand twitched. Lexi didn't flinch. "You are definitely your father's daughter."

"And my mother's," Lexi said. "Maybe you could give her some prison survival tips."

"You're here because you're useful." Braxton jabbed his finger toward her, stopping it just shy of her nose. Lexi resisted the urge to bite it. "I want your father. He'll come as long as I have you and as long as I keep you alive. Try remembering it before you mouth off next time."

"I hope I get to watch my dad kill you."

A growl escaped Braxton's sneering lips. He grabbed the upright of the chair and pushed, spilling Lexi onto her side. It hurt, but she didn't give the asshole the satisfaction of even a small grunt of pain. Her heart raced as Braxton glared down at her. Despite her defiance, Lexi knew how vulnerable she was lying trussed in a building full of men who didn't care much about her well-being. "I'll make sure you get a front-row seat when I kill him," Braxton said. "I'll do it nice and slow. You can agonize together. Then, you won't be useful anymore." He drew his foot back and kicked Lexi in the midsection. She couldn't suppress a sharp intake of breath at the added show of fury. Her ribs throbbed even as Braxton backed away and left the room.

She allowed herself a minute of relaxing breaths to ease the pain. Then, she went back to work on the knot.

TYLER SAT with Sara Morrison in Rollins' house. They brewed and drank a fresh pot of coffee. Neither attempted any small talk after Tyler told her the reason for his visit. Sara wished him good luck getting Lexi back and waited on the couch while Rollins drove to Baltimore.

A few minutes later, Tyler's phone buzzed with a video call from Rollins via an encrypted messenger. "How's it look?" Tyler asked.

"It's doable," Rollins said. "I'm kind of surprised someone like Braxton would use a place like this, honestly. I don't think it's easy to defend."

"What do you mean?"

"The first thing I noticed was the roads. You have some wide areas in the back for receiving, but it all empties into a narrow avenue. No better out front." He pointed past the row of buildings. "It's pretty easy to get penned in by a simple roadblock."

"I don't plan on blocking the street," Tyler said.

"It would also make it hard for them to bring in reinforcements," Rollins pointed out.

It was a fair point. Tyler figured all Braxton's men would be onsite, but what if they weren't? They could get past a roadblock, but delays mattered. "How about the interior? I have a rough idea of the layout."

"I'm not trying to get inside," Rollins said. "I brought thermals, though. Might tell you where more men are."

"Sounds good."

The video feed showed moving pavement as Rollins walked. He provided quiet narration. "I'm checking the back first." He went silent. "The roadway back here is really open. Not much cover."

"Good to know," Tyler said. A plan blossomed in his head. If Rollins could tell him where more men were located, it would help.

"The rear of this place is a lot bigger than the front. It's kind of an unusual layout. Looks like this is some kind of warehouse, but the front was a tire center."

"I'm sure Braxton took what he could find at the time." Rollins' conclusion was right, though. Tyler found the structure odd when he looked at the schematics. Such a large area would be difficult to secure. Braxton must have counted on anonymity.

"Putting thermals on," Rollins said. The screen went black. He must have set the phone down. "All right. It's not the best for figuring out who's inside at this distance. Best guess is three guys moving around the interior."

They must have stood close to the rear wall to be detected. Rollins padded around to the front. "I don't know if you'll pick up anyone," Tyler told him.

A few minutes later, Rollins confirmed this. "No heat signatures," he said. "I'm heading back to my truck. You need anything else?"

"I don't think so. Thanks for helping."

"You bet." Rollins hung up.

"You're going to get her?" Sara Morrison said.

Tyler nodded. "I think Braxton and I have moved past any pretense. We're down to brute force."

"You don't think he . . ."

"No. If he's going to kill her, he wants to do it in front of me. It's how he is."

Sara grabbed Tyler's hand and squeezed it. "Go get her."

Tyler looked down at her hand and grinned. "Yes, Madam Undersecretary."

TYLER WORE BLACK. Sweatshirt, pants, shoes, gloves, mask, face paint, even his bullet-resistant vest. If he'd gone with a camouflage color scheme, it would have felt like being in the Army again. He left the 442 about two blocks away in a parking lot off Holabird Avenue. Weapons check time.

Everything was good.

Tyler ducked and walked toward the former tire service center housing the remains of Braxton's operation. He hated conducting an operation in the afternoon, but every hour Lexi spent here diminished her chances of survival. He reached the far end of the building and turned toward the back. All the windows were dark. No one parked a car in the rear. A lot across the alleyway behind the building held a bunch of old junkers. Tyler crouched among them and surveyed his target. Rollins' warning proved prescient: other than the rust buckets where Tyler hid, very little back here could provide cover. He also remembered the tip about blocking the road.

Finding a vehicle which looked like it might still work proved a challenge. Tyler discovered an old Subaru whose body was a wreck, but the engine appeared solid. Sure enough, it turned over when he hot-wired it. Tyler pulled the battered car into the roadway. It prevented easy access or escape from the rear. He then returned to his post.

A minute later, a man appeared on patrol.

Tyler sank against the metal carcass of a minivan as best he could. The sentry looked in each direction, his M-16 following his head every time. The guy lit a cigarette. He turned to his right. Tyler made a slow and steady advance. He drew a knife. The sentry sucked in two lungfuls of poison and blew out a white cloud. Tyler crept close behind him and stood. The man gave no indication he knew anyone was on his exposed six. Tyler put his left hand over the sentry's mouth and drove the knife between two ribs and into his chest. He withdrew the blade. Blood pooled at the guard's feet as he went limp in Tyler's grip.

Setting the man down quietly, Tyler searched him for comms devices. He found a small radio on the dead man's belt and an earpiece in one ear. Tyler put the receiver in his own ear and slipped the radio into the back pocket of his pants. He scampered back to the automobile graveyard and waited for a minute. No activity from the building. If anyone knew the man out back was dead, nothing was done about it. The comms channel remained quiet.

Tyler made his way around to the front of the building. It afforded a little more cover, with leafy bushes adorning the area, which at least offered Tyler something to hide behind. He crouched behind the shrubbery and waited. No one came out of Braxton's building. All quiet on the earpiece. Tyler moved toward the building when the door opened. He scrabbled back to a bush near the side wall. Whoever walked out glanced in his direction. After a moment, the man muttered, "Damn cats."

He started off to the left away from Tyler. After walking about fifty steps, he turned around and did the same in the opposite direction. From behind the foliage, Tyler watched the man walk to the far end of the derelict structure next door before pivoting on his heel. His head turned as he glanced from side to side. His position behind the bush made it hard for Tyler to take this sentry out. If he moved too much—and crouching this long grew uncomfortable—the branches and leaves would make enough noise to give him away. This guy wouldn't attribute random sounds to a cat a second time.

When the guard walked past again, Tyler shifted so he could lean more against the building. The leaves made a little noise. The sentry never broke stride. He walked to the same spot as the first time, performed a sharp pivot, and came back toward Tyler.

Thirty feet. This was the distance from the sidewalk to the building. About twelve strides for someone of the guard's height. Tyler flattened himself as much as he could. His knees protested. The man drew closer, leading with his pistol. His eyes scanned the bushes. Tyler's black getup would be effective for blending into the darkness, but not the greenery. If this guy didn't know something was amiss, he soon would.

The sentry's gun poked into the foliage. One more step and Tyler could act. The shadows must have made him hard to spot.

The guard took the required stride. Tyler gripped the gun in one hand, stood up as fast as he could, and buried the knife under the man's chin. The blade wasn't long enough to make it fatal on its own, but it removed his ability to call out for help. Surprise and injury combined to loosen his grip, and Tyler wrested the gun from him.

Tyler then withdrew the blade and thrust it into the guard's chest. Blood trickled from the sides of his mouth. He slumped to the side. Tyler let him fall, then wiped the knife on the dead man's shirt. Two down. With the ones he'd already killed, Braxton couldn't have a lot left. Tyler scampered toward the old place next door and took out his phone. He dialed Rick Rust. "They're looking for you," he said when he picked up after four rings.

Tyler kept his voice to a whisper. "No doubt. By now, you know they have my daughter."

"Yeah. I'm sorry, man. I never thought it would go this far."

"I need some information. How many men are left?"

"Counting me, I think we have eight in here."

Which meant six. Tyler stared down worse odds before. "All right." He described his idea of the building's layout and where Braxton held Lexi. Rust confirmed the details. "Thanks. I'll text you when shit's getting real." Tyler put his phone away and took a deep breath.

Getting Lexi out remained the objective.

The fallen sentry carried a set of keys in a pocket. Tyler took them to the front door, and the second one he tried opened it. He stowed the keys and pushed the door open, his MII entering the foyer ahead of him. The area could have been a nice entryway for another company, even housing a reception desk. Instead, it sat empty. Twenty feet away, another door opened into the rest of the building. Tyler tested it. Locked.

He expected a keypad, but it was another basic mechanical lock. The pilfered keys got him past it. Tyler pushed the door open, moved to the side, and looked in. An empty hallway yawned in front of him. He moved through the door, pausing to let it hit his heel so it could close with minimal noise. Doors lined each side of the corridor and led to another area at the far end.

Tyler hugged the right-hand wall as he made a slow advance. He was about to open the door when his phone buzzed. A quick look around showed no one else, so he glanced at his phone. Rust. *I'm in 1st room on left.* Tyler moved to the opposite wall, opened the door, and peeked inside. Rust sat alone at a desk. "Where is everyone?" Tyler whispered.

"I've tried to keep tabs," Rust said, matching Tyler's lowered tone. "It's hard to snoop around without people being suspicious, though. Should only be one or two guys out here."

"Plus my daughter."

Rust nodded. "Everyone else should be in the back."

"Ready to take them out?" Tyler said.

"Let's go." Rust stood, grabbed his pistol, and followed Tyler into the hallway.

37

L exi worked on the knot. The big guy who tied it never served as a sailor. Lying on her side complicated the process, but she kept at it. She could feel it loosen beneath her fingers. One loop popped open, and she slid the rope through. Within a minute, she freed both her arms. She struggled to get the chair upright again before working on her legs. With all her limbs free, Lexi stood, hopped on the balls of her feet, and shook her arms. Feeling and circulation flooded back.

"You assholes!" she yelled as footsteps passed by. She got up and tried the door. Locked. Even if it were unlocked, where would she go? A bunch of men like the two who snatched her walked the halls. Replaying the scene spiked Lexi's heart rate. She glanced around the room. The only furniture was the chair she freed herself from. A creaky bookshelf stood against the far wall. She walked over to it. They'd left her a six-pack of bottled water and a box of granola bars.

Her father would be looking for her. Her abductors took her watch, so Lexi didn't know how much time had passed. Her dad would be coming. She knew it. He would find her. If she managed to get out of this room, she could help him. Her confines featured no windows, and only a single bulb overhead lifted the darkness. She needed a way out of here . . . past a locked door and an unknown number of trained men. As Lexi pondered the futility of her situation, she heard voices nearby. She padded to the door and knelt in front of it. Cupping a hand to her ear, she listened as best she could.

"What the hell are we doing with the girl?" a man said in a deep voice.

"Hell, I don't know," another said. He had a higher-pitched tone. "Especially after this morning." What happened? Lexi's heart pounded at the thought of Braxton killing her dad.

"I didn't sign up to be a goddamn babysitter."

"We ain't babysitting. She's in the room by herself."

"What about when she needs to use the can?" He paused. "I don't like this."

"Let's hope we don't get stuck with it for long. Braxton said her old man will come for her." He was still alive, then. Lexi released a breath she didn't know she'd been holding.

"What if her father comes in with his own bunch of guys?" the first man said. "Braxton ain't said much, but I know he's concerned."

"Either way, this gig still ends for us," the man said, "and the girl."

Lexi scooted away from the door. For the first time, she thought about what might happen if her dad didn't agree to whatever they wanted him to do. She took a deep breath, wiped her eyes, and scanned the room for something to use as a weapon. While she did, she heard a key in the lock. Before she could make it back to the chair, the large goon who threw her in here entered the room.

He didn't look happy at seeing her free.

～

EACH TOOK one side of the corridor—Tyler the right and Rust the left. The first six opposite rooms were empty. Rust checked the last on his side; he emerged a couple seconds later and nodded to indicate it was clear. Tyler opened the right-hand one. He saw Lexi standing beside a chair right away, but his eyes didn't linger on her long. Behind her, a guy who looked like he just stepped off the football field stood and reached for his gun.

Room dimensions were small. Firing a pistol would be loud and very close to Lexi. Tyler surged forward and drew his knife as he ran. Before the large man cleared his gun, Tyler stabbed him under the sternum, pulling the blade back and plunging it into the man's torso again and again until his eyes rolled back, and he sagged to the bloody floor.

Tyler glared at the fallen goon for a few seconds before calming himself and looking away. Lexi stared at him. Many girls—and boys—in her place would have been horrified at seeing their fathers stab a man to death. Lexi frowned, but she didn't look frightened, and her voice conveyed relief rather than fear when she talked. "I knew you'd come." She wrapped Tyler in a hug.

"Are you all right?" Tyler asked his concern. He squeezed Lexi for all he was worth. Tears welled in his eyes. "Did they hurt you?"

"I'm fine, Dad."

They held their embrace for several more seconds until Rust said, "We should probably get going."

Tyler released Lexi and smiled at her. She offered one in return. To Rust, Tyler said, "You have keys to one of the company vehicles?"

"Yes." He gave a set to Tyler. "Take this one. It's Maxwell's. Prick thinks he should get to drive a Tesla on the company dime."

In turn, Tyler gave them to Lexi. "Get in and go."

She stared at the keys in her hand and then gave Tyler a quizzical look. "What? Why would I leave?"

"Because it's going to get a lot worse around here," Tyler said. "Now, go. I intend to finish Braxton once and for all."

"But Dad—"

"No buts. Don't argue with me. Get in the Tesla and go."

She looked between the keys and her father again. "All right." She hugged Tyler again. "Be careful, Dad. That asshole hates you, and he still has a few guys."

"We'll be fine. Now, get out of here."

Lexi left the room and jogged up the hallway. Tyler and Rust watched her walk out the front door. A few seconds later, Tyler heard the muted sound of an electric vehicle driving away. Leave it to Maxwell to get himself a nicer ride than everyone else. He hadn't changed a bit since their days together in the unit.

"Ready to finish this?" Tyler said.

Rust leveled his pistol at Tyler. "I helped you get your daughter out of here," he said. "It was bullshit. Braxton shouldn't have done it." He shook his head. "But you killed Bobby. He was my friend. I liked him."

"Think about this."

"I've spent the last couple hours thinking about it." Rust took a step out of the room and waved the pistol, indicating Tyler should follow him. "Let's go see Braxton. I think the two of you will have a lot to talk about."

38

Tyler chided himself. He should have seen the betrayal coming. Rust seemed to care about his buffoonish partner Bobby. While he accepted Bobby's death with practicality in the aftermath, Tyler should have realized he'd harbor resentment. At least he ensured Lexi's safe exit. She'd be on the highway before long and wouldn't need to deal with Braxton and his mess anymore.

"You're making a mistake," Tyler said as Rust led him through the doors to the receiving area. Tyler counted four other guys. He recognized one: Ryan Anderson, always Braxton's most eager—and massive—sycophant. Anderson could've been a hell of a soldier and officer, but his commander's poisonous influence dragged him down and curtailed his career. Despite it all, the man remained loyal to Braxton to this day. Anderson smirked as Tyler entered. None of the others showed any reaction.

"I told you why I'm doing this," Rust replied. He jabbed the muzzle of his pistol into Tyler's back to encourage him forward.

"You die first," Tyler said. Rust took the M11, of course. The shotgun remained in the car. Tyler was left with a knife and his cunning. They would need to be enough.

The rear of the building looked like somewhere a business would receive and process inventory. Parts of the floor remained open, with only a few desks and partition walls scattered about. The right half held stacks of used pallets near the entrance and empty crates along the right-hand wall. Braxton got a shipment of something here. Probably weapons. His men would be well-armed. Both the normal and rollup doors at the back were closed.

"Sir," Anderson said, cementing himself as a suckup, "you'll want to see this."

A few seconds later, Braxton stepped out from behind a partition wall. "Well, well," he said. "I knew we'd see you soon. You're so predictable." Tyler remained silent. As usual, Braxton filled the gap with more self-important talking. "You probably came here to beg me for your daughter's life. I wonder what she would think of you, then. And if she'd beg me not to kill you." Tyler again said nothing. Neither did Rust, which came as a relief. "Shall we ask her?"

"I'll get her, sir," Anderson volunteered like the eager toady he was. Braxton nodded. While Anderson walked toward the entrance, Tyler took small steps back toward the wall. Rather than push the gun against him, Rust followed his lead. A door opened in the main part of the building. Anderson cursed. He came running in a few seconds later. "She's gone."

Braxton scowled at Tyler. "You got her out?"

"You really should hire better guards, Leo."

Anderson glared at Tyler and then stood beside his commander. Rust moved around to Tyler's front, keeping the muzzle of the pistol trained on his forehead less than a foot away. "I can finish him right now," he said.

"I wanted to make him suffer," Braxton said. "Still do. Bring him to me."

Rust frowned and turned to look at Braxton. Tyler went for the gun. He pushed down on Rust's fist and up with the frame. Rust's index finger snapped in the trigger guard. Tyler snatched the gun away, gripped it properly, and shot Rust between his surprised eyes. Tyler grabbed the body before it could fall and held it in front of him while the other men drew their weapons. A stack of pallets offered cover, but it lay ten feet away. Tyler backed toward it.

One of Braxton's men realized what he was doing and moved to intercept. "Cut him off," Braxton said as he scampered behind a nearby desk. Tyler, still holding Rust's Kevlar-clad corpse as a shield, leveled the pistol at the man trying to cut him off. They both fired. Rust's vest and body soaked up the impact of the incoming bullet. Tyler's shot took his adversary in the throat. He sank to the floor as blood poured from between his fingers.

Tyler made it behind the pallets. He fished his M11 out of the back of Rust's pants, then released the body. He had two pistols and three opponents—four counting Kent Maxwell, who'd yet to make an appearance. An opportunist like him would be waiting for the right time.

Compared to what he often faced in Afghanistan, Tyler liked these odds.

LEXI THOUGHT the Tesla Model X featured gull-wing doors, so she was a little surprised and disappointed to find the driver's side opened conventionally. She started the vehicle and marveled at how quiet it was without a conventional engine. After backing out of the spot, she pulled away. The electric torque hit immediately, and it shoved her back in the seat. Lexi smiled. She might have to keep the SUV when everything was over. After being abducted and held by Braxton's men, she couldn't wait to be free. She knew her dad would come for her. He'd been saving people or keeping them safe his whole life.

Lexi looked around to get her bearings. She was in Baltimore. Jimmy's Famous Seafood whizzed by on the left. According to the massive center screen, Dundalk Avenue lay not far ahead. She used her fingers to zoom out and saw the route home. But her dad would be stuck at Braxton's compound. Lexi wanted to call 9-1-1, but she realized she didn't have her phone. Whoever drove this SUV didn't leave one behind.

Should she abandon her dad? He'd be outnumbered. As capable as he was, he wasn't active duty anymore. And he was fifty. The men in the building may not be as good, but they were younger and more numerous. Even the guy who helped get her free could turn on him. Lexi witnessed the grunts and their fanatical devotion to Braxton.

A horn honked behind her, jarring Lexi from her thoughts. She made the left onto Dundalk Avenue and continued. A sign showed I-95 ahead via Eastern Avenue. She could take it and get home. There were probably more direct routes, but they'd require her to figure out the nav system on the fly. Lexi also considered turning around and going back for her dad. He'd come for her. How could she just drive away now regardless of what he told her to do? What would she do once she got there? She had a large vehicle but no phone and no weapon. She might only get in the way.

She might end up kidnapped again.

A half mile to the highway. Lexi churned the options through her mind. She might be a distraction, or she could make a difference. Her dad found her and got her out. Why should she abandon him now?

Lexi swung the SUV around, stomped on the accelerator, and headed back to the building.

39

Pallets wouldn't provide cover forever. Each bullet striking them splintered bits of wood onto the floor. Anderson and the other two men fanned out and fired from different angles. It was a good tactic. Braxton would occasionally yell something while staying behind cover. Still no sign of Maxwell.

A shadow shifted in the light. Tyler peeked out to his left. The gunman took a wider angle, hoping to come around the pallets and get a better shot. Tyler acted first, squeezing off two rounds from each pistol and dropping the man with four holes in his body.

One down.

Tyler glanced from side to side. No other cover nearby. The crates were stacked flat against the wall. Making it to the desks and cubicle partitions would get him shot. He needed to make his stand here.

He fired to the left the last time. Maybe Anderson and the other guy would expect him to immediately go the other way. People often alternated actions, even running in zig-zag patterns to elude pursuers. Tyler leaned out past the left edge of the pallets. No one was there. He inched his way to the front corner.

Tyler turned, dropped into a crouch, and fell onto his left side. The surprised goon looking back at him took four bullets center mass. Anderson scampered away when he saw what went on. He made it behind a desk before Tyler could get a shot off. The receiving area quieted. The acrid smells of blood and gunsmoke hung in the air.

"Sure you want to go through with this, Leo?" Tyler said, taking cover behind the pallets again. "Looks like it's down to you, your loyal toady, and your chief ass-kisser. I'm not sure which is Maxwell and which is Anderson."

"Screw you!" Anderson said.

"When did you get so sensitive, Anderson? Your lips have been glued to his ass for years. No reason to be embarrassed about it now."

"I was an *officer*."

"And still a sycophant," Tyler said. "You could have at least picked someone worth sucking up to."

Anderson answered with an inarticulate yell. Bullets slammed into the wood behind Tyler. A few bits flew off and landed on his head and neck. He brushed them away. "How did someone so touchy ever get to captain?"

"I'm tired of trying to deal with you, Tyler," Braxton said. "I'm sure Ryan is, too."

"I am, sir," Anderson said in agreement, even though his role in this conversational thread was superfluous.

"You got Lexi out. You've set me back years. Why don't we all just walk away?"

"You're not getting off so easy, Leo," Tyler said. "The only way you leave here is in a body bag. I'll let you decide how many pieces your corpse is in when it happens."

"You always thought you were such a badass," Anderson said, scowling at Tyler.

"And I was right," Tyler said. "Now, be quiet, Ryan. The grownups are talking."

"You're overrated. I always thought so."

"Good for you."

"Let's settle this, then," Anderson said. "You and me."

"Sure," Tyler agreed. "Step out so I can shoot you."

"I mean the old-fashioned way. Like men. We put our guns down and see who's better."

"Yeah, sure. And then your asshole boss shoots me. I'll pass."

"I won't interfere," Braxton said. "In fact, I'll wait outside. If Ryan wins, he and I drive away. And if you win, Tyler, then you and I finish this once and for all."

Anderson stepped out into the open. So did Kent Maxwell. It was just like him to wait to show himself. At least Maxwell would be a worthy opponent. He'd been loyal to Braxton, but he was his own man, too. Both held their guns at their sides. Maxwell, as usual, looked annoyed. He never seemed like he wanted to be anywhere. Maybe the proximity to a toady like Anderson made him sour. "Maxwell," Tyler said with a small nod. "You have some failure to make up for."

"Piss off, Tyler."

"You want to take Anderson's place in his deal?"

"Sure," Maxwell said. "I'll give you a better fight."

"Anderson," Tyler said, "you're big and dumb. Did you kidnap my daughter?"

"Yeah," he said. "What of it? Guess what else I did while I carried her inside?"

Before Anderson could answer his own rhetorical question, Tyler shot him in the head.

"Goddammit!" Braxton hollered as the body slumped to the concrete floor. "You didn't have to kill him."

"You didn't have to kidnap my daughter, Leo. Get over yourself. You're better off without such a turd, anyway."

"Same deal, sir," Maxwell said without turning to address his former commander. "You wait outside. Tyler and I will settle this."

"But Anderson . . ."

"We can hire an accountant."

Braxton's sigh filled the empty space. "Fine. I'll be outside. Kill this prick." The backdoor creaked open, and Braxton walked into the night. Tyler considered shooting him in the back. It would leave him open to Maxwell, however. An unacceptable risk; the man wouldn't miss at this range. A slam echoed in the room a moment later.

The idea of this fight was ridiculous. Why even consider it? Despite his sensible objection, Tyler pondered the idea. Maxwell was younger, slightly bigger, and probably stronger. Less so in all three areas than Anderson, but he still held advantages over Tyler. But he probably wasn't better. Tyler could take him, and then he'd walk outside, empty the magazine into Braxton, and go on his way. The alternative meant continuing this standoff. Two against one. Unless Braxton called anyone else. Then the odds could get much worse.

On top of it all, Tyler welcomed the thought of beating Maxwell's ass in a fight. Like most officers—especially those of the Leo Braxton Finishing School—he could stand to get knocked down a few pegs. "Fine," he said. "I have two guns, and I'll drop them one at a time. You so much as look at me funny, I shoot."

Maxwell still held his pistol at his side. He regarded Tyler with a wolfish grin. "You and me now, old man."

"Throw down your gun," Tyler said.

"You first."

Tyler set one down and nudged it behind the pallets. "One is all you get. I'm not leaving myself unarmed against you."

"Fine," Maxwell said. He set down the pistol he'd been holding and kicked it across the room. Then he unholstered a revolver at his ankle and pushed it in the same direction with his boot. "Now your other gun."

Tyler pondered shooting Maxwell where he stood, but he'd already done it to Anderson, who deserved it a lot more. He set his other pistol down and sent it the way of the other one. "All right, Maxwell," he said. "You think I've been overrated all this time, too?"

"I think you've always caused a lot more trouble than you're worth."

"Fair enough. Let's dance."

Maxwell advanced.

~

MAXWELL WAS STILL FAIRLY YOUNG . . . probably forty by now. He was a little taller and broader than Tyler, and his physique told everyone he kept himself in shape after leaving the service. A lot of people caught up in Braxton's web made involuntary exits from the Army; Tyler wondered if Maxwell earned the chance to leave on his own terms. If not, it would make the man's devotion to Braxton all the more puzzling. Why stay in league with someone who torpedoed so many careers through simple ambition and lies?

When Tyler knew him, he'd been a captain. He heard Maxwell got promoted to major just after Tyler left the unit and went on terminal leave. It didn't take long for everything to fall apart from there. Maxwell's dark hair remained untouched by gray, and in his time in the private sector, he'd discovered the joys of growing a goatee.

Tyler took a few steps forward and set himself, presenting his side to his opponent. Maxwell would be a trained fighter, too; he wasn't some chump like Bobby who got by on size and a mean glare. The two men circled each other, neither making a move. Maxwell broke the stalemate with a punch, which Tyler turned aside. Next came a kick, also repelled.

They weren't his best efforts. Tyler knew Maxwell was feeling him out. He tried not to show too much. Maxwell came in for another strike, but Tyler recognized the feint and extracted his arm from the nerve hold before Maxwell could get the necessary grip. Tyler launched a basic kick, turned away by Maxwell, then a volley of punches. A few connected and rocked the larger man back.

Maxwell answered with an elbow in Tyler's gut. He recoiled and sucked in a breath while his opponent pressed the advantage. A flurry of punches, elbows, and knees came in. Tyler couldn't stop them all. He staggered back yet couldn't gain any separation. As soon as he tried, Maxwell closed the gap. Tyler went for a headbutt, and Maxwell lunged away, leaned back in, and clobbered Tyler with a strong right hand. It spun him around and sent him crashing to the concrete floor.

Tyler only had time to raise himself to all fours before Maxwell was on him. He squatted over Tyler, putting his body weight on his opponent's back while cinching in a rear chokehold. Tyler struggled to keep from collapsing flat onto the floor. Maxwell got the hold in good. Tyler tried to pry the brawny arm away to no avail. Blackness crept in on the edges of his vision. His chest burned. He needed to free himself from the hold.

He tried to stand, but Maxwell's weight kept him in place. He knew how to use his mass and leverage. The grip made it impossible to roll over. Stars flashed before Tyler's eyes. His fingers fumbled for his belt buckle, undoing it and holding a short length in his right hand. Tyler snapped his wrist back, driving the metal into Maxwell's head. He grunted but didn't let go. Tyler did it again. And a third time. He put all he had left into the fourth. The buckle struck Maxwell's head with a satisfying crack, and he slumped to one side.

Tyler scampered free. His lungs drank in fresh air in a huge gulp. He needed a couple more breaths before he could roll over. Maxwell sat on the floor, bleeding from above his temple. He shook his head to clear it and rose to one knee. Tyler did the same. He wrapped the notched end of the belt around his hand and swung it in a wide, violent arc. The metal slammed into Maxwell's head with another satisfying crack, spiraling him once again to the concrete.

Maxwell didn't move. Tyler steadied his breathing. His lungs no longer felt like he'd stood at the edge of a volcano. He rose, wobbled a step or two, then found his footing. Maxwell stirred. Tyler held an end of the leather strap in each hand, crouched, and wrapped it around Maxwell's neck. He pulled it tight with all his strength, crossing his forearms behind his foe's head. Maxwell's hands tugged at his arms, but Tyler wouldn't let go. He understood how to use mass and leverage, too.

Maxwell made a few more attempts to pry his way loose but nothing more. The buckle to the head took a lot of the fight out of him. He succumbed to the strangulation, and Tyler let his body slump to the concrete. He rolled off and sat. Braxton waited outside. He'd kept his word, at least. Tyler stood, grabbed his M11, and headed for the warehouse door.

40

Braxton remained outside the whole time. Tyler put his hand on the knob. Would the disgraced colonel be an opportunist, waiting outside to shoot him? The door looked to be made of steel. It wouldn't stop a respectable bullet. Tyler glanced around the area. He found a metal pipe and carried it to the exit. With one hand on the knob, he crouched and used the pipe to push the door open.

No gunshots greeted him. He studied the rear of the building on his exposed side. No sign of Braxton or anyone else. Tyler inched into the opening. He tossed the pipe back inside, let the door stop against his knee, and drew his pistol. He held it before him in a two-hand grip, his right arm bent a little, and his left arm across his midsection. Leading with the M11, Tyler peeked around the door. He didn't see anyone. Tyler maintained his crouch and moved out onto the loading dock. He hugged the wall and kept searching for Braxton. The man had to be around somewhere.

Tyler took a few cautious steps to his left. With the sun behind the clouds and many shadows around, dimness prevailed behind the building. Even though the area lacked obvious hiding places, the low light would make spotting an adversary difficult. Braxton possessed the advantage—if nothing else, he heard the door open and knew Maxwell didn't walk out.

Something caught Tyler's eye. Movement? He raised the Mii, but it was too late. A gunshot blasted the stillness from the air and slammed into Tyler's lower left arm, which had been across his midsection. He cursed and dropped to the concrete. Pins and needles preceded numbness up and down the length of his arm, and moving his fingers proved impossible. Tyler ignored his arm, pointed his pistol where he thought he saw movement, and fired.

Silence was the only reply for a few seconds. "Did you think it would be so easy?" Braxton. Every time life took a shit on Tyler, Braxton was there. "I taught you well, Tyler. Did you really think I taught you everything I know?"

"Come over here, Leo. Let's end this."

"You took out Maxwell," Braxton said. Tyler couldn't locate his voice. "He's stronger and younger than either of us. I don't like my chances." He paused. Tyler felt exposed lying in the open with no cover. He needed to move, but doing so would require getting up and making himself an easier target. "I'd rather pick my spots."

"What happened to being a man?" Tyler taunted. He breathed in and out. The arm was broken. Ignore it. Don't go into shock. "You used to talk about it a lot. Was it just bullshit like so many other things you said?"

"You'll have to do a lot better to bait me. Guys in Leavenworth were pretty good at it."

"I wouldn't know." Tyler kept looking around. Where was Braxton hiding? And why didn't his voice give him away? It was hard to pin down, almost like it carried an echo.

Producing such an effect required specific spaces. The building walls on either side of the access road weren't tall enough. A small dumpster sat across the pavement. The fight with Maxwell afforded Braxton plenty of time to find an advantageous position. The small, enclosed area would certainly distort a voice and create the echo Tyler heard.

He leveled his pistol and fired five shots down the length of the dumpster. The high-pitched wail of bullets hitting the metal surface made Tyler wince. Even with his ears ringing, Tyler knew Braxton remained silent. Did those shots take him out? He lay on the concrete a minute. Nothing. Tyler got to his feet, not using his left arm at all. He hopped down from the deck. As he started toward the dumpster, he heard a noise behind him.

When he turned, Braxton clobbered him with a plank of wood.

Tyler hit the pavement hard, and the M11 clattered across the asphalt. The left side of Tyler's head and face throbbed. Stars danced before his eyes. He shook his head but couldn't clear the cobwebs. "Good guess," Braxton said. "I thought about hiding in there, but then I realized I didn't want to be in a goddamn dumpster. Funny thing. Little gap between the buildings there? You stand back a few feet, your voice echoes off the walls. I discovered it by accident but figured I could use it against you." Braxton strode up and hammered Tyler in the gut with the two-by-four. "I was right."

The vest took a little of the blow, but it was designed to stop high-velocity projectiles. It wouldn't be much good in this situation. Tyler tried to get to his feet, but Braxton battered him repeatedly. After a particularly hard shot blasted the wind from his chest, he sagged to the pavement and stopped trying. Maybe Braxton would start talking again. Tyler waited for an opening.

"All you had to do was walk away, *John*," Braxton said. "None of this happens if you mind your own business. But you're drawn to me. Maybe it's because we're so much alike."

Tyler rolled his eyes. "I'm nothing like you."

Braxton's first response was jabbing Tyler in the side with the two-by-four. A fresh wave of pain cascaded throughout Tyler's body. More of him hurt than didn't. He couldn't remember the last time he'd taken such a beating. "You're a lot more like me than you want to admit," Braxton said. "How did playing mechanic work out? You know who you are. Hate me all you want, but you know who you are."

"Go to hell, Leo."

Braxton raised the plank again and brought it down on Tyler's midsection three more times. Even breathing hurt at this point. "I probably will end up in hell," Braxton said, "if it even exists." He tossed the two-by-four down and took a gun from the back of his trousers. "But you're going there first."

41

L exi made her way back down Dundalk Avenue. The light at Holabird turned red, but she ignored it and barreled through to make the right turn. Some guy in a tiny car honked his wimpy horn in protest. Lexi ignored him and kept driving. A minute later, she turned into the parking lot.

She cruised past the front of the building and saw no activity. It made sense. Most of the men hung out in the large receiving area. She turned the SUV around and drove it as fast as she could toward the rear of the structure. Tires squealed as she made the first right turn, so she slowed a little for the second.

Ahead, she saw two figures on the access road. One raised a wooden plank and bludgeoned the other with it. As Lexi drove closer, she realized the man on the ground was her dad. "You are not killing him, you piece of shit!" she said to the empty passenger spaces. She cut the headlights and kept going. Braxton stood over her dad, tossed the two-by-four down, and replaced it with a gun. Lexi stepped on the accelerator, and the electric motors responded. She had to get there on time.

She veered a little to the left as she approached. Braxton half-turned. Lexi cut the wheel to the right. He pivoted all the way around, and his eyes got as big as Frisbees before the Tesla's smooth grill plowed into him. Lexi made sure to steer around her dad and hit the brakes. Braxton flew onto the windshield, cracking it in several places, then rolled off the hood, tumbled onto the asphalt, and lay still.

Lexi looked at the two fallen men. Her breaths came in rapid gulps. She'd just hit a man at high speed and sent him flying. Was he dead? She'd never thought of herself as a killer. Her father sat up, wincing the entire time. He kept his bloody left arm close to his body as he struggled to one knee. Lexi opened the door and sprinted the short distance to him. She hugged him harder than she'd ever hugged anyone before. "Oh, my god, Dad, are you all right?" Tears slid down her cheeks as her father gripped her tightly with his right arm.

"I thought I told you to leave," he said. She pulled away. He smiled at her. "I'm glad you came back. Thanks. Help me up, will you?" Lexi held out a hand, stepping rearward to pull her father to his feet as he grimaced through the pain it caused. He looked around and hobbled over to a pistol.

"Is he dead?" Lexi said.

"If not, he's about to be." Her dad approached Lexi and gently put his left arm around her. He kissed her forehead. "Thanks a lot, Lexi, but you don't need to see this."

"Yes, I do," she said. The edge in her voice surprised even her. "That bastard kidnapped me, and now he almost beat you to death. I want to watch him die."

After regarding her for several long seconds, her dad nodded. "Have it your way." He walked to Braxton, and Lexi trailed behind him. "You alive down there, Leo?"

Braxton stirred and grunted. His right leg lay at an awkward angle, and he bled from many cuts and scrapes. Leaving him here was probably enough to kill him. If someone heard anything and called 9-1-1, however, the bastard might live, and Lexi didn't want that.

"I'll take it as a yes." Her father pointed the gun at Braxton. "Goodbye, Leo. I probably will see you in hell, but you're getting a head start." Lexi covered her ears as eight shots thundered into the fallen Braxton before the slide locked. Blood poured from new wounds and pooled under the body. Lexi helped her dad limp to the SUV where he leaned against the hood.

"You need an ambulance," she said.

He shook his head. "Too many questions."

"You've been shot, and he beat you half to death. You need to go to the hospital."

Her dad looked at her but didn't say anything. His eyes took on a faraway look. When they glassed over, Lexi reached out and caught him before he slumped to the pavement. She sat him down against the front of the car, found his cell phone, and dialed 9-1-1.

TYLER HEARD the beeping before he woke up. His eyes opened. He lay in a hospital bed. Something pumped oxygen into his nose, and an IV bag stood at the right side of the railing. He checked his left wrist for handcuffs and found none. Score one for the good guys. Of course, the cast on his arm probably earned him a pass. Tyler's eyes settled on the guest chair where Lexi sat. She smiled and leaned forward. "Hey, Dad."

"You called the ambulance," said Tyler.

"You didn't give me much choice when you passed out."

Tyler nodded. The movement of his head sent waves of nausea rippling up from his core. "I guess you're right. How long have I been here?"

Lexi looked at her watch. "About six hours."

"Shit. Don't you need to get home? What about—"

"Dad. Chill. I'm fine. I've had food and coffee. What more do I need?"

"A security detail?"

"I don't blame you," Lexi said with a smile. "We talked about what might happen. Braxton kidnapped me. You're the one who got me out."

"And who didn't insist hard enough you go home," Tyler said.

"You're still alive because I'm hard-headed."

"You're definitely my daughter," Tyler said.

"Mom's too," Lexi said. "She could go toe-to-toe with you in a stubborn showdown."

Tyler grinned. He always enjoyed the back-and-forth with his daughter. "I feel like I need to argue about it to show how hard-headed I am."

"Don't." Lexi leaned back in the chair. "I don't enjoy picking on the weak."

"Laugh it up."

"I will," Lexi said.

"The cops been here?" Tyler asked.

Lexi bobbed her head. "They came by when you were still out cold. I told them to try again tomorrow."

Tyler glanced at a clock hanging near the wall-mounted TV. "It's almost oh-two-hundred. How are you still here?"

"I'm your daughter," Lexi said. "Considering the circumstances you came here under, they let me stay past visiting hours." She paused. "You look like hell, Dad. How do you feel?"

"Like I got shot in the arm and then bludgeoned with a board." He frowned. "I guess my arm is broken?"

"The doctor told me a fractured radius," Lexi said.

"He got technical with you?" Tyler said.

"I told him I was in nursing school." Lexi batted her

eyelashes. "He gave me the full rundown, and I just nodded at the interesting bits."

Tyler laughed but cut it short when his ribs barked in protest. "Thanks for coming in. You should get home, though. It's late, and you've had a rough go of it recently."

"I do like driving that Tesla. Gotta figure out a way to keep it." Tyler didn't say anything. He wanted her to keep the Accord Coupe they'd worked on together, but a final thumb in Kent Maxwell's dead eye held some appeal, too. "Anymore asshole former commanders who might want to kidnap me, Dad?"

"Can't think of any."

"That's a relief." She walked up to the bed, kissed Tyler on the cheek, and put her head on his chest. He gave her a one-armed hug.

"Be safe, kiddo. Love you."

"Love you, too, Dad."

Tyler watched her leave. He looked up at the ceiling and sighed. Braxton was dead. The whole mess was finally at an end. Soon, however, he'd have the cops crawling all over his hospital room and probably his house. Maybe they'd have the decency to wait until morning. At least the venue was in Baltimore. Whoever came to ask questions would probably owe some deference to Captain Leon Sharpe. Maybe the man himself would make an appearance.

Despite the time, he grabbed his cell and dialed Rollins. As always, he answered like he'd been awake and waiting to pounce on a ringing phone. Tyler wondered if the man ever slept. "I was starting to worry about you."

"I'm alive," Tyler said. "Braxton gave me his best, though."

"You in the hospital?"

"Yeah. There's a crucifix on the wall. Must be Saint Agnes."

"Lexi all right?"

"She's good. Just left."

"Hang on a minute," Rollins said. "I have orders to put you

on the phone." The line fell silent. It took more than a minute, but the next voice Tyler heard was Sara Morrison's.

"I understand you're in the hospital."

"If not for my daughter," Tyler said, "I'd probably be in the morgue."

"Braxton is dead?"

"Very much so. You can go back to living your life now, Miss Morrison."

"Sara, please. Thank you, Tyler. Do you know what kind of recovery you're looking at?"

"I have a fractured arm," he said. "A few other injuries, too, but nothing super serious. I'll probably be on light duty for a while."

"Glad to hear it," Sara said. She paused and sighed. "Braxton cut quite a wide swath of destruction. Did you know my deputy was recently found dead in his house?"

"No. Wow. Though I think he played a role in all this."

"Yes. I talked to Mister Smith. I was furious when I heard. Firing a government employee isn't always easy, but I would have ordered Arthur marched out with a bayonet up his ass."

"I'm sure it would have been worth seeing," Tyler said.

"You don't want a job, do you, Tyler?"

"I have one. I think."

Sara chuckled. "I hope you do. I'm glad you're all right. No offense, but I'm a little more glad Braxton is dead. Someone in his crew also murdered the man I'd been dating."

"I'm sorry to hear," Tyler said.

"Thanks," Sara said. "I've also ordered any of Braxton's men remaining in the Middle East rounded up. We think Victor White is there with them. Personally, I kind of hope they resist, but the official Pentagon line is we want them back alive."

Tyler smiled. "Considering their employer, I doubt you'll bat a thousand on your goal. You can get back to work, at least."

"Thanks to you."

"I'm glad I could get there when I did."

"When you're out of the hospital and recovered," Sara said, "give me a call. Maybe we can catch up."

"I will," Tyler said.

RICH FERGUSON APPROACHED the hospital with Captain Leon Sharpe. They walked in the front doors, received stick-on guest passes from the receptionist, and stepped into the elevator. Rich pushed the button for the fifth floor. "You ever meet Tyler?" Sharpe asked.

"In the service?"

"Anywhere?"

"You said he retired about eight years ago?" Sharpe bobbed his bald black head. "Our careers overlapped, but I never met him."

"He's something else." Sharpe adjusted his tie. "He was a sergeant when I was a specialist. Smart guy. Good soldier. Probably could have gone far in the officer ranks if he wanted, but he elected for a technical warrant rating."

The elevator dinged, and both men stepped out onto the fifth floor. "What was his expertise?"

"Wheeled vehicle mechanic," Sharpe said. "He was especially good at it for the promotion." They stopped near the nurses' station. Everyone must have been out on their rounds. "He didn't just instruct how to fix Jeeps and Hummers, though. Later in his career, he taught soldiers how to clear rooms and breach hostile compounds."

"Sounds like he had quite an interesting career," Rich said.

Sharpe nodded. "Ended before it should've, too."

"Bad?"

"You ever have a commander you didn't get along with?"

Rich smirked. "No . . . never."

"Very funny," Sharpe said. "His situation was bad, though. Shit got sideways. *Real* sideways."

"How bad are we talking?" Rich leaned his elbow on the counter once it became apparent Sharpe wasn't going to move anytime soon.

"The army investigated his colonel. Eventually, they charged him with a war crime, court martialed him, and threw him in Leavenworth. I couldn't believe he got out."

"What's all this have to do with the man we're going to talk to?" Rich asked.

"I'd just like you to take it easy." Sharpe moved his massive hands up and down slowly. "You get intense sometimes. Dial it back a little."

"Captain, it's likely this man killed a roomful of people . . . many of whom were fellow veterans."

"I know," Sharpe said. "What I'm telling you is we might not have the whole story. So we're going to listen to what he has to say. I'd appreciate it if you didn't give him the third degree."

Rich frowned but offered a slight bob of his head. "Fine."

"Good." Sharpe scanned the hallway and headed to the left. Rich followed him.

42

L ight fought through the blinds and blanketed half the room as Tyler awoke. He had a vague recollection of a nurse checking on him in the night. The clock mounted near the TV showed eight-fifteen. Tyler took in the room. The other bed remained empty. A cup of water sat on the small table beside him. Tyler drained it in one gulp.

The door opened a minute later. A pretty blonde nurse came in, smiled at Tyler, and checked his IV. "How are we feeling this morning?" she asked.

"Happy to be alive," Tyler said.

"Good. We'll get you some breakfast soon. The doctor will come by and check on you later. You might even be able to go home today."

"It'd be nice."

"Trying to get rid of me so soon?" the nurse inquired with a grin.

If Tyler were a younger man, he'd be keenly interested in her sticking around. Considering she looked like nursing school lay in her very recent past, however . . . Plus, after spending time with Sara Morrison, he liked her, despite the difficult circumstances of their meeting. "No offense," he said.

"I know. Everything looks good. You'll have some food soon." She walked out the door. A few minutes later, an older woman in dark scrubs came in carrying a tray. She set it on the table, regarded Tyler with a neutral expression, and left without saying anything. Tyler's ribs barked as he sat up. He grabbed the tray and set it on his lap.

"No points for presentation or delivery," he said to no one. The plate held scrambled eggs colored an unnatural yellow, home fries which needed a couple more minutes on the stove, and boring white toast. And coffee. Tyler expected it to be weak, but he drank it anyway. It was a little better than he thought. A respectable medium roast. Pretty mild, not too strong. Brewed for the masses.

Despite the unappealing look of the food, Tyler scarfed it all down. He would've eaten two more plates if given them. Getting shot and beaten worked up an appetite. After he finished breakfast, the door opened again. Leon Sharpe strode in wearing his captain's dress blues, and a plainclothes detective walked in behind him. The short hair, steady gaze, and posture marked the other man as former military. "Tyler," Sharpe said as they stopped at the foot of the bed.

"Leon."

"This is Rich Ferguson." The two men exchanged nods.

"Your name is John Tyler, correct?" Ferguson asked. Tyler remained silent. "You know why we're here?"

"You're eager to try the coffee?"

"A gunfight in Baltimore. I'm not going to dance with you and ask if you know anything about it. So let's cut to the part where you tell me what happened."

Sharpe cleared his throat. Ferguson kept looking at Tyler. "All right. A man I served under in the army started his own company after he got out of Leavenworth well short of his original sentence for war crimes. We clashed because he went after another soldier who served in his unit. He escalated things by kidnapping my daughter . . . I presume you've already talked to her." Neither policeman offered an acknowledgment. "I got her out. The guys trying to prevent her rescue didn't make it."

"That's it?" Ferguson asked a few seconds after Tyler lapsed into silence.

"It's the *Readers Digest* version."

"Give it to me unabridged."

"Detective, I—"

"Sergeant."

Tyler offered a fractional nod. "All right. Sergeant, I'm sure I'm not the first person you talked to. It's been, what . . . ten or eleven hours since this all went down? By now, you know how many bodies were there, and you probably know *who* they were." Ferguson again offered nothing in response. Someone else who liked to hold things close. "I told you the circumstances of my going there. You can connect the dots without anything else from me."

"We're being polite questioning you here," Ferguson said.

"What a good look for the department," Tyler said. "Dragging a veteran who'd been shot and beaten out of his hospital bed to your precinct. I'm sure your public relations people will have a grand old time cleaning it up." To Sharpe, he said, "You have good PR people on staff, Leon?"

"Sergeant Ferguson might be a little aggressive," Sharpe said. "He does have a point, though. A pile of people are dead, and no one else can give us the whole story. We need to hear some things from you."

"Fine. Fire away."

Ferguson said, "Did you kill Leonardo Braxton?"

"Yes."

"Ryan Anderson?"

"Yes."

"Kent Maxwell?"

"I can save you some time here, Sergeant," Tyler said. "My answer is yes to every body you found there."

"Why shouldn't we take you in for multiple murders?" Ferguson asked.

"Because I told you why I was there. By now, I presume you've spoken to my daughter. If you're industrious, you've also talked to a woman named Sara Morrison." Ferguson jotted a note. "If not, I recommend looking her up." He'd keep Rollins out of it if he could. "Miss Morrison can tell you about the charm of Leo Braxton as well as anyone."

"He kidnap her?" Ferguson said.

"Sent three assholes to kill her," Tyler said, "among other offenses."

"You stop them?"

"It happened well outside your jurisdiction. How much do you care?"

Sharpe frowned while Ferguson fell silent. "We'll reach out to Miss Morrison. Anything else you can tell us about Braxton?"

"Yes," Tyler said. "The world is no poorer for his absence. In fact, it's better. The sun is fractionally brighter today without him darkening the planet by existing. I know you understand this at least a little, Leon."

"Pretty harsh," Ferguson said.

"Miss Morrison can fill you in on the finer points of his personnel file."

"All right. I'm sure we'll be in touch. Don't leave the state."

"I'll do what I please unless a judge directs me otherwise, Sergeant. Have a good day." Ferguson stared at Tyler a few seconds before Sharpe nudged him, and they both walked out.

Tyler found the remote to his articulating bed and eased

himself from sitting to lying down again. The police wouldn't find much. They could verify everything he said about Braxton and his group. Tyler couldn't expect a medal to arrive in the mail—even though he deserved one—but he also didn't think they'd recommend any charges against him.

He waited for the doctor and hoped to go home.

JAKE EASED the borrowed Sentra into the parking lot. He stopped at the side of the building. *Smitty and Son Classic Car Repair.* The sign looked like he remembered. The shop itself appeared a little worse for wear, however. Dents in the siding, a broken window or two . . . probably vandalism by Braxton and his men. They were dead, thanks to the man his father hired. The whole chapter of his life was behind him now.

He needed to repair the relationship with his father.

Jake got out of his car and walked in the front door. He noticed the third desk had been cleared off and some papers sat atop it. His father worked in the bay, an old GTO up on the lift. "Be right there," he called without turning around. Jake moved behind the counter, past the desks, and into the shop.

His father turned and looked like he wanted to say something, no doubt about a customer being in the work area. His mouth hung open for a few seconds. Then, he walked to Jake and hugged him. Jake wrapped his arms around his father. They stood for a while until both men pulled back. "I missed you," his father said. "You had me worried."

"I know, Dad. I'm sorry. I . . . wanted to do the right thing, and it all fell to shit. Then, I just wanted to keep you safe and out of it."

"I understand. It ended up shitty, but I'm proud of you. Never doubt yourself when you do what you know is right."

Jake bobbed his head. "It's what you taught me. How's Mister Tyler?"

"Recovering," Smitty said. "You ready to get back to work?"

"I'd like to. I have to clear some things up with my reserve unit first. Then . . . sure. Only, not every day. This is your passion. I get it. You're really good at it. I like working on these cars, but I don't love it. I don't want to do it all the time."

"All right. We can work out a schedule for you."

"What about Tyler?"

His dad shrugged. "I owe him a debt I can't possibly repay. So do you. If he still wants to work here, I'll be glad to keep him on the payroll."

Jake inclined his head toward the GTO. "What are you doing here?"

"New rotors all around."

"I can handle it, Dad. Talk to Tyler. Maybe he's ready to come back to work, too."

"All right," his father said. "I will." He clapped Jake on the shoulder. "Welcome back, son."

"Thanks, Dad."

TYLER ENDED up staying one more night for observation. The following morning, the same smiling blonde nurse checked on him, the same dour woman delivered an identical breakfast, and a doctor gave him a final check-up. He discharged Tyler with a prescription for mild painkillers and an order to take things easy.

Lexi picked him up at the hospital. She drove Maxwell's Tesla SUV again. When she raised the wing door for Tyler to get in the more spacious back, he saw Zeke sitting on the other side. "Hi, Dad," he said.

"Twenty-four years in the Army and you barely get hurt," he said. "Now you've been shot and got your ass kicked."

"I'm glad you're doing well, too."

"How's being a mechanic treating you?"

Tyler smiled. He understood what his father told him when they met for dinner . . . back before everything went off the rails. *A man's gotta be who he is*. Tyler insisted he was a mechanic. Zeke saw through it. He could work on cars and be good at it, but there was more to him. The soldier. The killer. He was all those things. One dinner conversation with his father did more than his time on the couch with every shrink he saw—save the one who told him to paint. "Better than being an auto shop raider," Tyler said.

They drove to Tyler's neighborhood. When the SUV drove up his street, he saw the 442 sitting in its usual spot. "How did my car get here?" he wondered aloud as they pulled to the curb.

"Rollins dropped it off," Lexi said. "He called me yesterday."

"Thanks. I'm glad to see it here."

"Need help getting inside?"

"I think I can manage," Tyler said. His left arm was in a sling and would be for four weeks. Then the doctor would evaluate his recovery. If all went well, he'd wear a soft cast for two weeks, do some physical therapy, and then be back at full strength. He'd have a scar from where the bullet ripped into his flesh, but scars were good for showing off to dates.

Maybe he'd even get a chance to show Sara Morrison sometime.

"You staying, Dad?" Tyler said.

Zeke shook his head. "I need to get back. Lexi said she'd take me. You see the rear doors? Ain't this car some cool shit?"

"Sure. We just need to figure out how to keep it."

"Huh?"

"Long story," Tyler said. "Lexi can explain it to you on the drive." He bumped fists with Zeke and watched them drive away. After the warehouse and the drab hospital room, Tyler liked seeing the inside of his own house. He set his bag down, took a beer from the fridge, and opened it. Dos Equis Amber. He stuck to the traditional lagers and ambers. One time, he'd tried an IPA and came away thinking a half-hour of sucking a lemon would have been more pleasant.

He was finishing his beer when Smitty called for the second time. He picked up. "Jake's back."

"Good. I'm glad to hear he came home."

"He still wants to be a mechanic, though not full-time. I told him we'd need to figure out a schedule."

"You have your helper back. Getting the sign fixed would be good."

Smitty let out a dry chuckle. "I'll think about it. Listen, I was wondering if you still want to be on the schedule," Smitty said. "Can you stop in?"

"I think so," Tyler said. "Give me about an hour."

Tyler polished off the beer in three more swigs. He waited a few minutes, drank some water, and sat in his favorite recliner. The couch still showed the signs of Lexi fighting off her attackers. Tyler closed his eyes. The medication made him tired. About a half-hour later, his eyes fluttered open. He grabbed his car keys and drove to Smitty's shop. Inside, Smitty stood from behind his desk. He came around and bumped fists with Tyler. "Thanks for everything you did," he said.

Jake walked in from the shop. He and Tyler exchanged firm nods. "Haven't seen you in about ten years."

"After all I went through," Tyler said, "I might want to wait another ten before I see you again."

Jake smiled. "Like my dad said, thanks for everything you did."

"Sure."

"Jake, why don't you finish the car on the rack?" Smitty said. "Tyler and I have a couple things to talk about."

"All right." Jake and Tyler bobbed their heads at each other again. "Thanks. I hope I don't need you to do something like this for me in the near future."

Tyler shrugged his left shoulder, causing his arm to rise a bit in its sling. "If you do, you'll need to wait at least six weeks."

Jake headed back into the shop. Smitty waited for him to shut the door before saying anything. "I'm glad he's sticking around."

"Me, too."

"Truth is, though, I think you're a better mechanic than he is."

"Don't let him hear you tell me," Tyler said.

Smitty waved a hand. "It's fine. The boy's not passionate about it like I am. What I'm saying is I'd like you to stick around. You and Jake can both be part-time if you want. I suspect you'll be on light duty for a while."

Tyler nodded. "I don't think I'll be much good to you for a few weeks."

"You can work the counter."

Tyler chuckled. "You don't want me dealing with the public. The police are already investigating me for a building full of dead assholes in Baltimore. Let's not put any more on their plates."

Smitty smiled for the first time in Tyler's recent memory. "Fine. When your arm is better, then. We'll figure out a schedule."

"Do I get a raise?"

"No."

"My name on the sign?"

"No."

"Sounds perfect," Tyler said.

THE END

JOHN TYLER WILL RETURN with a new novel in the summer of 2021. In the meantime, you can read a free Tyler novella detailing his last job for Patriot Security by going to https://bit.ly/TylerPrequel.

AFTERWORD

If you enjoyed this book, I hope you'll leave a review. They help indie authors like me get our books noticed, meaning more readers like you can enjoy them. To leave a review, go to the book's sales page where you bought it, select your rating, and say a few words.

The John Tyler Thrillers

1. The Mechanic
2. White Lines (Summer 2021)

The C.T. Ferguson Crime Novels:

1. The Reluctant Detective
2. The Unknown Devil
3. The Workers of Iniquity
4. Already Guilty
5. Daughters and Sons
6. A March from Innocence
7. Inside Cut

While these are the suggested reading sequences, each novel is a standalone thriller or mystery, and the books can be enjoyed in whatever order you happen upon them.

Connect with me:

For the many ways of finding and reaching me online, please visit https://tomfowlerwrites.com/contact. I'm always happy to talk to readers.

This is a work of fiction. Characters and places are either fictitious or used in a fictitious manner.

"Self-publishing" is something of a misnomer. This book would not have been possible without the contributions of many people.

- The great cover design team at 100 Covers.
- My editor extraordinaire, Chase Nottingham.
- My wonderful advance reader team, the Fell Street Irregulars.
- Special thanks to crime fiction author and all-around good guy John D. Patten for helping me settle on the name John Tyler for this character.